Delinquency

and

Youth Crime

Fourth Edition

Delinquency
and
Youth Crime

Fourth Edition

Gary F. Jensen
Vanderbilt University

Dean G. Rojek
The University of Georgia

WAVELAND
PRESS, INC.
Long Grove, Illinois

For information about this book, contact:
Waveland Press, Inc.
4180 IL Route 83, Suite 101
Long Grove, IL 60047-9580
(847) 634-0081
info@waveland.com
www.waveland.com

Chapter Opener Photo Credits

Page 1, © Arthur Tress/Photo Researchers; page 25, © Corbis; page 67, © Jeff Greenberg/The Image Works; page 143, © 1998 Dick Hemingway; page 179, © David M. Grossman; page 311, © Jerry/Express News/Corbis Sygma; page 349, AP Photo/Gary Tramontina; page 387, © Eastcott-Momatiuk/The Image Works; page 421, © James Leynse/Corbis.

Printed in the United States of America

7   6   5   4   3   2   1

To Tanner, my link to immortality —*Grampa*

To Sheila, my sweet wife —*Gary*

Contents

Preface

This fourth edition of *Delinquency and Youth Crime* incorporates new research and new data that are unique to this textbook. For example, sufficient data on self-reports of delinquency over time are now available, enabling a thorough assessment of areas of agreement and disagreement among different measures. Another new feature is a critical assessment of claims that variation in gang activities are a product of "gang panic." Contrary to such claims, meaningful patterns can be discerned supporting the view that there were real increases and decreases over time, with media news stories following rather than preceding gang panics. We also incorporate a new approach to the "more guns, more crime" versus "more guns, less crime" debate.

While every chapter has been updated, the distinctive features of the text remain unchanged. We approach the study of delinquency and youth crime as *one* dimension of the crime problem—not necessarily the worst or even the most pressing concern. We focus on multiple sources of data relevant to the topic and attempt to arrive at tentative generalizations about consistencies across types of information as well as to explain inconsistencies. We encompass biological, psychological, and sociological perspectives and research as well as address the role of social forces and social institutions. Finally, we examine the full range of programs and philosophies involved in the attempt to moderate juvenile crime, devoting a full third of the text to such issues.

Juvenile delinquency and youth crime have been the subject of "scientific" research for nearly a century. This text attempts to capture and summarize the best of the research as well as to organize it in a manner that facilitates a comprehensive understanding of delinquency and juvenile justice. We deal with delinquency as (1) a sociolegal category invented in conjunction with the juvenile court, (2) a label applied to youth at the end of a chain of decisions involving the public, the police, and officials of the juvenile court, and (3) behavior that violates legal codes, regardless of its detection or processing.

The first four chapters deal with the "problem of delinquency" in these several different senses. Chapters 1 and 2 focus on delinquency as one dimension of the crime problem, as a central focus in the development of criminology in general, and as a sociocultural invention. In chapter 3 we examine the "images" of delinquency and youth crime conveyed by data compiled by officials. This provides a basis for comparison with chapter 4, which highlights images based on survey data. This fourth edition reveals continuities across types of data, including survey data relevant to gangs.

Chapters 5 through 8 encompass different approaches to "explaining" or "understanding" delinquency. In chapter 5 we try to provide an objective assessment of theory and research on biological and psychological correlates. Such research has grown increasingly sophisticated, reflecting the demise of a simplistic "nature-vs.-nurture" dichotomy and the emergence of modern research focused on the complex interplay of social psychological and biological processes. Chapter 6 addresses sociological theories as distinct schools of thought—sharing many basic assumptions but with contrasting emphases and themes sufficient to identify three basic causal approaches. We also explore recent reformulations, elaborations, and attempts at integrating theories.

Criminologists can become so enamored with theoretical distinctions that research on specific issues and social institutions of greater interest to the public is slighted. Chapters 7 and 8 deal with issues of enduring concern to students and the public. Chapter 7 addresses questions relevant to the role of the family, school, and peers in understanding delinquency. What role does the family play in generating or inhibiting delinquency? How do our educational institutions in general, and school experiences in particular, bear on the problem? To what degree is delinquency a problem of casual group behavior as opposed to gang activity? In chapter 8 we add religion, media, and guns to this set of concerns. Some of the research will strike many as yielding common sense conclusions, but some will generate controversy as well. For example, a careful inspection of research on the relationship between television violence and juvenile violence challenges much expert opinion. The section on guns may be unique to this textbook and incorporates a new approach to the topic, distinguishing between guns and gun cultures.

The definition of criminology as the scientific study of lawmaking, lawbreaking, and reactions to lawbreaking was proposed in Sutherland's pioneering textbook, *Principles of Criminology* (1924), and that definition still provides a basic framework for organizing a comprehensive treatment of delinquency and youth crime. The last four chapters cover basic and contemporary issues involving reactions to lawbreaking, including deterrence and labeling; imprisonment and alternatives; programmatic themes such as diversion, restitution, shock therapy, boot camps, and restorative justice; and prevention.

The text is designed for juniors and seniors as well as a general audience interested in delinquency as a social problem. While we have attempted to keep jargon to a minimum and to present both theory and research as simply and clearly as possible, it is a college textbook. We introduce students to complicated ideas, scientific and theoretical terms, and concepts that are crucial to debates and controversies in criminology as well as in society. While we feel it is important to present detail capturing the intricacies and evolution of theory and research, the chapter summaries "bring it all together," sparing the details. Many students have found it helpful to read the summary before tackling the more detailed discussion within the chapter. Students will also appreciate the new glossary of terms at the end of the book.

We are grateful for the support of two outstanding universities, the University of Georgia and Vanderbilt University. We have had a great working relationship with Waveland Press. Each edition has been improved through Laurie Prossnitz's attention to detail; this edition also benefited from Deborah Underwood's work on the graphics. We share Waveland's commitment to providing first-class textbooks at a reasonable cost.

one

Delinquency in Context

Jonesboro, Ark., Aug. 11, 2005

Jonesboro School Shooter Freed

(CBS/AP) Mitchell Johnson, one of the two boys convicted of what was at the time the worst school shooting on record, gets to walk away Thursday scot-free, reports CBS News Correspondent Lee Cowan. It was just seven years ago, when Johnson, then 13, and his companion, 11-year-old Andrew Golden, stole an arsenal of weapons and then opened fire on a courtyard full of students and teachers at an Arkansas middle school. Their ambush-style assault killed four young girls and an English teacher, who tried to shield her students from the barrage of bullets.

Under a now-changed Arkansas law, the boys were charged as delinquents, which meant they could only be held until they were 18. Federal prosecutors then stepped in with firearms violations which kept them in prison for three more years. But Johnson turns 21 on Thursday and cannot legally be held any longer. Many Jonesboro residents question whether justice has been served.

(CBS, 2005)

Introduction

The Jonesboro episode was one of a number of dramatic attacks on schoolmates and teachers that captured headlines between 1996 and 2007. In 1996 a student in Moses Lake, Washington, shot two classmates and a teacher. Three students were killed and five wounded in Kentucky, and a Mississippi student went on a shooting spree in 1997. In addition to Jonesboro, there was a similar school shooting in Oregon in 1998.

The most deadly episode of school violence occurred in 1999. At 11:30 AM on April 20, two teenagers dressed in black trench coats and black masks opened fire on their classmates and teachers at Columbine High School in Littleton, Colorado, a suburb of Denver. After killing 12 students and a teacher, and wounding 23 others, the two boys shot themselves. Hours earlier, Eric Harris, 18, and Dylan Klebold, 17, had gone bowling with their gym class.

There was a four-year lull in school shootings after Columbine, but new episodes of school violence were reported in 2003, 2005, 2006, and 2007. In 2003 two students were killed by a classmate at Rocori High School in central Minnesota. In 2005 two attacks took place, one on an Indian reservation in Minnesota. After killing his grandfather and his grandfather's girlfriend, donning his grandfather's bulletproof vest, taking his grandfather's guns, and driving his grandfather's squad car to Red Lake High School, a teenager killed a guard, a teacher, and five students, wounded thirteen others, and ended the spree by committing suicide. The second attack was in Jacksboro, Tennessee, where a 15-year-old boy, sent to the school office because of rumors he had a gun, shot and killed an assistant principal and seriously wounded two other administrators in the office. In 2006 another 15-year-old boy shot a school principal in Cazenovia, Wisconsin. The 2007 attacks involved an 18-year-old in Tacoma, Washington, and a 14-year-old in Cleveland, Ohio.

These events drew considerable media attention not only because of the loss of life and violence involved, but because they appeared quite distinct from the concerns about youth violence that had dominated the 1980s and early 1990s. Indeed, the third edition of this textbook began with an episode involving what a local paper referred to as "a simmering crack-cocaine turf war" and the "bloodiest ever gang fight" (Jensen and Rojek, 1998:2). The major focus between the second (1992) and third editions (1998) of this text was the escalation of violence, especially gang violence, among minority youth in America's major metropolitan areas.

Episodes such as Jonesboro, Columbine, Red Lake, and others were different. They did not involve warfare between rival gangs, attempts to control turf or drug markets, or robbery, and some of the youth committed suicide at the end of the massacre. Old clichés to "get tough" and use the death penalty could not be invoked for Columbine since the boys imposed the death penalty on themselves, as did the boys in the Red Lake and Cleveland episodes. Conceptions of delinquency and youth crime as products of poverty, urban decay, and inner city schools did not seem to apply.

The media and ideological pundits pointed to the "usual suspects" to explain these school shootings: widespread exposure to violence in films, television, and video games; a decline in religion; easy access to guns; and parental neglect. The subsequent debate about Jonesboro, Columbine, and the other school shootings also pointed a finger at the juvenile justice system. The boys involved ranged in age from 11 to 18. All but the 18-year-old fell in the age range under jurisdiction of the juvenile court, although after much debate over the appropriate jurisdiction, the 15-year-old boy in Tennessee was transferred to the adult system. As with prior episodes or "waves" of violence involving young people, the critical commentary about today's youth inevitably turned to the modern legal institution created to deal with the problems of youth—the juvenile justice system.

The Jonesboro shootings involved youth too young (11 and 13) to be dealt with by the adult criminal justice system, resulting in what many critics consider to be insufficient punishment. Those who lost children, spouses, and family members may legitimately feel that justice was not served, and that keeping the boys under the jurisdiction of the juvenile court meant that the punishment would not fit the crime. Although such dramatic cases actually are rare, the juvenile justice system tends to be judged based on their outcomes.

The Columbine shootings raised several issues involving the juvenile court. Harris and Klebold had been arrested as juveniles in 1998 for breaking into a van and stealing tools. Because of their age at that time, they were processed by the juvenile court and placed in a diversion program that required restitution and community service as opposed to time in detention or confinement in a correctional center (see chapter 9). Because juvenile court records are treated as confidential, details of their involvement were not revealed until a judge ordered the records released in 2002. The judge believed it was in the interest of the people of Colorado to assess whether this juvenile court program had failed.

Like juvenile court records, juvenile justice proceedings are not open to the public and the media for scrutiny, generating considerable suspicion about the system's effectiveness in dealing with the problems and offenses of juveniles. When episodes such as Columbine occur, all sorts of questions are raised. Were there no signs that the boys were headed for trouble? Could the juvenile court program have identified their problems and intervened to prevent escalation? In the wake of Columbine and the other school shootings, the juvenile justice system, schools, and parents were subject to critical scrutiny for failing to intervene more harshly when there were "obvious" clues that should have prompted intervention. After-the-fact analyses by criminologists revealed that at least six of eight offenders had made verbal threats prior to their actual crimes, had experienced some form of rejection, especially peer rejection, were interested in violent media of some kind, had been involved in prior violence, had expressed suicidal thoughts and thoughts of violence in their writings, and had a fascination with and access to guns (Kidd and Meyer, 2000). Many of these warning signs were known before the shootings, so why was there no intervention by schools, parents, or the juvenile justice system?

The answer rests with the frequency of such behavior among adolescents. Some of these warning signs are so common (see box 1-1) that most teenagers would become suspects. Many teenagers have felt rejected at some time, and sizeable numbers have an interest in some form of media with violent content. Approximately one in every five high school students has thought seriously about committing suicide in the span of a year (Centers for Disease Control and Prevention, 2000). Expressions of anger and threats of violence are quite common as well. About 14 percent of male seniors in high

Box 1-1   Warning Signs?

Criminologists can identify shared characteristics of those youths involved in school shootings. Why is it difficult to predict which specific youth are likely to be involved based on that information?

Source: Borgman © 1999 The Cincinnati Enquirer. Reprinted by permission of Universal Press Syndicate. All rights reserved.

school have been involved in a serious fight and 18 percent report having hurt someone seriously in the preceding 12 months (Johnston, Bachman, and O'Malley, 2005). In fact, such experiences are nothing new for high-school students (see chapter 4).

In the midst of the media frenzy and the desire to do something to prevent further violence, it is easy to lose sight of the fact that such events garner so much attention partly because they are rare. Indeed, the school shootings occurred in the context of an overall decline in school violence during the 1990s. Violent crimes against students ages 12 through 18 at school had declined from nearly 60 incidents per 1,000 students in 1993 to around 43 in 1998 (Small and Terrick, 2001:7). In fact, juvenile violence in general was declining during much of that decade (see chapter 3). Violence away from school had declined from about 70 incidents per 1,000 to 50 per 1,000. Moreover, when considered as a percentage of homicides involving juveniles, school fatalities accounted for between .4 to 1.5 percent of homicides during the 1990s. In sum, the surge in school shootings was not part of an ongoing or developing trend. In general, schools are relatively safe havens for most youth. In fact, 80 percent of schools studied by the National Center for Educational Statistics (2003) in an effort to measure the problem were found to have no episodes of serious violence in a given year.

Youth as a Perennial "Problem"

Expressions of concern and alarm about the behavior and offenses of youth, and a tendency to view the situation as progressively worse than in preceding generations, may be as old as written history. Consider, for example, the following anguished statement:

> Youth is disintegrating. The youngsters of the land have a disrespect for their elders, and a contempt for authority in every form. Vandalism is rife, and crime of all kinds is rampant among our young people. The nation is in peril. (Madison, 1970)

Although this lament appears to be a contemporary critique of youth in modern industrial society, it is alleged to date back some four thousand years to a despondent Egyptian priest.

During the Golden Age of Greece (500–300 BC), Socrates was quite disgruntled with the youth of his day, as evidenced by his claim that

> children today love luxury. They have bad manners, a contempt for authority, a disrespect for their elders, and they like to talk instead of work. They contradict their parents, chatter before company, gobble up the best at the table, and tyrannize over their teachers.

A seventeenth-century English philanthropist expressed these same concerns, lamenting the rudeness of young children who

> wrangle and cheat one another, and upon the least Provocation, swear and fight for a Farthing, or else shall be found whipping of Horses . . . or else shall be throwing of Dirt or Stones into Coaches, or at the Glasses. (T)hey have neither been taught their Duties either towards God or Man. (Jensen and Rojek, 1980:2)

At the turn of the twentieth century, youth were viewed as a problem requiring the invention of a new legal institution, the juvenile court. In that sense, juvenile delinquency is a relatively new dimension of the crime problem since juvenile courts and legislation dealing exclusively with the offenses of children are products of modern times. In the United States, Illinois was the first state to pass a juvenile court act (1899) and Wyoming the last to enact such legislation (1945). Toronto (1912) was among the first Canadian cities to establish a court for juveniles (Hagan and Leon, 1977). India passed its first juvenile statutes in 1920 (Priyadarsini and Hartjen, 1981). A major impetus for creating these new institutions was the perception that offenses of the young were a growing dimension of the crime problem requiring special legal attention. For some that special attention emphasized treatment and nonpunitive mechanisms for addressing troubled youth, but for others it was necessary because youth were not being treated early enough and harshly enough by the adult criminal justice system (see chapter 2).

In the 1950s, the billboard for the movie *Rebel without a Cause* depicted the James Dean character as a "teenager who thinks he has to be bad to make good." The film told the story of "a teenage kid caught in the undertow of today's juvenile violence." These are the same 1950s that often are depicted as "the good old days." In retrospect,

---

Box 1-2 The Perennial Problem of Youth and the Myth of the "Good Old Days"

When discussing the problems of youth, some span of time in the past is viewed typically as the "Good Old Days," and young people are viewed as worse than they have ever been. Have you experienced these themes while growing up and listening to parents, teachers, and others? Why do you think youth are viewed as a perennial threat?

Source: Hagar © King Features Syndicate. Momma © 1998 Mell Lazarus. Reprinted my permission of Mell Lazarus and Creator's Syndicate, Inc.

the 1950s were characterized by low crime rates, with Americans busy generating the baby boom that would become a social problem when the babies became teenagers in the 1960s. There was an upswing in the murder rate during this time as returning soldiers, lovers, and wives resolved their relationships, but delinquency was not the problem, at least statistically speaking. Yet, the same grave concerns and warnings about disintegrating society and rebellious youth were expressed in the 1950s as during other decades, and experts on youth mounted national movements to censor comic books, movies, and the newly emerging threat of television.

In the late 1960s the President's Commission on Law Enforcement and Administration of Justice concluded that "youth is responsible for a substantial and disproportionate part of the national crime problem," and that "America's best hope for reducing crime is to reduce juvenile delinquency and youth crime" (1967:169–70). The popular press depicted the problem even more dramatically, referring to the situation as the "youth crime plague" (*Time*, 1977:18) or as an example of remorseless teenagers "running amuck" (*Time*, 1989). Alfred Regnery, a past administrator of the Office of Juvenile Justice and Delinquency Prevention (OJJDP), viewed juvenile crime as a "grave problem on a national scale" with a "staggering" range and intensity (1985:65). In 1997, Congressman William McCollum of Florida was quoted for stating that young offenders today are ". . . the most dangerous criminals on the face of the earth" (Macallair and Males, 2000:1). In short, each new generation of adults reinvents the belief that the world is in the biggest mess it's ever been in, that youth are worse than in "the good old days," and that young people are the major contributors to the crime problem.

Juveniles in Conflict with the Law

It is a fact that a substantial proportion of young people have conflicts with the law before they reach adulthood. Based on several studies where youths' histories were compiled and analyzed, the National Center for Juvenile Justice estimates that about one-third of juveniles acquire a police record by the time they reach age 18. For example, by the time a cohort of boys born in Philadelphia in 1945 reached their 18th birthdays, 35 percent of them had acquired a record with the police (Wolfgang, Figlio, and Sellin, 1972). In a study conducted in rural Oregon, one-fourth of the males acquired records with the county juvenile department by that age (Polk, 1974). In Racine, Wisconsin, more than one-half of male youths born in either 1942, 1949, or 1955 had some contact with the police before they were adults (Shannon, 1982). In an urban, white, working-class London neighborhood, one-fourth of males born in 1953 had been convicted for "delinquency" by age 18 (West, 1982). Thus, based on studies in a variety of communities in more than one nation it is safe to conclude that a considerable proportion of youth do get into trouble with the law.

In some situations such trouble may be as much the rule as the exception. For example, in the Philadelphia cohort study about 50 percent of the nonwhite males, in contrast to nearly 30 percent of the white males, had acquired police records between ages 7 and 18. Such conflicts appear more likely for boys than for girls, for urban youths than for rural youths (Snyder and Nimick, 1983), and for youths in urban, industrialized societies than for youths in agrarian nations (Clinard and Abbott, 1973; Priyadarsini and Hartjen, 1981). Thus, while conflict with the law is quite common, it is more common in some settings and categories of youth than in others.

Undetected Lawbreaking

Although a sizable proportion of youth acquire an official record, an even greater proportion engage, without detection, in activities that are a potential source of conflict with the law. Data from a national survey of high school seniors showed that during 2005, 23 percent of girls and 27 percent of boys admitted shoplifting within the twelve months preceding the survey. Twenty-one percent of senior girls indicated having "taken something not belonging to you worth under $50" as did 34 percent of senior boys. Eighteen percent of senior boys reported having hurt someone badly enough that the person needed a doctor, compared to 6 percent of girls (Johnston, Bachman, and O'Malley, 2005). Involvement in some form of delinquency is common adolescent behavior and surveys over several decades suggest that it has been common for a considerable period of time.

Similar results have been reported in studies of youth in parts of London (West and Farrington, 1973) and other communities in England (Belson, 1978) as well as Canada (Hagan, Gillis, and Simpson, 1985), India (Hartjen and Kethineni, 1992), and Taiwan (Wang and Jensen, 2003). When youth are asked to report on their offense behavior they report much more delinquent activity than is ever reflected in police or court statistics. In fact, international self-report surveys have shown that youths in the United States do not dominate the statistics on property crime or drug use but do have unusually high prevalence of self-reported violence (Junger-Tas, Haen, and Ribeau, 2003).

Overrepresentation in Arrest Statistics

It is commonly observed that juveniles represent a disproportionate amount of arrests compared to adults. In table 1-1 we have summarized the percentage of arrests accounted for by people ages 10 through 17, as reported in the Federal Bureau of Investigation's Uniform Crime Report (UCR) for 2006. People ages 10 through 17 make up about 12 percent of the population, which means that when their offenses account for more than 12 percent of arrests they would be considered *overrepresented* in the arrest statistics. Table 1-1 shows that in 2006 offenses by youths ages 10–17 were clearly overrepresented by nearly two to four times in arrests for arson, vandalism, disorderly conduct, robbery, burglary, motor vehicle theft, larceny, and weapons offenses. They are somewhat overrepresented for liquor law violations, simple assaults, sex offenses other than rape, gambling, rape, and buying or possessing stolen property. They are about proportionately represented for aggravated assault. They account for 10 percent of arrests for murder and drug abuse and are underrepresented for the remaining offense categories. When all offenses are added together, juveniles account for more arrests than expected (16 percent). In short, despite the amount of attention paid to murder committed by juveniles, it is not disproportionately common. Among youths ages 10 through 17, theft of and attacks on property are the most distinctive.

It is common for people to believe that juveniles are getting worse and accounting for a growing share of the problem. The validity of that belief depends on the specific years compared. For example, in 1988 persons 10 through 17 years of age accounted for about 11 percent of arrests for murder compared to 15 percent in 1996. However, by 2002 it was back down to 11 percent and 9 percent by 2003. In 1988 juveniles

Table 1-1   Percent of Arrests Accounted for by Youths Age 10–17

Arson	46%	Rape	15%
Vandalism	38%	Vagrancy	14%
Disorderly	29%	Aggravated Assaults	13%
Robbery	28%	Drug Abuse	10%
Burglary	27%	Murder	10%
Motor Vehicle Theft	25%	Embezzlement	7%
Larceny	25%	Family and Children	4%
Weapons	23%	Forgery and Embezzlement	3%
Liquor Laws	22%	Drunkenness	3%
Simple Assaults	19%	Fraud	3%
Other Sex	18%	Prostitution/Vice	2%
Gambling	18%	Driving Under Influence	1%
Stolen Property	17%	**All Offenses**	**16%**

Source: Federal Bureau of Investigation. 2007. *Crime in the United States, 2006.*

accounted for 22 percent of robberies compared to 32 percent in 1996. Again, contributions to robbery arrests were down to 24 percent by 2003. Their overall contribution to arrests was 19 percent in 1996 compared to 14 percent in 1988, but was down to 16 percent by 2003. Juveniles accounted for a growing share of arrests for violent crimes in the early 1990s, but that surge was short-lived and had disappeared by the early twenty-first century. Some criminologists attributed that particular surge to the emergence of crack markets and measures taken by other youths to protect themselves from such violence (Blumstein, 1995).

We will consider variations in crime and delinquency over time in chapters 3 and 4, but it is important to note here that downturns are not accorded the same fanfare that surrounds upturns. When there is a surge in crime, there is a rush to attribute blame—violence in the media, the failure of juvenile justice, availability of guns, militarism, a decline in moral values, the breakdown of the family, and a variety of other possible causes. Criminologists are interested in both peaks and valleys, but the valleys are rarely the subject of popular or media discourse.

Juvenile Delinquency and Adult Crime

All of the foregoing observations—the enduring historical concern with the misbehavior of the young, the proportion of juveniles involved in illegal activities, the disproportionate contribution of juveniles to arrest statistics—have been the traditional justifications for devoting an extraordinary amount of attention to delinquency as a major aspect of crime in America. To put juvenile delinquency in proper perspective, however, we need to make some observations about juvenile crime in relation to the adult world and adult crime.

Overrepresentation of Young Adults in Violent Crime

Although government commissions, numerous politicians, and the popular press have dramatized the importance of addressing juvenile delinquency as America's "best hope" for reducing crime in general, this point of view has certain shortcomings. First, robbery is the only interpersonal offense that peaks among males under 18 years of age. Crimes of interpersonal violence peak among young people, but the peaks tend to occur in the young adult years. Moreover, it is important to remember that juveniles 10 to 17 years of age account for only 12 percent of the population. Their 16 percent share of arrests is higher than expected, but most crimes in America are committed by persons subject to the adult criminal justice jurisdiction.

Group Delinquency and Arrests

Second, the way in which arrest statistics are presented can affect images of the degree to which juveniles are responsible for crimes. Over two decades ago, Howard Snyder and Ellen Nimick argued that the UCR "has led to a distorted perception of the actual contribution of juveniles to serious crimes" (1983:49). Juveniles are more likely than adults to commit their crimes in groups and, hence, although one offense may be committed it may result in several arrests. Snyder and Nimick estimated that while people under 18 accounted for four of every ten *persons arrested* for serious property crime at that time, they actually accounted for about three in ten property *crimes cleared by an arrest*. Thus, the contribution of juveniles to crime statistics is more dramatic when number of persons arrested is considered than when crimes cleared by an arrest is the focus. The group nature of delinquency may exaggerate juvenile criminal activity and increase the visibility and hazard of arrest when juveniles commit offenses.

In response to such criticism, the UCR began reporting crimes cleared by an arrest of a juvenile or juveniles in addition to the percent of persons arrested (see figure 1-1). The traditional way of analyzing arrests shows persons under 18 accounted for 26 percent of persons arrested for the FBI's property crimes while about 19 percent of offenses were cleared by the arrest of someone in that age group. The figure for violent crime is lower when offenses cleared by an arrest is considered (13 percent) than when number of arrests is considered (16 percent).

The group nature of delinquency not only exaggerates arrest statistics but also may be relevant to understanding public fear of delinquency. Among the most readily dramatized crimes are those involving groups of youth attacking relatively helpless victims. Incidents of group attacks on randomly encountered victims, such as the "Central Park jogger" case in New York City, arouse great public concern and establish an image of delinquency as senseless violence by groups of youths. Most delinquency does occur in groups and most juveniles engage in some form of group delinquency at some time, but the outcome in terms of the proportion of crimes committed is not particularly dramatic compared to other age groups.

Changing Contribution to Arrest Statistics

Third, while increases in juvenile violence have received considerable publicity in the media, those changes should be put in perspective. Persons under 18 accounted for decreasing shares of property crime from the mid-1970s until 1990, when the percent

Figure 1-1   Percent of Offenses Cleared by Arrest of a Person Under 18 and Percent of All Arrests Accounted for by Persons Under 18

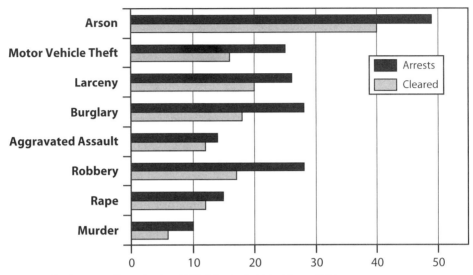

Source: Federal Bureau of Investigation. 2007. *Crime in the United States, 2006.*

of property crimes cleared by arrest of persons under 18 rose again. Similarly, the surge in juvenile violence in the 1990s brought their contribution back up to the level attained in the early 1970s. As the Office of Juvenile Justice and Delinquency Prevention recently observed, "Even with these large increases . . . juveniles are not responsible for most of the increase in recent years. If juvenile violence had not increased between 1988 and 1992, the U.S. violent crime rate would have increased 16 percent instead of 23 percent" (Snyder and Sickmund, 1995:iv).

Since the peaks in juvenile arrests in the 1990s, their rates for both property crime and violence have been declining and youth have been accounting for declining shares of the crime problem as measured by the FBI. The image of young people as "the most dangerous criminals on the face of the earth" is not consistent with available data on youth crime and delinquency.

Underrepresentation of Serious Adult Crimes

A fourth point concerning juvenile delinquency in relation to adult crime is that our major body of statistics on crime in the United States presents a biased picture of the crime problem. The FBI's annual Uniform Crime Report provides statistics on eight specific offenses—criminal homicide, forcible rape, robbery, aggravated assault, burglary, larceny, motor vehicle theft, and arson. Together these offenses constitute the **serious-crime index**. Four of the offenses included in the index (robbery, burglary, larceny, and motor vehicle theft) accounted for nearly 90 percent of all index crimes. Larceny (theft) alone accounted for nearly 60 percent of the index crimes in the United States. In sum, the index is heavily weighted with property offenses that are unusually common among juveniles.

Many crimes that are not included in the index of serious crime—for example, consumer fraud, fraud, child abuse, drunken driving, drunkenness, gambling, prostitution, and vice—are more characteristic of adults than juveniles. Further, there are innumerable offenses such as price fixing, income-tax evasion, and shoddy business practices that are not treated as criminal offenses. These offenses are not included in the serious-crime index because they are more likely to go unreported or because they are less reliably reported than other offenses. It seems clear, then, that there are grounds for challenging the view that adult crimes are "less serious" than those of juveniles.

Using the FBI's estimates of dollar costs of the four property offenses in 2002, the estimated loss due to juveniles ages 10–17 was about $5.5 billion in that year. This may strike people as a huge figure, but it has to be put in the context of adult-controlled crime. First, the loss due to adults for those same offenses is around $12 billion. However, the comparison becomes more dramatic when one considers losses due to such adult-dominated episodes as the failures of government-insured savings and loan institutions in the 1980s and 1990s. Considered "the biggest heist in U.S. history" (Pizzo, Fricker, and Muolo, 1989), the failures were as much a product of intentional fraud and illegal practices as of economic conditions. Politicians, banking executives, and entrepreneurs played a major role in deregulating the thrift industry while maintaining government insurance on deposits. They then took advantage of the deregulation through reckless and questionable loans, illegal appraisals, and collusion to artificially inflate their assets. When the outcome anticipated by opponents of deregulation occurred, the offenders escaped by taking advantage of bankruptcy laws and left the American public with the bill. The estimated loss for that scandalous episode was at least $500 billion (Calavita, Pontell, and Tillman, 1997). If the recent fraud scandal involving Enron, estimated to have resulted in losses to stockholders of $236 billion, and other ongoing cases of corporate fraud were added to this list, it is certainly safe to conclude that the cost of misappropriation of property by offenders "in the suites" exceeds the cost of juvenile misappropriations "in the streets" by many, many times. The two scandals alone equaled more than a hundred years' worth of juvenile property crime.

Organized crime is another costly enterprise run by and profitable for adults. Yet, organized crime activities are not likely to enter into crime statistics, and those caught engaging in such activities are not likely to be those who profit the most. Organized crime is involved in a host of illegal pursuits that ranges from fraud and corruption to murder. Organized crime's involvement in gambling alone is estimated to result in greater economic loss than all eight of the offenses in the FBI's serious-crime index. Moreover, organized crime uses the profits from the supply of illicit goods and services to gain control of other economic institutions and to corrupt the political system. Syndicated criminal organizations are not the domain of juveniles. Juveniles are found within these criminal confederations only at the "street level," where profits and power are minimal.

It is easy to show that adult-controlled crimes result in far greater economic losses than juvenile crime. It is much more difficult, however, to assess the amount of misery, pain, and suffering that adult-controlled crime may generate. How many Americans have suffered as a result of fraudulent health devices and misrepresented drugs? How many have suffered because of price fixing and its impact on everyday budgets?

How much do we suffer when government and big business violate or circumvent laws governing their activities? The public tends to react most severely to crimes involving direct attacks against people and property in which there are clearly defined victims and offenders. Yet, offenses that involve *indirect* and *collective* attacks against us all take a far greater toll.

To put juvenile delinquency in perspective, we also have to ask how fraud, corruption, and the violation of positions of trust affect attitudes toward law and authority. In the early 1940s Edwin Sutherland (1940) argued that white-collar crime or crimes committed by persons in violation of their positions of trust not only are a serious form of crime in terms of financial loss but, more importantly, also contribute to distrust on a wide scale. Unethical and illegal practices spread from person to person and from one business or occupational group to another, resulting in a general disrespect for the law by "noncriminals." Studies of occupational offenders indicate that while many feel *they* can violate the law with impunity ("business is business"), they also feel little shame in attributing the "crime problem" to others.

Another type of crime that began to generate increasing national concern in the last twenty-five years is child abuse. The image of the delinquent juvenile preying on a weaker victim is mirrored by parents who inflict considerable pain and suffering on their children. Despite the fact that most child abuse does not make its way into police statistics, close to 3 million children were estimated to be "maltreated" in 1993, about double the number of victims in 1986. By 2003 it was about 5.5 million (U.S. Dept. of Health and Human Services, 1996, 2003). An interview study of a nationally representative sample of 1,146 families with children ages 3 through 17 living at home measured violent acts that had a high probability of causing injury, and found that about 18 percent of mothers indicated at least one severe violent act towards one of their children (Gelles and Hargreaves, 1981). Richard Gelles and Murray Straus (1985) concluded that child abuse and neglect had reached epidemic proportions. Although this apparent surge has been found to be more a product of increased attention to the problem than of actual increases in abuse (see chapter 7), there are certainly grounds for alarm.

If speculation that abused children may be likely to become abusive parents is correct, then child abuse becomes part of a vicious cycle where violence breeds violence. There is already evidence which suggests that abused children are more likely to acquire an adult criminal record than nonabused children, including a higher frequency of arrest for violent crimes as adults (Widom, 1989). Moreover, such children report significantly more delinquency than found among nonabused children (Smith and Thornberry, 1995). In short, the problem of juvenile delinquency and youth crime appears to be linked with problems of parental adult violence.

Although a case can be made for the hypothesis that reductions in adult crime might lower juvenile delinquency, the more common argument is that "nipping it in the bud" early in a person's life would reduce the adult crime rate. This view strikes many as obvious because most adult offenders are found to have been juvenile offenders. Moreover, when the early intervention approach is advocated it tends to be accompanied by a "get-tough" perspective that assumes early punitive intervention would reduce the prospects of adult crime. If adult offenders were juvenile offenders, would not early punishment lower the prospects of adult crime?

At present, there is little or no evidence that a get-tough policy at the juvenile level will lower the odds of persistence in offending. Criminologists have noted the "paradox of persistence" (Cohen and Villa, 1996). The paradox is that when looking backward from adult offenders, there is a high probability of persistence. Yet, when looking forward, most juvenile offenders do not go on to adult criminal careers. This desistence may be due to **maturational reform** or changing social circumstances linked to age. It might even reflect the success of the juvenile court.

In a study of youths processed in California, Michael Ezell and Lawrence Cohen (2005) could find no evidence that the implementation of get-tough policies had the anticipated effect on the persistence of juvenile offenders. Those juveniles who committed offenses during times when punishments were relatively lenient had similar persistence rates to those committing offenses during more punitive times. Some criminologists have suggested that a tougher approach with a greater proportion of juvenile offenders could actually increase adult criminality (see chapter 11).

Public Opinion about Crime

Another justification for paying an inordinate amount of attention to juvenile crime might be public opinion. If there were a general consensus that the types of crimes disproportionately involving juveniles are the most serious crimes, then the severity of public condemnation would justify concentration on the topic. That, however, does not seem to be the case.

A 1984 study by the Bureau of Justice Statistics sought an answer to the question, "How do people rank the severity of crime?" They surveyed 60,000 people 18 years of age or older, assigning a base score of 10 to the following crime: "A person steals a bicycle parked on the street." Respondents were asked to assign scores to a wide range of crimes in comparison to that crime. The Bureau concluded:

> The overall pattern of severity scores indicates that people clearly regard violent crimes as more serious than property offenses. They also take white-collar crime and drug dealing quite seriously, rating two offenses of this type higher than some forms of homicide. One of the highest scores (39.1) is awarded to the factory that causes the death of twenty people by knowingly polluting the city water supply. (Bureau of Justice Statistics, 1984:5)

A legislator who accepts a bribe received a higher severity score than many of the FBI's so-called serious crimes. Doctors cheating on insurance claims received higher scores than most forms of larceny. The serious-crime index includes data on crimes which, it would seem, are considered less serious than several kinds of crime which are not reflected in crime statistics.

One component of public opinion that might help explain the attention given to juvenile crime is the early intervention philosophy, which suggests that by dealing with juvenile delinquency we are dealing with the roots of the crime problem. However, we can find as much justification for the position that an attack on adult-controlled criminal organizations would combat crime just as effectively. Delinquency and the transgressions of the young must be viewed in context. It is misleading to concentrate on relatively powerless segments of American society when crime is intimately linked to institutions that adults control and to values and practices that are passed from one generation to the next. The youth crime "plague" is paralleled by numerous other patterns of crime that can be presented in equally dramatic terms. White-collar crime can be depicted as a pernicious plague as can political corruption, organized crime, and child abuse.

It is understandable that indignation and concern are readily expressed about crimes in which there are clear-cut victims and offenders. Moreover, such crimes may be of particular concern when the offenders are young. It is important to note, however, that there are other criteria for assessing the seriousness of crime and a variety of reasonable arguments suggesting that juvenile delinquency may not be *the* most significant dimension of the crime problem.

Why Study Delinquency?

If we accept the argument that delinquency is not the most serious dimension of the crime problem, then why devote an entire textbook to it? In the preceding discussion we have tried to put delinquency in the context of other forms of crime. We have pointed out that there are grounds for arguing that crime involving adults is far more costly than crime involving juveniles and that delinquency qualifies neither as the most serious nor as the primary dimension of our crime problem. On the other hand, it is only through years of study that we can begin to question popular images and conceptions of the crime problem and to put juvenile delinquency in proper perspective. Delinquency is *one* dimension of our overall crime problem—one that has generated considerable public and political concern.

Moreover, while offenses among youth may be facilitated by the messages conveyed and institutions controlled by the adult world, the probability that people will commit common forms of adult crime is greater among people who had trouble with the law when young. In fact, the single best predictor of adult criminality is childhood or juvenile criminality (see Gottfredson and Hirschi, 1990). If the probability of juvenile delinquency is reduced, it could have an effect on subsequent adult crime. We cannot say whether this holds true for white-collar crime. Some theorists argue that children who are raised in families where parents wield power and authority are encouraged to take risks and that this orientation is reflected in common forms of undetected delinquency (i.e., shoplifting) as well as entrepreneurial risk-taking as adults (Hagan, Gillis, and Simpson, 1985). Such arguments imply a link between undetected delinquency among advantaged youth and white-collar crime. In sum, the correlation between delinquency and adult crime may be reciprocal, with each reinforcing the other.

In addition, delinquency is an illustrative subject matter for studying the forces that affect our laws and human behavior. Since the study of delinquency looks at activities, conflicts, and experiences that are familiar to most of us, it is also a convenient mechanism for studying ourselves and the everyday experiences affecting our lives. Self-understanding and insight into the operation of our social world can be rewarding in their own right. To the degree that each of us influences young people as parents, teachers, or friends, understanding the impact of different styles of family life, school experiences, and other circumstances which contribute to or inhibit delinquency can be useful for our own choices and personal policies.

Although few have challenged whether we need a criminal justice system, there is continual debate over whether we need a separate system for juveniles. The system has been criticized both for being too tough on juveniles and ignoring their rights and for being too soft and unconcerned with retribution or victims. Both positions have had their advocates throughout the history of the juvenile court. It is easy to lose sight of the social forces and arguments behind the development of a separate juvenile court system and to repeatedly discover the same inherent problems. Although an understanding of the system's history will not resolve the debate, it is worthwhile to discern what issues are of continuing concern. If the juvenile justice system generates debate because it is expected to serve a variety of conflicting goals, then mere recognition of this fact might facilitate more constructive discussions and proposals. The study of juvenile justice provides us with lessons in the politics and sociology of law and legal institutions.

Whether the student of delinquency is radical, liberal, moderate, or conservative, he or she is likely to view delinquency as a problem about which something should be done. There are many different opinions about what form that "something" should take. For some people part of the delinquency problem can be attributed to the nature of the laws that define delinquency as a legal category. The laws are vague and encompass behaviors and situations calling for social rather than legal intervention. To others the answer rests with identifying the causes of delinquent behavior. If generating forces or circumstances can be identified, then delinquency might be reduced by altering such circumstances.

Still others believe that part of the problem is attributable to inadequacies in the juvenile justice system and our reactions to it. Some think the system is too punitive and others think it is too lenient. Proposed solutions range from revolutionary change in our social-economical-political system to programs aimed at early identification and intervention. Whenever we choose among alternative solutions or merely declare that "something" ought to be done, we are making a moral decision. Hence, the study of delinquency forces us to consider our own moral and political beliefs and commitments, their implications for responding to delinquency, and their accuracy in relation to years of research on the topic.

Finally, the study of delinquency is central to the development of a scholarly tradition or field of study called **criminology**. As we study delinquency we will learn about criminology and a variety of possible careers. The study of delinquency has been particularly central to the development of sociological criminology as an academic field in American universities. This text examines delinquency in the context of the larger discipline of criminology and is organized in terms of the topics that have come to define that discipline. Hence, we will briefly discuss criminology and its relevance for organizing our study of delinquency.

Criminology and the Study of Delinquency

Criminology is most simply defined as the study of crime. Of course, the word "study" is a vague term that can encompass everything from a casual interest in crime to scientific research on determinants of criminal behavior. However, to most people the "... ologies" refer to fields of study involving specialists or people with special expertise on a topic.

The title "criminologist" is most likely to evoke an image of police investigators or forensic scientists analyzing evidence and solving crimes. Since crime is police business, the study of crime is typically thought of by the public as a police activity. Yet, when people go to college and take courses on crime and delinquency or decide to pursue advanced degrees in criminology they soon discover that there are a variety of specialists and a wide range of different "criminologies." This diversity is reflected in the membership of the American Society of Criminology, which includes sociologists, psychologists, anthropologists, biologists, economists, political scientists, lawyers, judges, police, and other professionals interested in crime.

One trait that most criminologists have in common is a commitment to the view that crime can be and should be studied following those standards or principles referred to as the **scientific method**. No matter what the particular discipline, criminology tends to be treated as a science, and such a designation has certain implications for the way in which criminology is approached. For one, as with any science, the aim is to discover and explain orderly patterns or regularities in the subject matter. A criminologist studying delinquency might be interested in whether certain types of delinquency are more common among central-city youth than youth in rural settings. Others might be interested in whether children with a measurable value in terms of a certain characteristic (e.g., low grades, child abuse) have a greater probability of involvement in delinquency than children with a different value for that characteristic (e.g., high grades, nonabuse). Some criminologists spend their time trying to account for changes in the extent or nature of different types of crime over time. Whatever the specific topic, criminologists share an interest in uncovering some type of meaningful order to the crime problem and explaining what generates that order. Some take the additional step of drawing implications about the alleviation of crime from such findings.

Modern criminologists are also committed to discerning such order and regularity through the systematic collection of data or evidence that can be verified by others. For much of the history of human discourse the standard for truth was the power or authority of the person making a declaration. There is always some tendency to accept declarations of truth when they are advanced by people we respect or admire, but the standard of truth in a science is verifiable evidence. For example, if a criminologist states that males commit more delinquent offenses than females, this statement should not be accepted merely because of the power or authority of the criminologist but on the basis of the data or information used to justify the claim. It should be verifiable in the sense that other people could gather and examine the same evidence and reach the same conclusion. The ability to do so may require some training, but that is exactly the purpose of this book.

Since much of the evidence used by criminologists is statistical in nature, it is common for people to claim that "you can say anything with statistics," implying that it is impossible to know when a researcher is lying or mistaken. If it is truly impossible, then there is no such thing as verifiable evidence and no way to decide what is truthful and what is not. However, if we really want to gain an understanding of crime, then our task is to learn abut the types of scientific evidence that are used to study crimes. With such knowledge, we can hope to be able to determine whether evidence is convincing given what we know about the problems encountered when using such data or evidence in the past. Thus, to approach a matter scientifically requires that it be approached very critically. Evidence must be assessed and questioned.

One of the early and most influential texts on the subject defines criminology as the scientific study of "the processes of making laws, of breaking laws, and of reacting toward the breaking of laws" (Sutherland and Cressey, 1974:3). Each of these areas is a source of public concern and each may be studied with a view toward discovering, explaining, and tracing out the implications of regularities. Each of the three may be approached as a target for change.

Lawmaking

Historically, the search for the causes, or **etiology,** of lawbreaking and for ways of dealing with lawbreakers (penology) have dominated criminological inquiry. The central questions were: (1) Why do some people become involved in crime or delinquency? and (2) What can we do about it either before or after the fact? In the 1960s, however, a growing number of people became interested in a third question: (3) Why do we have the laws we have? For these people the crime problem is, at least in part, a problem of **overcriminalization** (that is, treating too many types of behavior as crime) and the proliferation of laws "creating" crime. For example, after an extensive analysis of the drug problem in the United States, Erich Goode (1989) argued that our drug laws and their enforcement are primarily responsible for some of the most serious and harmful characteristics of the drug problem. By criminalizing drug use, the law can actually sustain a subculture, support an illicit market, drive users to crime, and create a host of other secondary problems. The view that laws exist to prevent or solve problems and to protect society has been countered with arguments that laws originally designed to cope with social problems may create new problems or may transform minor social problems into more serious ones (Rose, 1968).

In the 1970s critics of the juvenile justice system argued that too many kinds of youthful misbehavior were bringing youth to the attention of the court and that kids should be "left alone whenever possible" (Schur, 1973). A joint committee of the Institute for Judicial Administration and the American Bar Foundation (1977) advocated removing noncriminal behavior and victimless crimes from juvenile court jurisdiction as well. Some of these recommendations have been implemented (Holden and Kapler, 1995), reflecting perennial mandates to change the substance of laws as a remedy to some dimension of the delinquency problem.

Thus, at present, there appears to be widespread consensus that a comprehensive study of crime and delinquency requires consideration of the forces and processes involved in the making, as well as the breaking, of laws. Our attempts to explain lawbreaking are often based on *implicit* theories and assumptions about the nature of criminal law and the relation of people in a society to those laws. Therefore, in considering the sources and causes of criminal behavior, we are often assuming a certain perspective on the nature of laws whether or not we realize that fact.

Lawbreaking

The explanation of who becomes "delinquent" has been a persistent concern in criminological inquiry, dominating much of the earliest work and much, if not most, of the research over the last several decades as well. In pursuit of an explanation, criminologists have examined physical, biological, psychological, social, and cultural characteristics of people. Some criminologists have advanced explanations that stress abnormality, while others have suggested that criminal and delinquent behavior are learned and that the processes involved are basically the same as those through which all behavior and lifestyles are acquired. Detailed **case histories** and **ethnographies** carried out in the 1920s and 1930s supported the view that criminal behavior or delinquency is learned and not inherited (Thrasher, 1927; Shaw, 1930, 1931, 1938; Sutherland, 1937). More recent research has shown that whether we learn to be law-abiding or law-violating individuals, this learning process is essentially the same.

The roles of opportunities, values, and institutions such as schools, family, religion, and mass media in the causation of delinquency have been central foci in criminological research for several decades now. It is commonly presumed that if correlates or causes of lawbreaking can be identified, then one would be able to identify targets for preventive intervention or social change.

Reactions to Lawbreaking

We have already noted that an analysis of delinquency requires that we examine both lawmaking and lawbreaking. In addition, we should note that the study of law is one aspect of a larger concern—that is, the study of those forms of social control that involve "reactions to deviance." As Jack Gibbs has pointed out, a fundamental question in the study of social control is "What are the causes and consequences of variation in the character of reaction to deviance among social units over time?" (1972:4). The creation of laws or legal norms is one type of reaction to real or imagined problems and, hence, is a major aspect of the study of social control (Gibbs, 1989).

The dominant focus in the study of crime control has been **penology**—that branch of criminology concerned with the punishment and treatment of offenders and the administration of prisons. Although the study of prisons and other correctional programs remains a vital concern in criminology, social scientists have been increasingly concerned with the administration of justice in general and have been extending the study of crime control processes to include the police and the courts. Moreover, researchers have begun exploring community reactions to crime and the sources of public attitudes, beliefs, and fears about crime and crime control (Conklin, 1995:365–96). Numerous observers and researchers have pointed out that the public plays a key role in the implementation (or lack thereof) of **formal control processes** and that decisions to call the police, to press for action, and to provide testimony are problematic themselves (Black, 1970; Black and Reiss, 1970; Hawkins, 1973; Black, 1989). Thus, the study of reactions to crime and delinquency has been extended to encompass not only the operation of the justice system but the causes of public reaction to crime as well.

Organizing Our Inquiry

Our study of delinquency will be organized around the three basic issues defining the subject matter of criminology as already outlined: lawmaking, lawbreaking, and reactions to lawbreaking. In chapter 2 we will consider lawmaking. By exploring the nature, origin, and changes in juvenile law and juvenile justice we can gain an understanding of the forces that shape and sustain delinquency as a legal category and the juvenile court as a distinct legal institution.

In chapters 3 and 4 we will deal with *delinquent* and *delinquency* as labels applied to certain juveniles and certain behaviors by police and the courts. Given the existence of such a legal category as delinquency, how is it actually applied? Who gets labeled and why? Do data on officially labeled acts and persons give an accurate picture of the nature and distribution of delinquent activity? Criminologists must deal with such questions in order to assess the adequacy of certain bodies of data for reaching conclusions about delinquency.

Not everyone engages equally in the types of activities that are defined as delinquency, and students of crime and delinquency have come up with a wide range of explanations for this variability. Sociologists focus on the social and cultural environment as sources of variation. Others look to biological or genetic characteristics of individuals and groups. Still others have searched for the cause of delinquency in the individual's personality. Biological, psychological, and social psychological theory and research will be reviewed in chapter 5 and sociological perspectives in chapter 6.

While chapter 6 concentrates on theories and the research that supports them, chapters 7 and 8 summarize most of what is known about the role of the family, school, peers, religion, mass media, and the availability of guns in contributing to or inhibiting juvenile delinquency.

No study of delinquency is complete without a consideration of reactions to delinquency. At present, the issue of dominant concern to criminologists is the consequence of alternative reactions to delinquency. Does official processing, labeling, and punishment deter or encourage juvenile delinquency? Can community-based programs do a better job of inhibiting further delinquency than institutionalization of juvenile offenders? Can delinquency be reduced by diverting youth, making them compensate the victim or community, sending them to juvenile boot camps, or scaring them straight? In chapters 9, 10, and 11 we will explore these issues.

The concluding chapter will consider a much broader issue involving social policy and juvenile delinquency; that is, prevention. There we will grapple with complex and controversial issues: what meaning does all the research to date have for policy? If broad-scale change is called for, how far can we go and how far are we willing to go in dealing with the delinquency problem? What changes in our perspectives, values, and goals are we willing to consider? We cannot even take for granted that "something" must be done. Such decisions involve moral evaluations of delinquency and of the social arrangements that help produce delinquency.

Summary

Although juvenile delinquency as a legal category is a relatively recent invention, there is a long history of concern for the misbehavior of the young, as well as an enduring tendency to view crimes of the young as the major dimension of the crime problem. The view that certain categories of juveniles are quite commonly involved in crime is supported by police and court statistics and by behavioral reports in surveys of juveniles. However, it should be emphasized that (1) juveniles are most distinct in their high arrest rates for related property offenses, (2) the group nature of their offenses exaggerates their contribution to crime, (3) juvenile representation in arrest statistics has been declining in the last decade, and (4) juveniles are underrepresented in numerous types of crime that have a higher economic cost than juvenile property crimes. Delinquency is one dimension of the crime problem, but there are reasonable grounds for challenging the view that it is the most serious or primary dimension.

Yet, to study delinquency is to study an important element of the crime problem, particularly since adult crime and juvenile delinquency can reinforce one another. Such study also is a convenient vehicle for learning about ourselves and provides a foundation for making personal choices. Moreover, the study of delinquency has been central to the scientific discipline of criminology. Defining criminology as the scientific and critical study of lawmaking, lawbreaking, and reactions to lawbreaking, this text summarizes issues, theories, and research relevant to each of these topics in the study of juvenile delinquency and youth crime.

Discussion Questions

1. What was "unusual" about the dramatic attacks on schoolmates and teachers that captured headlines between 1996 and 2007? Were they part of a general trend toward increased violence in schools?

2. What feature of the juvenile justice system provokes suspicions about its role in society? Should the effectiveness of the system be judged based on the types of cases that draw media attention?

3. We tend to think of crime and delinquency as antisocial activities. In what sense are they antisocial? In what sense can it be said that juvenile delinquency is also a "social" activity?

4. What messages come to mind when examining the picture of the boy in the junkyard on the opening page of chapter 1?

5. How can the group nature of delinquency distort the image of the contribution of juveniles to the crime problem? What types of data on juvenile arrests illuminate that issue?

6. If all juvenile delinquency were to be eliminated would this solve our crime problem? Explain your answer.

7. For what types of crime are adolescents most overrepresented? For what types of crime are they underrepresented? What do you think accounts for these patterns?

8. What way of measuring delinquent behavior has shown it to be quite common in America? What proportion of youth would you guess have committed an offense for which they *could* have been arrested?

9. Identify and describe two different views of the relationship between adult crime and juvenile delinquency. Which affects the other?

10. What are the three topics encompassed by modern criminology? Give an example of how each topic is important for a thorough understanding of juvenile delinquency.

References

Bachman, J. G., L. D. Johnston, and P. M. O'Malley. 2004. *Monitoring the Future.* Ann Arbor, MI: Institute for Social Research.

Belson, W. A. 1978. *Television Violence and the Adolescent Boy.* Farnborough, England: Saxon House.

Black, D. J. 1970. "Production of Crime Rates." *American Sociological Review* 34 (August):733–48.

———. 1989. *Sociological Justice.* New York: Oxford University Press.

Black, D. J., and A. J. Reiss, Jr. 1970. "Police Control of Juveniles." *American Sociological Review* 35 (February):63–77.

Blumstein, A. 1995. *Violence by Young People: Why the Deadly Nexus?* National Institute of Justice, 229:2–9.

Bureau of Justice Statistics. 1984. "The Severity of Crime." *Bureau of Justice Statistics Bulletin,* NCJ–92326.

Calavita, K., H. N. Pontell, and R. Tillman. 1997. *Big Money Crime: Fraud and Politics in the Savings and Loan Crisis.* Berkeley: University of California Press.

CBS. 2005. "Jonesboro School Shooter Freed." August 11, 2005. [Online] http://www.cbsnews.com/stories/2005/08/11/national/main770335.shtml.

Centers for Disease Control and Prevention. 2000. "CDC Surveillance Summaries, June 9, 2000." *Morbidity and Mortality Weekly Report* 49 (No. SS-5):10.

Clinard, M., and W. Abbott. 1973. *Crime in Developing Countries: A Comparative Perspective.* New York: Wiley-Interscience.

Cohen, L. E., and B. J. Vila. 1996. "Self-Control and Social Control: An Exposition of the Gottfredson-Hirschi/Sampson-Laub Debate." *Studies on Crime and Crime Prevention* 5:125–50.

Conklin, J. E. 1995. *Criminology.* 5th ed. Boston: Allyn & Bacon.

Ezell, M. E., and L. E. Cohen. 2005. *Desisting from Crime: Continuity and Change in Long-term Patterns of Serious Chronic Offenders.* New York: Oxford University Press.

Federal Bureau of Investigation. 2007. *Crime in the United States, 2006.* Washington, DC: GPO.

Gelles, R. J., and E. F. Hargreaves. 1981. "Maternal Employment and Violence towards Children." *Journal of Family Issues* 2 (December):509–30.

Gelles, R. J., and M. Straus. 1985. *Is Violence Toward Children Increasing? A Comparison of 1975 and 1985 National Survey Rates.* Durham, NH: Family Violence Research Program.

Gibbs, J. P. 1972. "Social Control." New York: Warner Modular Publications, Module 1.

———. 1989. *Control: Sociology's Central Notion.* Urbana: University of Illinois Press.

Goode, E. 1989. *Drugs in American Society.* 3rd ed. New York: Alfred A. Knopf.

Gottfredson, M. R., and T. Hirschi. 1990. *A General Theory of Crime.* Stanford: Stanford University Press.

Hagan, J., A. R. Gillis, and J. Simpson. 1985. "Class Structure of Gender and Delinquency." *American Journal of Sociology* 90 (May):1151–78.

Hagan, J., and J. Leon. 1977. "Rediscovering Delinquency: Social History, Political Ideology and the Sociology of Law." *American Sociological Review* 42 (August):587–98.

Hartjen, C., and S. Kethineni. 1992. "Delinquency in Comparative Perspective: India." *International Journal of Comparative and Applied Criminal Justice* 16 (Fall):317–28.

Hawkins, R. 1973. "Who Called the Cops: Decisions to Report Criminal Victimization." *Law and Society Review* 7 (Spring):427–43.

Holden, G. A., and R. A. Kapler. 1995. "Deinstitutionalizing Status Offenders: A Record of Progress." *Juvenile Justice* 2 (Fall/Winter):3–10.

Institute for Judicial Administration and the American Bar Foundation. 1977. *Juvenile Justice Standards.* 24 vols. Cambridge, MA: Ballinger.

Jensen, G. F., and D. G. Rojek. 1980. *Delinquency: A Sociological View.* Lexington, MA: D. C. Heath.

———. 1998. *Delinquency and Youth Crime.* 3rd ed. Long Grove, IL: Waveland Press.

Junger-Tas, J., I. H. Marshall, and D. Ribeau. 2003. *Delinquency in an International Perspective: The International Self-Report Delinquency Study (ISRD)*. Monsey, NY: Criminal Justice Press.

Kidd, S. T., and C. L. Meyer. 2000. "Similarities of School Shootings in Rural and Small Town Communities." Paper presented at the Academy of Criminal Justice Sciences 38th Annual Meeting, Washington, DC.

Macallair, D., and M. Males. 2000. "Dispelling the Myth: An Analysis of Youth and Adult Crime Patterns in California over the Past 20 Years." San Francisco: Center on Juvenile and Criminal Justice.

Madison, A. 1970. *Vandalism: The Not-So-Senseless Crime*. New York: Seabury Press.

Maguire, K., and A. L. Pastore, eds. 2002. *Sourcebook of Criminal Justice Statistics, 2002*. U.S. Department of Justice, Bureau of Justice Statistics. Washington, DC: GPO.

National Center for Educational Statistics. 2003. *Violence in Public Schools: 2000 School Survey of Crime and Safety*. U.S. Department of Education.

Pizzo, S., M. Fricker, and P. Muolo. 1989. *Inside Job: The Looting of America's Savings and Loans*. New York: McGraw-Hill.

Polk, K. 1974. *Teenage Delinquency in Small Town America*. Research Report 5, Center for Studies of Crime and Delinquency. Rockville, MD: National Institute of Mental Health.

President's Commission on Law Enforcement and Administration of Justice. 1967. *The Challenge of Crime in a Free Society*. Washington, DC: GPO.

Priyadarsini, S., and C. A. Hartjen. 1981. "Delinquency and Corrections in India." In *Sociology of Delinquency*, edited by G. F. Jensen, 109–23. Beverly Hills: Sage.

Regnery, A. S. 1985. "Getting Away with Murder: Why the Juvenile Justice System Needs an Overhaul." *Policy Review* (Fall):65–68.

Rose, A. M. 1968. "Law and the Causation of Social Problems." *Social Problems* 16 (Summer):33–43.

Schur, E. 1973. *Radical Non-Intervention: Rethinking the Delinquency Problem*. Englewood Cliffs, NJ: Prentice-Hall.

Shannon, L. 1982. *Assessing the Relationship of Adult Criminal Careers to Juvenile Careers*. Washington, DC: U.S. Department of Justice.

Shaw, C. R. 1930. *The Jack-Roller*. Chicago: University of Chicago Press.

———. 1931. *Natural History of a Delinquent Career*. Chicago: University of Chicago Press.

———. 1938. *Brothers in Crime*. Chicago: University of Chicago Press.

Small, M., and K. D. Terrick. 2001. "School Violence: An Overview." *Journal of the Office of Juvenile Justice and Delinquency Prevention* 8:3–12.

Smith, C., and T. P. Thornberry. 1995. "The Relationship between Childhood Maltreatment and Adolescent Involvement in Delinquency." *Criminology* 33 (November):451–82.

Snyder, H. N., and E. H. Nimick. 1983. "City Delinquents and Their Country Cousins: A Description of Juvenile Delinquency in Metropolitan and Nonmetropolitan Areas." *Today's Delinquent* 2.

Snyder, H. N., and M. Sickmund. 1995. *Juvenile Offenders and Victims: A Focus on Violence*. Pittsburgh: National Center for Juvenile Justice.

Sutherland, E. H. 1937. *The Professional Thief*. Chicago: University of Chicago Press.

———. 1940. "White Collar Criminality." *American Sociological Review* 5 (February):1–12.

Sutherland, E. H., and D. R. Cressey. 1974. *Criminology*. New York: J. B. Lippincott.

Thrasher, F. M. 1927. *The Gang*. Chicago: University of Chicago Press.

Time. 1977. "The Youth Crime Plague." 11 July:18–28.

Time. 1989. "Our Violent Kids." 12 June:52–58.

U.S. Dept. of Health and Human Services, Administration for Children & Families. 1996. *Child Maltreatment, 1994*. Washington, DC: GPO.

———. 2005. *Child Maltreatment, 2003*. Washington, DC: GPO.

Wang, S. N., and G. F. Jensen. 2003. "Social Learning and Delinquency Behavior in Taiwan." In *Social Learning Theory and the Explanation of Crime: A Guide for the New Century*, edited by Ronald L. Akers and Gary F. Jensen, 65–83. New Brunswick, NJ: Transaction Books.

West, D. J. 1982. *Delinquency: Its Roots, Causes and Prospects*. London: Heinemann.

West, D. J., and D. P. Farrington. 1973. *Who Becomes Delinquent?* London: Heinemann.

Widom, C. S. 1989. "Child Abuse, Neglect, and Violent Criminal Behavior." *Criminology* 17 (2):251–72.

Wolfgang, M. E., R. Figlio, and T. Sellin. 1972. *Delinquency in a Birth Cohort*. Chicago: University of Chicago Press.

two

Juvenile Justice

> The powers of the Star Chamber were a trifle in comparison with those of our juvenile courts.
>
> (Roscoe Pound, former dean of Harvard Law School, 1937)
>
> Under our Constitution, the condition of being a boy does not justify a kangaroo court.
>
> (Supreme Court Justice Abe Fortas, 1967)

Introduction

The juvenile court was created in 1899 with the best of intentions, but over the years it has been attacked as "a scaled down second-class criminal court" (Feld, 1999). For some, it is an anachronistic social welfare agency that should be abolished. Others see it as too soft on juvenile offenders, "mollycoddling" junior thugs. Still others view it as too harsh and too much like the adult criminal justice system. Others call on the juvenile court to reclaim its historical position by "pursuing the best interests of the child" (Krisberg, 1988).

Both Dean Pound and Justice Fortas (see quotes above) were critical of the lack of due process in the juvenile court and railed against the unbridled discretion that was given to juvenile judges. The juvenile court was created to help, not punish, young offenders. While it was designed to be different from the criminal court, labeling it as a "Star Chamber" or a "kangaroo" court is a scathing indictment. A star chamber or kangaroo court is one that judges cases with little regard for rules of evidence or due process.

Because juvenile court proceedings are closed to the public, people tend to form opinions about the juvenile justice system based on sensational cases (such as those involving deliberations about remanding serious juvenile offenders to the adult system), media exposés of unpopular decisions, or political tirades about the system. It has become commonplace for critics of the system to argue that it was created to deal with less serious problems than confront the juvenile court today, and that we need to reassess the functions of the juvenile justice system in view of an "epidemic" of juvenile violence. However, such arguments are made with little recognition of the typical cases dominating juvenile court proceedings (i.e., property offenses), or the possible negative consequences of processing juveniles through the adult criminal justice system or incarcerating juveniles with adult offenders.

This chapter attempts to provide the historical background that led to the development of a juvenile court system. An understanding of the juvenile court in its historical context requires that we consider the broad social forces that shaped the evolution of a separate juvenile justice system in the nineteenth century and the social movements and political concerns (both progressive and conservative) that led to its invention. While a "child-saving" movement advocated a separate system to address the problems leading to youth crime, a separate system was also supported as an alternative to an adult criminal justice system that was heavily criticized and had a dubious record of rehabilitation. It is ironic that the contemporary juvenile court is under attack for being too lenient since one impetus for the separate juvenile system was that adult courts were viewed as inadequate for coping with the rising problems of the urban young. Contemporary critics who advocate turning juvenile offenders over to the adult system assume that the criminal justice system is working sufficiently well to solve the problem of crime. When viewed in historical context that is a dubious assumption.

A Brief Overview of Juvenile Justice

Juvenile justice systems are the legal institutions that handle offenses and problems of nonadults (generally persons under the age of 18). Such cases are handled in juvenile courts that are separate organizations within a state's court system, or in courts that are divisions of a larger court system. The full range of issues falling within the jurisdiction of a juvenile court will vary from state to state and county to county. Juvenile courts do not handle as wide a range of legal issues as do *family courts*, but they focus on a wide range of juvenile matters, only one of which is juvenile delinquency.

The organization of juvenile justice systems varies among jurisdictions, and similar procedures may be given different names. Figure 2-1 summarizes the major steps in a "generic" juvenile justice system and box 2-1 (on pp. 29–30) includes the definitions of important terms used in juvenile court. As seen in figure 2-1, the court process is very truncated compared to the adult system, but also seemingly contradictory. For example, nonpetitioned cases (no formal charges) ought to result in a high dismissal rate, but only 39 percent are dismissed. On the other hand, of those who are petitioned (given a formal charge), a third do not appear in court (not adjudicated). This is the world of civil court not criminal court, where the standards are less rigorous and the proceedings become a bit lax.

The terms used in juvenile court are different from those used in criminal court, though the ultimate outcome—such as probation or institutionalization—can be the same. Since the juvenile court is supposed to be helping, treating, or rehabilitating youth rather than punishing them, youth are not arrested but rather are "referred" to the court. Such **referrals** can come from agents of social control other than the police, such as school officials, social workers, and parents. Juveniles can be referred for specific activities that would not be criminal for an adult (e.g., truancy, smoking, runaway) as well as for vague patterns of activities (e.g., ungovernable, incorrigible). Such offenses are called **status offenses** because it is the juvenile's age status that warrants intervention by the juvenile justice system. Youth also are referred for offenses that are criminal for adults, but in the juvenile system these are called **delinquent acts**.

As noted above, a juvenile may be referred to the juvenile court by the police. Unlike the criminal justice system, however, virtually anyone can make a referral to the juvenile court. Overall, 84 percent of referrals are made by the police, but school authorities, parents, probation officers, social service agencies, and even victims can make a referral. In public order cases (disorderly conduct, liquor law violations, weapons offenses, and nonviolent sex offenses) nearly 40 percent of these referrals are from individuals or institutions other than the police (National Center for Juvenile Justice, 2003).

Juveniles are not indicted, but are issued a **petition** that infers that they will appear in court before a judge. As seen in figure 2-1, this does not always happen. Similarly, those who are not petitioned are not summarily released and can in fact be sent to an institution. Some juveniles can be waived to the adult court and tried as adults. A 13-year-old juvenile might be treated as an adult and given full rights of due process of law. As will be discussed later, the category of "other sanction" can be extremely problematic in juvenile court because juveniles are not protected by the Eighth Amendment

Figure 2-1 Juvenile Court Processing

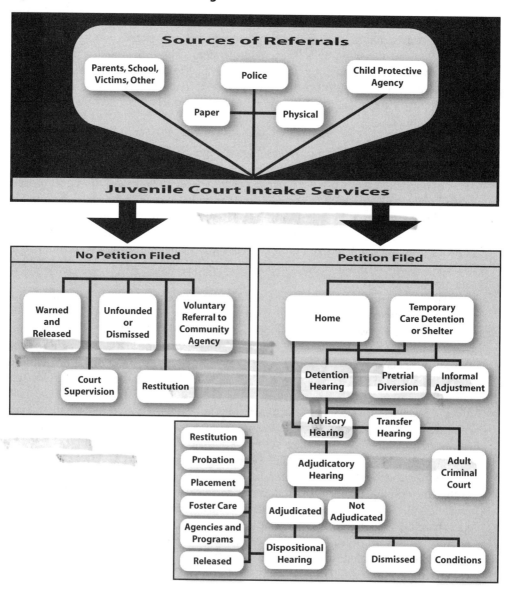

(no cruel or unusual punishments). Juvenile judges can issue a **disposition (similar to a sentence in adult court)** that could be considered unconstitutional in adult court.

The most common disposition is **probation**. Typically, youths on probation are under the supervision of a court official called a **probation officer**. The juvenile might otherwise be placed in an institution, treatment program, or foster home. It is interesting to note that of the 1.6 million cases referred to the juvenile court in 2000, less than a third were dismissed or, in essence, found not guilty.

In sum, consistent with the treatment-rehabilitation philosophy of the juvenile court, the terms used to describe the process do not carry the adversarial and combative connotations of terms for comparable procedures and decisions in the adult system. The juvenile court is presumed to be acting on behalf of youth. Hence, procedural *due process of law* safeguards taken for granted in the adult system have not been as prominent in the juvenile system.

Box 2-1   Glossary of Juvenile Justice Terms

Adjudicated: Judicially determined to be a delinquent, status offender, or dependent/neglected.

Adjudication Hearing: Hearing to determine whether a child should be adjudicated.

Advisory Hearing: A preliminary hearing to determine what subsequent actions are necessary.

Delinquency: Acts or conduct in violation of criminal law.

Delinquent Act: An act committed by a juvenile for which an adult could be prosecuted in a criminal court, but when committed by a juvenile is within the jurisdiction of the juvenile court. Delinquent acts include crimes against persons, crimes against property, drug offenses, and crimes against public order when such acts are committed by juveniles.

Dependent/Neglected: Those cases covering neglect or inadequate care on the part of the parents or guardians. They include lack of adequate care or support resulting from death, absence, or physical or mental incapacity of the parents; abandonment or desertion; abuse or cruel treatment; and improper or inadequate conditions in the home.

Detention: Temporary incarceration of a child who requires secure custody for his/her protection or protection of the community.

Detention Hearing: Hearing to determine whether a child is in need of secure detention.

Disposition: Definite action taken or a treatment plan decided upon or initiated regarding a particular case. Case dispositions are coded into the following categories:

Transfer to Criminal Court/Waive—Cases which were waived or transferred to a criminal court as the result of a waiver or transfer hearing.

Release—Cases dismissed (including those warned, counseled, and released) with no further disposition anticipated.

Probation—Cases in which youth were placed on informal/voluntary or formal/court-ordered probation or supervision.

Placement—Cases in which youth were placed out of the home in a residential facility housing delinquent or status offenders.

Other—A variety of miscellaneous dispositions not included above.

Disposition Hearing: A hearing held to determine what should be done after a child has been adjudicated.

Incorrigible: A juvenile law categorization in some jurisdictions encompassing youth who are repeatedly in conflict with authority.

(continued)

Informal Adjustment: Subject to court approval, after investigation in a delinquent or unruly referral, the designated court officer concluded that a child is within the jurisdiction of the court and undertakes to remedy the situation by giving counsel and advice to the parties with a view toward informal adjustment of the case. If the informal adjustment is not successful, the court officer may terminate the informal adjustment and file a petition.

Intake Officer: Probation officer who first reviews a referral and makes a recommendation on proper court action in a case.

Intake Services: Unit at juvenile court center where referrals are initially processed.

Juvenile Court: Any court which has jurisdiction over matters involving juveniles.

Petition: A document filed in juvenile court alleging that a juvenile is a delinquent, status offender, dependent, abused, or for a special proceeding (i.e., child support, legitimation) and asking that the court assume jurisdiction over the juvenile or asking that an alleged delinquent be transferred to criminal court for prosecution as an adult.

Referral: The filing of a complaint by a law enforcement officer; the child's parents, guardians, or custodians; the school system; a social service agency; or other individuals or agencies requesting the court to exercise its authority.

Restitution: Plan requiring offender to return property, make monetary compensation, or provide service to the victim and/or community to compensate for harm inflicted by the offender.

Source of Referral: The agency or individual filing a complaint with intake (which initiates court processing).

Status Offense: Behavior which is considered an offense only when committed by a juvenile (for example, running away from home).

Transfer Hearing: Hearing to determine whether a case should be remanded or waived to the criminal justice system.

Source: Compiled from J. Traugher, J. F. Lucas, and S. Parish, 1989, *Tennessee Juvenile Court Annual Statistical Report*; Pima County Collaboration for Children and Youth, 1980, *Juvenile Rights and Responsibilities*; Butts et al., 1994, *Juvenile Court Statistics, 1991*.

The organizational and procedural outgrowths of this treatment philosophy have come under attack by critics since the invention of the court. On the one hand, the treatment philosophy has been criticized for disguising a basically punitive system where the juvenile is neither helped nor protected by due process of law. On the other hand, the treatment philosophy and the leeway it accords intake officials, judges, and probation officers has been attacked for allowing lenient offender-centered decisions and dispositions.

An introduction to the history of this special legal institution and the controversies that perennially surround it should prompt questions about the diverse and contradictory expectations that different groups or "publics" have for the juvenile justice system. It is expected to deter, treat, and respond to the offenses of juveniles in a just manner. It likely cannot do all three equally well at the same time and can always be attacked for ignoring one goal while pursuing another. A review of the history of the juvenile court should make us aware of conflicting expectations and help us understand the basis for criticism.

Many features of the adult criminal justice system date to the eleventh century, while most features of the juvenile court system emerged only in the twentieth century. Indeed, the juvenile justice system can be considered to be in its infancy, with numerous issues of due process of law yet to be resolved.

The perceived need for a special court to deal with juvenile offenders was preceded by the development of conceptions of age categories between infancy and adulthood that required special attention. Whether this attention is good or bad from society's point of view or that of the people processed through the system remains a controversy. The debates concerning the merits of creating a juvenile court have reemerged in the past few years, reflecting a never-ending tension between the views that special consideration should be given to children, and that society should be protected from crime regardless of the age of the offender.

The Discovery of Childhood

It may seem ludicrous to propose that childhood was "discovered" just a few centuries ago, since the persistence of the human race obviously required that people had children. However, the number of stages that are acknowledged in human development varies among different societies and over time. For example, some historians argue that the concept of childhood as a socially distinct category developed sometime during the seventeenth century. Prior to that time, there were essentially two stages of life: infancy and adulthood. No one considered pre-adults to have any unique characteristics or position. Children were expected to work alongside their parents, and simply being young did not confer any special considerations. In fact, life was short, and with so many children dying in infancy, what appeared to be callousness toward children was a natural response to a highly precarious stage of existence. As late as the 1600s, two-thirds of all children died before the age of four (Bernard, 1992).

World population growth is a product of modern times, with little overall change until the eighteenth century. There were fewer than 300 million people on earth in the year 1000 AD compared to nearly 300 million presently in the United States and more that 6.3 billion in the world. Until recently, infant mortality (deaths of children under the age of one) was extremely high, with epidemics of plague and smallpox as well as such diseases as whooping cough, scarlet fever, diphtheria, typhus, dysentery, and measles serving as a natural check on population growth. Phillip Aries suggests in his book, *Centuries of Childhood*, "People could not allow themselves to become too attached to something that was regarded as a probable loss" (1962:38).

Researchers studying the fifteenth, sixteenth, and seventeenth centuries have noted that people tended to slow the rate at which they had children following disease epidemics (Wrigley, 1969). Some scholars suggest that plagues had devastating psychological as well as biological consequences and people were reluctant to bring new life into the world (Chambers, 1972). It was during such periods of stagnant population growth that the Catholic Church and numerous European governments mounted a campaign to encourage marriage and fertility and to discourage abortion, infanticide, and birth control.

Aries (1962) suggested that it was during this time period that the concept of childhood emerged. Based on an examination of family portraits, Aries argues that prior to the seventeenth century, all family members were represented as equals. Some members were tall and physically mature whereas others were short and somewhat scrawny, but there was no attempt to differentiate adults from children. Aries asserts,

"In medieval society, the idea of childhood did not exist" (1962:128). In fact, historians have noted that premodern people neither knew their ages nor celebrated their birthdays (Postman, 1994). But beginning in the seventeenth century, Aries noted a dramatic difference in family portraits, especially those depicted by Rubens and Van Dyck. Children ceased to be dressed like grown-ups and their placement in the portrait was typically of a dependent person held in the arms of his or her mother, or else sitting or leaning on an adult. Children wore clothing that set them apart from adults. Another historian suggested that "the decline in early mortality, therefore, can be seen as an independent variable that encouraged the deepening of emotional bonds between parents and children" (Zelizer, 1985:10).

Aries's interpretation of the discovery of childhood is a subject of debate and is not accepted by everyone. Linda Pollock (1983) argues that the assumption of indifference and neglect prior to the seventeenth century is exaggerated and based on inadequate documentary evidence. However, most historians agree that the cultural concept of childhood is a relatively recent invention. Once children emerged from infancy they were quickly integrated into the adult world without any need for formal education (Postman, 1994). Young children hauled water, split wood, and toiled in the fields alongside adults. Many children left home to work as servants or apprentices in the homes of others (Shorter, 1975). Aries (1962) points out that most children grew up quickly and participated in drinking and gambling in taverns, adult games and amusements, and witnessed or participated in sexual activity, "without any special efforts to protect their innocence from adult realities" (Feld, 1999).

Thomas Bernard sees the initial development of the concept of childhood around 1400 as "the first idea of childhood" (1992). With declining infant mortality, parents began to experience the joy and pleasure of having a child. The probability of the child surviving allowed parents to become attached to the child. Building on Aries's concepts, Bernard suggests that "the second idea of childhood" began around 1600 with the notion of the child as a potential adult. The Puritans stressed that children needed to be nurtured and taught. "Children could be shaped and molded and formed into righteous, law-abiding, God-fearing adults" (Bernard, 1992:52). This second concept of childhood implied certain obligations and roles that adults performed in order to properly socialize children.

The Discovery of Adolescence

The interim status between childhood and adulthood, which we call **adolescence**, was a term that came into use in the nineteenth century. Aries noted that in the French language there were three terms to denote age in the seventeenth century: childhood, youth, and old age, with youth signifying the prime of life. The word commonly used for referring to children from birth through their teens was "infant." Aries observed that the differentiation between infancy and childhood in the French language did not occur until the nineteenth century. In the sixteenth and seventeenth centuries aristocrats perceived a need to send their children to special schools for a classical education and, most importantly, for discipline, which was seen as an instrument of moral and spiritual improvement.

> A new moral concept was to distinguish the child, or at least the schoolboy, and set
> him apart: the concept of the well-bred child . . . (the concept) was the product of
> the forming opinions of an elite group of thinkers and moralists who occupied high
> positions in Church or State. The well-bred child would be preserved from the
> roughness and immorality which would become the special characteristics of the
> lower classes. In France this well-bred child would be the little bourgeois. In
> England he would be the gentleman, a social type unknown before the nineteenth
> century, and which a threatened aristocracy would create, thanks to the public
> schools, to defend itself against the progress of democracy. (Aries, 1962:327–28)

Aries tied the development or recognition of adolescence to the rise of an emphasis on militaristic discipline in the schools and the preparation of "boys of good family" for military careers. The adolescent was the young would-be soldier. Thus,
according to Aries, the idea of adolescence as a distinct age group began in Europe
and was related to the development of an educational system designed to produce disciplined, well-bred children whose further training in adolescence would prepare
them for military careers.

David Bakan (1971) has argued that "adolescence was added to childhood as a
second childhood in order to fulfill the aims of the new urban-industrial society which
developed so rapidly following the Civil War." Bakan's claim is that adolescence took
shape as a distinct sociolegal age category in the last two decades of the nineteenth
century in the United States as a result of three major social movements. These movements were aimed at (1) compulsory public education, (2) child labor legislation, and
(3) the establishment of a juvenile court. During the Progressive Era (1880–1920), the
state, according to Robert Bremner, became a kindly parent and the best interests of
the child coincided with the best interests of the state (1970).

According to Bakan, the term "adolescence" was an American discovery linked
specifically to G. Stanley Hall, one of the most prominent psychologists of the nineteenth century and the person who is considered the father of the study of adolescence. In an 1882 publication entitled *The Moral and Religious Training of Children*, Hall
compared the stage of adolescence to the evolution of the human species from sav-
agery into civilization. His so-called "storm and stress" hypothesis likened adolescence to a period marked by "a lack of emotional steadiness, violent impulses,
unreasonable conduct, the previous selfhood is broken up and a new individual is in
process of being born. All is solvent, plastic, particularly susceptible to external influence" (1882:29). While Hall's notion of adolescence as "a long pilgrimage of the soul"
has been severely criticized, his dramatic highlighting of this stage of child development added momentum to the call for greater care and concern for maturing children
in the late nineteenth century. Adolescents could be molded and shaped into responsible adults. Once they became adults they became set in their ways.

Social Change in the Nineteenth Century

The social movements of the nineteenth century reflected the transformation of
American society from a rural-agrarian economy to an urban-industrial one. This transformation took place as huge waves of immigrants poured into urban areas. Of particu-

lar importance were the reactions of the established Protestant middle and upper classes. It was from these ranks that the leaders of the social movements would emerge. In New York in the early 1800s and in Chicago in the late 1800s, upper- and middle-class social reformers worked to establish institutions and shape policies to socialize urban, lower-class immigrants into their conception of the American way of life.

The drive for compulsory public education of the young reflected the reformers' perceived need to integrate and control the masses and to prepare them for work. To acculturate the new Americans, children had to be taken out of the labor force and put in school. The importance of public education was also reinforced by an increasing industrial need for skilled labor and by the efforts of labor unions to gain control over working conditions. Cheap, readily available child labor was an impediment to successful unionization, and labor leaders were opposed to it on economic as well as social grounds. There also emerged a need to control the labor supply in the United States as unrestricted immigration and an increasing number of children began to produce a labor surplus. Thus, a concern for creating special institutions that could socialize and control emerging problem populations preceded the development of a special legal status for certain age groups.

In summary, the prolongation of childhood and the delineation of adolescence as a distinct age category were ultimately the products of social, economic, and technological change. Such change led to an increased emphasis on the uniqueness of children and the need for the state to take a more active role in the socialization of youth. Historian Christopher Lasch argues that Progressive reformers sought to shelter and preserve the family's influence on children, especially immigrant families, by creating new "agencies of socialized reproduction: educators, psychiatrists, social workers, and penologists" (1979:27). Lasch claims that these reformers sought to place the young under the benign influence of the state in order to insure the proper "American" socialization of children. Mary Carpenter, an influential penal reformer, stated in an 1875 address that it is the duty of the state to intercede and "stand *in loco parentis* and do its duty to the child and to society, by seeing that he is properly brought up" (Abbot, 1938).

Having considered the social forces at work, particularly in nineteenth-century America, we can now turn to an examination of the development of the juvenile court.

The Origins of Juvenile Justice

Several historical studies have dealt with the evolution of juvenile justice in the United States and Canada (Platt, 1969a; Bremner, 1988). In some of these studies there is disagreement on the sources or meaning of certain important developments in the processing of juveniles. For instance, a popular work by Anthony Platt focuses on the **child-saving movement** in the late 1800s as the key to the establishment of the first juvenile court in Chicago. In their histories of juvenile justice, Steven Schlossman (1977) and Harold Finestone (1976) describe the social developments and legal justifications that ultimately led to a separate juvenile justice system as occurring very early in the 1800s. Moreover, the social and religious forces of the late 1800s upon which Platt focuses are quite similar to the forces Schlossman and Finestone identify at earlier points in time. Schlossman and Finestone view the establishment of the juvenile court as a product of more benign forces than Platt, who suggests that such development was a reflection of pressure for increased social control by capitalists. As noted later in this chapter, an analysis of the history of Canadian juvenile court reform is critical of the vague references to the interests or needs of capitalists as the driving force behind the emergence of distinct juvenile laws and juvenile justice machinery. As we examine the development of the juvenile justice system it is important to recognize that there are conflicting interpretations of social history.

Compulsory Education and Houses of Refuge

An important development in the early evolution of juvenile justice in the United States was the establishment of the **house of refuge** in the 1820s by private philanthropists. John Sutton sees the house of refuge as the beginning of a juvenile justice system that represented "correctional segregation of the young that antedated their judicial separation" (1988:917). Such institutions were prison-like schools for juvenile offenders and impoverished children. They first appeared in New York and Boston in 1825, Philadelphia in 1828, and quickly spread to other major cities. Their development was intimately connected with the push for compulsory public education. It was argued that increasing delinquency was caused by "environmental corruption" caused by immigration, urbanization, poverty, and industrialization (Feld, 1999). Both compulsory education and the concept of the reformatory grew out of the efforts of middle- and upper-class reformers to deal with new problem populations through the extension of state control over children.

In 1838, a key court decision (*Ex Parte Crouse*), which concerned the constitutionality of incarcerating a child in a house of refuge without due process of law, drew on the arguments that reformers used to advance compulsory education, and helped establish the legal basis of the juvenile court. The case involved Mary Ann Crouse, who was committed to the Philadelphia House of Refuge on the basis of a complaint lodged by her mother. Her father did not find out about the action until after Mary was committed, and he subsequently sought to have Mary released on the grounds that her rights had been violated. The court decided that the Bill of Rights did not apply to children and that the house of refuge was merely a type of school for problem children. The court ruled:

> The object of the charity is reformation, by training its inmates to industry; by imbuing their minds with principles of morality and religion; by furnishing them with means to earn a living; and above all, by separating them from the corrupting influence of improper associates. To this end, may not the natural parents, when unequal to the task of education, or unworthy of it, be superseded by the *parens patriae*, or common guardian of the community? It is to be remembered that the public has a paramount interest in the virtue and knowledge of its members, and that, of strict right, the business of education belongs to it. (4 Wharton 9 at 11)

The concept of *parens patriae* (parent of the land), or the right of the state to care for minors and others who cannot legally take care of themselves, arose in fifteenth century English Common Law. The king, as parent of the land, was asked to become a guardian over those children whose natural parents were deceased. This legal right was used, ostensibly, to maintain the structure of feudalism and to assure the orderly transfer of feudal duties from one generation to the next. Similarly, the English Poor Laws of 1601 extended the original interpretation of *parens patriae* to allow the state to remove children from destitute parents and apprentice them to others. These children were forced to serve their masters as agricultural laborers or domestic servants until age 21. Thus, the Poor Laws and the *Ex Parte Crouse* case were predicated on the right of the state to intervene in the lives of children, even if the natural parents objected.

In the United States, the house of refuge movement and the establishment of reform schools for delinquent children used the concept of *parens patriae* as their legal foundation. It is also important to note that compulsory school attendance was being advanced at the same time, and this legal stipulation gave the state the right to mandate compulsory education for all children. According to Schlossman, the advocates of public education and reform schools:

> urged the judges to place both types of facility, public school and reformatory, under the safeguard of the *parens patriae* doctrine, and to establish once and for all time that the state's provision of education for the poor was a legitimate exercise of its police powers.
>
> The court agreed entirely with (this) point of view. A reformatory, it insisted, was nothing but a residential school for underprivileged children, a horizontal expansion of the fledgling public school system. A reformatory was "not a prison but a school." Its objectives were in the broadest sense educational: to train children in industry, morality, the means to earn a living, and most importantly, to isolate them from the "corrupting influences of improper associates." The court went on: "As to the abridgement of indefensible rights by confinement of the person, it is no more than what is borne, to a greater or less extent, in every school; and we know of no natural right to exemption from restraints which conduce to an infant's welfare." In sum, the court concluded, the government's right to incarcerate children who had not committed criminal acts was neither capricious nor vindictive, for the house of refuge was nothing but a residential public school for unfortunate youth. (Schlossman, 1977:10)

This characterization of reformatories was disputed in 1870 in Illinois in the case of *People v. Turner.* The case involved a boy who had been committed to the Chicago Reform School on vague charges that did not involve a definable crime. The state appellate court ordered the boy's release and questioned the analogy that had been drawn between reformatories and public schools, as well as the right of the state to intervene in violation of children's rights and parents' rights. However, as Schlossman has pointed out, this decision had little impact on the spread of reformatories or on subsequent court challenges. The movement to deal with problem populations through compulsory education and the extension of governmental control was too widely supported by reformers, industrialists, and the dominant ideology of the times to be overturned by a court decision.

Reform Schools

In the mid-1800s **reformatories** appeared as state-supported institutions for the care of young offenders. The first reformatories appeared in Massachusetts: the Lyman School for Boys in 1848 and the Lancaster School for Girls in 1855. Platt summarized the basic reformatory principles:

(1) Young offenders must be segregated from the corrupting influences of adult criminals; (2) "delinquents" need to be removed from their environment and imprisoned for their own good; (3) delinquents should be assigned to reformatories without trial; (4) sentences should be indeterminate; (5) reformation should not be confused with sentimentality; (6) inmates must be protected from idleness, indulgence, and luxuries through military drill, physical exercise and constant supervision; (7) reformatories should be built in the countryside; (8) labor, education, and religion constitute the essential programs of reform; (9) the value of sobriety, thrift, industry, prudence, "realistic" ambition, and adjustment must be taught. (Platt, 1977:54–55)

The goal of the reformatory was to isolate the young deviants from the evil influence of the city and provide a wholesome, pastoral setting. The *cottage plan* was introduced to provide some semblance of a stable family structure along with a program of vocational training. There was increasing uneasiness with large numbers of immigrants coming to America and bringing with them different languages, customs, and child-rearing practices. However, criticism of the custodial and repressive character of reformatories and houses of refuge appeared in the 1850s and 1860s as both correctional innovations failed to achieve their intended purpose (Watkins, 1998). As more and more children of immigrants and the poor populated the houses of refuge and reformatories, conditions deteriorated to the point that they were seen as warehouses for the untreatable or unmanageable (Rothman, 1980).

The "Placing-Out" System

In 1853 Charles Loring Brace, a Protestant minister, founded the Children's Aid Society in New York City. His intent was to send children of the "dangerous classes" to foster homes in the Midwest rather than place them in the long-term institutionalized care of houses of refuge. Brace organized what became known as *orphan trains*— large groups of vagrant and poor children that were gathered up and **placed out** with farm families. It is estimated that between 1853 and 1929 more than 125,000 children (some estimates are as high as 400,000) were sent from New York City to farm communities (Holt, 1992). Every two weeks, groups of children boarded trains and headed to Midwestern towns where Protestant clergy and prominent community leaders made arrangements for the arrival of these "orphan" children. The arrival of the orphan trains was advertised and families were encouraged to come and select one of these children to take home. Those children who were not selected boarded the train and moved on to the next town until all the children were finally placed. While these children were referred to as orphans, many simply came from poor, immigrant families, and the Children's Aid Society convinced parents that their children would be better off in what Brace called the "best of all asylums for outcast children, the farmer's home" (Lindsay, 1994:14).

Many criticisms arose regarding this placing-out system and the actual intentions of Brace and the Children's Aid Society. Some argued that the Society had a distinctive anti-immigrant tone, noting that a large portion of the children sent on the orphan trains were from Irish and Italian Catholic families. Henry Thurston observed that "the Society was the world of the old indenture philosophy of child labor in sheepskin disguise of a so-called Christian home" (1930:136). Brace's efforts were strongly criticized by Catholic groups. In 1863 a Catholic organization called the Protectory was organized to "rescue" Catholic children who might otherwise have fallen into the hands of the Children's Aid Society. The Protectory sought out Catholic homes and attacked Brace's apprenticing system as a process by which "every trace of their early faith and filial attachment will be rooted out . . . and effectually destroy every association which might revive in their hearts a love of their parents' religion" (Langsam, 1964:54). In 1869 the Sisters of Mercy, troubled by Catholic children being placed in Protestant homes, started their own "mercy trains" for Catholic children. Local Catholic priests would announce from the pulpit that a "mercy train" would be arriving, and those who wanted a child signed up for a boy or a girl.

Conflict between the Children's Aid Society and the Catholic Protectory continued well into the twentieth century. Follow-up examination of the placing-out system

---

Box 2-2   An Orphan Train

Charles Loring Brace, a Protestant minister, founded the Children's Aid Society in New York City and organized what became known as "orphan trains"—large groups of vagrant and poor children that were gathered up and "placed out" with farm families. Every two weeks, groups of children boarded trains and headed to Midwestern towns where Protestant clergy and prominent community leaders made arrangements for the arrival of these "orphan" children. The arrivals of the orphan trains were advertised and families were encouraged to come and select one of these children to take home.

What were the pros and cons of this approach for dealing with wayward and orphaned youth?

Source: Photo courtesy of the Kansas State Historical Society, Topeka.

found that in many instances children were placed with kind and caring farm families, but many of the placements occurred without a proper investigation of the foster-care family. Agents of the Children's Aid Society did attempt to conduct follow-up visits and in many instances this system worked reasonably well. Few of these children were ever found to be delinquent or sent to reform schools. However, Miriam Langsam reported that a high percentage of children under the age of thirteen remained with the family with whom they were placed, but those children who were older could not be found (1964). The suggestion is that many of these older children ran away from their foster homes, and some eventually returned to their biological families.

The Juvenile Court

The disillusionment with the house of refuge and reformatory movements and the endless squabbling between the Children's Aid Society and the Catholic Protectory, coupled with pressure from reformers, led to an expansion of state power in the late nineteenth century. Private philanthropic groups had attempted to solve the problem of juvenile delinquency but the state needed to step in and exert central control over these factionalized agencies. During the period from 1880 to 1920, often referred to as the **Progressive Era**, the nation was undergoing pervasive change. Increasing urbanization, a massive influx of immigrants, increasing labor violence, technological advances, and the concentration of wealth in the hands of a few meant that the laissez-faire posture of government prior to this time could no longer be tolerated. The power of government expanded significantly during the Progressive Era, creating the modern welfare state and the criminal justice system. Barry Krisberg and James Austin note that "during the Progressive Era, those in positions of economic power feared that the urban masses would destroy the world they had built. . . . From all sectors came demands that new action be taken to preserve social order, and to protect private property and racial privilege" (1993:27). It is no accident that the juvenile court emerged during this period, where optimism regarding the development of new correctional methods went hand-in-hand with the fear that social unrest could destroy all of society.

A number of factors converged in Chicago at the end of the nineteenth century to produce the first juvenile court. First, Chicago grew faster than any city in the world, reaching one million in 1890 and growing to two million by 1910 (Finestone, 1976). Second, more than 70 percent of the inhabitants of Chicago were immigrants. Third, the Chicago Bar Association was particularly concerned that Illinois had no reform schools and no power regarding the conduct of juveniles. With pressure from a coalition of reformers and the Chicago Bar Association, the Illinois legislature passed a bill in 1899 establishing the first juvenile court. The legislation formally established a separate system of juvenile justice that was to be essentially noncriminal and oriented toward treatment rather than punishment of juvenile offenders.

The new juvenile court was not to be a mere extension of the jurisdiction of the criminal court, but rather an independent court system with complete jurisdiction over the affairs of juveniles. The founders of the juvenile court envisioned it as the cornerstone of a comprehensive child care system. "It was designed to treat the youthful offender as a child primarily and only incidentally as a law violator" (Finestone, 1976:45).

Some observers view the motivation for the creation of the juvenile court as a product of the same conservative reformist concerns that resulted in the establishment of houses of refuge and reformatories. Anthony Platt described the conservative nature of reform during the late 1800s as follows:

> Contemporary programs of delinquency control can be traced to the enterprising reforms of the child-savers who, at the end of the nineteenth century, helped to create special judicial and correctional institutions for the labeling, processing, and management of "troublesome" youth. Child-saving was a conservative and romantic movement, designed to impose sanctions on conduct unbecoming youth and to disqualify youth from enjoying adult privileges. The child-savers were prohibitionists, in a general sense, who believed in close supervision of adolescents' recreation and leisure. The movement brought attention to, and thus "invented," new categories of youthful misbehavior which had been previously unappreciated or had been dealt with on an informal basis. Child-saving was heavily influenced by middle-class women who extended their housewifely roles into public service and emphasized the dependence of the social order on the proper socialization of children. (1969b:21)

Elsewhere in his writings, Platt (1974) extended his analysis to argue that the middle-class reformers were supported by an upper-class and industrial elite who would benefit from industrial discipline and who were concerned with establishing stability and order in a rapidly changing urban environment. Thus, Platt views the creation of the juvenile court as an outgrowth of middle- and upper-class interests, fears, and concerns that promoted an increase in the scope of state control.

In contrast to Platt, Schlossman and Finestone believe that the most distinctive or "progressive" feature of the juvenile court was its emphasis on probation and on the home and family as targets for treatment. According to Finestone, "Since the formation of the juvenile court represented the culmination and response to almost fifty years of criticism of the institutionalized handling of juvenile delinquents, it was primarily concerned with treatment in the community" (1976:45). Thus, the emphasis was on probation and the probation officer as an "agent of the court in the community." In an analysis of the development of juvenile court legislation in Canada, John Hagan and Jeffrey Leon presented a similar interpretation (1977:597). They argued that an emphasis on probation and the family as the focus of treatment was central to such legislation. They also argued that the link emphasized by Platt between the interests of industrialists and other elites and the invention of the juvenile court are purely inferential, and that most claims about the consequences of its invention are wrong.

Whether the creation of the juvenile court was progressive or conservative, or motivated by humanitarian concerns or class interests, is a continuing source of controversy. However, there does appear to be agreement that the gap between the promise of the juvenile court and its actual implementation was considerable. Platt argued that treatment for lower-class youths took the form of *training schools* built as prisons and based on the principle of reform through militaristic discipline and forced labor. The noncriminal nature of its proceedings gave the court greater control over the lives of juveniles in that it could deal with behavior that was not criminal but was defined as "bad" by the reformers. In his analysis of the operation of the Milwaukee Juvenile Court in the early 1900s, Schlossman reported that (1) relations between the court and clientele "were generally hostile and always superficial," (2) the court showed little concern with fair proceedings, and (3) actual operations were infused with a view of youth (particularly lower-class immigrant youth) as threatening and perverse (1977:167).

Overall, it appears that the establishment of the juvenile court represented a combination of humanitarianism and an anti-institutional ideology that emphasized probation and represented a fervent desire to disassociate the juvenile from common law doctrine in criminal justice (Watkins, 1998). However, its popularity, support, and implementation also reflected anti-urban, anti-Catholic, anti-immigrant, and anti-lower-class biases; in short, a concern with gaining better legal control over threatening categories of people. Humanitarianism demanded that children be "saved" from the brutal realities of the adult criminal justice system, but at the same time many adults felt that they needed to be saved from the children of the "dangerous" classes. The adult justice system was not controlling such youth effectively. Judges were reluctant to deal with youth in the same fashion as adults, and were releasing them back to the streets. Something had to be done. That "something" was the creation of a separate justice system for juveniles that encompassed a far wider range of offensive behaviors than the adult criminal justice system.

Parens Patriae and Due Process of Law

The move toward separate legal institutions for juveniles was justified as an "obvious" extension of the doctrine of *parens patriae*. This legal concept is reflected in virtually all juvenile codes and serves as the legal rationale for both the form and substance of juvenile justice in the United States. The major consequence of applying this concept to juvenile justice is that the court, acting on behalf of the state, can become the legal guardian of all juveniles in its jurisdiction and can thereby limit and possibly terminate the guardianship and custody rights of parents. "Juvenile court judges directed their attention first and foremost to the 'whole' child rather than to the specific crime. It was not his act but his soul that was at issue" (Feld, 1999:67).

Under the common law in England and the United States, a child under 7 years of age could not be charged with a criminal offense. Between the ages of 7 and 14, the child was normally not considered responsible for violations of criminal law. Exceptions could occur if it were shown that the child understood the nature of the offense and could distinguish between right and wrong. Thus, it was conceivable that under common-law principles, juveniles between the ages of 7 and 14 could be found responsible and sentenced to prison or execution as if they were adult offenders. However, the evidence is extremely weak that such punishments were actually carried out in England (Sanders, 1945) or in the United States (Platt, 1969a).

Nonetheless, the possibility of indiscriminate punishment and imprisonment of both juvenile and hardened adult offender alike in the criminal justice system was often cited in the first efforts to establish houses of refuge in New York, Boston, and Philadelphia. The argument was used again in the crusade for the creation of the juvenile court later in the nineteenth century. The amplification of the *parens patriae* doctrine in the United States allowed the relaxation of procedural safeguards and enabled the juvenile court to operate as a civil court, not a criminal court, allowing far greater discretion in dealing with juveniles.

Under the spirit of *parens patriae*, the American juvenile court emerged and spread to every state within a few decades. The phenomenal spread of the juvenile court ideology serves as testimony to the reform movement of the anti-institutionalists and the organizing efforts of upper-class women, who were in the forefront of the child-saving movement. Between 1899 and 1909, thirty-four states enacted some form of juvenile court law. By 1927, all but Maine and Wyoming had some form of juvenile court, but they were far from being identical. In an extensive historical analysis of the diffusion of juvenile court reform, Sutton (1988) found the states that most rapidly innovated were those with large urban populations, well-developed educational systems, and relatively decentralized political systems. Proximity to Chicago was a major influence on the rapid innovation of the North Central states. These also were states in which the Progressive ideology was strong.

Although states varied in the implementation and use of the system, the basic features were well-established quite rapidly. A President's Commission on Law Enforcement and Administration of Justice summarized the basic features of the system as follows:

> The juvenile court, then, was born in an aura of reform and it spread with amazing speed. The conception of the delinquent as a "wayward child" first specifically came to life in April 1899, when the Illinois legislature passed the Juvenile Court Act, creating the first statewide court especially for children. It did not create a new court; it did include most of the features that have since come to distinguish the juvenile court. The original act and the amendments to it that shortly followed brought together under one jurisdiction cases of dependency, neglect, and delinquency—the last comprehending incorrigibles and children threatened by immoral associations as well as criminal lawbreakers. Hearings were to be informal and nonpublic, records confidential, children detained apart from adults, a probation staff appointed. In short, children were not to be treated as criminals nor dealt with by the processes used for criminals.
>
> A new vocabulary symbolized the new order: petition instead of complaint, summons instead of warrant, initial hearing instead of arraignment, finding of involvement instead of conviction, disposition instead of sentence. The physical surroundings were important too: they should seem less imposing than a courtroom, with the judge at a desk or table instead of behind a bench, fatherly and sympathetic while still authoritative and sobering. The goals were to investigate, diagnose, and prescribe treatment, not to adjudicate guilt or fix blame. The individual's background was more important than the facts of a given incident, specific conduct relevant more as symptomatic of a need for the court to bring its helping powers to bear than a prerequisite to exercise of jurisdiction. Lawyers were unnecessary—adversary tactics were out of place, for the mutual aim of all was not to contest or object but to determine the treatment plan best for the child. That plan was to be devised by the increasingly popular psychologists and psychiatrists; delinquency was thought of almost as a disease, to be diagnosed by specialists and the patient kindly but firmly dosed. (1967:3)

Early Critics

From the outset, critics of the juvenile court questioned the concept of *parens patriae* as an adequate legal precedent. Because the notion had applied to protecting the property of children (Tappan, 1949), it was not a purely logical or automatic outgrowth of English Common Law tradition. Rather, the concept was extended by analogy as a legal basis for the court. The early critics challenged its constitutionality on the grounds that its application by the juvenile court violated notions of due process of law. Timothy Hurley, who was influential in establishing the Chicago juvenile court, lamented in 1905 that the property rights of children had been clearly established but the legal rights of the child as a person were ignored. Similarly, Thomas Eliot criticized the juvenile court as becoming a "department of maladjusted children" and for attempting to become "all things to all men" (1914:16). However, because the juvenile court defined its procedures as civil rather than criminal, constitutional guarantees of due process were not applicable.

Of course, the denial of due process was not entirely unique to the juvenile justice system. "State Court systems were relatively free to operate as they wished, bound only by their own constitutions and State Court interpretations" (Glen and Weber, 1971:1). The autonomy of state courts allowed considerable variation in the extension of due-process guarantees to adults who were being processed for criminal offenses. Extension of guarantees of due process to minors began much later and is still in process. States have had considerable autonomy in the handling of juveniles, and in the 1940s and 1950s some began to extend due-process protections to juveniles (Glen and Weber, 1971). During those years, Wisconsin, Minnesota, Oregon, and California revised or rewrote their juvenile codes to extend greater due-process guarantees to juveniles. However, for the most part the juvenile court was considered to be concerned with rehabilitation rather than punishment, and thus the trappings of criminal law and procedure were shunned.

Juvenile Justice and Key Court Cases

No sooner had the court been established than dissatisfaction arose with the juvenile justice system. For example, the Illinois legislature voted in 1912 to abolish the court, but the governor vetoed the measure (Decker, 1984). Robert Mennel (1973) cites several instances where the doctrine of *parens patriae* was challenged immediately after the juvenile court was created, but in each case there was a gradual strengthening of the powers of the court. It was not until 1966 that the United States Supreme Court handed down its first ruling that bore on the constitutionality and legal foundation of juvenile court proceedings. Since that time, the court has examined several matters that deal with the rights of juveniles and has questioned the absolute authority of the juvenile court. However, compared to the voluminous decisions that have been made in hammering out the legal rights of adults, we have only a handful of decisions that relate to juveniles.

Kent v. United States, 383 U.S. 541 (1966)

The *Kent* case is a most significant decision because it was the first time that the U.S. Supreme Court agreed to hear a case regarding a juvenile. As late as 1955 the Court refused to rule on the issue of due process of law for juveniles, stating that "since juvenile courts are not criminal courts, the constitutional rights granted to persons accused of crime are not applicable to the children brought before them" (*In re*

Holmes, 1089A, 2d 523). The Supreme Court argued that the juvenile court, operating under the doctrine of *parens patriae*, does not punish children but acts on their behalf. Due process of law does not apply to juveniles since the juvenile court is not a criminal court and the juvenile is not charged with committing a criminal act.

In 1966 the Court reversed its stand on the negation of due process in juvenile matters by ruling on the case of Morris A. Kent, Jr. The specifics of the case were as follows: (1) Kent, first arrested in 1959 at the age of 14 for housebreaking, was freed on probation; (2) in 1961 during the investigation of a theft, Kent's fingerprints were found at the scene of the crime; (3) the juvenile judge, after considering the charges against Kent, decided to waive jurisdiction and transferred the case from juvenile to adult court without stating a reason to the youth or his parents; (4) Kent stood trial as an adult and received a sentence of thirty to ninety years in prison. If Kent had appeared in juvenile court, the maximum sentence for the 16-year-old boy would have been five years (the court's jurisdiction does not extend beyond age 21).

The *Kent* case was appealed to the Supreme Court, and in 1966 the Court ruled that Kent's right of due process had been violated. In handing down its decision, the Supreme Court ruled that (1) a hearing must be held in juvenile court on the issue of remanding or transferring a juvenile case to an adult court; (2) the juvenile is entitled to counsel at the waiver proceeding; (3) counsel is entitled to have access to all the social records of the juvenile prepared by the staff of the court in presenting its decision to waive jurisdiction; (4) it is incumbent upon the juvenile court that a statement of reasons accompany the waiver order.

Although this 1966 decision was confined only to matters of waiver of jurisdiction, it marked the first significant step toward a review of the juvenile justice system. The Supreme Court appeared to open the door for further litigation by emphasizing the need for due process and fair treatment in the juvenile court. Justice Fortas added his personal observations to the *Kent* decision with the following statement:

> While there can be no doubt of the original laudable purpose of juvenile courts, studies and critiques in recent years raise serious questions as to whether actual performance measures well enough against theoretical purposes to make tolerable the immunity of the process from the reach of constitutional guarantees applicable to adults. There is much evidence that some juvenile courts, including that of the District of Columbia, lack the personnel, facilities, and techniques to perform adequately as representatives of the state in a *parens patriae* capacity, at least with respect to children charged with law violation. There is evidence, in fact, that there may be grounds for concern that the child receives the worst of both worlds; that he gets neither the protection accorded to adults nor the solicitous care and regenerative treatment postulated for children. (383 U.S. 541-555-56, 1966)

This poignant statement emphasized the Supreme Court's concern that the right to representation is "not a grudging gesture to a ritualistic requirement" but is the essence of justice. The *Kent* ruling set the stage for the landmark *Gault* case that was acted upon the following year.

In re Gault, 387 U.S. 1, 55 (1967)

On June 8, 1964, the sheriff of Gila County, Arizona, arrested 15-year-old Gerald Gault. The sheriff was acting on a complaint from a neighbor, Mrs. Cook, that Gerald and another boy had made lewd and indecent remarks to her on the telephone. Gerald was taken to the local detention facility, and his parents, who were both at work, were not informed of the arrest until later that evening. On June 9 an adjudication hearing was held, at which time Gerald and his parents were informed of the nature of the complaint. Mrs. Cook, however, did not appear. This hearing was conducted without any formal notice of charges, without legal counsel, without the presence of any witnesses, and without any record or transcript of the hearing. The dispositional hearing was held on June 15, and the juvenile court reported that "after a full hearing and due deliberation the court finds that said minor is a delinquent child, and that said minor is of the age of 15 years." The juvenile judge committed Gerald as a juvenile delinquent to an institution for boys "for the period of his minority"—that is, until Gerald was 21 years of age. As a juvenile, Gerald was sentenced to six years; had he been an adult, the maximum penalty would have been a fine of $50 or a jail sentence of not more than two months.

Arizona law permitted no appeal in juvenile cases. Instead, a petition for a *writ of habeas corpus* was filed with the Supreme Court of Arizona on August 3, 1964. Such a writ, in effect, demands that reasons be given concerning the detention of any individual. The writ was based on an alleged denial of the following rights: (1) notice of the charges, (2) right to counsel, (3) right to confrontation and cross-examination, (4) privilege against self-incrimination, (5) right to a transcript of the proceedings, and (6) right to appellate review.

The Supreme Court of Arizona dismissed the writ and each of the six allegations. This court argued against the first charge of denial of notice of charges by stating that the Gaults knew of the nature of the charges against Gerald by virtue of their appearance at the two hearings. Furthermore, the court stated that specific written charges are not necessary because "the policy of the juvenile law is to hide youthful errors from the full gaze of the public and bury them in the graveyard of the forgotten past." The court rejected the second charge of denial of counsel by arguing that "the parent and the probation officer may be relied upon to protect the infant's interests." In addition, the court maintained that the juvenile court has the discretion, but not the duty, to allow legal representation. The third and fourth charges (lack of cross-examination and protection from self-incrimination) were dismissed on the grounds that "the necessary flexibility for individualized treatment will be enhanced by a rule which does not require the judge to advise the infant of a privilege against self-incrimination." The final two charges concerning appellate review and a transcript of the proceedings were also denied. The court argued that Arizona law permitted no appeal of a juvenile court decision and that since juvenile proceedings are confidential, any transcript would have to be destroyed in due time.

The *Gault* case was then appealed to the U.S. Supreme Court, and on May 16, 1967, the Court reversed the decision of the Supreme Court of Arizona. The Supreme Court reexamined each of the six charges and found that the juvenile court's unbridled discretion "however benevolently motivated, is frequently a poor substitute for principle and procedure." Due process of law is provided for by the Constitution and "the condition of being a boy does not justify a kangaroo court."

The Supreme Court specifically stipulated: (1) Notice of charges must be given sufficiently in advance of juvenile court hearings to permit time to prepare for the court proceedings. (2) The probation officer cannot act as counsel for the child because he or she is in fact acting as the arresting officer. In any juvenile proceeding that may result in commitment to an institution, the juvenile and his or her parents must be notified of the child's right to be represented by counsel; if they are unable to afford counsel, the court must appoint an attorney to represent the juvenile. (3) Confrontation and sworn testimony by witnesses available for cross-examination are essential in delinquency hearings. Any order of commitment to a state institution cannot be sustained in the absence of these fundamental principles of the adversary process. (4) Although a juvenile hearing may in fact involve civil rather than criminal proceedings, the privilege of the right to remain silent as stipulated in the Fifth Amendment nonetheless applies in juvenile matters. The Constitution guarantees that no person shall be compelled to be a witness against her/himself when threatened with deprivation of liberty. The Supreme Court argued that juvenile proceedings that may lead to commitment to a state institution must be regarded as criminal hearings for the purposes of the privilege against self-incrimination.

The Supreme Court did not rule on the fifth charge, denial of the right to a transcript at juvenile hearings. Although such a practice is desirable, particularly in reconstructing the record in an appeals process, the Court did not enforce this procedure. Finally, regarding the sixth charge of denial of appellate review, the Supreme Court chose not to rule on the constitutionality of the Arizona statute that denied appeal in juvenile cases.

The importance of the *Gault* decision in the extension of juvenile rights cannot be minimized. Although it neither overturned the juvenile court system nor invalidated questionable procedures in dealing with the rights of juveniles, it did introduce the concept of due process of law into the juvenile court system. Feld (1999) points out that prior to *Gault* fewer that 5 percent of juvenile cases had legal representation, but even since *Gault* less than half of juveniles receive assistance of counsel. However, the Supreme Court heavily qualified the capacity of the doctrine of *parens patriae* to be the all-pervading philosophy of the juvenile court. The *Gault* decision also challenged the common assumption that juvenile court proceedings are noncriminal. In sum, this decision was not so much a culmination of the fight for juvenile rights as a call to arms in recognizing the dignity and respect that individuals under the age of majority must be accorded.

In re Winship, 397 U.S. 358 (1970)

The third case regarding juvenile rights came before the U.S. Supreme Court in 1970. A 12-year-old boy named Samuel Winship had been charged with stealing $112 from a woman's purse. This act, if committed by an adult, would constitute a crime of larceny, and the probable punishment would not be particularly severe. As a juvenile, however, Winship was ordered to be placed in a training school for a period of six years. The judge in the juvenile court relied on a provision of New York state law which states that proof of the matter in a juvenile case need not be established beyond a reasonable doubt but simply that an adjudicatory hearing be based on the civil law's standard of a "preponderance of the evidence."

The case was appealed to the U.S. Supreme Court on the grounds that the essentials of due process had been violated. In addition, the appellant contended that when a juvenile is charged with an act that would constitute a crime if committed by an adult, proof must be established beyond a reasonable doubt. The Court ruled that proof of a criminal charge beyond a reasonable doubt is constitutionally required for juveniles, as well as adults. Further, the Court argued, despite the rhetoric of the juvenile court, a delinquency adjudication is a conviction, and its proceedings are criminal. "Civil labels and good intentions do not themselves obviate the need for criminal due process safeguards in juvenile courts." The problem with the *Winship* case is that it refers to criminal acts, not status offenses or what are called PINS cases (persons in need of supervision). Further, Bernard (1992) argues that in everyday practice, juvenile court judges routinely disregard the evidentiary burden of *Winship* with impunity.

McKeiver v. Pennsylvania, 403 U.S. 528 (1971)

What appeared to be a steady progression of Supreme Court rulings extending the provisions of the Bill of Rights to juveniles received a temporary setback with the 1971 *McKeiver* ruling. The case involved a 16-year-old boy, Joseph McKeiver, who had been charged with three felonious acts in juvenile court. At the time of his adjudication hearing, a request made for a jury trial was denied, and McKeiver was adjudged delinquent and placed on probation. The case was appealed to the Supreme Court on the grounds that it violated the Sixth Amendment's guarantee of the right to an impartial jury and the Seventh Amendment's stipulation of the right to a trial by jury.

After a careful review of previous decisions relating to juvenile matters, the Court concluded that the right to a trial by jury in the juvenile court's adjudication stage is not a constitutional requirement. The precise reasons set forth entail the transformation of the juvenile proceeding into an adversarial process that would jeopardize the "idealistic prospect of an intimate, informal protective proceeding." Justice Blackmun, who delivered the decision, stated: "If in its wisdom, any State feels the jury trial is desirable in all cases, or in certain kinds, there appears to be no impediment to its installing a system embracing that feature. That however, is the State's privilege and not its obligation." The essence of this decision is the Supreme Court's refusal to equate juvenile proceedings with the proceedings of the adult criminal justice system. The Court believed that such an equation would negate "every aspect of fairness, of concern, of sympathy, and of paternal attention that the juvenile court system contemplates." Barry Feld (1999) asserts that the Court was convinced that a formal hearing might preclude a therapeutic orientation for the juvenile court but the Court did not present any evidence that a confidential proceeding is more efficacious.

Breed v. Jones, 421 U.S. 519 (1975)

In 1971, a 17-year-old Los Angeles juvenile was arrested on the charge of robbery with a deadly weapon. The juvenile was ordered detained pending adjudication on the delinquency petition. The juvenile court sustained the delinquency petition, finding that the juvenile had committed the robbery, and ordered that the proceedings be continued for a dispositional hearing. At this subsequent hearing, the juvenile judge ruled that this juvenile was "not amenable to the care, treatment and training program of the juvenile court" and therefore remanded the juvenile to the adult criminal court for a new trial. Despite the defendant's objections that such an action would constitute double jeopardy, the juvenile was tried in the adult criminal court and found guilty of committing a felony.

A petition was filed in the federal district court on the grounds that the juvenile hearing and the adult trial on the same criminal act had placed the defendant in double jeopardy. The district court denied the petition, stating that the juvenile proceeding was civil and not criminal in nature, and that if the juvenile court had to follow the rigorous rules and formalities regarding double jeopardy, it would be deprived of its ability to function. The case was then taken to the court of appeals, which ruled that the double jeopardy clause of the Fifth Amendment is fully applicable to juvenile court proceedings. Furthermore, the court ruled that the application of the double jeopardy guarantee in the juvenile court would not interfere with that court's goal of rehabilitation. In 1975 the decision of the court of appeals was appealed to the U.S. Supreme Court. In a unanimous decision, the Court upheld the ruling of the appellate court.

In handing down its decision, the Supreme Court broadened the concept of double jeopardy beyond its traditional meaning of double punishment to include the "potential or risk of trial and conviction." The Court argued that the juvenile was put in double jeopardy even though the juvenile hearings did not run their full course and did not arrive at a final disposition. Although sentenced for punishment only at the adult criminal trial, the juvenile was subjected to the burden of two trials for the same offense and twice had to marshal resources against the state. The effect of this ruling was to require that decisions about the transfer of jurisdiction be made before the juvenile or criminal proceedings are initiated.

Swisher v. Brady, 438 U.S. 204 (1978)

It is not unusual to find in many states substitute judges or referees who assist the actual judge in hearing cases. In Maryland, such a referee is called a *master* and actually hears delinquency cases and rules on the matter. However, in actuality the master submits his or her recommendation to the juvenile judge who officially rules on the matter. The *Swisher v. Brady* case involved a master who heard a case and found the juvenile not to be delinquent. The "official" judge of the juvenile court reviewed the case and allegedly obtained new information that was not discussed in the juvenile's hearing before the master. The juvenile judge overruled the master and found the juvenile to be delinquent.

This case was appealed to the Supreme Court on the grounds that it constituted double jeopardy and was in violation of the Court's position taken in the *Breed v. Jones* case. However, the Supreme Court ruled that the juvenile was subjected to only one hearing under the Maryland system. The Court reasoned that the juvenile judge's review of the record constituted a continuation of the original hearing before the master. Rather than being placed in jeopardy a second time, the master's findings are advisory only, subjected to final approval by the juvenile judge. In contrast, both California and Illinois have ruled that reversal by a juvenile court judge of a referee's dismissal of charges constitutes double jeopardy if the charges are heard again (Guggenheim and Sussman, 1985:54–55). It is important to note that a master or substitute judge typically assumes the posture of the official juvenile judge and the decision rendered is not official until the duly appointed juvenile judge approves the decision of the substitute judge.

Schall v. Martin, 467 U.S. 253 (1984)

Gregory Martin, a 14-year-old, was arrested in 1977 for first-degree robbery, second-degree assault, and criminal possession of a weapon. He lied to the police, giving a false name and a false address. Between the time of his arrest and fact-finding hearing, he spent a total of 15 days in detention. He was adjudicated a delinquent and placed on two years' probation. His attorney filed an appeal, contesting that his preventive detention was a violation of the due process. A lower-court ruled that the judge lacked the technical ability to predict future criminal conduct and the detention constituted punishment before trial. This court argued that "the vast majority of juveniles detained either have their petitions dismissed before an adjudication or are released after adjudication" (467 U.S. at 262). The Supreme Court ruled that juveniles do not enjoy the same liberties as adults and that "juveniles are always in some form of custody . . . if parental control falters, the State must play its part as *parens patriae*" (467 U.S. at 265). Feld asserts that the Supreme Court "resurrected 'paternalistic' assumptions and *parens patriae* ideology with the conclusory assertion that children have minimal rights . . . and thereby allowed states to abridge juvenile's liberty interests more readily than those of adults" (1999:139). Many critics of preventive detention assert that the juvenile court has no meaningful standards and too many juveniles are placed in detention who pose no threat to themselves or others. In the adult courts the standard for preventive detention is very high, stipulating that the arrestee presents a demonstrable danger to the community.

Fare v. Michael C., 442 U.S. 707 (1979)

The applicability of *Miranda* (a Supreme Court decision extending certain rights to suspects in the process of arrest) to juvenile proceedings has never been ruled upon by the Supreme Court. Considerable disagreement exists whether a juvenile is competent to waive his or her *Miranda* rights or whether a parent or an attorney must be present (Davis, 2000). In California a 16-year-old boy with a prior record was arrested and read his *Miranda* rights. Since the boy was already on probation, he asked to see his probation officer. He informed the arresting officer that he was instructed to contact his probation officer if he ever got into any difficulties. The police officer said the juvenile could not see his probation officer but he could see an attorney. The boy chose not to see an attorney but repeatedly asked for his probation officer and finally confessed to the crime. The California Supreme Court ruled that the request for a probation officer was an invocation of his Fifth Amendment right. The U.S. Supreme Court ruled that a probation officer is not an attorney but an officer of the law and as such cannot give advice. Further, the boy was an "experienced, older juvenile who knew what he was doing" when he confessed to the crime. Justice Marshall vehemently disagreed with this decision. He stated that the "juvenile reached out for an adult to obtain advice . . . it is absurd to think that a juvenile would know an attorney." Justice Marshall also pointed out that the "record indicates he was immature and uneducated and vulnerable to pressures of interrogation." However, the Court held that the 16-year-old's waiver of counsel was valid and his confession was admissible.

Under the *Miranda* ruling, once an individual requests to see an attorney, this constitutes an invocation of the Fifth Amendment and any statement made thereafter is inadmissible. But as stated in *Fare v. Michael C.,* the juvenile must specifically request an attorney. Some courts have stated that a request by a juvenile to see a parent also invokes the Fifth Amendment. The difficulty with the issue of requesting counsel is that it must be done with "sufficient clarity." If the juvenile's utterances are ambiguous regarding a request to see a parent or an attorney, the police may proceed with the interrogation. In a 1987 case, a juvenile confessed to a crime but was not advised that his mother was at the police station asking for him. The court ruled that the police had no obligation to tell the juvenile of the mother's presence, but accepted his confession.

New Jersey v. T.L.O., 105 S. Ct. 733 (1985)

The Fourth Amendment right regarding protection against unreasonable search and seizure has always been problematic for juveniles. This is compounded by the fact that juveniles are also students and the doctrine of *in loco parentis* asserts that school officials take the place of parents and as such can claim parental immunity from Fourth Amendment limitations. In essence this means that school officials in many states can search lockers for drugs; trained dogs can be used to sniff out drugs in lockers; and in certain situations, school officials can search students without a search warrant. This issue becomes quite complex because the courts have made distinctions between searches of lockers, which are jointly controlled by the student and the school, and the distinction of a teacher as a government representative and surrogate parent. Generally speaking, the limitations of the Fourth Amendment apply to law enforcement officials, not to private citizens.

The *New Jersey v. T.L.O.* case is a significant decision regarding school searches. The case arose out of an incident in which a teacher found two girls smoking in a lavatory. Because this violated school policy, the girls were taken to the assistant principal's office. The vice-principal then examined one of the girl's purse and found a pack of cigarettes but then also found marijuana, marijuana paraphernalia, a substantial quantity of money, index cards that appeared to be a list of students who owed the girl money, and two letters implicating the girl as a marijuana dealer. At the trial court level, the argument was made that the evidence was obtained illegally and therefore must be suppressed. The judge denied the motion to suppress stating that the school official acted in a reasonable manner. Upon appeal to the New Jersey Supreme Court, this court argued that the search violated the girl's constitutional rights and the evidence was not admissible. Finally, the case was appealed to the U.S. Supreme Court.

The Supreme Court stated that the *in loco parentis* (teachers acting in the place of parents) doctrine is suspect and such reasoning is "in tension with contemporary reality and the teachings of this Court." Secondly, the Court argued that when teachers conduct searches of students, they cannot claim parental immunity from Fourth Amendment restrictions. Teachers are acting as representatives of the state and they are subject to Fourth Amendment limitations. However, the Court adopted a "reasonable ground" standard by asserting that school personnel may have to conduct searches in order to maintain safety, order, and discipline in the school. The test for reasonableness according to the Supreme Court is twofold: (1) was the action "justified at its inception," and (2) was the search "reasonably related in scope to the circumstances which justified the interference in the first place."

What is not known is just how far the "reasonable suspicion" standard extends. The Court left unresolved whether school personnel must have individualized suspicion before searching a student or whether the standards change if school personnel act as agents of the police. The Court did acknowledge that students are indeed entitled to some protection under the Fourth Amendment but "the Court conceded the school has a need to maintain discipline in classrooms and on school premises, and some flexibility is needed in order to maintain order without being unduly restricted . . . the warrant requirement of the Fourth Amendment is too stringent to apply to school personnel" (Davis, 1996:3–22).

Stanford v. Kentucky, 492 U.S. 361 (1989) and *Missouri v. Wilkins*, 492 U.S. 361 (1989)

In 1989, the Supreme Court ruled on the issuance of a death sentence for two individuals under the age of 18. The petitioners claimed that they had a right to treatment in the juvenile justice system since they were 16 (Wilkins) and 17 (Stanford) years of age, and a death sentence constitutes cruel and unusual punishment. Stanford and an accomplice repeatedly raped and sodomized a gas station attendant during a robbery, drove the victim to a secluded area, and shot her point blank in the face. In the second case, Wilkins robbed a convenience store and repeatedly stabbed the victim, leaving her to die on the floor. As stated in their petition, the petitioners argued that the death penalty is contrary to the "evolving standards of decency that mark the progress of a maturing society."

What makes this case so fascinating is that in 1988 the Court in *Thompson v. Oklahoma* ruled that Oklahoma's imposition of a death sentence on an individual who was 15 years old at the time he committed the offense should be set aside. In this case it was argued that since Oklahoma did not have a minimum age for capital punishment they could not sentence a juvenile to death. Of the thirty-eight states that permit capital punishment, one state (Arkansas) allows it for youth aged 14, one state (Virginia) allows it for youth aged 15, ten states allow it for youth aged 16, and four allow it for youth aged 17. Interestingly, eight states (Arizona, Idaho, Montana, Louisiana, Pennsylvania, South Carolina, South Dakota, and Utah) have no minimum age specified. Finally, thirteen states and the federal system have 18 as the minimum age for capital punishment. Writing for the majority, Justice O'Connor stated that "the Eighth and Fourteenth Amendments prohibit the execution of a person who was under 16 years of age at the time of his or her offense" (487 U.S. 815, 838).

The Supreme Court consolidated the two cases under the caption of *Stanford v. Kentucky*, made no direct reference to the *Thompson* case of a year earlier, and rejected outright any notion that 16- or 17-year-old youth cannot be held responsible for their behavior and cannot be deterred. Further, the Court argued that no historical or current societal standard forbids the imposition of capital punishment for a person who murders at 16 or 17 years of age. Writing for the majority, Justice Scalia rejected the contention that the Court should look to other nations to discern a standard of decency and finding no national consensus regarding the death sentences of 16 or 17 year-olds, he upheld the original death sentences.

Qutb v. Strauss, 11 F.3d 488 5th Cir. (1993)

The Dallas City Council enacted a juvenile curfew ordinance that prohibited persons under 17 years of age from remaining in a public place or establishment from 11 PM until 6 AM on week nights and from 12 midnight until 6 AM on weekends. A public place was defined as any place to which the public has access like streets, hospitals, or office buildings, and an establishment was a privately owned business. A person under the age of 17 did not violate curfew if he or she was accompanied by a parent or guardian, was on an errand for a parent or guardian, was traveling to or from work, or was involved in a religious, school, or civic organizational function. Violation of curfew could result in a fine not to exceed $500 for each separate offense.

Elizabeth Qutb charged that this ordinance was unconstitutional and the Texas courts agreed. The matter then went to the Fifth Circuit Court of Appeals, which reversed the lower court. The appellate court argued that the state has a "compelling interest in increasing juvenile safety and decreasing juvenile crime." It found that the ordinance was constitutionally overbroad in that it allowed for exceptions including emergencies. The court argued that this ordinance represented only a minimal intrusion into the rights of parents.

The Qutb case resulted in the widespread passage of curfew ordinances in cities throughout the United States. In Bloomington, Minnesota, the Mall of America—the largest mall in the country—imposed curfews on unchaperoned teenagers. Persons under 16 years of age will not be permitted in the mall on Fridays and Saturdays after 6 PM unless accompanied by a parent or someone over 21. Similarly, Washington DC enacted an ordinance for persons under 17 from 11 PM to 6 AM on weekdays and midnight to 6 AM on weekends. However, a Federal District Court ruled that this curfew was unconstitutional. The judge based his ruling on the question of whether young people commit more crimes or become crime victims more often during the hours of curfew. The judge went on to state that the law was not narrowly tailored enough for the "court to sanction the government's erosion of one of the most comprehensive and valued liberty interests afforded citizens of a civilized society—the cherished freedom of movement." This latest ruling by the Federal District Court applies only to Washington DC and does not apply to the city of Dallas or to the Qutb case.

The American Civil Liberties Union asserted that "this ruling makes it clear that curfew laws violate the constitutional rights of children and parents, while doing nothing to make our streets safer." Statistics from cities suggest that very few juvenile crimes occur in public places during curfew hours (see box 2-3). Some argued that the home can be more dangerous than the streets in cases of children with abusive parents. Finally, others argued that curfews invited harassment by the police, who are not automatically able to tell the age of a young person. It was argued that curfews are enforced in an arbitrary and discriminatory manner. The ACLU argued curfews divert attention from real crime prevention. "If police officers are checking the IDs of every teenager walking a dog at 10 PM, and then driving those kids to police stations to be held until parents arrive, the police department's resources are diverted from dealing with real crime." To date, the legality of curfew ordinances has not been reviewed by the Supreme Court.

Box 2-3   Do Curfews Curb Delinquency?

The curfew statute in Dallas was defended using data on the time of day when violent victimizations occurred with no detail on differences between juveniles and adults. When are most juvenile offenses committed? How would you use these data in challenging the curfew statute?

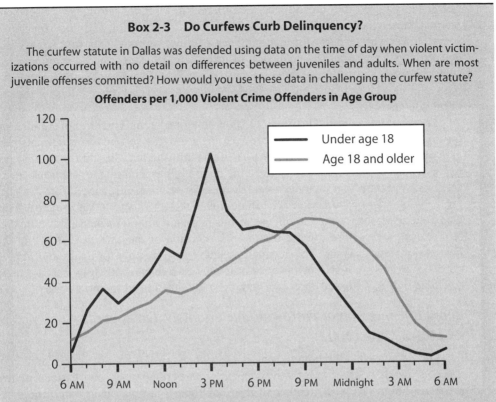

Offenders per 1,000 Violent Crime Offenders in Age Group

Source: Adapted from H. Snyder and M. Sickmund. 2006. *Juvenile Offenders and Victims: 2006 National Report*, chapter 3. Washington, DC: Office of Juvenile Justice and Delinquency Prevention.

Vernonia School District 47J v. Acton, 115 S. Ct 2386 (1995)

James Acton, a seventh-grader, signed up to play football but was denied participation because he refused to sign a drug-test consent form. His parents filed a court action arguing that this constituted an invasion of privacy and was in violation of the Fourth and Fourteenth Amendments to the U.S. Constitution. The Ninth Circuit Court agreed that this did indeed violate the Fourth and Fourteenth Amendments as well as certain provisions of the Oregon constitution. The matter was then appealed to the U.S. Supreme Court, and by a 6–3 decision the Court vacated the Ninth Circuit Court's judgment.

The Supreme Court argued that while state-compelled urinalysis for drugs is a search within the meaning of the Fourth Amendment, the search is reasonable. However, Justice Scalia, writing for the majority, argued that while a search required a warrant based on probable cause, this requirement was impracticable in the public schools. Basing his opinion on *New Jersey v. T.L.O.*, Justice Scalia stated that in "special needs" cases the Court has approved searches based on reasonable suspicion. While children do not "shed their constitutional rights at the schoolhouse gate," Justice Scalia asserted that those rights are different in a school setting than elsewhere. Schoolchildren have a reduced expectation of privacy at school, and this expectation is even lower with respect to student athletes. "School sports are not for the bashful," declared Justice Scalia. The collection of urine samples constituted a minimal invasion of privacy for student athletes. He also argued that drug use by athletes poses a particular danger and noted that student athletes also serve as role models for the rest of the student body.

The Vernonia School District in Oregon developed a precise series of stipulations for drug testing. If the drug sample proves to be positive, a second test is administered as soon as possible. If this test is negative, no action is taken. Should this second test prove to be positive the student is given the option of participating for six weeks in an assistance program that includes weekly urinalysis or being suspended from athletics for the remainder of the season. The student would then be retested at the start of the next athletic season. A second offense results in an automatic suspension for the current season, and a third offense results in suspension of the current season and the next two athletic seasons. This testing procedure is to be only for drugs and not for other conditions such as pregnancy or disease. The results of the drug tests are to be disclosed only to a limited class of school personnel on a need-to-know basis.

Board of Education of Pottawatomie County v. Earls, et al. 242 F.3rd 1264 (2002)

The Tecumseh, Oklahoma, School District required that all middle and high school students consent to urinalysis in order to participate in any extracurricular activity. Lindsay Earls, a member of the show choir, the marching band, the Academic Team, and the National Honor Society, brought action against the school district arguing that mandatory urinalysis violates the Fourth Amendment. Further, Earls argued that the school district had not demonstrated any significant problem with drugs and therefore this policy "neither addresses a proven problem nor promises to bring any benefit to students or the school." The U.S. District Court for the Western District of Oklahoma rejected the claim in 2000.

At the Supreme Court, Justice Thomas wrote for the majority, stating that the Vernonia case upheld suspicionless drug testing for athletes. Further, Justice Thomas argued that finding of probable cause is unnecessary in a public school context because it would "unduly interfere with the maintenance of swift and informal disciplinary procedures." A student's privacy interest is limited in a public school where students are required to submit to physical examination and vaccinations, and students who participate in extracurricular activities voluntarily subject themselves to more intrusions of their privacy. Justice Thomas asserted that some clubs require off-campus travel and communal dress, and they have rules and regulations which are a further intrusion upon normal rights. It was also found that some students appeared to be under the influence of drugs, a drug dog found marijuana in a school parking lot, and the people of the community were calling on the school board to discuss the drug situation. Justice Thomas concludes, "We find that testing students who participate in extracurricular activities is a reasonably effective means of addressing the school district's legitimate concerns in preventing, deterring, and detecting drug use."

Justice Ginsburg in a scathing dissent argued that "the particular testing program upheld today is not reasonable, it is capricious, even perverse: petitioners' policy targets for testing a student population least likely to be at risk from illicit drugs."

Roper v. Simmons 112 S. W. 3d 397 (2005)

Christopher Simmons at age 17 stated he wanted to murder someone because he could "get away with it." Simmons and two others broke into the house of Shirley Crook at 2:00 AM, covered her eyes and mouth with duct tape, and drove her in her minivan to a state park. After tying her hands and feet, the three threw Mrs. Crook from a railroad trestle into the river below, where she drowned. The next day, Simmons bragged about the killing. The police arrested him and Simmons confessed to the crime. The State of Missouri charged Simmons with murder and he was tried as an adult. At his trial the jury found him guilty and the judge imposed the death penalty. After the trial, the case was appealed to the Missouri Supreme Court, which set aside the death sentence and resentenced Simmons. The case then went to the U.S. Supreme Court, where by a 5–4 vote they affirmed the Missouri Supreme Court's decision based on the Eighth Amendment's prohibition of "cruel and unusual punishment" of a 17-year-old. Writing for the majority, Justice Kennedy, who had voted in favor of the death penalty in the Stanford case, changed his opinion. "From a moral standpoint," Justice Kennedy wrote, "it would be misguided to equate the failings of a minor with those of an adult, for a greater possibility exists that a minor's character deficiencies will be reformed." He further stated that "our determination finds confirmation in the stark reality that the United States is the only country in the world that continues to give official sanction to the juvenile death penalty." Justice Kennedy argued that there is a "national consensus against the death penalty," and stated that the governor of Kentucky decided to spare the life of Kevin Stanford (the 1989 *Stanford v. Kentucky* case) by commuting his sentence to life imprisonment. The governor had argued that "we ought not be executing people who, legally, were children." Justice Kennedy stated that the age of 18 is where "society draws the line . . . between childhood and adulthood. It is, we conclude, the age at which the line for death eligibility ought to rest."

In a scathing dissent, Justice Scalia dismissed Justice Kennedy's arguments by taking the unusual approach of reading from the bench his dissent. Justice Scalia called the decision a "mockery" and found "on the flimsiest of grounds" that a national consensus exists against the death penalty. "The Court thus proclaims itself the sole arbiter of our Nation's moral standards" argued Justice Scalia, and takes "guidance from the views of foreign courts and legislatures." Justice Scalia vehemently objected to the fact that the "subjective views of five members of this Court" can change the meaning of the U.S. Constitution. He asserted, "By what conceivable warrant can nine lawyers presume to be the authoritative conscience of the Nation?" Justice Scalia further argued that "our country has not reached a national consensus on the [death penalty] question" and is it absurd to think that "approval by other nations and peoples should buttress our commitment to American principles." He concluded his lengthy dissent by stating "this is no way to run a legal system."

Justice Scalia took his strong objection to the Simmons case public when he gave an address two weeks later. He criticized the "evolving notions of decency" argument as "simply a mask for the personal preferences of the five-member majority." He clearly objected to what is called an *activist judiciary*, which renders decisions based not on the Constitution but on personal opinion. Justice Scalia, in delivering this address at the Woodrow Wilson Center in Washington DC, blamed Chief Justice Earl Warren for the increased political role of a Supreme Court that seemed more interested in personal policy preferences than interpreting the law. Justice Scalia dismissed the whole argument presented in *Roper v. Simmons* by saying that the Supreme Court exists to ensure that legislation and executive actions comply with the spirit and intent of the Constitution. "The Court does not exist to decide cases are nebulous as an evolving notion of decency." The narrow 5–4 vote, the changing face of the Supreme Court, and Justice Scalia's blistering attack on *Roper v. Simmons* suggest that this matter will be examined again by the Supreme Court.

Overview: The Extension of Juvenile Rights

Starting with the 1966 *Kent* decision, the U.S. Supreme Court extended to juveniles some basic constitutional rights that restrict the open-ended authority derived from the doctrine of *parens patriae*. Although the Court did not radically alter the juvenile justice system, it introduced the concept of due process of law for children and adolescents. In most of its decisions regarding the rights of juveniles, the Court expressed a growing disenchantment with numerous aspects of the juvenile justice system. Although the Court did not fully endorse the procedural rights of juveniles regarding a criminal hearing, it seriously challenged the noncriminal nature of juvenile court proceedings. The Court has hesitated to negate what it feels is a unique function of the juvenile court system; it has not, however, specified the precise advantages of that system. In fact, recent Court decisions endorse aspects of the juvenile system that would not be acceptable in criminal justice procedures.

It is hazardous to predict what future constitutional rights will be extended to juveniles. Significant gains have been made, but the basic doctrine of *parens patriae* will inevitably continue to produce legal difficulties in the future. Many questions pertaining to the rights of juveniles are still unanswered: the use of questionable search and seizure practices (Fourth Amendment rights), speedy and public hearings (Sixth Amendment rights), cruel and unusual punishments (Eighth Amendment rights), vague and ambiguous definitions of delinquency, and the precarious balance between the social work and legal posture of the juvenile court. Indeed, it is not even clear whether juveniles technically can be arrested. In most states the phrase "take into custody" is used rather than "arrest." Because of this, the Supreme Court has never ruled on the applicability of the *Miranda* decision in the juvenile system.

It should also be noted that the rights the Supreme Court has extended to juveniles involve rules of evidence and due process at the adjudicatory hearing stage. Thus, when the juvenile stands accused he or she is now entitled to remain silent; to have an attorney (at state expense, if necessary); to be advised of his or her rights, notice of charges, and proceedings; and to subpoena witnesses. In addition, Court decisions suggest that rights to a transcript and appellate review are desirable. However, at the disposition stage the judge is not bound by the rules of evidence nor is the juvenile entitled to have an attorney. Some commentators (Glen and Weber, 1971) view the dual character of the juvenile justice system (that is, different standards for the adjudication hearing and the disposition hearing) as a means of protecting the rights of juveniles and at the same time serving the treatment aims of the court. Others (Krisberg and Austin, 1993; Feld, 1999) feel that the rights of children should be protected at all stages of the proceedings and advocate ensuring due process at points beyond the adjudication hearing.

The Supreme Court has always sought to preserve the noncriminal nature of the juvenile court and has never stated that a juvenile hearing must conform to all the requirements of a criminal trial. In light of the current criticism of the adult criminal justice system, this brand of justice may not be the ideal model. The adult system has been depicted (with considerable justification) as a system of "bargain-counter" justice in which notions of due process and the adversary roles of defense and prosecution are secondary to efficiency and mass production (Blumberg, 1970). Platt and Friedman (1968) found that in the Chicago juvenile court, private attorneys for juveniles, even after the *Gault* decision, tended to be small-fee lawyers who neither represented their clients in an adversarial fashion nor negotiated for their clients. Similarly, public defenders appeared to spend very little time on behalf of their juvenile clients (Platt, Schecter, and Tiffany, 1968). On the other hand, Spencer Cox (1967) reported that in Philadelphia the percentage of juveniles represented by counsel increased from 5 percent to 40 percent following the *Gault* decision. Cox noted that this increase had a number of consequences for the processing of juveniles: (1) a reduction in detention before hearings, (2) a drop in commitment to institutions, and (3) a staggering backlog of cases awaiting disposition. It is important to note that *Gault* applies to alleged delinquents who are faced with potential commitment. It does not apply to instances of status offenders (noncriminal offenses like truancy, running away, or ungovernability), or stages other than adjudication, such as intake, detention, or disposition (Wadlington, Whitehead, and Davis, 1983).

More recent analyses of juvenile court processing reveal that many, if not most, juveniles are not represented by attorneys even at the adjudication stage. Feld (1984) reports that in the decades following the *Gault* decision the promise of counsel has not been realized. In an analysis of court cases for Nebraska, Minnesota, and North Dakota, at least 50 percent of delinquents and status offenders did not have lawyers (Feld, 1988). However, it did not appear to work to a youth's advantage to have a lawyer. Feld found that "representation by counsel rebounds to the disadvantage of juveniles" (1988:419). Youths with representation did worse in terms of outcomes than youths without lawyers. Feld suggested a number of explanations for this perplexing finding, including the possibility that the lawyers were unskilled, inclined to go along with the judge, or prone to bad plea bargains. Then again, youths without lawyers might also have been less serious offenders.

The juvenile court, like the criminal court, is a system with characteristics and practices that are dictated by concerns for the efficient processing of thousands of cases rather than by legal notions of due process of law. It is one thing to read the lofty ideals of the juvenile court set forth in the juvenile code and in Supreme Court decisions, but it is another matter to view the system in operation. The modern juvenile justice system is fraught with judges who have an enormous backlog of cases, probation officers who carry an enormous caseload, parents who do not want to get involved, and detention and juvenile institutions that are typically filled to capacity. Feld argues that the juvenile court rarely attracts the most brilliant legal minds. "A juvenile court appointment constitutes either a stepping-stone to a more desirable judicial post or the end of the line of an undistinguished career" (Feld, 1999:133).

Current Definitions of Delinquency

While due process and the procedural rights of juveniles are in a state of flux and the subject of legal battles, legal definitions of what constitutes delinquent behavior have been criticized for their lack of precision and rigor as well. Even the meaning of the term "delinquent" is ambiguous and varies from jurisdiction to jurisdiction. For example, if we try to specify a legal definition of delinquent that would be generally applicable throughout the United States, all we can state is that a delinquent is a nonadult or a child who commits an offense against a law of the state. In some instances these offenses may be criminal acts and in other cases these behaviors may be noncriminal offenses such as running away from home.

The glossary of terms presented at the beginning of this chapter represents the current trend in defining delinquency. It is now common to maintain a distinction among categories and to limit the term "delinquent" to offenses that would be criminal if the youth were an adult. Moreover, patterns of conflict or misbehavior that could be the basis for deeming a youth "incorrigible" or "ungovernable" may now fall within the category of *status offenses*, together with the specific activities typically included (e.g., runaway, smoking, drinking). Such differentiation between criminal offenses and status offenses grew out of recommendations by two national commissions and subsequent federal legislation (see chapter 11) encouraging the diversion of status offenders from regular juvenile court processing. In the 1970s critics of the juvenile court (Lerman, 1971) were reporting that status offenders were dealt with as harshly as (or even more harshly than) youths who had committed criminal offenses. The lack of differentiation was particularly disadvantageous to girls, since a larger proportion of their offenses were status offenses. A major theme characterizing juvenile justice reform in the late 1970s and 1980s was to differentiate among offenders and to reserve forms of confinement for serious offenders. Currently, however, many people view juvenile offenders as "hardened criminals." According to Bernard (1992), the get-tough movement now dominates the response to delinquency, and juvenile offenses and criminal offenses are virtually synonymous.

The definition of nonadult varies from state to state, with age 18 the most common cutoff point between adult and nonadult. Table 2-1 lists the **jurisdictional age** (that is, the age *below which* a person is subject to juvenile court jurisdiction) for each of the fifty states plus the District of Columbia. In some states the cutoff point is as low as age 16, while in most states it is 18. The minimum age limit of children subject to the juvenile court's jurisdiction is rarely specified, although Massachusetts and New York require a child to be at least 7 years of age, and Colorado, Mississippi, Vermont, and Texas set the minimum age at 10. However, common-law traditions have in essence set an operational lower limit of at least 7 years of age. A person younger than

7 is presumed not to be responsible for his or her actions. In some states a child under 8 years of age who enters the juvenile justice system may be dealt with as a dependent, rather than a delinquent, child.

The second column in table 2-1 lists the waiver or transfer age whereby juveniles may be tried as adults in criminal court. Some states list no age and two states do not provide for a waiver hearing. In those states where a waiver hearing is permitted, generally there is an added stipulation that the child must have committed a serious felony or that the child had been adjudicated for a previous juvenile offense. In a few instances the waiver criteria are exceedingly complex and the listing of such states in table 2-1 may be oversimplified. For example, in Connecticut a child may be transferred to the adult court if he or she is 14 and is charged with a serious juvenile offense. A waiver is mandatory for those 14 or older charged with murder or those who have been previously adjudicated for a serious felony offense and are being charged for a second felony offense. The criteria for a waiver standard are generally vague, simply stating that the child is "not amenable to treatment or rehabilitation."

The third column in the table indicates the type of jurisdiction the juvenile court enjoys. In most instances the juvenile court has *exclusive jurisdiction*, which means that no other court can rule on the matter, regardless of the nature of the offense. The juvenile court generally has exclusive jurisdiction over delinquent behavior that is in violation of the criminal codes. The juvenile court will also have jurisdiction over noncriminal acts that constitute status offenses. Some states refer to such offenders as Persons in Need of Supervision (PINS) or Children in Need of Supervision (CHINS). Some states also extend juvenile court jurisdiction to children who are "in danger of leading an idle, dissolute, lewd, or immoral life" or "those who are a danger to themselves or others."

Finally, the juvenile court has jurisdiction over a broad range of neglect and abuse situations. Such children are those who are without a parent or who have been abandoned or abused, or who lack adequate parental care or supervision. Depending on the state, such a child may be referred to as *dependent, deprived,* or *neglected.* In those states where the jurisdictional age listed in the table is younger than 18, it invariably rises to 18 for abused, dependent, or neglected children. In instances of abuse or neglect, the juvenile court may place the child in a temporary shelter care or foster care home; in instances of serious mistreatment the court may terminate the parental rights of the child's parents.

The scope of juvenile court jurisdiction has often been criticized as vague. For example, it is not clear what a California statute means when it makes reference to a child under the age of 18 "who from any cause is in danger of leading an idle, dissolute, lewd, or immoral life." Similarly, a Texas statute describes as delinquent a child who "habitually so deports himself as to injure or endanger the morals or health of himself or others." These statutes are exceedingly broad and very subjective. Challenges to such statutes have been made but no court has found them to be unconstitutional. In one instance a three-judge federal panel found the phrase "in danger of leading an idle, dissolute, lewd, or immoral life" to be vague but the U.S. Supreme Court vacated the judgment.

In some states, more than one court has jurisdiction over juveniles. *Concurrent jurisdiction* means that the juvenile court shares jurisdiction with the criminal court. In

Table 2-1   Jurisdiction of the Juvenile Court

State	Jurisdiction Age	Waiver Age	Type of Jurisdiction	Offenses Excluded
Alabama	18	14	Exclusive	None
Alaska	18	None stated	Exclusive	None
Arizona	18	None stated	Concurrent	None
Arkansas	18	14	Concurrent	None
California	18	16	Exclusive	None
Colorado	18	12	Concurrent	None
Connecticut	16	14	Exclusive	Capital offenses
Delaware	18	16	Exclusive	Capital offenses
DC	18	15-felony 16-under commitment	Concurrent	None
Florida	18	14	Concurrent for death or life imprisonment	None
Georgia	17	15	Concurrent for death or life imprisonment	Burglary if over 15
Hawaii	18	16	Exclusive	Serious felonies
Idaho	18	14	Exclusive	Capital offenses
Illinois	17	13	Exclusive	Serious felonies
Indiana	18	14-mandatory if serious felony	Exclusive	Serious felonies
Iowa	18	14	Exclusive	None
Kansas	18	any age	Exclusive	Age16, 2 prior felonies
Kentucky	18	14	Exclusive	None
Louisiana	17	14	Concurrent	Serious felonies
Maine	18	None stated	Exclusive	None
Maryland	18	15	Exclusive	Serious felonies
Massachusetts	17	no provision	Exclusive	None
Michigan	17	14	Exclusive	None
Minnesota	18	14	Exclusive	None
Mississippi	18	13	Exclusive	Capital offenses
Missouri	17	12	Exclusive	None
Montana	18	16	Exclusive	None
Nebraska	18	No provision	Concurrent for felonies	None
Nevada	18	14	Exclusive	Murder

State	Jurisdiction Age	Waiver Age	Type of Jurisdiction	Offenses Excluded
New Hampshire	17	None given	Concurrent for felonies	None
New Jersey	18	14	Exclusive	None
New Mexico	18	No provision	Exclusive	None
New York	16	No provision	Exclusive	Serious felonies
North Carolina	16	13	Exclusive	Capital offenses
North Dakota	18	14	Exclusive	None
Ohio	18	15	Exclusive	Serious felonies
Oklahoma	18	None stated	Concurrent	Serious felonies
Oregon	18	15	Exclusive	None
Pennsylvania	18	14	Exclusive	Murder
Rhode Island	18	Any age	Exclusive	None
South Carolina	17	Any age	Exclusive	None
South Dakota	18	None stated	Concurrent for felonies	None
Tennessee	18	16	Exclusive	None
Texas	17	15	Exclusive	None
Utah	18	none given	Exclusive	Serious felonies
Vermont	18	10 for serious felonies	Concurrent	Serious felonies
Virginia	18	14	Exclusive	None
Washington	18	None stated	Exclusive	None
West Virginia	18	14	Exclusive	None
Wisconsin	17	15	Exclusive	None
Wyoming	18	None stated	Concurrent	None

Source: S. M. Davis. 2000. *Rights of Juveniles: The Juvenile Justice System.* New York: Clark Boardman. Reprinted with permission Clark Boardman Callaghan.

Arkansas the criminal and juvenile courts have joint jurisdiction over all children under age 18. In other states the jurisdiction is concurrent only for offenses that are punishable by death or life imprisonment (Florida and Georgia) or when the juvenile has committed a serious felony offense (Nebraska, New Hampshire, South Dakota). In these situations, the prosecuting attorney generally decides to which court the juvenile will be referred.

The last column in table 2-1 lists those states which exclude certain offenses from the jurisdiction of the juvenile court. Until recently, nearly every state gave the juvenile court full jurisdiction over all offenses. In the past few years, there has been a growing trend to exclude serious offenses from the jurisdiction of the juvenile court. There is increasing discussion in state legislatures to mandate the hearing of serious felony cases in criminal court and completely bypass the juvenile court.

Continuing Controversy

The juvenile court will continue to be a source of controversy because it deals with people who are not quite adults and not quite children. There will be those who will resist extending to juveniles all of the rights of adults. At the same time, however, when youths commit serious offenses there will be pressure to treat them like adults. Feld suggests that "substantive and procedural reforms have converted the historical ideal of the juvenile court as a welfare agency into a quasi-penal system that provides young offenders with neither therapy nor justice" (1999:3).

Certain activities that are legally acceptable for adults will continue to be legally unacceptable for youth. In fact, to deal with alcohol consumption, states have uniformly raised the legal drinking age. To keep youth in school, state lawmakers are contemplating legislation that would deny driving licenses to dropouts. Such actions are based on the presumption that the state has more leeway to regulate and control the behavior of juveniles than the behavior of adults, and that juveniles do not have the right to resist such efforts. Thus, the ambiguous status of youth creates a double bind in that there is pressure to treat them as adults when dealing with their transgressions but to deny them a full range of rights in other regards.

As the composition of the Supreme Court changes, so will interpretations of the nature of "rights" and "due process of law" for both adults and juveniles. In reality, rights are not stable, constant, and unambiguous but are instead subject to human interpretation. Krisberg and Austin summarize the situation as follows:

> The juvenile court presents us with a curious mixture of uplifting ideology and harsh daily realities. Its rhetoric is steeped in concepts such as "compassionate care" and "individualized treatment." Yet, too often the reality is assembly line justice in which large numbers of youngsters and their families are quickly "disposed of" through a limited set of options that rarely are adequately funded. Conservatives consistently have attacked the juvenile court for its leniency, but liberals likewise have criticized the court for its excessive use of detention and jailing for minor offenses. (1993:1–2)

Even if standards of due process are clearly defined and extended to minors who have committed criminal offenses, a significant proportion of adolescents—incorrigible youths and status offenders—will continue to be processed through the juvenile court system without having committed a criminal offense. Rather than reducing the involvement of the court in the lives of youth, as was intended by many advocates of diversion, an increasing number of programs have been developed to deal with a growing range of youthful misbehavior, leading one critic of the juvenile justice system to ask whether youth are "being abused at higher prices?" (Schwartz, 1989). While some court processes are reserved for the most serious offenders, the juvenile justice system has been dealing with a wider range of youth with the implementation of diversion programs. The proliferation of such programs has generated new controversies involving the same perennial conflicts—due process and justice for juveniles versus the government's right to control the behavior of youth.

Thomas Bernard argues that solving the problem of juvenile delinquency "cannot be accomplished by introducing a new juvenile justice policy. Rather it requires changing the larger social conditions that gave rise to the problem in the first place" (1992:186). The juvenile court cannot solve the problems of delinquency without changing the social environment and this calls for radical change beyond the capacity of the juvenile court. The juvenile court itself is in need of transformation from its nineteenth-century origins, but no degree of structural or legal change in the juvenile court will ultimately solve the problem of delinquency.

The behavior and attitudes of the young should be understood in the context of a largely adult-controlled and adult-defined world. Children can easily become scapegoats for the grief and woes of modern industrial society. In America today, adolescents are seen as the cause of many of society's shortcomings. Crimes against persons and property, drug-related problems, lack of respect for authority, overweening ambition, greed, and widespread apathy are considered unique problems of youth; in fact, they are as much, if not more so, the problems of American society as a whole.

Summary

The origin and development of the juvenile justice system was influenced by a confluence of social forces including declining infant mortality rates, industrial development, urbanization, immigration, and such reform movements as compulsory public education, child labor legislation, and houses of refuge. Such forces helped establish childhood, adolescence, delinquents, and status offenders as bio-social-legal categories between birth and legal adulthood.

The legal groundwork and philosophical precedents of the juvenile court can be traced to the development of houses of refuge and reform schools for troublesome youth in the early and mid-1800s. The legal doctrine invoked in establishing such institutions was *parens patriae*, the concept that the state has the right to act as a parent. However, the establishment of houses of refuge and reform schools, the later "anti-institutionalist" movement, and the eventual creation of the juvenile court did not flow purely from humanitarian concerns; these movements also reflected the religious, ethnic, and class prejudices of the time.

The debate among scholars about the forces that shaped the juvenile justice system has not been resolved. Anthony Platt interprets the emergence of the juvenile court in the late 1800s as an extension of religious and class conflicts. In contrast, Schlossman, Finestone, and Hagan and Leon argue that the emergence of the juvenile court reflected an anti-institutional ideology that stressed probation, the home, and the family as targets of treatment. Scholars do agree, however, that there was and remains a considerable gap between the professed aims and the actual operation of the juvenile justice system.

Although the first juvenile court was established in 1899, it was not until 1966 that the U.S. Supreme Court first ruled on a constitutional issue relating to juvenile court proceedings. In a modest number of cases since 1966, the Supreme Court extended several rights of due process to juveniles at the adjudicatory level. These rulings do not, however, apply to the pre- or post-adjudicatory stages of the juvenile justice system. Moreover, the Court has not addressed several of the constitutional protections extended to adults in terms of their applicability to juveniles. Whether the

Court's decisions have had a significant impact on juveniles processed through the system is still a subject of dispute. The mass-processing aspects of the administration of justice, whether for adults or for juveniles, may make Supreme Court decisions irrelevant to the everyday operation of juvenile justice systems.

The creation of a separate juvenile court was more than a matter of instituting new procedures and new terminology. It involved the extension of state control over a wider range of activities than criminal law had ever encompassed. An examination of current statistics shows several overlapping categories of activity or problems that can bring a juvenile to the attention of the juvenile court. The nature of the offense alone does not automatically enable us to decide whether a youth is a delinquent, a status offender, or a dependent. Such categorization may also depend on age, gender, past behavior, and community reaction. Moreover, while distinctions between categories are made in statutes, the relevance of these distinctions for the actual processing and ultimate disposition of cases remains a subject of debate (see chapter 11).

Despite evidence of similarities in outcomes when comparing adult and juvenile justice systems, the juvenile court will continue to be attacked by some factions as harsh and repressive and by others for being lenient and sympathetic. Justice Blackmun's remarks in the *McKeiver* decision seem to echo the uncertain fate of the juvenile court:

> If the formalities of the criminal adjudicative process are to be superimposed upon the juvenile court system, there is little need for its separate existence. Perhaps that ultimate disillusionment will come one day, but for the moment we are disinclined to give impetus to it. (*McKeiver v. Pennsylvania*, 403 U.S. 528 1971)

Discussion Questions

1. Compare the terms used to describe the processing of juvenile offenders with those used for adult offenders. What is the purpose of that difference in language?

2. What is the juvenile justice system expected to do? Do you think all of these expectations can be effectively achieved at the same time? How do these multiple goals explain perennial unhappiness with that system?

3. Historians and other scholars argue that "childhood" and "adolescence" were age categories that had to be invented or discovered. How are these developments important for understanding the development of the juvenile justice system?

4. What social forces and social movements of the nineteenth century led to the development of the juvenile court?

5. Some scholars view the origins of the juvenile justice system as a progressive concern for child welfare and treatment, while others view it as basically conservative, aimed at control and punishment. Discuss how elements of each orientation are featured in the early operation of the juvenile justice system.

6. What is the meaning of the term *parens patriae* and what role did it play in the development of the juvenile justice system? Is it still reflected in decisions involving juvenile rights?

7. What major legal issues *have not been resolved* by the U.S. Supreme Court in the handling of juvenile offenders?

8. Can you see any trend or pattern to the Supreme Court's rulings on juvenile matters? Have additional rights been extended in the last twenty years?

9. Do you think mental age should be a consideration in determining the legality of the death penalty? What has been the Supreme Court's position on this issue?

10. Juveniles represented by attorneys in juvenile court seem to fare worse than those without representation. Develop two possible explanations for this disparity.

References

Abbot, G. 1938. *The Child and the State.* Vols. 1 and 2. Chicago: University of Chicago Press.

Aries, P. 1962. *Centuries of Childhood.* New York: Vintage Books.

Bakan, D. 1971. "Adolescence in America: From Idea to Social Fact." *Daedalus* (Fall): 979–95.

Bernard, T. J. 1992. *The Cycle of Juvenile Justice.* New York: Oxford University Press.

Blumberg, A. S. 1970. *Criminal Justice.* Chicago: Quadrangle Books.

Bremner, R. H. 1970. *Children and Youth in America: A Documentary History.* Vols. 1 and 2. Cambridge: Harvard University Press.

———. 1988. *American Philanthropy.* Chicago: University of Chicago Press.

Chambers, J. D. 1972. *Population, Economy and Society in Pre-Industrial England.* London: Oxford University Press.

Cox, S. 1967. "Lawyers in Juvenile Court." *Crime and Delinquency* 13 (October): 488–93.

Davis, S. M. 1996, 2000. *Rights of Juveniles: The Juvenile Justice System.* New York: Clark Boardman.

Decker, S. H. 1984. *Juvenile Justice Policy, Analyzing Trends and Outcomes.* Beverly Hills: Sage.

Eliot, T. D. 1914. *The Juvenile Court and the Community.* New York: Macmillan.

Feld, B. C. 1984. "Criminalizing Juvenile Justice: Rules of Procedure for Juvenile Court." *Minnesota Law Review* 69:141–276.

———. 1988. "*In re Gault* Revisited: A Cross State Comparison of the Right to Counsel in Juvenile Court." *Journal of Research in Crime and Delinquency* 34 (October): 393–424.

———. 1999. *Bad Kids: Race and the Transformation of the Juvenile Court.* New York: Oxford University Press.

Finestone, H. 1976. *Victims of Change.* Westport, CT: Greenwood Press.

Glen, J. E., and J. R. Weber. 1971. *The Juvenile Court: A Status Report.* Washington, DC: Center for Studies of Crime and Delinquency.

Guggenheim, M., and A. Sussman. 1985. *The Rights of Young People.* New York: Bantam Books.

Hagan, J., and J. Leon. 1977. "Rediscovering Delinquency: Social History, Political Ideology and the Sociology of Law." *American Sociological Review* 42 (August): 587–98.

Hall, G. S. 1882. "The Moral and Religious Training of Children." *Princeton Review* (January): 26–48.

Holt, M. H. 1992. *The Orphan Trains: Placing Out in America.* Lincoln: University of Nebraska Press.

Hurley, T. D. 1905. "Necessity for the Lawyers in the Juvenile Court." *Proceedings of the National Conference of Charities and Correction,* 173–77.

Krisberg, B. 1988. *Rethinking the Vision: The Future of the Juvenile Court.* San Francisco: National Council on Crime and Delinquency.

Krisberg, B., and J. Austin. 1993. *Reinventing Juvenile Justice.* Newbury Park, CA: Sage.

Langsam, M. 1964. *Children West: A History of the Placing Out System of The New York Children's Aid Society.* Madison, WI: State Historical Society.

Lasch, C. 1979. *Haven in a Heartless World: The Family Besieged.* New York: Basic Books.

Lerman, P. 1971. "Child Convicts." *Trans-Action* 8 (July/August): 35–45.

Lindsey, D. 1994. *The Welfare of Children*. New York: Oxford University Press.

Mennel, R. M. 1973. "Origins of the Juvenile Court: Changing Perspectives on the Legal Rights of Juvenile Delinquents." *Crime and Delinquency* 68:18–36.

National Center for Juvenile Justice. 2003. *Juvenile Court Statistics, 1998*. Washington, DC: Office of Juvenile Justice and Delinquency Prevention.

Platt, A. 1969a. *The Child Savers: The Invention of Delinquency*. Chicago: University of Chicago Press.

———. 1969b. "The Rise of the Child-Saving Movement: A Study in Social Policy and Correctional Reform." *Annals of the American Academy of Political and Social Science* 381 (January): 21–38.

———. 1974. "The Triumph of Benevolence: The Origins of the Juvenile Justice System in the United States." In *Criminal Justice in America,* edited by R. Quinney, 356–89. Boston: Little, Brown.

———. 1977. *The Child Savers: The Invention of Delinquency*. 2nd ed. Chicago: University of Chicago Press.

Platt, A., and R. Friedman. 1968. "The Limits of Advocacy: Occupational Hazards in Juvenile Court." *Pennsylvania Law Review* 116:1156–84.

Platt, A., H. Schecter, and P. Tiffany. 1968. "In Defense of Youth: A Case Study of the Public Defender in Juvenile Court." *Indiana Law Journal* 43:619–40.

Pollock, L. A. 1983. *Forgotten Children: Parent-Child Relationships from 1500 to 1900*. New York: Cambridge University Press.

Postman, N. 1994. *The Disappearance of Childhood*. New York: Vintage Books.

President's Commission on Law Enforcement and Administration of Justice. 1967. *Task Force Report: Juvenile Delinquency and Youth Crime*. Washington, DC: GPO.

Rothman, D. J. 1980. *Conscience and Convenience*. Boston: Little, Brown.

Sanders, W. B. 1945. "Some Early Beginnings of the Children's Court Movement in England." *National Probation Association Yearbook* 39:58–70.

Schlossman, S. L. 1977. *Love and the American Delinquent*. Chicago: University of Chicago Press.

Schwartz, I. M. 1989. *(In)justice for Juveniles: Rethinking the Best Interests of Children*. Lexington, MA: D.C. Heath.

Shorter, E. 1975. *The Making of the Modern Family*. New York: Basic Books

Snyder, H., and M. Sickmund. 2006. *Juvenile Offenders and Victims: 2006 National Report*. Washington, DC: Office of Juvenile Justice and Delinquency Prevention.

Sutton, J. R. 1988. *Stubborn Children: Controlling Delinquency in the United States, 1640–1981*. Berkeley: University of California Press.

Tappan, P. W. 1949. *Juvenile Delinquency*. New York: McGraw-Hill.

Thurston, H. 1930. *Dependent Children: A Story of Changing Aims and Methods in the Care of Dependent Children*. New York: Columbia University Press.

Wadlington, W., C. H. Whitehead, and S. M. Davis. 1983. *Cases and Materials on Children in the Legal System*. Mineola, NY: Foundation Press.

Watkins, J. C. 1998. *The Juvenile Justice Century: A Sociolegal Commentary on American Juvenile Courts*. Durham, NC: Carolina Academic Press.

Wrigley, E. A. 1969. *Population and History*. New York: McGraw-Hill.

Zelizer, V. 1985. *Pricing the Priceless Child: The Changing Social Value of Children*. New York: Basic Books.

three

Images of Delinquency
Police and Juvenile Court Statistics

In a recent wave of the National Youth Survey (NYS), we showed all respondents their rap sheets and asked them to confirm each arrest record. Many were shocked, some became angry, and others volunteered that we had missed an arrest or two. Overall, 27 percent of arrests were challenged by our respondents. In most cases, respondents acknowledged the arrest event, but claimed that it was unfounded, a mistake of some kind, and that they were told these charges had been dropped and they never went to court. I recall that one school teacher in Kansas was horrified, claimed the charge was unfounded and was dropped, and said if the local board of education found out she had an arrest record, she could lose her job. Another young man told us that he had purchased a motorcycle from a private party and had an accident on his way home. He was unconscious at the scene and was taken to the local hospital. The next day two police officers came to arrest him for vehicular theft as they could find no evidence that he owned the motorcycle. They then called the original owner and verified his story. He never heard anything more about it until we showed him his rap sheet with an arrest for vehicular theft. When we checked again with the relevant police agency, we were told that his story might well be true as they almost never clean records from their files or correct them to reflect such an outcome, and at this point in time they had no way to verify what happened.

(Delbert Elliott, "Lies, Damn Lies and Arrest Statistics," The Sutherland Award Presentation at the American Society of Criminology meeting, Boston, 1995)

Introduction

In this chapter and the next, we focus on images of delinquency rather than facts about delinquency because use of the word "facts" implies a degree of certainty that cannot be justified when examining available data on delinquency. In contrast, the word "image" suggests a perspective that might be distorted or a view that might be presented in a way that emphasizes certain dimensions of reality and downplays others (Jensen and Rojek, 1998). Claims about "facts" can be based on the vested interests of persons or agencies that collect them (O'Brien, 2000) or the degree to which they fit our preconceptions and stereotypes. Because measurement always involves a filter or a lens that captures some features of the subject, complete objectivity is not possible.

Official statistics on juvenile delinquency are the product of a complex reporting system influenced by local citizens (when there is a victim) who may or may not lodge a complaint with the police, the police themselves who may or may not act on a citizen's complaint, and a juvenile court, which may or may not rule on the acceptability of that particular juvenile behavior (Karmen, 2001). More specifically, any behavior can be viewed from different perspectives; likewise, the eventual reporting of that behavior can vary widely depending on the social characteristics or background of the observer. For example, eyewitness testimony in a court of law is normally viewed as problematic because different eyewitnesses can see the same event but arrive at different conclusions. A simple auto accident in which one car hits another may generate as many different interpretations as there are witnesses. People do not agree on basic facts because we all wear a set of lenses that makes us see different elements of a particular social phenomenon.

Interpreting Crime and Delinquency Data

In 1927 Werner Heisenberg presented an observation that shook the world of physics to its core (Cassidy, 1992). Heisenberg argued that the conditions necessary for precise or certain measurement of a subatomic particles' position created uncertainty in determining the same particle's momentum. This paradox became known as the Heisenberg uncertainty principle, which expresses a limitation of simultaneous measurement of subatomic particles' position and momentum. Similarly, measuring the subatomic particle's velocity will distort its direction. In other words, the act of measuring one dimension of a subatomic particle alters the measurement of another dimension. The very act of measurement becomes an intrusion on the natural state of a subatomic particle.

When attempting to measure delinquency, efforts to assure the anonymity and confidentiality of respondents who answer questionnaires either in private or in mass settings may lead to inaccuracies because the researcher cannot elaborate on the meaning of items in the survey. Conversely, interviewing youth one-on-one about offenses may increase the accuracy of what they report, but inhibit their willingness to answer questions honestly. Far from discovering "facts," measuring delinquency with one method only increases the uncertainty about the accuracy of other methods.

If we decide to measure criminal or delinquent acts using police reports, we may increase our certainty that something worthy of official attention has been measured, but decrease our certainty that all of the relevant "hidden" events have actually been detected. For offenses with victims, a cast of characters is involved in transforming events into an accurate measure of delinquency. Victims may not report their victimizations to the police, or may report differentially based on characteristics of the offense and offender. The police may respond differently over time and among different groups, which increases our uncertainty that they have provided an accurate, unbiased estimate of criminal and delinquent offenses and offenders. We can shift to self-report or victimization measures to avoid some of these problems, but as noted above such techniques may increase our uncertainty about other dimensions of delinquency.

It should be apparent, then, that a fundamental problem in the study of delinquency is uncertainty about the best way to measure delinquent behavior (Walker and Katz, 2002). Do we measure delinquency as interpreted by the juvenile offender, the juvenile offender's victim, or the police? Each party to the act might be only partially correct. Thus, we use the concept of the "image" of delinquency as portrayed by police statistics, the juvenile offender (self-report data), and the victim (victimization surveys). These three perspectives have some similarities, but just as many dissimilarities. There is not one perfect measure of delinquency but three different data sets that do not triangulate perfectly; however, when agreement occurs across these three measures, we can have some confidence that a real underlying pattern exists.

Uniform Crime Reports: The Crime Index

In the 1920s the International Association of Chiefs of Police appointed a committee to develop a system for gathering crime data in the United States. This committee developed what became the basis for the FBI's Uniform Crime Report (UCR) by 1929. The FBI began publishing monthly data by 1930, quarterly data by 1932, and prepared its first annual report in 1958 (Federal Bureau of Investigation, 2004). This annual report contains two major categories of information: "crimes known to the police" and "persons arrested." Arrest statistics will be discussed in a later section.

Because the UCR includes only those offenses that are reported or detected and designated as a crime by police, most events and people who *could* enter into official statistics do not, because they go undetected or unreported. A major reason many criminal victimizations never become crimes recorded by the police is that the victims do not take the initial step of reporting the crime (see chapter 4). Since most police activity is in response to public complaints, the public's willingness to report crimes is a major factor affecting the number of youths who are caught and processed through the juvenile justice system.

Why do people choose *not* to report crimes against them? The most common reasons given by respondents to the National Crime Survey vary by offense. For personal victimizations, between 20 and 25 percent of respondents indicated the offense was not reported because it was a "private or personal matter" (Maguire and Pastore, 2004: table 112). For the crime of rape, 54 percent of African-American respondents indicated the victimization was not reported due to perceptions of the police as "inefficient, ineffective, or biased" (Maguire and Pastore, 2004: table 113). "Lack of proof" and the view that "police would not want to be bothered" were common reasons for failure to report thefts.

The first category of the UCR, **crimes known to the police**, provides statistics on the serious-crime index. Seven crimes were selected in 1929 to be in this index: murder, rape, aggravated assault, robbery, burglary, larceny-theft, and motor vehicle theft. An eighth offense, arson, was added to the serious-crime index in 1978, but reports do not include arson in the overall crime index because of difficulties and uncertainties about accuracy in its measurement. Whether these seven offense categories, and only these seven, are in fact the most serious crimes occurring in the United States is a matter of contention (Reiman, 2003). For example, drug offenses, bribery, white collar crime, and fraud, to mention but a few, are not part of this crime index. The number of offenses and the calculation of the crime rate per 100,000 population are summarized in box 3-1.

A cursory inspection of the number of offenses reported reveals that larceny-theft dominates the FBI's crime index (around 7 million arrests), and a goodly proportion of thefts are shoplifting. Homicide, clearly the most serious offense, contributes relatively little to the crime index (around 16,000 arrests). A major criticism of the crime index is that it is strongly influenced by property offenses (burglary, larceny-theft, and motor vehicle theft), whereas the four violent crimes (murder, forcible rape, robbery, and aggravated assault) have at best a moderate influence on the crime index (Felson, 1994).

Figure 3-1 (on p. 72) graphs the property crime rate and the violent crime rate together and separately. Property crimes dominate the overall crime index, and trends

Box 3-1   Crime Rates in the United States

The crime rate reported by the FBI in its annual Uniform Crime Report (http://www.fbi.gov/ucr/cius2006/data/table_01.html) divides the number of crimes "known to the police" by the U.S. population as estimated by census data (299,398,484 in 2006). Because those rates would be very small, they are multiplied by 100,000, yielding the number of crimes "per 100,000" people. The number of crimes known for 2006 is listed below. Compute the crime rate per 100,000 for each offense category.

Offense	Number Known to Police	Rate per 100,000
Murder	17,034	
Rape	92,455	
Robbery	447,403	
Aggravated Assault	860,853	
Burglary	2,183,746	
Larceny	6,607,013	
Motor Vehicle Theft	1,192,809	
Total	11,401,313	

Do you think crimes per 100,000 people is the most appropriate base for computing rates for offenses such as motor vehicle theft and rape? Why transform crime into a "rate"? Why is it important for studying variations over time or comparing cities and states?

in violence look trivial when they are plotted together (top graph). When plotted on separate scales (middle and bottom graphs) it is easier to discern shared trends. There was a strong increase in both property and violent crime rates from the late 1950s through the 1960s, with a brief leveling in the early 1970s and early 1980s for property crime rates. In general, the upward trend for violent crime continued to the mid-1990s. There were remarkable decreases beginning in the early to mid-1990s.

Explaining Variations over Time

A variety of factors have been cited as responsible for these trends (Blumstein and Williams, 2000). For example, the baby boom of the late 1940s and 1950s produced a large teenage population in the 1960s, whereas the "graying of America" in the 1990s resulted in a higher proportion of older people who are less likely to engage in crime. Numerous other explanations have been posited—such as high incarceration rates in the 1990s, a strong economy, reduced unemployment, crackdowns on some forms of crime based on the so-called "broken windows" approach (see chapter 6), lower reporting of crime, and changes in illicit drug markets. Some have even suggested the manipulation of crime statistics.

The most controversial explanation is offered by Steven Levitt and Stephen Dubner in *Freakonomics* (2005). They argue that the 1973 *Roe v. Wade* decision permitting legalized abortion reduced the future at-risk criminal population fifteen to eighteen years later. In other words, the crime rate dropped in the 1990s because lower-class women had access to abortion in the 1970s and 1980s. The authors claim that the generation of teenagers in the 1990s included a smaller proportion from crime-prone

Figure 3-1   Crime Rates per 100,000 Population (1960–2006)

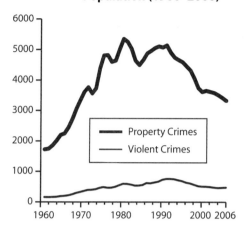

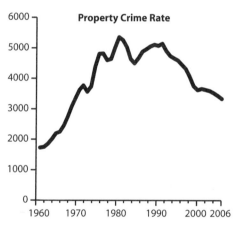

Property Crime Rate

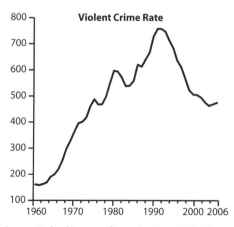

Violent Crime Rate

Source: Federal Bureau of Investigation. 2007. *Crime in the United States, 2006.*

groups due to legalized aborting of unwanted children years earlier.

Criminologist James Q. Wilson (2005) has reviewed Levitt and Dubner's research and concludes that "as of now, no one is entitled to decide who is correct." A key criticism is that homicide rates fell for age groups that were far too old to have been affected by the *Roe v. Wade* decision, as well as for younger age groups. As Philip Cook and John Laub observe, "The timing of the downturn is simply wrong for legalized abortion to be the driving force" (2001:23). Levitt and Dubner's argument implies a unique reduction in crime in the late 1980s and early 1990s (fifteen to eighteen years after *Roe v. Wade*) because the proportion of "unwanted" (aborted) children declined. The decline in crime may have been more prominent for juvenile age groups, but the declines are found for cohorts that should have included sizeable proportions of unwanted children (non-aborted) as well. Moreover, there was no actual measure of variation in legal abortions relative to live births over time. Levitt and Dubner argue that within the time span they studied, crime dropped fifteen to eighteen years after the decision. However, the number of abortions relative to live births surged right after *Roe v. Wade*, leveled off, and began declining within a short span of time. If their argument is correct (i.e., a reduction in crime occurs fifteen to eighteen years after abortions increase), then the decline in abortions relative to live births should have led to an increase in crime beginning in the mid-1990s. Yet, murder rates declined during that time span. Finally, Levitt and Dubner's argument is based upon a span of fifteen to eighteen years before the effect is realized. During the time, many alternative events occurred that could be advanced as explanations for variation in the crime rate (e.g. post-Vietnam War increases in divorce or family breakdown). Several scholars have presented evidence challenging Levitt and Dubner's arguments (see Foote and Goetz, 2005).

To further illustrate the problems associated with interpreting crime data, refer to figure 3-2, which plots homicide rates over a 100-year span. The issues suggested by such data can be summarized as follows: (1) There was a huge decline in homicide during the Great Depression, a time when marriages and births declined due to economic hardship. The legal status of abortion was relatively unchanged during that time span. Indeed, the decline in marriage and births should have meant fewer unwanted children; yet, there is no unusual decrease in homicide fifteen to eighteen years later. (2) The post-World War II surge in homicide rates is coterminous with a surge in divorce rates, marriage rates, and birth rates. People wanted to get married and start families following the war. It is very questionable that this return to routine after the depression and World War II was associated with an increase in abortion. (3) The time period fifteen to eighteen years after *Roe v. Wade* actually witnessed an upturn in homicide rates. The decline begins more than 20 years after the decision. The longer the intervening time lag, the more questionable the argument becomes. (4) When government data on legal abortions relative to live births are considered, the brief upsurge following *Roe v. Wade* is found to have leveled out in the late 1970s, and began declining in the 1980s. The correlation is actually a positive one, with high abortion rates associated with higher homicide rates. We are not suggesting that a positive correlation indicates that high abortion rates "cause" high murder rates, but are merely pointing out that a variety of counter arguments are possible.

Figure 3-2   Homicide Rates (1900–2006)

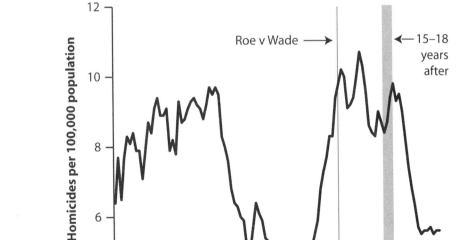

Source: Homicide data for 1900 through 1932 based on Eckberg (1995). Homicide data after 1932 are based on the FBI's Uniform Crime Reports.

Crime Rates as a Quality-of-Life Measure

One use of the crime index outside of law enforcement is determining the best and worst cities in which to live. A key component to this rating system is the FBI's crime index for a particular city. If the overall crime index is 4,063 crimes per 100,000 people, then a city with a crime rate that is significantly above the national average would be considered undesirable, while a city significantly below the national average would be desirable. Bismarck, North Dakota, had a crime index of 3,744 per 100,000 in 2003 and Green Bay, Wisconsin, had a crime index of 3,652 per 100,000. Conversely, for the same year Atlanta's crime index was 11,368 per 100,000 and St. Louis had 14,285 crimes per 100,000. On the surface, St. Louis and Atlanta appear to be cities to avoid. However, recall that the key component of the crime index is larceny-theft, which accounts for nearly 60 percent of crimes in the index. Atlanta and St. Louis are southern cities, which means the weather permits more shopping, more bicycles left on the front lawn, and more year-round outdoor activity, factors that can inflate larceny-theft rates. On the other hand, the weather in Bismarck and Green Bay produces what is termed "target hardening" by virtue of the fact that in the winter months doors and windows tend to be closed and locked and there is less mobility outside of the house.

Box 3-2   Atlanta's 1996 Olympic Bid: Enhancing the Image of a City

Cities that bid to host the Olympic Games have been known to use all forms of persuasion, ranging from exaggerations of the number of hotel rooms to outright bribes. In 1990, the city of Atlanta was actively pursuing the bid for the 1996 Olympics. Gifts were given to members of the International Olympic Committee (IOC), ranging from an $800 bulldog to a $10,000 bus for a delegate from Peru. The head of the Atlanta Olympic Committee stated, "Although we occasionally exceeded the IOC's guidelines, our work was always done with honest intent." Congressional investigators reported that thirty-eight individual gifts were given to International Olympic Committee members that exceeded the $200 per-gift limit. These included golf clubs, surgical instruments, complimentary airline tickets, a carburetor kit for a luxury car, a scholarship to Georgia Tech for an official's daughter, a tennis scholarship to the University of Georgia for another official's daughter, and undetermined sums of money.

More amazing was the "cleansing" of certain records. For example, it was reported to the IOC that the average temperature in Atlanta in August was 75 degrees (records indicate 85 to 90 degrees would be more accurate) and no mention of exceedingly high humidity levels. Moreover, despite Atlanta's consistent ranking as first or second in the FBI's crime index, it was reported that Atlanta was a very safe city. The mayor boasted of a decline in crime, but it was found that in one year alone, 22,000 police reports were missing and crime incidents were downgraded, underreported, or discarded. The city evicted 30,000 residents of low-income housing to improve the image of Atlanta, and detained 9,000 homeless people during the games. The city passed "public nuisance" ordinances including panhandling, window washing, loitering, lying down in a public park, urban camping, and cutting through a parking lot but not owning a vehicle. An elite drug squad, the Red Dogs, was ordered to arrest anyone who looked homeless and had less than ten dollars. All storm-sewer drainage lines had steel grates to prevent individuals from living in them. Finally, city officials devised a strategy to give the homeless a one-way bus ticket to any city.

Go online and try to find crime statistics for Atlanta. How do they compare to other cities in the southern United States?

While there is a common assumption that juveniles drive the crime rate up or down, there is in fact no information from the serious-crime index that would allow us to determine what role adolescents play in influencing crime rates and, by extension, quality-of-life issues. We can infer that the increase in crime in the 1960s may have been influenced by the baby boomers who moved into their adolescent years. Similarly, the leveling off of crime in the late 1970s and 1980s may imply that the baby boomers moved into adulthood, while the declines of the 1990s and 2000s are a reflection of the "graying" of the baby boom generation. However, no information is gathered regarding the age of the offender. All that is reported is that a crime occurred; the crime index does not report the characteristics of the offender. Thus, the crime index is not a very useful measure of criminal involvement by adolescents although there is an assumption that juveniles are a primary reason why the crime index for a particular locale is high or low (Snyder and Sickmund, 2006).

Uniform Crime Reports: Arrests

The second part of the Uniform Crime Report contains information regarding arrests. This section of the UCR is much more revealing of juvenile activity because it lists twenty-nine different offenses and presents arrests by age, sex, race and ethnicity, and geographic location (state, city, suburban, or rural area). The first eight offenses in the arrest table are often referred to as **Part I offenses**. Generally speaking, these are felony offenses. The remaining twenty-one offenses are referred to as **Part II offenses** and include many misdemeanor offenses. It is important to note that even though the UCR lists twenty-nine different arrest violations, there are still many offenses that are omitted. For example, so-called white-collar crimes such as insider trading, income tax cheating, or illegal business practices are not recorded.

It often surprises people to learn how modest the number of arrests is for juveniles compared to adults. The vast majority of arrestees are adults (84%). Moreover, adults comprise the bulk of arrests for the most serious crimes. For Part I offenses, adults constitute the vast majority of those arrested for murder, rape, robbery, and aggravated assault. The percent of juveniles who are arrested for the four property offenses—burglary, larceny-theft, motor vehicle theft, and arson—is higher, but only in the case of arson does it come close to 50 percent. For Part II offenses, all of the arrests are overwhelmingly of adults with the exception of runaways and curfew, which are status offenses and by definition could only be juvenile arrests. Thus the first "image" we have of juvenile delinquency using police statistics is that adults are highly involved in criminal activity and juveniles account for a modest number of arrests. Of course, as was noted in chapter 1, juveniles may be overrepresented in some offenses and underrepresented in others.

Returning to table 1-1 in chapter 1, the general pattern based on arrests reveals that juveniles tend to be arrested primarily for property offenses like arson, vandalism, and motor vehicle theft but have relatively small percentages of arrests for murder, forcible rape, and aggravated assault. It is noteworthy that juveniles constitute a tiny percent of the arrests for driving under the influence. Since young teenagers cannot obtain a driving license, this low percentage should not be surprising, but the media often portray DUI offenders as juveniles.

In trying to determine whether a particular offense is disproportionately adult or juvenile, we need to determine what percent of the U.S. population falls within the "juvenile" classification. Normally the cutoff age is 18, but this is not true in every state. Many states have age 17 as the cutoff, and still others have different ages for different offenses. However, by way of convention, a person 17 or under is normally considered a juvenile and those 18 and older are considered adults. A second problem is determining the lower age limit of a juvenile. According the U.S. Census Bureau (2000), 26 percent of the inhabitants of the United States are under the age of 18, but this encompasses ages 0 to 17. Very few children under the age of 10 ever appear in UCR statistics, so this age range is too broad. The age range of 10 to 17 has been arbitrarily set as the "at-risk juvenile population." Even this age range may be too broad since 10- and 11-year-olds are rarely arrested. However, in juvenile delinquency estimates, this is considered to be the at-risk age group. Using this restricted age range, the Census Bureau reports that about 12 percent of the U.S. population is between the ages of 10 to 17. Thus, juveniles are low in homicide arrests, slightly higher in rape and aggravated assault, but significantly overrepresented for robbery and the four property offenses of burglary, larceny-theft, motor vehicle theft, and arson. Considering Part II offenses, most of these arrests are adults, with the exception of curfew and runaway offenses which are by definition only applicable to juveniles.

Of course, as noted in chapter 1, the number of arrests made by law enforcement agencies can bias the image of the juvenile contribution to crime since the arrest data do not reveal the number of people arrested or the number of crimes committed. The number of arrests is not equivalent to the number of people arrested. Some youths are arrested more than once in a given year. Moreover, a single crime may result in the arrest of more than one person. Thus, 10 million arrests might represent far less than 10 million people arrested. We need to be extremely careful not to equate one arrest as the arrest of one person, or conclude that one crime is the product of a single person. This problem is very relevant to the study of juvenile delinquency because juveniles tend to associate with other juveniles, and a significant proportion of juvenile crime is committed by groups of juveniles. A further problem is that the FBI reporting procedure states that an arrest is classified by the most serious offense. For example, a youth charged with aggravated assault, possession of marijuana, and shoplifting will be coded as an arrest for aggravated assault. Thus, the approximately 61,000 juvenile arrests for burglary in 2006 mean that burglary was the most serious violation but there could have been other less serious charges.

Another way to approach the problem of the number of arrests and the number of offenses committed is to examine what are referred to as "clearance rates." When a crime is reported to the police and an arrest for that crime takes place, the crime is solved, or in the jargon of law enforcement, the crime is "cleared." A single arrest may solve or clear multiple offenses reported to the police. For example, one arrest for burglary might result in the offender admitting to dozens and dozens of burglary offenses. The phenomenon of plea bargaining encourages offenders to cooperate or aid law enforcement personnel by admitting to other criminal acts in exchange for a reduced sentence.

As was noted in chapter 1, there are more arrests than there are crimes for juvenile offenders. For example, 16 percent of arrests for violent crimes were juvenile offenders, but this cleared 13 percent of the violent crimes. More dramatically, 26 percent of all arrests for property offenses were juveniles, but this only cleared 19 percent of the reported property offenses. Juveniles tend to commit offenses in the context of a group and the number of arrests overestimates the actual number of offenses. Burglary, robbery, and motor vehicle theft provide the most dramatic examples of juveniles being arrested in relatively high numbers, with a smaller proportion of offenses cleared. Clearance rates show that juveniles are responsible for far fewer criminal acts than what is given by arrest data. Moreover, the tendency for juveniles to commit group offenses may make them more vulnerable to an arrest.

Changes in Arrest Data over Time

Figure 3-3 shows the juvenile arrest rates for a twenty-five year span for the four violent offenses and four property offenses. There has been remarkable fluctuation in the arrest rates, but in every instance there is a dramatic decline from 1995 to 2005. Contrary to public perception, juveniles typically are not involved in homicide cases.

Figure 3-3   Arrests per 100,000 Persons Ages 10 through 17 (1980–2005)

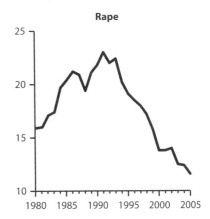

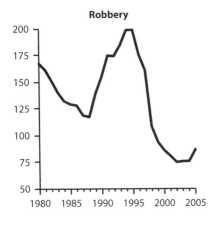

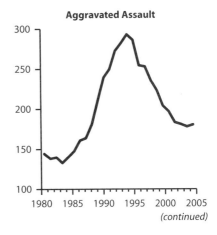

(continued)

Figure 3-3   *(cont'd.)*

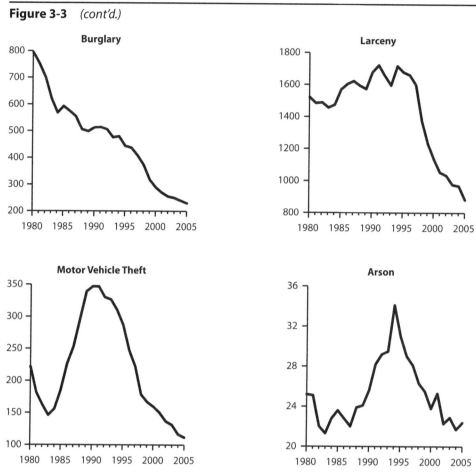

Source: H. Snyder and M. Sickmund, *Juvenile Offenders and Victims: 2006 National Report.* http://ojjdp.ncjrs.org. Accessed March 19, 2007.

However, of those juveniles who were arrested for murder, we see an arrest rate that more than doubled from approximately 6 per 100,000 in 1980 to slightly more that 14 per 100,000 in 1993, before a long steady decline to about 3 per 100,000 in 2005. Forcible rape is also disproportionately an adult offense, with 83 percent of those arrested for rape being adult. As shown in figure 3-3, the arrest rate for rape went from 17 per 100,000 in 1980 to a peak of 23 per 100,000 in 1991, and then the rate declined to 12 per 100,000 in 2005. The rates for robbery followed a different pattern, with an arrest rate of approximately 170 per 100,000 in 1980, a steady decline to 120 per 100,000 in 1988, followed by a surge to 200 per 100,000 in 1994. Beginning in 1995 there was a steady decline in juvenile robbery arrests to 75 per 100,000 in 2003 with an upturn to 87 per 100,000 in 2005. Finally, for aggravated assault, the arrest rate of slightly less than 150 per 100,000 in 1980 doubled to nearly 300 per 100,000 and then declined to 180 per 100,000.

Juveniles are far more likely to be arrested for property offenses. The arrest trend for burglary shows a steady decline from 1980 to 2005. Nearly 30 percent of burglary arrests are juvenile, so this decline represents a significant reduction in the overall burglary rate. Clearly the highest arrest rate within the crime-index offenses for juveniles is for larceny-theft, and the arrest trend from 1980–2005 indicates nearly 30 percent of larceny-theft arrests were juveniles. Larceny-theft rates were 1,500 per 100,000 in 1980, increased to nearly 1,750 in 1991 and, beginning in 1997, sharply declined to 880 per 100,000 in 2005. Motor vehicle theft is also disproportionately a juvenile offense, with 30 percent of those arrested being juveniles. The rate for motor vehicle theft in 1980 was approximately 220 per 100,000 juveniles, decreased to 150 per 100,000 in 1983, more than doubled to 350 per 100,000 in 1991, and then steadily declined to 112 per 100,000 in 2005. Finally, the trends for arson show a modest increase from 1980 to 1994 and then a gradual decrease to 2005. The FBI does not normally report arson cases because unless there is a careful determination by a skilled arson investigator, it is difficult to determine whether a crime occurred.

Changes in Arrest Rates by Gender

Crime is overwhelmingly a male phenomenon. Of all arrests, over three-fourths are males and about one-fourth are female. More importantly, the more serious the offense, the more likely the perpetrator is to be a male. For murder, rape, robbery, aggravated assault, burglary, motor vehicle theft, and arson, 80 percent or more of the offenders are male. The only exception was larceny-theft, where about 70 percent of those arrested were male and 30 percent were female. For Part II arrests, males dominant every category except for fraud (55 percent), forgery (60 percent) and in only two instances do females represent the majority—prostitution (64 percent) and runaways (59 percent). Crime is clearly a male activity, particularly in the case of violent crime.

In figure 3-4 arrest rates for males and females are plotted together and on separate scales to illustrate differences in rates as well as shared or disparate trends. For example, both property crime and violent crime arrest rates for females surged upward from the mid-1980s to the mid-1990s and began dropping after that point. For males, violent crime also surged from the mid-1980s to the mid-1990s, but there was little change in property crime arrest rates during that period. Both property crime and violent crime arrest rates declined beginning in the mid-1990s for boys and girls.

Figure 3-5 plots the ratio of male to female arrest rates for three violent crimes and three property crimes. For five of six offenses, girls have been closing in on boys. The ratio for burglary arrest rates has fallen from 14 to 1 to about 7 to 1. The ratio for motor vehicle theft has fallen from over 8 to 1 to 4.5 to 1. The ratio of boys' to girls' arrest rates for larceny is down from about 2.6 to 1 to 1.4 to one. Ratios for aggravated assault and robbery are both down as well.

Overall, the ratio of boys' to girls' property crime and violent crime arrest rates has nearly been cut in half over the last quarter of a century. The one exception is murder, where the male ratio surged to almost twice that of females, from about 8–10 to 1 in the early 1980s to about 20 to 1 in the early 1990s. However, by 2000 the ratio was back down to 8 to 1. Thus, for most offenses there is evidence that female adolescents have been catching up with their male counterparts, but the gap between male and female arrests is quite prominent for the most serious crimes.

Figure 3-4   Arrests per 100,000 Males and Females Ages 10–17 (1980–2005)

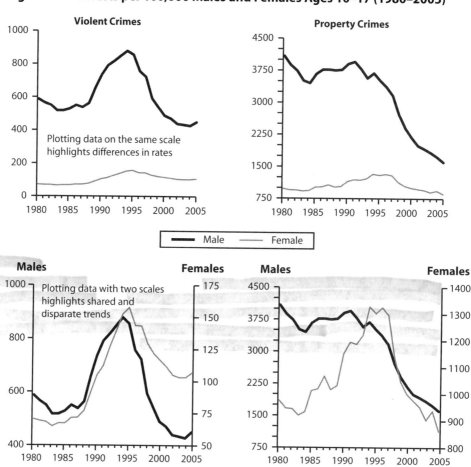

Source: H. Snyder and M. Sickmund, *Juvenile Offenders and Victims: 2006 National Report.* http://ojjdp.ncjrs.org. Accessed March 19, 2007.

Self-report data to be addressed in chapter 4 suggest that the decline in the gender ratio is a reflection of real changes in the behavior of girls and not merely a change in the way in which girls are treated by law enforcement. The decline in the gender ratio for violence is about the same using self-reports as the decline using arrest rates. However, changes in the treatment of girls can not be ruled out as a possible explanation of some of the convergence. As will be noted in the final section of this chapter, some studies have suggested that girls are treated more severely than boys for status offenses, but boys are treated more severely than girls for delinquent offenses. Shifts toward more uniform treatment of males and females may have lowered the gender ratio over time.

Figure 3-5   Ratio of Male to Female Arrest Rates, Ages 10–17 (1980–2005)

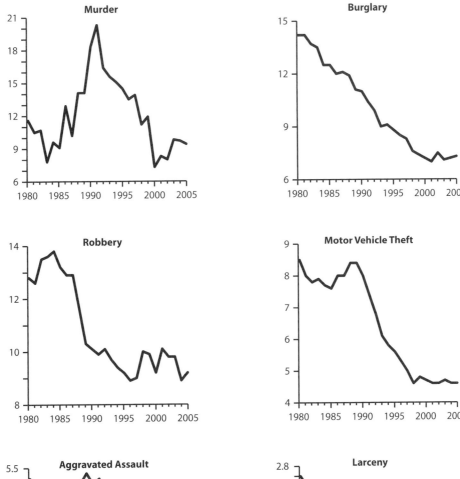

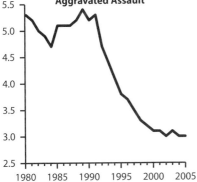

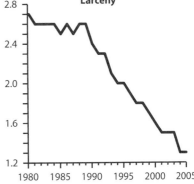

Source: H. Snyder and M. Sickmund, *Juvenile Offenders and Victims: 2006 National Report.* http://ojjdp.ncjrs.org.
Accessed March 19, 2007.

Changes in Arrest Rates by Race

UCR statistics categorize ethnicity as white, black, American Indian, or Asian. While Latinos are currently the largest minority group in the United States, arrest statistics do not have a separate classification for Latinos. Generally, they are lumped into the category of white. The composition of the U.S. juvenile population by race or ethnicity is 78 percent white, 16 percent black, 4 percent Asian/Pacific Islander, and 1 percent American Indian. The group that tends to be disproportionately overrepresented in arrest statistics is African Americans. Arrest data for juveniles in 2006 show that 47 percent of arrests for violent offenses were white youth, 51 percent were black youth, 1 percent was Asian youth, and 1 percent was American Indian youth. White youth were underrepresented in arrest data and black youth were overrepresented by more than three times. For property offenses, the proportions for black youth were 31 percent and for white youth 66 percent. The most glaring differences between black and white youth were for violent offenses. According to the National Center for Juvenile Justice (2006), in 2005 the arrest rate for black youth was 850 per 100,000, three times the 283 per 100,000 arrest rate for white youth.

Figure 3-6 plots the arrest rates for the violent crime and property crime indices for black and white youths ages 10 to 17. The top charts plot black and white rates on the same scale to highlight the differences in rates, while the bottom charts use two scales to allow a comparison of patterns over time. As will be elaborated below, the overall property crime arrest rates are narrowing, with relatively flat rates from 1980 through 1995 and a downturn shared by both black and white youth after that point. Blacks and whites followed somewhat similar paths for violent crimes, with relative stability through the mid-1980s, a rapid acceleration to the mid-1990s, and a decline from that point forward. In fact, the decline has been somewhat more dramatic for blacks than whites.

Figure 3-7 (on p. 84) summarizes the ratio of black to white arrest rates between 1980 and 2005. The ratio of blacks to whites declined for three offenses—larceny, robbery, and burglary—during the 1980s, with a sustained decline for robbery to the end of the 1990s. The ratio for murder surged from the mid-1980s to the mid-1990s, returning to the ratios experienced in the early 1980s during the early 2000s. With the exception of larceny, a new upturn in the black-to-white ratio has characterized the early years of the new century. The ratios are particularly prominent for violent offenses, with the smallest ratios found for larceny and burglary.

More detailed analyses of the homicide rate show that "all of the increase in youth homicide was a result of guns, while the non-gun homicide rate remained essentially constant" (Cook and Laub, 2001:2). Moreover, the growth in the gender ratio and the black-white ratio from the mid-1980s to the mid-1990s is consistent with arguments that a new form of cheap cocaine led to violent competition and a proliferation of weapons for self-protection among those not involved with the drug. At least one criminologist has argued that the escalation of homicide burned itself out through the violence-induced attrition of offenders (Karmen, 2000:235-38). After considering a variety of explanations, Cook and Laub state that "the appeal of what has become the conventional explanation, the introduction of crack cocaine in one city after another across the nation, is that it has the right timing and can accommodate all these facts" (2001:28).

Figure 3-6   Arrests per 100,000 Black and White Youths Ages 10–17 (1980–2005)

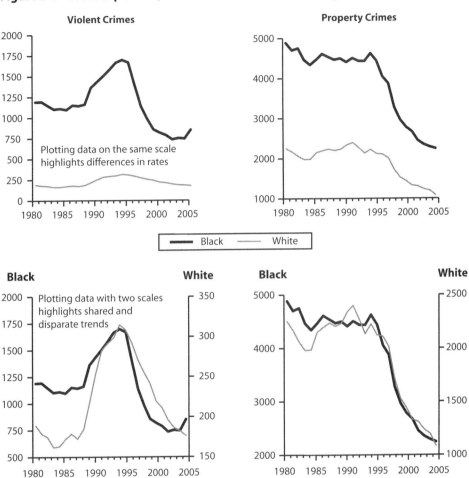

Source: H. Snyder and M. Sickmund, *Juvenile Offenders and Victims: 2006 National Report*. http://ojjdp.ncjrs.org. Accessed March 19, 2007.

The Implications of Co-Offending

As mentioned earlier, research has consistently shown that juveniles tend to commit offenses in the company of their peers (Conway and McCord, 2002). The period of adolescence is a time of intense interaction with peers, and this group behavior distorts the true meaning of arrest statistics. The phenomenon of group participation in adolescent criminal activity is referred to as **co-offending**. Unfortunately, police data typically do not record co-offending rates but only single instances of arrest. Hence, we do not know to what degree co-offending manifests adolescent behavior or how co-offending varies by age or by offense.

Figure 3-7   Ratio of Black Arrest Rates to White Arrest Rates Ages 10–17 (1980–2005)

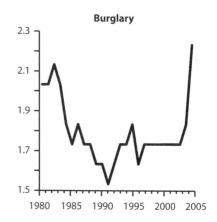

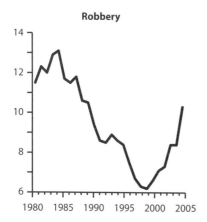

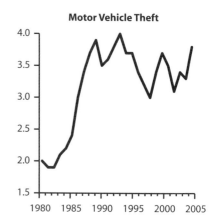

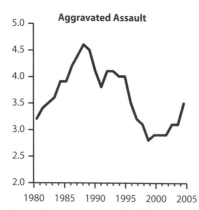

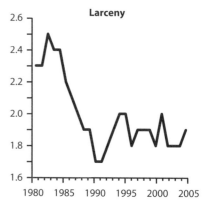

Source: Based on an analysis of data from H. Snyder and M. Sickmund, *Juvenile Offenders and Victims: 2006 National Report*. http://ojjdp.ncjrs.org. Accessed March 19, 2007.

Fortunately, Kevin Conway and Joan McCord (2002) have examined co-offending and patterns of juvenile crime in Philadelphia. In figure 3-8, co-offending and solo offending are graphed by the offender's age for property and violent offenses. Co-offending for violent offenses rises steadily from age 12 to 17, and is considerably higher than solo violent offending. Similarly, co-offending for property offenses rises markedly from ages 12 to 15 and is significantly greater than solo property offending. What is different about co-offending for property offenses is the dramatic decline after age 15, a pattern that is not seen with co-offending for violent offenses. For 16- and 17-year-old offenders, violent crimes were twice as likely to be co-offending offenses as solo offenses. Thus, co-offending has serious implications for understanding juvenile criminal activity.

The second issue that Conway and McCord (2002) examine is age at first offense. They found that young offenders committed most of their crimes with accomplices, but at ages 16 to 17 the incidence of co-offending to solo offending was approximately equal. For a first arrest of a 12-year-old, less than 10 percent would be solo crimes while 90 percent would be co-offending or mostly co-offending. At ages 13 to 15 for a first arrest, solo criminal activity doubles to nearly 20 percent, and co-offending or mostly co-offending is at 80 percent. Finally, at ages 16 to 17 for a first arrest, solo and co-offending rates are somewhat comparable. Thus, there is clear evidence that co-offending is more prominent for younger than older first-time offenders.

Co-offending also has implications on learning violent propensities. "Interaction among delinquent peers apparently encourages and escalates their proclivity to commit crimes" (Conway and McCord, 2002:11). Adolescents learn criminal behavior

Figure 3-8   Crime, Age, and Co-Offending

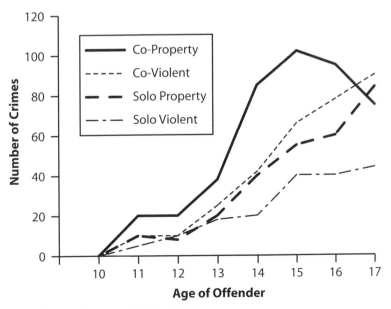

Source: Based on data from Conway and McCord, 2002.

from their accomplices, and those adolescents who co-offend with a violent partner or partners manifest a stronger tendency to become violent themselves.

Victimization data also show race to play a significant role in co-offending. For white offenders, 63 percent of crimes were reported to be committed by a lone offender, but for blacks the percent of all crimes of violence committed by a lone black offender was only 21 percent. This suggests that blacks have a higher rate of co-offending than whites and that the disproportionate amount of criminal behavior attributed to blacks is distorted by co-offending. Police data unfortunately do not routinely record whether an arrest was in the context of a group or an event involving a single person. However, in assessing the implications of police data, the confounding influence of adolescent co-offending needs at least to be acknowledged, even if the data are missing.

Juvenile Court Statistics

The UCR provides a breakdown of police disposition of juvenile offenders who are **taken into custody**. Normally, this would be a more accurate measure than those "arrested," but this breakdown is shown only for those reporting agencies that actually report on processing. Some 9,000 agencies report arrest by age, but only 6,000 agencies report how juvenile cases are handled. Thus, there is no perfect measure of juveniles taken into custody.

Another data source that can be of use to examine juvenile delinquency is *Juvenile Court Statistics*, published by the National Center for Juvenile Justice. Although the bulk of juvenile arrests will be referred to the juvenile court (70 percent), some 20 percent of juvenile cases will be handled within the police department, 7 percent will be referred to adult court, 1 percent referred to a welfare agency, and another 1 percent referred to some other police agency. In other words, police departments exercise discretion in their handling of juvenile cases, and the number who are arrested is not the number who appear in juvenile court.

Unlike criminal court cases where a formal arrest has to occur before someone appears in court, referral sources to the juvenile court include law enforcement agencies, social service agencies, schools, parents, probation officers, and victims. For example, in the year 2000, 84 percent of delinquency cases were referred by law enforcement agencies, but this ranged from a high of 92 percent for property offenses to a low of 63 percent for public order offenses such as disorderly conduct, liquor law violations, and obstruction of justice.

Juvenile court statistics use the case as the unit of count; that is, a case represents a juvenile processed by the juvenile court on a specific referral, regardless of the number of law violations contained in the referral. A juvenile arrested for a burglary, weapons offense, shoplifting, and drinking under age would represent one case. The juvenile court also uses the term "disposed" to refer to a precise court action as a result of a referral. It does not mean that the case is closed or terminated but that a plan of action was taken. For example, a case is often disposed with a probation sentence that may last for an extended period of time. The case was disposed but in a sense the juvenile is still under the jurisdiction of the juvenile court.

Figure 3-9 shows the number of delinquency cases referred to the juvenile court from 1939 to 2002. It needs to be emphasized that the term "delinquency offense" in the context of the juvenile court refers to an offense against the criminal code. As seen in figure 3-9, juvenile court referrals peaked in 1996–1997 at a rate of about 63 per 1,000 youth under its jurisdiction, which was about six times greater than the rate of 10 per 1,000 in 1939. It should be noted that the same downturn in the mid-1990s observed in UCR "crimes known" and "arrest rates" is also found in juvenile court statistics. As we will discover in the next chapter, this same pattern is uncovered when using self-report survey data.

Because the data are based on those apprehended, referred, or processed by juvenile courts, the interpretation of trends is even more problematic than encountered when using UCR data. For example, increases in referrals to juvenile court may be affected by variations in space available for processing cases. Since its creation in 1899, as the juvenile court's *capacity* to handle cases increased, the actual use of the system also increased. There are always more cases that *could* be turned over to the juvenile system than are actually referred, and thus any increase in capacity will be used. Thus, referral rates seem to grow more uniformly with less dramatic fluctuations than found using UCR statistics.

Juvenile Court Statistics began providing breakdowns by type of offense about two decades ago and reports rates for offenses against persons, property, drug law violations, and public order offenses. Each of the four categories is shown separately in figure 3-10. For crimes against persons, the case rate almost doubled since 1985 from a rate of 7 per 1,000 to more than 13 per 1,000. This includes homicide, rape, robbery, aggravated assault, and simple assault. Collectively, crimes against persons amounted

Figure 3-9   Juvenile Court Referrals per 1,000 Youth (1939–2002)

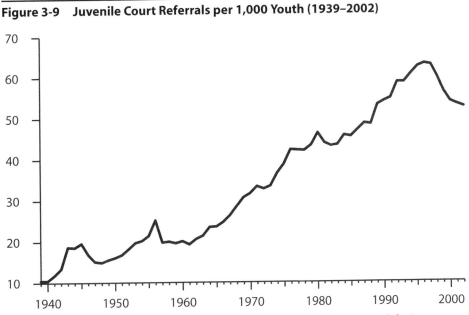

Source: Based on issues of *Juvenile Court Statistics*, with adjustments for 1985 changes in definition.

to between 20–25 percent of the delinquency cases. Similar to UCR data, rates peaked in the mid-1990s and were somewhat lower in the early years of the twenty-first century.

Property offenses include burglary, larceny-theft, motor vehicle theft, vandalism, and other property-related offenses. As was the case with FBI data, juvenile court data confirm that juveniles most typically commit property offenses. About 40 percent of all delinquent offenses are property offenses. As indicated in figure 3-10, referral rates for property crimes increased from 1985 to a peak in the early 1990s, and have been declining since the mid-1990s. Again, the pattern is quite similar to UCR data.

Referral rates for drug violations increased dramatically during the 1990s, from about 3 cases per 1,000 to more than 6 cases per 1,000. The total number of cases soared from 65,000 in 1991 to nearly 200,000 in 1997. While drug law violations

---

Figure 3-10   Referral Rates per 1,000 Youth by Type of Offense

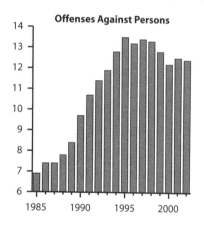

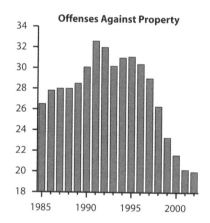

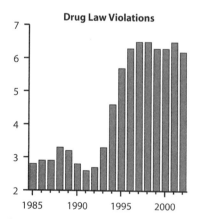

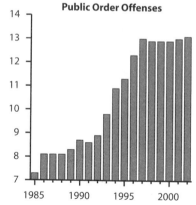

Source: Based on data from Anne L. Stahl, Charles Puzzanchera, Anthony Sladky, Terrence A. Finnegan, Nancy Tierney, and Howard N. Snyder. 2005. *Juvenile Court Statistics 2001–2002*. Pittsburgh, PA: National Center for Juvenile Justice.

encompass a wide array of drugs such as cocaine, heroin, barbiturates, and amphetamines, the number one drug in this offense category is marijuana. Drug offenses constituted 12 percent of all juvenile cases in 2000. As will be discussed in chapter 4, the "war on drugs" may have led to increasing juvenile court referrals but with no evidence of a corresponding decline in drug use. Trends in referral rates appear to parallel trends in self-reported use of marijuana (see chapter 4).

Finally, public order offenses include a wide array of behaviors such as obstruction of justice, disorderly conduct, weapons offenses, and liquor law offenses. Public order offenses constituted over 20 percent of all cases in 2000, with the rate almost doubling between 1985 and 2002.

The juvenile court may also be required to deal with status offenses, but in many jurisdictions other community agencies are responsible for these cases. For example, family crisis units, county attorneys, and social service agencies may be involved with such cases. As a result, there are no accurate statistics on status offenses, but estimates approach 160,000 cases nationally, with the percentage breakdown as follows: liquor law violations (28 percent), truancy cases (24 percent), runaway cases (16 percent), and ungovernable cases (12 percent). The number of status offense cases increased during the 1990s, with liquor law violations accounting for the greatest increase. The case rates for black juveniles were significantly higher than for whites in runaway, truancy, and ungovernability cases. However, blacks had an exceedingly low liquor law case rate, with 91 percent of all liquor violation cases involving white offenders and 4 percent involving black youth. Finally, while males accounted for 77 percent of all delinquency cases, females accounted for 61 percent of status offense cases. Chapter 6 will explore the unique role that status offenses play in launching delinquent careers according to modern feminist theories of juvenile delinquency.

For one final look at statistics, refer to figure 3-6 comparing black and white arrest rates for violent crimes. The graph shows a more dramatic surge for blacks, peaking in the mid-1990s, and a much more dramatic decline for black youth compared to white youth. What do we find using juvenile court referral rates for offenses against persons? The same pattern. The referral rates are higher for blacks than for whites, but to allow a comparison of trends, we plot them on different scales in figure 3-11. Comparing the trends for both groups, there was both a more dramatic upward trend for blacks and a more significant decline. Thus, although there is a tendency to emphasize disparities in different bodies of data on delinquency, patterns that persist across a variety of different measures also point to "real" and meaningful variations. This comparison will continue in the next chapter where we will discover numerous shared patterns across diverse measures.

Discretion and Discrimination

Many critics of the juvenile justice system in the United States charge that lower-class youth and minorities are sanctioned more severely and more frequently than middle or upper-class white juveniles and that discrimination is pervasive in police and court processing of juvenile offenders (Tonry, 1995). Differential enforcement of the law infers that the juvenile justice system is biased, and serious miscarriages of jus-

Figure 3-11   Trends in Juvenile Court Referral Rates for Black and White Youth

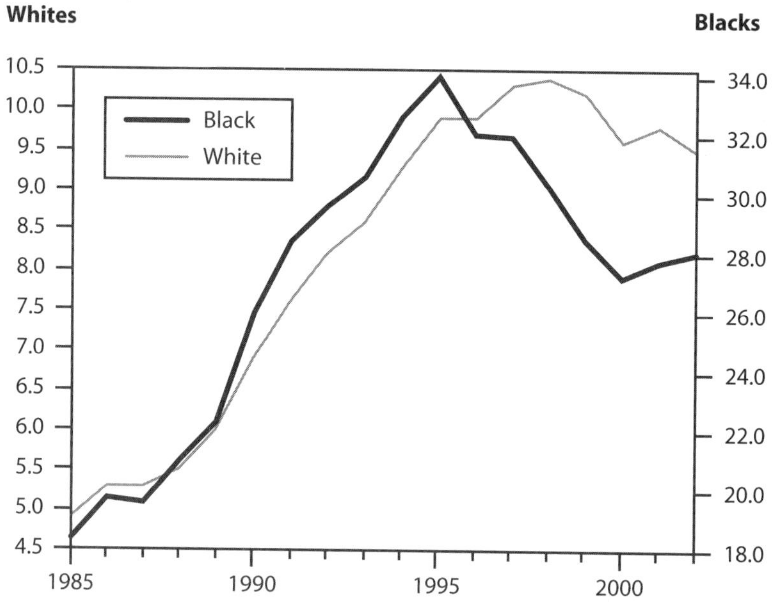

Source: Based on data from A. Stahl, C. Puzzanchera, A. Sladky, T. Finnegan, N. Tierney, and H. Snyder. 2005. *Juvenile Court Statistics 2001–2002*. Pittsburgh, PA: National Center for Juvenile Justice.

tice are inflicted upon the poor and certain minority groups. Despite the volumes of articles and books that have been written on this topic, the allegation of discrimination is a complex topic and no single, simple conclusion can be drawn at present.

In a classic study of police discretion, Donald Black and Albert Reiss (1970) found that most police encounters with juveniles do not result in an arrest. When arrests do occur, the police are responding to citizens' complaints rather than acting on their own initiative. Black and Reiss refer to this as **reactive policing** rather than **proactive policing.** The police are far more likely to apprehend a juvenile when citizens lodge a complaint, and this citizen complaint restricts police discretion. Several studies of police behavior show that less that 15 percent of juveniles get arrested when the police are in a proactive mode (Black and Reiss, 1970; Myers, 1999). When citizens lodge a complaint, the police officer seems to function more as a public servant and accedes to the wishes of the complaining citizen. Thus, the decision to arrest can be influenced by legal factors, which are based on legitimate legal considerations, and nonlegal factors that are difficult to analyze since they are based on personal bias or prejudicial attitudes.

Legal Factors

Nearly every study of police encounters with juveniles seems to cite the *seriousness* of the offense as the primary explanation for an arrest. Robert Terry (1967), along with Black and Reiss (1970), concluded that the likelihood of an arrest increases with the seriousness of the offense. In addition to seriousness, other factors can play an important role in the arrest decision, such as the presence of a weapon, the degree of premeditation (as opposed to a spontaneous act), and the sophistication of the offense (as opposed to a childish prank) (Myers, 1999; Goldman, 1963).

A second legal predictor of a juvenile arrest is the presence of a prior arrest record. Terry (1967) found that first offenders were arrested 38 percent of the time, but only 7 percent were actually referred to the juvenile court. On the other hand, juveniles who had five or more arrests were referred to the juvenile court 66 percent of the time. Aaron Cicourel (1976) found that having a prior record could transform a relatively minor offense into an arrest.

A third legal issue is the presence of evidence. Kenneth Novak and colleagues (2002) found that the stronger the evidence, the higher the probability of an arrest. The quality of the evidence, the victim's ability to identify a suspect, the officer's observation of the crime being committed, and corroborating witnesses all contribute to the probability of an arrest (Mastrofski, 2000).

Nonlegal Factors

Research on the legal factors that predict the probability of an arrest suggests that arrest decisions are affected by the strength of a particular case. However, nonlegal considerations can enter into the decision to arrest, which give rise to claims of police bias or police discrimination. Of course, when discussing juvenile court processing it has to be recognized that the underlying philosophy of juvenile justice has been that the disposition or treatment of a case *should* vary depending on factors other than the specific legalities of the case. In terms of the philosophy invoked to justify a separate justice system for children, the juvenile court is *supposed* to take a juvenile's background and home life into account in deciding what action to take.

The controversy concerning **discrimination** centers around *acceptable* criteria for that differential processing of cases. The most attention has been devoted to discrimination on the basis of race, but there has been increasing concern over the influence of social class, gender, age, and other attributes. For example, coming from a single-parent home may affect a juvenile court disposition, and the way a youth interacts with the police—his or her demeanor—may affect the probability of arrest. To the police and the courts, such considerations may seem completely legitimate, while to others they may appear completely arbitrary and unfair. That the law should treat girls differently than boys may seem mandatory to some and totally discriminatory to others.

Use of the word "discrimination" implies differential treatment of people on the basis of characteristics that are defined by law or interest groups as inappropriate as a basis for differential discretion. Our review of discrimination against juveniles will concentrate on three particular background characteristics that have been studied as sources of bias—race, social class, and gender.

Differential Processing by Race

There is a long history of research on discrimination by race in the criminal justice system and a growing number of studies of bias in the processing of juveniles. Patterns suggesting racial bias are found often enough to justify continuing concern about discrimination. In one review of racial bias, Marjorie Zatz (1987) identifies four "waves" of research since the 1950s. The first wave of research published from the 1950s through the mid-1960s reported clear and consistent biases. A second wave of research published between the mid-1960s and into the 1970s found little evidence of discrimination. The next wave of research (conducted in the 1970s and 1980s) reported complex findings that stressed the indirect and cumulative ways in which racial bias could operate. Finally, some of the most recent research has reported evidence of bias. A sample of such studies is summarized in the following discussion to illustrate the complexity and range of findings on the topic.

Nathan Goldman (1963) conducted a study on police decisions to refer apprehended juvenile delinquents to court in Allegheny County, Pennsylvania, in the late 1940s. He found that 65 percent of African-American juveniles were referred to court but only 34 percent of white juveniles. But for more serious offenses he found no evidence of racial bias. In Philadelphia, Terence Thornberry (1973) found significant racial differences in the processing of juvenile offenders. Seriousness of the offense was positively related to the severity of the disposition, but even when taking seriousness of the offense into consideration, racial differences were quite apparent. Theodore Ferdinand and Elmer Luchterhand (1970) found that African-American youths who were first offenders were referred to juvenile court more often than their white counterparts. Irving Piliavin and Scott Briar (1964) argued that the police look for clues as to the personal character of the alleged offender as a "good boy" or "bad boy." White juveniles were often seen as "good boys" who were cooperative and often were not arrested. However, African-American youth were often seen as hostile, uncooperative "tough guys," and thus were more often arrested. Piliavin and Briar also noted the police routinely patrolled the inner-city areas more than middle- or upper-income areas and this may also have generated higher arrests.

Respect toward the police has been found to be a critical factor in explaining why an arrest takes place. Black and Reiss found that juveniles who were antagonistic toward police officers had a higher probability of arrest. Stephen Mastrofski (2000) argues that it is not hostility alone that leads to an arrest, but hostility when others are present, most particularly other officers. Black and Reiss (1970) found that when police acted on their own initiative, without the presence of a complainant, the probability of an arrest is low. However, when a complainant was present, the probability of an arrest increased. Further, Black and Reiss found that African-American complainants pressed for an arrest more often than white complainants. Thus, citizen expectations or demands can influence whether officers make an arrest.

James Q. Wilson (1968) examined the style of organization of police departments and delineated two models that he labeled as "fraternal" and "professional." The professional police department was a paramilitary organization that strictly enforced rules, closely supervised police officers, and was highly bureaucratized. This style of police organization produced a high number of arrests, minimal discretion by the "cop on the beat," but less evidence of discriminatory arrest practices. The fraternal department was highly decentralized, placed less emphasis on strict procedures, but had greater evidence of discriminatory arrest practices. The highly bureaucratic police department reduced police discretion and thereby reduced discriminatory arrest practices. However, with reduced discretion, officers on the beat had less ability to weigh the circumstances of the offense, and routinely arrested far more individuals.

There is evidence that discrimination may vary by the seriousness of the offense. For felony offenses police discretion may be reduced in that every offender who has committed a homicide, robbery, or serious assault will be arrested. However, with petty offenses, the police officer can exercise significant discretion and this in turn can lead to differential arrests. Michael Tonry (1995) argues that the "war on drugs" has been directly primarily against African Americans. According to Tonry, this so-called war and the set of harsh crime-control policies it spawned were

> launched to achieve political, not policy objectives, and it is the adoption of political purposes of policies with foreseeable disparate impacts, the use of disadvantaged black Americans as a means to the achievement of politicians' electoral ends, that must in the end be justified and cannot. (1995:123)

The focus in law enforcement on crack cocaine, used primarily by African Americans, rather than powdered cocaine used in the white community has led to sky-rocketing arrest rates for drugs in the African-American community and a marked decline in drug arrest rates in the white community (see chapter 4).

Many studies point out that discrimination occurs not only at the point of arrest but throughout the juvenile justice process. McCord and Margaret Ensminger's research (2003) has shown that African Americans are slightly more likely to be arrested, slightly more likely to be detained, slightly more likely to be referred to juvenile court, and slightly more likely to be sent to a juvenile institution. The end result is that significantly more African-American youth are confined in institutions than whites. Discriminatory practices can occur at all stages of juvenile processing and the cumulative effect of modest discrimination may produce a sizeable gap between African-American youth and white youth at the end of the whole process.

Overall, no single conclusion is justified by the research on racial bias. Robert Agnew (2005) has differentiated between discrimination that is direct or indirect. Direct discrimination is relatively easy to examine in terms of arrest statistics, detention rates, institutionalization, and length of sentence. But indirect discrimination is more subtle. Coming from a single-parent, female-headed household may produce a bias in how a juvenile judge decides a case. Living in a poor, inner-city neighborhood can be a liability in the eyes of the juvenile court. Similarly, not achieving acceptable grades in school, or not participating in "acceptable" after-school programs, athletic activities, or social activities can also be viewed as risky behavior. Thus, discrimination can be the product of direct and indirect factors. It is difficult to pinpoint precisely where and to what extent discrimination occurs in the juvenile justice system, but there is sufficient evidence to suggest that African-American youth are often treated more harshly than their offenses or history would lead us to expect.

Differential Processing by Social Class

There has been less research on the influences of social class than on race-based discrimination, but while the evidence is somewhat mixed, there are a number of studies that point to discrimination based on social status. George Bodine (1964) examined police disposition of juveniles by the social status of the neighborhood and found that juveniles from lower-class areas had higher referrals to juvenile court. A decade later, Thornberry (1973) also found that social class had a strong effect on police disposition of juvenile offenders. More recently Robert Sampson (1986) and Miriam Sealock and Sally Simpson (1998) suggested that discrimination against lower-class juveniles may exist in certain communities.

Other studies have found no significant evidence of discrimination by social status. Researchers found that what appeared to be racial bias in some police encounters was generated by neighborhood characteristics (Smith, Visher, and Davidson, 1984). People in poor neighborhoods were more likely to be arrested than people in more prosperous neighborhoods. The fact that more African Americans lived in the poorer neighborhoods accounted for their greater susceptibility to arrest. The researchers pointed out that it was not individual status or class that determined the greater risk but the characteristics of neighborhoods themselves. Living in the wrong place resulted in a higher probability of arrest.

Similarly, Sampson concluded, "Apparently, the influence of SES [socioeconomic status] on police contacts with juveniles is contextual in nature, and stems from an ecological bias with regard to police control, as opposed to single individual-level bias against the poor" (1986:884). In other words, juveniles who live in lower-status neighborhoods that have been identified as crime-prone areas are more likely to come into contact with the police who patrol these areas more heavily. Cicourel (1976) suggested that the police feel that parents do not play a strong disciplinary role in lower-class neighborhoods and police therefore must play a stronger role in such neighborhoods compared to middle- or upper-class neighborhoods.

Differential Processing by Gender

In the 1950s it was suggested that a "chivalry factor" played a role in juvenile processing, whereby the police treated females more leniently than their male counterparts. Otto Pollak (1950) argued that females do not commit fewer crimes than their male counterparts but that they "get away" with more because their criminal behavior is less likely to be reported than male crimes (e.g., shoplifting), and they receive a form of paternalistic treatment by the criminal justice system. Pollak believed there was a marked reluctance to arrest females, to handcuff them and force them into a police car, and to refer them to juvenile court.

This chivalry hypothesis has been countered in more recent years by claims that females are treated more harshly than boys for some offenses because of a "double standard of justice" that allows "boys to be boys" but holds girls to a higher standard of behavior. Rita Simon (1975) noted that an alternative to the preferential treatment model is the view that women receive more punitive treatment than males because their criminal behavior is more "out of line" with social expectations than male crime. In other words, involvement in crime and delinquency is a greater departure from the ideals of how a female should act than it is for males. If we were to accept this hypothesis, we would assume that girls who violate the law and are caught receive harsher treatment than their male counterparts. There is evidence that when juvenile female offenders are apprehended for violating "traditional" gender roles, they may be treated more harshly by the juvenile justice system (Chesney-Lind, 1974; Terry, 1967). Merry Morash (1986) found that females are more likely to be arrested for status offenses than males but males are more likely than females to be arrested for "typical male" delinquency. Similarly, Christy Visher (1983) found that girls who do not meet the police officers' role expectations are more likely to be arrested than older females. Meda Chesney-Lind and Randall Shelden (2004) suggest that when the police or the juvenile courts encounter status offenses that are associated with sexual behavior or the possibility of sexual behavior on the part of females, there is a need to be more concerned and to protect the well-being of the female. When the perpetrator is a juvenile male, this sense of paternalism does not seem to be present. One study reports a tendency for girls to be "overarrested" for runaway and incorrigibility, suggesting that some form of the chivalry factor still exists (Teilman and Landry, 1981).

Overall, there appears to be a tendency for boys and girls to be treated differently for different offenses. When girls run away, this behavior seems to be taken more seriously than when boys do the same thing. On the other hand, there is a tendency to respond more severely to males who commit nonstatus offenses. There is also some evidence to suggest that females who do not conform to gender stereotypes, such as respect or deference to the police, may be more likely to be arrested than males.

Summary

Proclamations about the problem of juvenile delinquency typically cite a body of "facts" about youth crime or "facts" about delinquency. It is more appropriate to discuss "images" of delinquency since there are multiple sources of information that may yield divergent observations. Many criminologists have questioned whether police and court statistics can give us the real or true facts about delinquency in that these statistics are the outcome of numerous behaviors and decisions by the public and by agents of the law. Thus, such data are influenced by a wide range of factors other than the behavior of juveniles. Whether an event is recorded as a crime is a product of both public and police action and the interaction between the two.

Whether suspects become statistics as criminals or delinquents depends on such contingencies as the offense committed, offense history, complainant preference, the manner in which suspects and complainants interact with the police, and the organization and operational practices of police departments. Despite these complexities, the image of delinquency suggested by police and court data is in many ways consistent with public stereotypes, but with numerous qualifications.

Since so many factors other than offense activity alone can affect the chances of becoming an official statistic, some criminologists choose to view such data as merely a reflection of stereotypes and biases rather than "real" behavioral variations among categories of youth. However, the more common contemporary approach to such data is to study delinquent behavior as a product of a variety of influences and to gather data by other means as well. In the next chapter we will look at alternatives to official statistics, some of which are thought to more directly tap the real behavior of offenders. But as we shall see, those methods have their shortcomings as well, and critics challenge whether any technique short of direct observation can give us an accurate or valid picture of delinquency.

The UCR serious-crime index ("crimes known") tells us little about juvenile crime since the age of the offender is not reported. Arrest statistics are somewhat more meaningful since the police record the age, sex, and race and ethnicity of the person. However, they suggest that juveniles have relatively low arrest rates for the most serious violent offenses but high arrest rates for property offenses. The probability of a juvenile committing murder is quite low; he or she is much more likely to commit vandalism, burglary, or motor vehicle theft. Second, there has been a steady decline in juvenile offenses since the early to mid-1990s. Third, the ratio of male to female arrest rates appears to be declining for many kinds of offenses, a trend that may reflect changes in the processing of girls, but is also quite consistent with patterns based on self-reports. Fourth, both back and white juvenile arrest rates have been dropping in the past ten years but the decline in black arrests has been more dramatic than for whites.

Finally, juvenile court statistics give us another glimpse of the official processing of the juvenile offender. Delinquency cases have been increasing steadily since the 1940s, with a decline beginning in 1996. However, property offenses constitute the bulk of these cases. This corresponds to police arrest data. Juvenile cases for drug law violations have increased most dramatically since the early 1990s. Because status offenses are handled differently from state to state, the figures on status offense cases are a bit suspect. But it appears that there is an increase in the number of status offense cases referred to juvenile court, and liquor law violations constitute the greatest number of status referrals. Race is significant in that black youth have higher referrals to juvenile court for runaway, truancy, and ungovernability cases, but white youth have a far higher referral rate for liquor law cases than black youth.

Police and juvenile court data will always be an undercount of the true amount of juvenile crime. As we will see with victimization data, significant numbers of crime victims simply do not call the police. Further, there is always the issue of police discretion that infers social class or race bias. However, police are public servants and as such enforce local community standards. The local community can influence police behavior, and police statistics may reveal community pressure to arrest or not arrest. The importance of police data is that it reveals who gets arrested and for what offenses. Police data reveal the tolerance or intolerance of various communities to certain forms of adolescent behavior, the reactions to certain acts of deviance, and the processing of juvenile offenders.

Discrimination by the police is alleged in numerous studies, but controls for other factors that affect arrest decisions can alter those conclusions. There is evidence that differentials in arrest and processing are generated by seriousness of the offense committed and the prior record of the offender, the preference of the complainant, and the demeanor of the juvenile. Some of these may be linked to race. The allegation of social class bias may be confounded with police assessment of the criminality of the offender's neighborhood and increased police patrol. Females may receive preferential treatment for some offenses but be held to a higher standard for status offenses.

It may be a disappointment that the allegation of police bias needs to be placed in the context of the arrest situation or may vary from community to community, and there is no simple conclusion to be drawn. Delinquency is the product of a multitude of social circumstances and it may be that a long causal string of social forces is the explanation. Subtle but pervasive social issues may have a cumulative effect on the eventual determination of who is and who is not delinquent. The police might contribute to this process, but they are not the sole explanation for who gets arrested and why marked differentials exist between African Americans and whites, or males and females.

Discussion Questions

1. Why are chapters 3 and 4 titled "Images of Delinquency . . ." rather than "Facts about Delinquency"?

2. In what sense might it be correct to observe that the victims of crime determine the magnitude of the official crime rate each year?

3. In their book *Freakonomics*, Steven Levitt and Stephen Dubner argue that the 1973 *Roe v. Wade* decision permitting legalized abortion reduced the future at-risk criminal population fifteen to eighteen years later. Examining variations in murder rates over time, critically assess their argument.

4. Identify the two major sources of data on crime and delinquency in the United States. Specify what types of information are provided in each and the shortcomings of each for reaching conclusions about the nature and extent of delinquent behavior.

5. Suppose someone did a careful survey of two communities and found that the actual rates of criminal and delinquent behavior were the same in each but that the crime rates using police statistics were dramatically different. How is this possible? What specific points could be raised to explain this disparity?

6. In what way is it misleading to claim that crime peaks in adolescence? In what sense is this claim correct?

7. Identify three observations about female as compared to male crime and delinquency based on police and court statistics.

8. On what grounds does your text state that no single, simple conclusion can be reached concerning discrimination against black American youth by police and courts?

9. Several popular articles on female delinquency argue that there is a "double standard" for the handling of female as compared to male offenders. What do studies actually show concerning the treatment of the two sexes?

10. What finding based on police and court statistics did you find most interesting? Why was it interesting to you?

References

Agnew, R. 2005. *Juvenile Delinquency: Causes and Control.* Los Angeles: Roxbury.

Black, D. J., and A. J. Reiss, Jr. 1970. "Police Control of Juveniles." *American Sociological Review* 35 (February): 63–77.

Blumstein, A., and J. Williams. 2000. *The Crime Drop in America.* Cambridge, England: Cambridge University Press.

Bodine, G. 1964. "Factors Related to Police Dispositions of Juvenile Offenders." Paper presented at the annual meeting of the American Sociological Association.

Cassidy, D. C. 1992. *Uncertainty: The Life and Science of Werner Heisenberg.* New York: W. H. Freeman & Co.

Chesney-Lind, M. 1974. "Juvenile Delinquency: The Sexualization of Female Crime." *Psychology Today* (July): 44–46.

Chesney-Lind, M., and R. G. Shelden. 2004. *Girls, Delinquency, and Juvenile Justice.* Belmont, CA: Thomson/Wadsworth.

Cicourel, A. 1976. *The Social Organization of Juvenile Justice.* New York: John Wiley.

Conway, K. P., and J. McCord. 2002. "Longitudinal Examination of the Relation between Co-Offending with Violent Accomplices and Violent Crime." Washington, DC: U.S. Department of Justice.

Cook, P. J., and J. H. Laub. 2001. "After the Epidemic: Recent Trends in Youth Violence in the United States." NBER Working Paper No. W8571, October. Available at SSRN: http://ssrn.com/abstract=288484.

Eckberg, D. 1995. "Estimates of Early Twentieth-Century U.S. Homicide Rates: An Econometric Forecasting Approach." *Demography* 32: 1–16.

Federal Bureau of Investigation. 2007. *Crime in the United States, 2006.* Washington, DC: GPO.

Felson, M. 1994. *Crime and Everyday Life.* Thousand Oaks, CA: Pine Forge.

Ferdinand, T. N., and E. G. Luchterhand. 1970. "Inner-City Youths, the Police, the Juvenile Court, and Justice." *Social Problems* 17 (Spring): 510–27.

Foote, C. L., and C. F. Goetz. 2005. "Testing Economic Hypotheses with State-Level Data: A Comment on Donohue and Levitt." Federal Reserve Bank of Boston Working Paper 05-15, November 22, 2005.

Goldman, N. 1963. *The Differential Selection of Juvenile Offenders for Court Appearance.* New York: National Council on Crime and Delinquency.

Jensen, G. F., and D. G. Rojek. 1998. *Delinquency and Youth Crime.* 3rd ed. Long Grove, IL: Waveland Press.

Karmen, A. 2001. *Crime Victims.* 4th ed. Belmont, CA: Wadsworth.

Levitt, S. D., and S. J. Dubner. 2005. *Freakonomics: A Rogue Economist Explores the Hidden Side of Everything.* New York: William Morrow.

Maguire, K., and A. L. Pastore, eds. 2004. *Sourcebook of Criminal Justice Statistics—2003.* Washington, DC: U.S. Department of Justice.

Mastrofski, S. D. 2000. "The Police in America." In *Criminology: A Contemporary Handbook,* edited by Joseph F. Sheley, 405–45. Belmont, CA: Wadsworth.

McCord, J., and M. E. Ensminger. 2003. "Racial Discrimination and Violence: A Longitudinal Perspective." In *Violent Crime: Addressing Race and Ethnic Differences,* edited by D. F. Hawkins, 319–30. Cambridge, England: Cambridge University Press.

Morash, M. 1986. "Gender, Peer Group Experiences, and Seriousness of Delinquency." *Journal of Research on Crime and Delinquency* 23: 43–67.

Myers, S. 1999. *Police Encounters with Juvenile Suspects: Explaining the Use of Authority and Provision of Support.* Washington, DC: National Institute of Justice.

Novak, K., J. Frank, B. Smith, and R. Engel. 2002. "Revisiting the Decision to Arrest: Comparing Beat and Community Officers." *Crime and Delinquency* 48: 70–98.

O'Brien, R. M. 2000. "Crime Facts: Victims and Offender Data." In *Criminology,* edited by J. Sheley, 59–83. Belmont, CA: Wadsworth.

Piliavin, I., and S. Briar. 1964. "Police Encounters with Juveniles." *American Journal of Sociology* 70 (September): 206–14.

Pollak, O. 1950. *The Criminality of Women.* Philadelphia: University of Pennsylvania Press.

Reiman, J. 2003. *The Rich Get Richer and the Poor Get Prison.* 7th ed. Boston: Allyn & Bacon.

Sampson, R. J. 1986. "Effects of Socioeconomic Context on Official Reaction to Juvenile Delinquency." *American Sociological Review* 51: 876–85.

Sealock, M., and S. Simpson. 1998. "Unraveling Bias in Arrest Decisions: The Role of Juvenile Offender Type-Scripts." *Justice Quarterly* 15: 427–57.

Simon, R. J. 1975. *Women and Crime.* Lexington, MA: D. C. Heath.

Smith, D., C. A. Visher, and L. A. Davidson. 1984. "Equity and Discretionary Justice: The Influence of Race on Police Arrest Decisions." *The Journal of Criminal Law and Criminology* 75 (Spring): 234–59.

Snyder, H. N., and M. Sickmund. 2006. *Juvenile Offenders and Victims: 2006 National Report.* Washington, DC: U.S. Department of Justice.

Stahl, Anne L., Charles Puzzanchera, Anthony Sladky, Terrence A. Finnegan, Nancy Tierney, and Howard N. Snyder. 2005. *Juvenile Court Statistics 2001–2002.* Pittsburgh, PA: National Center for Juvenile Justice.

Teilman, K. S., and P. H. Landry. 1981. "Gender Bias in Juvenile Justice." *Journal of Research in Crime and Delinquency* 18 (January): 47–80.

Terry, R. M. 1967. "Discrimination in the Handling of Juvenile Offenders by Social Control Agencies." *Journal of Research in Crime and Delinquency* 4 (July): 218–30.

Thornberry, T. 1973. "Race, Socioeconomic Status, and Sentencing in the Juvenile Justice System." *Journal of Criminal Law and Criminology* 64 (March): 90–98.

Tonry, M. 1995. *Malign Neglect: Race, Crime, and Punishment in America.* New York: Oxford University Press.

Visher, C. 1983. "Gender, Police Arrests, and Notions of Chivalry." *Criminology* 21 (February): 5–28.

Walker, S., and C. Katz. 2002. *The Police in America.* 4th ed. New York: McGraw-Hill.

Wilson, J. Q. 1968. "The Police and the Delinquent in Two Cities." In *Controlling Delinquents,* edited by S. Wheeler. New York: John Wiley.

———. 2005. Review of *Freakonomics* by Steven D. Levitt and Stephen J. Dubner. *Commentary Magazine.* July/August. Electronic version accessed at http://www.commentarymagazine.com/cm/main/viewArticle.html?id=9926.

Zatz, M. 1987. "The Changing Forms of Racial/Ethical Biases in Sentencing." *Journal of Research in Crime and Delinquency* 24 (February): 69–92.

four

Images of Delinquency
Survey Data

(S)elf-reports, whether by offenders or victims, are an essential research tool for determining the extent of youth violence. They furnish a window into violent behavior that never reaches the police. For example, the National Crime Victimization Survey reveals that the majority (58 percent) of serious violent crimes committed by youths are not reported to the police (Snyder and Sickmund, 1999). A large fraction of the crimes that are reported never result in an arrest. Estimates indicate that only 6 to 14 percent of chronic violent offenders are ever arrested for a serious violent crime.

(Youth Violence: A Report of the Surgeon General, 2001)

Everyone Does It! I Just Got Caught!

How often have you heard someone say, "Everyone does it. I just got caught!"? How often have you said that yourself? This statement highlights not only the focus of this chapter but also a major research issue in criminology. Criminologists have long recognized that those individuals who are caught are not necessarily a **representative sample** of the total population of people who have done things for which they *could* have been arrested and punished. Statistics about people who are caught reflect the behavior of the public, police, prosecutors, judges, and attorneys as well as characteristics of offenses, offenders, and victims.

Criminologists ask to what degree are the cases that appear in police and court statistics representative of offenders? Are those who get caught a biased sample of those who commit offenses? Are comparison groups of people who do not have records representative samples of noncriminals and nondelinquents? Or, are many of them simply offenders who did not get caught? The general issue is one of **sampling bias**. A variety of characteristics other than offenses committed might bias data on those caught. Some variations among categories of youth may be products of their race, gender, appearance, or mannerisms rather than their offense behavior alone.

Variations in crime over time may reflect changes in victim reporting and rates of apprehending and responding rather than actual changes in rates of offending. If a greater proportion of rapes are reported to the police and treated seriously, then rape can appear to be increasing when actual rates of offending remain the same. An official crackdown on crime may lead to a greater proportion of crimes making their way into statistical reports, much like the "war on drugs" increased the proportion of drug offenses captured in police statistics. Because official statistics are affected by more than criminal or delinquent activity, criminologists have tried to develop alternative sources of data that allow comparisons among measures. The two major alternative sources of information are self-report surveys and victimization surveys.

Self-report surveys attempt to measure offense behavior through interviews or questionnaires by asking individuals about the extent of their criminal or delinquent involvement. **Victimization surveys** attempt to measure the extent of certain types of crime through interviews or questionnaires dealing with the individual's experiences as the victim of a crime. Although both of these techniques for assessing the extent and correlates of crime and delinquency have been criticized, they do overcome some of the shortcomings of police and court statistics. They tap into "hidden" crime and delinquency and allow an assessment of behavior that escapes detection or is not recorded by justice officials. By considering several different sources of information, even though each has its limitations, we can begin to formulate a fuller, more accurate image of delinquency.

Self-Reports of Delinquency

The most widely used alternative to police and court statistics in the study of delinquency is the self-report survey, in which people are asked to report on their own delinquent activity. Such surveys date back to the 1940s (Porterfield, 1946; Murphy, Shirley, and Witmer, 1946), but the technique gained popularity in the late 1950s with the work of F. Ivan Nye and James F. Short, Jr. (1957). The self-report technique became the dominant method of studying delinquency in the 1960s and 1970s and was given a major boost by the most cited work in criminology in the twentieth century, Travis Hirschi's *Causes of Delinquency* (1969). Although the book focused on white male youth in junior and senior high schools in Contra Costa, California, its use of self-reports to test competing theories of delinquency prompted a sizeable wave of self-report questionnaire studies. In fact, the self-report survey developed into the most common method among criminologists for testing theories about the characteristics of samples of youth that correlate with delinquency. Because it focuses on delinquency as reported by youth rather than on those youth who are arrested, cited, or referred to juvenile court, the method avoids some of the biases that might be reflected in official processing.

Such self-report surveys have taken two basic forms. One form is the **interview**, in which the subject is questioned about his or her background, opinions, and delinquent activities. The second is a **checklist** or **questionnaire** that the subject fills in or completes. Some researchers believe that the interview method reduces error because the interviewer can explore a respondent's answers and gather more detail when needed. On the other hand, the interview makes it more difficult to assure the respondent of anonymity because he or she can be identified by the interviewer. Interviews also are more costly than surveys because surveys can be administered to large groups of people all at once. The questionnaire method is useful both for gathering information from large samples and for assuring anonymity, but it does not allow for detailed elaboration of answers or the ability to clarify certain questions. The questionnaire method also assumes that subjects can read reasonably well and can follow written directions.

Although the self-report method emerged in an attempt to find measures of criminal and delinquent behavior that would improve upon police and court statistics, the method has had numerous critics. It is only in the last few years that sufficient consensus on their reliability and validity has emerged to justify their inclusion in major government assessments of youth violence. In 1993 a major presidential task force (Reiss and Roth, 1993) totally ignored self-report survey methods as a tool for measuring violence, a stance that was severely criticized in an address by Delbert Elliott to the American Society of Criminology in 1994. Later, as senior scientific editor of the 2001

Surgeon General's report on youth violence (see quote heading this chapter), Elliott incorporated self-report survey data as an acceptable and valuable technique for measuring delinquency and youth crime.

Reliability and Validity of Self-Report Surveys

In their attempts to provide accurate, valid measures of delinquent behavior, self-report methods assume that: (1) the behavior in question can be clearly and precisely described in a manner that yields the same "meaning" or interpretation for respondents as intended by the researcher, (2) people will remember their transgressions, (3) they will give honest answers to queries about their behavior, and (4) they can follow directions, read, and understand the questions. If these requirements are not met, then the reliability and validity of the data can be seriously questioned.

Reliability and validity are two distinct criteria for evaluating the adequacy of the self-report technique. When addressing the **reliability** of a measurement technique, the basic issue is whether repeated measurements would yield consistent results. If repeated measures using a particular technique yield inconsistent results (when there is no reason to believe that the phenomena being measured have changed), then that technique is considered unreliable. They do not have to yield perfectly consistent results, but they should yield a high degree of consistency in both absolute terms and as compared to survey data measuring other phenomena in the social sciences.

A number of studies have tested the reliability of the self-report technique by comparing the results of measurements at different points in time, by examining the results of different ways of measuring the same thing, and by scrutinizing the consistency of responses to different questions in the same survey. Such tests suggest that in terms of prevailing standards for assessing reliability, self-reports yield consistent, reliable data on delinquency (Hindelang, Hirschi, and Weis, 1981; Thornberry and Krohn, 2001). Some researchers argue that interviews provide more reliable data than questionnaires (Elliott and Ageton, 1980) because questions can be explained and answers elaborated, but the evidence to date suggests that the differences are minor (Thornberry and Krohn, 2001; Krohn, Waldo, and Chiricos, 1975). Anonymous questionnaires yield data of comparable reliability to interviews.

The validity of self-reports as measures of delinquent behavior has been a more controversial issue than their reliability. A measure is considered to have **validity** when it can be shown to measure what it is supposed to measure. A measure may yield the same results time after time, but can be measuring something other than what was intended. If youth exaggerate their involvement in delinquency to be "cool," then their "attitude" is being measured rather than their offense behavior. If youth fail to report delinquent activity because they fear being caught, then fear of apprehension may be what is being measured. The data might be reliable, yielding the same responses each time, but not measure what was intended.

A variety of problems can affect validity, including difficulty in defining "real" delinquent events using ordinary language. Researchers concerned with measuring behavior that is in violation of the law are confronted with the fact that laws are imprecise and ambiguous. For example, it is common in self-report studies to ask "During the past year, how many times have you taken a car without permission (not parents' car)?" The question was intended to measure events that could end up in police statistics as motor vehicle theft. However, such circumstances as who took it from whom, for what reason, and for how long would affect whether an event made its way into motor vehicle theft statistics. Similarly, surveys often ask "During the past year, how any times have you run away from home?" Such events could be labeled as acts of incorrigibility, truancy, curfew violation, or runaway. Once again, depending on the circumstances, a single event could be handled officially in numerous ways. Even questions about "getting into a fight" can refer to quite different events for girls and boys. For some youths it may mean a verbal, shouting, name-calling episode while for others it may mean a physical altercation. In short, although behavioral events described in self-reports are often imprecise and may encompass activities that have little chance of prompting police or court action, so too the laws defining activities that can result in legal action are broad and imprecise.

Since researchers cannot validate their measurement of delinquency by direct observation of the delinquent behavior, how can the validity of self-reports be assessed? In his study of delinquency in Flint, Michigan, Martin Gold assessed the validity of his self-report survey by interviewing the teenaged acquaintances of his respondents who were most likely to have information about the respondents' delinquent behavior (1970:19–24). Thus, Gold could compare what the respondents in his study admitted with what the informants said about them. He found that his self-report interviews underestimated delinquent behavior by about 30 percent, but that there were no marked differences in concealment across categories of sex, race, and social status. Although the self-reports underestimated delinquency, they did so to such comparable degrees for different groups that differences among groups could be plausibly interpreted as reflecting real differences in delinquent behavior rather than differences in honesty or memory.

Numerous studies have shown involvement in delinquency as measured by self-reports to be highly correlated with police, court, and institutional statistics (Nye, 1958; Erickson and Empey, 1963; Hirschi, 1969; Elliott and Voss, 1974; Hindelang, Hirschi, and Weis, 1981). We have already noted that memory, honesty, and understanding may preclude a perfect match between self-reports and police statistics, but it is also important to recognize that what appears to be the "same" event may have quite different meanings to the offender and the police. Dean Rojek (1983) compared youths' reports and police reports of offenses over a six-month period and found that they matched only 46 percent of the time. Mismatches were due to errors in youths' recollections of when events took place, differences in what they remembered being arrested for and what the police recorded, and uncertainties about arrests in situations with multiple arrests. In some instances the events were interpreted differently:

> A field encounter between a police officer and a juvenile may not have resulted in an arrest, but perceived through the eyes of a juvenile he or she was "busted" by the police. Further, the categorization of the deviant act may be unduly complex because of multiple offenses and differing levels of seriousness for each offense. The juvenile may perceive a police encounter in terms of an arrest for a particular behavior, while the police officer may view the encounter as a "police contact" for a different act of deviance. (1983:73)

Thus, the issue is not necessarily a matter of one body of data being the correct standard against which to judge the validity of another. The police officer sees "reality" from one perspective in defining delinquent events and it does not necessarily correspond with the adolescent's perspective.

Measuring Violence

Some prominent criminologists remain critical of the utility of the self-report method for studying violence and propose that the method is best suited for the study of common property crime. For example, Steven Messner and Richard Rosenfeld state that "because serious offending is engaged in by small numbers of people, it is difficult to study via survey research methods that have been favored by recent generations of researchers" (2001:43). In fact, self-report studies have not dealt with offenses such as murder and rape. Not only are there reservations about honesty in reporting such offenses, but such events are sufficiently rare that they would not show up very often even in large surveys. Unless one used a huge sample, it is unlikely that there would be enough cases involving certain specific offenses for any meaningful analysis.

However, the most common forms of violence (fights, assaults, robberies) do occur with sufficient frequency to allow analysis, and as one of the most prominent survey researchers, Elliott (1994) has shown that survey data can be used to arrive at meaningful generalizations about sources of variation in the general category of "serious violent offenses." Furthermore, as will be documented in the section on patterns over time, an analysis of self-reported violence over time using survey data suggests considerable consistency between official and survey data for violent offenses involving youths (see Jensen, 2003; 2006).

Patterns Based on Self-Reports

Police and court statistics, as well as self-reports, have their limitations. Different people will accept or reject the "facts" suggested by each method, depending on the weight that they assign to those limitations and how well the "facts" mesh with their own preconceptions. So-called experts who are committed to the assumption that social status is an important correlate of delinquency are more likely to doubt the results of self-report research than are those committed to theories that do not assume such a correlation. Those who argue that the justice system discriminates against minorities are more likely to accept results that seemingly minimize real behavioral differences among groups. Those who believe minorities are "the problem" are more likely to accept police arrest data. Those who believe that only males are "real" members of gangs are likely to challenge any source of data that is contrary to that impression.

On many topics, self-report data and police data are typically less disparate than they seem, and data produced by both types of studies yield a surprising number of comparable findings. When different ways of measuring a phenomenon yield similar patterns, then we tend to have greater confidence that the patterns are real and not merely artifacts of one particular methodology. When different data sources yield disparate results, the challenge to criminologists is to propose and, ultimately, test hypotheses about the reasons for such variation.

Frequency of Delinquent Behavior

Self-report surveys have been conducted in a number of different nations, with literally hundreds having been carried out in the United States. In table 4-1 we have summarized the results of a survey conducted among a representative sample of high school seniors in the United States in 2005 (Johnston, Bachman, and O'Malley, 2005). When asked how many times they had engaged in each form of behavior in the last twelve months, a surprising proportion of youth admit to delinquent behavior. About 27 percent of senior males have shoplifted as have 23 percent of senior girls. Considering the fact that the questions asked about offenses in the prior 12 months, it would be safe to conclude that most youths have done so at some time.

Sizeable percentages report other offenses as well, although males tend to dominate, especially for the most serious offenses. About 18 percent of senior males report having damaged school property on purpose, compared to about 6 percent of senior females. About 12 percent of senior males have stolen something worth more than $50 compared to about 6 percent of senior girls. About 18 percent of males have hurt someone badly enough that they needed bandages or a doctor while only 6 percent of females report hurting someone that badly.

Not only has self-report research shown the extent of involvement in delinquency to be far greater than many people might anticipate, but research encompassing junior as well as senior high school students suggests that a surprising proportion of preadolescent youths are involved. For example, in a study of drug use among junior and senior high school students in Georgia (Rojek, 1996), students were asked, "Have you ever gotten really drunk in the past twelve months?" More than 8 percent of sixth-graders, 16 percent of seventh-graders, and 26 percent of eighth-graders report being intoxicated at least once in the preceding twelve months. When one considers that sixth-grade students are about 12 years old, these results are quite startling. The percentage increases steadily by grade to the point where close to 60 percent of seniors report getting really drunk in a twelve-month period. Alcohol use remains the number one drug problem among youth.

Changes over Time

Self-report data are not available for the long span of years encompassed by the Uniform Crime Reports, but the Institute for Social Research at the University of Michigan has conducted an annual survey each year since 1975 that includes self-reports of offenses and victimizations. That project, Monitoring the Future, was designed to explore changes in values, behaviors, and attitudes of American youth based on a sample of about 15,000 high school seniors from approximately 125 schools. About 2,500 high school seniors answer questions about their offense behavior and about 14,500 answer questions involving drug use. A second national survey has been carried out by the Centers for Disease Control (CDC) in odd numbered years since 1991, which greatly limits its use for making statements about variation over time. With data available for only a few points in time, it will be many years before we can assess the correspondence between the CDC data and other sources of data.

Of course, the use of the Monitoring the Future (MTF) surveys to study variation over time has obvious limitations. It is quite reasonable for criminologists to have major reservations about self-report data as an authoritative source of information on

Table 4-1   Percent of High School Seniors Self-Reporting Delinquent Involvement in Last Twelve Months

	Male	Female	White	Black	Hispanic
Gotten into a serious fight in school or at work					
Not at all	86.1	90.7	90.7	79.2	83.8
Once	7.5	6.0	6.1	10.0	9.2
Twice or more	6.4	3.3	3.7	10.8	6.9
Taken something not belonging to you worth under $50					
Not at all	65.5	78.8	72.3	75.6	66.3
Once	15.0	10.2	13.4	8.5	14.0
Twice or more	19.2	10.9	14.3	15.9	19.8
Taken something from a store without paying for it					
Not at all	72.7	77.0	76.8	72.2	65.3
Once	12.1	10.8	10.2	10.8	15.4
Twice or more	15.1	12.3	13.0	17.0	19.3
Taken a car that didn't belong to someone in your family without the owner's permission					
Not at all	92.7	97.0	96.0	95.0	90.3
Once	3.3	1.7	2.3	2.3	3.9
Twice or more	4.0	1.3	1.7	2.7	5.8
Gone into some house or building when you weren't supposed to be there					
Not at all	69.1	78.5	73.3	80.0	66.7
Once	13.9	11.0	13.6	7.3	14.0
Twice or more	17.0	10.5	13.1	12.7	19.4
Damaged school property on purpose					
Not at all	82.5	93.5	88.3	89.2	83.7
Once	8.5	3.1	6.3	4.6	6.6
Twice or more	9.1	2.9	5.4	6.2	9.7
Taken part in a fight where a group of your friends were against another group					
Not at all	77.8	84.2	82.8	73.1	77.7
Once	12.8	10.0	10.4	16.2	12.7
Twice or more	9.4	5.8	6.8	10.8	9.6
Hurt someone badly enough to need bandages or a doctor					
Not at all	82.1	94.3	90.1	80.7	84.6
Once	9.4	3.7	5.4	9.7	10.0
Twice or more	8.5	2.0	4.5	9.7	5.4
Used a knife or gun or some other thing (like a club) to get something from a person					
Not at all	94.9	98.9	97.8	95.0	94.2
Once	2.3	0.6	1.1	1.6	2.7
Twice or more	2.8	0.6	1.1	3.5	3.1
Taken something not belonging to you worth over $50					
Not at all	88.3	94.4	92.4	88.8	86.1
Once	5.6	2.8	3.8	5.8	5.0
Twice or more	6.1	2.8	3.8	5.4	8.9

Source: Johnston, Bachman, and O'Malley, Monitoring the Future, 2005.

patterns of violence among sociodemographic categories of youth, and it is even more reasonable to have doubts about such data from high school seniors as a source of information on crime over time. Even in large samples, the number of youth reporting the most serious offenses will be small and there will be marked and possibly meaningless fluctuations in the rates based on these small numbers. A few extra cases can look like a major change when in fact the numbers may be fluctuating randomly. Because the surveys are limited to high school seniors, the most violent youth may not be in the sample. It is likely that a disproportionate share of the most violent youth will have dropped out of school and that the MTF surveys reflect the behavior of those youth who made it that far in the educational system. In short, they likely underestimate the most serious offenses.

Yet, many of these criticisms have little bearing on whether the self-report data that do exist can yield meaningful statements about violence over time. Self-reports may not be perfectly reliable and valid, but if reliability and validity were to be relatively stable over time, self-report data might tap trends or variations in violent events over time. If sources of error are relatively stable over time, then variation in self-reports may capture variations in actual offending over time. Similarly, while some of the most serious offenders may have dropped out before their senior year, variations over time in the reports of new cohorts of high school seniors may still capture underlying currents of behavior. Dropouts may have higher rates of violence than those who stay in school, but patterns over time could still parallel one another if it were possible to compare offense rates for dropouts and rates for those still in school. The rates may be lower for high school seniors than for more representative samples, but fluctuations and trends may be quite similar.

One of the most recent attempts to document trends in youth violence is Philip Cook and John Laub's article in *Crime and Justice*, which uses UCR arrest data and victim reports from the National Crime Victimization Surveys (NCVS) as "two indicators of the underlying phenomenon (i.e. serious violence committed by juveniles)" (2002:1–37). Based on these two sources of data, they conclude that an unprecedented "epidemic" of youth violence "began in the mid-1980s . . . peaked in 1993–94, and . . . has receded since" (2002:2).

Would we have been badly misled had MTF data on self-reported violence been used to identify these same patterns over time? Figure 4-1 graphs the sum of the averages for number of times that high school seniors indicated having hurt someone badly, used a weapon to rob someone, or been in a group fight between 1975 and 2005, and also graphs an equation that captures the general pattern. The average number of violent self-reported offenses between 1975 and 2005 varies in approximately the same manner as police arrest rates for violent offenses among juveniles. Whether using UCR "crimes known" or juvenile arrest rates, the same basic observations about trends in violence over this span of time can be made. To paraphrase Cook and Laub, self-reports of violence by high school seniors suggest that an epidemic of youth violence began in the mid-1980s, peaked in the mid-1990s, and receded through the remainder of the 1990s. In short, quite comparable statements about violence could be made using the self-report data.

Would we have made radically different statements about property crime over time using MTF data as compared to juvenile arrest rates? The two sets of data do not

Figure 4-1   Average Number of Violent Offenses, Self-Reports of MTF Seniors (1975–2005)

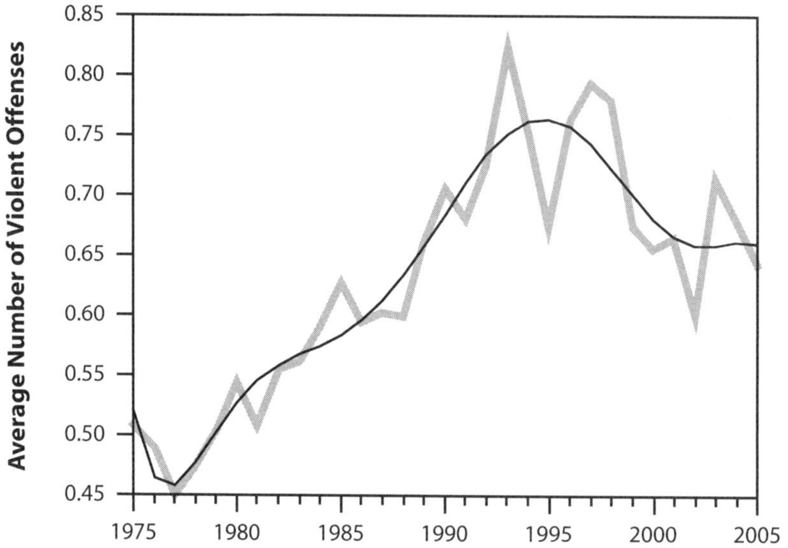

Source: Based on calculations using Monitoring the Future surveys by Johnston, Bachman, and O'Malley (odd years) and Bachman, Johnston, and O'Malley (even years).

necessarily encompass the same activities, so some variation should be expected. The MTF surveys do not measure burglary, but ask about going into a house or building "when you weren't supposed to be there." Taking a car without the owner's permission is the proxy for motor vehicle theft. The MTF surveys distinguish between thefts over and under $50, but also ask about shoplifting. The same event may be reported by the respondent more than once (theft and shoplifting). In its report titled *Juvenile Crime, Juvenile Justice*, the National Research Council and Institute of Medicine note that thefts over $50 can increase due to inflation regardless of any changes in offense behavior (McCord, Widom, and Crowell, 2001). The FBI ceased making such a distinction over thirty years ago when it was found that crime rates were being manipulated by underestimating the value of items so they would not enter the UCR index. At that time, the larceny index was limited to thefts over $50. In short, we cannot create a measure of property crime that is identical to the UCR.

Although we should not be surprised if major disparities in temporal patterns are found when comparing different types of data, the overall patterns appear quite comparable in most instances. Figure 4-2 includes five MTF offenses that parallel the UCR. The property crime arrest rates for persons 15–17 and 18–20 are included in the graphs as well. Three offenses that would be classified as "larcenies" (shoplifting, theft under $50, theft over $50 adjusted for inflation) declined between 1975 and 1985, increased from the early to mid-1990s, and declined thereafter.

The only item approximating the circumstances for burglary is trespass, and it follows the same pattern as theft and shoplifting. However, this pattern contrasts with that

Figure 4-2   Average Number of Property Offenses and Best Equation, Self-Reports of MTF Seniors and FBI Arrest Rates (1975–2005)

Theft over $50
(Adjusted for inflation)

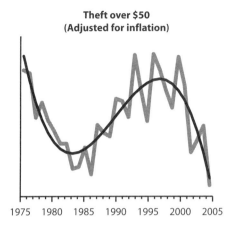

Theft under $50
(Adjusted for inflation)

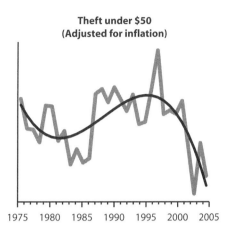

Shoplifting

Taking a Car

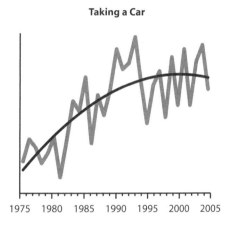

Trespass
(Breaking and Entering)

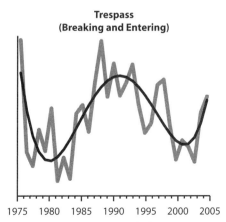

Arrest Rate for Property Crime

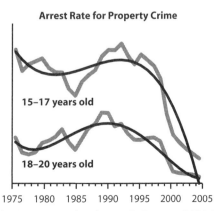

15–17 years old

18–20 years old

Source: Self-reports based on calculations using Monitoring the Future surveys by Johnston, Bachman, and O'Malley (odd years) and Bachman, Johnston, and O'Malley (even years). Arrest rates from FBI Uniform Crime Reports.

noted in chapter 2, where burglary showed a steady decline over the last twenty-five years. Of course, the MTF item is very broad and may encompass parties, drinking, or any activity that would involve entering a structure without permission. It should also be noted that burglary is the only offense in the arrest data that exhibits that trend. All others follow a pattern similar to the survey data. This exceptional pattern may reflect greater specificity over time in what counts as a "burglary" in the UCR.

Another exception in temporal patterns is the item asking about taking a car without permission. Self-reports for that item follow an upward trend, flattening out after the mid-1990s. In contrast, arrest data show motor vehicle theft to be declining in the early 1980s, increasing to the early 1990s, and declining thereafter (see chapter 2). Again, such disparities may reflect differences in perceptions of events in the minds of respondents to the MTF surveys as compared to events that result in arrest or are classified as thefts by the police. For those offenses involving the least ambiguity in terms of UCR classifications, the patterns revealed for both violent and property offenses are quite comparable.

Self-Reports of Illicit Drug Use

Although there was an enduring reluctance to use self-report data in the study of trends in violence and serious crime until recently, the MTF data on drug use have been used regularly to track trends over the last several decades. They have been a common source of news reports on drug use among youth and receive considerable publicity each year. In fact, the main aim of the MTF surveys has been to compile detailed data on the use of illicit drugs and they include more items dealing with aspects of drug use than any other issue.

Figure 4-3 summarizes data on different forms of self-reported drug use for the years 1975 through 2006, yielding several important observations. First, as most people would expect, alcohol is the preferred drug among high school students in the United States. Three-fourths of high school seniors report drinking alcohol. However, alcohol use has declined, with 85 to 90 percent admitting drinking in the 1970s as compared with 70 to 75 percent in the 1990s and early 2000s. One explanation proposed for this decline is the fact that the legal drinking age was 18 in most states when the MTF surveys began, but was gradually raised to 21 in all states. Self-reported alcohol use declined steadily as the drinking age was raised, leveling out in 1992. After a brief upturn in the mid-1990s it continued to decline. It is interesting to note that use of marijuana and a variety of other drugs followed a similar path during that span of time, suggesting that factors other than any specific effect of legal drinking age on alcohol use have to be considered. It may be that enforcement of the laws governing alcohol use increased the odds that youth would be caught using other drugs as well, and that an increase in general risk of apprehension led to a general decline in the most commonly used drugs.

After prompting concern of an epidemic in the early 1980s and rising sharply in the mid-1980s, cocaine use declined each year between 1986 and 1992, beginning a new upward trend in that year. A similar pattern can be noted for the use of marijuana, tranquilizers, and hallucinogenic drugs (e.g., LSD). After fourteen years of stability (1975–1988), alcohol use began declining in the late 1980s.

Figure 4-3   Percentage Self-Reporting Drug Use (1975–2006)

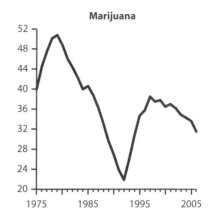

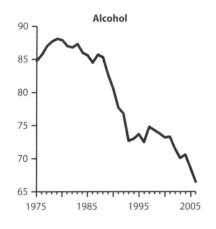

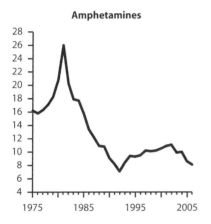

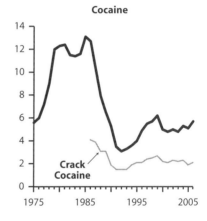

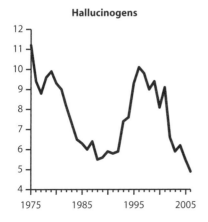

(continued)

Figure 4-3   *(cont'd.)*

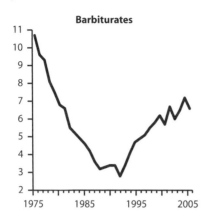

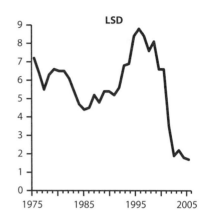

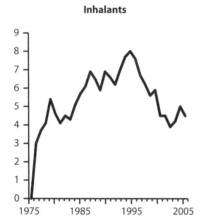

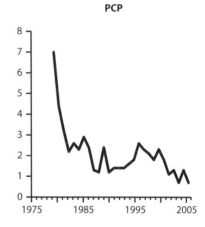

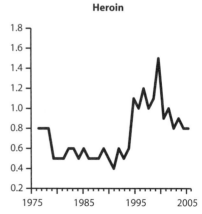

Source: Self-reports based on calculations using Monitoring the Future surveys by Johnston, Bachman, and O'Malley (odd years) and Bachman, Johnston, and O'Malley (even years).

The one form of drug use that followed a sustained upward trend for two decades is inhalant use, which reached an all-time high in 1995. In a survey of Georgia youth (Rojek, 1996), nearly 30 percent of seventh-graders used inhalants while the percentage steadily declined to 14 percent for seniors. Inhalants are incredibly dangerous, causing damage to the nasal passages, trachea, and lungs as well as oxygen deficiency to the brain. Moreover, such substances are cheap and readily available to younger adolescents. Older adolescents have the social contacts and the money to procure more "traditional" drugs like alcohol and marijuana. Fortunately, inhalant use began declining in the mid-1990s and is now at the level it was almost thirty years ago.

One factor contributing to marked declines in many forms of drug use in the 1980s was changing attitudes about the health hazards of drugs. Changes in perception of harm were particularly prominent for cocaine, with a sudden downward shift in reported cocaine use between 1986 and 1987. In 1986, Len Bias, a college basketball player headed for the professional ranks, died of complications attributed to cocaine, and the national publicity surrounding this case may have helped generate this sudden shift. Tragic real-world events such as Len Bias's death may have had more consequences for drug use than any government policy. Moreover, the effect of the sudden shift in perceived harm in 1986–87 may have eroded over time as fewer and fewer youth in each subsequent senior cohort would be cognizant of such events. By 1992 the high school seniors being surveyed would include youth who were only 11 or 12 years of age when the publicity revolving around cocaine-induced deaths occurred. The 1995 cohort of seniors includes youth who were around 8 years of age in 1986. Unfortunate real-world lessons that receive considerable media attention appear to lose their impact with the passage of time.

It is important to recognize that some downward trends have been relatively long term. The first official "drug czar," William Bennett, often cited intensive patrol efforts and law enforcement crackdowns as the explanation for the types of decreases reported above. Yet, some forms of drug use had been declining for a decade prior to the establishment of Bennett's position as Director of the Drug Enforcement Administration in 1989 and President George Bush's "war on drugs." In fact, illicit drug use increased in the 1990s despite increases in government funding and increasing drug arrest rates. Highly publicized tragic events such as Bias's death likely had more to do with the 1986–87 downturn in cocaine use than any activities under the auspices of the drug czar. This critical observation does not mean that laws and their enforcement are totally ineffective. Laws and risk of punishment probably do affect choices (see chapter 9). However, young people appear to react quickly to events that dramatically illustrate realistic dangers of drug use.

Another possible explanation of the shared patterns across numerous forms of drug use is drug education. Nancy Reagan's "Just Say No" program began in 1986, the same year as Bias's death. Moreover, there were increases in the percentage of students reporting drug education programs in schools around that time. In 1985 about 70 percent of seniors reported having had drug education classes. This percentage increased to 81 percent by 1990. The percentage fell over the next several years, but was back up again by the end of the 1990s. About 75 percent of seniors reported such classes in the MTF survey in 2004. The arrest rate for juveniles did not follow a pattern that could explain these trends, but the educational aspects of the war on drugs may have been effective.

Spatial Distribution

In our discussion of official statistics in chapter 3, we noted two aspects of the spatial distribution of delinquency that are of interest to criminologists: the distribution of delinquency in areas of cities and variations among communities of different size. Indeed, one of the earliest theories of delinquency (Shaw and McKay, 1942) argued that rapid change or succession in the racial or ethnic composition of a neighborhood prevented or disrupted the development of conventional institutions or organizations in the area. This resulted in social disorganization, which in turn led to a high delinquency rate. This explanation fit their information on the distribution of officially recorded delinquency.

Although no self-report study exactly parallels studies of the spatial distribution of delinquency that are based on police and court data, there are some studies examining characteristics of neighborhoods in relation to self-reported delinquency. Focusing on African-American adolescent males in the San Francisco-Oakland metropolitan region, Robert Kapsis (1978) examined rates of self-reported and official delinquency in three neighborhoods that were at varying stages of racial change. Kapsis found that according to both measures of delinquency, the delinquency rate was highest for males living in neighborhoods with the highest racial succession and lowest in the most stable neighborhoods. Moreover, this pattern held true even when measures of socioeconomic status, family structure, and educational performance and commitment were taken into account.

A study of "Neighborhood and Delinquency" (Simcha-Fagin and Schwartz, 1986) collected data from 553 urban adolescent males between 11 and 18 years of age as well as from their mothers or female guardians. They also collected census data on neighborhoods. After several preliminary stages of analysis, they examined the relation between measures of self-reported delinquency and residential stability, community economic well-being, level of organizational participation, and a measure of community disorder and criminal subcultures. The level of organizational participation in a neighborhood was found to affect adolescent delinquent behavior while the extent of disorder and the existence of criminal subcultures were more relevant to official reactions to delinquency. Residential stability affected delinquency as well but indirectly through its relation to attachment to school. In neighborhoods with a lot of turnover, children were less likely to form bonds in school and more likely to engage in delinquency as a result.

Two recent studies have used self-report survey data to identify features of neighborhoods that affect juvenile offending. One study found that neighborhoods with high levels of professional sector employment had significantly lower rates of self-reported violence (Bellair, Roscigno, and Vélez, 2003). Researchers interpret this finding as evidence that employed professionals are role models for youth in a neighborhood. In turn, the availability of professional role models was found to affect violence through several social learning mechanisms (see chapters 5 and 6). The availability of such models enhanced family well-being, led to fewer encounters with negative peers, and reduced the risk of learning violent attitudes.

In another study of neighborhoods, D. Wayne Osgood and Amy Anderson (2004) found that rates of what they called "unstructured socializing with peers" affected rates of delinquency. They determined that such unstructured socializing was a product of low parental monitoring. These findings about neighborhoods are consistent with a variety of sociological theories that were originally developed to explain rates of delinquency using police and court statistics.

Self-report studies bearing on rural/urban differences have been conducted as well. In one such study, researchers found that although the rural farm community they studied tended to rank lowest in self-reported delinquency, there was actually very little overall difference between adolescents in a rural farm community and adolescents in urban settings (Clark and Wenninger, 1962). Compared with (1) youth in an industrial city of 35,000, (2) youth in a lower-class urban neighborhood, and (3) youth in a wealthy Chicago suburb, rural youth ranked last for fourteen of thirty-eight offenses studied. However, for those fourteen offenses, the average percentage difference between the rural youth and each of the three urban samples was only 4.7 percent. The greatest urban/rural differences involved sneaking into theaters, curfew violations, major theft, borrowing money without intending to pay it back, drinking, using slugs in vending machines, and truancy. Major theft was the only serious offense for which the average difference between the rural youth and the three urban samples exceeded 10 percent. For violent offenses, arson, many forms of vandalism, trespassing, breaking and entering, and hanging around or entering adult-only establishments, the rural sample ranked first or second.

In their 1967 national survey of youth, Gold and coauthor David Reimer (1974) found that central-city youths reported an average of 8.6 delinquent offenses during the three years preceding the interview, compared to 7.5 for suburban youths. In 1972 the comparable rate was 7.8 for central-city youths, 6.0 for suburban youths, 7.1 for youths in small cities and towns, and 4.5 for rural youths. Overall, the differences by residence were small and varied over the years of Gold and Reimer's study.

The Monitoring the Future surveys provide more recent data and reveal little variation by city size or urban/suburban location. The disparity between official statistics and self-report surveys may reflect differences in the manner in which youthful violence is responded to in different settings or the fact that youths who make it to their senior year are similar across settings. Or, as was noted in chapter 3, both members of the community and police may handle situations informally in settings where people know one another, which would generate a greater difference using police data than self-report data. Moreover, actual fights and interpersonal violence may be quite common in settings where people have developed traditions of resolving conflicts directly rather than through law enforcement officials.

Gender Differences

One of the most studied topics in criminology since the mid-1970s has been the gender difference in delinquency. Whether using police, court, or self-report data, the general conclusion is that males are more involved in delinquency than females. Beyond that observation there is considerable disagreement. Some criminologists argue that self-report data show less dramatic differences than official statistics and give the impression that the gender difference is quite small. For example, based on her analysis of self-report data on middle-class youth, Pamela Richards argues "There is little evidence that there are marked differences in the delinquent activities reported by girls and boys" (1981:453). Yet, in another self-report study, the authors conclude that "gender is a strong and consistent correlate" (Hagan, Gillis, and Simpson, 1985:1151). In short, scholars do not agree on the magnitude and importance of the gender difference, although they do agree that males are more delinquent.

Some self-reported acts are so common (e.g., petty theft, shoplifting, defying parents, and so on) that the sex difference will appear smaller in self-report studies because the measures used are heavily weighted with those offenses where sex differences are the least prominent. In fact, one analysis (Jensen, 1985) has shown when acts that rarely enter into official statistics are eliminated and the samples are matched for jurisdiction, age, and setting, estimates of the sex difference based on official statistics are remarkably similar to estimates based on self-reports. The ratio of male to female delinquency for FBI index crimes in a 1976 survey in Tucson, Arizona, was 2.5 to 1 for juvenile court statistics, 2.6 to 1 when youths were asked to report on arrests and referrals, and 2.4 to 1 when self-reports were used, with smoking, drinking, and disobedience or defiance of parents excluded from the measure of total delinquency.

Data from a nationwide survey yield similar results (Elliott, Huizinga, and Ageton, 1985). When only FBI index crimes are counted, the 1978 National Survey of Youth yields a male to female ratio of about 3.9 to 1. The ratio using FBI data on arrests of persons under 18 for that same year is 3.2 to 1, and the ratio using national juvenile court statistics is 3.2 to 1. Whether ratios of this magnitude are evidence of strong or marked differences is simply a matter of judgment. Compared to social class, broken homes, time spent watching television, and all sorts of other variables to be reviewed in this and subsequent chapters, the differences observed by gender are impressive.

In an attempt to explain the gender difference in delinquency, Gary Jensen (2003) found that the gender ratios were quite comparable for official and self-report measures when using the average number of offenses. For example, among Seattle youth studied (Hindelang, Hirschi, and Weis, 1981), the gender ratio for the average number of officially recorded offenses was 3.2 to 1; that is, just over three male offenses to every female offense. When the same procedure is used for self-reported "UCR type" offenses, the ratio was about 4.6 to 1. The results suggest that when using police records and self-reports for the same sample, the gender ratio is at least as prominent using survey data as police data.

In further analysis of three data sets (Monitoring the Future 2003, the Seattle Survey 1979, the Richmond Youth Study 1965), Jensen (2006) found the average gender ratio using self-reports was 4.9 to 1 for white youth and 2.6 to 1 for black youth. Because there has been very little research on the interaction of race and gender in the generation of delinquency, there is no empirically verified explanation of the greater disparity for white youth than black youth. It may be that styles and types of interaction are more similar for black males and females than for white males and females.

Another topic where different impressions abound is the magnitude of gender differences over time. Box 4-1 includes a plot of the ratio of male to female delinquency for violent offenses using averages from the Monitoring the Future surveys. Although there are fluctuations up and down, there is an overall trend in the data. In the 1970s the ratio of the male average to the female average was about 8 to 1. By the turn of the century the ratio was about 4 to 1. Consistent with arrest data, girls are becoming more like boys. The ratio has been declining for theft offenses as well, but not as dramatically as for violent offenses.

Box 4-1   The Gender Ratio

The graph below plots the ratio of the male average to the female average for self-reports of hurting someone badly enough that they needed bandages. A trend line shows the ratio declining over the years of the MTF surveys. What do you think accounts for that decline? Are girls simply more likely to report activities that they concealed in the past? Or are girls becoming more like boys?

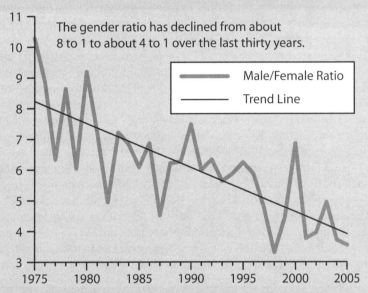

The gender ratio has declined from about 8 to 1 to about 4 to 1 over the last thirty years.

Male/Female Ratio
Trend Line

Source: Based on Monitoring the Future surveys by Johnston, Bachman, and O'Malley (odd years) and Bachman, Johnston, and O'Malley (even years).

A quite plausible explanation of this convergence is that girls are being raised more similarly to boys over time in terms of involvement in activities that require aggression and physical contact. In fact, the Monitoring the Future Surveys ask questions about taking risks and enjoying dangerous activities and, consistent with the view that boys and girls are being raised more alike, a growing percentage of girls respond positively to those types of questions. Moreover, over time there has been a declining gender differentiation in all sorts of activities that may increase the odds of violence. Yet, it is important to note that the difference is far from disappearing altogether. The gender ratio has been declining, but boys are still far more likely to commit the most serious offenses. We will deal with this issue further in subsequent chapters when we consider the characteristics of youth that help account for gender variation.

Racial Differences

Whether or not there are racial differences in delinquency rates is a complex and extremely controversial issue. Although about 15 percent of the juvenile population in the United States is African American, they account for close to 30 percent of arrests and about 50 percent of juveniles sentenced to incarceration. The disproportionate representation of African-American youth at each stage of processing has led to accusations that extralegal factors play a major role in decisions to process. Indeed, some early self-report findings found race to be of little relevance to delinquency compared to police and court data. However, as discussed earlier, these self-report studies have been criticized for focusing too heavily on petty offenses and ignoring serious offenses.

More recent self-report studies find African-American youth to be somewhat more involved in some forms of delinquent behavior than white youth. The most intensive analysis of variations in self-reported violence by race is Elliott's (1994) National Youth Survey (NYS). The NYS is a longitudinal study of a national sample of 1,725 youths who were between 11 and 17 years of age in 1976. By age 27, 42 percent of males and 16 percent of females had committed at least one serious violent offense. The black-white ratio was about 5 to 4. This ratio using arrest statistics at that time was about 5 to 1 for violent offenses.

One of the major studies assessing the validity of self-reports found African Americans to be only slightly more delinquent than whites using self-report data (Hindelang, Hirschi, and Weis, 1981). When juvenile court records were searched to verify the accuracy of the respondents' answers, they found that white respondents reported 90 percent of the offenses on their records, while African Americans reported only 67 percent of their official record. Further, they found that the race difference was related to the seriousness of the offense, with African Americans tending to underreport such offenses as burglary, vehicle theft, and weapons offenses. The precise reason for this underreporting is not clear. The researchers speculated that it might be intentional underreporting, a product of poor reading ability, social desirability, lower saliency of events, or higher rates of forgetting. However, they were unable to arrive at any precise explanation. Moreover, a more recent study did not find this disparity in the validity of survey data among racial groups (Farrington et al., 1996).

Average self-reports of serious violence for black and white seniors as well as the ratios of black averages to white averages are plotted in figure 4-4. They reveal a pattern that fits the descriptions of variation over time emphasized in various discussions of the "epidemic" of youth violence in the 1990s. Self-reported violent offenses surged for both blacks and whites during that span of time, with the ratio increasing from about 1 to 1 in the early 1980s to close to 2 to 1 in 1994. The ratio declined in the late 1990s but may be moving up again in the early twenty-first century.

When averages for major theft are plotted (see figure 4-5 on p. 122), they show whites exhibiting higher rates in some years and blacks exhibiting higher rates in others. White theft exceeded black theft during the 1980s, but a huge surge in self-reported theft by black seniors occurred in the 1990s. After its peak in the mid-1990s, the black average fell below the white average by 2002. There may be the beginning of a surge in 2005, but it could be a temporary anomaly. In short, self-reports of violence follow a pattern over time that is more consistent with police statistics than are self-reports of major theft, but the same surge appears for the 1990s, and we may be approaching another upturn for black growth in the early twenty-first century.

In an attempt to explain these patterns, Jensen (2006) has hypothesized that the disparities between black and white youth using different bodies of data may be due to the limitation to high school seniors in the MTF surveys. Analyzing two other surveys

Figure 4-4   Self-Reports of Violence and Black/White Ratio for Black and White MTF Seniors (dashed lines are the best-fitting equations)

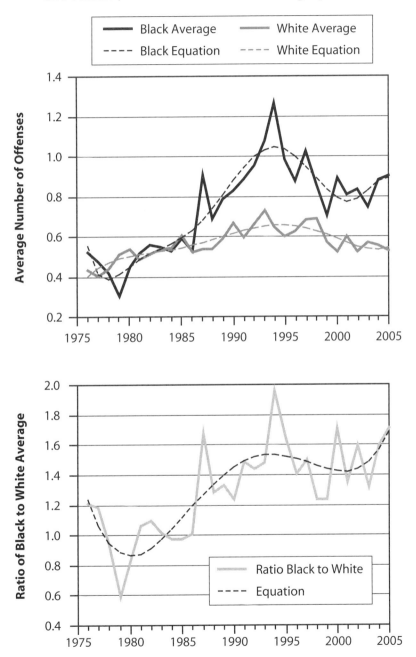

Source: Self-reports based on calculations using Monitoring the Future surveys by Johnston, Bachman, and O'Malley (odd years) and Bachman, Johnston, and O'Malley (even years).

that encompassed youth at different grade levels, he found that the black average was lower than the white average among seniors (a ratio of 0.9 to 1), but was about 1.4 to 1 for sophomores and juniors. The same pattern was found in a second survey encompassing school youth 12 through 19 years of age. The ratio was about 1.1 to 1 among

Figure 4-5   Self-Reports of Major Theft (adjusted for inflation) and Black/White Ratio for Black and White MTF Seniors

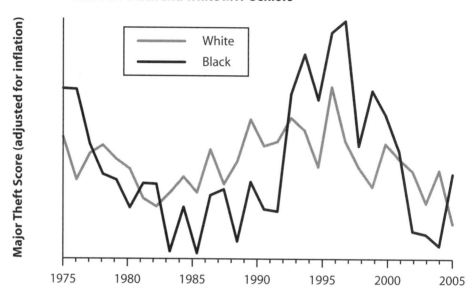

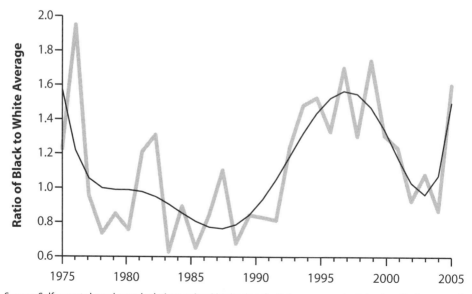

Source: Self-reports based on calculations using Monitoring the Future surveys by Johnston, Bachman, and O'Malley (odd years) and Bachman, Johnston, and O'Malley (even years).

youths at least 17 years of age as compared to 2 to 1 for younger youth. Since youth can drop out of school when they reach age 16 in most states, the decline in those ratios may reflect differential dropout rates by race. Because of differential dropout rates, black seniors are a more select sample of black youth than is the case for white seniors.

It is important to note that such findings do not preclude the use of data on seniors to study patterns over time. The same surge or "epidemic" is found in survey data as in police data even among seniors. The surge would likely have been much greater were the surveys to have encompassed youth the same age who had dropped out of school. So, while temporal patterns may be somewhat muted by the limitation of self-reports to high-school seniors, the marked surge in violence in the late 1980s into the mid-1990s and the subsequent decline can be discerned even in that select group.

Typically, the drug problem in America is depicted as a "black problem," but that image is not sustained in national surveys. For example, the 2003 National Survey on Drug Use and Health (Office of Applied Statistics, 2004) found self-reported driving under the influence of alcohol to be more common among whites (16.5 percent) than Hispanics (10.3 percent) or blacks (9.8 percent). The same pattern was found for driving under the influence of illicit drugs. The same survey in 2004 reported that the rate of current illicit drug use is highest among American Indians or Alaska Natives (26 percent), followed by youth indicating two or more races (12 percent), whites (11 percent), Hispanics (10 percent), blacks (9 percent), and Asians (6 percent). In short, black youth are not found to use illicit drugs more than white youth, and several surveys suggest that use is greater among whites. This pattern is not consistent with arrest statistics, which show markedly higher rates for black youth.

This disparity may be a product of several factors. For one, there may be bias in drug law enforcement, with black youth arrested and apprehended more than white youth. Moreover, because surveys focus on users more than sellers it may be that those most involved in street-level activity and sales do not end up being respondents in national surveys. In a study of "Race, Drugs, and Policing" (Beckett, Nyrop, and Pfingst, 2006:129), the authors found that the majority of those who delivered methamphetamine, ecstasy, powder cocaine, and heroin in Seattle were white, while blacks were in the majority for only one drug, crack cocaine. Participation in the predominately white drug market did not lead to arrests to the same degree as participation in the more racially diverse minority market. Close to two-thirds of those arrested for delivering drugs were black. Among the factors generating this disparity was the "outdoor" visibility of the crack trade and extraordinary law enforcement attention to racially diverse markets as compared to predominately white markets. The study's authors conclude that "the overrepresentation of blacks and underrepresentation of whites among those arrested for delivering illegal narcotics does not appear to be explicable in race-neutral terms."

The confluence of drugs, violence, and gangs has tended to dominate the image of the drug problem in the United States. The surge of violence involving young black males between the 1980s and the 1990s can be considered a "real" behavioral wave in that it shows up in police data, self-reports, and victim surveys. This surge is often attributed to the development of "crack"—a version of cocaine that is relatively cheap for the intense highs it generates. The emerging demand for crack, which can be sold in small quantities on the street, led to violent competition for the market, with youth arming themselves for self-protection even when not involved in the trade. Roland Fryer and colleagues (2005) argue that this surge in the demand for and sale of crack was the major factor responsible for the upswing in homicide among black youth, both directly through conflict and indirectly through the wide range of social problems generated by crack use itself. They argue that the decline in violence beginning in the mid-1990s was associated with the decline in crack use and crack wars and the attenuation of problems associated with its use. The fact that illegal activity associated with the crack trade was mirrored in all the statistics seems to lend support to the conclusion of Beckett, Nyrop, and Pfingst that the crack trade received much more law enforcement attention than did drug markets predominately involving whites.

Although it is common for drug surveys to consider minority groups other than African-American youth, only a few local studies of self-reports have differentiated minority groups other than African Americans, and very little is known about the self-reported delinquency of Asian, Hispanic, or Indian American youth. One survey in Seattle (Chambliss and Nagasawa, 1969) reported that 36 percent of Japanese youths admitted to some delinquent activity compared to 52 percent of whites and 53 percent of African Americans. Only 2 percent of Japanese youth had been arrested, compared to 36 percent of African Americans and 11 percent of whites. Leroy Gould (1969) also reported lower rates for Asian Americans than for African-American or white youths.

An Arizona survey of high school students (Jensen, Stauss, and Harris, 1977) found that Indian youths attending public high schools had higher rates of self-reported delinquency than white or Hispanic youths, and further analysis (Jensen, 1985) indicated a slightly higher overall involvement in delinquency for Hispanics than for whites. However, the differences between whites and Hispanics were quite small and more prominent for fighting and assault than for property offenses. These results are similar to those reported for African-American youths in the National Survey of Youth. Crimes involving interpersonal conflict are indicated more often by African-American and Hispanic youths than white youths.

Age

In our summary of police and court records in chapter 3, we noted that arrest rates for the types of offenses that disproportionately involve juveniles tend to peak during middle adolescence and that the more serious offenses tend to peak in the early adult years. The drop in arrest rates for the over-25 age group is quite dramatic.

Self-report studies of delinquency have tended to suggest a similar pattern with regard to overall involvement. Hirschi (1969) found the greatest proportion of youths self-reporting delinquent acts were in grades nine and ten. In a national survey of youth that encompassed only those ages 13 through 16, self-reported delinquency was found to be more frequent and more serious the older the age category of the respondent (Williams and Gold, 1972).

On the other hand, Stuart Fors and Dean Rojek (1983) examined sixth- through twelfth-graders and found that property offenses and "traditional" drug involvement increased with age but certain activities were more prevalent in younger age categories. For example, running away, assault, inhalant use, and school suspension were significantly higher in middle school (grades 6 through 8) than in high school.

In their study of self-reported criminality in a three-state sample of persons age 15 and older, Charles Tittle and Wayne Villemez (1977) presented data that are essentially consistent with the view that young persons account for a disproportionate share of most offenses. Data from that study show that persons 15 through 24 years of age reported the highest rates for four offenses (minor and major theft, assault, and marijuana use) out of the six examined. Gambling and cheating on one's income tax were most common among persons age 25 through 44. For all six offenses, persons over 65 had the lowest rates. Finally, for all age groups and offenses, males tended to report more criminality than females.

Elliott's NYS data indicate that serious violence peaks at age 17 for males and age 15 for females. This is a different pattern than found using arrest data, where rates tend to remain high in the young adult years. The NYS suggests that the age-specific prevalence of violence accelerates from age 12 and decelerates to about age 22, where it flattens out. For females the rate at age 21 is about the same as at 12 years of age, while for males it reaches the level for 12-year-olds at about age 22. Hence, survey data suggest a greater concentration of violence in the teenage years than do arrest data. This disparity may reflect differences in the types of violent offenses that lead to arrest as compared to those asked about in the survey.

Social Status and Social Class

Since the advent of self-report surveys, the relationship between social status and delinquent behavior has been one of the most studied relationships in delinquency research. In the mid-1930s Sophia M. Robinson (1936) investigated "hidden" delinquency in New York City. On the basis of self-reported data, Robinson argued that juvenile court statistics were unduly biased toward lower-class children; that the differentials between lower-class youths and middle- and upper-class youths reflected the greater availability of noncourt resources for more affluent children. A few years later Edward Schwartz (1945) conducted a similar study in Washington DC and found far more delinquency in the middle and upper classes than was recorded in official statistics.

In his pioneering study of college students in Fort Worth, Texas, Austin Porterfield (1946) found that despite self-reports of a great number of delinquent offenses, virtually none of them had been brought to the attention of the police or the courts. Porterfield interpreted his findings as the result of a differential application of the law that works against lower-class youths. He suggested that adolescents from economically deprived areas or families are observed more closely than juveniles from higher status backgrounds. Porterfield also concluded that juveniles from the lower socioeconomic strata are dealt with in a more punitive manner than upper-class youth.

The research conducted by Short and Nye in the late 1950s was a major contribution to the study of hidden delinquency. These investigators measured delinquency by using a list of twenty-three delinquent behaviors, with offenses ranging from driving without a license to grand larceny to drug use. The data were gathered with anonymous questionnaires in high schools and in correctional training institutions in several western and midwestern communities. Short and Nye (1958) found that nearly all of the institutionalized youths were from the lower socioeconomic strata, in contrast to only 53 percent of the total high school population. However, when the high school samples were analyzed, the overall results showed essentially no consistent relationship between delinquency and social class. In a few instances some differences were found to be significant but, out of a total of 756 tests for differences by socioeconomic status, only 33 were found to be significant. The researchers concluded that juvenile delinquency is not linked to class and that much middle- and upper-class delinquent behavior goes undetected.

These early studies examining the relationship between social class and delinquency challenged the popular notion that lower-class adolescents were more deviant than middle- or upper-class youth. During the decades of the 1960s and the 1970s, a plethora of studies were conducted on the issue of social class and delinquency that seemed to suggest that there was either no association, or, at best, a very weak relationship. However, the debate has never been settled, and presently there is renewed interest in this controversial topic.

From a methodological perspective, two questions have been asked: (1) How does the way in which delinquency is measured affect the class-delinquency relationship? and (2) How does the way that class is measured affect the relationship? Serious law breaking is relatively rare, and unless the sampling frame is very large, it is not inconceivable that serious delinquent acts will not be detected. Some research of social class and delinquency may be problematic because of an undersampling of serious acts.

Similarly, the measurement of social status may be flawed. Some measures are very crude: for example, placing people in a threefold class category, such as high, middle, or low. Other measures may mask important distinctions within their ranking scheme. Johnson (1980) argues that the crux of the issue is not the lower class per se, but a particular range of the lower class called the "underclass." This underclass is distinguished from what Johnson calls the "earning class" in terms of unemployment, poverty level, and welfare eligibility. "When the truly lower-class adolescents are sampled, they are usually not identifiable as a distinct group when respondents are stratified by socioeconomic status of fathers' occupations" (1980:87). The lower class can contain a wide range of blue-collar or manual trade categories that are economically secure as well as those who are destitute or impoverished because of underemployment.

It is generally agreed that in the area of relatively minor misbehavior, which is extremely commonplace, there is no evidence of a class-linked relationship (Tittle, Villemez, and Smith, 1978). But when attention is focused on serious and repetitive delinquency, there is some evidence that it is class-linked (Hindelang, Hirschi, and Weis, 1979). Elliott and Huizinga examined the results from the National Youth Survey administered from 1976 through 1979 to youths age 11 to 17 and concluded that middle-class youth commit fewer offenses than do working- or lower-class youth. "Not only are these class differences statistically significant, they are also substantial, with lower- and working-class male rates ranging between two and ten times those of middle-class males" (1983:164). One again, it needs to be emphasized that the bulk of delinquent behavior involves petty property offenses that are equally common to all social classes. But in those instances where serious offenses such as felony assault and robbery are differentiated, there are significant class differences. Moreover, while the ratio between middle-class and lower-class delinquency may be two to ten times greater for lower-class youth, these ratios are based on very small numbers of lower- or working-class youths involved in serious delinquency.

Because of the methodological difficulties associated with the measurement of social class and delinquency, it is reasonable to assume this controversy will continue. Even if there are differences between the lower class and upper class, it may be that in terms of explaining crime, these class differences are still not crucial. Richard Johnson (1979) expended great effort to examine the relationship between social class and delinquency only to find that there are other more critical forces at work, such as delinquent associates, success in school, perceived risk of apprehension, and susceptibility to peer influence.

The most recent approach to the study of class variations is to consider characteristics of different categories of youth that may counterbalance one another, generating smaller relationships than are expected when the sole focus is on the criminogenic circumstances faced by the disadvantaged. Indeed, some prominent theorists have made the iconoclastic claim that advantaged youth in capitalist societies have higher rates of delinquency than disadvantaged youth (Hagan, Gillis, and Simpson, 1985; 1987). Why? Because they are less likely to believe they will be caught, are less likely to be suspected, are raised to take risks, and are, in many ways, freer to commit delinquent acts with impunity. One reason for the small variations traditionally found may be that the relationships are nonlinear; that is, those at the top may be freer to engage in delinquency without major consequences than youth on the bottom of the socioeconomic ladder, while the most disadvantaged youth may have more criminogenic pressures. If there are countervailing influences, the lowest rates may be found in the middle.

A recent study in New Zealand reports results that may help explain the mystery of social class and delinquency (Wright et al., 1999). As summarized in box 4-2 on the following page, Bradley Wright and his colleagues found that certain characteristics of youth with high economic standing encourage delinquency, while other characteristics of youth with low economic standing also encourage delinquency. It is easy to forget that many activities that require economic resources (sports, cruising, parties, etc.) also provide freedom from adult control, and studies have shown that such freedom facilitates delinquency (see Jensen and Brownfield, 1986; Osgood et al., 1996; Osgood and Anderson, 2004).

Victimization Surveys

The victimization survey is another tool for measuring the extent and nature of crime in the United States. Self-report surveys ask people to report their own involvement in criminal and delinquent activity, while victimization surveys ask people to report on experiences as victims of such activity. The best known victimization survey is the National Crime Victimization Survey (NCVS), an annual survey administered by the Bureau of Justice Statistics, with interviews conducted by the Census Bureau. The NCVS interviews approximately 76,000 persons 12 years of age or older in 42,000 randomly selected households.

Whereas the anonymous, self-response questionnaire has been the most common technique in self-report research on delinquency, the preferred technique in victimization surveys has been the in-person interview. This technique is preferred because it yields a high response rate from representative samples of households. Victimization surveys seek a great deal of specific information from victims, and interviewers can probe answers and clarify questions. However, the NCVS also uses computer-assisted telephone surveys to measure victimization.

Box 4-2   Countervailing Social Forces

In "Reconsidering the Relationship between SES and Delinquency: Causation but Not Correlation" (1999), Bradley R. Entner Wright, Avshalom Caspi, Terrie E. Moffitt, Richard A. Miech, and Phil A. Silva report on a study of New Zealand youth that may explain why so many studies suggest a small or weak relationship between socioeconomic status (SES) and delinquency despite common theories predicting strong relationships. They propose that

> this apparent contradiction between theory and data may be reconciled by recognizing that SES has both a negative and positive indirect effect upon delinquency that, in tandem, results in little overall correlation between the two. We tested this proposal with longitudinal data from the Dunedin Multidisciplinary Health and Development Study. We used measures of parental SES recorded at study members' birth through age 15, social-psychological characteristics at age 18, and self-reported delinquency at ages 18 and 21. We found that low SES promoted delinquency by increasing individuals' alienation, financial strain, and aggression and by decreasing educational and occupational aspirations, whereas high SES promoted individuals' delinquency by increasing risk taking and social power and by decreasing conventional values. These findings suggest a reconciliation between theory and data, and they underscore the conceptual importance of elucidating the full range of causal linkages between SES and delinquency. (Wright et al., 1999)

What characteristics or circumstances experienced by advantaged youth in the United States might encourage delinquency? What characteristics of disadvantaged youth might discourage it? Some criminologists argue that the lower classes and upper classes should have the highest rates, with youth in the middle having the lowest rates. Can you think of reasons why such a pattern might be found?

Because they are based on information provided by respondents, the same limitations of self-report questionnaires apply to victim surveys. Respondents may not remember events or may get the time period wrong. Some observers suggest that the problem of "telescoping" may inflate victimization rates by as much as 20 percent, leading to higher estimates of crime than actual rates (Brantingham and Brantingham, 1984). Moreover, respondents are often asked questions about victimizations of others in the household, but may not have such information. Some may exaggerate their experiences or those of household members while others may choose not to report such experiences (Savitz, Lalli, and Rosen, 1977).

Victimization researchers have tried to cope with these problems by limiting the time period covered by the survey (for example, the NCVS asks about incidents occurring in the preceding six months to help avoid memory decay and telescoping), by carefully describing criminal victimizations, and by cross-checking reports by different members of households.

Limitations of Victimization Survey Data

As with police and court data and self-report studies, victimization surveys have certain drawbacks. First, if we wish to focus exclusively on juvenile delinquency, victimization surveys are quite limiting. While the age of the victim can be ascertained, the age of the offender can only be estimated where there was face-to-face contact. Of course, in those instances where knowledge of the offender is a complete unknown, such as in most property theft, there is no way of determining the age of the offender.

A second major problem with NCVS data is that it focuses exclusively on Part I offenses (with the obvious exclusion of homicide). That is, questions deal only with rape, robbery, assault, burglary, personal and household larceny, and motor vehicle theft. Victimless crimes, such as drug abuse, prostitution, and gambling are excluded. Similarly, all Part II offenses are excluded (such as fraud, embezzlement, forgery, and driving under the influence of drugs). Thus, NCVS offenses are heavily geared toward those offenses that are perceived by the FBI to be "serious." Conversely, such white-collar offenses as income tax evasion, price-fixing, or shoddy business practices are completely ignored.

The NCVS focuses exclusively on offenses involving members of a household or offenses against the household. The initial surveys included commercial establishments, but those were dropped in 1977. Hence, the NCVS omits a huge volume of offenses where the targets are not individuals, but commercial establishments. Shoplifting accounts for a sizeable proportion of larcenies, but does not involve household members as victims. Hence, a huge volume of behavior tapped in self-report surveys never makes it into the victimization surveys. Moreover, only robberies with individuals as victims enter into the NCVS. Robberies occurring on the streets or at residences account for about 56 percent of robberies, so 44 percent do not appear in the NCVS. Thirty-two percent of burglaries are nonresidential and thus will not make their way into victimization surveys (Federal Bureau of Investigation, 2002).

An analysis of the NCVS by David Finkelhor and Richard Ormrod found

> substantial underreporting to police of violent and property crimes against youth (age 12 to 17) compared with the reporting of such crimes against adults. This underreporting is not explained by the crimes involved being less serious, being committed by juvenile perpetrators, or by any other aspect of the crimes for which NCVS information is available. (2001:219)

We should add that, not only does it appear that the NCVS disproportionately misses juvenile victimizations, but that it does not get the information directly from children in the home when the parent or adult authority decides to provide the data. Finally, children under 12 are not included in the assessment. In sum, there are major differences between the offenses (victimizations) measured by the NCVS and both police and self-report survey data. Each measures different aspects of the crime problem in different ways.

Patterns Based on Victimization Data

Recognizing the limitations of victim surveys for the study of delinquency, researchers nonetheless acknowledge that any thorough treatment of the difficulties of measuring crime must pay attention to such data. Victimization data are increasingly cited by news media and are often the source for statements about trends in crime.

Volume

Most researchers agree that the NCVS records fewer victimizations than actually occur. Memory decay, embarrassment in reporting crimes, coding errors, and other limitations mean that NCVS data do not provide a totally accurate picture of crime. However, even though it excludes commercial crimes, the NCVS reveals far more victimization than is picked up in the Uniform Crime Reports. In 2004 the NCVS recorded 24 million victimizations. There were about 21.4 violent victimizations per 1,000 people and 161 property offenses per 1,000 households.

A sizeable proportion of these victimizations do not make their way into Uniform Crime Reports as "crimes known to the police." According to the 2004 NCVS findings, about 50 percent of all violent crime victimizations were reported to the police and about 39 percent of property victimizations. NCVS victims indicated that they were most likely to report a completed motor vehicle theft (85 percent). Even in instances of extremely serious crimes, some victims were reluctant to report these to the police. For example, only 36 percent of rapes or sexual assaults were reported.

In general, data gathered from respondents to the NCVS over the years suggest that people do not report offenses to the police because (1) the item involved was recovered without calling police, (2) the crime was reported to some official other than police, (3) "lack of proof," (4) the crime was a private matter, or (5) the police would not want to be bothered or could do nothing anyway. Since there is always a huge number of unreported victimizations, changes in public tendencies to report crimes can lead to artificial increases or decreases in crime. Increases in insurance coverage of rental and homeowner property, improved police-community relationships, and even changes in the demographic composition of the population can increase the percent of total victimization reported to police.

Time

Because victimization survey data have been collected systematically on a national scale only since 1972, such data are not available for those time periods during which police data indicate sizeable increases in crime in the United States (see chapter 3). Moreover, a major redesign of the NCVS in 1992 means that some changes in victimization rates may reflect changes in the questions asked in the survey. The Bureau of Justice Statistics has compiled data on property victimizations adjusting for such differences. It typically surprises people to learn that the long-term trend in property crime rates based on NCVS data has been downward for the last several decades. This pattern is not found in "crimes known to the police," arrest rates, or self-reports of property offenses. The exception is the period from the mid-1990s through 2004 where all indicators of property crime suggest a decline. When specific forms of property crime are considered, victimization data and "crimes known" rates are quite comparable over time; for example, burglary (correlation = +.96) and motor vehicle theft (+.76). In contrast, larcenies reported to the police and NCVS reports of theft are weakly related (+.26). Of course, the NCVS does not include shoplifting or thefts that do not victimize a household. The two different techniques do not measure exactly the same activity and thus may reflect quite different patterns over time.

Figure 4-6 summarizes MTF data from high school seniors and NCVS estimates of violent victimizations for youths 12–15 and 16–19. The Monitoring the Future data

Figure 4-6   MTF and NCVS Violent Victimizations (1975–2004)

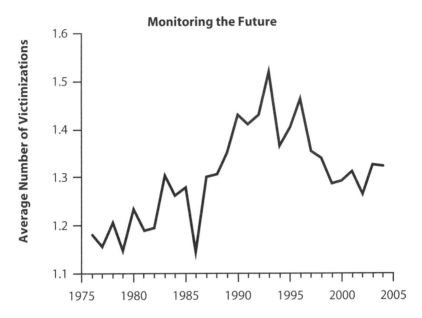

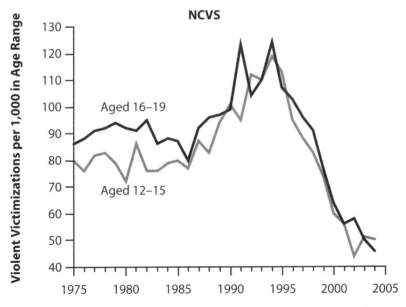

Source: Self-reports based on calculations using Monitoring the Future surveys by Johnston, Bachman, and O'Malley (odd years) and Bachman, Johnston, and O'Malley (even years). NCVS estimates from Child Trends Data Bank.

show an upward trend from the late 1970s onward, with a dip in the mid-1980s, and then a downturn from the peaks in the mid-1990s. In contrast, NCVS rates were relatively flat until the mid-1980s. However, all three series suggest similar trends after the mid-1980s. Victimizations escalated rapidly to a peak in the mid-1990s and have exhibited a downward trend after that point. This basic pattern was found for self-reported violence and a variety of police measures as well.

Space

Victimization survey data have been computed for urban, suburban, and rural areas. The risk of personal and household victimization is greatest for urban residents, with little difference between suburbanites and rural residents. This has not always been the case. In general, suburban settings had higher victimization rates than rural areas for most of the history of the NCVS. By 2000 the rates had converged. This convergence reflects the fact that the declines in victimization were more prominent for suburban than rural areas. Rather than concluding that rural areas were getting worse, it appears that suburban rates were falling faster. Victimization in urban settings was declining as well, but the gap between the urban and other settings persists.

Perceived Gender, Age, and Race of Offenders

The National Crime Victimization Surveys have gathered data on perceived characteristics of the offender(s), but because such information depends on victims' perceptions, it is subject to greater error and distortion than other victimization survey findings. Such perceptions do, however, provide another source of data in constructing an image of crime and delinquency. Needless to say, no information can be gathered on property offenses where the offender is not known.

Consistent with police statistics and self-report survey data, victimization data show the vast majority of offenders in personal crimes of violence to be male. Males were perceived to be the offender in 82 percent of the crimes and females 18 percent of the time. The ratio is about 4.5 to 1, which is not dramatically different than the 4 to 1 ratio found for self-reports of violence. Moreover, consistent with arrest and self-report data, the percentage of offenders perceived to be female has increased. In 1988, 13 percent of offenders in lone victimizations were perceived to be female, compared to 18 percent in 2003. The percentage female among multiple offenders has been increasing as well. However, it is important to remember that while the gap has narrowed, females still account for a small proportion of perceived offenders and that all three types of data show that the more serious the offense, the greater the gender ratio.

The offender is perceived to be between 12 and 20 years of age for about 29 percent of single-offender violent victimizations and 32 percent of multiple-offender victimizations. This is at least twice the proportion that would be expected by their percentage of the population. Juveniles and young adults are clearly overrepresented as perceived offenders. Moreover, youth are about four times more likely to account for multiple-offender events than persons over age 30. Victimization data and UCR data both support the contention that youthful offenders are more likely than older offenders to commit offenses in groups.

Victimization data on the perceived race of offenders show African Americans to be disproportionately identified as offenders. Although about 12 percent of the population is African American, the offender is perceived as African American in about 40 percent of robberies, 24 percent of rapes and sexual assaults, 23 percent of aggravated assaults, and 19 percent of simple assaults. Similar patterns are found for multiple offender victimizations.

NCVS data also show that crimes of violence are predominantly intraracial; that is, African Americans tend to victimize African Americans, and whites victimize whites. In those instances where a white person was a victim of violence, 73 percent of the time the offender was white. Similarly, when an African-American person was the victim, 75 percent of the time the offender was African American. Although African Americans have higher than expected rates of offending and higher than expected rates of victimization, it is still the case that most interpersonal violence tends to be an intraracial phenomenon.

Who Are the Victims?

In addition to providing another source of information on the distribution of crime and delinquency and a means of assessing the perceived characteristics of offenders, victimization data have been central to the growth of interest in **victimology**; that is, the study of victims. A considerable amount of descriptive detail is now available on the characteristics of victims. In fact, so much detailed information is available that it is not possible to summarize all of it in this text. The information provided by the U.S. Department of Justice suggests that victims of crime tend to be young rather than old, male rather than female, African American rather than white, poor rather than rich, and of low educational status rather than high educational status.

Analyses of victimization data have noted the similarity or homogeneity in the backgrounds of victims and offenders. The most highly victimized groups (the young, African Americans, males, people of low income and with little education) tend to be the same groups with high offense rates. Conversely, the least victimized categories (older, white, female, high income and education) tend to have the lowest offense rates as well. Some theorists have argued that this similarity reflects the tendency of people with certain characteristics to come into close proximity with offenders (Cohen, Kluegal, and Land, 1981). An analysis of the Monitoring the Future data (Jensen and Brownfield, 1986) found that much of the sex difference in victimization reflects sex differences in delinquent activities. Self-admitted involvement in delinquent activities is one of the strongest correlates of victimization. The high risk of victimization encountered by males appears to be associated with high male involvement in risky and deviant routines. The types of situations providing the opportunities and situational pressures conducive to offense activity also provide a high risk of victimization. That study suggests that the explanation of victimization involves some of the same circumstances and variables as explanations of offending.

Survey Research and the Study of Gangs

One of the reasons that sociology became the discipline most intensively involved in the study of delinquency (see chapters 6 and 7) was the observation that delinquent behavior most often occurs in the company of other youths. This observation does not mean that most delinquent activity is "gang" activity but, rather, that it tends to be peer-group activity. To some, any group of youth that engages in some form of delinquency while together might qualify as a "gang." Using such a broad definition a huge proportion of youth would qualify as members of gangs.

Research definitions of gang membership and gang offenses range from very broad and inclusive definitions to very selective definitions. For example, in Terence Thornberry and James Burch's Rochester Youth Development Study (1997) a gang member was defined as anyone who reports having been a member of a street gang or "posse" at any point prior to the end of high school, and a gang offense is any offense ever committed by those respondents. In contrast, Malcolm Klein (1997) and Sanders (1994) adopt very narrow and exclusive structural definitions. Sanders defines a gang as "(A)ny trans-personal group of youths that shows a willingness to use deadly force to claim and defend territory, and attack rival gangs, extort or rob money, or engage in other criminal behavior as an activity associated with its group, and is recognized by itself and its immediate community as a distinct and dangerous entity" (1994:20).

Use of an inclusive definition led Thornberry and Burch to conclude that about 30 percent of their sample were gang members and that girls (29 percent) were almost as likely as boys (32 percent) to indicate having been a gang or "posse" member. When longevity as a member is taken into account, however, none of the girls in the study had been a member of a gang for four years while 7 percent of the boys indicated such stable membership. The prevalence of gang delinquency drops as restrictive criteria are imposed.

When juveniles in high-risk neighborhoods of Denver were asked questions about their membership in gangs, about 5 percent of the sample indicated they were gang members in a given year (Esbensen and Huizinga, 1993). The researchers estimate that between the ages 12 and 18, about 7 percent of juveniles will have belonged to a gang in these inner-city, high-risk zones. In the Denver study, gang members had to acknowledge gang membership as well as indicate gang involvement in any one of the following offenses: car theft, selling dope, gun thefts, burglary, robbery, gang fights, assaults, or drive-by shootings. Because these studies have been conducted in different cities and samples we do not know whether the high rates for the Rochester study reflect a worse gang problem or differences in the criteria imposed.

Beth Bjerregaard (2002) has shown that the criteria imposed have a major effect on the estimated magnitude of the gang problem as well as variations by gender. Analyzing data from a survey conducted in four states, she found that about 17 percent of females indicated gang membership compared to 25 percent of males when the sole criterion was self-acknowledged membership. However, when restricted by the additional criteria used in the Denver study, the percentages fell to about 10 percent for females and 19 percent for males. Finally, when respondents were asked additional questions about "gang structure" such as gang/group size, name, leadership, regular meetings, special clothing, and turf, the percentages fell to about 4 percent for girls and 11 percent for boys. In short, the gang problem could be depicted as four times greater for girls using the unrestricted option compared to the organized gang option, and over twice as serious for boys using the unrestricted versus the organized gang option. Moreover, the gender ratio increases as increases in restrictions are imposed.

Another means of assessing the presence of a gang problem or changes therein has been to survey police departments, asking for estimates of the magnitude of the gang problem. For purposes of the survey, the National Youth Gang Center (Egley and Major, 2004) defines a gang as "a group of youths or young adults in your jurisdiction that you or other responsible persons in your agency or community are willing to identify as a 'gang'." Hate groups, prison gangs, motorcycle gangs, and gangs with solely adult members are excluded.

Many jurisdictions use a scoring system to determine whether a youth should be considered a gang member (see box 4-3). For example, in Tennessee a youth must score at least ten points on the state's rating scale to be classified as a member of a gang. Self-acknowledgment is worth eight points and other criteria such as a gang name, gang tattoos, and identification by other gang members can quickly move the youth beyond the ten-point cutoff. The National Youth Gang Survey allows officials in each jurisdiction to make their estimate and no specific scoring system is required.

Results from that survey are quite dramatic. For example, reporting on the results for the 2002 survey, Arlen Egley and Aline Major state that "youth gangs were active in more than 2,300 cities with a population of 2,500 or more and in 550 jurisdictions served by county law enforcement agencies" (2004:2). They note that 731,500 gang members and 21,500 gangs were active in the United States in 2002. Of course with over 40 million youths 15 through 24 years of age in the U.S. population in that year, the law enforcement estimate would mean that less than 2 percent of all youths in that age range would be deemed gang members. In fact, when the size of the population in the 15–24 age range is considered, the number of gang members was less than one-half of one percent in the 1970s and 1980s and 2.2 percent at its peak in the mid-1990s.

There are no systematic survey data based on youths' self-reports that would allow any statements about the magnitude of gang involvement over long spans of time. However, the Monitoring the Future surveys have asked high school seniors to report the number of times they were involved in altercations where one group of youths got into a fight with another group. While such data do not include dropouts or provide detail on the meaning of group fights, we can compare the variations over time for these survey data with the estimates from FBI youth gang murder rates and the national police surveys. Since the "gang epidemic" was also a growing news theme during the 1980s and 1990s, we also should consider the volume of news stories about gangs, reported by Randall Shelden and colleagues (2001:3). They state that the gang problem as depicted by shifts in gang-related articles in newspaper and magazines "does not always conform to reality," referring to a decline in news coverage "in recent years" despite what they believe to be a "steady growth in the number of gangs and the number of gang members" in "surveys of law enforcement agencies." Of course, the actual estimates through surveys of law enforcement agencies did point to a decline.

Equations based on these four estimates of the gang problem are plotted in box 4-4 (on p. 137). Several observations about patterns over time are suggested by the four different sources of data. First, the FBI and self-report data followed nearly identical paths, both accelerating from the mid-1980s to the mid-1990s and declining thereafter, with a possible upturn after 2001. Second, gang news stories follow a similar pattern, but "lag" behind the trends in events captured by the FBI and self-report data.

Box 4-3   How Do We Define a Gang Member?

The form below is used by law enforcement in Tennessee to maintain a database on gangs and subversive groups. A score of 10 or more qualifies an individual as a "confirmed gang member." How do these criteria compare with those used in survey research on gangs?

Gang / Subversive Group Information

In order to submit the name of the GANG / SUBVERSIVE GROUP to the database, the gang itself must meet requirements of Guideline OJP 4600.1.B Criminal Intelligence Systems Operation Policies (Title 28 Code of Federal Regulations Section 23) and be based on reasonable suspicion of their involvement in criminal activity and be multi-jurisdictional in nature.

An individual will be considered a confirmed gang member when he/she achieves 10 or more points from the below criteria. Indicate each appropriate category listed below and total the number of points accrued.

9 Points _____ Subject admits gang affiliation (DESCRIBE IN NARRATIVE)

8 Points _____ Subject has gang-related tattoos/brands (ATTACH PHOTO)

3 Points _____ Subject uses hand signs, uses or possesses symbols or is in possession of or has participated in graffiti of which clearly indicates gang affiliation (LIST SPECIFIC SYMBOLS/SIGNS USED)

1 Point _____ Subject wears "colors," gang clothing, gang paraphernalia in such a way that indicates gang affiliation (LIST SPECIFIC ITEMS AND COLORS IN NARRATIVE)

8 Points _____ Subject's name appears on a gang roster, hit list or gang-related graffiti (DESCRIBE IN NARRATIVE)

3 Points _____ Possession of gang documents—roster, procedures, by-laws, etc. (DESCRIBE IN NARRATIVE)

1 Point _____ Possession of commercial gang-related publications (DESCRIBE IN NARRATIVE)

8 Points _____ Participation in gang publications—submitting articles, illustrations, etc. (DESCRIBE IN NARRATIVE)

2 Points _____ Consistent, observed contact with confirmed gang members (DOCUMENT OBSERVATIONS-DESCRIBE IN NARRATIVE)

9 Points _____ Subject identified as a gang member by a reliable informant

8 Points _____ Subject identified as a gang member by another gang member (DOCUMENT THE CONTACT AND LIST CONFIRMED GANG NAME)

8 Points _____ Subject involved in criminal gang incidents (DESCRIBE IN NARRATIVE)

5 Points _____ Subject's victims or targets of crime are members of a rival gang (DOCUMENT THE VICTIM AND LIST CONFIRMED GANG NAME)

1 Point _____ Known contact with confirmed gang members (DOCUMENT THE CONTACT AND LIST CONFIRMED GANG MEMBER)

2 Points _____ Participating in photo with confirmed gang member (ATTACH PHOTO OR DESCRIBE IN NARRATIVE)

5 Points _____ Outside jurisdiction information / documents (DOCUMENT CORRESPONDENCE)

3 Points _____ Sending / receiving correspondence to / from confirmed gang members (DOCUMENT CORRESPONDENCE)

8 Points _____ Named a gang member in correspondence (DOCUMENT CORRESPONDENCE)

10 Points _____ Subject identified as a gang member by another law enforcement agency (OUTER DEPARTMENTAL CONFIRMATION MUST ADHERE TO 28 CFR)

Total Points _____

News stories peak a year later. Finally, the police estimates follow a similar pattern but with an even longer lag, peaking in 1997. It is true that the police estimates do not always coincide with "reality" but they do follow a similar pattern over time, with a decline evidenced by the late 1990s. It appears that those agencies had a delayed response to real events, with little evidence that they created a panic for the sake of budget increases.

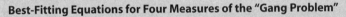

Box 4-4   Four Different Measures of the Gang Problem

The graph below plots four equations estimating trends in "gang" activity in the United States based on four different ways of measuring the problem. FBI youth gang murder rates and MTF self-reported group fights exhibit very similar trends. These two measures of offense events appear to be followed by similar trends in gang news stories, and gang news stories appear to be followed by similar trends in police perception of the magnitude of the gang problem in their jurisdictions. What implications do these patterns have for the view that the media or overzealous police dramatized or fabricated the gang problem? What do the data suggest about the validity of survey data for measuring violent behavior?

Best-Fitting Equations for Four Measures of the "Gang Problem"

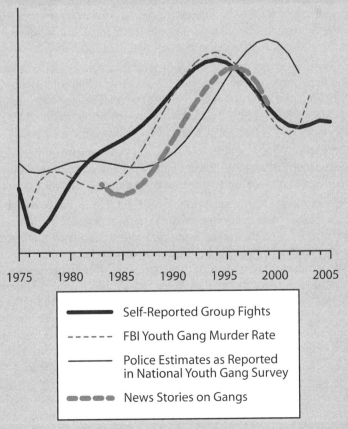

Summary

In this chapter we have tried to summarize a body of self-report survey research, as well as a body of research based on a more recently developed technique for studying crime—the victimization survey. Some conclusions suggested by the data produced by these two research methods conflict with patterns suggested by police and juvenile court statistics. However, there is also a surprising amount of consistency in some of the patterns of variation suggested by different bodies of data. Following are several statements that are consistent with at least two types of data. We deem these statements to be "consistent with the data" rather than "supported" or "demonstrated" by the data because they often go beyond the specific information available. For example, victimization survey data do not bear directly on statements about delinquency; this is often the case for national crime statistics as well. Thus these statements are not statements of fact but, rather, tentative generalizations that appear at this time to be justified:

1. Of all of the characteristics of youth, gender is the most strongly correlated, with the greatest disparities for serious and violent offenses. Although the ratio has declined considerably over the years, the gender gap still persists.

2. Offense rates tend to be highest among youths in large cities and changing or unstable neighborhoods and communities, but the difference appears greater using police data than self-report or victimization data.

3. Offense rates vary among racial or ethnic categories, with the most prominent and consistent pattern involving higher rates of interpersonal violence among African Americans and higher rates of alcohol-related offenses and most forms of drug use for whites. Asian Americans tend to have the lowest rates and Hispanics tend to fall between white and African-American youth.

4. Estimates of the magnitude of the gang problem over time follow similar patterns using FBI and self-report data, with gang news stories following a similar, but delayed pattern, and police survey estimates following behind the news.

We present these statements with the warning that further research may negate or further qualify each and every one of them. However, these patterns or images have been suggested in enough studies using different methods to qualify as some of the strongest candidates for "facts" about juvenile delinquency.

It is also important to recognize that there are a variety of theories that attempt to make sense of or explain these facts. We were dealing with some basic theories relevant to these "facts" whenever we asked if the patterns observed reflected differences in behavior or differences in the public and police response over time, among territories, or in dealing with different categories of people. When we find that news stories and police estimates of the gang problem follow behind youth gang murders and reports of group fights, those patterns have implications for theories that media and police generate variations by their attention to the problem. If anything, it appears that their estimates lag behind the problem as measured by other methods. Attempts to explain discrepancies between data sources (e.g., larger racial differences using arrest than survey data) typically take the form of "labeling" or "conflict" theory (see chapters 6 and 9), which propose that some youth are more liable to arrest and prosecution than others because of characteristics other than their offenses. The theories that assume the variations over time, space, and among social categories reflect "real" differences in behavior are quite diverse as well and will be summarized in chapters 5 and 6. Research on delinquent gangs will be addressed again in chapter 7 when we deal with the family, school experiences, and peer groups as the three most significant social institutions shaping a youth's behavior. Other relevant social influences include religion, media, and America's gun culture, which will be discussed in chapter 8.

Discussion Questions

1. Why did social scientists devise survey methods for measuring crime and delinquency when police and court data were already available?

2. What are the major assumptions underlying the use of self-report survey methods? Do you think that research can live up to these assumptions?

3. Discuss the advantages and disadvantages of the in-person interview and the self-completed questionnaire for measuring delinquency.

4. What are the issues involved when the *reliability* and *validity* of self-reported delinquency are questioned? Which seems to be the more controversial issue of the two, and why is it difficult to resolve the controversy?

5. Other than problems of reliability and validity, what are *two* other criticisms of self-report techniques? How can the self-report technique be defended against these criticisms?

6. In his book on *The Criminality of Women*, Otto Pollak argued that women are really just as involved in crime as men but the crime rate is lower because their crimes go unreported or undetected. Given what you have learned based on self-report research and victimization data, assess the adequacy of this argument, making sure to cite specific findings.

7. Compare and contrast the results of research on social class and delinquency using self-report techniques versus police and court statistics. Suggest a possible explanation for disparities or inconsistencies using the two measures.

8. Summarize the results of victimization research concerning any *two* of the following: (1) trends over time, (2) spatial distribution, (3) gender, (4) age, or (5) race.

9. State an observation concerning delinquency that is consistent with all three techniques for studying its social distribution (police data, self reports, and victimization surveys). Identify an apparent disparity or inconsistency using the three different measures.

10. Describe how measures of (1) FBI juvenile gang violence, (2) survey measures of group violence, (3) police estimates of the gang problem, and (4) gang news stories are related to each other. Which two measures follow the most similar path over time and what are the implications for arguments that survey data cannot measure serious offenses?

References

Bachman, J. G., L. D. Johnston, and P. M. O'Malley. Even years since 1975. *Monitoring the Future.* Ann Arbor: Institute for Social Research, University of Michigan.

Beckett, K., K. Nyrop, and L. Pfingst. 2006. "Race, Drugs, and Policing: Understanding Disparities in Drug Delivery Arrests." *Criminology* 44:105–37.

Bellair, P. E., V. J. Roscigno, and M. B. Vélez. 2003. "Occupational Structure, Social Learning, and Adolescent Violence." In *Social Learning Theory and the Explanation of Crime: A Guide for the New Century,* edited by Ronald L. Akers and Gary F. Jensen. Advances in Criminological Theory, Vol. 11. Edison, NJ: Transaction Publishers.

Bjerregaard, B. 2002. "Operationalizing Gang Membership: The Impact Measurement on Gender Differences in Gang Self-Identification and Delinquent Involvement." *Women & Criminal Justice* 13:79–97.

Brantingham P., and P. Brantingham. 1984. *Patterns in Crime.* New York: Macmillan.

Bureau of Justice Statistics. 2002, 2003, 2004. *National Crime Victimization Survey.* Statistical Tables. Washington, DC: U.S. Dept. of Justice.

Chambliss, W. J., and R. H. Nagasawa. 1969. "On the Validity of Official Statistics: A Comparative Study of White, Black and Japanese High School Boys." *Journal of Research in Crime and Delinquency* 6 (January):71–77.

Child Trends Data Bank. www.childtrendsdatabank.org. Accessed March 17, 2006.

Clark, J. P., and E. P. Wenninger. 1962. "Socioeconomic Class and Area As Correlates of Illegal Behavior Among Juveniles." *American Sociological Review* 27 (December):826–34.

Cohen, L. E., J. E. Kluegal, and K. C. Land. 1981. "Social Inequality and Criminal Victimization." *American Sociological Review* 46 (October):505–24.

Cook, P. J., and J. H. Laub. 2002. "After the Epidemic: Recent Trends in Youth Violence in the United States." *Crime and Justice* 29:1–37.

Egley, A., Jr., and A. K. Major. 2004. *Highlights of the 2002 National Youth Gang Survey.* OJJDP Fact Sheet. April, 2004, Number 1.

Elliott, D. S. 1994. "Serious Violent Offenders: Onset, Developmental Course, and Termination." *Criminology* 32:1–21.

Elliott, D. S., and S. Ageton. 1980. "Reconciling Race and Class Differences in Self-Reported and Official Estimates of Delinquency." *American Sociological Review* 45 (February):95–110.

Elliott, D. S., and D. Huizinga. 1983. "Social Class and Delinquent Behavior in a National Youth Panel, 1976–1980." *Criminology* 21:149–77.

Elliott, D. S., D. Huizinga, and S. Ageton. 1985. *Explaining Delinquency and Drug Use.* Beverly Hills: Sage.

Elliott, D. S., and H. L. Voss. 1974. *Delinquency and Dropout.* Lexington, MA: DC Heath.

Erickson, M. L., and L. T. Empey. 1963. "Court Records, Undetected Delinquency and Decision-Making." *Journal of Criminal Law, Criminology and Police Science* 54 (December):456–69.

Esbensen, F.-A., and D. Huizinga. 1993. "Gangs, Drugs, and Delinquency in a Survey of Urban Youth." *Criminology* 4:565–89.

Farrington, D. P., R. Loeber, M. Stouthamer-Loeber, W. Van Kammen, and L. Schmidt. 1996. "Self-Reported Delinquency and a Combined Delinquency Seriousness Scale Based on Boys, Mothers, and Teachers: Concurrent and Predictive Validity for African-Americans and Caucasians." *Criminology* 34:501–25.

Federal Bureau of Investigation. 2002. *Crime in the United States.* Washington, DC: GPO.

Finkelhor, D., and R. K. Ormrod. 2001. "Factors in the Underreporting of Crimes Against Juveniles." *Child Maltreatment* 6(3):219–29.

Fors, S. W., and D. G. Rojek. 1983. "The Social and Demographic Correlates of Adolescent Drug Use Patterns." *Journal of Drug Education* 13:205–22.

Fryer, R., P. Heaton, S. Levitt, and K. Murphy. 2005. "Measuring the Impact of Crack Cocaine." National Bureau of Economic Research Working Paper 11318:1–65.

Gold, M. 1970. *Delinquency Behavior in an American City.* Belmont, CA: Wadsworth.

Gold, M., and D. J. Reimer. 1974. "Changing Patterns of Delinquent Behavior Among Americans 13 to 16 Years Old, 1967–1972." Ann Arbor: Institute for Social Research, University of Michigan.

Gould, L. 1969. "Who Defines Delinquency: A Comparison of Self-Reported and Officially Reported Indices of Delinquency in Three Racial Groups." *Social Problems* 16 (Winter):325–36.

Hagan, J., A. R. Gillis, and J. Simpson. 1985. "The Class Structure of Gender and Behavior." *American Journal of Sociology* 90:1151–78.

———. 1987. "Class in the Household: A Power Control Theory of Gender and Delinquency." *American Journal of Sociology* 92 (January):788–816.

Hindelang, M. J., T. Hirschi, and J. Weis. 1979. "Correlates of Delinquency: The Illusion of Discrepancy Between Self-Report and Official Measures." *American Sociological Review* 44:995–1014.

———. 1981. *Measuring Delinquency.* Beverly Hills: Sage.

Hirschi, T. 1969. *Causes of Delinquency.* Berkeley: University of California Press.

Jensen, G. F. 1985. "The Truth about Sex and Crime." Paper presented at the Annual Meeting of Arizona Justice Educators, Arizona State University, Tempe.

———. 2003. "Self-report Data on Youth Violence over Time: Surprising Results Using Monitoring the Future Surveys." In *Public Health and Criminal Justice Approaches to Homicide Research*, edited by C. R. Block and R. L. Block. Chicago: HRWG Publications.

———. 2006. "Correcting the Surgeon General's Report on Youth Violence." Paper presented at the annual convention of the American Sociological Association, Montreal, Canada.

Jensen, G. F., and D. Brownfield. 1986. "Gender Lifestyles and Victimization: Beyond Routine Activity." *Victims and Violence* 1 (2):85–99.

Jensen, G. F., J. H. Stauss, and V. W. Harris. 1977. "Crime, Delinquency, and the American Indian." *Human Organization* 36:252–57.

Johnson, R. E. 1979. *Juvenile Delinquency and Its Origins.* New York: Cambridge University Press.

———. 1980. "Social Class and Delinquent Behavior: A New Test." *Criminology* 18:86–93.

Johnston, L. D., J. G. Bachman, and P. M. O'Malley. Odd years since 1975. *Monitoring the Future: Questionnaire Responses from the Nation's High School Seniors.* Ann Arbor: Institute for Social Research, University of Michigan.

Kapsis, R. E. 1978. "Residential Succession and Delinquency: A Test of Shaw and McKay's Theory of Cultural Transmission." *Criminology* 15 (February):459–86.

Klein, M. 1997. *The American Street Gang: Its Nature, Prevalence, and Control.* New York: Oxford University Press.

Krohn, M., G. Waldo, and T. Chiricos. 1975. "Self-Reported Delinquency: A Comparison of Structural Interviews and Self-Administered Checklists." *Journal of Criminal Law and Criminology* 65:545–55.

McCord, J., C. S. Widom, and N. A. Crowell, eds. 2001. *Juvenile Crime, Juvenile Justice.* Commission on Behavioral and Social Sciences and Education. National Research Council and Institute of Medicine. Washington, DC: National Academy Press.

Messner, S. F., and R. Rosenfeld. 2001. *Crime and the American Dream.* 3rd. ed. Belmont, CA: Wadsworth.

Murphy, F. J., M. M. Shirley, and II. L. Witmer. 1946. "The Incidence of Hidden Delinquency." *American Journal of Orthopsychiatry* 16 (October):686–95.

Nye, F. I. 1958. *Family Relationships and Delinquent Behavior.* New York: John Wiley.

Nye, F. I., and J. F. Short, Jr. 1957. "Scaling Delinquent Behavior." *American Sociological Review* 22 (June):326–31.

Office of Applied Statistics. 2004. *Results from the 2003 National Survey on Drug Use and Health: National Findings.* DHHS Publication No. SMA 04-3964, NSDUH Series H-25. Rockville, MD: Substance Abuse and Mental Health Services Administration.

Osgood, D. W., and A. L. Anderson. 2004. "Unstructured Socializing and Rates of Delinquency." *Criminology* 42 (3):519–49.

Osgood, D. W., J. K. Wilson, J. G. Bachman, P. M. O'Malley, and L. D. Johnston. 1996. "Routine Activities and Individual Deviant Behavior." *American Sociological Review* 61:635–55.

Porterfield, A. L. 1946. *Youth in Trouble.* Fort Worth, TX: Leo Potishman Foundation.

Reiss, A. J., Jr., and J. A. Roth, eds. 1993. *Understanding and Preventing Violence.* Washington, DC: National Academy Press.

Richards, P. 1981. "Quantitative and Qualitative Sex Differences in Middle-Class Delinquency." *Criminology* 18:453–70.

Robinson, S. M. 1936. *Can Delinquency Be Measured?* New York: Columbia University Press.

Rojek, D. G. 1983. "Social Status and Delinquency: Do Self-Reports and Official Reports Match?" In *Measurement Issues in Criminal Justice,* edited by G. P. Waldo. Beverly Hills: Sage.

———. 1996. *A Longitudinal Analysis of Attitudes and Behaviors Related to Drug Involvement.* Department of Sociology, University of Georgia.

Sanders, W. B. 1994. *Gangbangs and Drive-Bys: Grounded Culture and Juvenile Gang Violence.* Hawthorne, NY: Aldine de Gruyter.

Savitz, L. D., M. Lalli, and L. Rosen. 1977. *City Life and Delinquency: Victimization, Fear of Crime and Gang Membership.* Washington, DC: Office of Juvenile Justice and Delinquency Prevention.

Schwartz, E. E. 1945. "A Community Experiment in the Measurement of Juvenile Delinquency." In *Yearbook, National Probation Association, 1945.* New York: National Probation Association.

Shaw, C. R., and H. D. McKay. 1942. *Juvenile Delinquency and Urban Areas.* Chicago: University of Chicago Press.

Shelden, R. G., S. K. Tracy, and W. B. Brown. 2001. *Youth Gangs in American Society.* Belmont, CA: Wadsworth.

Short, J. F., Jr., and F. I. Nye. 1958. "Extent of Unrecorded Juvenile Delinquency: Tentative Conclusions." *Journal of Criminal Law, Criminology and Police Science* 49 (November–December):246–302.

Simcha-Fagin, O., and J. E. Schwartz. 1986. "Neighborhood and Delinquency: An Assessment of Contextual Effects." *Criminology* 24 (November):667–704.

Snyder, H. N., and M. Sickmund. 1999. *Juvenile Offenders and Victims: 1999 National Report.* Washington, DC: U.S. Dept. of Justice, Office of Justice Programs, Office of Juvenile Justice and Delinquency Prevention.

Thornberry, T. P., and J. H. Burch II. 1997. *Gang Members and Delinquent Behavior.* Juvenile Justice Bulletin, Office of Juvenile Justice and Delinquency Prevention. Washington, DC: U.S. Dept. of Justice.

Thornberry, T. P., and M. D. Krohn. 2001. "The Self Report Method for Measuring Delinquency and Crime." In *Measurement and Analysis of Crime and Justice: Criminal Justice 2000,* Vol. 4, edited by David Duffee. Washington, DC: National Institutes of Justice.

Tittle, C. R., and W. J. Villemez. 1977. "Social Class and Criminality." *Social Forces* 56 (December):474–502.

Tittle, C. R., W. J. Villemez, and D. Smith. 1978. "The Myth of Social Class and Criminality." *American Sociological Review* 43:643–56.

Williams J. R., and M. Gold. 1972. "From Delinquent Behavior to Official Delinquency." *Social Problems* 20 (Fall):209–29.

Wright, B. R. E., A. Caspi, T. E. Moffitt, R. Miech, and P. Silva. 1999. "Reconsidering the Relationship between SES and Delinquency: Causation but Not Correlation." *Criminology* 37 (1):175–94.

Youth Violence: A Report of the Surgeon General. 2001. Washington, DC: U.S. Dept. of Health and Human Services.

five

Explanations of Delinquency
Biology, Psychology, and Learning

> At the sight of that skull, I seemed to see all of a sudden, lighted up as a vast plain under a flaming sky, the problem of the nature of the criminal—an atavistic being who reproduces in his person the ferocious instincts of primitive humanity and the inferior animals. Thus were explained anatomically the enormous jaws, high cheekbones, prominent superciliary arches, solitary lines in the palms, extreme size of the orbits, handle-shaped or sessile ears found in criminals, savages and apes, insensibility to pain, extremely acute sight, tattooing, excessive idleness, love of orgies, and the irresistible craving of evil for its own sake, the desire not only to extinguish life in the victim, but to mutilate the corpse, tear its flesh and drink its blood.
>
> (Cesare Lombroso, *Crime, Its Causes and Remedies*, 1911)

Introduction

Cesare Lombroso's dramatic description of the nature of the criminal as a throwback to more primitive life forms strikes most college students as humorous. Yet, Lombroso is accorded the title "father of scientific criminology" since his research in the 1890s was one of the earliest attempts to develop a theory of criminality founded on the scientific approach of gathering data and carefully examining measurable characteristics that differentiate criminal offenders from the "normal" population. The "enormous jaws, high cheekbones . . . handle-shaped sessile ears" became the cornerstone of a theory called *Italian positivism*. In the early twentieth century Lombroso's theory and methods were on the cutting edge of science. However, the scientific method also requires ongoing research and a constant evaluation of the data and procedures used in forming any conclusion. It is ironic that Lombroso's own insistence on scientific rigor led to the discrediting of his theory.

Much of the early theory and research in criminology reflected an expectation that some key characteristic of criminals would be found that would distinguish them from the rest of humanity. Potential offenders therefore could be easily identified and either isolated or controlled. It is not surprising that features of the body and the mind would be the first to be proposed in that search, in view of the growing prestige of the medical professions and spectacular progress in the scientific understanding of disease in the latter part of the nineteenth century. Human mental and behavioral aberrations were symptomatic of some underlying disease or malady, it was thought, and medical procedures and diagnostic instruments could be used to discern their biological roots and even possibly correct them.

In contemporary criminology the search for a few simple psychological or physiological characteristics that could conclusively distinguish between offenders and honest citizens has given way to a more realistic emphasis on interwoven biological, psychological, and social variables that increase or decrease the probability of criminal or delinquent conduct. Criminologists accept that even the best-regarded theories will yield predictions that are fraught with error. Unlike the "laws" of physics where there is high predictive power, trying to predict human behavior produces not laws but theories that might explain a modest amount of human behavior. Certain measurable characteristics of people and their social environments significantly affect the odds of offending, but a sizeable proportion of people defy those odds. This indeterminacy is frustrating for anyone who expects science to provide precise answers and straightforward cures.

This chapter will examine attempts to explain crime and delinquency that focus on the biophysiological, mental, and social learning processes that affect behavior. While much of the early theory and research may seem naive and seriously inadequate in view of modern scientific standards, the critiques of this early research were crucial to the development of a "methodological toolkit" to be used in the assessment of more contemporary research. A distinct set of issues must be raised in evaluating research, and the greater the attention to such issues the greater confidence we can have that the information presented is an accurate description of reality.

Searching for Answers

In order to evaluate theory and research on delinquency effectively, we need to ask how we should go about finding answers. Some people believe we can arrive at the answers by asking people their opinions or by discussing the issues. Some believe we can find answers by talking with those in law enforcement who have firsthand knowledge of delinquency. Others believe that such questions can only be answered by conducting extensive research, like a scientist in a laboratory setting. However, people have different expectations about what constitutes a satisfactory explanation, and understanding those expectations will help us understand different ways of seeking answers. Lombroso was seeking answers in a manner he considered to be scientific and objective when he had his flash of insight into "criminal atavism." Yet in terms of the standards for good research in contemporary criminology, his work has not withstood critical evaluation.

Public Opinion

Most of us are familiar with public opinion polls that attempt to assess the beliefs, attitudes, and values of the American populace. Often we consider public opinion to be an important assessment of what is true or accurate. But consider, for example, the responses made by the general public to the following question: "Is there more crime in the U.S. than there was a year ago, or less?" (Gallup Poll, 2006). Sixty-seven percent responded that there was more crime than in the previous year. Most people think crime is increasing regardless of actual increases and decreases. In fact, both victimization and FBI data have been trending downward for many years.

Box 5-1 reveals another feature of public opinion that complicates its acceptance as a reflection of reality. When asked about the role of violence on TV and in video games, respondents from different age groups had markedly different views on whether such violence was a major cause of youth problems. Different publics appear to harbor different beliefs. Do we consider the opinions of youth to be closer to the truth or the opinions of the elderly? It should also be noted that no scientific research has found a relationship between *actual rates of violent crime* and the amount of violent content on television (see chapter 8). The murder rate was as high in the 1930s before the invention of television as it is now.

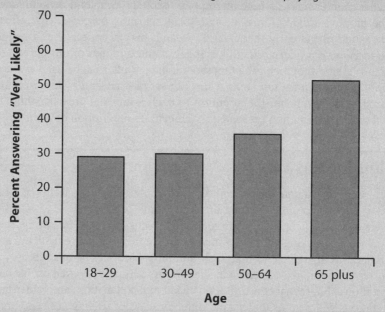

Box 5-1   Opinions About TV Violence

The chart below reveals the percent of respondents in an opinion poll indicating that problem behavior of youth is "very likely" caused by "watching violent TV or playing violent video games."

Why are younger age groups less likely than older age groups to see violence on TV and in video games as causes of problem behavior in youth? Whose opinion do you accept as the "truth"?

Source: Davis and Smith, 2002.

Expert Testimony and Practical Experience

When a news reporter sets out to get information on a topic, the opinion of experts is likely to be a major source. Some people are considered experts because of the positions they occupy, regardless of any additional qualifications based on experience. Yet the criminal trial of O.J. Simpson seriously eroded public confidence in expert testimony when it was seen that forensic scientists failed to follow standard procedures. Similarly, the allegation that the FBI Crime Lab tainted the findings to help the prosecution raises questions about expert evidence.

A second rationale for according expert status to some people is the amount of practical experience they have. The assumption that experience will provide wisdom has its shortcomings as well. For example, J. Edgar Hoover was the first director of the FBI, serving in that position from 1935 to 1972. While there was mounting evidence that organized crime and Mafia activities were a major dimension of the crime problem in the United States, Hoover viewed such beliefs as "baloney" and claimed the conception of organized crime as a national problem was the invention of imaginative crime writers. One crime historian contends that when faced with mounting evidence of mob activities on a national scale, the FBI started referring to organized crime as "La Cosa Nostra" in order "to get Hoover off the hook" (Hammer, 1989).

Government commissions often seek information on topics by soliciting expert testimony, but such solicitations can be stacked for or against a particular viewpoint. For example, the 1986 report on pornography issued by the U.S. Attorney General came to a very different conclusion than a 1970 report by the Commission on Obscenity and Pornography. The 1986 commission, unlike the 1970 commission, saw pornography as inherently harmful and called for the vigorous enforcement of pornography laws. While the 1970 commission had a budget of $2 million and spent two years on its report, the 1986 commission had a budget of only $500,000 (sixteen times less than the 1970 commission expressed in 1970 dollars) and spent one year conducting community town-hall meetings. The 1986 commission pointed with pride to the fact that it obtained information from "experienced" authorities in public hearings organized in six U.S. cities. The witnesses included a nude dancer, a concerned parent, the chaplain of the U.S. Senate, police officers, postal inspectors, and psychologists. This 1986 commission was criticized for "stacking the deck" by selecting eleven commission members whose opinions coincided with the administration's views and for soliciting written statements from individuals and organizations who were staunchly opposed to pornography. Thus, the quality of being "experienced" is highly subjective and, as exemplified by the two different pornography commissions, the conclusions reached by experts and experienced professionals can be radically different.

Qualities of a Sound Causal Theory

If public opinion, expert testimony, and practical experience are not sufficient for identifying causes of crime and delinquency, then how do we decide between conflicting points of view? While there is considerable debate and controversy over the whole issue of causation, there does seem to be some agreement in the sciences and criminology that certain minimum requirements must be met before any argument regarding a causal influence can be accepted as convincing. Ideally, such claims should be derived from or fit with a larger body of systematically ordered and logically consistent propositions that constitute a theory.

If the theory is to be deemed a **scientific theory** it should be constructed in a manner that allows specification of the findings that would *disconfirm* the theory. A scientific theory is never *proven* to be true in that some future test could always disconfirm the theory. However, a good theory is one that has survived numerous tests over time. When the criterion of ultimate testability is applied, it places great restraints on theories. For example, if someone wants to claim that offenders are "biologically inferior" to nonoffenders or that offenders are "psychopathic," the underlying theoretical constructs will have to be clearly defined and the type of measures that would constitute an acceptable test specified. In other words, if someone wants to develop a theory of delinquency based on demon possession, he or she will have to specify how such demons can be seen or measured and shown to be more common among delinquent than nondelinquent youth. A sound scientific theory must be stated in a manner that allows empirical testing.

While theories or explanations should be evaluated in terms of issues of logical consistency among their claims, the validity of their constructs, and their amenability to testing, there are some basic requirements for making causal claims that are often overlooked in criminological research. We must always ask whether (1) an *association* or relationship has been found, (2) whether that relationship might be *spurious*, (3) whether there has been a convincing empirical or theoretical rationale provided for claiming a specific *causal order*, and (4) whether *specification* of how the theory operates in terms of time or circumstances surrounding an event has occurred. Each issue will be illustrated below with examples from criminological research.

Association

In an observational study of urban gangs, *Islands in the Street* (1991), Martín Sánchez Jankowski proposes that gang youth exhibit a social character that he labels "defiant individualism." Defiant individualism is proposed to emerge among youth as a product of intense competition for scarce resources, and gang youth are supposed to exhibit that social character to a greater degree than other youths in such environments. Moreover, several characteristics often cited as causes of gang delinquency are dismissed as irrelevant. For example, Jankowski argues that

> . . . it is important to dismiss a number of the propositions that have often been advanced. The first is that young boys join gangs because they are from broken homes. . . . In the ten years of this study, I found that there were as many gang members from homes where the nuclear family was intact as there were from families with the father absent. (1991:39)

He dismisses dropping out of school because there were *only slightly more* members who dropped out than who finished school.

While this research provides excellent descriptive information on gang members, there is no comparable information provided on nondelinquent or nongang youth to justify claims that one variable is related to another. In order to make claims about relationships (i.e., that defiant individualism is more characteristic of gang youth than nongang youth) or the lack of a relationship (i.e., that coming from a broken home or dropping out of school does not affect the odds of gang membership), we need a comparison between gang and nongang youth. It may be the case that broken homes or dropping out characterized only half the gang members, but these figures are several times higher than ordinarily found for nondelinquent or nongang youth. A demonstration of **association** requires evidence that youth who vary on one characteristic have greater or lesser odds of exhibiting some other characteristic. We can neither uncover correlates or relationships nor dismiss them based on data from offenders alone (see box 5-2).

Criminologists are interested in identifying factors or conditions that increase the probability of crime or delinquency in a certain population. The fact that many gang members came from intact homes and many had not dropped out of school does not allow those experiences to be dismissed as relevant correlates, but it does indicate that we must explore other variables. Defiant social attitudes may be part of the explanation (see Jensen, 1996), but we need data on the distribution of such attitudes among gang and nongang youth. In short, theoretical claims about relationships require comparison.

Box 5-2   Is There an Association?

The following data are based on a survey of high school students. Is the probability of delinquency affected by band membership? Is band membership a causal force inhibiting delinquency in this high school?

© Batom, Inc. North America Syndicate.

Percent of Band and Non-Band High School Students Reporting at Least One Delinquent Offense

	Band	Non-Band
Theft	37%	52%
Vandalism, fights, joyriding	37%	52%
Hard drugs	13%	21%
Marijuana	40%	57%
Drunk	40%	56%
Smoking	41%	49%
	(N = 67)	(N = 161)

Nonspuriousness

Another requirement for building a sound scientific theory is to rule out the possibility that the association observed between two variables is **spurious**; that is, a product of coincidental or shared connections with other variables. An example of spurious association is the tradition in the notorious Al Capone gang in the 1920s of rubbing bullets with garlic. The argument was that garlic acted as a poison and when a person was shot, death was most certain. The Capone gang also began using Thompson submachine guns and they found that after riddling a person with thirty or forty bullets rubbed with garlic, the person invariably died. The connection of death with garlic-rubbed bullets was clearly spurious. Had garlic been delivered by some less traumatic means it would not have had the same effect. Garlic-free bullets would likely have worked just as well. Of course, the belief that garlic helped kill opponents might have made the Capone gang appear more effective as killers.

A famous example of a spurious relationship in early delinquency research was the finding that middle children did not have higher rates of delinquency when family size was controlled. While some theorists had argued that middle children had higher rates of delinquency because they were squeezed between older and younger siblings who received more parental attention, Travis Hirschi (1969) noted that larger families had more middle children. When he isolated the effects of birth order from family size, birth order made no difference.

Whenever a claim is made that one variable is causally relevant to the explanation of another, we should consider the alternative possibility that they are both functions of other circumstances. For example, if someone argues that watching violence on television increases the odds of violent behavior, it would be legitimate to propose that watching violence on television and violent behavior could appear correlated because they are both reflections of parental attitudes and behavior. If poor grades are correlated with delinquency, then we should discuss whether family circumstances generated both poor grades and involvement in delinquency. The scientific method requires that we raise alternative possibilities, propose ways to test such alternatives and, when possible, carry out such tests.

Causal Order

Another issue that should always be raised in assessing scientific claims that one circumstance or variable is causally relevant or antecedent to another is **causal order**. Causal theories identify **independent variables** that account for change in **dependent variables**. For example, we might argue that delinquency depends on delinquent friends, low self-esteem, and poor parental supervision. The latter three variables are the independent variables when this argument is made because we are not addressing how they are determined. Of course, when the theorist addresses the relationships among these variables (e.g., the effect of poor supervision on acquiring delinquent friends) we specify a complex causal model with independent variables, a series of intervening variables, and ultimately a dependent variable.

The difficulty with conducting research is that humans cannot be manipulated like rats in a maze to see how one variable impacts another variable. Federal requirements regulate research on human subjects so that no harm can be inflicted on research subjects, and there must be fully informed consent from the subjects themselves. The classic argument of whether capital punishment has a deterrent effect on murder rates could be tested by executing all homicide offenders in one state, putting all homicide offenders in prison in another state, and setting all homicide offenders free in a third state. Research such as this would be unethical and federal guidelines would prevent it. Thus, researchers are bound by guidelines that prevent the manipulation of human subjects, meaning that basic questions of how a certain variable impacts another variable often remain unknown.

A second limitation to research is the need for observation over an extend period of time. Suppose a researcher finds interrelationships between low self-esteem, neglectful parents, delinquent friends, and delinquent behavior, but these are all observed at the same point in time. Such research is very common in criminology and such designs are called cross-sectional. To defend any particular causal sequence we need information on change over time or some form of longitudinal research design. We could follow our subjects for years, measuring changes in each variable even though we did not actually manipulate the causal variables ourselves. Tests of theories based on panels of subjects followed over many years are increasingly common in criminological research. Delbert Elliott's National Youth Survey is an example. The difficulty with longitudinal research is that it is extremely expensive. Moreover, the need for researchers to follow individuals or groups of individuals over time can be problematic in our mobile society, where a sample assembled at the start of a research project may rapidly dwindle as subjects move to another locale.

In some instances a presumed causal order may be defensible based on general information or theoretical consensus. For example, since gender identity is established quite early in life, few people would seriously challenge the causal primacy of gender in the explanation of delinquency. Of course, there will be debates about the way in which a person's gender ultimately affects involvement in delinquency (i.e., opportunity, temperament, attitudes, parental control, etc.), but the issue at that point is not the causal priority of gender. When we try to determine which qualities of gender affect future involvement in delinquency we are looking for the **intervening mechanisms** that link gender to delinquency. The attempt to identify intervening causal mechanisms is distinct from the concern about spuriousness in that the existence of a causal link is not at issue. Rather, the issue is the sequence of ways in which a variable (i.e., gender) has ultimate (indirect) consequences for behavior. When we argue that a relationship is spurious we are questioning whether there is any direct, indirect, or remote causal linkage at all. When we argue about causal order in a complex explanation we are concerned about sequences of effects.

Some models of delinquency are unidirectional or linear, with one variable impacting a second, and then these jointly impacting a third variable, until we reach the end state of delinquent behavior. But more sophisticated models argue that human behavior is not the result of a simple linear progression of events but of **reciprocal causation**. Association with delinquent friends may cause delinquency, but being engaged in more and more delinquent behavior may result in the acquisition of more delinquent friends. Family conflict may facilitate delinquency, but involvement in delinquency may be a major source of conflict with parents.

Specification

A good scientific causal theory will generally specify the limitations of the theory or the circumstances under which the theory applies. For example, most sociological theories were developed to explain male delinquency. As feminist critics have argued (see chapter 6), we cannot be certain that theories elaborated and tested among males will necessarily apply to females. In short, the statements made about male delinquency may not be generalizable to female delinquency. Theories that seem to explain delinquency in American society may not explain delinquency in other societies. In fact, there will be instances summarized in subsequent chapters where relationships found in one region of the United States are not found in other regions.

One way of making sense out of conflicting research findings is to identify the circumstances of sample, time, method, and setting that may affect the nature of the relationships found. The more precise and careful a scientist is in specifying the circumstances that can influence findings, the better the chances of accumulating meaningful knowledge about crime and delinquency.

Our Methodological Toolbox

In chapters 3 and 4 we discussed notions of validity, reliability, and representative versus biased samples. If claims are made about characteristics of youth that affect the odds that they will engage in delinquent behavior, then we should expect valid, reliable measures of "delinquent behavior" and a reasonably representative sample of "youth." In addition to expectations that researchers will use valid, reliable measures of their concepts and gather data from cases that are representative of the populations under study, we also expect that they demonstrate nonspurious associations, address the issue of causal order, consider the mechanisms generating observed relationships, and attempt to specify the circumstances that might limit the generalizability of their results. All of these issues constitute a critical methodological toolbox from which we can draw in our review of criminological research and in our search for possible "causes" of delinquency. We should have greater confidence in claims advanced after attending to such issues than in claims advanced with blatant disregard for such expectations.

Biological Schools of Thought

For much of the history of Western civilization, people have been viewed as occupying a special, unique niche in the universe by virtue of a soul, free will, and reason. Some of the earliest systematic thought about crime and criminal justice was based on such a premise. The **classical school** of criminology (prominent during the 1700s and represented by such philosophers as Montesquieu, Voltaire, Marat, Beccaria, and Bentham) believed that the law and criminal justice should be predicated on the view of people as rational, thinking beings. This school argued that human behavior is based on hedonism and that the pleasure-pain principle should serve as the guide for social control. Individuals choose actions that give pleasure and avoid those that give pain. Punishment should fit the crime and be certain, severe, and swift enough to deter a rational human being. According to the classical school of criminology, law-breaking is due to free and rational decision making; therefore, laws need to be clear and simple. Deterrence comes not from severe punishment but from punishment that is appropriate, prompt, and inevitable.

The founder of the classical school of criminology was Cesare Beccaria (1738–1794), an Italian mathematician. Beccaria felt that the laws and the enforcement of law in Europe were arbitrary, capricious, and irrational. He published a small book, less than 100 pages, *On Crime and Punishments*, challenging the legal practices of his day. Because he felt his ideas were so radical, the book was published anonymously. Beccaria argued that the legal system needs to be rational and fair. Crime is the result not of bad people but of bad laws. His principal argument was that punishment should not exceed that which is necessary to prevent the offender from committing the crime. People are rational and intelligent beings who weigh the costs and benefits of their behavior. Punishment that is applied fairly and impartially will serve as a deterrent to criminal behavior. He argued for the prevention of crimes rather than for punishment. *On Crimes and Punishments* became one of the most influential books ever written, leading to massive legal reforms in Europe, and ultimately becoming the foundation for the deterrence school of thought that will be discussed later.

Jeremy Bentham (1748–1832) was a prolific writer who took up the cause espoused by Beccaria. Bentham introduced the notion of the *hedonistic calculus*, which was predicated on the principle of pleasure versus pain. If people are rational, thinking beings, then they will choose pleasure over pain. Human behavior is based on human calculations of seeking pleasure and avoiding pain. Thus, criminal law should be based on the notion of punishment outweighing the profit derived from crime. Further, punishment must be increased in proportion to the severity of the crime. Like Beccaria, Bentham saw the purpose of punishment as deterrence, not vengeance. The question was not why some people committed crime and others did not; rather the focus of attention was on social control as a product of a rational and fair legal system. Bentham's ideas radically transformed the English code, often referred to as "The Bloody Code," because brutal punishments, most notably executions, were inflicted for minor offenses.

By the mid-1800s, however, with the development of biology and theories of natural selection and evolution, the "uniqueness" of humankind was being called into question. If Charles Darwin's theories of evolution were correct, human beings could be viewed as one stage in the evolution of organic life and, as such, humans were neither perfect nor complete but were evolving into higher organic forms. The most famous criminological work along this line was carried out in Italy in the late 1800s and early 1900s and is referred to as **Italian positivism**. The term "positivism" is derived from the Latin word *positivus* which means that which is laid down and can be found by rational insight and observation. That is, explanations for criminal behavior can be discovered by gathering facts and using the scientific method to discover clues about relationships.

Cesare Lombroso (1835–1909)

The name most prominently associated with the positivistic school is that of the Italian physician Cesare Lombroso. Using data from government agencies, anthropological measurements, and tools of the medical sciences, Lombroso sought to discover the "causes" of crime. While Lombroso considered a wide range of social and societal forces that might contribute to crime (for example, population density, the price of bread, wealth, education, unemployment, newspaper crime coverage, and so on), he is best known for his view of the "born" criminal, or innate criminal types. Lombroso argued that a large proportion of criminals (he estimated 40 percent) were **atavistic**— that is, genetic throwbacks. He reached this conclusion on the basis of observations of the physical and biological characteristics of criminals. The preface to this chapter is a statement from Lombroso after he examined the skull of a notorious Italian criminal. Lombroso believed his observations revealed an unusual number of criminals to be more akin to lower forms of life and to primitive humans than to "civilized" people (see box 5-3).

Lombroso was inclined to advocate biological interpretations of differences that could have been given sociological interpretations. For example, when confronted with the fact that women had lower rates of crime than men, Lombroso argued as follows:

> That women less often engaged in highway robbery, murder, homicide, and assault
> is due to the very nature of the feminine constitution. To conceive an assassination,

---

Box 5-3   "Criminal Man"

Applying Lombrosian methods, Gina Lombroso-Ferrero (1911, reissued 1972) described the physical characteristics of male criminals:

Eyes: The eyebrows are generally bushy in murderers and violators of women. Ptosis, a paralysis of the upper lid, which gives the eye a half-closed appearance, is common in all criminals.

Nose: In thieves the base of the nose often slants upwards, and this characteristic of rogues is so common in Italy that it has given rise to a number of proverbs.

Jaws: Enormous maxillary development is one of the most frequent anomalies in criminals and is related to the greater size of the zygomae and teeth.

Chin: This part of the face, which in Europeans is generally prominent, round and proportioned to the size of the face, in degenerates as in apes is frequently receding, flat, too long or too short.

Height: Criminals are rarely tall. Like all degenerates, they are under medium height.

HEAD OF CRIMINAL

Can you describe what you think the "typical" delinquent looks like? What sort of image comes to mind? Where do you think such images originate? Can you look around your classroom and spot offenders using these descriptions?

---

to make ready for it, to put it into execution demands, in a great number of cases at least, not only physical force, but a certain energy and a certain combination of intellectual functions. In this sort of development women almost always fall short of men. It seems on the other hand that the crimes that are habitual to them are those which require a smaller degree of physical and intellectual force, and such especially are receipt of stolen goods, poisoning, abortion, and infanticide. (1911:184–85)

Lombroso depicted women as inferior to men, lacking the intellectual and constitutional ability to carry out the same acts as men. If women did commit crimes, it was because they had "masculine" characteristics. He typically proceeded by discovering a fact based on available statistics and then provided an interpretation that made the fact fit his theory. Since no predictions or hypotheses were ever presented before assessing the facts, Lombroso's theory could be bent to explain anything.

There are good grounds for criticizing the "savage" image of primitive humanity and lower forms of life in Lombroso's comparisons as well. For example, most aggression in animals takes the form of "posturing" and "bluffing," with the winner scaring off the loser. The ultimate outcome of animal aggression is rarely lethal.

Lombroso's work also can be criticized in terms of the criteria of causality that we discussed earlier in this chapter. For one, Lombroso did not establish an association between physical attributes ("biological inferiority," or "degeneracy") and the probability of criminal activity. The most he could say (and even that is debatable) is that he found some physical differences between incarcerated or dead Italian convicts and a sample of Italian soldiers. Moreover, once Lombroso had developed his working hypothesis that criminals tended to be atavistic, he selectively searched for and highlighted slight differences. He did not state in advance of his search any criteria for identifying atavism or biological inferiority but, rather, defined atavism in terms of whatever differences he found. Many of the traits he assumed to be inherited are not necessarily genetically determined—for example, heads too small or too large, short legs, sloping shoulders, flat feet, distinctive hair, eyes, nose, ears, lips, or jaw. Many of these traits could be caused by diet or the environment; circumstances that resulted in poor health care.

As a result of his positivistic or scientific approach, Lombroso's ideas on crime causation underwent revision, and by the time of his death in 1909 he increasingly took social and environmental factors into account. He argued that scientists should remain neutral to societal values and maintain total objectivity by sticking to the facts. Lombroso described himself as a "slave to facts," and is referred to as "the father of modern criminality." Finally, Lombroso suggested that crime was determined by causal forces often beyond the awareness of individuals involved, not the expression of free will as depicted by the classical theorists. Since crime was caused rather than freely committed, it would not deserve punishment. The Lombrosian outlook allied itself with the reformatory movement of the nineteenth century, which favored rehabilitation rather than retribution. Indeterminate sentences, probation, and prisons with educational or vocational programs became the norm.

Charles Goring (1870–1919)

In *The English Convict*, published in 1913, English physician Charles Goring delivered a devastating critique of Lombroso's work. Goring argued that Lombroso had not provided adequate statistical evidence of the differences claimed and that his theoretical biases had colored his interpretation of the data. Rather than merely criticize, however, Goring gathered data on three thousand convicts and compared types of offenders within that sample. He then compared those findings to data available for the general population on ninety-six traits. Goring could find no evidence of Lombroso's criminal types. However, he did find differences between convicts and nonconvicts in the English population in terms of stature and measures of intelligence. Convicts were shorter, weighed less, and were classified as lower in intelligence than the general population. While Goring concluded that "there is no such thing as a physical criminal type" (1913:173), his findings led him to conclude that convicts were "inferior" to nonconvicts and ultimately agreed with Lombroso that criminals are born with criminal traits.

E. A. Hooton (1887–1954)

Although Goring's work has been described as dealing a "crucial blow to Lombrosian theory" (Quinney, 1970:69), the controversy over Lombroso's work did not end there. In a work entitled *Crime and the Man* (1939), American anthropologist E. A. Hooton attacked Goring on much the same grounds as Goring had attacked Lombroso. Hooton was a Harvard anthropologist who felt that Goring had been biased against Lombrosian theory and had interpreted his data in the manner least favorable to Lombrosian notions. After comparing data from more than 17,000 individuals, including convicts, college students, police officers, and mental patients, Hooton concluded that criminals are organically inferior and that this inferiority is genetically inheritable. He took his argument to its logical conclusion: "It follows that elimination of crime can only be effected by the extirpation of the physically, mentally, and morally unfit, or by their complete segregation in a socially aseptic environment" (1939:41).

Hooton argued that "our information definitely proves that it is from the physically inferior element of the population that native born criminals from native parentage are mainly derived" (1939:309). Taking elaborate measurements of his subjects, he concluded that in nineteen out of thirty-five measurements there were significant differences between offenders and nonoffenders. According to Hooton, criminals had low foreheads, crooked noses, thin lips, long thin necks, narrow jaws, and several other distinctive features.

Hooton's work met with severe criticism because of his lack of representative control groups, blatant deficiencies in his methodology, and his failure to demonstrate how physical deviations are in any way indicative of inferiority. A reviewer of Hooton's book called it "the funniest academic performance that has appeared since the invention of movable type" (Reuter, 1939). Hooton's research is now only of historical importance. However, the basic premise of Italian positivism was well entrenched in the first half of the twentieth century.

William Sheldon (1898–1977)

Drawing on earlier work by the German psychiatrist Ernst Kretschmer, William Sheldon, a physician and professor of psychology, proposed a *constitutional psychology* in which the body is the starting point for understanding personality and behavior (*Varieties of Delinquent Youth*, 1949). Sheldon's focus was on body type, or *somatotype*, which he defined as "a quantification of the primary components determining the morphological structure of the individual." A person's type was determined by the predominance of structures associated with digestion and assimilation of food (**endomorphy**), by the predominance of bone, muscle, and connective tissue (**mesomorphy**), or by the predominance of skin, appendages, and the nervous system (**ectomorphy**).

Sheldon's hypothesis was that there would be differences between the somatotypes of delinquent boys and the somatotypes of the rest of the population, although he could not predict in advance what those differences might be. Bodies were somatotyped by measuring the intermixture of the three types of structures. According to Sheldon, every physique can be calibrated into three components on seven-point scales, with one as the lowest value and seven as the highest. A three-digit number based on the estimate of endomorphy, mesomorphy, and ectomorphy was created. Sheldon's data were based on two hundred youths who were wards of a home for delinquent boys in Boston between 1939 and 1942. The measurements for the delinquent youths were compared with measurements for four thousand college students drawn primarily from Harvard University, the University of Chicago, and Oberlin College. Compared to the college sample, the sample of delinquent youths tended to be mesomorphic. Sheldon concluded, "So far as the somatotype is concerned our sample of delinquents, far from being weaklings, are a little on the hefty and meaty side" (1949:730). In contrast to Hooton's criminal sample, Sheldon's delinquents were not shorter than the general population.

Although Sheldon showed, at best, a difference in body build between some delinquent youths and a college sample, he presumed that such data are relevant to understanding delinquent behavior in general. In fact, he claimed that further exploration of constitutional differences could "cure the lust for war and delinquency" and proposed a nationwide compilation of biological profiles in order to "find out who are the biological best" (1949:879). He did not examine the possibility that the differences between his two samples might have been related to differential selection by the institutions from which the samples were drawn. He also did not address the social meaning or cultural relativity of "inferiority," the social meaning of different body builds, and the differences in social experiences that might result from differences in physical appearance. Rather, he argued that different body types are reflected in different personality types and, ultimately, in behavior. Sheldon's data are inadequate for substantiating his more grandiose arguments for unique temperamental traits that were ascribed to the three somatotypes.

Sheldon concluded that the tendency to become criminal is hereditary. This led him to argue for eugenics, or selective breeding. "Our best stock tends to be outbred by stock that is inferior to it in every respect" (1949:45). He began to urge the government to adopt strict birth-control programs that would prevent "bad stock" from reproducing. However, Sheldon's technique of somatotyping, of arriving at this crucial three-digit score, was quite unsophisticated and arbitrary. Edwin Sutherland reanalyzed Sheldon's data using more objective measures of delinquency and reported, "The general conclusion is that in this group of two hundred youths the variations in civil delinquencies are not significantly related to variations in Sheldon's indexes of constitutional psychology" (1951:11).

Sheldon Glueck (1896–1980) and Eleanor Glueck (1898–1972)

The last of the classic works dealing with bodily constitution and delinquency that we will review here is a study by Sheldon and Eleanor Glueck (*Unraveling Juvenile Delinquency*, 1950). This study involved five hundred delinquent youths and five hundred relatively nondelinquent youths in the Boston area. The groups were matched as well as possible in terms of age, general intelligence, ethnicity, and residence in an underprivileged neighborhood. The study gathered data on a wide variety of social, psychological, and physical characteristics.

The Gluecks found no significant differences in health between their two samples but did report that a greater proportion of delinquent youths than of nondelinquent youths had been "restless" children. They also reported that the delinquents were "superior" to nondelinquents in body size and conformity to a "masculine" physical type. As in William Sheldon's research, delinquent boys were found to be more mesomorphic than the control group of nondelinquents.

No one has explained why there is an unexpected proportion of mesomorphic boys among official delinquents. It may be that boys with such builds are reacted to as dangerous or threatening. If the "masculine" build is overrepresented because of reactions rather than some temperamental, neurological, or physiological difference, then body build should not be related to self-reports of delinquency. There has been one study of body type in relation to self-reports of delinquency and that study reports no significant correlation (McCandless, Persons, and Roberts, 1972). Thus, even if other criticisms of the Glueck's research are ignored (see Cortes and Gatti, 1972), a persistent finding about body type among boys in institutions tells us little about differences in behavior.

Chromosomal, Glandular, and Neurological Variables

While early research focused on physical characteristics of people and observable external characteristics that were thought to correlate with variations in internal processes of some kind, more contemporary research has examined variations in chromosomal abnormalities and in glandular and neurological functioning. Some of the traits studied have been found to be too uncommon to explain much crime, and the causal role of others has not yet been established.

Chromosomal Abnormality

There are 23 pairs of chromosomes in humans that carry the biological structures responsible for the transmission, development, and determination of inherited characteristics. Of these 23 pairs or 46 chromosomes, two determine the sex of the person. The male chromosome configuration is recorded as 46, XY and the female as 46, XX. In the process of human conception, the female contributes 23 chromosomes and the male also 23 chromosomes. If the male contributes an X chromosome, this unites with the X of the female and a female offspring will ensue. Conversely, if the male contributes a Y chromosome, this unites with the X of the female and a male offspring is created. Thus, the male determines the sex of the child.

In 1961 researchers discovered instances of chromosomal abnormalities. For example, males can have an additional chromosome (47, XXY) which results in **Klinefelter's syndrome**, a condition in males that causes certain female characteristics such as diminished facial hair, increased breast tissue, and lower testosterone levels. The converse of this abnormality is the 47, **XYY syndrome**, which results in males who are tall and "presumably" unusually prone to violence. Such cases were suspected of being "supermale."

In 1965 a British research team headed by Patricia Jacobs (1965) reported that 7 out of 197 mentally abnormal males in a prison hospital had an extra Y chromosome. Through the use of the *buccal mucosa smear technique*, in which cells are scraped from the inside of the cheek to determine chromosomal content, it has been found that only one out of every thousand males is XYY. Thus, 7 out of 197 (3.6 percent) is unexpectedly high. However, the characteristic is sufficiently rare among inmates that it can explain very little variation. Moreover, chromosomal abnormalities are associated with a higher than expected probability of property crime, not violence (Price and Whatmore, 1967). The popular assumption was that the trait creates an extra dose of maleness and the carrier would be inclined toward violence.

In 1977, more than thirty-one thousand Danish men who were tall were checked for chromosome composition (Witkin et al., 1976; Mednick and Volavka, 1977). While researchers found only twelve men with the XYY abnormality, five of the twelve had records. If the probability of acquiring a record were the same as for XY males (9 percent), only one should have been found to have a record. Moreover, consistent with the British study, it was property crime and not violent crime that was overrepresented.

The infrequency of this chromosomal abnormality suggests that even if a connection could be established between the XYY syndrome and crime, it could only account for a small fraction of crime that is committed. Certain chromosomal abnormalities can affect physical and mental functioning and, hence, it is plausible that they might also affect probabilities of criminality. However, the XYY syndrome cannot take us very far in the explanation of crime and delinquency (Trasler, 1987). It can offer no explanation for female crime and we are still left with the fact that the vast majority of crimes are committed by normal XY males. Moreover, as documented in chapters 3 and 4, girls are becoming more like boys with no evidence of change in the gene pool.

Endocrinology

Another possible source of some variations in human behavior is the functioning of the endocrine glands. These glands, including the pituitary, adrenals, thyroid, and gonads, secrete hormones that affect such body functions as metabolism, emotions, and sexual processes. Secretions by the endocrine glands have been shown to affect emotional states, but the connection between endocrine abnormalities and criminal behavior is not clearly established.

For example, abnormal secretions of **testosterone**, a male steroid hormone, have been hypothesized as a possible cause of criminal aggression. Some research has shown that testosterone levels are higher among offenders who have committed violent crimes than among those committing nonviolent crimes. However, research on testosterone levels and aggressiveness is quite contradictory on this point (Mednick and Volavka, 1980).

The best evidence of a connection between testosterone levels and crime and delinquency is a study by Alan Booth and D. Wayne Osgood (1993). Using self-reports of delinquency and adult deviance collected by the Centers for Disease Control as part of the Vietnam Experience Study, Booth and Osgood found a "moderately strong and significant" relationship between testosterone levels and both prior delinquency and adult deviance. They concluded: (1) "Testosterone is one of a larger constellation of factors contributing to a general latent propensity toward deviance, and (2) the influence of testosterone on adult deviance is closely tied to social factors" (1993:93).

High levels of testosterone tended to inhibit the formation of stable social bonds that in turn increased the odds of deviance. Booth and Osgood also note that while high levels of testosterone have been suspect as potential correlates of male crime and delinquency, variation in testosterone levels may affect female behavior as well (see Udry, 1988). Anthony Walsh concluded that "no reputable researcher . . . claims that high levels of testosterone *cause* aggressive or sexual behaviors, only that they *facilitate* such behavior" (2000:192).

Some work has also been conducted on the female menstrual cycle. According to Saleem Shah and Loren Roth (1974), the four premenstrual days and the four days of menstruation itself account for 29 percent of the days in the typical lunar month. However, during these eight days, some 50 to 80 percent of female suicide, violence, depression, crime, and admittance to mental institutions occurs. Some attention has been given to premenstrual syndrome or PMS, which manifests itself in *some* women in terms of tension, fatigue, headaches, cramps, and depressed moods. As with the XYY hypothesis, the PMS hypothesis far exceeds its scientific evidence. Rather than PMS causing criminal behavior, it has been suggested that criminal behavior or stress can trigger early menstruation. The evidence to date does not support the conclusion that women are antisocial during menstruation or that it is the cause of female crime.

Autonomic Nervous System

The autonomic nervous system (ANS) controls the physiological activity associated with emotions and is often referred to as the involuntary nervous system. There are two systems involved, the sympathetic nervous system and the parasympathetic nervous system. The **sympathetic nervous system** is activated when anger, fear, or anxiety is being experienced and it influences heart rate, blood pressure, sweating, and changes in galvanic skin response (changes in the saline content of perspiration). The **parasympathetic nervous system** is activated after the sympathetic and induces a state of quiescence and relaxation. For normal individuals, encountering a stressful situation activates the sympathetic nervous system and the arousal of human emotions can be detected with the use of the polygraph or "lie" detector, which measures changes in the ANS. However, there are some individuals who cannot experience an ANS arousal and for these people polygraph results are meaningless. Individuals who are referred to as sociopaths are alleged to be incapable of experiencing fear or anxiety. The notion of a "cool and calculating killer" may be indicative of a person who has a sympathetic nervous system that does not respond to fear or anxiety. For some of these individuals, adrenaline injections lower the threshold of the sympathetic nervous system and they can experience anger, guilt, or fear.

The basis of biosocial theory in explaining antisocial behavior is that individuals who cannot experience the dissipation of fear or anxiety have difficulties learning (Mednick and Volavka, 1980). Mednick and associates (1982) describe this process as follows:

1. Child A contemplates aggressive action.

2. Because of previous punishment or the threat of punishment he suffers fear.

3. Because of fear he inhibits aggressive response.

4. Because he no longer entertains the aggressive impulse, the fear will begin to dissipate, to be reduced. Fear reduction is the most powerful, naturally occurring reinforcement that psychologists have discovered. The reduction of fear (which immediately follows the inhibition of the aggression) can act as a reinforcement of this inhibition and will result in learning inhibition of aggression (1982:39–40).

The faster that fear can be reduced, the faster the delivery of the reinforcement. A person who has an ANS that recovers quickly from fear or anxiety will receive immediate rewards from inhibiting the aggression and in the process will learn socially approved behavior quickly. On the other hand, the slower the ANS recovery, the less the reward factor from the parasympathetic system and, therefore, the less learning that takes place. Gordon Trasler, in reviewing the work done by Mednick, finds his results to be "excessively optimistic" but concludes that "the research which has been stimulated by Mednick's work promises major gains" (1987:205).

It is also important to remember that the initial connection between fear and rule breaking may not be established because no aversive consequences were experienced. A youth with a responsive ANS in an environment where parents are unaware or unresponsive to initial rule breaking or where rule breaking is more rewarding than alternatives, will not be inhibited by autonomic reactions. The types of conditioning that establish fear reactions may never have occurred. At present no one has untangled the effects of learning environments and contingencies from the responsiveness of individuals to learning in those environments. Mednick has obtained supportive results but a common refrain has been that these results are inconclusive.

Genetics and Inherited Dispositions

A common observation in the history of criminology has been that the criminality of one member of a family is related to the criminality of other members of a family. Early research focused on "criminal families" (Dugdale, 1877; Estabrook, 1916) while more recent research examines the behavior of twins, siblings, and the correlation between the criminality of adopted children and their adoptive and biological parents' criminality. Some of the most recent research uses measures of self-reported delinquency and attempts to estimate the "heritability" of criminality by controlling for social relationships.

Twin Studies

One way of examining the possible impact of biological factors on human behavior is the study of identical or **monozygotic twins**. Identical twins develop from a single female egg and have no hereditary differences. Fraternal or **dizygotic twins** are produced when two eggs are fertilized and have only half of their genes in common. If heredity plays a role in explaining criminal behavior, then monozygotic twins should have a higher **concordance rate**, or similarity of deviant behavior, than dizygotic twins. The earliest of these studies conducted in the United States, Europe, and Japan between 1929 and 1962 found concordance rates for identical twins to be as high as 70 percent, while those for fraternal twins were between 15 to 20 percent. However, because of numerous methodological problems in these early studies (such as the use of official definitions of crime, the nonrepresentativeness of the samples, and the higher probability that identical twins are more likely to be treated similarly than fraternal twins), these studies are suspect (Pollock, Mednick, and Gabrielli, 1983).

Some of the best twin studies focusing on recorded criminality were conducted by Karl O. Christiansen (1977) in Denmark. He tried to overcome some of the methodological shortcomings of the earlier studies by examining all twins, not just those found in institutions, and by taking into consideration more background variables. His studies support the notion of a higher concordance rate between identical than fraternal twins. He found that if one identical twin had a criminal conviction, the other twin also had a conviction in 35 percent of the cases. The concordance rate for fraternal twins was only 12 percent. But even Christiansen warned that his findings do not offer convincing proof that heredity is the basis for higher concordance for identical twins. The unique life experiences of identical twins—being dressed alike, treated alike, confusion as to which one is which, the social environment of identical twins—may differ significantly from fraternal twins. The greater concordance rate for identical twins may have much more to do with their social environment than genetics. Michael Gottfredson and Travis Hirschi (1990) examined the Danish studies and found serious flaws in the research. They concluded that the evidence is very small that inherited traits played a role in delinquency.

David Rowe (1986, 1987, 1990) has used complex forms of statistical analysis in studying antisocial behavior in twins and his research suggests a genetic basis for delinquent behavior (see box 5-4). Using self-reports of delinquency from twins in high schools throughout Ohio, Rowe compared the similarity in delinquency of identical twins and nontwin siblings from a single high school in Ohio. Since he also measured respondents' perceptions of family environment and associations with delinquent peers, he was able to examine the similarity in behavior of twins when controlling for environmental sources of delinquency. The greater similarity in the behavior of identical twins than in fraternal twins or nontwin siblings persists despite controls for other variables when using self-report measures. The correlations are similar for fraternal twins and nontwin siblings. Rowe argues that it is not that genetic factors directly cause delinquent behavior, but rather that there is a genetic basis for temperamental traits such as aggressiveness, anger, impulsivity, and dishonesty, or genetic variation in capacities to learn. His work suggests some form of "heritability" of individual characteristics that correlate with delinquency. On the other hand, Jones and Jones (2000) argue that identical twins are more susceptible to a "contagion effect" in that identical twins tend to be more associated with each other than fraternal twins.

Box 5-4   Self-Report Studies of Twins

(MZ = Monozygotic, DZ = Dizygotic)

Hypothesis: If the greater similarity in self-reported delinquency among twins is due to shared social circumstances, then statistical controls for social variables will eliminate the effect of the twin factor. Social variables would be the "intervening mechanism" through which shared genetic traits affect delinquency.

MZ/DZ → Social Bonds → Delinquency

If it does not do so, then we have to conclude that being an identical twin has an impact of its own above and beyond shared social circumstances. That direct effect may be the "heritability" or genetic factor working through other mechanisms such as ANS, intelligence, cognitive functioning, and temperament (ANS= autonomic nervous system).

→ Social Bonds →
MZ/DZ → Other Variables → Delinquency
→ Heritability →

Research Conclusion: The greater similarity in MZ behavior cannot be explained by social variables because the similarity persists when such variables are statistically controlled.

Plausible Explanation: There is a hereditary factor at work.

Source: Derived from research by David Rowe, 1986.

Adoption Studies

Because of the difficulty in differentiating between social and genetic influences in twin studies (see Walters and White, 1989), some researchers have turned to the study of adoption as a more meaningful way of assessing the impact of biological factors on human behavior. By comparing the criminal behavior of adopted children to that of their biological parents and their adoptive parents, researchers can arrive at better estimates of the impact of inheritance. Mednick and Volavka (1977) conducted such a study in Denmark for all adoptions between 1924 and 1947. Denmark is often the site of such adoption studies because Danish records of vital statistics including adoptions have been meticulously kept since the 1890s. In a study of more than 14,000 adoptions, Mednick and Volavka found that children who had biological parents with criminal convictions had a far greater chance of being involved in deviant behavior than those who had noncriminal biological parents. Figure 5-1 shows the percentage of adoptees who had a criminal conviction in the four possible combinations of adoptive and biological parents with or without criminal convictions.

Among adoptees whose adoptive and biological parents had no criminal convictions, only 13.5 percent of these had a criminal conviction. Of those whose adoptive and biological parents had a criminal conviction, 24.5 percent had a criminal conviction. A biological influence is suggested by the two off-diagonal cells. About 15 percent of sons had a criminal record when their adoptive parent had a criminal conviction and the biological parent did not. In contrast, 20 percent of those with a convicted biological parent and a crime-free adoptive parent had a conviction. While the percent difference is not dramatic, having parents with a criminal conviction increases the chances that a child will also have a criminal conviction. Serious methodological problems cloud the overall findings from adoption studies. For one, the definitions of criminal behavior vary from study to study. A second problem is the amount of time children spend with their biological parents before being adopted. A third problem is that adoptive parents are screened. In the Danish study adoptive parents could not have a criminal record for the preceding five years. Thus the findings from adoption studies must be cautiously reviewed.

Figure 5-1   Percent of Sons with Criminal Records by Criminal Conviction of Parents

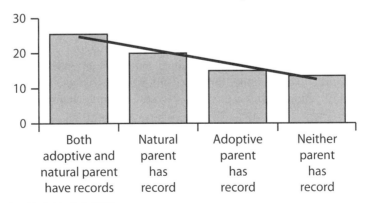

Source: Based on Mednick et al., 1984.

Neurological Functioning

Recent attempts to differentiate between persistent and nonpersistent offenders have prompted new arguments about neurological and cognitive functioning in relation to delinquency. Terrie Moffitt (2003) differentiates between two types of offenders, those youth whose offenses primarily occur in adolescence (adolescent-limited offenders) and those that offend throughout the life course (life-course persistent). Moffitt suggests that it is within this second type of offender that some underlying biological or neurological characteristic may operate. If offending is persistent across the life course, then it is plausible to hypothesize that some characteristic that persists across the life course, such as neurological problems, should be considered.

Cauffman, Steinberg, and Piquero (2005) attempted a test of Moffitt's argument by examining cognitive functioning, autonomic reactivity, and other biological factors among serious offenders being held by the California Youth Authority (CYA) and adolescents attending public schools in northern California. They were especially interested in deficits in the prefrontal lobe that affect "executive functioning" (i.e. impulse control, affect regulation, attention, and planning). Deficiencies in such functioning are suspect as correlates of delinquency. They report support for the argument that serious CYA offenders had poor scores on tasks involving the prefrontal cortex. In contrast, variation in delinquency among the public high school students was unrelated to frontal lobe functioning.

Their findings suggest that there may be a small category of serious offenders in which cognitive functioning may play a role in persistent offending. However, as they note, differences were found for some measures of cognitive functioning but not others. Moreover, the tests were administered among current CYA and high school youth, raising issues of causal order. Abuse, violence, diet, and a variety of traumas may have led to problems in cognitive functioning. In short, although the research provides an interesting perspective on different types of offenders, the unique causal relevance of cognitive functioning has not been established. On the other hand, neither has it been shown to be irrelevant.

Biology and Delinquency: An Overview

Modern biological explanations of crime have far surpassed the unscientific assertions of the early biological school. However, despite the enormous advances in understanding the role of human biology, its relationship to crime is still uncertain. For some, biology might play a limited but essential role. Fishbein, for example, argues for the role of a conditional free will which "postulates that individuals choose a course of action within a preset, yet to some degree changeable range of possibilities" (see Rojek and Jensen, 1996:104). On the other hand, Gottfredson and Hirschi looked at the evidence of biology and crime and found no convincing evidence whatsoever that biology has any significant role to play in explaining delinquency (see Rojek and Jensen, 1996). Glenn Walters and Thomas White reviewed an exhausting list of studies on crime and heredity and concluded that "genetic factors are undoubtedly correlated with various measures of criminality, but the large number of methodological flaws and limitations in the research should make one cautious in drawing any causal inferences at this point in time" (1989:478). In a later study, Walters (1992) concluded, after examining different studies on biological explanations, that the supporting findings were quite weak. Acknowledging the limitations of research on biological and genetic determinants of predispositions to crime, Rowe concludes: "The existence of a modest genetic influence on variation in criminal disposition is perfectly consistent with simultaneous influence of the social environment" (2002:15). Finally, Ronald Akers and Christine Sellers concluded:

> There is little to disagree with in the assertion that biology interacts with the environment. The real question involves the nature of that interaction and the extent to which crime is influenced by biology or environment. If a theory proposes that biological defects or abnormalities are the direct cause of all or most criminal behavior, it is not likely to be supported by empirical evidence. (2004:64)

Psychological Schools of Thought

In our review of biological perspectives, we noted the gradual shift away from the assumption that lawbreakers are born criminals to the notion that there are biological factors that can predispose a person to antisocial behavior when certain environmental conditions exist. Beginning with the work of Sigmund Freud (1856–1939), a new perspective for understanding human behavior emerged. This perspective attributed troublesome behavior to psychological problems anyone could encounter in the course of human development. Leading further away from the notion of born criminal types, the new perspective emphasized experiences that anyone might have and learning processes that anyone might experience.

The Psychoanalytic Approach

The shift away from the assumption that people who break the law are biologically or constitutionally different from others is reflected in the work of Sigmund Freud and other psychoanalysts. Freud was not particularly concerned with explaining criminal behavior but, rather, with advancing his ideas on mental illness. However, the Freudian psychoanalytic approach opened a new dimension to the study of deviant behavior by proposing that problem behavior reflects problems in personality development.

Freud postulated that the human personality can be conceived of in terms of three basic forces. At birth the only force that functions is the **id**. The id is concerned with immediate gratification and is concerned only with pleasure. As the child grows, an **ego** develops that is in close contact with social reality. The ego attempts to curb the drives and urges of the id and to direct behavior in a way that is consistent with physical and social reality. The **superego**, the last element of the personality to develop, captures the idea of a conscience that attempts to restrain the id. Freud introduced the concept of the unconscious by describing the id and superego as basically unconscious elements of the personality and the ego as the conscious part.

From the Freudian perspective, the human personality is characterized by a struggle between the creative urges of the id and the constraining forces of the ego and the superego. The "healthy" personality achieves a balance between these forces. Personality disorders arise when one of the forces is too dominant. For example, domination of the id could be reflected in criminal activities, and an overdeveloped superego could result in anxiety neurosis. Normal socialization processes are conducive to healthy personality development, but if the socializing agents are punitive, inconsistent, or arbitrary, the child's personality may get out of balance. Thus, from the psychoanalytic view, delinquent behavior can be symptomatic of deep emotional conflicts and unconscious motivations. All people are seen as antisocial by nature, but through balanced, proper socialization they become law-abiding citizens.

From a psychoanalytic perspective, what are the deficiencies that can result in delinquency? An almost endless list of specific problems could be compiled. There are, however, some basic categories of problems that psychoanalysts stress. One category centers around the development of the superego. Normal personality development supposedly entails incorporation of ego ideals—that is, identification with the social and ethical standards of conduct of significant people in one's environment. If experiences or circumstances interfere with superego development, or if ego ideals are themselves criminal, then delinquency can result.

Another cause of delinquency from the psychoanalytic perspective is inadequate ego development. The infant is depicted as guided by the pleasure principle in seeking gratification of instinctive needs. However, normal personality development involves learning to take reality into account (the reality principle). To achieve normal development, the ego must learn to sacrifice immediate pleasures in order to achieve pleasure in the future. Thus, from the psychoanalytic perspective, the inability to defer gratification is indicative of disturbed ego development and is a potential source of delinquency.

The normal personality is characterized by harmony, or balance, between instinctive needs, reality, and the conscience. If the ego and superego are unable to control instinctive needs, the individual is likely to get into trouble with others in his or her environment. On the other hand, if such needs are denied or repressed by an overly rigid ego or superego, the individual may develop mental and behavioral problems that are a reflection of the inner tension or conflict. In Kate Friedlander's words, "Generally speaking, delinquent behavior is the result of a disturbance in the relative strength of the three domains of the mind—the id, the ego, and the superego" (1947:185).

The proof that psychoanalysts offer for these theories is very different from that demanded by social scientists. Psychoanalysts support their arguments with case histories of individuals who come to their attention. If a person is experiencing some sort of mental, emotional, or behavioral difficulty, analysts attempt to identify the source of the problem by encouraging the person to talk freely about past experiences that may have caused unconscious conflicts. Thus, causes are discovered "after the fact." Rather than identifying those conditions thought to generate delinquency, measuring them, and assessing whether or not such conditions increase the probability of delinquency, psychoanalysts point to cases that support their notions. It is unlikely that psychoanalytic theories will ever be tested in terms of the standards of causation that are central to the social sciences. In the psychoanalytic view, causes are unknown to the subject and can only be discovered with the help of experts who have special psychoanalytic training. Thus, there is no way for an outsider to prove or disprove the validity of psychoanalytic explanations. The "data" that support psychoanalytic theories are events and experiences that only the expert is qualified to interpret. The inference of unconscious motives is often made through techniques that are largely subjective and susceptible to multiple interpretations such as dream analysis, hypnosis, and Rorschach test. Donald Shoemaker concludes that "the field of psychotherapy thus becomes based more on art than on science" (2000:58).

On the other hand, some basic psychoanalytic notions are quite compatible with the sociological explanations that we will consider in the next chapter. For example, the assumption that the attempt to maximize pleasure can lead to conflict with the law if not checked by socialization is quite compatible with a brand of sociological theory known as social control theory. The emphasis in psychoanalytic theory on relationships with parents and identification with adult ego ideals is quite compatible with the emphasis of some sociological theories on the family in delinquency causation. However, sociological theorists are at odds with psychoanalytic explanations that attribute crime and delinquency to hidden mental conflicts because only the therapist is able to determine when these unconscious urges are operative. The focus in sociological explanations is on more observable and more readily measurable aspects of the external social environment and the groups to which an individual belongs. Moreover, although the psychoanalytic approach acknowledges that human social adaptation is a continuous, lifelong process, it focuses extensively on early childhood experiences and maternal relationships. Both may be important for understanding delinquency, but sociologists tends to focus more extensively on institutions that a child enters in later childhood and adolescence, such as the school and adolescent society. The sociological focus includes forces that are not likely to be recognized when the emphasis is on early childhood—for example, limited economic opportunity, legitimacy of the law, and social standing.

Sociologists also question the cultural biases that tend to be implicit in psychoanalytic notions. What is "normal" personality development? The answers depend on the norms or standards of the system being studied. Psychoanalytic theory maintains that learning to defer gratification in the short run for the sake of gratification in the long run is a normal, healthy stage in human social adaptation. But what if a child is born into an environment where the likelihood of gratification in the long run is extremely uncertain? Children in economically secure, predictable environments where parents and other agents insure future gratification, have reason to follow such a pattern of adaptation. Under different circumstances, focusing on immediate gratification may be normal. Such sayings as "Live for today and let tomorrow take care of itself" were not necessarily originated by people with "abnormal" personalities.

Psychopathology

Psychiatrists, psychologists, and some sociologists have used the concept of the **psychopath** in dealing with criminality. This concept grew out of the notion that some criminals are so depraved, so bad, or so "morally insane" that they stand out from the ordinary criminal population. The psychopath has been depicted as having a complex of character traits that supposedly makes him unique among criminals. Sociologists William and Joan McCord have described the psychopath as follows:

> The psychopath is asocial. His conduct often brings him into conflict with society. The psychopath is driven by primitive desires and an exaggerated craving for excitement. In his self-centered search for pleasure, he ignores restrictions of his culture.

The psychopath is highly impulsive. He is a man for whom the moment is a segment of time detached from all others. His actions are unplanned and guided by his whims. The psychopath is aggressive. He has learned few socialized ways of coping with frustration. The psychopath feels little, if any, guilt. He can commit the most appalling acts, yet view them without remorse. The psychopath has a warped capacity for love. His emotional relationships, when they exist, are meager, fleeting, and destined to satisfy his own desires. These last two traits, guiltlessness and lovelessness, conspicuously make the psychopath as different from other men. (1964:16)

The term *psychopath* is used interchangeably with the more recent terms *sociopath* and *antisocial personality*. Collectively, the three terms are used by various psychiatrists in describing individuals who are unsocialized, irresponsible, and unable to feel guilt or learn from experience or punishment, as defined in the *Diagnostic and Statistical Manual of Mental Disorders*.

Attempts to use the concept of the psychopath to explain illegal behavior can easily result in a circular argument. Illegal behavior is taken as symptomatic of some deeper psychopathology, but the evidence for that pathology is the very behavior to be explained. If a person commits irresponsible acts, then is the behavior explained by deeming that person "irresponsible"? To argue that a person commits antisocial, aggressive, and impulsive acts because he or she is antisocial, aggressive, and impulsive is hardly a satisfactory explanation.

Diagnoses as psychopathic have been criticized as a basis for predicting future dangerousness. William McCord and Jose Sanchez (1983) followed children over a twenty-five year period who were diagnosed as psychopathic at two juvenile institutions. They found very little evidence to suggest that these children were any more crime prone than other delinquents who were not considered to be psychopaths.

As a further example, in 1966 the Supreme Court ordered that 967 patients who were considered dangerous and institutionalized in a mental hospital for the criminally insane be transferred to regular mental hospitals (Steadman, 1973). The Court found that the procedures for labeling individuals "dangerous" were quite arbitrary. Of the 967 patients, only 26 (2.7 percent) were ever returned to a hospital for the criminally insane. One-half of the original group was eventually discharged within a relatively short period of time and of those released, over 80 percent had no further arrests.

Seymour Halleck's query about whether psychopathy is a "form of mental illness, a form of evil, or a form of fiction" (Kittrie, 1971:170) has yet to be answered. Many feel the term is overused and too readily applied to any offender who has committed a serious or violent offense. Katz and Chambliss (Sheley, 1995) conclude that it is impossible to define psychopathy. The term is so broad as to be applied to any and all criminals and ought to be eliminated in any discussion of criminal behavior. The Gluecks found that nondelinquents were more neurotic than delinquents and that nearly half of the delinquents had "no conspicuous pathology" as compared to 56 percent of the nondelinquents (Glueck and Glueck, 1950).

Personality Research

Some psychological researchers have attempted to provide empirical support for the notion that certain personality types are unusually prone to delinquency. Personality traits such as impulsiveness, aggressiveness, sensation-seeking, and rebelliousness are commonly viewed as characteristics of deviant personality traits. Two popular personality tests used in the study of delinquency are the *Minnesota Multiphasic Personality Inventory* (MMPI), a self-administered inventory of 550 items with several subscales to measure different personality traits, and the *California Personality Inventory* (CPI), composed of 480 items.

The basic approach in using MMPI or CPI inventories is to measure variations in personality traits such as tolerance, sociability, dominance, and socialization. It is suggested that nondelinquents and delinquents differ in terms of personality traits, and the MMPI or CPI can therefore be used to predict delinquent behavior. Consider, for example, the following items from the CPI and what they purport to measure:

Scale	*Item*	*Purpose*
Self-control	I would do almost anything on a dare.	To assess self-regulation and freedom from impulsivity.
Sense of well-being	I am afraid to be alone in the dark.	To discriminate individuals feigning neurosis from normals and psychiatric patients.
Tolerance	I feel sure there is only one true religion.	To identify accepting, non-judgmental social beliefs and attitudes.
Femininity	I would like to be a nurse.	To define a continuum of psychological femininity.

The validity and reliability of such personality inventories have been highly criticized. The scales were developed using small samples, generally less than fifty people. Second, the labeling of a set of responses as "self-control," or "tolerance" is open to debate. Third, the redundancy among such scales as sociability, social presence, socialization, or communality is of dubious scientific value. Fourth, the scales were developed by comparing the responses of psychiatrically diagnosed individuals with those of "normal" individuals. What constitutes a "normal" individual is open to debate, and psychiatric diagnoses of what constitutes mental impairment vary by hospital or clinic. Whatever findings emerge using the MMPI or CPI must be very cautiously interpreted.

It has been argued that a subscale known as the *psychopathic deviate scale* (Pd scale) on the MMPI can differentiate delinquents from nondelinquents. However, at least fourteen items in the MMPI inventory actually measure self-reported delinquency, and one item in the psychopathic deviate scale calls for a response to the statement, "I have never been in trouble with the law." We have already seen that the concept of psychopath does not get us very far in explaining delinquency since the definition of psychopath includes reference to the very behaviors that the concept is meant to explain. Similarly, the Pd scale itself includes measures of the very behavior that the scale is introduced to explain. In other words, the scale may show nothing more than that adolescents who have been in trouble with the law are more likely than those who have not been in trouble with the law to indicate they have been in trouble with the law! We have to conclude that such tests do not tell us much about the causes of delinquency.

The overall results of using personality traits as a discriminant characteristic that differentiates delinquents from nondelinquents have not been impressive. Daniel Curran and Claire Renzetti (1994) argue that most delinquents are psychologically normal. If you use the analogy of delinquency as drift—with juveniles drifting or flirting with the law and then drifting out of delinquency—this would infer that most of the time even serious delinquents are not involved with law-violating behavior. Therefore, most of the time delinquents can be law abiding and not psychologically impaired. A second problem is that delinquent behavior is not a dichotomy, that is, deviant or not deviant, but a continuum. There are degrees of seriousness, but personality inventories see delinquency as an either/or situation. Akers (1994) concludes that studies based on personality characteristics "have not been able to produce findings to support personality variables as major causes of criminal and delinquent behavior" (1994:88).

Learning Theories

Much of the biological theory and research as well as most psychological theories previously summarized assume that delinquents and criminals are somehow deficient in ways that affect their ability to learn—whether that deficiency is a result of temperament, irritability, mental ability, conditionability, or cognitive functioning. However, there are several different learning processes that can affect behavior, and several learning mechanisms have been introduced in the explanation of delinquency. The emphasis in some theories is on how delinquency and crime can result from *normal learning* processes rather than deficiencies in learning.

Classical Conditioning

Most college students have heard of Russian physiologist Ivan Pavlov and of "Pavlov's dogs." Pavlov conducted experiments in which he rang a bell before giving a dog a piece of meat. Pavlov found that after he had repeated this procedure 30 or 40 times, the dog began to salivate at the sound of the bell even when it was not given meat. The dog's salivation was a *conditioned response* to a stimulus (the bell) that had come to signal, or cue, the presentation of food. Over time, if the bell was not followed by food, the response gradually faded (*extinction*), although it could reappear (*spontaneous recovery*). Pavlov also found that such learned associations or conditioned responses could be transferred to new but similar situations and stimuli (*generalization*).

Building on the work of psychologist Hans Eysenck, Gordon Trasler applied some of Pavlov's classic principles of learning to the explanation of criminality. Trasler (1962) argued that learning experiences when we are very young affect the probability of delinquency and crime later in life. For example, when parents respond negatively to a child's breaking rules at home, the child will experience anxiety, an involuntary reaction like the salivation of Pavlov's dogs. Such anxiety can become a conditioned response to a variety of similar situations. Since anxiety is viewed as a state that people like to avoid, people supposedly avoid or escape situations that cause anxiety. Thus, Trasler's theory is that conformity is *escape-avoidance behavior* and the inhibition of criminality is a learned, conditioned response that is strongly resistant to extinction because it functions to reduce anxiety. Trasler did introduce personality notions into his theory when he argued that some people are more resistant to such conditioning than others—specifically, people who are outgoing and crave excitement (extroverts) are resistant to escape-avoidance conditioning, while people who are quiet, self-controlled, and introspective (introverts) readily subject to such conditioning. The most central principle in Trasler's theory, however, is the idea that cues in learning situations come to be coupled with reactions of the involuntary nervous and glandular system and that these conditioned reactions come to act as a barrier to crime.

Trasler illustrated his concept of *passive avoidance conditioning* with experiments in which rats were given an unpleasant stimulus when they touched a lever that normally released food pellets. Even after the negative reinforcement was removed, the rats still would not touch the lever. The "anxiety" that the rats had acquired in anticipation of punishment continued, even though the punishment no longer existed. Similarly, if an individual is conditioned to experience punishment for wrongdoing during early years of socialization and thereby acquires anxiety, the individual will experience anxiety in contemplating delinquent behavior, even when the actual probability of punishment is remote. In this fashion, deviant behavior is avoided.

Operant Conditioning

Operant theory is another brand of learning theory that has been applied to the study of crime and delinquency. Operant theory draws on the theoretical formulations of B. F. Skinner (1904–1990), acclaimed as the most influential psychologist of the twentieth century. Rather than focusing on ill-defined concepts of personality or on involuntary conditioned reactions, operant theorists focus on behaviors that are considered to be voluntary and controlled by the central nervous system. For Skinner, learning takes place by trial and error. *Operant behavior* is behavior that is controlled by its consequences. Stimuli that increase or strengthen the behavior are called *reinforcers*, and stimuli that decrease or weaken the behavior are known as *punishers*. Stimuli that become learned cues associated with reinforcement or punishment are called *discriminative stimuli*. In classical conditioning, as with Pavlov's dogs, the organism is passive and simply learns what to expect from the environment; that is, a stimulus leads to a response. However, in operant conditioning, the organism is active and learns how to get what it wants from the environment.

The emphasis in operant theory is on behavior and the explanation of behavior in terms of observable aspects of the individual's environment. Radical behaviorists feel that such concepts as personality are unobservable artifacts that contribute nothing to the explanation of behavior but, rather, hinder scientific progress. Skinner (1971) was particularly adamant in attacking theories that assume the existence of autonomous human beings who act of their own free will. Skinner believed that a science of behavior will be achieved only if such notions as free will and personality are abandoned.

According to the principles of **operant conditioning**, juvenile delinquency is a learned behavior. If a delinquent act results in positive feedback (praise, admiration, envy), the behavior will be strengthened. If the delinquent act results in negative feedback or punishment, the behavior will decrease. For Skinner, behavior is controlled by the environment, not by internal forces. Behavior is modified by changing the reward system, such that delinquent acts receive negative rewards and law-abiding behavior receives positive rewards. Whether deviant behavior or conforming behavior persists depends on the rewards or punishments for the behavior. In his book *Beyond Freedom and Dignity* (1971), Skinner dismissed the notion of individual freedom and argued that our actions are nothing more than a set of behaviors shaped by the environment.

Differential Association Theory

We noted in chapter 1 that as early as 1896, American sociologists had postulated that criminal or delinquent behavior is learned behavior. A formal statement of this position—known as the differential association theory of criminal behavior—was first presented by Edwin Sutherland in 1939. Sutherland's basic premise was that deviant behavior was not the product of some sort of Freudian unconscious drives or Lombrosian biological factors but simply was behavior that was the product of social interaction. His first edition of *Criminology*, published in 1924, was a modest attempt to refute the theories of heredity. The second edition appeared in 1934, but it was in his third edition in 1939 that the concept of differential association appeared. Sutherland further modified his theory in 1947 and the theory has remained unchanged since that edition. He named the perspective **differential association theory** because delinquency was attributed to the balance of associations with people who defined lawbreaking in favorable and unfavorable terms. The most central learning process was normative—delinquency was a product of an excess of "definitions" favorable to lawbreaking as compared to definitions unfavorable to lawbreaking. Such definitions were learned in social interaction in intimate groups.

From this perspective delinquency did not result from deficiencies in learning, but rather, reflected the successful learning of values, norms, and beliefs which encouraged delinquency. Fundamental to differential association theory is the view that deviant behavior is learned in much the same way as conforming behavior. Sutherland stated that "criminal behavior as human behavior, has much in common with non-criminal behavior, and must be explained within the same general framework used to explain other human behavior" (Sutherland and Cressey, 1970:73). In other words, delinquency was not an inherited trait but like any other behavior, it involved socialization. A person must learn how to commit a delinquent act and must acquire the necessary attitudes, motives, and rationalizations conducive to the violation of legal norms. Sutherland's conception of crime as conformity to deviant norms rather than abnormality directed attention away from pathological conditions to more normal and natural factors. It provided an explanation of crime and delinquency in diverse social settings and cultures. As a social psychological theory, differential association theory explains why adolescents become drawn into criminal behavior. As a structural theory, it explains why crime rates vary in different parts of the community. For his contribution, Sutherland is referred to as the "Dean of American criminology."

Differential Reinforcement Theory

In an effort to provide a more precise specification of learning theory, Robert Burgess and Ronald Akers formulated what they called **differential association-reinforcement theory** (1966). Their purpose was to reformulate Sutherland's approach in terms of general principles of behaviorism. In their original formulation of the theory the emphasis was on delinquency as "operant" behavior; that is, involvement in delinquency could be explained by the reinforcing or punishing consequences in the environment. In some instances, the behavior could be explained by its nonsocial reinforcement. If a person is hungry and alleviates that hunger by stealing food and eating it and experiences few negative consequences for doing so, then the behavior is likely to be repeated. Its frequency is affected by its nonsocial outcomes.

While incorporating nonsocial reinforcement, greater emphasis is placed on variations in the reactions of others, and the theory has come to be referred to as a "social learning" theory of delinquency. As summarized by Akers and his colleagues:

> The primary learning mechanism in social behavior is operant (instrumental conditioning in which behavior is shaped by the stimuli which follow, or are consequences of the behavior). Social behavior is acquired through direct conditioning and through imitation or modeling of others' behavior. Behavior is strengthened through reward (positive reinforcement) and avoidance of punishment (negative reinforcement) or weakened by averse stimuli (positive punishment) and loss of reward (negative punishment). (Akers et al., 1979:637)

The person first learns the behavior in question through processes of imitation or through observing consequences experienced by others (vicarious reinforcement). The behavior is then maintained by rewards and punishments from the group. The family, peers, and significant others such as teachers are especially important for both imitation and differential reinforcement of behaviors. This theory has been tested in hundreds of articles dealing with drug use, delinquency, and a wide range of law-breaking behaviors and has fared quite well. It appears safe to conclude that the probability of delinquency for any given individual is affected by the behavior and reactions of significant others, and that imitation, differential reinforcement, and the values, norms, and beliefs that people learn in the process each seem to play a role in explaining delinquency. Since this theory has been elaborated by sociologists as well as psychologists, we will return to some issues involving the theory in chapter 6.

Differential reinforcement theory has focused on the mechanisms that explain how individuals learn deviant and conforming behavior and, for much of its history, paid relatively little attention to identifying the specific social environments where these processes generate one or the other form of behavior. However, as will be elaborated in chapter 6, Akers (1998) has formulated a version of learning theory that he calls "social structure/social learning theory," which encompasses such issues.

Explicitly or implicitly, the sociological perspectives that we will consider in the following chapter make assumptions about the conditions affecting the differential reinforcement of criminal and conforming behavior. For example, "social disorganization" perspectives attribute variation in crime to variation in the vitality of certain institutions that have traditionally rewarded conformity and punished deviance (such as the family, the neighborhood, the church, and the school). If these social institutions are "disorganized" due to such factors as population change, urbanization, and industrialization, the probability that crime will be punished and conformity rewarded may be quite low. Similarly, the "strain" theorists argue that when people find that the legitimate opportunity to obtain certain goals or rewards is limited, they are likely to explore or invent illegitimate alternatives. If specific social groups come to approve illegitimate avenues for achieving success, or if new standards of conduct and order emerge where conventional institutions have failed, crime and delinquency may then become subculturally acceptable ways of behaving. Thus, variable crime rates may reflect normative conflict, which is the central tenet of the "cultural conflict" theories we will consider later.

Social learning theories are quite compatible with sociological perspectives since they postulate that other people play a major role in the process through which individuals learn delinquent behavior. They also attempt to delineate the nature of learning processes, which sociologists have taken for granted. On the other hand, sociologists have been more concerned than psychologists and learning theorists with identifying the social conditions that structure the distribution of differential learning processes. As Akers has noted:

> The general culture and structure of society and the particular groups, subcultures, and social situations in which the individual participates provide learning environments in which the norms define what is approved and disapproved and the reactions of others (for example, in applying social sanctions) attach different reinforcing or punishing consequences to this behavior. In a sense, then, social structure is an arrangement of sets and schedules of reinforcement contingencies. (1977:64)

We turn to such perspectives in the next chapter, where we consider theory and research that attempt to explain delinquency by focusing on the structural, cultural, and group characteristics that shape learning processes.

Summary

We began this chapter by outlining the different sources people rely on in seeking answers to questions about the causes of delinquency—public opinion, expert testimony, and experience. As an alternative to these sources, social scientists have attempted to gather and analyze data on crime and criminals and on delinquency and delinquents, with the aim of identifying characteristics of people or their environments that increase the probability of crime and delinquency. In the course of these efforts, scientists have developed a set of standards for assessing claims that some characteristic or condition is a cause of crime or delinquency. Such standards require that causal claims be backed up with evidence that (1) shows an association, (2) eliminates the possibility of spuriousness, and (3) establishes a causal order. Causal claims should also be preceded by a concerted effort to acquire data representative of the populations under study and to create valid, reliable measures of variables. Even when these standards have been taken into account, there may be divergent views concerning the mechanisms or processes through which the causal relationship is established. Different theorists may identify different intervening variables. Finally, it is also vital to specify the circumstances of sample, setting, and time that may affect the relationships observed. It is important to have a rudimentary understanding of these issues because most criticisms of research focus on failures to take one or more of them into account.

The early biological research we reviewed was often characterized by sampling bias, ill-defined or underdefined concepts, possibilities of spuriousness, alternative causal orders, and failure to consider nonbiological interpretations. On the other hand, more recent biological studies overcome many of these criticisms and have yielded results suggesting possible genetic, hormonal, or neurological correlates of criminal and delinquent behavior.

The development of psychoanalytic and psychological schools of thought represented a shift away from the assumption that criminals and delinquents are basically different types of organisms to the view that they are simply people who have encountered problems while in the process of developing into social beings. The standards of proof for such theories are very different from those expected in the social sciences. We cannot judge whether psychoanalytic perspectives are correct or incorrect explanations of delinquency since they have not been tested in terms of the standards of causation that are central to the social sciences.

The concept of the psychopath and attempts to measure the dimensions of the psychopathic personality have not advanced our understanding of crime and delinquency. Definitions of the concept, as well as scales that are presumed to measure it, actually include reference to the very phenomenon to be explained. We certainly do not doubt that people's feelings, attitudes, and beliefs are correlated with their behavior, but we do question whether the search for personality differences has in any way provided scientifically adequate or consistent evidence about such correlations.

One issue on which sociological and psychological theories are likely to agree is that much (if not most) delinquent behavior is learned behavior. Psychologists and social psychologists vary in the learning processes that they emphasize and in the degree to which they incorporate notions of personality into their theories. Some focus on principles of classic conditioning and involuntary anxiety reactions, while others focus on operant conditioning that involves voluntary behavior and on the interplay between behavior and its consequences. Sociologists have actually used principles of operant conditioning to restate sociological theory. Such efforts show lines of convergence between sociological and psychological perspectives, with the latter identifying learning processes and the former identifying characteristics of society, culture, or groups that structure distribution of those learning processes.

Discussion Questions

1. Suppose someone claims that television violence is a cause of delinquency as evidenced by the fact that youths with delinquent records watch more television than youths without such records. Evaluate the statement based on the requirements for making causal claims.

2. Given that more than one study has found a difference in body type when comparing delinquent and nondelinquent boys, what keeps us from automatically accepting this finding as evidence of a genetic, physiological, or biological cause of delinquency?

3. Do you have an image of what a "delinquent" looks like? Do you have any ideas about the origins of such images? What consequences might your image have for the way you react to certain people?

4. Research on identical twins has shown that they exhibit more nearly similar behavior than fraternal twins even when environmental or social factors have been controlled. Does this prove that tendencies toward criminality are inherited? Defend your view.

5. What emphases in psychoanalytic theory are compatible with sociological perspectives? What characteristics contrast with sociological perspectives?

6. On what grounds do your text's authors take the position that the concept of psychopath as used cannot take us very far in the explanation of crime and delinquency?

7. Which particular personality inventory has most consistently differentiated between delinquents and nondelinquents? Does this test enable us to conclude that researchers have isolated a personality trait that is causally related to delinquency? Justify your answer.

8. Recent attempts to differentiate between persistent and nonpersistent offenders have prompted new arguments about neurological and cognitive functioning in relation to delinquency. Describe what is known at this point in time.

9. What is "social" about social learning theory? How do modern reformulations compare with Sutherland's original formulation of differential association theory?

10. Compare classical conditioning theory with operant learning theory. Give an example of how each could be applied to the explanation of delinquency.

References

Akers, R. L. 1977. *Deviant Behavior.* Belmont, CA: Wadsworth.

———. 1994. *Criminological Theories: Introduction and Evaluation.* Los Angeles: Roxbury.

———. 1998. *Social Learning and Social Structure: A General Theory of Crime and Deviance.* Boston: Northeastern University Press.

Akers, R. L., M. D. Krohn, L. Lanza-Kaduce, and M. Radosevich. 1979. "Social Learning and Deviant Behavior: A Specific Test of a General Theory." *American Sociological Review* 44:636–55.

Akers, R. L., and C. S. Sellers. 2004. *Criminological Theories: Introduction, Evaluation and Application.* 4th ed. Los Angeles: Roxbury.

Booth, A., and D. W. Osgood. 1993. "The Influence of Testosterone on Deviance in Adulthood: Assessing and Explaining the Relationship." *Criminology* 31:93–117.

Burgess, R. L., and R. L. Akers. 1966. "A Differential Association-Reinforcement Theory of Criminal Behavior." *Social Problems* 14 (Fall): 128–47.

Cauffman, E., L. Steinberg, and A. R. Piquero. 2005. "Psychological, Neuropsychological and Physiological Correlates of Serious Anti-Social Behavior in Adolescence: The Role of Self-Control." *Criminology* 43:133–76.

Christiansen, K. O. 1977. "A Preliminary Study of Criminology among Twins." In *Biosocial Bases of Criminal Behavior,* edited by S. Mednick and K. Christiansen. New York: Gardner Press.

Cortes, J. B., and F. M. Gatti. 1972. *Delinquency and Crime.* New York: Seminar Press.

Curran, D. J., and C. M. Renzetti. 1994. *Theories of Crime.* Needham Heights, MA: Allyn & Bacon.

Davis, J. A., and T. W. Smith. 2002. *General Social Survey.* Chicago: National Opinion Research Center (machine-readable data file).

Dugdale, R. L. 1877. "The Jukes: A Study in Crime." In *Pauperism, Disease, and Heredity.* 4th ed. New York: Putnam.

Ellis, L. 1982. "Genetics and Criminal Behavior." *Criminology* 20:43–66.

Estabrook, A. H. 1916. *The Jukes in 1915.* Washington, DC: Carnegie Institute.

Friedlander, K. 1947. *The Psycho-Analytic Approach to Juvenile Delinquency.* New York: International Universities Press.

Gallup Poll. 2006. Gallup Poll New Service, Social Series Crime. October 9–12.

Glueck, S., and E. Glueck. 1950. *Unraveling Juvenile Delinquency.* New York: Commonwealth Fund.

Goring, C. 1913. *The English Convict.* London: His Majesty's Stationery Office.

Gottfredson, M., and T. Hirschi. 1990. *A General Theory of Crime.* Palo Alto, CA: Stanford University Press.

Hammer, R. 1989. *The Illustrated History of Organized Crime.* Philadelphia: Running Press.

Hirschi, T. 1969. *Causes of Delinquency.* Berkeley: University of California Press.

Hooton, E. A. 1939. *Crime and the Man.* Cambridge: Harvard University Press.

Jacobs, P. A., M. Brunton, M. M. Melville, R. P. Brittain, and W. F. McClemont. 1965. "Aggressive Behavior, Mental Subnormality, and the XYY Male." *Nature* 208 (December): 1351.

Jankowski, M. S. 1991. *Islands in the Street: Gangs and American Urban Society.* Berkeley: University of California Press.

Jensen, G. F. 1996. "Defiance and Gang Identity: Quantitative Tests of Qualitative Hypotheses." *Journal of Gang Research* (Summer): 13–29.

Jones, M., and D. Jones. 2000. "The Contagious Nature of Antisocial Behavior." *Criminology* 38:25–46.

Kittrie, N. N. 1971. *The Right to Be Different: Deviance and Enforced Therapy.* Baltimore: Johns Hopkins Press.

Lombroso, C. 1911. *Crime, Its Causes and Remedies.* Boston: Little, Brown.

Lombroso, C., with G. Lombroso-Ferrero. 1911/1972. *Criminal Man.* Montclair, NJ: Patterson Smith.

McCandless, B. R., W. S. Persons, and A. Roberts. 1972. "Perceived Opportunity, Delinquency, Race and Body Build Among Delinquent Youth." *Journal of Consulting and Clinical Psychology* 38:281–91.

McCord, W., and J. McCord. 1964. *The Psychopath: An Essay on the Criminal Mind.* Princeton: Van Nostrand.

McCord, W., and J. Sanchez. 1983. "The Treatment of Deviant Children: A Twenty-Five Year Follow-Up Study." *Crime and Delinquency* 29:238–53.

Mednick, S. A., W. F. Gabrielli, and B. Hutchings. 1984. "Genetic Influences in Criminal Convictions: Evidence from an Adoption Cohort." *Science* 224:891–94.

Mednick, S. A., V. Pollock, J. Volavka, and W. F. Gabrielli. 1982. "Biology and Violence." In *Criminal Violence*, edited by M. E. Wolfgang and N. A. Weiner. Beverly Hills: Sage.

Mednick, S. A., and J. Volavka. 1977. "Biology and Crime." In *Biosocial Bases of Criminal Behavior*, edited by S. Mednick and K. Christiansen. New York: Gardner Press.

———. 1980. "Biology and Crime." *In Crime and Justice: An Annual Review of Research*, edited by N. Morris and M. Tonry. Chicago: University of Chicago Press.

Moffitt, T. 2003. "Life-Course-Persistent and Adolescent-Limited Anti-Social Behavior: A 10-Year Research Review and a Research Agenda." In *Causes of Conduct Disorder and Juvenile Delinquency*, edited by Benjamin B. Lahey, Terrie Moffitt, and Avshalom Caspi. New York: Guilford Press.

Pollock, V., S. Mednick, and W. Gabrielli, Jr. 1983. "Crime Causation: Biological Theories." In *Encyclopedia of Crime and Justice*, Vol. 1, edited by S. H. Hadish. New York: Free Press.

Price, W. H., and P. B. Whatmore. 1967. "Behavior Disorders and Patterns of Crime among XYY Males Identified at a Maximum Security Hospital." *British Medical Journal* 1:533–37.

Quinney, R. 1970. *The Problem of Crime.* New York: Dodd, Mead.

Reuter, E. B. 1939. "Review of E. A. Hooton, Crime and the Man." *American Journal of Sociology* 45:123–26.

Rojek, D. E., and G. F. Jensen. 1996. *Exploring Delinquency: Causes and Control.* Los Angeles: Roxbury.

Rowe, D. C. 1986. "Genetic and Environmental Components of Anti-Social Behavior: A Study of 265 Twin Pairs." *Criminology* 24:513–32.

———. 1987. "Resolving the Person-Situation Debate: Invitation to an Interdisciplinary Dialogue." *American Psychologist* 42:218–27.

———. 1990. "Inherited Dispositions for Learning Delinquent and Criminal Behavior: New Evidence." In *Evolution, the Brain, and Criminal Behavior: A Reader in Biosocial Criminology,* edited by L. Ellis and H. Hoffman. New York: Praeger.

Shah, S. A., and L. H. Roth. 1974. "Biological and Psychophysiological Factors in Criminology." In *Handbook of Criminology,* edited by D. Glaser. Chicago: Rand McNally.

Sheldon, W. H. 1949. *The Varieties of Delinquent Youth.* New York: Harper.

Sheley, J. F. 1995. *Criminology: A Contemporary Handbook.* Belmont, CA: Wadsworth.

Shoemaker, D. 2000. *Theories of Delinquency: An Examination of Explanations of Delinquent Behavior.* 4th ed. New York: Oxford Press.

Skinner, B. F. 1971. *Beyond Freedom and Dignity.* New York: Alfred A. Knopf.

Steadman, H. J. 1973. "The Psychiatric as a Conservative Agent of Social Control." *Social Problems* 20:263–71.

Sutherland, E. H. 1951. *Principles of Criminology.* 3rd and 4th eds. Philadelphia: J. B. Lippincott.

Sutherland, E. H., and D. Cressey. 1970. *Criminology.* 8th ed. Philadelphia: J. B. Lippincott.

Trasler, G. 1962. *The Explanation of Criminality.* London: Routledge & Kegan Paul.

———. 1987. "Biogenetic Factors." In *Handbook of Juvenile Delinquency,* edited by H. C. Quay. New York: John Wiley.

Udry, R. 1988. "Biological Predispositions and Social Control in Adolescent Sexual Behavior." *American Sociological Review* 53:709–22.

Walsh, A. 2000. "Behavior, Genetics and Anomie/Strain Theory." *Criminology* 38: 1075–1108.

Walters, G. 1992. "A Meta Analysis of the Gene Crime Relationship." *Criminology* 30: 595–613.

Walters, G., and T. White. 1989. "Heredity and Crime: Bad Genes or Bad Research?" *Criminology* 27:455–85.

Witkin, H., et al. 1976. "Criminality in XYY and XXY Men." *Science* 193 (August):547–55.

six

Explanations of Delinquency
Structure, Culture, and Interaction

> The individual person is more intrinsically a specimen of any group of which he is a member than is a plant or animal of its biological species. The plant or animal is a specimen of botanical or zoological species, because through heredity there is transmitted a uniform morphological and physiological pattern. The human being as a member of a social group is a specimen of it, not primarily, if at all, because of physique and temperament but by reason of his participation in its purposes and activities. Through communication and interaction the person acquires the language, tradition, standards, and practices of his group.
>
> (Clifford Shaw, *The Jack-Roller: A Delinquent Boy's Own Story*, 1930:186)

Sociology and the Study of Delinquency

In the last chapter we considered the ideas and research of a variety of physicians, biologists, psychologists, and learning theorists about how and why individuals come to be involved in crime and delinquency. To some, the answers can be found in properties of the body or physiological processes. To others, the answers reside in properties of the individual mind or personality. And to yet other scholars, the behavior of individuals is explained by contingencies of reward and punishment in the external world. In each instance, the explanation focuses on the behavior of individuals. One academic tradition, sociology, stresses ways of thinking about delinquency that focus our attention on aspects other than the individual or individual behavior.

Although the study of delinquency has become an interdisciplinary enterprise with scholars from a variety of academic fields involved, for much of the twentieth century the scientific study of delinquency (and crime) was dominated by scholars who are identified as "sociologists." **Sociology** is typically defined as the scientific study of social systems, and such systems can range from small groups of interacting individuals to nations and international systems. In the attempt to understand delinquency, one of the central premises characterizing a sociological approach has been that delinquency is more than the behavior of individuals. As noted in chapters 1 and 3, delinquency often is group behavior. In fact, some prominent early sociologists specifically excluded the explanation of individual lawbreaking from their theories. For example, Clifford Shaw and Henry McKay (1942) developed a theory of delinquency during the 1920s and 1930s that they intended to apply "primarily to those delinquent activities which become embodied in groups and social organization."

Moreover, many of the terms used in chapters 3 and 4, such as the "incidence" and "prevalence" of delinquency or a "crime rate," refer to characteristics of populations, territories, communities, or socially differentiated categories of people. Such measures involve the behavior of individuals but are viewed by sociologists as characteristics of social systems to be examined in relation to other properties of those systems. When we ask questions about variations in delinquency rates over time and social space, and begin to think of other characteristics of social systems that make sense of such variations, then we are asking distinctively sociological questions (see box 6-1).

Conceptions of Delinquency

The focus of many sociologists on the social nature of delinquency does not mean that such scholars have no interest in the behavior of individuals. In fact, a review of the sociological literature would show at least three distinct treatments of the subject

---

Box 6-1   What Is the Relationship?

Sociologists and sociologically oriented criminologists are interested in crime and delinquency along a number of dimensions: as individual and group behavior, as labels applied to individuals and groups, and as rates characteristic of territories and time periods. In the graph below each dot represents a county. In this instance, the state is Tennessee. The vertical axis (the "Y" axis) is the motor-vehicle theft rate per 100,000 population for each county in the year 2000. The horizontal axis (the "X" axis) is per capita income for each county in the year 2000. The straight line is called a regression line and gives you an idea of the nature of the relationship.

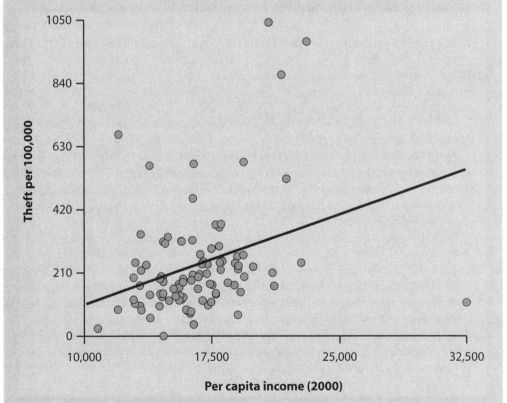

Describe the relationship between per capita income and rates of motor vehicle theft among counties. Do these data mean that rich people are more likely to steal cars? Can you think of any reasons why counties with high per capita income tend to have higher rates of motor vehicle theft?

Source: Federal Bureau of Investigation. 2002. *Crime in the United States.*

matter. First, delinquency can be conceived of as an activity involving a specific type of group—the **delinquent gang**. For much of the 1950s and 1960s, the nature and origins of delinquent gangs was the dominant focus among sociologists studying delinquency, and gangs were viewed as a particularly serious dimension of the crime problem.

A second conception of the delinquency problem, closely associated with the emphasis on gangs, stressed subcultures or contracultures. Delinquent **subcultures** consisted of youth with shared traditions or systems of values, norms, and beliefs passed on from one generation to another which facilitated trouble with the law. Such subcultural traditions were the subject matter of theories of gang delinquency since one of the distinct defining characteristics of such groups was, presumably, the criminogenic perspective shared by members of such groups. Different types of subcultures were thought to emerge in different types of urban settings. Delinquent **contracultures** were systems of values, norms, and beliefs shared by youth who rejected conventional culture and adopted contrary standards. Some youth were merely doing what was expected in their social world (a subculture), while others were depicted as rebelling against a conventional adult culture by constructing an oppositional or contracultural system of values, norms, or beliefs.

In the 1970s sociological theory and research shifted away from the study of gangs and the presumption of subcultural or contracultural traditions to a third conception of delinquency. Delinquency was simply *behavior in violation of the law.* Such behavior could occur in gangs but most of it involved casual groups of youth who did not fit the image of delinquent gangs. Rather than seeking an explanation of the origin and perpetuation of certain types of groups, subcultures, or contracultures, the focus shifted to the contribution of group processes and variable values to delinquent activity in a wide range of social settings among rather ordinary youths. However, the surge in youth and gang violence (see chapter 4) from the mid-1980s to the mid-1990s was accompanied by a resurgence of interest in delinquent gangs. This resurgence was prompted by a real increase in gang violence beginning in the mid-1980s. Although that "epidemic" peaked in the mid-1990s, the renewed interest in gangs has continued into the twenty-first century.

That resurgence should not lead us to believe that gang delinquency is the primary form that delinquency assumes as a type of peer group behavior. Delinquency tends to be peer group behavior, but the dominant conceptions of the subject matter have vacillated over time. As noted in chapter 4, the magnitude of the gang problem varies greatly depending on whether researchers use a broad definition encompassing a wide range of peer group behavior, or a very restrictive definition of what constitutes a gang. Although it is true that gang youth account for more than their share of serious delinquency, many common forms of delinquency and much serious delinquency involve casual peer groups as well as individuals acting alone.

The Subject Matter of Theories

Sociologists continue to debate which theory offers the best, most sociological, and most comprehensive view of delinquency. For purposes of this text, we are merely concerned that the reader recognize the distinctions among conceptions and the possibility that a theory which explains delinquent behavior does not necessarily apply to delinquent gangs. Moreover, a theory relevant to delinquent behavior in general may not incorporate exactly the same explanatory variables as a theory focusing on ordinary **peer group** delinquency or on specific types of delinquency (e.g., drug use). On the other hand, most theories have been applied explicitly or implicitly to the concept of delinquency as a group phenomenon and to the concept of delinquency as behavior that is in violation of the law. Similarly, most theories have been applied to explaining how individuals come to be involved in delinquency, as well as to explaining variations in delinquency rates among different groups or settings.

Sociological Schools of Thought

There are several different ways to summarize the body of theory in a field. We could present the field in historical sequence, in terms of specific contributions of specific theorists, or in terms of schools of thought. At the risk of oversimplification, we will take the latter approach and attempt to summarize three systems of ideas that have dominated sociological theory and research on juvenile delinquency. No one theorist necessarily addresses all the issues or assumptions characteristic of a particular perspective, but certain similarities in fundamental assumptions tend to locate theorists in one or another school of thought. Moreover, theorists may draw on more than one system of ideas to explain delinquency. By approaching sociological perspectives on delinquency as schools of thought, we will discover areas where the theories are in marked conflict, as well as areas where they are in agreement.

We will find that theorists often focus on distinctively different questions. For example, when attempting to understand specific instances of delinquency, most people are interested in questions such as "Why did he or she do it? What was the motive?" These are reasonable questions to ask, but are not as central to some types of theories as to others. Some theorists assume the motives or "reasons" to be so common and obvious that they do not really explain why some youth commit delinquent offenses and others do not. It is safe to propose that most of us have wanted to hurt someone at some time, to sneak something out of a store without paying for it, to see what a "high" is like, or to join in with our peers even when it involves lawbreaking. Common forms of delinquency are likely to involve very common motives, leading some theorists to propose that the real question is "Given the prevalence of motives, why *don't* people break laws?" Theories focusing on barriers are sometimes called **amotivational theories**. They are also called *control* theories because the focus is on the absence or breakdown of mechanisms that discourage or constrain delinquent choices. Theorists who focus on limits on the opportunity to commit offenses as the key to understanding crime and delinquency put little emphasis on any specific motivation as well. If there are few cars to steal in an area, people living there may have low rates of auto theft, not because they are unusually virtuous, but because targets are not readily available. Hence, so-called *opportunity* or *routine activities* theories tend to be amotivational as well.

Theorists addressing the issue of motivation differ widely on the nature and origins of motives as well. For example, some theorists introduce sequences involving specific frustrations and problem-solving responses to those frustrations. While control theorists focus on barriers, *strain* theorists focus on problems that delinquency can alleviate when other ways of solving problems are limited. As an example, most students understand the motivation to cheat when someone is heading for poor grades and is confronted with mounting pressure to get good grades. If the good grades were already achieved, pressure to get good grades would not necessarily lead to cheating. Moreover, poor grades would not matter if there were no pressure or expectations to get high grades. The combination of pressure and poor grades is a "problem," and cheating might be seen as one solution. Strain or frustration theories emphasize problems that generate pressures resulting in delinquency and frame delinquency as "problem-solving" behavior.

Some theorists answer questions about motivation by focusing on how that behavior came to be rewarded as opposed to sanctioned, and do not require that a specific or special form of motivation be introduced. The behavior may be rewarding because it solves a problem, but the behavior may be rewarding in other ways as well. For example, giving in to peer pressure solves a problem (the pressure goes away when you go along with the group), but youth can be rewarded in a variety of ways without experiencing any pressure. Youths may imitate their friends or experience social reinforcement in the form of camaraderie and fun. They may have learned that "this is the way we do things" and no pressure is needed to explain such routine group behavior. This second type of motivational theory asks both why we do it and why we do not. The most recent version of this type of theory is called social structure/social learning theory and focuses on differentials in a variety of learning processes that can constrain or facilitate delinquent or criminal behavior and how those processes are distributed across time and space.

Shared Assumptions

Since the views that we will consider are all sociological, they do share certain basic assumptions. One basic assumption (shared by several psychological perspectives as well) is that delinquency can be best understood if it is approached as *learned*, rather than biologically determined, behavior. This assumption is closely linked to a second assumption, which is that as learned behavior, delinquency is not totally random or unpredictable, but is, instead, more common in some circumstances than in others. What those exact circumstances are varies from one sociological theory to another, but all such theories share the view that it is dimensions of the *social environment* which explain the distribution of delinquency and the probability that individuals will learn delinquent behavior. Important aspects of the social environment are its values, norms, beliefs, and technical knowledge (i.e., how to do things, including crime). These cultural patterns are variably learned, depending on the nature and operations of such socializing forces as the family, school, church, community, and peer groups (each of these will be dealt with in chapters 7 and 8). Learning also depends on the *structure of opportunities* for engaging in delinquent and nondelinquent activities.

Thus, the basic sources of delinquency are viewed as *originally external* to the individual. People are not born delinquent but are born into circumstances or have experiences that are conducive to delinquency. Individual values, beliefs, and conceptions of right and wrong become part of the individual's personal makeup, or self, through processes of social learning and socialization. This argument does not mean that genetic or biological factors are totally irrelevant to explaining delinquency. Instead, it reflects a belief that delinquency can be more adequately predicted and explained by considering (1) the influences of relationships with other people and institutions, (2) the values, norms, beliefs, and techniques learned as a product of such relationships, and (3) variations in the opportunity to commit offenses.

In the sections to follow we will concentrate on three basic *systems of ideas* that have been applied to explaining variations in the distribution of delinquency in different settings and among categories of people, as well as to explaining individual behavior and the development of delinquent gangs. These three systems of ideas or schools of thought will be referred to as *social disorganization/social control, structural strain/status frustration*, and *normative conflict/differential association* theories. Each type of theory has a long history and each has been reformulated or modified in a variety of ways in the last few decades.

Social Disorganization/Social Control Theory

The concept of social disorganization was widely used in early American sociology and criminology to refer to the unsettled conditions of urban life generated by growth and change. It is not surprising that the notion came into use among sociologists at the University of Chicago in the early 1900s, since Chicago was a booming industrial city increasingly populated by recent immigrants of diverse racial and ethnic backgrounds. Such conditions were viewed as contributing to a breakdown in the teaching and learning of "social rules" that previously had inhibited crime and delinquency (Thomas and Znaniecki, 1918). Robert Park argued that city life is characterized by a breakdown in the traditional schemes of control that have always depended on intimate personal relationships, such as occur in "the home, neighborhood, and other communal institutions" (1952:58).

Clifford Shaw (1929) and Edwin Sutherland (1939), both Chicago sociologists, used the concepts of social disorganization and social control to develop theories of delinquency. Shaw argued:

> Under the pressure of the disintegrative forces which act when business and industry invade a community, the community thus invaded ceases to function effectively as a means of social control. Traditional norms and standards of the conventional community weaken and disappear. Resistance on the part of the community to delinquent and criminal behavior is low, and such behavior is tolerated and may even become accepted and approved. (1929:204–5)

Thus, the expansion of business and industry, coupled with immigration, growth, mobility, and cultural diversity, was seen to weaken or inhibit certain traditional forms of control, which, in turn, facilitated high rates of delinquency.

Social disorganization theories attribute variation in crime and delinquency over time and among territories to the absence or breakdown of communal institutions (e.g., family, school, church, and local government) and communal relationships that traditionally encouraged cooperative relationships among people. The concept is defined in terms of the absence or breakdown of certain types of relationships among people, and is intimately tied to conceptions of those properties of relationships that are indicative of social or communal "organization." Relationships among people in a given territory are presumed to be especially organized when there are high levels of involvement across age-levels in activities coordinated by representatives of communal institutions (e.g., family-heads, pastors, school organizations, and local officials). Such organized interaction is presumed to be closely and reciprocally associated with the development of a sense of community or communal bonds among people in close geographic proximity to one another. The concept was developed to refer to the absence of organization among people in relatively small ecological units (neighborhoods, census tracts, communities), but has been used to explain variations in crime among larger units (e.g., counties, states, and nations) as well as variations over time.

The value of the concept of social disorganization for explaining crime and delinquency has been challenged on grounds of *circularity*: crime and delinquency have often been cited as indexes of social disorganization as well as phenomena to be explained by social disorganization. It is meaningless to argue that crime and delinquency rates are high because communities are "disorganized" and, then, to turn around and cite high crime rates as a measure of such disorganization. Moreover, since there is generally some order to social life even under the most dire circumstances and even when it is organized around illegal activities, the concept of social disorganization can be misleading. As we have noted before, delinquency itself has social qualities.

Although the concept itself may be vague and difficult to use in a noncircular fashion, it ties together a variety of explanations of crime and delinquency that focus on the social conditions that affect conventional social institutions, as well as the bonds between people and those institutions. Moreover, some theorists have reintroduced the same central arguments using somewhat different terms to refer to the same causal processes at the ecological level. They hypothesize that the "social integration" of communities is inhibited by population turnover and cite supporting evidence to explain variation in crime rates among cities (Crutchfield, Geerken, and Gove, 1982:467–82; Stark et al., 1983:4–23). The greater the mobility of the population in a city, the higher the crime rates. Further, Rodney Stark and colleagues argue that population turnover is a satisfactory inferential measure of variation in social integration and provide supporting evidence from numerous states (1983:4–23). The greater the proportion of a state's population that consists of newcomers or transients, the higher the crime rate. These arguments are identical to those proposed by social disorganization theorists, and the supporting evidence is as indirect as the evidence cited by social disorganization theorists. But, by referring to the positive end of a continuum (social integration rather than disintegration), such research has not generated the same degree of criticism as social disorganization theory. Others have used or proposed a variety of measures of social integration that are distinct from crime and delinquency, including measures of informal neighboring, organizational involvement, social networks, and communal perceptions of collective efficacy (Simcha-Fagan and Schwartz, 1986; Taylor and Covington, 1988; Bursik, 1988; Taylor, 2001; Sampson, 2002).

As expressed by Robert Bursik (1988:521), social disorganization theory is the "group-level analogue of control theory." Both social disorganization theory and social control theory focus on barriers to crime and delinquency and the absence or breakdown of social institutions as correlates of crime and delinquency at either the ecological level or among persons. They both presume that crime is most probable when those institutions and control mechanisms that ordinarily function to reinforce conformity are weak or disrupted. Both focus on failures or inconsistencies in the socialization of the young as part of the underlying causal process when explaining delinquency, but disorganization theory highlights the ecological variables assumed to generate those inconsistencies and failures.

Social control theories accord primacy to relationships, commitments, values, norms, and beliefs that are purported to explain why people do not break laws. The most prominent social control theorist in the twentieth century, Travis Hirschi viewed the motivations as so natural to human beings that no special forces were necessary to explain lawbreaking. Lawbreaking is often the most immediate source of gratification or conflict resolution, and no special motivation is required to explain such behavior. Human beings are active, flexible organisms who will engage in a wide range of activities, unless the range is limited by processes of socialization and social learning. On the other hand, many control-oriented theorists do introduce motivating forces, pressures, and pulls into their explanations. However, such motivations are viewed as sufficiently common, diverse, transitory, and situational that a more complete understanding of delinquency is to be gained from focusing on the barriers or constraints that inhibit lawbreaking rather than attempting to discern specific motivating forces. Rather than being generated by one or a few dominant forces, the motives for delinquency are depicted as quite diverse, ranging from instrumental needs (stealing when one is poor and hungry) to emotional rage, frustration, and sheer thrill and excitement. However, since most people are motivated to break laws at one time or another, a focus on motives does not explain who will commit criminal and delinquent acts (Briar and Piliavin, 1965).

Social control theory, like social disorganization theory, has been criticized for circularity. In one of the first systematic presentations of a social control theory of delinquency, A. J. Reiss, Jr., wrote:

> Delinquency may be defined as the behavior consequent to the failure of personal and social controls to produce behavior in conformity with the norms of the social system to which legal penalties are attached. Personal control may be defined as the ability of the individual to refrain from meeting needs in ways which conflict with the norms and rules of the community. Social control may be defined as the ability of social groups or institutions to make norms or rules effective. (1951:196)

The difficulty with such statements is that delinquency is by definition behavior that does not conform with certain norms. Thus, the statement can appear circular: "Failure to abide by norms occurs when people fail to abide by norms." However, when we consider the specific conditions cited or measured in the development of social control theories, we find that they are not necessarily circular. For example, Reiss went on to identify the failure of such primary groups as the family to provide reinforcement for nondelinquent roles and values as a crucial variable in the explanation of delinquency. Such conditions can be defined and measured in different terms than the delinquent behavior they are supposed to explain.

Another theory emphasizing the lack of constraints is **drift theory**, which derives from David Matza's work on *Delinquency and Drift* (1964). Matza saw the delinquent as an "actor neither compelled nor committed to deeds nor freely choosing them: neither different in any simple or fundamental sense from the law-abiding, nor the same; conforming to certain traditions in American life while partially unreceptive to other more conventional traditions" (1964:28). The word "drift" does convey some of the distinctive characteristics of social control theory. According to Matza the delinquent "flirts" with criminal and conventional behavior. It is essentially an amotivational perspective—that is, rather than seeking an answer to the question of what *motivates* adolescents to commit delinquent acts it seeks to discover what *prevents* adolescents from committing such acts. If an adolescent has few stakes in conformity, then she or he is freer to break rules than the adolescent who has high stakes in conformity.

We noted in chapter 1 that different sociological theories take quite different stands on the role that values and norms play in explaining crime and delinquency. Social disorganization/social control theorists have taken a variety of positions on the issue. According to Hirschi (1969), there is a general consensus in American society that criminal and delinquent activities involving personal harm and loss or damage to property are improper or immoral. By "consensus," Hirschi did not mean that everyone feels equally strong about the impropriety of lawbreaking. Some people accept the law as more morally binding than do other people, and are therefore less likely to break it. Nevertheless, Hirschi argued against the notion that any sizable racial, ethnic, or status groups in America have subcultural systems of values and norms that require criminal or delinquent behavior.

Matza and Gresham Sykes have observed that although "official" proclamations and conventional institutions stress the importance of obeying the law, "subterranean" traditions are conducive to crime (1961). Supposedly law-abiding citizens accord respect and admiration to the person who "pulls off the big con," who takes risks and successfully engages in exciting, dangerous activities, whether legal or illegal. Movies and television programs about this type of risk-taker or maverick are popular among all groups and classes of people, which reflects a widespread ambivalence toward the law. Sykes and Matza (1957) have also pointed out that although conventional institutions prevail upon us to not break the law, other social norms tell us that breaking the law is not so bad under certain circumstances: when the victim "had it coming" (denial of an innocent victim); when those supporting the law are not morally pure themselves (condemnation of the condemners); when the offender "had no choice" (denial of responsibility); when "no one was hurt" (denial of injury); or when the offense was motivated by social purposes more important than the law (appeal to higher loyalties). Such beliefs, or **techniques of neutralization**, can be learned in quite conventional contexts. They are reflected in legal codes as "extenuating circumstances" and in the public's reaction to certain types of crime. In this view, delinquency is not the result of different, subcultural values but, rather, is facilitated by specific beliefs that reduce the impact of more general moral commitments or by sporadic endorsement of deviant values hidden beneath the surface of society's traditional normative order.

Thus, some social control theorists view delinquency as a reflection of rather pervasive beliefs that encourage illegal and immoral activities. For them, delinquency reflects an ambivalence about lawbreaking or the lack of a consistent moral stance against lawbreaking. Other social control theorists merely emphasize the lack of commitment to the law: the person who is not morally bound to the law is freer to violate the law.

In sum, social disorganization/social control theorists generally believe that social conditions that attenuate or inhibit bonds to conventional institutions are the cause of individual and gang delinquency. To paraphrase Jackson Toby (1957), "The uncommitted adolescent is a candidate for gang socialization." Harold Finestone has characterized this view of the delinquent as a "dissatisfied" drifter (1976:10). This image of the individual delinquent is consistent with the social control perspective on the nature of delinquent gangs; uncommitted or disaffiliated adolescents are seen as drifting together to form tenuous, unstable aggregates, which Lewis Yablonsky (1959) has labeled **near groups**. Gangs, or near groups, are held together by lack of alternatives and conflict with authority, not by loving social bonds. In contrast to other sociological schools of thought, the social control perspective views the gang delinquent as "committed to neither delinquent nor conventional enterprise" (Matza, 1964:1).

Structural Strain/Status Frustration Theory

A second major perspective on delinquency first emerged in the late 1930s and grew in popularity during the 1950s through the mid-1960s. This perspective is referred to as **structural strain theory** because it relates crime and delinquency to a combination of Americans' cultural emphasis on high levels of financial "success" with social structures in which the realistic possibilities of attaining such success are limited for a sizeable proportion of the population. Four sociologists were especially prominent in the development of this perspective: Robert Merton, Albert Cohen, Richard Cloward, and Lloyd Ohlin.

According to the French sociologist Émile Durkheim, "No living being can be happy or even exist unless his needs are sufficiently proportioned to his means" (1951:246). Writing in the late 1800s and early 1900s, Durkheim argued that some forms of suicide occurred when needs and means were badly out of alignment. Extending Durkheim's ideas, Merton (1957) believed that deviance of various kinds could be attributed to the disparity between the cultural emphasis on success (leading to cultural needs or goals) and the actual opportunity to achieve success (means). When people learn that they should strive for certain goals and there is not equal opportunity or ability for everyone to realize them, then some portion of people are going to be frustrated. This disparity, coupled with a weakening of norms defining what forms of behavior are acceptable means of achieving success, prompts people to innovate and consider illicit means of obtaining their goals. Merton viewed crime and delinquency as **innovation**, a type of behavior that is most characteristic of lower-class people. The lower-class concentration of crime allegedly reflected the combination of limited opportunity coupled with a commitment to success and weak acceptance of the norms embodied in the law. People who are strongly bound to norms precluding criminal or delinquent behavior can respond to disparities between valued goals and limited opportunity by giving up their aspirations and conforming in a "ritualistic" fashion. Merton viewed **ritualism** as a common lower-middle-class adaptation to problems that generate crime and delinquency in the lower classes. He also argued that some people give up the pursuit of success and reject conventional norms. Their behavior is characterized by drug use, alcoholism, and vagrancy. Merton referred to this type of adaptation as **retreatism**. Finally, other people may adopt new goals and norms and rebel against the existing system. **Rebellion** is yet another way to deal with strain.

The disparity between success and opportunity can have consequences for people of every social standing. However, in Merton's view, criminal and delinquent behavior is a lower-class response to this type of social disorganization because the lower-class child is more thoroughly socialized to aspire toward success than to abide by legal norms. Under such circumstances, conventional norms are likely to be ignored, and new ways of getting ahead considered.

In his classic work *Delinquent Boys* (1955), Cohen's explanation of delinquency was strongly influenced by Merton's version of strain theory. However, Cohen believed that Merton's conception of the process did not explain the emotion involved in many delinquent activities. Cohen concluded that delinquent behavior represents a collective effort by juveniles to resolve adjustment problems caused by their loss of social status in American society. The lower-class child is constantly measured by the "middle-class measuring rod," which is discriminatory because socialization experiences differ according to class. Lower-class youth are not adequately socialized to fulfill the status requirements of middle-class society. Differential socialization experiences result in what Cohen referred to as **status frustration**. Status frustration is supposedly most common among boys from lower- or working-class families, since the middle-class measuring rod stresses characteristics that working-class socialization does not (for example, thrift, neatness, the ability to defer gratification, and good manners).

When status problems are experienced collectively—that is, by a number of adolescents who interact with one another—one outcome may be the creation of an alternative set of criteria for determining status. According to Cohen, delinquents create a new set of standards *contrary* to those emphasized in middle-class institutions. Thus, Cohen viewed delinquent gangs as a contracultural phenomenon. As noted earlier, the concept of contraculture refers to a system of values that are in opposition to dominant standards and that are the result of problems experienced in trying to obtain status while abiding by such standards. Delinquent activities are supposedly marked by a repudiation of middle-class standards and the adoption of nonutilitarian, malicious, rebellious attitudes. Although Cohen refers to a delinquent "subculture," the term "contraculture" conveys the sense of his explanation much better (Yinger, 1960).

Another elaboration of structural strain theory is found in Cloward and Ohlin's *Delinquency and Opportunity* (1960). Cloward and Ohlin argued that the motivation to deviate is provided when one accepts culturally prescribed goals of success and finds that legitimate avenues for achieving such goals are limited. However, they attempted to merge Merton's strain theory with approaches that emphasize illegal opportunity and criminal traditions. They argued that the consequences of strain depend on the availability of the illegitimate opportunities in a given setting. If status problems are experienced in a setting in which criminal activities are well organized and involve adult criminal role models, then involvement in a criminal subculture characterized by **criminal gang** activities such as theft is a likely resolution to a youth's problems. If no such well-organized illegitimate activities are available, then gang life centered around conflict, fighting, or violence may be the collective resolution to status problems. This response is called a **conflict gang** subculture. Finally, youth who are ill-equipped for organized criminal activity or for a gang life oriented toward conflict may withdraw into a **retreatist gang** subculture organized around drug use.

Although the structural strain/status frustration theorists reviewed are at odds on a number of points (for example, whether delinquent behavior is irrational and malicious or rational and utilitarian), they all emphasize a particular type of motivation: status problems induced by discrepancies between conventional culture and limits imposed by our social structure. Strain theorists argue that rates of crime and delinquency are highest in those categories of the population in which such discrepancies are most likely to occur. Delinquency is viewed as a form of social behavior that functions to solve the status problems. Thus, strain theorists introduce a special motivation to explain delinquency: structurally induced status frustration.

Strain theorists also share the view that people born into our society *at least initially* want to conform to the conventional standards that are reflected in the law. According to Cohen, before they hit upon delinquent alternatives, lower-class boys try to live up to the standards of middle-class adults but are unable to do so. Alternatives are explored after status problems are experienced. Strain theorists depict people as basically moral in the sense that they are always trying to be honorable, whether by adhering to conventional norms and values or by elaborating new norms that define delinquency and crime as good and acceptable. Cohen introduced the psychological defense mechanism of **reaction formation** to explain this reversal.

In describing the delinquent as a "frustrated social climber," Finestone (1976:2) summed up the strain theorists' image of delinquent youth. Delinquency, especially gang delinquency, is viewed as a solution to status problems. The gang delinquent is a problem solver who is involved in a problem-solving contracultural or subcultural system. As Cohen (1955) expressed it, "The same value system, impinging upon children differently equipped to meet it, is instrumental in generating both delinquency and respectability." The strain theorists' image of the delinquent, then, is that of an essentially moral, striving human being who has been forced by circumstances beyond his or her control to explore new ways of attaining respect and self-esteem. Group delinquency is depicted as problem-solving behavior.

Normative Conflict/Differential Association Theory

Thus far we have considered theories that view delinquency as a product of (1) freedom from or inconsistencies in conventional socialization and control, and (2) status problems generated by disparities between cultural aspirations and social reality. A third perspective is characterized by the argument that in certain social contexts, delinquency and crime are approved, required, or expected behaviors. Some advocates of this last position have specifically repudiated the basic assumptions of strain theory. For example, Walter Miller has argued that the strain theorists' image of a delinquent subculture is erroneous (1958). Miller does not believe that the value systems of lower-class gangs are contracultural (that is, a rejection of dominant middle-class values). Rather, Miller has argued, the values, or focal concerns, of gang members are a product of "the lower class community itself—a long established, distinctively patterned tradition with an integrity of its own" (1958:5–6). According to Miller, the gang boy conforms to the values or standards of a larger subculture that is generally linked to regional, racial, or social status. Thus, delinquency is supposedly a reflection of the values, norms, and beliefs of large, but distinct, segments of the population.

From the **normative conflict** perspective, the basic source of variation in delinquency rates is subcultural diversity in standards of right and wrong. When a region of the nation, particular sections of a city, or particular groups or categories of people have high crime rates, cultural conflict theorists posit that the values, norms, and beliefs of those particular segments of the population differ from the standards embodied in the law. Contrary to the strain and control theorists, normative conflict theorists view society as characterized by quite diverse standards of right and wrong, with some standards more likely than others to be expressed in the law. Groups or segments of the population whose cultures are in conflict with the law are more likely to come into actual conflict with the law. Sutherland and Donald Cressey have noted that the "principle of normative conflict . . . makes sense out of variations in crime rates by observing that modern societies are organized *for* crime as well as against it," and then observing further that "crime rates are unequally distributed because of differences in the degree to which various categories of persons participate in this normative conflict" (1974:89). This concept of normative conflict differs from the concept of subterranean values in that it attributes the values that are conducive to delinquency to disadvantaged groups whose cultures are in conflict with the dominant middle class. In contrast, the type of inconsistency or conflict that Matza and Sykes have described as "subterranean" characterized the value systems of the dominant groups in society.

Once such cultural conflict, or diversity in standards of right and wrong, is assumed, then the process of learning delinquency becomes one of **differential association** with different standards. Hence, the basic principle of Sutherland and Cressey's differential association theory is that "a person becomes delinquent because of an excess of definitions favorable to violation of law over definitions unfavorable to violation of law" (1974:75–77). The emphasis is on the learning of normative or cultural standards, some of which define lawbreaking in favorable terms while others define it in unfavorable terms. The principle of normative conflict at the collective level sets the stage for differential exposure to different standards at the individual level.

From a cultural conflict perspective, delinquency is explained by the same processes as is lawfulness. The motivation for delinquency, like the motivation for lawfulness, is quite natural—the human tendency to live up to the expectations of significant others. Children ultimately become involved in delinquency because the standards they learn are in conflict with the standards reflected in the law. As John DeLamater has noted, cultural deviance (in this case delinquency) "occurs through the normal process of social learning" (1968:447). Thus, cultural conflict theorists view deviance as a product of successful **subcultural socialization**; strain theorists view it as a product of **resocialization** through the collective development of contracultural standards; and control theorists view it as a product of failures or inconsistencies in conventional socialization. Because they see delinquent behavior as conforming behavior that is only deviant from some other group's perspective, normative conflict/differential association theorists need posit no special motivation for deviance. Youths are merely doing what is expected in their immediate environment.

Since this school of thought defines delinquency as conforming behavior that is shaped by normative standards and the expectations of others, its image of the delinquent differs from the images of the other two perspectives that we have reviewed. Delinquents tend to be depicted as among the most able, persevering, and gregarious members of their particular communities. For example, Miller has argued that to become a gang member, a boy must be able to subordinate individual preference to group interest and that lower-class gang members "possess to an unusually high degree both the capacity and motivation to conform to perceived cultural norms" (1958). From such a perspective, it is the best products of a lower-class culture, rather than the worst, who are likely to become delinquent. Those most sensitive to the opinions and expectations of members of their subculture are those most likely to become involved in delinquency. To borrow Hirschi's term, the image of the delinquent is one of "hypermorality" (1969). The delinquent is a conformist in a subculture whose standards are in conflict with the law.

Sociological Theories and Delinquency: An Overview

Several sociologists have summarized different perspectives on deviance, crime, and delinquency, and we can get a good overview of the three approaches outlined above by drawing on their works. Table 6-1 describes these three approaches in terms of causal forces, socialization processes emphasized by each, their images of the delinquent and of the law and moral standards, and their views of culture and motivation. Many of their characteristics were discussed previously, but this chart helps to highlight unique characteristics of distinct schools of thought.

Referring to table 6-1, the three classic causal perspectives on criminal and delinquent behavior evoke a causal process that operates on a macro, or societal, level as well as on a micro, or individual, level. On the societal level disorganization/control theory attributes variation in crime and delinquency to variations in the collective ties

Table 6-1   Characteristics of Major Causal Theories

	Social Disorganization/ Social Control	Structural Strain/ Status Frustration	Normative Conflict/ Differential Association
Causal factor at societal level	Social disorganization	Structural strain	Normative conflict
Causal factor at individual level	Weak conventional bonds	Status frustration	Differential association
Role of socialization	Failure or inconsistencies	Resocialization	Differential socialization
Image of offenders	Drifter	Problem solver	Conformist
View on law and morality	Low acceptance of conventional	Initial acceptance, strain-induced rejection	Conflicting definitions
View of culture	Infraculture	Contraculture	Subculture
Motivation	Natural, diverse, situational	Special status problems	Natural, social, cultural

to traditional institutions of social control and the strength of those institutions. Strain theory attributes variation in crime among and within societies to the malintegration of cultured ambitions and opportunity to achieve conventional success goals. Cultural conflict theory assumes the presence of multiple cultures or subcultures within a particular society such that some segments of society run afoul of the law by merely living up to the expectations of significant others in their immediate social world.

At the individual level, control theory focuses on barriers to delinquency in the form of attachments to conventional people, values, norms, and beliefs. Strain theory translates social strain into status frustration, which occurs when individuals cannot attain prescribed goals. Finally, cultural conflict theory introduces the concept of differential association to explain how members of differing subcultures acquire and maintain attitudes and behaviors that nonmembers of the subcultural groups view as deviant.

DeLamater (1968) has delineated three perspectives on the deviant "socialization" process and each fits best with one of the three classic sociological perspectives. DeLamater observes that becoming deviant may reflect: (1) inadequate socialization into conventional norms, (2) initial socialization into deviant subcultural norms, or (3) problem-solving resocialization. Control theorists tend to emphasize failures or inconsistencies of socialization into what they deem to be conventional norms while cultural conflict theorists tend to focus on successful subcultural socialization. Finally, the third process, resocialization, fits strain theory because the abandonment of conventional norms and the creation and adherence to a "new" system that helps solve status problems reflects a change in the content of the socialization process or resocialization. The individual initially learns conventional standards and tries to abide by them. If such attempts lead to frustration, then the individual may turn to delinquency and the creation or adoption of alternative standards.

Hirschi (1969) and Finestone (1976) have dealt with the general image of the delinquent suggested by different theories. In the social control perspective, the delinquent is "dissatisfied" (Finestone) or "amoral" (Hirschi). By amoral, Hirschi means that the delinquent is less bound to conventional moral standards and can therefore deviate more freely, with fewer moral complications and less guilt. According to this view, delinquent youth are also "uncommitted" (Matza, 1964). From a cultural conflict perspective, delinquent youth are actually "hypermoral" (Hirschi) in the sense that they make the greatest effort to live up to expectations in their subcultural environment. They are conformers. Finally, from the perspective of strain theory, those youths who initially try to adhere to conventional standards, but fail to get ahead by doing so, seek moral solutions to their status problems. Finestone has depicted this image as one of "frustrated social climber." Group delinquency can become a solution for youths who lack conventional status resources.

Each theoretical approach is also characterized by a particular image of the law and moral standards. Cultural conflict theorists stress normative conflict in society and a view of the law as representative of the standards of certain powerful segments of society. In this view, society is characterized by dissection and conflict between the standards of some sizable subcultures and the standards that are reflected in the law. In contrast, both control and strain theorists view society as characterized by consensus regarding the impropriety of most types of crime and delinquency. Hirschi has noted that control theory assumes "a common value system within the society whose norms are being violated" and that "deviance is not a question of one group imposing its rules on the members of another group" (1969). Control theory does not deny that traces of deviant values are buried or embedded within our culture. These subterranean values occasionally serve as convenient rationalizations for delinquent behavior or neutralize the inhibiting impact of other standards. Strain theorists also assume that there is a common value system, as well as basic agreement on the impropriety of criminal and delinquent activity, but that those who experience frustration may construct an alternative moral order (contraculture) to cope with such problems.

Cultural concepts are used differently in each of these theories as well. For example, Milton Yinger (1960) has noted that the concept of the delinquent subculture characteristic of Cohen's strain theory is really that of a contraculture—a system of values, norms, and beliefs that specifically develops in reaction to problems in coping with the dominant system. In contrast, the cultural conflict theorists use the concept of subculture in a more conventional way. Their focus is on a system of values, norms, and beliefs that is in conflict with standards reflected in the law but that exists as an enduring set of traditions characteristic not merely of delinquent gangs but of whole subpopulations, communities, or neighborhoods. Finally, for control theorists like Hirschi, such concepts as contraculture or subculture are not necessary for understanding delinquency, since an overall cultural consensus regarding moral standards is assumed and delinquency is seen as resulting from freedom from moral constraints.

Lamar Empey (1967) has noted that control theorists have advanced a third concept of American culture characterized by an **infraculture**, the system of subterranean values, norms, and beliefs that we discussed earlier. According to this concept, certain values, norms, and beliefs are conducive to delinquency but are part and parcel of the dominant cultural system rather than the standards of specific subgroups. Such infracultural aspects of American culture are not viewed as requiring crime but as tending to neutralize abstract moral commitments to the law. For example, we might all agree that "honesty is the best policy," but also applaud those who carry off clever heists or steal from the rich to give to the poor.

This idea has not been incorporated specifically into any explanatory theory. To be relevant to explaining variation in delinquent activity, subterranean beliefs would have to be viewed as "variably" learned aspects of American culture and some effort made to identify the circumstances associated with such learning. On the other hand, to the degree that **subterranean beliefs** are viewed as neutralizing the moral constraints of the dominant system and freeing the individual to deviate, the concept fits quite well with control theory.

We earlier discussed the way each of the three perspectives differs in its approach to the issue of motivation. Cultural conflict theory and control theory focus on quite "natural" motives, while strain theory is characterized by a "special motivation" (Hirschi, 1969). Cultural conflict theory focuses on the natural tendency of people to abide by the cultural expectations and normative standards prominent in their own social environments. (In other words, delinquents learn the delinquent standards of their particular subcultural environments.) For control theorists, motives are natural in a very different sense. Hirschi did not feel that control theory need pay any attention to the motivational issue (1969:33), while control theorists who have focused on motivation have merely outlined short-term, situationally induced desires experienced by all youths. The motives for delinquency are diverse, situational, and so common that they have little explanatory power. In contrast, the strain theorist identifies a very special, structurally induced type of motive: status frustration. People have to be forced to deviate by circumstances largely beyond their control. The introduction of a special force is necessary in neither cultural conflict theory nor in control theory.

Contemporary Causal Theories

The basic perspectives discussed above have not been stagnant and unchanging, and distinct contemporary theories both reflect basic themes from the earlier perspectives and apply new twists to them. In table 6-2 we have categorized "modern" theories in terms of their answers to three simple questions, the first of which is: Does the theory incorporate or require some form of imbalance, strain, stress, or frustrated pursuit of conventional or widely shared goals? If so, it is classified as falling within the strain/frustration tradition. Many modern extensions are classified as integrated theories because they incorporate ideas and concepts from other perspectives. But, the fact that they introduce specific forms of motivational pressure generated by some form of imbalance or discrepancy in the achievement of widely shared goals distinguishes them as a strain/frustration theory.

New or reformulated versions of the normative conflict/differential association school of thought do not necessarily share all of the assumptions outlined in table 6-1 and may, in fact, allow the alleviation of status problems to be one source of reinforcement for delinquency (a strain theory characteristic), but that motivation is not introduced as a key feature of new extensions. If a contemporary theory incorporates variations in normative orientations, emphasizes a wide range of quite normal learning processes, and incorporates a youth's peers or companions as a key feature of the theory, then we classify it in the normative conflict/differential association tradition. If the following question is answered in the affirmative, it is located in that tradition: Does the theory focus on normal learning processes, including socially structured schedules of reward and punishment, variable values, norms, and beliefs, and associations with people who both encourage and discourage crime and delinquency? If so, the theory fits better with the normative conflict/differential association category than the other two systems of ideas. Social learning variations do not require that normative systems be in conflict, although it is historically anchored in that tradition.

Finally, does the theory assume that the absence of constraints or limits on opportunity for crime is key to explaining crime and delinquency? If "motivation" refers to characteristics of humans considered to be quite natural when social, cultural, or opportunity constraints are absent such that no special pressure is required, then it falls in the social control tradition.

We will also discuss three sociological theories that are classified in contemporary criminology as "life-course" theories. Life-course theorists focus on processes that vary by age and/or the relevance of different causal processes by age. However, when they focus on these issues they tend to apply one or another of the basic systems of ideas outlined above. Some fall closer to the social disorganization/social control end of the continuum and some fall closer to the normative conflict tradition. If a theorist

Table 6-2   Modern Reformulations

Type of Theory	Social Disorganization/ Social Control	Structural Strain/ Status Frustration	Normative Conflict/ Differential Association
Societal level	Collective efficacy (Sampson and others)	Institutional anomie (Messner & Rosenfeld)	Social structure/social learning (SSSL) (Akers)
	Broken windows (Wilson & Kelling)	Code of the streets (Anderson)	
	Social support (Cullen)		
	Routine activities (Cohen & Felson)		
Individual level	Social support (Cullen)	Integrated strain-bond (Elliott)	Social learning (Akers)
	Self-control (Gottfredson & Hirschi)	General strain (Agnew)	Interactionist (Thornberry)
	Life-course/informal control (Sampson & Laub)	Self-derogation (Kaplan)	Life course-social learning (Warr)
		Defiant individual-ism (Sánchez-Jankowski)	
		Control balance (Tittle)	

emphasizes variable relations with peers as a key feature of an age-graded theory, it falls closer to the normative conflict/differential association end of the continuum. If a theory incorporates age-graded variations in goals and frustrations in achieving goals, the life course theory would fall in the strain/frustration category.

Extensions or Reformulations in the Social Disorganization/Social Control Tradition

Ideas proposed by six theorists can be classified as variants based on features of a social disorganization/social control framework: (1) routine activities theory, (2) broken windows theory, (3) self-control theory, (4) social support theory, (5) life-course theory/informal control, and (6) collective efficacy theory. We cannot do justice to all of these variations in an introductory text on delinquency and youth crime, but we can highlight their central characteristics and explain why we locate each in one of the basic traditions. It is much easier to remember and understand features of theories when they can be discussed in terms of traditional schools of thought and understood through contrasts and comparisons with basic themes.

Routine activities theorists propose that variations in crime can be explained by variations in routine activities of everyday life that affect the availability and vulnera-

Box 6-2   Routine Activities Theory

This cartoon illustrates a theme in routine activities theory. What variable is represented in the warning sign? If unemployment increases the probability of an unemployed owner being home, what would that theory predict about the effect of unemployment on burglary rates?

bility of people and property as targets (Cohen and Felson, 1979; Cohen, Kluegal, and Land, 1981; Felson, 1998). For example, a shift to small television sets during some years would make it easier to steal such sets while an increase in size would make it more difficult. More women traveling to work would increase their availability as targets of street violence. Since burglars prefer to carry out their offenses when no one is home, more people at home protecting or guarding their property should reduce burglaries. Thus, temporal variations in crime rates can reflect increases or decreases in the availability of unprotected targets.

Variations in risks of victimization by people living in an area can be explained by the convergence of attractive targets, lack of guardians, and availability of motivated offenders. The fact that motivated offenders are included might suggest that the theory is a motivational one. Yet, we classify routine activities as a perspective in the social disorganization/social control tradition. Why? Because the theory does not introduce any form of "pressure" to explain variation in crime and pays little attention to actual motivation. Indeed, the motives tend to be depicted as quite routine and normal. In fact, some criminologists (see Akers and Sellers, 2004) discuss routine activities together with perspectives that assume offenders are merely making "rational choices" to maximize reward/cost ratios. An offender is part of the equation generating victimizations, but the source of offender motivation is either quite normal or unspecified.

The original formulation of routine activities did not focus on social learning mechanisms, and even recent extensions of the theory that claim to encompass "unsupervised peer group activities" as part of routine activities theory locate it in the social disorganization/social control tradition. It should be noted that the addition of social learning processes involving peers and the extension of the theory to include "deviant" routines would move the theory into the differential association tradition.

Broken windows theory was proposed by James Q. Wilson and George Kelling in 1982 and had a major impact on the operational theories of many police departments in the United States. The theory is based on the idea that when there are observable signs of "social disorder" in an area, such as broken windows, graffiti, and abandoned cars, these can encourage crime, while removing such signs can inhibit crime. Moreover, by attacking what might appear to be minor problems such as vandalism and loitering, more serious forms of crime could be affected. Although critics have challenged the view that crime can be inhibited by merely attending to its "signs" rather than the underlying social disorder, the logic of the theory is a social disorganization logic. Crime and delinquency can be reduced by removing the circumstances that help sustain an image of an area as disorganized or disordered.

In a widely cited and controversial book advocating a **general theory of crime**, Michael Gottfredson and Hirschi (1990) proposed that variations in crime, delinquency, and other forms of rule breaking can be explained by variations in the sheer possibility of engaging in an activity (opportunity) together with variations in a characteristic of individuals referred to as **self-control**. In this version of control theory, external forces work in two ways. First, there are structured variations in the opportunities to commit some forms of crime (e.g., teenagers are unlikely to be involved in corporate fraud). Second, external variations in parental supervision and socialization are viewed as the source of variations in self-control. In their perspective, self-control is an internal characteristic of individuals established to varying degrees at a relatively young age and reflected in behavior throughout the individual's life course. The strength of self-control affects the odds that individuals can establish stable relationships in their adult life, their susceptibility to spontaneous peer pressures, and the nature of reactions to frustrations. Self-control is introduced as the master *mediating variable* explaining the impact of all other variables. This theory follows a control theory logic, but accords self-control a key role in explaining all forms of force and fraud.

Another perspective falling within that tradition is Francis Cullen's **social support theory** (1994). Cullen defines social support as "the perceived or actual instrumental or expressive provisions supplied by the community, social networks, and confiding partners." *Instrumental* support is assistance in providing life's material necessities, while *expressive* support is assistance in providing emotional needs. Support can be provided through interaction between individuals, by social networks and communities, and by both formal agencies (e.g., educational, government, religious, and justice institutions) and through informal associations (e.g., friends and neighbors). This perspective falls in the social disorganization/social control tradition because the focus is on the prevalence or absence of supportive relationships of several kinds and does not introduce special problem-solving mechanisms. Social support overlaps with "social bonds" or formal and informal social controls in other versions of the theory, and a system lacking in supportive relationships would qualify as "socially disorganized."

Robert Sampson and John Laub (1993) propose a **life-course/informal control** theory of crime and delinquency that addresses persistence and desistence in offending based on an age-graded theory of informal social control. It is called a life-course theory because it focuses on how people change over time. Sampson and Laub acknowledge that changes in peer relationships (central to social learning theory) play a role and such an acknowledgement might lead us to classify them as differential association theorists. However, we classify their theory as a version of social control for several reasons. First, their research focuses on the role of conventional institutions and investments in explaining age variation. They focus on marriage and jobs as important factors to explain desisting from crime. Second, they emphasize "informal control" and conventional social bonds. As is the case with most theories, they may incorporate ideas from other theories, but they avoid calling their theory a "social learning" theory and adopt the terminology of social control theory instead.

Sampson and various colleagues (Sampson, Raudenbush, and Earls, 1997; Sampson and Bartusch, 1998; Sampson and Raudenbush, 1999, 2004; Sampson, 2002) as well as Ralph Taylor (2001:128–29) introduce a new concept, **collective efficacy**, as the key to understanding ecological variations in crime and delinquency. Thus, they emphasize the positive end of a social organization—disorganization continuum. Social disorganization is high for a locale when residents do not get along with one another, do not belong to local organizations geared to the betterment of the community, and are unlikely to intervene when they encounter wrongdoing. In contrast, the opposite end of the continuum is collective efficacy. When residents do get along, work through local organizations to better the community, and take steps to informally control trouble in their neighborhood, they are high in collective efficacy. This perspective is very similar to Cullen's social support theory and falls within the social disorganization tradition.

Extensions or Reformulations in the Structural Strain/Status Frustration Tradition

There are also contemporary twists on strain/status frustration theories: (1) self-derogation theory, (2) integrated strain-bond theory, (3) general strain theory, (4) control-balance theory, and (5) institutional anomie theory. Such theories are classified here as part of the strain tradition because they all include an imbalance of some kind that provides the motivation for violating laws. Offending is a response to some pressure generated by frustrated expectations or a discrepancy between what youths have and what they dream of achieving. In general, offending is supposed to help resolve the problem and alleviate the pressure.

Howard Kaplan (1975, 1980) and Delbert Elliott and colleagues (Elliott, Huizinga, and Ageton, 1985) were the first theorists to propose an integrated theory in which variables from strain, social control, and differential association theory all played a role in the explanation of delinquency. However, we classify their perspectives in the strain/frustration tradition because they focus on frustrations in goal attainment as the catalyst setting youth in search of a solution. For Kaplan, attaining and maintaining self-esteem is a major driving force among humans as social beings, and threats to self-esteem provide the motivational pressure leading to delinquency. This perspective is reflected in the title of his major work, *Deviant Behavior in Defense of Self* (1980). The central theme in his **self-derogation theory** is that when youth lack resources to attain esteem in conventional ways and interact with youth who have adopted delinquent resolutions to status problems, delinquency becomes a problem-solving response. Although variables from other theories are incorporated, the emphasis on deviance as "a defense of self" and threats to self-esteem as the major source of motivational pressure justifies classifying it in the strain/frustration tradition.

Elliott's **integrated strain-bond theory** is properly classified under the strain/frustration logic as well in that it requires a special motivational force to initiate the process that leads to delinquency. Some form of discrepancy between aspirations and achievement leads to a decline in conventional control (e.g., attachment to school), which in turn leads to formation of bonds to delinquent peers and, ultimately, delinquent behavior. Elliott viewed his perspective as an integration of strain and social control theory, while others (Akers and Sellers, 2004) view the theory as quite compatible with differential association and social learning theory. In contrast, we classify a theory as an extension or reformulation of the strain tradition when it accords the major motivational role to frustrated attainment of goals, which is certainly the case for Elliott's integrated theory.

The title of Robert Agnew's most recent work is *Pressured into Crime* (2005), which explains why we have categorized his reformulation as an extension of a strain/status frustration logic. Neither social disorganization/control theory nor cultural conflict/differential association theory require a "pressure" to explain crime. Control theorists contend that we learn more about crime and delinquency by studying variable constraints rather than sources of motivation, and cultural conflict theorists do not require any unusual pressure since offenders are merely living up to the expectations of others in their sociocultural environment or joining with peers through routine learning processes. **General strain theory** is a motivational theory and introduces pressures as a major source of motivation for crime and delinquency.

It is called a "general" strain theory because it is not limited to the specific types of frustrated goal achievement emphasized in the original development of the theory; that is, failure to achieve positive goals. For example, Agnew argues that youth have the right to expect that their parents will not abuse them. Violation of such expectations should, he argues, generate stress and anger. This type of disparity involves an undeserved exposure to negative stimuli. The more unjust the experience, the greater the delinquency. He also includes losses of positively valued stimuli, such as breakups with boyfriends and girlfriends, loss of a loving parent, being kicked out of school. All of these can generate strain and provide the motivational pressure to become involved in delinquency. Agnew is careful to point out that such an outcome is not automatic and that variables emphasized by other theories may shape the response to strain. However, it is clear that the theory falls in the strain/frustration tradition.

Charlie Tittle (1995) has developed a very elaborate theory of deviance in general he terms **control-balance theory**. Because it includes control in its title it may be tempting to categorize it with social control theory. But consider the following statement: "Deviant behavior is interpreted as a device, or maneuver, that helps people escape deficits and extend surpluses. An unbalanced control ratio, in combination with a desire for autonomy and fundamental bodily and psychic needs, predisposes an individual to act deviantly" (1995:142, 147–48). Early strain theorists emphasized failures to achieve widely shared success goals, and Tittle incorporates problems in achieving more basic human needs or goals as providing motivation or the predisposition for deviant action. The emphasis on escape carries a connotation that fits strain-theory logic. Like Agnew, Tittle incorporates variables from a variety of theories to help explain when predispositions result in actual deviant behavior.

In *Crime and the American Dream*, Steven Messner and Richard Rosenfeld (2001) propose yet another version of a strain/frustration theory—an **institutional anomie theory** in which economic dominance is the cause of high crime rates in the United States compared to other nations. In an earlier article they argued as follows:

> Economic dominance occurs when: (1) economic goals are assigned high priority in comparison to non-economic goals; (2) the claims of economic roles are typically honored at the expense of non-economic roles when conflicts occur; (3) social standing tends to be highly dependent on the performance of economic roles than of non-economic roles; and (4) the calculating, utilitarian logic of the marketplace penetrates other institutional realms.
>
> Economic dominance leads, in turn, to high rates of crime via two complementary processes. First, this type of institutional imbalance provides fertile soil for the growth of the anomic cultural pressures associated with market arrangements. This is because the non-economic institutions that bear primary responsibility for cultivating respect for social norms, such as families and schools, are less capable of fulfilling their distinctive socialization functions. Second, economic dominance weakens the external controls associated with institutional attachments. When the economy dominates the institutional balance of power, non-economic roles become relatively unattractive. The result is relatively tenuous institutional engagement, weak social control, and high rates of crime. (1997:1396–97)

While the theory is clearly anchored in the anomie-strain tradition, as evidenced by its focus on "the growth of the anomic cultural pressures associated with market arrangements," the mediating mechanisms linking economic dominance to crime are quite compatible with social disorganization/social control theory. Not only do anomic "cultural pressures" directly facilitate crime, but they also weaken (or prevent the development of) other social institutions as sources of informal social control. Messner and Rosenfeld's "macro-level" strain theory is very similar to Elliott's "micro-level" theory in that both view strain-theory motivational forces as undermining conventional institutions leading to increases in crime rates (Messner and Rosenfeld) or delinquent behavior (Elliott).

We classify Martin Sánchez-Jankowski's *Islands in the Street* (1991) and Elijah Anderson's *The Code of the Street* (1999) in the strain tradition because the character traits or "codes" they identify as characteristic of gang youth are not viewed as a reflection of a wider subculture passed on through normal processes of socialization from generation to generation, but as a response to limited resources or the irrelevance of more conventional culture to life on the streets. Based primarily on observational or ethnographic evidence, Sánchez-Jankowski argues that the key to understanding movement into gangs is a type of social character called **defiant indi-**

vidualism. Although defiant individualism sounds like a psychological trait, Sánchez-Jankowski views it as a functional type of social character emerging most distinctively in environments where people are in intense competition for scarce resources. When a theorist emphasizes defiance, it implies more of a contraculture than a subculture. Anderson reintroduced the notion of an oppositional subculture where self-respect requires a demonstration of toughness, and maintenance of honor requires physical violence. Although the **code of the street** is identified as most relevant to black youth, Sánchez-Jankowski's version is relevant to gang members in a wide range of ethnic groups, including whites.

It should be noted that codes and characters can become subcultural if they become an enduring tradition passed on through normal learning processes in an area. For example, the code of the street is depicted as widely known among urban blacks and this code is "adjusted to" even among those who do not embrace it. However, the fact that it is depicted as acknowledged rather than embraced and in conflict with a more conventional culture shared by most blacks suggests that it could qualify as a subcultural orientation in conflict with a wider conventional black and white culture. On the other hand, as long as there is an emphasis on a character or code that originates with and is sustained by those having problems with a wider conventional culture and social system, such a perspective fall closer to strain theory's problem-solving interpretation of subcultures as contracultures.

Extensions or Reformulations in the Normative Conflict/Differential Association Tradition

The most prominent elaboration of ideas that has been linked with the normative conflict/differential association theory is Ronald Akers's social learning theory, discussed in chapter 5. However, it is vital to point out that social learning theory is not a simple outgrowth of that tradition in that it includes both normative and non-normative learning processes. Social learning theorists believe that although definitions play a role in the learning of conventional and unconventional behavior, such definitions do not capture all ways of learning delinquency. For example, peer pressures to "go along" can, it is argued, increase the odds of delinquency even when a youth defines the activity as wrong. Concern about parental reaction can inhibit delinquency even when a youth does not define the activity as something they ought not do. In short, social learning theory, in contrast to normative conflict/differential association theory, stresses non-normative as well as normative learning mechanisms that can lead to or inhibit delinquency. Social learning theory does fit with normative conflict/differential association theory in that the learning processes are normal and can involve learning of expectations that conflict with the law.

Moreover, the perspective has been expanded to include both micro and macro issues and is now called a **social structure/social learning (SSSL) theory**. It has been extended to apply to variations among societies as well as variations among socially differentiated categories of people within societies (see Akers, 1998; Jensen and Akers, 2003; Akers and Jensen, 2006). Like other contemporary theories, social learning theory grew out of ideas expressed in a particular type of sociological theory, but has been modified or reformulated to encompass a variety of learning processes. For example, when attempting to explain variations among nations, a SSSL theorist would focus on variation in cultural or normative traditions, opportunity to commit crimes, and the strength of conventional institutions (Jensen and Akers, 2003).

When the causal logic of social learning theory is extended to the macro-level and applied to violence, the resulting perspective would focus on characteristics of societies that impede or undermine (1) cultural and political consensus and (2) conventional institutional relationships, but enhance (3) unregulated interaction in peer groups, (4) situational opportunities to engage in, or be a victim of, crime, and (5) the development of sustained tendencies for people to resolve interpersonal conflicts through violent action. The emphasis on "heterogeneity," "weak social support networks" and "collective inefficacy" in contemporary versions of social disorganization theory is quite compatible with the first two characteristics, while the third is compatible with claims by Sampson (2002) and Osgood and Anderson (2004) about the impact of unsupervised youth groups as a central mediating variable at the neighborhood level. The fourth characteristic reflects either "availability" of a behavioral choice in social learning theory, or "opportunity" as specified by routine activities theory. Social learning theory differs from routine activities theory through its specification that involvement in certain types of routines are both more "criminogenic" and more "victimogenic" than others (Jensen and Brownfield, 1986). Finally, the fifth characteristic allows for variations that are generated and sustained by cultural or subcultural tolerance or ambivalence concerning appropriate means of resolving interpersonal disputes (see Luckenbill and Doyle, 1989). Such tolerance is especially likely when agents of formal control are not accorded authority to intervene (Sampson and Wilson, 1995).

Two life-course theories can be considered part of this tradition as well. Terence Thornberry (1987) proposed an **interactionist theory** that he believes integrates social control and social learning theory. We classify it as a life-course theory in the social learning tradition because the factors that influence delinquency and crime are supposed to vary by age and the stage in a delinquent career from initiation to persistence to desistence. Mark Warr (1993, 2002) has elaborated a **life-course/social learning** perspective that specifically incorporates ideas, concepts, and propositions from differential association and social learning theory. While Sampson and Laub focus on family and jobs as key to the explanation of age gradations in crime and delinquency, Warr argues that the impact of variables such as marriage for desistence from offending can be explained by the shift in balance of associations. As children age, peers grow in importance in their social lives—a pattern that helps explain increases in delinquency with age. As they move into adulthood, peers are still important, but variables such as marriage and employment begin to impact time spent with peers. Sampson and Laub locate their theory in the social control tradition while Warr anchors his theory in the differential association-social learning tradition.

Theory-Related Research

Each of the three sociological schools of thought that we have reviewed developed in an attempt to make sense out of presumed "facts" about delinquency and crime. Arrest rates were highest in the areas surrounding the central business district of cities and decreased in zones outside of the city center. Why did rates vary in such a fashion? Social disorganization/control theorists attributed such variation to the deleterious effect of growth and change on conventional institutions. Structural strain/status frustration theorists argued that people living in areas with the highest arrest rates are those most likely to experience a disparity between aspiration and reality. Cultural conflict theorists argued that such areas are characterized by enduring cultural traditions that define lawbreaking in favorable terms. In short, all three perspectives explain commonly believed "facts" about delinquency.

Each of the major theories of delinquency can make sense out of variations in delinquency by setting, social class, age, and gender. However, each does so using different concepts and assumptions about people, culture, and society. Hence, tests of sociological theories have come to concentrate directly on the causal mechanisms generating delinquency. If high delinquency rates are attributable to subcultural normative traditions passed on through socialization in specific territories or collectivities of people, then research should uncover systematic differences in such traditions by territory or collectivity. If gang delinquency grows out of failure in the conventional system and repudiation of conventional values and norms, then there should be evidence of an oppositional value system among gang youth as compared to nongang youth. If delinquency is most probable when youth develop few stakes in conventional institutions, then we should expect that youths who are relatively free of conventional entanglements will be freer to violate rules of all sorts. Theory-oriented research concentrates on bringing evidence to bear as directly as possible on the specific causal mechanisms and assumptions of one or more theories of delinquency.

It is not a simple matter to do such research since theorists are typically quite vague on the exact meaning of concepts and only rarely provide guidelines for actually measuring them. Moreover, scholars disagree on the actual significance or meaning of findings for the validity of a theory. A piece of research viewed as contrary to a theory by one scholar may be viewed as irrelevant by another or even as supportive evidence by yet another. In addition, delinquency can be conceived of and measured in several different ways, and an explanation of delinquency conceived in one fashion may not adequately explain delinquency conceived of in a different fashion. Thus, any review of research bearing on theory is open to challenge, and the conclusions are largely based on the judgment of the reviewer. Moreover, a considerable amount of research has focused on specific social institutions such as the family, media, education, and religion, rather than on testing hypotheses derived specifically from the theories summarized above. Research on such specific topics will be addressed in chapters 7 and 8.

Structural Strain/Status Frustration Theory

The original formulations of structural strain/status frustration theory in sociology focused on gangs and subcultures, attributing the nature and distribution of delinquent gangs to the existence of delinquent subcultures that have distinctive values, norms, and beliefs. Thus, Cohen claimed to be explaining the "content" of a delinquent gang subculture, or contraculture. Hence, the first major studies testing such theories focused on the values, norms, and beliefs of gang youth. For example, Short and Strodtbeck (1965) compared gang boys in Chicago with lower-class and middle-class nongang boys in terms of their evaluations of conventional images (for example, "someone who works for good grades at school," "someone who saves his/her money") and deviant images (for example, "someone who is a good fighter with a tough reputation," "someone who knows where to sell what he/she steals"). They found that all of their samples evaluated middle-class, conventional images in equally high terms. Moreover, each sample ranked conventional images more highly than any of the unconventional images. Gang boys did tend to tolerate deviant lifestyles or images more than nongang boys, but there was no evidence of a reversal in evaluations of different lifestyles. Several early studies (Gordon et al., 1963; Lerman, 1968; Gold, 1963) found that gang boys evaluate deviant and conventional behaviors in terms of their "goodness" much the same as do nondelinquents.

Whether applied to gangs or delinquent behavior in general, strain theory also introduced "blocked ambitions" as a key motivation for delinquency as problem-solving behavior. Those categories of youth with the highest collective levels of strain were predicted to have the highest rates of delinquency. Some researchers have assumed that this argument can be tested by measuring perceived opportunities for success, and have reported that rates of delinquency are higher for youths who perceive their opportunities as limited than for those who anticipate no barriers to success (Cernkovich, 1978; Aultman, 1979). However, while these findings are consistent with strain theory, they do not provide crucial support in that they are consistent with other theories as well. Youths who do not anticipate achieving certain success goals may not be committed to such goals and therefore experience little or no frustration. A social control theorist could argue that they merely have less to lose by involvement in delinquency. A cultural deviance theorist could argue that deviant routes to success are accorded respect in the wider subcultural community and that youths who perceive conventional opportunity as limited are not frustrated.

It is blocked opportunity *coupled* with commitment to certain success goals that characterizes the logic of the strain explanation of delinquency. "Strain" is defined in terms of a discrepancy between a person's ambitions and opportunity; not opportunity alone. Because a disparity between ambition and reality is central to strain theories of delinquency, some researchers have predicted that the highest rates of delinquency should be found among youths who have high ambitions but do not expect to realize them. Their rates should be higher than those for youths who neither expect to achieve nor care about such conventional goals. The latter youth should not be frustrated since they do not have blocked ambitions. In actual research, the highest delinquency rates are found among boys who have both low aspiration *and* low expectations (Hirschi, 1969; Short, Rivera, and Tennyson, 1965). Reanalysis of one of these studies (Jensen, 1986) indicates that boys low in both aspirations and expectations are not significantly higher in delinquency than boys in the high strain category (i.e., high aspirations, low expectations). Such a finding is contrary to strain theory predictions that the highest delinquency rates should be found among boys experiencing frustrated ambitions.

Several scholars have suggested that an adequate test of strain theory requires consideration of goals that are important and meaningful in the everyday lives of teenagers. While an initial examination of such a possibility suggested that anticipated failure in the achievement of immediate goals was related to delinquency (Quicker, 1974), reanalysis of such data (Greenberg, 1979a, 1979b) and two additional studies (Elliott and Voss, 1974; Agnew, 1984) have failed to provide support for strain theory. In his early research, Agnew actually argued that there is a sufficient range of goals for adolescents to allow them to achieve at least some of them, and hence, strain theory may be unable to explain delinquency because "very few adolescents are strained" (1984:446). Rather than doggedly contemplating failure in the pursuit of unrealistic goals, teenagers are likely to shift goals and concentrate on those they can achieve.

When applied to the explanation of delinquency, problem-solving versions of strain theory imply that, given the right circumstances, such activities are part of a "solution" to the problems generating them. For example, Cohen depicts a delinquent contraculture as a collective solution to status problems:

> The delinquent subculture, we suggest, is a way of dealing with the problems of adjustment we have described. These problems are chiefly status problems: certain children are denied status in respectable society because they cannot meet the criteria of the respectable status system. The delinquent subculture deals with these problems by providing criteria of status which these children *can* meet. (1955:121)

Other theorists have expressed similar arguments in which the specific problem prompting a search for a solution is damaged self-esteem. Kaplan (1975) argues that a wide variety of deviant behaviors are "defenses of self," prompted initially by social rejection. Sociologists advancing such arguments have focused specifically on participation in delinquent groups as a means of acquiring status and self-respect.

Research on status problems and delinquency has yielded mixed results with regard to the role delinquency plays in solving those problems. Two studies have found that when youths are followed over time, those who initially have low self-esteem have a subsequently higher probability of delinquency, and that self-esteem appears to increase after such involvement (Kaplan, 1980; Bynner, O'Malley, and Bachman, 1981). In contrast, two other studies report no significant enhancement of self-esteem following participation in delinquency (McCarthy and Hoge, 1984; Wells and Rankin, 1983). One of the studies supporting the problem-solving argument also reports that it applies only to certain categories of boys who lack other means of coping with or mitigating rejection (Kaplan, 1980). As matters stand today, we cannot say for certain that delinquency solves status problems, but neither can such a possibility be dismissed. Moreover, none of these studies specifically examines group delinquency, and it is the allocation of status by other similarly situated youth which helps solve status problems, according to sociological brands of strain theory.

One study has specifically addressed the relevance of perceptions of gender-based barriers to achievement on female delinquency. Stephen Cernkovich and Peggy Giordano (1979) analyzed self-report data from 1,355 male and female high-school students and found perception of blocked opportunity based on gender to be unrelated to delinquency among girls. More general perceptions of blocked opportunity also were unrelated to delinquency among girls. In contrast, such general perceptions were a significant correlate of delinquency for boys. Thus, strain-theory notions may be more relevant for boys than girls (as Cohen originally proposed). However, it is important to remember that without data on the aspirations or ambitions of youth, the perception of limited opportunities is not necessarily indicative of frustration. Those who perceive limited opportunity may or may not be ambitious and may or may not be frustrated. At any rate, there is little evidence that strain theory applies to girls and, currently, there is a lack of crucial support among boys.

Most recent research has concentrated on Messner and Rosenfeld's or Agnew's versions of strain theory rather than the classic versions that focused on gangs and subcultures. For example, Messner and Rosenfeld (1997, 2001) propose that societies characterized by economic dominance with a weak governmental "safety net" will have higher rates of homicide than nations with a strong safety net. Dominance of economic institutions and economic goals are hypothesized to increase crime by undermining conventional institutions such as the family and by generating economic pressures on people who have restricted opportunity. Messner and Rosenfeld analyzed homicide data among nations and their research indicates that nations such as the United States with a relatively weak welfare system have significantly higher rates of homicide than nations with strong welfare safety nets (e.g., Scandinavian nations). However, other analyses have shown that when nations have a strong governmental safety net, other institutions such as the family and religion are weaker, not stronger as implied, and that property crime rates are actually higher in the nations with the stronger nets (see Jensen, 2002). Moreover, the impact of the safety net variable has been found to disappear when other variables are introduced (Jensen and Akers, 2003; Jensen, 2006).

Agnew's theory has received some support in that several studies have found that measures of "stress," "anxiety," or "anger" are positively correlated with delinquency when other correlates are controlled (e.g., see Agnew and White, 1992; Paternoster and Mazerolle, 1994; Piquero and Sealock, 2000; Jensen, 2003). One of the most recent tests of the theory examines the impact of a variety of negative experiences (e.g., emotional abuse, unemployment, homelessness). Such experiences were associated with a high level of anger among youth and that anger was a significant correlate of crime (Baron, 2004). However, such findings are problematic for any problem-solving version of strain theory. If delinquency is a means of alleviating stress or anxiety, then delinquency should not be related to stress; that is, the response, delinquency, should have solved the problem. On the other hand, such findings are consistent with a version of strain theory where stress and anxiety provide part of the impetus for delinquency, but where delinquency does not eliminate the specific problem generating it.

Social Disorganization/Social Control Theory

The most significant development in the study of social disorganization is research measuring characteristics of neighborhoods in Chicago through a combination of videotapes, surveys, census data, and police data. Sampson and Raudenbush (1999:603) used these data to test a theory of collective efficacy, defining collective efficacy as "cohesion among residents combined with shared expectations for the social control of public space." They found that "collective efficacy explains lower rates of crime and observed disorder after controlling neighborhood structural characteristics." In contrast, using videotapes to rate street segments in terms of the observable features of neighborhoods emphasized in broken windows theory, they found very little support for that perspective.

Sampson and Bartusch (1998) also found little support for theories that depict the normative orientations of blacks and Latinos as encouraging crime. They report that "contrary to received wisdom, we find that African Americans and Latinos are less tolerant of deviance—including violence—than whites" (1998:777). Such findings are problematic for versions of normative conflict theory such as Miller's, in which sizeable segments of whole communities or neighborhoods share normative orientations conducive to lawbreaking. Sampson and Bartusch did find pervasive cynicism about the law and dissatisfaction with the police among minorities, but those findings are not evidence of a criminogenic subculture. In short, the research by Sampson and colleagues is consistent with common themes in social disorganization/social control perspectives.

Control theorists focus on barriers to involvement in delinquency and have argued that the search for underlying motivation will not get us very far in understanding delinquency. The most important question is not why youths commit offenses, but rather why *don't* youths commit offenses? Briar and Piliavin challenge the view that there are measurable, long-term motives of the sort emphasized when structural strain or subcultural value systems are introduced to explain delinquency:

> Because delinquency behavior is typically episodic, purposive, and confined to certain situations, we assume that the motives for such behavior are frequently episodic, oriented to short-term ends, and confined to certain situations. That is, rather than considering delinquency acts as solely the product of long-term motives, deriving from conflicts or frustrations whose genesis is far removed from the arenas in which the illegal behavior occurs, we assume these acts are prompted by short-term situationally induced desires experienced by all boys to obtain valued goods, to portray courage in the presence of, or be loyal to, peers, to strike out at someone who is disliked, or simply to "get kicks." (1965:36)

The support for social control theorists' challenge to the significance of motivation has been rather indirect. For one, the *lack* of research to support arguments that emphasize structurally and culturally induced motives has been interpreted as an indication that the motives must be much more diverse and difficult to predict than motivational theories suggest. Second, the fact that delinquency itself is episodic and sporadic, occupying very little time (even among gang delinquents), has been cited as support for the idea that the motives are similarly sporadic and episodic. Finally, the fact that delinquent activity is so common suggests that the motives are quite commonly experienced and not concentrated in any one social class or social setting.

Martin Gold's research into the degree of premeditation involved in delinquent behavior, as well as the intensity of delinquent participation, led him to compare delinquency to a "pickup" game of basketball or football (1970). Such games are casual, unplanned, and short term. Some youngsters are strongly committed to the game, but many are indifferent or unwilling to play. With the proper combination of time and place, a game can be organized, but in many instances sufficient catalyzing forces do not emerge. If and when the stage is set and the game begins, performance becomes an important aspect. The fact that a group of friends is present is not so important as the notion of the performance. In other words, Gold sees delinquency as a spontaneous, unplanned event with certain members of the group performing as players and others being more passive and performing as the audience. Gold believes that the image of delinquency as an impromptu performance is closer to the truth than the image of the delinquent as a chronic offender or disturbed adolescent. Thus, Gold's findings support social control theory's downplaying of motivational factors and strong emphasis on the situational nature of delinquent behavior.

Research studies have shown significant relationships between involvement in delinquency and attachment to conventional others, values, and institutions. Youths who identify with their parents, care what their teachers think about them, aspire toward high occupational or educational status, and respect the law and its agents are significantly less likely to commit delinquent acts than are youths with fewer "stakes in conformity" (Hirschi, 1969; Hindelang, 1973; Jensen, 1972; Hepburn, 1976). However, the most recent studies following youth over a period of time suggest that the impact of such stakes in conformity may have been exaggerated in research examining such relationships at single points in time (see Agnew, 1985; Elliott, Huizinga, and Ageton, 1985; Liska and Reed, 1985). Since youths' relationships with conventional people, values, and institutions can be affected by their past misbehavior, some of the association between such variables and delinquency may be a product of the impact of misbehavior on such relationships rather than the inhibiting impact of those relationships. Those studies suggest that delinquent peers and variation in conventional and unconventional beliefs may have the greatest impact on delinquency and that other circumstances such as family and school relationships affect delinquency through their impact on association with such peers and beliefs.

The studies following youths over time involve a relatively short period of their lives and tend to involve youths at or past the peak ages for delinquency. These characteristics of the studies are important to our interpretation of results because the relevance of such variables as relationships with parents may rest with responses to behavior in childhood socialization. Youths who do not care about their parents' reactions or whose parents do not detect or react to misbehavior in early childhood are likely to get into difficulties at school and in the community. Research to be summarized in chapter 10 shows that changes in parental response to behavior can impressively alter their children's behavior as well. In sum, while some studies are challenging the relevance of social control variables to delinquency, there is considerable counter evidence that parental attempts at control and socialization are relevant to the behavior of children.

Control theory is at odds with strain theory over the relationship between conventional aspirations and delinquency. As already noted, strain theorists argue that high aspirations coupled with limited opportunity generate status problems and that such problems are concentrated in the lower or working classes. On the other hand, some control theorists (Hirschi, 1969) believe that conventional aspirations constitute a "stake" in conformity and therefore act as a barrier to delinquency.

As noted in the discussion of strain theory, ambitious youth who anticipate failure do not appear to be significantly more delinquent than unambitious youth. However, neither has it been conclusively shown that high conventional aspirations inhibit delinquency regardless of realistic expectations. For example, some of the findings that Hirschi uses to challenge strain theory also show that youths who do not expect to achieve high status have high delinquency rates, whether or not they aspire to such status (1969:172). Some of these youths may have abandoned any commitment to conventional success as a result of anticipated failure, and many of them may never have had such aspirations. However, such findings constitute a problem for the control theorists' argument that aspirations act as a barrier to delinquency, regardless of youths' expectations.

The scope of factors that control theory presents as barriers to delinquency is quite broad. For example, Briar and Piliavin (1965) have cited the following barriers: (1) fear of material deprivations and punishments, (2) protection of self-image, (3) maintenance of valued relationships, and (4) preservation of future status and activities. Hirschi has differentiated four dimensions of the "social bond" between youths and conventional society that act as a barrier to delinquency: (1) attachment or identification; for example, with parents, (2) commitment to conventional goals; such as high occupational status, (3) belief in the legitimacy of conventional norms, and (4) involvement in conventional activities.

Several studies of involvement in conventional activities have failed to support the predictions of control theory. Hirschi found that participation in work, sports, recreation, and hobbies were unrelated to delinquency (1969:189–90). Robin reported that involvement in antipoverty job corps or neighborhood youth corps programs had no significant impact on delinquent behavior during or after participation in the programs (1969:323–31). Schaefer found no significant relationship between participation in interscholastic athletics and delinquency when controlling for grade-point average and social class (1969:40–47). Even the amount of time under direct parental control or surveillance has been found to be only weakly related to delinquency. On the other hand, involvement in some academic activities has been shown to be negatively related to delinquency (Hirschi, 1969:191–92; Hindelang, 1973:481–83). In short, although control theory predicts that participation in conventional activities should deter delinquency, many forms of participation do not. There is little overall support for the folk belief that "idle hands are the devil's workshop." Those forms of participation that are related to delinquency (for example, time spent on homework) are those that are likely to reflect real commitment and valued relationships. Control theorists have not been able to predict what forms of participation are important barriers to delinquency.

Research also has failed to support some control theorists' claims that attachment to others is a barrier to delinquency even if those others are involved in delinquency. One of the most prominent control theorists has argued that "we honor those we admire not by imitation, but by adherence to conventional standards" (Hirschi, 1969:152). This argument represents an extreme version of control theory in which it does not matter to whom a person is attached. The actual support for that argument is very weak, and there are several studies whose findings are to the contrary. Hirschi reported a weak negative correlation between "wanting to be like one's friends" and delinquency, even for youths with several delinquent friends. However, further analysis of the same body of data (Jensen and Erickson, 1977) showed no significant association between peer commitment and delinquency among African-American youths. Moreover, at least four studies have reported positive associations—that is, the greater the attachment to peers, the greater the delinquency (Empey and Lubeck, 1971; Hindelang, 1973; Erickson and Empey, 1965; Elliott and Voss, 1974). Linden and Hackler report that the characteristics of the peers to which a youth is attached do affect the relevance of peer attachment to delinquency (1973:43). Boys with weak ties to conventional associates but with moderate or strong ties to deviant peers are more involved in delinquency than are boys who are not tied to their delinquent peers.

Giordano, Cernkovich, and Pugh (1986) argue that delinquents are not lone wolves whose only personal relationships are manipulative and exploitative. Rather, they argue that the friendship patterns of delinquent youth are quite like those of non-delinquent youth. The bulk of the research at present is consistent with this view, suggesting that there are weak but positive associations between attachment to peers and delinquency, and that boys who are "tied," "committed," or "attached" to their delinquent peers are more likely to be involved in delinquency than those who are not so committed. However, contrary findings have yet to be explained and will no doubt be the subject of further research.

Control theory variables have been introduced in the attempt to explain the gender difference in delinquency with some success. Boys and girls differ in the strength of familial bonds, in degrees of parental control, school performance, endorsement of conventional beliefs, and in their perceptions of risk of punishment. In that sense, girls have more stakes in conformity than boys. Furthermore, variations in such variables have been shown to explain much of the gender difference in delinquency (Jensen and Eve, 1976; Hagan, Gillis, and Simpson, 1985, 1987). However, association with delinquent peers has been found to be relevant to the sex difference as well, and such associations are not central to some versions of control theory.

Gottfredson and Hirschi's self-control theory has generated new research in criminology, but it should be noted that at the time the theory was proposed there was already evidence that youth who acknowledged having difficulty controlling their temper were more likely to report delinquent acts than other youth, controlling for a variety of variables (Jensen, 1973). People low in self-control are "free to enjoy the quick and easy and ordinary pleasures of crime without undue concern for the pains that follow from them" (Hirschi and Gottfredson, 2001:90). People who learn to consider the long-term consequences of their acts have self-control. Variations in self-control are established through interaction and socialization processes involving parents who care about their children, monitor their activities, recognize transgressions when they occur, and take steps to correct their children. In the process, "the child learns to avoid acts with long-term negative consequences" (2001:90).

This perspective is not a mere extension or reformulation of Hirschi's social control theory. As presented in *A General Theory of Crime* (1990), and subsequent explications of that theory, Gottfredson and Hirschi's self-control theory is a major departure from Hirschi's social bond theory as presented in *Causes of Delinquency* (1969). Most of the features of social bond theory that made it appealing to sociologists have been abandoned. In fact, self-control theory is subject to all of the criticisms Hirschi leveled against psychological theories in *Causes of Delinquency*. In his earlier work, Hirschi challenged theories that focused on internal, unchanging motivations or constraints. In his new work with Gottfredson, the central focus is on just such states. Hirschi challenged perspectives that lumped conceptually distinct social bonds together as well as theories that transformed disparate barriers or constraints into simple latent constructs. Yet, in *A General Theory of Crime* internal barriers are lumped together under the rubric of self-control. In short, the arguments concerning the primacy of self-control presented in *A General Theory of Crime* are directly contrary to the arguments presented when advocating social bond theory. In his earlier work, Hirschi demonstrated the distinct relevance of different types of bonds, whether conceived of as social or personal aspects of the self. But in his later work with Gottfredson, Hirschi explains variation in criminality by one inclusive, psychological construct, self-control. Absence of self-control explains continuity in crime among individuals over the life course, with the form of crime varying by the age-related structure of criminal opportunity.

There have been two types of research relevant to self-control theory. In one line of research, self-control is inferred to be the stable underlying factor that explains the continuity of deviant behavior or conformity over the life course. The correlation between childhood transgressions and more serious offenses later in life is taken as evidence of an underlying lack of self-control. In contrast, conformity at various ages is attributed to the early establishment of self-control. The second line of research attempts to more directly test the theory by operationalizing "low self-control" and relating it to lawbreaking, with other criminogenic variables controlled. According to Gottfredson and Hirschi, "people who lack self-control will tend to be impulsive, insensitive, physical, risk-seeking, short-sighted, and nonverbal" (1990:90–91). The opposite set of characteristics applies to people with high self-control. The attempt to specify the indicators of "low" self-control differentiates Gottfredson and Hirschi's self-control theory from social bond theory in that it introduces quasi-motivational sources of variation (i.e., impulsivity and risk-taking), relevant to the question of why people break laws.

Research attempting to measure self-control directly (e.g., Grasmick et al., 1993) has used survey data assessing attitudes of respondents that are thought to tap variations in these traits. The most recent review of such research concludes that measures of self-control are significantly related to lawbreaking, but that the theory can be challenged as a general theory of crime. Variables central to differential association and social learning theory affect lawbreaking, regardless of variations in self-control (Pratt and Cullen, 2000). At present, self-control theory has not been shown to have superior explanatory power over Hirschi's earlier social bond theory.

There is a mounting body of research drawing on social bond theory to argue that discontinuities between juvenile and adult crime are a product of variations in new social bonds. In an award-winning research monograph, *Crime in the Making: Pathways and Turning Points through Life* (1993), Sampson and Laub challenge Gottfredson and Hirschi's theory and report that, consistent with social bond theory, such variables as marital attachment and stable employment explain discontinuities in deviance. Discontinuities can be explained by social bond theory, social learning theory, and a variety of new theories categorized under the rubric of life-course perspectives.

Normative Conflict/Differential Association Theory

Normative or cultural conflict theory assumes that society is characterized by socially differentiated groups who have conflicting definitions of right and wrong, and that delinquency is the product of differential learning of conflicting definitions. Paul Lerman has captured the essence of cultural conflict theory, noting that "in a traditional conflict of conduct codes, it appears that one of the codes prescribes explicitly illegal behavior while the other proscribes it" (1968:235). Research, however, has failed to reveal the types of class-linked definitions that cultural conflict theorists posit.

In his study of white youths in California, Hirschi (1969) compared the sons of fathers in lower-class occupations with the sons of semi-skilled, white-collar fathers, and those of professional fathers. He found no significant differences among these groups in attitudes that supposedly characterize lower-class youths (for example, an expedient attitude toward the law, admiration of "sharp" operators, or sensitivity to adult criticism). He did find that the sons of professionals were less likely to feel fatalistic (that is, "there is no sense looking ahead since no one knows what the future will be like") than sons of fathers in other occupations. However, when Hirschi took measures of academic success or failure into account, he also found that the academically incompetent middle-class child was much more likely than the academically incompetent lower-class child to exhibit fatalistic attitudes. Thus, Hirschi suggested that fatalistic attitudes, rather than being an enduring aspect of a class culture, are anchored in experiences that may be more common in the lower than in the middle classes. In short, even the minimal differences in attitudes that Hirschi observed may be produced and reproduced through socially structured experiences rather than through cultural transmission.

Another set of research findings tends to contradict the argument that the **focal concerns** of lower-class culture lead to lawbreaking. Studies of attachment to or identification with parents have consistently shown that children attached to their parents are less likely to be delinquent in a variety of different samples and settings (Glueck and Glueck, 1950; Hindelang, 1973; Elliott and Voss, 1974) and regardless of social class (Hirschi, 1969). If lower-class focal concerns are conducive to delinquency, then adolescents who are most sensitive to the opinions of lower-class adults should be most likely to violate the law. Research has yet to support this argument.

The finding providing the most support for differential association theory has been the observed relationship between delinquent peers and involvement in delinquency. Adolescents with delinquent friends are themselves more likely to get into trouble with the law or report involvement in delinquency than are adolescents without delinquent friends (see Warr, 2002 and Akers and Jensen, 2006 for summaries of relevant research). This relationship is one of the strongest and most persistent in delinquency research.

For most of the history of research on delinquent peers and delinquency, it was not possible to claim that association with delinquent peers actually preceded involvement in delinquency, since it was also conceivable that youths involved in delinquency drifted together (i.e., birds of a feather flock together). It was also possible that the relationship was due to some common connection with circumstances affecting both the nature of one's friends and one's behavior. For example, youths with poor grades might be more prone to trouble and more prone to drift into delinquent groups. However, research studying panels of adolescents over time has shown that association with delinquent peers does affect a youth's subsequent probabilities of delinquency (Elliott, Huizinga, and Ageton, 1985; Paternoster and Triplett, 1988).

Another issue in normative conflict theory involves its emphasis on "definitions" as the most crucial variable in the explanation of delinquency. While delinquent peers are central to learning delinquency, it is the values, norms, and beliefs acquired through such associations that explain such group influences. When people break the law, it must be because they have learned a set of moral standards that require lawbreaking or because they have learned an "excess of definitions favorable to the violation of the law." Definitions control behavior to such a degree that what appears to be deviant behavior is really conforming behavior. People are always doing what they believe to be morally correct. This characteristic of normative conflict/differential association theory sets it apart from social learning theory (see chapter 5). According to social learning theorists, delinquency can be learned through imitation, differential reward and punishment, and "normative" socialization.

It does appear that variations in moral beliefs about the law and the impropriety of lawbreaking are affected by delinquent friends, and one study reports that such friends have their impact through such normative or definitional learning processes (Matsueda, 1982). Other studies suggest that while definitions and delinquent associations are key to understanding delinquency, delinquent friends may affect delinquency through group processes and pressures other than normative learning (Akers et al., 1978; Elliott, Huizinga, and Ageton, 1985; Paternoster and Triplett, 1988). Youths who "go along with their friends" may be rewarded by others for such conformity and thus do what their friends are doing even though they define such activity as wrong. However, there is also a general tendency for people to seek consistency between their moral beliefs and behavior. It may be that youths become involved in delinquency due to friendships, conflict at home and school, and a variety of circumstances, and subsequently develop a moral code that legitimizes their behavior.

Social learning theory has been the subject of a considerable volume of research. In fact, the theory has been tested in relation to a wider range of forms of deviance, in a wider range of settings and samples, in more different languages, and by more different people, has survived more "crucial tests" against other theories, and is the most strongly and consistently supported by empirical data than any other social psychological explanation of crime and deviance (see Akers, 1998; Akers and Jensen, 2003). Akers and Jensen (2006) have accessed the research relevant to the theory and conclude:

> The great preponderance of research conducted on social learning theory has found strong to moderate relationships in the theoretically expected direction between social learning variables and criminal, delinquent, and deviant behavior. When social learning theory is tested against other theories using the same data collected from the same samples, it is usually . . . found to account for more variance in the dependent variables or have greater support than the theories with which it is being compared . . . (W)hen social learning variables are included in integrated or combined models that incorporate variables from different theories in the same sample with the same data, it is the measures of social learning concepts that have the strongest main and net effects . . . Cross-cultural studies have found that social learning theory is not society or culture bound but is well supported by research in other societies. (2006:10)

In prior editions of this text we were critical of social learning theory because it did not deal with the macro issues that other theories addressed. However, Akers began addressing such issues under the rubric of a social structure/social learning theory (SSSL). His basic argument is that social learning mechanisms are key to explaining variations by race, class, gender, and location. Since his elaboration of the theory in 1998, tests of the SSSL model have been conducted for delinquency, substance use, elderly alcohol abuse, rape, violence, and binge drinking by college students. Also,

Akers and Jensen (2003) found that social structural and cultural factors derivable from social learning principles did a better job of explaining variation in homicide rates among nations than the institutional anomie theory. These and other findings are consistent with the SSSL model.

Research specifically addressing SSSL theory has been shown to be relevant to understanding the distribution of violence among neighborhoods. Bellair, Roscigno, and Velez argue that, in contrast to other theories emphasizing social disorganization, violence among adolescents "has its roots in local labor market conditions and opportunity" (2003:199). They use a SSSL model to explain the "spatial concentration of violence among adolescents," introducing a variable that they believe is more relevant to SSSL theory than more traditional variables—the availability of professional role models in an area or neighborhood. They show that structural effects are explained or mediated by social learning mechanisms, and further, at the macro-level it is the prevalence of professional sector employment that is most intimately tied with such mechanisms. They argue that the structural distribution of violence reflects the "absence in the community of professional role models and a decline in employment opportunities" rather than the traditional measures of the concentration of disadvantage. Thus, not only are social learning mechanisms key mediators, but the macro-level condition that is most important is the presence of professional role models. In short, opportunities for modeling at the structural level are central to the explanation of the spatial distribution of violent crime.

Jensen (2003) has addressed the gender difference in delinquency by testing the hypotheses derived from a variety of theories using data collected from youths in Seattle by Hindelang, Hirschi, and Weiss (1981). The gender difference in either self-report or police data for serious offenses (including violence) was found to be fully explained by three sets of variables: (1) gender-linked self-images, (2) acceptance of conventional moral standards, and (3) interaction with delinquent peers. Although some of these findings can be argued to fit with other theories as well, social learning theory is the only one to encompass all of them. The results are consistent with Akers's SSSL theory in that the social learning mechanisms are the mediating mechanisms that explain the most prominent difference in delinquency by social background.

Additional Perspectives

We argue that when carefully analyzed and compared, sociological theories about delinquency and youth crime tend to fall in one or another of the traditions outlined earlier. Three types of theorists, however, have been very critical of those traditions and the research they have inspired. We will now examine these three perspectives that challenge the traditional sociological explanations of delinquency: Marxist, feminist, and social constructionist theories.

Marxist Theory

Several theorists, including David Greenberg, Herman and Julia Schwendinger, Richard Quinney, Jock Young, and others have proposed perspectives that draw on or reformulate prior theoretical notions in terms of ideas developed by German social philosopher Karl Marx (1818–1883). In **Marxist theory** the economic system is central to understanding all other aspects of society and culture, and people's lives revolve around economic production. Marxist theorists focus on the control of economic production and work in societies, and locate the origins of social problems in the contradictions that characterize capitalism as a form of political-economic organization. For example, in capitalist societies and in societies colonized or under development by capitalist societies, it is to the advantage of those who control economic development to have a large, readily available, surplus labor force. Cheap, available labor helps keep costs down and profits up. Moreover, to generate profits, the products of economic production must be sold. There must be a market for them. People must want both the necessities and luxuries produced. Of course, the generation of a large surplus labor force that is often unemployed and underemployed, combined with the emphasis on consumption, creates the same condition emphasized by strain theory—sizeable segments of society with needs that cannot be realized.

When applied to the explanation of delinquency, Marxist theory views young people as particularly likely to experience such a strain or contradiction. In fact, as noted in chapter 2, Marxist theorists argue that the category of "juvenile delinquent" itself was invented to cope with the problem behaviors generated as the marginal period of life (between childhood and incorporation into the economy) grew. A central concept in some Marxist perspectives on delinquency is **marginality**. Categories of people who exist on the periphery of the economic system as an unemployed or underemployed surplus population or labor force are marginal categories. Youth as a whole are marginalized, although many will move into the mainstream economy with age. Marxists attribute the high crime rate of youth to their status as a marginal category, and variations within the adolescent world reflect variations in marginality (see Schwendinger and Schwendinger, 1976; Greenberg, 1979a). The Schwendingers (1985) claim that it is in the best interest of the state and dominant economic classes to maintain such marginal categories as a ready pool for low-paid manual labor.

The exact nature of variations among adolescents and the processes operating at the individual level in the determination of delinquency have not been clearly specified by Marxist theorists, and scholars claiming a Marxist heritage for their theories make contradictory claims. For example, the emphasis on marginality implies that the most marginal young people and those with the least hope of escaping marginality with age will have the highest delinquency rates. Yet, John Hagan and colleagues (1985) predict that children whose parents control other workers will be raised to take risks and to believe that they are relatively free from the control of others and, hence, will engage in more delinquency than lower-status youth. Those youth who are least marginal in terms of potential dominance of others and occupational power are predicted to have the highest rates, rather than those on the periphery. Those youth are posited as "freer" to break laws with impunity. Hagan, Gillis, and Simpson (1985) hypothesize that power decreases the probability of being caught and punished, and hence, increases rather than decreases most common types of delinquency.

In contrast, Mark Colvin and John Pauley (1983) propose a *structural Marxist* approach to delinquency, predicting an inverse relationship between parent's occupational power and children's delinquency. According to their theory, parents tend to reproduce the authority relations they experience at the workplace in the home; therefore, the coercive social milieu that most workers find themselves in leads to authoritarian relationships at home. Coercive and authoritarian family relationships allegedly undermine affection and intimate bonds to parents, leading to a higher probability of delinquency than nonauthoritarian and noncoercive familial relationships. Thus, while Hagan, Gillis, and Simpson predict that those parents who are most controlled and dominated in the workplace will have children who are controlled, and hence, less likely to break laws, Colvin and Pauley predict that such control undermines social bonds and increases the odds of delinquency. The predictions are the exact opposite although they both propose to be structural Marxist theories.

In their award-winning book, *Adolescent Subcultures and Delinquency* (1985), the Schwendingers propose a different approach that combines notions of symbolic interactionism with Marxist theory in the explanation of delinquency. The focus in *symbolic interaction theory* is on the formation and selection of symbolic identities that occur in interaction with other people. In their theory, adolescent subcultures are organized around certain common identities that youths can take on and those identities are more important for understanding delinquency than parental class. Indeed, the Schwendingers predict small but negative relationships between parental status and delinquency. In contrast, youths who belong to certain *stradoms* (stratified peer-group domains) are predicted to vary in delinquency and school misconduct. Data on delinquency and membership in different stradoms support their argument. They found the lowest rates of delinquency among "Brains" and "Athletes" and the highest rates among streetcorner types of youth referred to as "Hodads" or "Greasers." "Socialites" and "Surfers" were more likely to be involved in delinquency than "Brains" or "Athletes" as well. The stradom a youth falls in is affected by parental status but determined by other variables as well, such that the relationship between parental status and delinquency may be quite weak while the relationship between stradom membership and delinquency may be quite strong. In this theory it is stratification and lifestyles in the adolescent social world that are central to understanding delinquency.

At the individual level, Marxist theorists introduce variables much like those stressed in other criminological theories. Why don't people break laws more often since the economic system is not serving their interests? Some Marxists will emphasize fear of legal punishment in answering this question. Powerful groups determine the nature of laws defining crime, and law enforcement serves to control marginal groups (see Quinney, 1980; Chambliss and Mankoff, 1976; Taylor, Walton, and Young, 1973). Fear of punishment is central to explaining crime and delinquency in deterrence theory, a classical criminological perspective which we will discuss in chapter 9.

In his presentation of a "Working-Class Criminology" (1975), English criminologist Jock Young argues that people are inhibited by a conservative ideology of law and order that is maintained through educational institutions and which does, to some degree, appeal to working-class and marginal groups who need protection from crime. Compulsory education helps insure a common exposure to a belief system stressing the virtue of conformity to law, patience in the pursuit of material and social success, and the horrendous personal and social costs of lawbreaking. Thus, variations in crime and delinquency can reflect variations in acceptance or internalization of beliefs that inhibit lawbreaking, a notion consistent with several traditional theories.

Another variable introduced in the discussion of capitalism and social problems is **alienation**. This concept is widely used by sociologists and has been used in a variety of studies of delinquency (see Menard and Morse, 1984; Engstad and Hackler, 1971; Stinchcombe, 1964). The *Dictionary of the Social Sciences* defines alienation as "an estrangement or separation between the parts or whole of the personality and significant aspects of the world of experience" (1964:19). The concept originally referred to aspects of economic production under capitalism wherein people became "estranged" from the products of their labor (e.g., mass assembly lines where each worker performs a repetitive, specialized task and neither owns nor controls the final product). However, it is widely used to refer to estrangement from society in general or specific institutions such as the school. For example, modern mass education is often depicted as "alienating" and those youths who are most alienated from such institutions are predicted to be the most likely to get into trouble. There are several studies supporting such arguments (e.g., Stinchcombe, 1964; Engstad and Hackler, 1971). Moreover, research taken as support for social control theory is also consistent with this argument in the sense that youths who are not attached to conventional people and institutions can also be considered to be estranged or alienated from those institutions.

Another individual cause of delinquency and crime emphasized by the Marxist theorist William Bonger (1916) was **egoism**. According to Bonger, people in a capitalist society are encouraged to pursue satisfaction of ever-expanding desires for wealth and status with little regard for the well-being of others. Such egoism is viewed as common to most people in such societies and even more common among the relatively advantaged classes than among the disadvantaged. However, while egoism provides a motivating force for delinquency, Bonger argues that the children of the well-to-do are watched more closely and prevented from associating with "bad society" and, thus, are less likely to commit delinquent acts.

In sum, it is difficult to discern one consistent set of specific predictions about such basic issues as the relation between social class and delinquency that could be considered *the* Marxist perspective. Furthermore, the processes operating at the individual level are similar to those characterizing strain, cultural conflict, control, and deterrence theories of criminality. The most distinctive claim is that societies characterized by capitalism or capitalist colonization should have higher rates of delinquency than societies characterized by socialist or communist forms of economic organization (Chambliss and Mankoff, 1976). Due to international variations in crime statistics and the lack of comparative data on actual rates of delinquent activity among distinctive societies, that claim is still a hypothesis to be tested. Moreover, some Marxist theorists (Quinney, 1977) would not necessarily accept that variations in crime and delinquency among *existing* societies are relevant to the view that a "true" socialist society would have low crimes rates, for the simple reason that the principles of a true socialist state have not been realized in existing societies. Hence, the fact that advanced capitalist economies do not have invariably high delinquency rates (e.g., Japan, Switzerland) may be irrelevant to such theories. As we will note in chapter 12, such theories make claims about the future that are not necessarily anchored in existing variations. That fact does not make them wrong, but means that verification of the theory can only occur with the future realization of alternative forms of economic organization.

Feminist Theory

Of all the background characteristics of youths studied by criminologists, the most impressive and persistent differences in crime and delinquency across different societies, different measures of crime, and different times are gender differences. Yet, the gender difference has not been as prominent as class differences as a historical focus for sociological theories of crime and delinquency. Even contemporary theories that highlight its importance introduce gender in the context of the study of class variations rooted in classical Marxist theory.

Advocates of **feminist theory** have been critical of several features of criminological theory and research that they argue reflect a male bias. For one, there has been little research on forms of delinquency where females have rates comparable to or exceeding male rates, such as running away (Chesney-Lind, 1989). Since the most serious female status offenders are more likely than male status offenders to come from families where they have been the victims of male sexual abuse, the role that male dominance over women (i.e., patriarchy) can play in generating female delinquency is slighted. Second, variables that might help explain low female rates of delinquency that are specific to females have been ignored. For example, fear of rape among girls and their parents may be a powerful constraint on female involvement in activities that increase the odds of victimization and the odds of delinquency, but such fears have never been included in any specific formulation of conventional criminological theories. Feminist critics advocate the development of theories that more directly address the dimensions of the female world and female experiences than has been the case in criminology thus far. Finally, several critics have discussed more subtle biases in male criminological theory that transform pain and suffering into positive forms of behavior (see Jensen, 1988; Chesney-Lind and Shelden, 1992). Activities where males predominate become forms of innovation or group conformity while female deviance falls within categories of escapism and retreatism. One recent theory depicts female conformity as unimaginative "submission" in contrast to male conformity, which is depicted as a reasoned choice among multiple options (Tittle, 1995). Male behavior is the tacit positive norm whether deviant or conforming.

Although gender has been moving closer to center stage in theoretical criminology, the actual amount of empirical research testing theories of gender variation is quite limited. There has been an increasing amount of research on the gender difference but few, if any, new gender-based variables have been introduced. Nor has any specific theory of delinquency that would be unique to girls been proposed and tested either by feminist criminologists or traditional criminologists. However, when applied to the gender difference, several traditional theories have helped to make sense of those differences.

Social Constructionist Theory

A third perspective that challenges the dominant focus of criminology on finding causes and testing causal theories is called **social constructionism**. Social constructionism has been the dominant perspective among sociologists interested in the study of social problems and deviance during the last decades of the twentieth century and the initial decades of the twenty-first century.

There is no single authoritative definition of that perspective, but its basic characteristics are widely understood by sociologists. First, the focus in social constructionism is on the way in which problems and problem groups come to be defined as such. Rather than asking why some people or groups do things that upset others, the fundamental question is why do some behaviors come to be defined as problems.

A very simple definition of social constructionism in the study of deviance is expressed in Rubington and Weinberg's statement that social constructionists view deviance as "subjectively problematic" as opposed to "objectively given" (2005:1–2). The typical approach to delineating the features of the constructionist perspective is to contrast it with an opposing, traditional, and quantitative alternative. These traditional alternatives are referred to using terms such as "absolutism," "realism," "naturalism," or "positivism." So, for example, a positivist takes for granted that the problems or problem people studied really exist and that people are placed in such judgmental categories because they have violated widely accepted societal norms. The social constructionist emphasizes the aspects of crime and criminals that are created as a product of panic and prejudice. In contrast, because these problems and problem-people are real to the positivists, they ask what other measurable characteristics of people or their social world determined that reality.

One of the most common types of evidence used to highlight the constructionist position is any indication of a tenuous or fabricated "reality" as the impetus for defining a social problem, defining problematic people, or applying definitions and labels to specific people. In fact, the most impressive "deconstruction" of a problem from such a perspective is a demonstration that the alleged reality is a total fabrication or a dramatic distortion of some real-world events. Socially constructed myths can be exposed when information on the actual events that prompt the moral enterprise defining a problem can be shown to be an overdramatization or an overreaction to those events.

For example, a common research theme in constructionist research is to examine the role of the media or the use of the media by various interest groups in the invention or definition of a social problem. Social constructionists can make a strong case for the view that "reality depends on perspective, and perspective is to a degree arbitrary" by demonstrating disparities among measures of reality. For example, Shelden, Tracy, and Brown (2001:3) state that data on gang-related articles in newspapers and magazines "demonstrates that media reporting of events does not always conform to reality." The specific pattern leading to that conclusion was the decline in news coverage "in recent years," coupled with "steady growth in the number of gangs and the number of gang members" in "surveys of law enforcement agencies." The gang problem could be interpreted as declining according to one source of subjective imagery while remaining constant, or even increasing, using data pertinent to an alternative subjective reality.

In fact, the concept of a **moral panic** was introduced by social constructionists to encompass situations where the public, political, and media reactions to a troublesome event or "problem" appear to far exceed the actual magnitude or any changes in the magnitude of the problem (Goode and Ben-Yehuda, 1994). The rediscovery of the gang problem in the 1980s is depicted by McCorkle and Miethe under the rubric of *Panic: The Social Construction of the Gang Problem* (2002), and their analysis emphasizes the fabrication of many aspects of the problem. News about cocaine use among athletes is depicted by other researchers as a problem fabricated through media hype with little or no relation to actual drug use (Reinarman and Levine, 1989). Similar arguments have been proposed for problems ranging from the search for Satanists and witches in preschools (Richardson, Best, and Bromley, 1991) to child abuse data (Best, 1990) to the "crack-baby panic" (Logan, 1999).

However, in the process of highlighting the "fabricated" dimensions of many social problems, constructionists tend to minimize the relevance of any discernable variations in the magnitude of underlying events or behaviors. Whenever a claim is made that a particular situation is a moral panic or a fabricated problem, it is incumbent upon those making such claims to clearly demonstrate that there was no actual surge of real-world events to prompt such a panic. Similarly, it is incumbent upon sociologists using positivist methods to ask to what degree a public or media reaction was an overreaction to any discernible change in behavior. Both perspectives require attention to data of some kind (see box 4-4 as an illustration).

Summary

This chapter outlined theories developed by sociologists to explain the distribution of delinquency and summarized much of the research carried out to test such theories. Sociological approaches have been most distinct from psychological or biological perspectives when treating delinquency as a type of group behavior, a distinctive subcultural orientation, or as a characteristic of neighborhoods, communities, or territories. Moreover, years of research have shown delinquency to be an eminently sociological subject matter in that it is generally a group activity. The fact that most delinquency occurs among youths interacting with other youths has been established in numerous studies and is true for both boys and girls and in a variety of different settings.

While much of the chapter concentrated on the contrasts among theories, it is important to remember that the theories do share certain broad assumptions in common, enabling us to classify them as sociological in orientation. They all assume that delinquency is acquired or *learned* behavior and that the probability that such behavior will be acquired varies, depending on cultural patterns, social institutions and groups, and the structure of legal and illegal opportunities. Different sociological theories are characterized by different ideas about the exact nature and relative importance of different environmental circumstances. Three theories that differ sufficiently to be considered unique schools of thought are (1) social disorganization/social control theory, (2) structural strain/status frustration theory, and (3) normative conflict/differential association theory.

Contemporary reformulations of traditional sociological perspectives are classified in terms of three basic questions. Does the theory incorporate or require some form of imbalance, strain, stress, or frustrated pursuit of conventional or widely shared goals? If so, it falls in the structural strain tradition. Does the theory assume that the absence of constraints or limits on opportunity for crime plays a key role in explaining crime and delinquency? If "motivation" refers to characteristics of humans considered to be quite natural when social, cultural, or opportunity constraints are absent such that no special pressure is required, then it falls in the social disorganization/social control tradition. Does the theory focus on normal learning processes, including socially structured schedules of reward and punishment; variable values, norms, and beliefs; and associations with people who both encourage and discourage crime and delinquency? If so, the theory fits better with the normative conflict/differential association category than the other two systems of ideas.

Has any one theory fared better than others in research? In general, the social learning perspective has been subjected to more tests than any other theory and has fared quite well. Moreover, when features of the theory that are not central to the logic of strain or social control theory have been considered (e.g., the influence of peers, contingent effects of attachment to parents, separable influences of normative and non-normative learning processes), social learning theory has fared very well. Does its comparative success mean that the other perspectives are totally wrong? Of course not. Anger and frustration can lead to delinquency. Under some circumstances, delinquency may become a "defense" of self. Low self-control can facilitate delinquency. On the other hand, as a general theory that can encompass anger, frustration, and self-control, we have to give the edge to social learning theory.

Further progress in the explanation of delinquency is likely to require that more attention be paid to several issues that have been raised repeatedly over the decades but have rarely been investigated in a systematic fashion. Specifically, we need to learn far more about the relevance of different variables at different times in history, for specific groups and settings, for different types of offenses, and for group as opposed to individual delinquent activities. This issue will become even more obvious in the chapters to follow, which deal with the relevance of family, schools, peers, religion, media, and guns. The same limitations characterizing tests of theory apply to seemingly straightforward studies of the relevance of specific social variables to the explanation of delinquency.

Discussion Questions

1. Because the theories discussed in this chapter are all "sociological," what assumptions do they share?

2. Your text indicates that the motivation for delinquency from a cultural conflict perspective is "natural." Yet, the motivation for delinquency in social control theories is called natural as well. Explain how these two contrasting theories can both view motivation as natural.

3. On what grounds do control theorists argue that an emphasis on motivation will not take us very far in understanding delinquency?

4. What do you consider to have been important barriers to delinquency in your life? Do you think your experience can be generalized to other groups and settings?

5. Use the ideas associated with strain theory to explain the higher rate of delinquency among males than females. Do you think today's teenage girls are more likely to experience the problems discussed by strain theorists than teenage girls in the 1950s?

6. Certain folk sayings parallel theories of delinquency; for example, "birds of a feather flock together" and "a rotten apple spoils the barrel." Discuss these two examples in relation to theories of delinquency.

7. Explain the classification of any two of the following contemporary reformulations of the three major theories in criminology: (1) self-control theory, (2) broken windows theory, (3) general strain theory, or (4) institutional anomie theory.

8. Cultural conflict theorists assume that normative socialization involving definitions of right and wrong conduct explain why friends and parents influence behavior. Are there ways friends and parents might influence a youth's behavior regardless of their definitions? What processes have social learning theorists suggested?

9. Which type of sociological theory most stresses the view that deviance is "subjectively problematic" as opposed to "objectively given." What does that statement mean and why are this text's authors critical of the perspective?

10. What do so-called feminist and Marxist theories share in common? How do they differ?

References

Agnew, R. 1984. "Goal Achievement and Delinquency." *Sociology and Social Research* 68(4):435–51.

———. 1985. "Social Control Theory and Delinquency: A Longitudinal Test." *Criminology* 23:47–61.

———. 2005. *Pressured Into Crime: An Overview of General Strain Theory.* Los Angeles: Roxbury.

Agnew, R., and H. R. White. 1992. "An Empirical Test of General Strain Theory." *Criminology* 34:475–99.

Akers, R. L. 1998. *Social Learning and Social Structure: A General Theory of Crime and Deviance.* Boston: Northeastern University Press.

Akers, R. L., and G. F. Jensen. 2003. *Social Learning Theory and the Explanation of Crime.* Vol. 11 of *Advances in Criminological Theory.* New Brunswick, NJ: Transaction Books.

———. 2006. "Empirical Status of Social Learning Theory: Past, Present and Future." In *Taking Stock: The Status of Criminological Theory,* edited by Frances T. Cullen, John Paul Wright, and Kristie R. Blevins, 37–76. Vol. 15 of *Advances in Criminological Theory.* New Brunswick, NJ: Transaction Books.

Akers, R. L., M. D. Krohn, L. Lanza-Kaduce, and M. Radosevich. 1979. "Social Learning and Deviant Behavior." *American Sociological Review* 44 (August):636–55.

Akers, R. L., and C. Sellers. 2004. *Criminological Theories: Introduction, Evaluation, and Application.* Los Angeles: Roxbury.

Anderson, Elijah. 1999. *Code of the Street: Decency, Violence, and the Moral Life of the Inner City.* New York: W. W. Norton.

Aultman, M. 1979. "Delinquency Causation: Typological Comparisons of Path Models." *Journal of Criminal Law and Criminology* 70:152–63.

Baron, S. W. 2004. "General Strain Theory, Street Youth and Crime: A Test of Agnew's Revised Theory." *Criminology* 35:457–83.

Bellair, P. E., V. J. Roscigno, and M. B. Velez. 2003. "Occupational Structure, Social Learning, and Adolescent Violence." In *Social Learning Theory and the Explanation of Crime: A Guide for the New Century,* edited by Ronald L. Akers and Gary F. Jensen, 197–226. Vol. 11 of *Advances in Criminological Theory.* New Brunswick, NJ: Transaction Books.

Best, J. 1990. *Threatened Children: Rhetoric and Concern About Child Abuse.* Chicago: University of Chicago Press.

Bonger, W. 1916. *Criminality and Economic Conditions.* Boston: Little, Brown.

Briar, S., and I. Piliavin. 1965. "Delinquency, Situational Inducements, and Commitments to Conformity." *Social Problems* 13(1):35–45.

Bursik, R. J., Jr. 1988. "Social Disorganization and Theories of Crime and Delinquency: Problems and Prospects." *Criminology* 26 (November):519–51.

Bynner, S. M., P. M. O'Malley, and J. G. Bachman. 1981. "Self-Esteem and Delinquency Revisited." *Journal of Youth and Adolescence* 10:407–44.

Cernkovich, S. A. 1978. "Evaluating Two Models of Delinquency Causation." *Criminology* 16:335–52.

Cernkovich, S. A., and P. C. Giordano. 1979. "Delinquency, Opportunity and Gender." *Journal of Criminal Law and Criminology* 70 (Summer):145–51.

Chambliss, W. J., and M. Mankoff, eds. 1976. *Whose Law? What Order?* New York: John Wiley.

Chesney-Lind, M. 1989. "Girls' Crime and Woman's Place: Toward a Feminist Model of Female Delinquency." *Crime and Delinquency* 35:150–68.

Chesney-Lind, M., and R. Shelden. 1992. *Girls, Delinquency and Juvenile Justice.* Pacific Grove, CA: Brooks Cole.

Cloward, R. A., and L. E. Ohlin. 1960. *Delinquency and Opportunity.* New York: Free Press.

Cohen, A. K. 1955. *Delinquent Boys.* New York: Free Press.

Cohen, L., and M. Felson. 1979. "Social Changes and Crime Rate Trends: A Routine Activity Approach." *American Sociological Review* 46 (October):505–24.

Cohen, L., J. Kluegal, and K. Land. 1981. "Social Inequality and Predatory Criminal Victimization: An Exposition and Test of a Formal Theory." *American Sociological Review* 46 (October):505–24.

Colvin, M., and J. Pauley. 1983. "A Critique of Criminology: Toward an Integrated Structural Marxist Theory of Delinquency Production." *American Journal of Sociology* 89:513–55.

Crutchfield, R. D., M. R. Gerken, and W. Gove. 1982. "Crime Rate and Social Integration: The Impact of Metropolitan Mobility." *Criminology* 20:467–78.

Cullen, F. T. 1994. "Social Support as an Organizing Concept for Criminology: Presidential Address to the Academy of Criminal Justice Sciences." *Justice Quarterly* 11:527–59.

DeLamater, J. 1968. "On the Nature of Deviance." *Social Forces* 46 (June):445–55.

Durkheim, É. 1951. *Suicide.* Translated by J. A. Spaulding and G. Simpson. New York: Free Press.

Elliott, D. S., D. Huizinga, and S. S. Ageton. 1985. *Explaining Delinquency and Drug Use.* Beverly Hills: Sage.

Elliott, D. S., and H. L. Voss. 1974. *Delinquency and Dropout.* Lexington, MA: Lexington Books.

Empey, L. T. 1967. "Delinquency Theory and Recent Research." *Journal of Research in Crime and Delinquency* 4 (January):32–42.

Empey, L. T., and S. G. Lubeck. 1971. *Explaining Delinquency.* Lexington, MA: Lexington Books.

Engstad, P., and J. C. Hackler. 1971. "The Impact of Alienation on Delinquency Rates." *Canadian Journal of Criminology and Corrections* 13 (April):1–8.

Erickson, M. L., and L. T. Empey. 1965. "Class Position, Peers and Delinquency." *Sociology and Social Research* 49 (April):268–82.

Federal Bureau of Investigation. 2002. *Crime in the United States.* Washington, DC: GPO.

Felson, M. 1998. *Crime and Everyday Life.* 2nd ed. Thousand Oaks, CA: Pine Forge Press.

Finestone, H. 1976. *Victims of Change: Juvenile Delinquents in American Society.* Westport, CT: Greenwood Press.

Giordano, P., S. Cernkovich, and M. Pugh. 1986. "Friendships and Delinquency." *American Journal of Sociology* 91:1170–1202.

Glueck, S., and E. Glueck. 1950. *Unraveling Juvenile Delinquency.* Cambridge: Harvard University Press.

Gold, M. 1963. *Status Forces in Delinquent Boys.* Ann Arbor: Institute for Social Research, University of Michigan.

———. 1970. *Delinquent Behavior in an American City.* Monterey, CA: Brooks Cole.

Goode, E., and N. Ben-Yehuda. 1994. *Moral Panics: The Social Construction of Deviance.* Oxford: Blackwell.

Gordon, R. A., J. F. Short, Jr., D. S. Cartwright, and F. L. Strodtbeck. 1963. "Values and Gang Delinquency." *American Journal of Sociology* 69 (September):109–18.

Gottfredson, M. R., and T. Hirschi. 1990. *A General Theory of Crime.* Palo Alto, CA: Stanford University Press.

Grasmick, H. G., C. R. Tittle, R. J. Bursik, Jr., and B. J. Arneklev. 1993. "Testing the Core Empirical Implications of Gottfredson and Hirschi's General Theory of Crime." *Journal of Research in Crime and Delinquency* 30:5–29.

Greenberg, D. 1979a. "Delinquency and the Age Structure of Society." In *Criminology Review Yearbook,* edited by S. Messinger and E. Bittner. Beverly Hills: Sage.

———. 1979b. *Mathematical Criminology.* New Brunswick, NJ: Rutgers.

Hagan, J., A. R. Gillis, and J. Simpson. 1985. "The Class Structure of Gender and Delinquency: Toward a Power-Control Theory of Common Delinquent Behavior." *American Journal of Sociology* 90:1151–78.

———. 1987. "Class in the Household: A Power Control Theory of Gender and Delinquency." *American Journal of Sociology* 92 (January):788–816.

Hepburn, J. R. 1976. "Casting Alternative Models of Delinquency Causation." *Journal of Criminal Law and Criminology* 67 (December):450–60.

Hindelang, M. J. 1973. "Causes of Delinquency: A Partial Replication and Extension." *Social Problems* 21 (Spring):471–87.

Hindelang, M. J., T. Hirschi, and J. Weiss. 1981. *Measuring Delinquency.* Beverly Hills: Sage.

Hirschi, T. 1969. *Causes of Delinquency.* Berkeley: University of California Press.

Hirschi, T., and M. Gottfredson. 1983. "Age and the Explanation of Crime." *American Journal of Sociology* 89:552–84.

———. 2001. "Self-Control Theory." In *Explaining Criminals and Crime,* edited by Raymond Paternoster and Ronet Bachman, 81–96. Los Angeles: Roxbury.

Jensen, G. F. 1972. "Parents, Peers and Delinquent Action: A Test of the Differential Association Hypothesis." *American Journal of Sociology* 78 (November):562–75.

———. 1973. "Inner Containment and Delinquency." *Journal of Criminal Law and Criminology* 64 (December):464–70.

———. 1986. "Dis-Integrating Integrated Theory." Paper presented at the Annual Convention of the American Society of Criminology, Atlanta, Georgia.

———. 1988. "Mainstreaming and the Sociology of Deviance: A Personal Assessment." In *Changing Our Minds: Feminist Readings in the Transformation of Knowledge,* edited by K. Andersen et al. Albany: State University of New York Press.

———. 2002. "Institutional Anomie and Societal Variations in Crime: A Critical Appraisal." In *Talking about Violence: Building a Foundation for Scientific Discourse through Common Definitions and Measurements,* edited by Carolyn Rebecca Block, 45–74. Vol. 22 of the *International Journal of Sociology and Social Policy.*

———. 2003. "Gender Variation in Delinquency: Self-Images, Beliefs, and Peers as Mediating Mechanisms." In *Social Learning Theory and the Explanation of Crime: A Guide for the New Century* edited by Ronald L. Akers and Gary F. Jensen, 151–78. Vol. 11 of *Advances in Criminological Theory.* New Brunswick, NJ: Transaction Books.

Jensen, G. F. 2006. "Religious Cosmologies and Homicide Rates among Nations." *The Journal of Religion and Society* 8:1–13.

Jensen, G. F., and R. L. Akers. 2003. "Taking Social Learning Global: Micro-Macro Transitions in Criminological Theory." In *Social Learning Theory and the Explanation of Crime: A Guide for the New Century*, edited by Ronald L. Akers and Gary F. Jensen, 9–38. Vol. 11 of *Advances in Criminological Theory*. New Brunswick, NJ: Transaction Books.

Jensen, G. F., and D. Brownfield. 1983. "Parents and Drugs: Specifying the Consequences of Attachment." *Criminology* 21 (November):543–54.

———. 1986. "Gender, Lifestyles and Victimization: Beyond Routine Activity." *Violence and Victims* 1(2):85–99.

Jensen, G. F., and M. L Erickson. 1977. "Peer Commitment and Delinquency: New Tests of Old Hypotheses." Unpublished manuscript.

Jensen, G. F., and R. Eve. 1976. "Sex Differences in Delinquency." *Criminology* 13 (February):427–48.

Kaplan, H. 1975. *Self-Attitudes and Deviant Behavior*. Pacific Palisades, CA: Goodyear.

———. 1980. *Deviant Behavior in Defense of Self*. New York: Academic Press.

———. 1984. *Patterns of Juvenile Delinquency*. Beverly Hills: Sage.

Lerman, P. 1968. "Individual Values, Peer Values and Subcultural Delinquency." *American Sociological Review* 33 (April):219–35.

Linden, E., and J. C. Hackler. 1973. "Affective Ties and Delinquency." *Pacific Sociological Review* 16 (January):27–46.

Liska, A. E., and M. D. Reed. 1985. "Ties to Conventional Institutions and Delinquency." *American Sociological Review* 50:547–60.

Logan, E. 1999. "The Wrong Race, Committing Crime, Doing Drugs and Maladjusted for Motherhood: The Nation's Fury over Crack Babies." *Social Justice* 26:115–38.

Luckenbill, D. F., and D. P. Doyle. 1989. "Structural Position and Violence: Developing a Cultural Explanation." *Criminology* 27:419–36.

Matsueda, R. 1982. "Testing Control Theory and Differential Association." *American Sociological Review* 47:489–504.

Matza, D. 1964. *Delinquency and Drift*. New York: John Wiley.

Matza, D., and G. M. Sykes. 1961. "Juvenile Delinquency and Subterranean Values." *American Sociological Review* 26 (October):712–17.

McCarthy, J. D., and D. R. Hoge. 1984. "The Dynamics of Self-Esteem and Delinquency." *American Journal of Sociology* 90 (2):396–410.

McCorkle, R. C., and T. D. Miethe. 2002. *Panic: The Social Construction of the Street Gang Problem*. Upper Saddle River, NJ: Prentice-Hall.

Menard, S., and B. J. Morse. 1984. "A Structural Critique of the IQ-Delinquency Hypothesis: Theory and Evidence." *American Journal of Sociology* 89:1347–78.

Merton, R. K. 1957. *Social Theory and Social Structure*. New York: Free Press.

Messner, S. F., and R. Rosenfeld. 1997. "Political Restraint of the Market and Levels of Criminal Homicide: A Cross-National Application of Institutional Anomie Theory." *Social Forces* 75:1393–1416.

———. 2001. *Crime and the American Dream*. 3rd ed. Belmont, CA: Wadsworth.

Miller, W. 1958. "Lower Class Culture as a Generating Milieu of Gang Delinquency." *Journal of Social Issues* 14:5–19.

Osgood, D. W., and A. L. Anderson. 2004. "Unstructured Socializing and Rates of Delinquency." *Criminology* 42:519–49.

Park, R. E. 1952. "Community Organization and Juvenile Delinquency." In *Human Communities: The City and Human Ecology*, edited by E. C. Hughes, et al. Glencoe, IL: Free Press.

Paternoster, R., and P. Mazerolle. 1994. "General Strain Theory and Delinquency: A Replication and Extension." *Journal of Research in Crime and Delinquency* 31:235–63.

Paternoster, R., and R. Triplett. 1988. "Neighborhood Changes in Ecology and Violence." *Criminology* 26 (November):591–620.

Piquero, N. L., and M. D. Sealock. 2000. "Generalizing General Strain Theory: An Examination of an Offending Population." *Justice Quarterly* 17:449–84.

Pratt, T. C., and F. T. Cullen. 2000. "The Empirical Status of Gottfredson and Hirschi's General Theory of Crime: A Meta-Analysis." *Criminology* 38:931–64.

Quicker, J. C. 1974. "The Effect of Goal Discrepancy on Delinquency." *Social Problems* 22 (October):76–86.

Quinney, R. 1980. *Class, State and Crime.* 2nd ed. New York: Longman.

Reinarman, C., and H. Levine. 1989. "The Crack Attack: Politics and Media in America's Latest Drug Scare." In *Images of Issues: Typifying Contemporary Social Problems*, edited by Joel Best, 115–37. New York: Aldine de Gruyter.

Reiss, A. J., Jr. 1951. "Delinquency as the Failure of Personal and Social Controls." *American Sociological Review* 16:196–207.

Richardson, J. T., J. Best, and D. G. Bromley. 1991. *The Satanism Scare.* New York: Aldine De Gruyter.

Robin, G. D. 1969. "Anti-Poverty Programs and Delinquency." *Journal of Criminal Law, Criminology and Police Science* 60 (Fall):323–31.

Rubington, R., and M. Weinberg, eds. 2005. *Deviance: The Interactionist Perspective.* Boston: Allyn & Bacon.

Sampson, R. J. 2002. "Transcending Tradition: New Directions in Community Research, Chicago Style." *Criminology* 4:213–30.

Sampson, R. J., and D. J. Bartusch. 1998. "Legal Cynicism and (Subcultural?) Tolerance of Deviance: The Neighborhood Context of Racial Differences." *Law and Society Review* 32:777–804.

Sampson, R. J., and J. H. Laub. 1993. *Crime in the Making: Pathways and Turning Points through Life.* Cambridge, MA: Harvard University Press.

Sampson, R. J., and S. W. Raudenbush. 1999. "Systematic Social Observation of Public Spaces: A New Look at Disorder in Urban Neighborhoods." *American Journal of Sociology* 105:603–51.

———. 2004. "Seeing Disorder: Neighborhood Stigma and the Social Construction of 'Broken Windows.'" *Social Psychology Quarterly* 67:319–42.

Sampson, R. J., S. W. Raudenbush, and F. Earls. 1997. "Neighborhoods and Violent Crime: A Multilevel Study of Collective Efficacy." *Science* 277:918–24.

Sampson, R. J., and W. J. Wilson. 1995. "Toward a Theory of Race, Crime, and Urban Inequality." In *Crime and Inequality*, edited by John Hagan and Ruth Peterson. Palo Alto, CA: Stanford University Press.

Sánchez-Jankowski, M. 1991. *Islands in the Street: Gangs and American Urban Society.* Berkeley: University of California Press.

Schaefer, W. E. 1969. "Participation in Interscholastic Athletics and Delinquency: A Preliminary Study." *Social Problems* 17 (Summer):40–47.

Schwendinger, H., and J. R. Schwendinger. 1976. "Marginal Youth and Social Policy." *Social Problems* (December):84–91.

———. 1985. *Adolescent Subcultures and Delinquency.* New York: Praeger.

Shaw, C. 1929. *Delinquency Areas.* Chicago: University of Chicago Press.

———. 1930. *The Jack Roller.* Chicago: University of Chicago Press.

———. 1969. *Juvenile Delinquency and Urban Areas.* Rev. ed. Chicago: University of Chicago Press.

Shaw, C., and H. McKay. 1942. *Juvenile Delinquency and Urban Areas.* Chicago: University of Chicago Press.

Shelden, R., S. K. Tracy, and W. B. Brown. 2001. *Youth Gangs in American Society.* 2nd ed. Belmont, CA: Wadsworth/Thomson Learning.

Short, J. F., R. Rivera, and R. A. Tennyson. 1965. "Perceived Opportunities, Gang Membership and Delinquency." *American Sociological Review* 30 (February):56–67.

Short, J. F., and F. L. Strodtbeck. 1965. *Group Processes and Gang Delinquency.* Chicago: University of Chicago Press.

Simcha-Fagan, O., and J. E. Schwartz. 1986. "Neighborhood and Delinquency: An Assessment of Contextual Effects." *Criminology* 24 (November):667–703.

Stark, R., W. S. Bainbridge, R. D. Crutchfield, D. P. Doyle, and R. Finke. 1983. "Crime and Delinquency in the Roaring Twenties." *Journal of Research in Crime and Delinquency* 20 (January):4–23.

Stinchcombe, A. L. 1964. *Rebellion in a High School.* Chicago: Quadrangle Books.

Sutherland, E. H. 1939. *Principles of Criminology.* Philadelphia: J.B. Lippincott.

Sutherland, E. H., and D. R. Cressey. 1974. *Criminology.* 9th ed. Philadelphia: J. B. Lippincott.

Sykes, G. M., and D. Matza. 1957. "Techniques of Neutralization: A Theory of Delinquency." *American Journal of Sociology* 22 (December):664–70.

Taylor, I., P. Walton, and J. Young. 1973. *The New Criminology.* New York: Harper and Row.

Taylor, R. B. 2001. "The Ecology of Crime, Fear, and Delinquency: Social Disorganization versus Social Efficacy." In *Explaining Criminals and Crime*, edited by R. Paternoster and R. Bachman, 124–40. Los Angeles: Roxbury.

Taylor, R. B., and J. Covington. 1988. "Neighborhood Changes in Ecology and Violence." *Criminology* 26 (November):553–89.

Thomas, W. I., and F. Znaniecki. 1918. *The Polish Peasant in Europe and America.* New York: Alfred A. Knopf.

Thornberry, T. 1987. "Towards an Interactional Theory of Delinquency." *Criminology* 25:863–91.

Tittle, C. R. 1995. *Control Balance: Toward a General Theory of Deviance.* Boulder, CO: Westview Press.

Toby, J. 1957. "Social Disorganization and Stake in Conformity: Complementary Factors in the Predatory Behavior of Hoodlums." *Journal of Criminal Law, Criminology and Police Science* 48:12–17.

Warr, M. 1993. "Age, Peers, and Delinquency." *Criminology* 31:17–40.

———. 2002. *Companions in Crime: The Social Aspects of Criminal Conduct.* Cambridge: Cambridge University Press.

Wells, L. E., and J. H. Rankin. 1983. "Self-Concept as a Mediating Factor in Delinquency." *Social Psychology Quarterly* 46:11–22.

Wilson, J. Q., and G. Kelling. 1982. "Broken Windows." *Atlantic Monthly* (March):29–38.

Yablonsky, L. 1959. "The Delinquent Gang as Near-Group." *Social Problems* 7:108–17.

Yinger, M. 1960. "Contraculture and Subculture." *American Sociological Review* 25:625–35.

Young, J. 1975. "Working-Class Criminology." In *Critical Criminology,* edited by I. Taylor, P. Walton, and J. Young. London: Routledge and Kegan Paul.

seven

Contexts for Socialization
Family, School, and Peers

Adolescents in the United States live their daily lives in two social worlds with two different masters. At school and in certain activities outside of school, they observe and participate in the culture of their peers, a culture with its own rules of dress, music, speech, and behavior, and an emphasis on popularity, physical attractiveness, and athletic success. . . . From this culture they move regularly to the environment of home and family, which may complement or clash with that of school and peers.

(Mark Warr, "Parents, Peers, and Delinquency," 1993)

Introduction

In chapter 6 we outlined the similarities and differences among the major sociological theories examining the causes of delinquency. One of the common themes characterizing those theories is that most human behavior, including delinquent behavior, is *learned* and that the major source of human learning involves interaction with other people. People become human beings through processes of social interaction and social learning that are referred to as *socialization*. Socialization takes place in a variety of settings. For a child growing up in a developed, industrial society like that of the United States, the family, school, and peer groups are viewed as particularly crucial to socialization, with each emerging to dominate in shaping behavior in just that sequential order (i.e. family, school, and peers). These three social institutions or groups have received the bulk of attention in criminological theory and research, and we will summarize the relevant literature in this chapter.

The Family

The family is viewed as the most critical institution in our society for shaping a child's personality, attitudes, and behavior. At the same time, however, many social commentators have noted a decline in the range of functions performed by the family. Some seventy years ago, William Ogburn (1938) observed that of seven functions served by the family throughout history (economic production, status allocation, education, religious training, recreation, protection, and provision of affection), only the family's role in providing affection was not declining. Although the family may have been a more important social institution at earlier points in history, most scholars are still willing to accept that it remains a major setting for socialization in American society.

Harry Harlow's (1962) classic work with the rhesus monkey dramatically illustrated the importance of parents to young infants. Harlow raised monkeys in isolation from their parents and replaced the parents with a variety of surrogates made of wire or terry cloth; some with a bottle for feeding and others with none. He found that infant monkeys preferred the cloth surrogate mother that offered no milk over the regular feeding provided by the bare-wire surrogate. Infant monkeys appeared to have an innate need for warmth and closeness rather than simply food. Harlow also found that infant monkeys raised in isolation were aggressive and unsociable in the presence of other monkeys. These isolated and orphaned monkeys did not know how to play, how to interact, or even how to mate. Perhaps what was most significant was that their poor social development could not be easily remedied by placing them back into a normal social environment.

If generalized to humans, the monkey experiments suggest that normal behavior is dependent on meaningful parent-child relationships and that inadequacies in early childhood socialization can have ramifications later during the period of adolescence and adulthood. Similarly, the discovery of **feral children**, children who were isolated from human contact, analogous to Harlow's monkeys, attest to the critical need for meaningful social interaction at an early age. Feral children are often the result of an illegitimate birth and are hidden from public view. One such child called "Anna" was kept in an attic for her first six years. When discovered, she was unable to walk, talk, or display normal human emotions. Despite intensive care and attention, "Anna" could not attain the status of a normal child, and in fact died at the age of 10 (Davis, 1947). While Harlow's monkey experiments and the few cases of feral children are extreme examples of defective parental socialization, they do point to the critical need for a warm and meaningful parent-child relationship. When this is absent, the child may suffer permanent deficiencies.

Importance of Early Childhood Socialization

Jean Piaget (1896–1980), perhaps the most influential child psychologist in the twentieth century, extended Harlow's research on infant monkeys by studying early childhood socialization. While earlier researchers had placed great importance on the latter stages of adolescent development, the interaction with peers, and school experiences, early childhood was assumed to be of relatively minor importance. Piaget argued that the formative years from early infancy to ages 4 or 5 were critical. In fact, he noted, much of the foundation for later life begins in these early formative years. The child is not simply amassing facts but rather employs what Piaget called the "discovery method," where the child gets an opportunity to apply developing ideas and test their limitations. Parents become a guide to discovery, not a force-feeder of facts and ideas. Piaget observed infants and young children and tried to understand how children perceive the world and how their thought processes evolve. Parents play a critical role during this early stage of development. The foundation for intellectual understanding, muscular development, coordination, and the development of the self are all tied to parent-child interaction. Piaget's research documents the vital role that parents play in early childhood socialization. Like Harlow, Piaget suggested that children who are deprived of warm, caring, interactive parents can be deprived of vital nurturing. This first stage of childhood socialization sets the stage for later growth and development. According to Piaget, effective parenting begins at the moment of birth.

More recent research on early brain development emphasizes the importance of human development from conception to the third birthday. The brain is the only organ in the human body that is incomplete at birth. After birth, the brain continues to develop through wiring and re-wiring of the synapses in the brain. Early experiences for the infant, both negative and positive, have a dramatic effect on the development of these synapses. Research supports the "use it or lose it" principle wherein only those pathways that are used frequently are retained (Lally, 1998). As early as three months of age, the infant can distinguish spoken sounds and the brain organizes itself to recognize those sounds. Children living in **sensory-deprived environments** like orphanages have been found to have smaller brains than those who grow up in a sensually rich environment. Similarly, children who are rarely touched or spoken to have smaller brains than those children reared in a loving and interactive environment. Of all the sensory experiences, touching and holding the infant are the most critical (Shonkoff and Phillips, 2000). Researchers also have learned that the more words the infant hears, the more brain connections that are made; thus, children who are read to regularly make more connections in the brain (Porter, 2006). In summary, the experiences of early childhood are closely related to brain development and this is a period of time when families have virtually complete control over the infant and directly contribute to brain development. There is evidence to suggest that the family may play a far more important role during early childhood and early adolescence than in middle or late adolescence when children are more subject to peer influences (Patterson et al., 1992).

The Family in Major Theories

The family also occupies a key position in many of the theories of delinquency that we summarized in chapter 6. For example, strain theory emphasizes such variables as aspirations, limited opportunities for success, status frustration, and delinquent subcultures. The family plays a role in the strain theory of delinquency insofar as it determines a youth's social standing, his or her chances of getting ahead by legitimate means, and, hence, the probability of status problems. In Robert Merton's version of strain theory (1957), the family also is important in that working-class children are depicted as more thoroughly socialized to aspire toward culturally prescribed goals of success than to accept norms limiting the means to do so. In Robert Agnew's (1992) revised strain theory, neglect and abuse in the family can be a source of the anger that can motivate delinquency.

The role of the family in normative/cultural conflict perspectives varies from one theorist to another. Edwin Sutherland and Donald Cressey (1974) have argued that the family is important to the degree that it affects the chances of exposure to definitions favorable and unfavorable to lawbreaking. In cultural conflict theory, such definitions are always intervening to explain the impacts of various institutions on delinquency. Walter Miller's (1958) emphasis on lower-class focal concerns suggests that the lower-class family facilitates delinquency insofar as the values conveyed by adults lead to trouble with the law. However, like Sutherland and Cressey, Miller contended that it is the "one-sex peer unit" and not the two-parent family unit that is most relevant to understanding the behavior of members of the lower-class community. Miller argued that such peer units are especially salient for understanding adolescent males who come from female-based households since it is within peer groups that they solve problems of sex-role identification and learn the "male" role.

Social control theory accords relationships with parents a central role in the explanation of delinquency. If parents supervise their children and parent-child ties are strong, then the probability of delinquency is greatly reduced. Children refrain from delinquency not only to avoid their parents' ire but also because of the values, aspirations, and beliefs learned in interaction with their parents (Hirschi, 1985). This inhibiting effect is presumed to occur in all social categories and settings—among males and females, minority and nonminority, rural and urban youth.

Social learning theory also accords a major role to parents and the family in the explanation of delinquency. The processes of imitation, differential reinforcement, and normative learning so central to this theory all involve parents and other members of the family. In most instances it is assumed that parents will try to shape their children's behavior and beliefs in ways that will keep them out of serious trouble. It is in the world of their peers that contrary behavior is likely to be rewarded. However, children also can learn to violate rules from their parents—either directly or indirectly. If parents smoke, drink, or use drugs, then the probability that their children will do so is significantly greater than if they do none of these (Jensen and Brownfield, 1983). In fact, strong ties to parents are not likely to discourage deviance in children if parents themselves are known to engage in the same behavior. Admonishments to "do as I say, not as I do!" are often used by parents in the attempt to overcome imitation effects, but it is doubtful that they can be truly effective considering the contradictory messages communicated (see box 7-1).

A more recent attempt to incorporate family variables into the explanation of delinquency is called power-control theory (Hagan, Simpson, and Gillis, 1985, 1987). As posited by John Hagan and associates, **power-control theory** specifically addresses

Box 7-1   Conflicting Messages

What does this cartoon suggest about parental values and child rearing? What conflicting social learning processes are reflected in Snuffy's attitudes and behavior?

the gender difference in delinquency and links it to the class status of mothers and fathers in the household. The difference between girls and boys is predicted to be greatest in households where (1) fathers are in occupations where they dominate or control others, and (2) mothers are either housewives or in occupations where they are controlled by others. Such households are classified as high in *patriarchy* (i.e., father rule). In such households girls are thought to be treated very differently than boys. Girls are closely supervised and raised to avoid taking risks while, allegedly, boys are raised to take risks and are relatively free to do what they want. In contrast, households where mothers and fathers are in similar occupational categories are classified as *egalitarian* or balanced in terms of male-female power. In such households girls and boys, it is argued, are subject to more nearly comparable degrees of adult control and encouragement of risk-taking. Hagan, Simpson, and Gillis provide some research support for their theory (1987), but their power-control explanation of the gender difference has not been shown to be superior to other sociological explanations of the gender difference (Jensen, 2003). However, their theory reflects the continuing centrality of the family in sociological theories of delinquency.

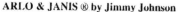

Research on the Family and Delinquency

There are literally hundreds of studies dealing with various aspects of family life and delinquency. We have organized our presentation around certain aspects of the family that have been the subject of considerable research. First, we will consider certain structural characteristics of the family and a child's place in the family: the broken home, ordinal position, and family size. Then we will turn to research concerning actual relationships among family members; that is, affective relationships between parents and between parents and child, methods of parental control, and parental supervision. The concept of *parenting* encompasses all of these issues and "good" parenting has come to mean attempts to establish and enforce rules; to convey knowledge, values, and norms appropriate to the age of the child; to take part in family activities; to provide basic needs and appropriate supervision, and to accomplish all of this in a loving family environment. No wonder good parenting is very difficult.

ARLO & JANIS ® by Jimmy Johnson

Arlo and Janis: © Newspaper Enterprise Association, Inc.

The "Broken" Home

A very common claim about juvenile delinquency is that it is the result of a **broken home**. The departure of a parent, typically the father, is assumed to disrupt the life of the child and hamper the effective socialization and supervision of children. One hundred years ago, less than 5 percent of marriages ended in divorce. Currently about 50 percent of marriages end in divorce, and about one-third of white children and three-fourths of African-American children can expect to live in a single-parent family at some time. Hence, it is no longer an easy matter to define the "normal" or "typical" family.

Figure 7-1 shows the divorce rate in the United States over the past one hundred years. In the early part of the twentieth century the divorce rate was low; it made a dramatic jump after World War II and then declined. Beginning in the 1960s the divorce rate began to rise sharply, peaking in the early 1980s. In 2005 there were 2.3 million marriages (7.8 marriages per 1,000 population) and 1.1 million divorces (3.7 divorces per 1,000). Candice Batton and Gary Jensen (2002) have analyzed fluctuations in homicide rates and report that divorce rates are significantly related to homicide rates in the second half in the twentieth century when other relevant variables are controlled. They suggest that in the first half of the twentieth century, fluctuations in homicide rates were products of prohibitionist legislation, depression-level unemployment, massive waves of new immigrants, and mob activity, but that divorce replaced unemployment as a source of high homicide rates following World War II. In other words, family breakdown became more common and more relevant for explaining homicide rates after the war. It should also be noted that the decline in the divorce rate corresponds fairly well with the decline in youth violence.

Figure 7-1   Divorce Rate per 1,000 Population

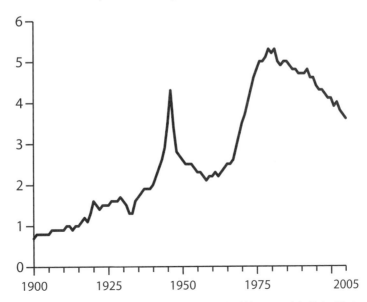

Source: 1900–1970, U.S. Census Bureau, 1975; after 1970, *Statistical Abstracts of the United States.*

Divorce can be a way of resolving a marital situation that is marked by intense dislike, chronic conflict, and total incompatibility. Some children might be living in a more wholesome situation living with one parent rather than in an "intact" family amidst an atmosphere of severe marital tension. Constance Ahrons (1995) argues that in some situations, divorce results in what she calls the "binuclear family" that spans two households, with each parent continuing to meet the needs of the child. On the other hand, divorce can have pervasive negative consequences for children, affecting numerous variables that affect delinquency. Ronald Simons and colleagues (2004) found that divorced parents make fewer demands on their children, provide less supervision, display more hostility toward their children, and use less effective disciplinary techniques than married parents. Paul Amato (1993) found that children of divorced parents had lower academic achievement, more behavior problems, lower self-esteem, and poorer social relations; however, the differences were not great. Others have suggested that for many children of divorced parents, problems existed *before* their parents divorced, suggesting that the problem is not divorce but poor marriages (Cherlin et al., 1991). Marital discord and a high level of conflict in the home may have a pronounced negative effect on children. Amato (1993) found that if parental conflict continues after a divorce, this may have demonstrable negative consequences for the child. Remarrying after divorce may not eliminate the negative effects of divorce. Children raised in stepfamilies do less well in school, appear to have more adjustment problems, and are more likely to engage in delinquent behavior than children in never-divorced families (Simons et al., 2004). Research seems to suggest that a broken home with good family relations is less conducive to delinquency than an intact home with poor family relations.

In the latter part of the twentieth century, single-parent families increased dramatically. Single-mother families increased from 3 million in 1970 to 10 million in 2003 (26 percent of families with children), while the number of single-father families increased from less than half a million to slightly more than 2 million (6 percent of families with children). Conversely, the number of two-parent families declined from 87 percent in 1970 to 68 percent in 2003 (U.S. Census Bureau, 2004). The relevance of single-parent homes to delinquency has varied in research, depending on whether other characteristics of families have been taken into account, how the concept of broken/nonbroken is calibrated, as well as on the way delinquency is measured. For example, Patricia Van Voorhis and colleagues (1988) found it was the quality of the home environment that led to delinquency, regardless of whether the family was intact or not. Single-parent families are not distributed equally across racial and ethnic groups. Approximately 23 percent of white children, 37 percent of Latino children, and 65 percent of African-American children are being raised by a single parent (ChildStats.Gov, 2005). Further, the poverty rate for single parents is nearly five times higher than for two-parent families (ChildStats.gov, 2004). Thus, the relationship between broken homes (and specifically single-parent families) and delinquency may be mediated by economic factors. Poverty, unemployment, economic despair, and a myriad of social hardships may cause family problems and delinquent behaviors.

The early studies of broken homes and delinquency strongly suggested there was a link between the two, but these were based on records of police, juvenile courts, and correctional facilities. For example, children living in something other than an intact family were found to be disproportionately represented in juvenile court statistics (Chilton and Markle, 1972). In his classic work, *Causes of Delinquency* (1969), Travis Hirschi found that both African-American and white boys from single-parent homes were more likely to have police records than boys from intact homes. However, when their self-reported delinquent acts were considered, boys from homes with a stepfather had the highest rates.

When self-report techniques are used to measure delinquency, the differences in offending between those from broken and intact homes have been quite small (Gove and Crutchfield, 1982; Rosen and Neilson, 1982). Based on interviews of self-reported delinquent behavior conducted with 1,725 youths between ages 11 and 17, Rachelle Canter (1982) notes that youths from broken homes reported more delinquent acts than youths from intact homes, but when comparing averages the differences are far from striking. The small differences in results using official and self-report techniques prompted Richard Johnson to conclude,

> It is very tempting to conclude that the official system is indeed responding differently to similar behavior by adolescents from different types of families—families which do not otherwise differ in expected ways along several dimensions presumed to relate to delinquent behavior. (1986:77)

As we examine the issue of the family and delinquency, it is critical to bear in mind the data source we are using to measure delinquency. The police and juvenile court officials may take into consideration the parents' marital status, and children of divorced parents may be seen as coming from a "troubled" background that results in official court action.

It should also be noted that as self-report surveys have become more sophisticated, complex patterns have been found. For example, researchers tested the hypothesis that single-parent homes would have no impact on delinquency as long as the child was strongly attached to the custodial parent (Rankin and Kern, 1994). They found that such households were moderately associated with delinquency because there is only one parental attachment. In other words, the risk of delinquency increases in single-parent homes because parental monitoring, supervision, and discipline may be weaker.

A more recent study attempted to determine whether a child's gender makes a difference in terms of the impact of paternal absence on a child's behavior (Mott, Kowaleski-Jones, and Menaghan, 1997:103). Using data collected from mothers about their children at several points in time to examine that issue, they found that paternal absence was more consequential for boys than girls in terms of problem behaviors. However, when they took "a new man in the home" into account, they found that paternal absence was not a crucial factor; rather, the fact that a new man was added to the household often led to an increase in problem behaviors. This finding is very similar to results reported by Hirschi (1969) three decades earlier that male youths from homes with a stepfather had the highest rates of self-reported delinquency.

David Farrington and Rolf Loeber compiled a summary of findings from three major longitudinal studies in Denver, Pittsburgh, and Rochester and concluded that "multiple family transitions are a risk factor for delinquency" (2000:6). Defining transitions as "changes in the family structure caused by events in the parenting figures' lives such as divorce, separation, death, or long term hospitalization" (2000:31), they report that there was a consistent relationship between such experiences and delinquency and drug use among girls and boys. Juby and Farrington (2001) studied variation among types of disruptions among boys and found that disruptions caused by death were less consequential than disruptions caused by parental disharmony.

At present, there is consensus that disruptions in family structure affect the odds of delinquency to some degree, with variations depending on other characteristics of family life such as resources to cope and the amount of conflict. Some studies have found effects for a variety of family disruptions, but the most commonly noted pattern seems to be that children in **stepfamilies** or **reconstructed families** are statistically more likely to have a variety of problems compared to children in families that have not experienced disruptions (Comaner and Philips, 2002; Rebellon, 2002).

Ordinal Position

While the single-parent home has historically been a dominant focus in relating family characteristics to delinquency, there has been periodic interest in the impact of **ordinal position**, or birth order, in relation to juvenile delinquency. For example, an early study in England found that intermediate children who had older and younger siblings tended to be overrepresented among delinquents (Lees and Newson, 1954). The explanation posited for this finding is that the firstborn sibling lives the first years as an only child and receives the undivided attention and affection of his or her parents. The child born last enters into a firmly established family situation with parents who are experienced in raising children and older siblings who function as role models. The intermediate sibling may get "squeezed out" of affection and may gravitate into delinquent behavior for attention.

Research in England and the United States suggests that the higher delinquency rates for middle children may actually be an artifact of family size (Loeber and Stouthamer-Loeber, 1986). Obviously, families with only one or two children have no middle children and small families have lower delinquency rates than large families. Hence, any study of ordinal position must examine the impact of birth order in families with three or more children and exclude smaller families from the analysis. When Hirschi took family size into account in his research on youth in the San Francisco Bay area he could find no evidence that middle children are more likely to commit delinquent acts than youngest or oldest children. West and Farrington (1973) report the same results for British youth. Ordinal position was not associated with delinquency when family size was taken into account.

With the shrinking size of families any discussion of birth order effects may be moot. For example, the average size of families in the United States decreased from 3.24 in 1970 to 2.57 presently. Furthermore, only 9 percent of families have more than five members, 3 percent have more than six members, and only 1.8 percent has seven or more members (U.S. Census Bureau, 2004). Childbearing in the United States over the last twenty years has been at its lowest level in history. Some 200 years ago the number of births per woman in America was around eight, today it is 1.8. A search for articles on delinquency and birth order produced one scholarly article on the topic, and this was based in locales in France. The "baby bust" in recent years has negated much discussion of first born, last born, and intermediate siblings.

Family Size

While variations by birth order may be the product of family size, several issues involving family size and delinquency have not been settled. For one, to isolate the independent relevance of family size means that other variables that correlate with family size and delinquency have to be taken into account (e.g., racial/ethnic status, unemployment, social class). Not only might family size be confounded with other variables, but the relevance of family size may vary depending on other circumstances such as economic advantage. For example, British research suggests that family size is related to delinquency but that the connection is quite weak for middle-class families compared to lower-class families (Rutter and Giller, 1984). For example, rural families tend to be larger than urban families but urban delinquency rates tend to be higher than rural. It may be that the number of children does not affect delinquency when families have sufficient economic resources to manage a large household.

Hirschi (1969) examined the relationship between family size and delinquency using self-report data and controlling measures of academic performance, parental supervision, and emotional attachment. Regardless of such controls, family size appears related to delinquency. He notes, however, that the mechanisms generating the effect have not been identified. Other researchers suggest that it is not family size that contributes to delinquency but rather having delinquent siblings (Loeber and Stouthamer-Loeber, 1986). In other words, in large families there are more siblings and if one sibling is delinquent, there is a higher probability that another sibling will be delinquent. However, as with birth-order effects, the gradual demise of large families due to a declining birth rate indicates that the relevance of family size to delinquency is not likely to be a major research topic in coming years.

Family Relationships

During the *blitzkrieg* of London in World War II, British officials built large nurseries in the rural countryside where infants and young children could be safely cared for by nannies and child care personnel, while their parents continued the war effort in urban areas. Despite the professional care that was ministered to these children, many of them appeared to have physical and psychological difficulties. Listlessness, emotional outbursts, and mental aberrations seemed to be the result of maternal deprivation. Elaborating on this observation, John Bowlby (1951) attempted to determine the importance of the maternal relationship for juvenile delinquency. Studying a group of juvenile delinquents drawn from patients at a child guidance center, Bowlby found a relationship between the absence of the mother and delinquent behavior. He concluded:

> On the basis of this varied evidence it appears that there is a very strong case indeed for believing that prolonged separation of a child from his mother (mother-substitute) during the first five years of life stands foremost among the causes of delinquent character development and persistent misbehavior. (1951:11)

Despite the popular acceptance of this observation, Bowlby's findings have been severely criticized, and no supporting evidence has been provided to substantiate his theory of maternal deprivation. Research has suggested that it is not the absence of a parent per se that results in delinquency, but the quality of the relationship that exists between the child and the remaining parent. In recent years, the **maternal deprivation hypothesis** was altered to suggest that working mothers contribute to their children's chances of becoming delinquent. The concept of the **latchkey child** (the child who comes home to an empty house and carries the key to the house on a string around his or her neck) has come into popular usage. However, Hill and Stafford (1979) reported that some working mothers compensate for being away from home by reducing their leisure time in order to spend time with their children. Generally, studies examining the effect of mothers' employment on delinquency find little evidence of any type of an impact (Hayes and Kamerman, 1983; Loeber and Stouthamer-Loeber, 1986). Hirschi (1985) suggests that supervision is the key explanatory variable, and when working mothers can provide supervision for the child, there is no increased likelihood of delinquency. Kalmijn (1994) found that mothers who work in high status jobs lead to positive school effects for their children. These children performed better academically, were more likely to complete high school, and more like to attend college and eventually graduate.

Vander Ven and Cullen (2004) used multiple regression techniques to analyze data from the National Longitudinal Survey of Youth (NLSY) in an attempt to learn whether the occupational status of mothers had effects on criminality during adolescence and early adulthood. They report that "after tracing the effects of maternal resources, work hours, and occupational controls to criminality, . . . cumulative time spent by mothers in paid employment had no measurable influence on criminal involvement." Thus the alleged effect of mothers' employment on delinquency appears to be a myth.

It is also important to note that unemployment of fathers is typically viewed as a "cause" of delinquency because of its presumed consequences for family well-being. In the past, when fathers were supposed to be the sole breadwinners, deviations from that standard were viewed as problematic. When women's roles were linked primarily to the home, working mothers were believed to be a source of problems. Yet, to the degree that working mothers can contribute to the well-being of families, their employment might lower the odds of delinquency by increasing opportunities for success and educational aspirations. Moreover, to the degree that unemployed fathers might help supervise children, their unemployment might reduce the odds of delinquency. In sum, the relationship between parental employment outside of the home and delinquency may be weak or nonexistent either because such circumstances make no difference or because of such counter-balancing mechanisms.

Though employment status may have a negligible impact on delinquency, research has consistently shown that children who feel unwanted by their parents are more likely to report involvement in delinquency (McCord, 1984; Pulkkinen, 1982). These results appear to hold whether the rejection was by a mother or a father. Several studies also show that if children rejected their parents, this also can be related to delinquency (Loeber and Stouthamer-Loeber, 1986). Patterson (1980b) compared parents of children who steal with the parents of law-abiding children and found that the former set of parents lacked basic parenting skills. These parents failed to be assertive, failed to punish, and perhaps most importantly failed to interact and show concern.

Many intact families are in fact "broken" in terms of the actual relationships among family members. Atlas (1984) found that family tensions and parental discord greatly contribute to delinquent behavior and that divorce or separation can some-times reduce hostility and enhance the emotional needs of children. Long-term ten-sion supposedly reduces family cohesiveness and impairs the parents' ability to provide an atmosphere conducive to meaningful adolescent growth and development. If the family environment is disruptive and unstable, and parents display constant hos-tility toward one another, it is doubtful they will be able to exert a positive influence on their children. Amato and Keith (1991) reviewed the literature on divorce and fam-ily conflict and found that although divorce is harmful to children, family conflict has a more negative impact. A British study provides further support for that hypothesis in that boys from conflictual but intact families were not markedly different from boys in disrupted families (Juby and Farrington, 2001).

Power and colleagues (1974) showed that more delinquents from unhappy homes became *recidivists* (habitual offenders) than did delinquents from single-parent homes. Stouthamer-Loeber and colleagues (1984) found that unhappily married mothers supervised their children significantly less well than did happily married mothers. Hir-schi (1969) has argued that an affective tie between parent and child is one of the strongest convention-inducing variables in delinquency research. The weaker the bond between parent and child, the greater the probability of delinquent behavior. Hirschi found a consistent pattern of a lack of attachment and poor communication between delinquent children and their parents. For example, among boys reporting lit-tle intimate communication with their fathers, 43 percent reported committing at least two delinquent offenses. On the other hand, only 5 percent of boys with a high level of communication with their fathers reported such delinquent behavior. Joan McCord (1991) found that caring mothers who are affectionate, nonpunitive, and assertive were able to insulate their children from delinquency in even the most debilitated and crime-prone urban ghettoes.

Utilizing a social learning perspective, Rand Conger argued that "willingness to respond positively to one's children will raise the reinforcement value of the home and increase the rate of interaction from juvenile to parents as well as increase the probabil-ity that a juvenile will emulate conventional parental patterns of behavior" (1976:31). Conger found that communication between parent and child acts as a barrier to delin-quency only if the interaction is positive. Thus, communication in an excessively puni-tive home does not act as a barrier to delinquency. In a similar vein, Jensen and Brownfield (1983) reported that attachment to nondrug-using parents inhibits chil-dren's drug use, while attachment to drug-using parents either makes no difference or encourages children's drug use. Another study found that parents who use drugs serve as poor role models and can affect children's drug use (Dembo et al., 1986). No matter how strong the degree of attachment between parent and child, if parents are involved with drugs the chance that the child may also use drugs is enhanced.

One recent study has attempted to distinguish the relevance of "emotional sup-port" from the relevance of "parental supervision" (Wright and Cullen, 2001). Researchers found that delinquency was reduced by three aspects of the family envi-ronment: parental attachment, household rules, and parental supervision. In short, they propose that effective parenting is more than control and that constructing a home environment that discourages delinquency requires attention to emotional sup-port as well.

Parental Control, Discipline, and Punishment

It is well-established that parental efforts to monitor or supervise their children tend to be associated with reduced rates of delinquency. A more controversial issue is whether parental use of physical or corporal discipline inhibits or facilitates delinquency, especially forms of delinquency involving interpersonal violence. **Corporal punishment** refers to attempts to control or change a child's behavior through the physical implementation of pain, including spanking, hitting, slapping, shoving, and the use of implements such as belts, paddles, switches, hairbrushes, and sticks. Most parents have spanked their children at some time, believing that pain will help to deter further misbehavior. Such a belief is certainly consistent with various learning theories and deterrence theory (see chapter 9). Anticipated pain can lower the odds of behavior that has elicited such a response in the past. However, social learning theories also imply that physical punishment can have consequences that increase the odds of future misbehavior through processes of imitation. For example, if family problems are dealt with through some form of physical violence, then a child may learn to deal with daily problems in other settings through force and violence. Thus, while potentially inhibiting some forms of misbehavior, physical punishment might increase other forms through imitation.

Moreover, if punishment is administered in a manner that weakens bonds to parents, the net impact could be an increase rather than a decrease in misbehavior. Therefore, while the use of physical means of punishment may be common and widely accepted as necessary by parents, there are reasons to be concerned about its possible negative consequences. Murray Straus (1991) found a strong relationship between exposure to physical punishment and the child's later aggression throughout life. The child learns in the home that physical punishment is a way of resolving problems and takes this learning outside the home using aggression to solve his or her problems.

As Agnew (1983) points out, criminological research on the topic has not been perfectly consistent. The most common finding has been that physical punishment by parents is positively associated with both official and self-reported measures of delinquency. However, some research has also suggested that physical punishment can reduce the odds of delinquency (McCord, McCord, and Howard, 1961) or has no effect (Nye, 1958) *if it is consistently applied*. In the United States 80 percent of adults agree with the statement, "It is sometimes necessary to discipline a child with a good, hard spanking" (Flynn, 1994). Steinmetz (1987) argues that because of the frequency and intensity of violence in the home, the family can become the training ground for violence. All studies agree that inconsistent or erratic discipline is positively associated with delinquency, and that the combination of physical punishment and inconsistency may make physical punishment appear to be positively related to delinquency.

Agnew (1983) provides further support for the argument that the impact of physical punishment depends on consistency of discipline. Using data from a nationally representative sample of over 2,000 tenth-grade boys, Agnew found that physical punishment, intermittent (erratic) discipline, and inconsistent demands by parents as perceived by youth each increased the odds of self-reported delinquency (1983). However, physical punishment increased delinquency the most among parents whose children perceived inconsistent demands. Physical punishment slightly decreased delinquency for children whose parents were perceived to be consistent in their demands. Since few parents fell in the highly consistent category, physical punishment increased the odds of delinquency for most youth.

The most detailed study of the issue of corporal punishment in American families is Straus's *Beating the Devil Out of Them* (1994). Based on over 4,000 cases, Straus found that adults who recollected corporal punishment as a child had higher levels of violence of all kinds when they were older. He found this to be the case despite controls for a variety of variables that might have generated a spurious relationship. In contrast, other researchers have reported that quality of parental involvement is more important than spanking in the explanation of delinquency (Simons, Johnson, and Conger, 1994).

Family Violence

The family is typically studied as an agency of conventional socialization and control, thereby inhibiting delinquency. The research summarized above substantiates its importance in understanding delinquency. Yet the family also has been depicted as "a cradle of violence" (Steinmetz and Straus, 1973). Beatings, stabbings, burnings, and chokings are surprisingly common events within some families. While the home is typically thought of as synonymous with safety, security, and love, in some instances it may be more dangerous than walking the streets in a tough neighborhood. It is not surprising that the emotional environment of the family generates both love and anger. In fact, it can be argued that societies that accord importance to the family but where government institutions provide a relatively weak safety net outside of the family will have higher rates of family violence than found in societies with strong welfare systems and a weaker commitment to family (Jensen, 2001).

The U.S. Surgeon General has ranked abuse by husbands and partners as the leading cause of injuries to women ages 15 to 44 (Ingrassia and Berk, 1994), and the American Medical Association has estimated that as many as one in three women will be assaulted by a domestic partner in her lifetime (Blackman, 1994). In the *Annual Review of Psychology*, researchers conclude that "family violence is the most relevant form of violence in this country" (Tolan, Gorman-Smith, and Henry, 2006:559).

One particular type of violence that has received increasing publicity and concern is parental violence against children. In 2003, the National Clearinghouse on Abuse and Neglect reported that more than 900,000 children were victims of abuse or neglect—and these figures are limited to those who came to the attention of officials. These numbers translate into a rate of about 12 victims per 1,000 children. However, the National Family Violence Survey (Straus, Sugarman, and Giles-Sims, 1997) estimated a rate of 49 per 1,000 children when self-reports of physical "conflict tactics" reported by parents is considered. A report from the Bureau of Justice (Durose et al., 2005) summarized the magnitude of the problem with the following observations:

- A total of 3.5 million violent crimes occurred in the family between 1998 and 2002.

- Twenty-two percent of murders were family murders.

- Nearly a quarter of all murder victims under age 13 were killed by a family member.

- The average age of children murdered by a parent was 7 years.

- Only 60 percent of family violence is reported to the police.
- Of family violence cases reported to the police, only 36 percent resulted in an arrest.

Child abuse cuts across all categories of race, sex, social class, religion, and ethnicity, but it does appear that lower-class families are subjected to more stress and have fewer coping techniques than higher-class families, resulting in higher rates of child abuse. Abusive parents are often experiencing stress and cope by taking it out on others, including their children (Gelles, 2007:409). If children of abusive parents grow up to be abusive parents themselves, then we may be faced with a perpetual cycle of violence (Gelles and Cornell, 1985).

The legacy of child abuse is not just the physical scars that children carry with them. The consequences of violence and abuse produce innumerable problems. Some researchers feel that abused children have a higher probability of growing up to be delinquents and have less respect for the conventional order (Steinmetz, 1987). In fact, Carolyn Smith and Terence Thornberry (1995) studied 1,000 seventh and eighth-grade students in Rochester, New York, and found that 69 percent of youths who were "maltreated" as children reported involvement in violence as compared to 56 percent who had not been maltreated. For youths who experienced multiple forms of maltreatment, 78 percent self-reported violence. In sum, family violence doubled the risk of self-reported violence.

Increasing attention to family violence has been accompanied by increasing concern for sexual abuse of children. Upwards of 130,000 cases of child sexual abuse are reported each year, but this is most likely a gross underestimate. Estimates of the prevalence of sexual abuse range between 3 and 36 percent of children, depending on the way the measure is constructed (Finkelhor et al., 1997). Dr. James Hopper reports that approximately one in four girls is sexually abused by age 14 and one in three by age 18. He also reports that one in six boys is sexually abused before age 16 (Hopper, 1997). While it is impossible to arrive at precise figures, many authorities suggest that perhaps one in ten boys and one in three girls have been victims of sexual exploitation. Father or stepfather/daughter incest is found to be the most common form of child sexual abuse.

Although the National Clearinghouse statistics have shown increasing numbers of cases of child abuse brought to official attention over time, Straus (2001) reports that National Family Violence Surveys have shown decreasing abuse. Parents were less violent toward children over the years encompassed by the surveys. Declines in severe and very severe violence directed toward children are particularly notable and statistically significant. This same study also surveyed rates of marital violence and the data suggest that husbands were less violent toward their wives over time. Straus and Gelles (1990) suggest that the greatest declines in family violence are found for those forms that have received the greatest attention and where the most change in law enforcement has occurred.

Support for and use of corporal punishment has been declining as well. Straus notes that in 1968, 94 percent of Americans believed that spanking was "sometimes necessary," but that figure had dropped to 55 percent by 1999. Although he found no significant change in the use of physical tactics in disciplining toddlers, he did find a sizeable reduction (from about 50 percent to about 35 percent) for youths 13–14 years of age. Parents are showing signs of a movement away from hitting, slapping, or more severe forms of violence over time, but such tactics are still very common (about 95 percent for toddlers). Juvenile violence has been declining for about the past fifteen years, so it does not appear that sparing the rod threatens to increase juvenile violence. Indeed, it is conceivable that it has the opposite effect.

The School

While the range of functions served by the family has been declining, the importance of the school as a context for socialization has been growing. What was viewed as a luxury for the affluent during the seventeenth and eighteenth centuries has grown to encompass a greater and greater proportion of the entire population. For example, in 1870, 57 percent of youth ages 5 to 17 were enrolled in school, and only 1.2 percent were in high school. By 2005, 97 percent of children between the ages of 5 and 17 were enrolled in school: 95.4 percent of 5- and 6-year-olds, 98.6 percent of 7- to 13-year-olds, 98 percent of 14- and 15-year-olds, and 95.1 percent of 16- and 17-year-olds (U.S. Census Bureau, 2005). Several decades ago, completion of elementary school was considered a significant educational attainment. Today, completion of high school is seen as virtually mandatory for even the most menial of jobs, and it is becoming increasingly expected that a college degree is the appropriate level of educational attainment for many entry-level positions.

Since so much of the average American's teenage life is encompassed by school, it is hardly surprising that schools should be viewed as central to an understanding of delinquency. According to some versions of strain theory (see chapter 6), adolescents are driven to delinquency as a way of rebelling against school authority (Elliott and Voss, 1974) or as a way of solving status problems generated by school experiences. The school is also central in social control theory, which generally views the school as an institution designed to encourage conventional attitudes and behavior. Hirschi views the role of the school in the following manner:

> Between the conventional family and the conventional world of work and marriage lies the school, an eminently conventional institution. Insofar as this institution is able to command his attachment, involvement, and commitment, the adolescent is presumably able to move from childhood to adulthood with a minimum of delinquent acts. (1969:110)

While the strain theorist views school experiences as a source of frustration and rebellion, the control theorist views school experiences as important in the sense that they represent bonds to an eminently conventional institution. The person who is not attached, involved, or committed to school or concerned about the teachers' opinions is "freer" to drift into delinquency.

From a normative conflict/differential association perspective, the school is a source of definitions "unfavorable" to lawbreaking, and from a social learning perspective it is a major setting for the reinforcement of rule-abiding conduct. In short, while they may differ in the specific mechanisms involved, the major theories all accord experiences at school a critical role in the explanation of delinquency.

Social learning theory emphasizes several learning processes that involve school as well. Despite the recent publicity about teachers engaging in illegal sexual activities with students, teachers tend to act as conventional role models and generally attempt to teach values and attitudes that are believed to inhibit deviance. High grades earned in school are a form of social reinforcement for approved academic behavior, while youths with poor grades have less to lose by violating school rules and committing delinquent acts. Despite widespread publicity, the school shootings in the 1990s and 2000s are aberrations; school is a relatively safe place to be as compared to cruising the streets or hanging around with friends or fellow dropouts outside of school.

Research on the School and Delinquency

According to Walter Schaefer and colleagues, schools have become the primary instruments of socialization for youth, the "basic conduit through which the community and adult influences enter into the lives of adolescents" (1972:13). They listed the following as "defects in the schools that heighten educational failure and deterioration, and hence delinquency":

1. belief in the limited potential of disadvantaged pupils
2. irrelevant instruction
3. inappropriate teaching methods
4. testing, grouping, and "tracking"
5. inadequate compensatory and remedial education
6. inferior teachers and facilities in low-income schools
7. school-community distance
8. racial and economic segregation

While plausible arguments concerning the contributory influence of these conditions to the advent of delinquency have been advanced, there is not a large body of research that relates specifically to each of these points. Some studies have, however, dealt with delinquency in specific relation to school achievement, attachment to teachers and school, dropping out of school, tracking, and intelligence tests. In addition to these studies, we will consider some research on the association between characteristics of schools, victimization rates, and violence in schools.

Achievement

One of the most persistent findings concerning the school and delinquency is that students who are not doing well in school have higher rates of delinquency than those who are faring better. For example, Johnson (1979) examined the causal connection between parents, school, and delinquent associates as primary agents in explaining delinquent behavior, and found success in school and attachment to school to be of utmost importance. Students who experience success in school have higher occupational expectations, fewer delinquent associates, and become more attached to school. Stronger attachment to school means fewer delinquent values, which ultimately means less delinquent involvement. Thus, school achievement can serve as a crucial background variable in the long causal chain affecting delinquency. As we shall see in the section on peers, delinquent associates appear to be the most critical factor in the understanding of delinquency, but school achievement and attachment to school serve as counteracting forces in the development of delinquent associates. Johnson argues that schools become "the central arena for the shifting and sorting of adolescent companionships, which prove to be so relevant to delinquent behavior" (1979:109).

Jensen (1976) found that achievement level is significantly related to delinquency status and that the relationship persists regardless of socioeconomic status and racial classification. Among whites and nonwhites, the higher the achievement, the lower the odds that a youth will acquire a delinquent record before his or her eighteenth birthday. The findings also suggested that differences in delinquency status occur only when we move beyond the lowest levels of achievement. Similarly Frease (1973) reported that no student with a grade-point average of 3.0 (B) or better had a police record, but that the arrest rate was as high as 75 percent among boys with the lowest grades.

Farrington (2005) suggests that there is a constellation of childhood indicators that predict delinquent behavior. Low school achievement emerges as one of the most critical indicators of subsequent delinquent behavior. However, the most recent study of the issue suggests some major qualifications of the achievement-delinquency link. Felson and Staff (2006) found that it was youths who paid attention and were orderly in class that had the best grades and the least involvement in delinquency. Thus, rather than achievement being an investment or accomplishment that acted as a barrier to delinquency, they argue that the relationship is spurious and attribute it to the self-control of youth. Teachers favor those students who exhibit control in the classroom. Teachers play a role in their explanation, but, allegedly, are reacting to characteristics established outside of the school or in early childhood socialization.

Attachment to Teachers and School

As we noted earlier, both control and social learning theory emphasize the strength of the bond between students and their school and teachers as an important barrier to involvement in delinquency. Further, as discussed in the previous section, students who do not achieve good grades do not develop strong emotional ties or a sense of attachment to school. There is, in fact, persistent evidence that students who do not like school or their teachers, and who do not take their educational responsibilities seriously, are more likely to report delinquency than those who are more strongly attached to their teachers and school (Jensen, Erickson, and Gibbs, 1978; Hirschi, 1969; Hindelang, 1973; Thornberry et al., 1991). Students who disrupt class and upset teachers at an early age are more likely to get into trouble with the law in later years (Spivack and Cianci, 1987). Goldman (1961) found that schools which manifest a close relationship between teachers and students have low levels of school vandalism, whereas schools that are cold and institutional are continually plagued with broken windows, graffiti, and "trashing." The evidence to date strongly suggests that students who are not bonded to their school tend to have higher rates of delinquent behavior than those who see their school as a warm and meaningful part of their lives.

School Dropouts

Schools play a significant role in channeling youth into the higher-status positions in society. Conversely, school performance also sorts out those who will occupy the lower rungs on the occupational ladder. The chances of making it in American society without the proper educational credentials are remote. For example, according to U.S. Census Bureau statistics (2005), people 21 to 64 years of age with less than eight years of education earned $21,332 a year, four years of high school produced an income of $27,351, college graduates earned $42,877, and those with advanced degrees earned on the average $55,242. Individuals who do not complete at least high school will be severely disadvantaged. In the United States, nearly 10 percent of whites age 25 or older do not have a high school diploma; for African Americans it is 20 percent, and for Hispanics it is 42 percent. The current official dropout rate for 16- to 24-year-olds is 10 percent for whites, 12 percent for African Americans, and 24 percent for Hispanics. However a recently published report, *The Silent Epidemic*, funded by the Bill and Melinda Gates Foundation, challenges these official estimates (Bridgeland, Dilulio, and Morison, 2006). The authors estimate that the dropout rate is between 29 and 32 percent, with African Americans and Hispanics having as high as a 50 percent dropout rate. They argue that dropout rates are underestimated and graduation rates are overestimated in official reports.

> Many schools in America can't tell us on any given day who's in school and who's not, nor in any given year how many students have successfully made it through their four years of schooling to graduate and how many have dropped out.
> (Eugene Hickok, Deputy Secretary of U.S. Dept. of Education, quoted in Bridgeland, Dilulio, and Morison, 2006)

Delbert Elliott (1966) followed several cohorts of boys over a period of time and kept track of the delinquency referral rates of boys who eventually graduated from high school and of those who dropped out. Data on the dropouts included delinquency rates while in school and afterward. Elliott found that lower-status youths who eventually dropped out had a higher rate of delinquent referrals than lower-status youths who eventually graduated. While still in school, these eventual dropouts had the highest delinquency referral rate of all groups studied. However, after dropping out, the referral rate for lower-status dropouts was actually the lowest of all the groups studied. This finding is contrary to the expectation that school dropouts will continue or perhaps escalate delinquent activities once they are out of school. Elaborating on these findings, Elliott and Harwin Voss (1974) found that while future dropouts were in school, there was a progressive escalation of their delinquency rates: before they dropped out, their police contact rate was anywhere from four to nine times greater than the rate of those who graduated. However, after dropping out, their referral rates fell off dramatically.

Elliott and Voss interpreted this pattern as support for a strain-frustration delinquency argument. They suggested that students who eventually drop out of school grow increasingly frustrated the longer they are in school and that their increasing referral rates reflect their increasing frustration. Dropping out alleviates their school-generated frustrations, and (so the argument goes) their involvement in delinquency diminishes. Of course, there are other possible interpretations that do not require that the potential dropout be viewed as frustrated. We could argue that the school experiences that weaken the student's bond to the school and lead to dropping out progressively "free" the student to violate the law. After dropping out, new bonds (for example, marriage, a job) are formed, and the delinquency rate therefore drops. However, whether delinquency and dropping out of school are viewed as results of frustration or progressive detachment, Elliott and Voss's findings support the argument that school experiences are important in explaining involvement in delinquency.

A more recent study of the issue suggests that rather than decreasing the probabilities of future crime, dropping out increases the chances of future trouble. In a study of a 10 percent sample of the 1945 Philadelphia cohort discussed in chapter 1 and throughout this text, researchers found that both the short-term and long-term effects of dropping out were higher probabilities of further criminality (Thornberry, Moore, and Christenson, 1985). This finding applied to both minority and majority groups and to youths from blue-collar backgrounds. The odds of greater crime were increased regardless of later marital or employment status. They note that the results are consistent with social control theory and contrary to Elliott and Voss's strain theory predictions. Similarly, Marvin Krohn and his associates (1995), using data from the Rochester Youth Development Study, also found that teens who dropped out of school committed more crimes, took more drugs, and suffered from myriad other social problems than high school graduates. They argue that problems that began in school continued after the juvenile left school. The evidence strongly suggests that dropping out is associated with low-paying jobs, high unemployment, and higher chances of deviant activity.

Tracking

One educational technique that has received a significant amount of attention as a potential contributor to delinquency is the use of educational "tracks" or ability groups for students of varying intellectual capabilities. In general, **tracking** refers to a method of curriculum assignment that places students in an educational program according to scores on intelligence tests and levels of academic achievement. The criticism of such an educational classification scheme is that students assigned to the lower track are accorded second-class status. It may also be the case that students who are not placed in higher tracks are denied opportunities for achievement and success, and that slow bloomers are not given the opportunity of being transferred to the upper track.

Schaefer, Olexa, and Polk (1972) gathered data on the impact of track placement on academic achievement and delinquency. They found that students in the college-bound track achieved far better grades than those in the noncollege track. While 37 percent of the students in the college track placed in the top quarter of their class and only 11 percent fell in the bottom quarter, students in the noncollege track achieved significantly lower grades: only 2 percent in the top quarter and 52 percent in the bottom quarter. If students who are not in college tracks are simply less intelligent than those who are, the results of this study are not particularly disturbing. However, Schaefer and associates also analyzed their data controlling or holding constant father's occupation, IQ scores, and grade-point average for the last semester of junior high school. They found that significant differences still persisted between the two tracks. Of the students in the college track, 30 percent fell in the top quarter and only 12 percent in the bottom quarter, whereas 4 percent of students in the noncollege track placed in the top quarter and 35 percent in the bottom quarter. The researchers concluded that assignment to the noncollege track has a pronounced negative effect on grades.

These researchers also found that track assignment was associated with dropping out, lack of participation in school activities, and delinquency. Students in the noncollege track tended to be less involved in extracurricular activities during high school than students in the college track, and far more of them dropped out of high school. Finally, track position appeared to be a powerful explanatory variable in predicting deviant behavior. The researchers found that although students in the noncollege track comprised 29 percent of their sample, they accounted for 53 percent of all students disciplined once, 70 percent disciplined three or more times, and 51 percent of those who were suspended from school. Similarly, they were more than twice as likely as students in the college track to have a juvenile court record. The researchers argued that the alienation, frustration, and stigma caused by this second-class citizenship may have been partly to blame for the marginality of this group (Schaefer, Olexa, and Polk, 1972).

Other research on tracking has supported the notion that school status is a far more important determinant of delinquent behavior than the traditional variable of parental social class. David Hargreaves (1968) studied an English secondary school and found that boys in the lowest "stream" tended to be social isolates and were more involved in delinquent activities than were those in higher streams. Kelly and Balch (1971) put forth a "school status" theory of delinquency, arguing that one's location in the reward structure of the school is an important predictor of delinquent involvement. In further analysis, Kelly (1974) found that track position, compared to gender and social class, emerged as the strongest predictor of some twenty-five different forms of delinquent activity.

Such findings have been interpreted as the results of a self-fulfilling prophecy. According to this interpretation, students in the low or basic tracks do not do as well as they should because school personnel expect them to do poorly. In one of the several experiments that have explored self-fulfilling prophecies, Rosenthal and Jacobson (1968) gave three kinds of IQ tests to 650 elementary school students. They told the teachers that these tests would predict which children were about to "bloom" or "spurt" intellectually. After administering the tests, the researchers merely selected at random a certain proportion of students as intellectual bloomers regardless of their IQ scores. The teachers assigned to these students were told to expect them to make marked intellectual gains. The remaining children constituted a control group, with no purported intellectual superiority. At the end of the first year, the IQ gains of the "intellectual bloomers" greatly exceeded the gains of the control group; the same results occurred at the end of the second year. Rosenthal and Jacobson published their findings in a book entitled *Pygmalion in the Classroom*, borrowing from the story of a Greek king named Pygmalion who brought to life a statue of a beautiful woman. Hence, the phrase **Pygmalion effect** became associated with this work.

As engaging as these findings are for delinquency research, there have been numerous criticisms of the Rosenthal and Jacobson study (Thorndike, 1968; Snow, 1969) and not all studies of teacher expectations have obtained the same results (Boocock, 1978). However, a large number of studies with various methodologies have obtained results similar to Rosenthal and Jacobson's, indicating that the process they identified seems to occur. Subsequent studies suggest that teachers' expectations as well as those of parents and peers have dramatic effects on how much students learn (Oakes, 1994; Eder, 1981). Jeannie Oakes (1985), in a highly acclaimed study titled *Keeping Track: How Schools Structure Inequality*, suggests that low-track students are being exposed to material that is qualitatively different from the educational material presented to high-track students. Tracking retards the academic progress of certain students, lowers self-esteem and career aspirations, and encourages racial and economic segregation. Oakes found that low-track students are being taught how to fill out forms and write checks while high-track students are reading Shakespeare and learning analytic geometry. She asks:

> Could it be that we are teaching kids at the bottom of the educational hierarchy— who are more likely to be from poor and minority groups—behaviors that will prepare them to fit in at the lowest levels of the social and economic hierarchy? And, at the other extreme, are we teaching kids at the top of the schooling stratification system behaviors that are most important for professional and leadership roles? In essence, are we teaching kids at the bottom how to stay there and kids at the top how to get ahead? (1985:91)

Gamoran (1992) argues that schools need to create educational tracks that are flexible, allowing student mobility within and between tracks. Those schools with rigid, inflexible tracks will produce inequalities between tracks. Schools must be concerned with overall achievement and minimize the potential inequality that is an inherent risk with any tracking system.

Intelligence Tests

Intelligence tests of one kind or another are used in schools to channel youth into different educational programs. They are accorded significance by educational institutions and, in general, those youth who do poorly on such tests also have high rates of delinquency.

Albert Binet, the creator of the first IQ test, wrote in 1905 that an **IQ score** should only be used as a rough guide for identifying mildly retarded and learning disabled children who needed extra help in school. He emphatically stated that the test "does not permit the measure of intelligence because intelligence is not a single scalable thing like height" (quoted in Gould, 1981:151). Binet argued that the IQ score was intended to be a rough guide, constructed for a limited practical purpose.

A social movement in the late 1800s and early 1900s known as **eugenics** claimed that one's IQ was inherited. Proponents said that by allowing individuals with low IQs to reproduce, we were weakening our "human stock." In 1927 the U.S. Supreme Court supported this view by upholding Virginia's compulsory sterilization law in the *Buck v. Bell* case. More than thirty states enacted such laws, with Virginia ordering more than 7,500 compulsory sterilizations. In 1927, Carrie Buck's test scores caused her to be labeled feeble-minded and she had an operation, supposedly for a ruptured appendix. She never was informed that her fallopian tubes were severed until it was discovered in 1980. She was reexamined by psychologists in 1980 and found to be of normal intelligence (Gould, 1981). Thus, IQ tests have been used in highly questionable ways, and for many, the deification of the IQ score is quite unpalatable.

No test can measure native intelligence because "IQs always are based on the individual's interactions with the environment" (Sattler, 1982:64) and no matter how carefully the questions are written, there is always a cultural bias to such tests. It is generally agreed that IQ tests are a better indicator of a child's background and learning environment than of his or her natural intelligence. Further, it has been shown that test scores can be influenced by test readiness, test anxiety, motivation, perceived test payoff, and even the race of the test administrator. However, for all the negative features of IQ tests, they still predict academic success better than any other tool. What they do measure is a combination of factors including intelligence, knowledge, middle-class language patterns and experiences, motivation, and test readiness, to name but a few of the test dimensions.

While not a perfect measure and clearly culturally biased toward white, middle-class standards, IQ tests do give some indication of how well a student will perform in school. Immigrants typically score low on IQ tests but their descendants score considerably higher—not because of a change in innate ability but because of familiarity with white middle-class norms, behaviors, and values. However, attempting to measure "native intelligence" is extraordinarily difficult. Consider, for example, some possible IQ items:

1. If you throw the dice and 7 is showing on the top, what is facing down?

   (a) Seven   (b) Snake eyes   (c) Boxcars   (d) Little Joes

2. The Percheron is a kind of

   (a) Goat   (b) Horse   (c) Cow   (d) Sheep

3. Christy Mathewson is famous as a

   (a) Writer   (b) Artist   (c) Baseball player   (d) Comedian

4. The Chicano term for the police is

   (a) La migra   (b) La chota   (c) El gabacho   (d) El pachuco

Most "streetwise" kids would know the answer to number one is seven. People growing up on a farm would know a Percheron is a horse. Baseball card collectors would know Christy Mathewson as a member of the Hall of Fame. Finally, most Hispanic kids would know that the Chicano term for the police is *la chota*. So what constitutes intelligence?

No matter what our interpretation of IQ tests, we should expect a relationship between IQ test performance and delinquency. Wolfgang, Figlio, and Sellin's (1972) study in Philadelphia found that the average IQ of boys who had been stopped by the police was 101 compared to 108 for those not stopped. A study in England also found that the average IQ of boys age 8 to 10 who would later become delinquent was 95, while it was 101 for those who did not become delinquent (West, 1982). Hirschi and Hindelang (1977) also pointed to the small but consistent difference of about nine points between the IQs of delinquents and nondelinquents.

It is quite reasonable from a sociological perspective to expect that all sorts of measures of ability, achievement, and intelligence may be related to delinquency. Students who do not fare well in terms of the criteria that a particular institution uses to evaluate people are likely to be less sensitive to the emphases and concerns of that institution. The reason they do not do well in terms of those criteria can be debated. However, it would be surprising to find anything other than lower test scores among delinquents since school experiences are important in the explanation of delinquency. And, as Hirschi and Hindelang concluded in their review of the literature, the relationship between IQ test performance and measures of official delinquency is at least as strong as relationships found for social class and race. Hirschi and Hindelang's research indicted that IQ affects delinquency through its association with school performance—that is, students who do not score well in terms of grades and academic achievement have a higher probability of involvement in delinquency.

Menard and Morse are highly critical of any attempt to suggest that IQ is an important variable in explaining delinquency. They argue that delinquent behavior is a consequence of social institutional practices rather than individual characteristics. Thus:

> Access to desirable social roles and positive labeling in the school, the home, and society in general mutually reinforce one another and lead to commitment to the legal and social norms of society. Commitment, in turn, leads to nondelinquent, conforming, or prosocial behavior. Negatively, the absence of access to desirable social roles plus premature and/or inappropriate negative labeling mutually reinforce one another and lead to alienation, a rejection of rejecters. Alienation, in turn, leads to delinquent behavior. The behavior generated by institutional structures through opportunity and labeling may then feed back into the institutional structure, generating responses which reinforce that behavior. (1984:1349)

In other words, rather than suggesting that IQ exerts any direct causal impact on delinquency, these authors argue that differences in IQ may lead to differences in institutional responses, and these responses may stimulate delinquency. While they are critical of Hirschi and Hindelang's research, their conclusion is basically the same: IQ tests gain their significance from the meaning accorded them by educational institutions and through their correlation with other measures of achievement and academic success at school.

Crime in School

In the past several decades a great deal of attention has been given to the problem of order and personal safety within the American school system. In 1974 Congress required the Department of Health, Education and Welfare to study the extent of crime in American schools, and in 1978 a report entitled *Violent Schools—Safe Schools* was published (Boesel, 1978). In this study, thousands of teachers and students reported their experiences in school and how their lives and property are in jeopardy. While this study sensitized the nation to the problem of crime in the school, it has been highly criticized for slipshod and unsophisticated analysis (Baker and Rubel, 1980; Gottfredson and Gottfredson, 1985).

Sensationalized accounts of murder and mayhem reached such a crescendo in California that the Attorney General sued the Los Angeles school district for not providing a safe environment for students. The suit, based on the shaky legal ground that requiring students to attend schools that were unsafe constituted cruel and unusual punishment, was dismissed by the trial judge. In 1982 California amended its state constitution to read:

> Right to Safe Schools. All students and staff of public primary, elementary, junior high and senior high schools have the inalienable right to attend campuses which are safe, secure and peaceful. (Article I, section 28C)

Citizens and parents should expect not only safe schools but also access to information on school safety. Tools in the pursuit of that goal are the studies of school crime and safety by the National Center for Education Statistics and the Bureau of Justice Statistics. A series of reports on *Indicators of School Crime and Safety* have drawn from such sources as surveys of school principals; household surveys; National Crime Victimization surveys; and teacher and student surveys.

In chapter 1, we noted that the much-publicized school shootings occurred in the context of a declining rate of overall school violence, an observation yielded by the *Indicators of School Crime and Safety.* Nonfatal victimization rates in schools have been declining and the rate for serious violent crimes in 2005 was about 5 per 1,000 students at school compared to 10 per 1,000 away from school. Out of about 2,400 children ages 5 to 19 who were victims of homicide, there were 33 committed at school (less than 1.5 percent). Schools are generally safer environments than the community or even families.

The fact that violence in schools is declining and that schools are relatively safe places does not mean that school violence should be ignored. Indeed, one effect of the school shootings has been a proliferation of school violence prevention programs. These programs will be considered in chapter 12's discussion of prevention. There is mounting evidence that certain kinds of school-based intervention programs designed to reduce school violence have been effective.

Moreover, while students may be less likely to be victims of serious violent crimes at school than away from school, they are more likely to have things stolen at school (see figure 7-2). For crimes of theft the rate in 2005 was 33 thefts per 1,000 students at school and 23 thefts per 1,000 students when away from school (National Center for Education Statistics, 2007). The evidence from the school crime reports indicates that school crime, like crime in the community, is fairly widespread but at the same time is essentially nonviolent (Short, 1990). Teachers and students are in much greater danger of losing their property through theft than of being assaulted or robbed. Middle schools were more likely than primary or secondary schools to report racial tensions, bullying, verbal abuse of teachers, and disorder in the classrooms. Nearly a third of students at urban schools reported the presence of street gangs in school. In grades 9 through 12, 29 percent of students reported that someone had offered, sold, or given them an illegal drug on school property. Seventeen percent of students in grades 9–12 reported they carried a weapon, but only 6 percent reported bringing a weapon to school.

Jackson Toby (1983) suggests that the teacher and student victimization rates may not be as dramatic as the *perception* of fear of crime in school. In the largest cities, 7 percent of senior high school students said they stayed home from school out of fear at least once in the month before the survey, as did 8 percent of the junior high students. Among the teachers in the largest cities, 28 percent said they hesitated to confront misbehaving students in the month preceding the survey out of fear for their own safety.

Toby suggests that schools mirror the local community or neighborhood in the volume and type of crime. "Some schools become virtual jungles from the point of view of student and staff safety and wastelands from the point of view of education" (1983:76). Toby sees the major problem of crime in school to be compulsory attendance. He suggests that a uniform age of compulsory attendance be set at 15 years, and disruptive or unruly students who are 15 years of age or older would simply be expelled from school.

Gottfredson and Gottfredson (1985) are not convinced by Toby's argument. They argue that the average school is not "the hotbed of violence and disorder that popular accounts suggest" (1985:1). Teachers are exposed to a wide variety of personal indignities, the least frequent being rape or assault and the most common being verbal abuse. Students are rarely robbed or assaulted but do experience a fair amount of petty theft. Hence, the major problem in schools, according to the Gottfredsons, is the frequency of minor victimizations and personal indignities. They see school size as the critical variable. When teachers have extensive contact with a limited number of students, social control is at the optimum level. In exceedingly large schools, the educational climate becomes impersonal and disruptive as teachers are exposed to large numbers of different students who are rotated through an endless series of classes. Second, the Gottfredsons suggest that rules must be clear and enforced, not with an emphasis on authoritarian rule but fair and predictable school policies. Third, schools located in areas characterized by high poverty, unemployment, and female-headed households will manifest high crime rates in the schools. Policies calling for more integration in the community itself are imperative. Finally, the Gottfredsons are not convinced that if compul-

Figure 7-2   Victimization per 1,000 Students At and Away from School

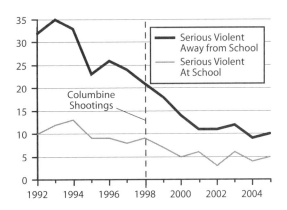

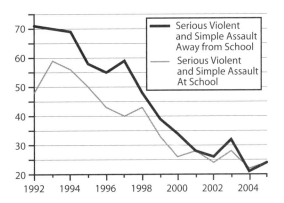

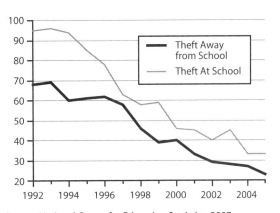

Source: National Center for Education Statistics, 2007.

sory education laws were uniformly lowered to age 15 that the crime rate in school would be improved in any significant way.

The Peer Group

We noted in chapter 6 that several sociological theories attempt to explain the emergence and persistence of delinquency in terms of gangs rather than individual delinquent behavior. In fact, one of the reasons sociology was prominent in the academic foundation of American criminology was that it focused on social systems or social "organizations"—everything from groups to nations. Some criminal activities were clearly "organized" whether that organization took the form of an adult crime syndicate such as the Mafia or attempts to maximize corporate profits through price-fixing or fraudulent accounting and company reports. Similarly, while thought of as antisocial behavior, delinquency was also "social" behavior in the sense that it typically occurred in groups of youths of similar age and social characteristics. Delinquent behavior was and remains an activity that tends to occur in groups, and that is true in all settings and categories of youth studied.

The term "gang" is likely to be used in everyday depictions of what may be nothing more than garden-variety peer group delinquency. Since that term evokes images of an identifiable set of violent youths with a common identity as members of a named group controlling a certain territory or turf, other terms have been used as well to convey other senses in which delinquency is peer group behavior—for example, delinquency as "a pickup game," "law-violating youth groups," and "near groups." Even the term "gang" can be qualified based on the degree of organization involved. Some researchers believe that the focus on gangs characterizing criminology in the 1960s helped perpetuate a "gang myth hysteria" and ignored the essentially spontaneous and casual nature of delinquency in very loosely organized play groups. To fully understand the group nature of delinquency requires recognition of its most common form as well as its more dramatic, but less common, form—the street gang.

Peer Group Delinquency as a Pickup Game

Many sociologists have criticized an exclusive focus on gangs because it limits the study of delinquency to one type of group that accounts for a small amount of the total volume of delinquency in America (Hirschi, 1969:52–53). This point of view is expressed by Martin Gold, based on research on delinquency in Flint, Michigan:

> The "gang" image seldom fit the teenage groups involved in delinquent behavior. That is, the groups did not regularly and frequently commit delinquent acts together; their members did not characterize themselves as especially delinquent compared with other teenagers; and their behavior together was not usually delinquent. Rather, the groups of teenagers who committed delinquent acts consisted usually of two or three youngsters who often hung around together, and from time to time engaged in delinquent behavior. From the point of view of even the most delinquent boys, their companions in crime were drawn from the ranks of the many fellows they knew and spent time with; seldom were any particular boys ever consistent fellow offenders. More important than the particular company was the

presence of an opportunity for delinquency at a time when everyone's mood was ripe for the action.

Perhaps gang delinquency, not much a part of the Flint (Michigan) scene, is more characteristic of the hearts of great cities where teenagers may stick closer together with fewer friends than they do in Flint, and where the delinquent opportunity and the daring-defiant mood are more often coincident. Yet observers of delinquency in the inner-city slums of London and New York report that the gang image is much overblown even there.

Delinquent behavior, as our data describe it, is more casual, spontaneous, and loosely organized than the gang myth would lead us to believe. We have suggested that delinquent activity more closely resembles the pickup games of ball we used to get into at the park or on the street, when someone showed up with a bat and ball, the environment provided an adequate setting, and we had the spirit for the game. (1970)

The image of delinquency presented by Gold and others emphasizes spontaneity and a certain element of play. When the stage is set and the right combination of youth get together, the odds of delinquency may be enhanced; but such activity is not the premeditated aim of such groups. Moreover, most such collections of youth lack the features that would justify calling them a gang. Gold's research supports the conclusion that delinquency is most often a spontaneous activity in ordinary peer groups. There is no planning, no serious premeditation, no specific agenda—things "just happen."

Gender and the Group Nature of Delinquency

When conceived of as spontaneous peer group activity, delinquency is a social event for both girls and boys. The fact that true delinquent gangs are rare among girls has led some scholars (see Cloward and Piven, 1979) to depict female delinquency as individualistic and lacking in the social solidarity of male delinquency. However, at least three studies have examined the relation between gender and peer delinquency and all three report the same results (see Erickson and Jensen, 1977). Girls are just as likely or even more likely than boys to indicate that they were with others when they engaged in delinquent action. This finding should not be surprising since no one has ever demonstrated greater sociability, solidarity, or engrossment in intimate peer group relationships for boys than for girls. As summarized in chapters 3 and 4, girls are less likely than boys to engage in most forms of delinquency and have especially low rates for the most serious offenses. However, when they do commit delinquent acts, they are as likely to commit them with company as are boys.

The fact that delinquency is as likely to be a social activity for girls as for boys does not mean that there are no differences in the group nature or organizational nature of crime and delinquency by gender. Darrell Steffensmeier (1983) has studied "institutional sexism" in the underworld of crime and proposes that sex segregation is particularly prominent for organized, professional, and high-risk, high-gain criminal activity. Since most juvenile delinquency is spontaneous, nonprofessional, and low in profit, the gender difference in delinquency should not be as distinct as it is for more highly structured crime. Moreover, the gender difference in structural gang membership should be greater than the difference in more casual and spontaneous peer group activity. The gender difference should also be lower for the least dangerous and lowest risk group activities. Thus, the difference between males and females varies depending on the organization of the activity but, in general, both male and female delinquency are forms of social action.

The National Youth Gang Survey reported that 39 percent of all youth gangs have at least some female members, but only 2 percent of current gangs are predominantly female (Egley, 2002). Moreover, similar to findings for boys, those girls who are members of gangs tend to be far more involved in delinquent behavior than are nongang females. However, female gang members commit fewer violent crimes than male gang members, and tend to commit property and status offenses. Further, female gang members tend not to carry weapons, do not engage in drug sales, and do not commit serious property crimes. A significant finding indicates males tend to be less delinquent in male-majority gangs, but in sex-balanced gangs, males seem to experience a status threat and become more prone to delinquency (Peterson et al., 2001). Thus, gangs that consist of both males and females tend to be more delinquent than majority or all-male gangs.

Gangs, Near Groups, and Law-Violating Youth Groups

Some peer groups involved in delinquency are more structured and have features that justify the term "gang." However, there is great variation in the features of groups thought of as gangs, and the degree to which gangs are responsible for serious crime and delinquency depends on the definition used. As a reflection of this diversity, criminologists have used a variety of terms to refer to gang-like peer groups.

A study of youths in Philadelphia found that police records of gang membership were not adequate for assessing the extent of gang delinquency (Savitz, Lalli, and Rosen, 1977:49). Thus, researchers chose to gather information on delinquent gangs through interviews. They defined the gangs in two different senses. Drawing on William Arnold's work, they classified youths as either structural gang members or as functional gang members. A **structural gang member** belonged to a group with "acknowledged leadership, common gang meeting place, and a territory or turf within which the group feels safe and where entry by others can provoke the group to violence." Such gangs were defined solely on the basis of their structural characteristics and not according to whether they actually engaged in aggressive behavior. A **functional gang member** was one who belonged to a group that got into fights with other groups and that expected fighting of its members.

Among males with delinquent records, structural gang membership was quite rare. Of African Americans with delinquent records, 16 percent were classified as structural gang members, as were 22 percent of whites. While few youths belonged to structural gangs, a greater proportion indicated that their group of friends fought with other groups and that they were expected to join in the fighting. This type of functional gang membership was true of 44 percent of the African Americans with records and 68 percent of the whites (Savitz, Lalli, and Rosen, 1977). In short, the territorially based gang with acknowledged leadership was relatively rare, even among youths with records. It was even rarer among Philadelphia youths who did not have official records (11 percent of African Americans and 14 percent of whites).

The Philadelphia data are essentially consistent with the arguments of Lewis Yablonsky that gangs are misconceived as having a measurable number of members, clearly defined membership, specific roles for different members to play, a set of norms that are mutually agreed upon, and a definite leadership structure. Yablonsky (1959) argued that a more accurate image is that of a "near group." Such a group is characterized by (1) diffuse role definitions, (2) limited cohesion, (3) impermanence, (4) minimal consensus of norms, (5) shifting membership, (6) disturbed leadership, and (7) limited definition of membership expectations. From this perspective, even identifiable gangs in large cities would be viewed as falling somewhere between the structural gang, a true social group, and a totally unorganized, unstructured mob. Hence, Yablonsky uses the term "near group" to emphasize the point that the typical juvenile gang is more than a disorganized mob but less than a highly organized social group.

The finding that gang membership was more characteristic of white youth than African-American youth in Philadelphia in the 1970s is consistent with the view that the association between African-American and Hispanic minority status and the gang problem emerged sometime after the mid-1970s. In fact, if we were to measure "gang conflict" using the answers of high school seniors to the question about how many times they have been in a fight involving contending groups, the predominance of African-American youth in such activity emerges some time in the early 1980s. When the *Monitoring the Future* surveys were first conducted, white youth tended to exceed African-American youth in group conflict. In the most recent surveys, African-American youth have much higher average involvement than whites.

While there needs to be a clear delineation between a group and a gang, the precise definition of a gang is illusive. Walter Miller has attempted to delineate gangs as just one type of **law-violating youth group**. He defines youth gangs as

> . . . a self-formed association of peers, bound together by mutual interests, with identifiable leadership, well-developed lines of authority, and other organizational features, who act in concert to achieve a specific purpose or purposes which generally include the conduct of illegal activity and control over a particular territory, facility, or type of enterprise. (1980)

Bursik and Grasmick (1993) argued that "groups are ephemeral, with no elaborate organizational structure, name, or sense of turf, . . . as opposed to gangs that have elaborate organization, names, a sense of corporate identity, and identification with particular territories."

Gangs are viewed by criminal justice, youth service, and other local officials as a serious problem in most major cities in the United States. The number of gangs in the United States is open to speculation. In the 1970s, the number of gangs and gang membership was modest. In the 1980s, estimates of gang membership began to exceed 100,000, and in the 1990s the number of gang members was estimated in the range of 500,000. The actual number of gangs varies and presently it is estimated there are 24,000 gangs with a membership of 760,000 (Egley and Ritz, 2006). Malcolm Klein (1995) estimates that Los Angeles alone has nearly 1,000 gangs. All evidence suggests that gang activity increased in the 1980s and 1990s, but national data is more impressionistic than factual. What is known about gang activity is localized. It does appear that gang members account for far more than their share of violent offenses and that they are a significant dimension of the crime-delinquency problem in certain settings. However, it is also important to remember that most delinquency is a peer group activity more akin to Gold's "pickup game" than the routine activities of identifiable and structured gangs.

Perhaps some of the best documented evidence on gangs was provided by Short and Strodtbeck's Chicago studies in the mid-1960s. Detailed records were maintained of the day-to-day activities of gangs. The researchers found little evidence of tightly structured gangs with narrowly focused behavioral patterns. Rather, they concluded that gangs were loosely organized with enormous behavioral versatility. The major offense for many of the gangs involved drinking and disturbing the peace (1965).

Klein sees gangs as more casual and less crime prone than the standard portrayal of street gangs. He argues:

> Street gangs through the years have done nothing more often than they have done something exciting. Their most customary activities are sleeping, eating, and hanging around. Criminal acts are a minority of the activities they engage in, and violent acts are a minority of those. We must remember that despite the drama and lethality of gang violence, its prevalence does not deserve using the label *violent gang*. (1995:28–29)

Characteristics of Contemporary Gangs

Gangs are difficult to define and study because they take on so many different styles and appearances. For example, Fagan (1989) categorizes four styles of gang activity:

1. **Social gangs**: A social group with minimal delinquent activities. Involvement in drugs is limited to alcohol and marijuana.

2. **Party gangs**: Tend to focus on drug use and drug trafficking but limited involvement in other types of delinquent activities.

3. **Serious delinquent gangs**: Limited involvement in drug use but heavy involvement in serious delinquent activities.

4. **Organized gang**: Heavy involvement in delinquent activity and drug use and sales. Well organized and clear authority structure that hovers close to becoming a formal criminal organization.

Others have come up with different classification schemes that highlight the fact that gangs are not unidimensional. They take on different characteristics in different cities, respond to different needs, and manifest different degrees of delinquent behavior. Maxson and Klein (1995) classify gangs differently than Fagan, looking at size, duration of existence, and criminal behavior. Their categorization scheme includes:

1. *Traditional gangs*: well-defined turf, large, well-established

2. *Neotraditional gangs*: small, newer territorial gang, less organized

3. *Compressed gangs*: small, narrow turf, narrow age range

4. *Collective gangs*: large but no specialization, no distinguishing characteristics

5. *Specialty gangs*: small, crime focused, specializes in a particular form of deviant behavior, e.g., drugs

Contemporary studies show the majority of American street gangs to be African-American, Asian, or Hispanic. Klein (1995) reports that of the nationwide survey of gangs that he conducted, less than 10 percent of gangs are white. Street gangs have become a haven for the underclass, the poor, the "truly disadvantaged" members of society. Julius Wilson's book *The Truly Disadvantaged* (1987) addresses the emergence of an urban underclass that is living in a persistent and pervasive state of poverty. The industrial base of many urban centers has disappeared, leaving significant unemployment problems, low-paying service jobs in the fast-food industry, and underemployment. Wilson argues that there has been massive movement out of the central city by the upper and middle classes and what remains are "the people left behind." Education, housing, health care, personal safety, and recreation all suffer. Others use the term *deindustrialization* (Hagedorn, 1988), which refers to the out-migration of industry to other parts of the country or to foreign nations, leaving behind the so-called "rust belt" cities. Out of this growing problem of decay and despair in the inner city, street gangs emerge to provide a way of survival, prestige, and camaraderie.

Gangs and Drug Trafficking

Some gangs are sufficiently structured and organized that they approach the status of what one criminologist refers to as "corporate" gangs (Taylor, 1990). Enduring, structured gangs have been particularly notable in Chicago (e.g., the Cobras, El Rukns, Vice Lords) and Los Angeles. Two of the largest gangs in the U.S. are the Bloods and the CRIPS (Community Revolution in Progress), both founded in Los Angeles in the late 1960s–early 1970s. Each is estimated to have 30,000 members (Egley and Ritz, 2006). While clearly the province of the young, the proportion of gang members who are juveniles is estimated to be about 35 percent. The "original gang members" (known as OGs in the gangs) are now adults in their 50s. The hard core members, "gangsters," range from age 16 to 22. While the gangs include "baby" and "tiny" gangsters, it is important to remember that the types of offenses that are drawing national attention are the same ones that have peaked in the young adult years among nongang offenders.

There have been some changes in gang activity in terms of frequency, characteristics of participants, and in targets. It is estimated that one in four homicides in Los Angeles is gang-related. Moreover, the participants are thought to be older than they were two or three decades ago (Taylor et al., 2007). While the targets of gang violence in the past were typically other gang members who had impugned the honor or invaded the territory of rival gangs, the killings in recent years have been less direct. Most victims were members of rival gangs, but were not targeted specifically because of an affront or personal vendetta. Rather, they were casualties of increased competition among gangs for control of the drug market. Based on their study of gang homicides in Los Angeles, Maxson and associates conclude that 54 percent of gang homicides show no evidence of a prior personal contact: "In these gang homicides, the relationship between opponents appears to be based on gang affiliation rather than enmity between familiar individuals" (Maxson, Gordon, and Klein, 1985). They also report that "in spite of rising public concern about innocent bystander victims, we found mention of only four such cases—all gang-related" (1985). Gang homicides dealt with by Los Angeles county sheriffs disproportionately involved Hispanic suspects compared to nongang homicides, while gang homicides dealt with by the city police department disproportionately involved African-American suspects. Out of a total of nearly 700 gang homicides, less than 1 percent involved white suspects. In contrast, about one-quarter of nongang homicides involved whites. Only 3 percent of gang homicide suspects were female compared to about 15 percent of nongang homicides. Gang violence appears to be more distinctively a minority group and male activity than is nongang violence.

In his discussion of inner-city gangs, Jeffrey Fagan suggests that gangs may have become "quasi-institutionalized" in some inner cities, ghettos, and barrios. By this he means that they compete for status and authority with other social institutions in an area such as church, school, and family. "If schools, families, and legal institutions are weak in inner cities, gangs have a near monopoly on status-conferring activities" (Fagan, 1990). Moreover, in areas where they control some portion of the drug market, they can become the most lucrative "employer" as well.

Esbensen and Huizinga (1993) argue that there is little evidence that gang members are heavily involved in drug activity, suggesting that less than one-third sell drugs. Yet, the movement of some gangs into the drug trade has been accompanied by an escalation of violence as rival groups and dealers battle for control of the market. Guns are vital to gaining and maintaining that control. The use of guns escalates and spreads to younger members and peripheral youth both for self-protection and as a source of status. A shift to more and more lethal weapons transforms fights and assaults into homicides.

In the third edition of this text, we noted that there is reason to believe that the violence associated with gang drug wars might stabilize and decline in future years. Violence is particularly likely when rival gangs are attempting to gain control over the same market. When rival criminal syndicates were battling for control of bootlegging, prostitution, or other illegal markets in American cities in the 1920s and 1930s, mob violence was quite common. In a sense, it was when "organized" crime was "disorganized" that violence was most likely. Profits are likely to be maximized when illicit goods and services are provided in an organized manner and when criminal organizations operate in a businesslike manner. Excessive violence draws attention and is likely to lead to crackdowns that increase the cost of doing business.

To some degree gang violence may reflect the effect of successful law enforcement efforts to disrupt the leadership of criminal organizations such as the Mafia. Disruption of traditional syndicates, the expansion of trade routes for drugs, and the availability of cheap crack-cocaine has increased the number of competitors for control of the drug market. When the market is divided in an organized manner and original gang members and leaders begin operating as a business, the overall extent of violence associated with the drug trade may decline. Violence associated with gang activities will never disappear but the history of criminal organizations suggests that overall violence could very well decline.

Is the Gang Problem Declining?

In chapter 4, we noted that a variety of different measures of the gang problem suggest a decline in gang violence beginning in the mid-1990s, with declines in violence preceding a decline in gang news stories, and a decline in gang news preceding a decline in law enforcement estimates. Four different "measures" of the problem point to a decline within that span of time.

However, we also noted that the magnitude of the gang problem depends on the criteria adopted to define someone as a gang member. Thornberry and Burch's Rochester study (1997) defined a gang member as anyone who reports having been a member of a street gang or posse at any point prior to the end of high school, and a gang offense is any offense ever committed by those respondents. Use of an inclusive definition leads Thornberry and Burch to conclude that gang members account for "the lion's share of delinquent acts." When applied to offenses such as homicide, the more restrictive definitions show gangs to be responsible for a disproportionate share of crime, but far less than the lion's share (Miethe and Recoeczi, 2004; Maxson and Klein, 1995).

The difficulty in accessing the magnitude of the gang problem is reflected in Curry and Decker's book, *Confronting Gangs*. After a thorough review of research on "the link between gangs and crime," they conclude that (1) "gang members participate in a large number of serious delinquent and criminal acts" (1998:29) and (2) "gang members are responsible for more crime and delinquency than their nongang counterparts" (1998:59). Whether the failure to address the gang problem would, as Thornberry and Burch argue, "result in failure to make substantial progress in the nation's efforts to reduce serious, violent, and chronic delinquency" (1997:3) depends on how large those numbers are and the share of crime attributable to members of gangs. Information on those specific details varies greatly, depending on definitions and measures of the gang problem.

While it is clear that variations in the definitions used can affect conclusions about the magnitude of the gang problem, the proliferation of distinct definitions and methods of measurement has not been accompanied by systematic research on relationships among such measures. Gang researchers involved in local studies use one specific technique such as responses to survey questions, participant observation, informant perceptions, or police classifications. On a national scale, measures of the gang problem are limited to responses of law enforcement personnel to survey questions asking them to report on aspects of the gang problem in their jurisdictions. The only measure of self-reported offending available on a national scale is the "group fighting" question in the Monitoring the Future surveys of high school seniors, and many criminologists would challenge this item as a measure of the gang problem.

Adolescent Society

It is widely accepted that delinquency is a peer group activity and that the odds of a youth engaging in delinquency are much greater for youth with delinquent friends than those with only conventional friends. Youths asked to report on how they initially got involved in delinquency are likely to mention friends, just as peer pressure is acknowledged as a source of initial experimentation with drugs. The characteristics and activities of a youth's peers are important for understanding her or his own behavior.

Some theorists dealing with the world of adolescent peer groups present an image of adolescent society *in general* as essentially unconventional and in conflict with the norms and laws of parents. Some years back, Ralph England (1960) suggested that rapid urbanization and industrialization in the nineteenth century resulted in the marginalization of youth. That is, they were neither adult nor child, but an isolated group of individuals who became extremely hedonistic and materialistic. It is alleged that in the twentieth century, teenagers began to express their independence from adult society by adopting distinctive and faddish dress and hairstyles, entertainment idols, dance steps, musical tastes, and even a distinctive language (VanderZanden, 1986).

These external symbols were suggestive of what many perceived to be a definitive break from the larger culture and the inculcation of a distinct youth culture (Richards, 1988). In one of the best-known works on adolescent society, James Coleman wrote:

> Our adolescents today are cut off, probably more than ever before, from the adult society. They are still oriented toward fulfilling their parents' desires, but they look very much to their peers for approval as well. Consequently, our society has within its midst a set of small teenage societies which focus teenage interests and attitudes on things far removed from adult responsibilities, and which may develop standards that lead away from these goals established by the larger society. (1961:9)

The fact that teenage groups have emerged does not necessarily mean that involvement in such groups is conducive to delinquency, but the imagery of pursuing goals "different from" those of the larger society suggests such a possibility. Bell (1983) indicated that a distinctive style and taste develop within a youth culture such that teens share more with each other than with their parents or other adults. Covington (1982) takes the youth culture argument directly into the realm of delinquency. She states that because adolescence is a transitional stage between childhood and adulthood, it must have its own set of norms, values, and expectations. Parents create conflict by expecting adolescents to subscribe to the same set of standards and values as when the youth was a child. The adolescent finds such norms and values to be unfulfilling and unchallenging. The adolescent begins to question parental norms and values, turns to his or her peers for guidance and meaning, and in the process an adolescent deviant subculture arises.

The emphasis on the unconventional aspects of youth culture has not gone unchallenged. For example, in an article entitled "The Myth of Adolescent Culture" (1955), Frederick Elkin and William A. Westley argued that the distinctiveness of youth culture has been overexaggerated. They suggested that adolescents are far more conventional than the youth culture stereotype allows. Other scholars have attacked the emphasis on the distinctiveness of youth culture by arguing that the adult world is not as prudish and square as it is commonly depicted. Bennett Berger (1963) pointed out that many adults share the values and interests of adolescents regarding cars, sports, and romance, as well as their emphasis on status, popularity, and anti-intellectualism. John Coleman (1980) suggests that when conflict occurs between parents and teenagers, it is usually over trivial matters, not debates over morality or ideology. Coleman also points out that teenagers in his study saw their parents more positively than they saw themselves in terms of honesty, reliability, unselfishness, and patience. Finally, Cohen (1980) found that early adolescents do gravitate away from their parents, but as the adolescent moves through high school peer acceptance becomes less salient and the importance of family becomes more apparent.

Compared to the amount of research on families, schools, and gangs, we actually know very little about the distinctiveness of adolescent society in comparison to the adult world. Moreover, there is relatively little research on variations within the adolescent world. Race, socioeconomic status, age, sex, and educational attainment most likely cut across adolescent society, creating a plurality of group memberships, values, and attitudes. Several questions have not been asked about adolescent subcultures. For example, do adolescents in general (1) repudiate the dominant culture of their parents and create a contraculture, (2) differ in degree as to basic values and ideals and constitute a subculture, or (3) merely differ in some respects, ultimately subscribing to the same value system? Raymond Eve (1975) found support for the third view. He reported statistically significant differences between students and teachers for drinking, but in other areas both groups were quite similar. Eve concluded that students' values differ only in a small degree from the adult value system. Similarly, Smeja and Rojek (1986) found that college students who use marijuana but not hard drugs like barbiturates, amphetamines, cocaine, or narcotics were eminently conventional. They exhibited respect for and endorsement of the social order in every way except for the regulation of marijuana. On the other hand, nonusers of drugs and marijuana-only users were quite distinct from regular users of hard-core illicit drugs like narcotics, barbiturates, and amphetamines. The fact that adolescents behave somewhat differently or are somewhat rebellious does not mean that they subscribe to a value system that is radically different from their parents'. There is marked heterogeneity in American society on a number of dimensions, but there can still be a basic endorsement of a common set of values and beliefs.

The importance of peers in the lives of adolescents and the existence of youth culture are two quite distinct issues. At present, there is little support for the argument that adolescents in general share values, norms, or beliefs that conflict with or cut them off from the adult world. Nonetheless, there are ways in which participation in peer group activities can facilitate delinquency. For one, although the majority of adolescents may express quite conventional values and beliefs, their structural position in modern America gives them considerable leisure time and freedom from many types of conventional social bonds. They are not children, but neither are they adults. This marginality, coupled with the age-grading of schools, sets the stage for a high level of peer group interaction and considerable free time. While the popular literature would suggest that adolescents become involved in a tug-of-war between the values of their parents and the values of their friends, the truth lies somewhere in between. Recall Matza and Sykes's (1964) concept of subterranean values. There is a certain allurement or excitement associated with deviant activities, but that does not require rejection of the dominant culture. Adolescents, like adults, can appear entrenched on the side of law and order and still transgress the law. Adolescents typically engage in behavior that is acceptable for adults but considered inappropriate for juveniles. It is not that adolescents want to reject adult society; rather they want to embrace it.

Jensen and Erickson (1978) attempted to assess the impact of incorporating elements of conflict into questions about peers. Students were asked whether they would "go along with their friends" or join their families if their families were planning to go to a show. There was no significant relationship between a student's answer to this question and self-reported delinquency (although a slightly greater proportion of those who indicated they would go along with friends did report delinquent activities). On the other hand, when an element of conflict was introduced by asking them whether they would go riding around with friends after school if their parents had told them never to do that, there was a sizable relationship: students who indicated they would disregard parental authority reported significantly more delinquency. Similarly, students who indicated they would go along with peers in situations involving conflict with the law reported significantly more delinquency than did those who indicated they would not go along. Several different variables are intertwined in these types of measures (peer commitment, attachment to the law, attachment to parents), precluding any simple conclusion that peer commitment encourages delinquency.

In considering socialization within the context of adolescent society, it is important to ask the following questions: How often do adolescents experience conflict between peers and conventional authority? What are the general tendencies of adolescents in making such choices? In general, research suggests that adolescents and parents tend to get along reasonably well. Hill states:

> The psychoanalytic position that rebelliousness is normal during adolescence enjoys considerable support from those who work with troubled and troublesome young people. Studies of more representative samples of the population, however, do not support this position. Adolescence is not, in general, a period of overt rebelliousness and familial conflict in industrial societies according to representative samples of parents and their adolescent offspring. (1980:38)

In those situations where there is a question of peers versus parents, Brittain (1963) found that parents have more influence in those issues that involve future plans such as education or occupation, while peers have more influence in the more mundane aspects of daily life such as dress, grooming, and music. Jensen and Erickson (1978) found that the tendency of the adolescent to go along with peers is highly variable and depends on the choice. In general, adolescents chose to go along with their friends when the degree of conflict with their parents was minimal.

Overall, it does not appear that adolescent society *in general* is characterized by values, norms, and beliefs that clearly cut them off from the adult world or that facilitate delinquency. However, as a leisure class or as a large segment of the population with time to bide, adolescents have considerable freedom to commit delinquent acts. Moreover, those most involved in the activities that, in the eyes of adults, characterize adolescent society are those most likely to become involved in delinquency. When adolescents choose to please their peers despite the possibilities of conflict with authority, the probability of their involvement in delinquency is very high.

Mutual Interdependence, Independence, and Causal Sequences

Although we have dealt with family, school, and peers individually, it is important to recognize that social reality involves an interrelated web of influences. At several points in the discussion, we commented on the difficulty of isolating the impact of one specific characteristic of a situation that intertwines many other characteristics. Experiences and relationships in one setting are shaped and influenced by experiences and relationships in other settings. The complexity of these interrelationships is what makes it so difficult to differentiate causal relationships from spurious relationships and to decide between causes and effects.

Consider, for example, the relationship between conditions of family life and experiences at school. The stronger the bond between parents and child, the stronger the bond between the child and teachers. Of course, there are numerous exceptions to that observation, but there is definitely an association between the two variables. Similarly, the stronger the bond between a youth and school, or between a youth and parents, the weaker the chances that he or she will acquire delinquent friends or choose to go along with peers in situations that conflict with authority.

While most scholars would agree that experiences in different settings are interrelated, there are several different positions taken in the literature on a number of other issues. For example, Hirschi (1969) reports that experiences within school and the family as well as associations with delinquent peers *each* help explain delinquency; that is, experiences in a variety of settings are each *independently* relevant to explaining delinquency. Other scholars posit causal sequences where the influence of some experiences are *indirect* through their association with other experiences. Some of these models borrow from several different theories and put the variables in specific sequence.

For example, Johnson (1979) constructed a general model to explain delinquent behavior by starting with parental affection for the child, which leads to parental attachment, then attachment to school. These variables then influence the selection of delinquent friends, which ultimately impacts delinquent behavior. Moreover, delinquent values are strengthened by having delinquent associates but weakened by strong attachment to school. Finally, delinquent behavior is positively influenced by having delinquent associates and acquiring delinquent values. Marcos, Bahr, and Johnson (1986) developed a similar model to examine the causal forces leading up to adolescent drug use. They found as did Johnson that friends are the most influential factor in delinquent behavior, but the acquisition of delinquent friends is influenced by parental attachment and school attachment.

The exact causal sequence among these forces is still a subject of debate as is the simple question of cause versus effect. While social scientists tend to think of family life, school experiences, and peer relationships as sources or causes of delinquency, it is widely recognized that experiences in each can be *affected by* delinquency and troublemaking as well. Youths who get into trouble may be judged more harshly at school and be disliked by teachers. They may upset their parents and break down family bonds. They may come to associate with other kids in trouble and come to define lawbreaking in favorable terms. In sum, delinquency might precede and account for the circumstances presumed to generate it.

In one study Liska and Reed (1985) used data from a large sample of boys gathered at two points in time and found that involvement in delinquency affected how attached they were to teachers and school, but that relations at school did not have much relevance to predicting delinquency. They concluded that "delinquency appears to be more of a cause than a consequence of school attachment" (1985). Of course, findings on attachment to school do not necessarily apply to school performance and there are research results supporting the view that school failure precedes delinquency (Phillips and Kelly, 1979). Moreover, while low school attachment did not appear to precede delinquency, attachment to parents did. Liska and Reed conclude that their findings "suggest that parents, not school, are the major institutional sources of delinquency control" (1985). At present there are conflicting points of view about the relevance of each of these institutions to delinquency and their direct independent effects versus indirect effects as well as whether they follow or precede delinquency. Some of the results summarized in subsequent chapters suggest that parents can influence their children's troublemaking by changing their own behavior, and that school programs can influence student behavior as well. Thus, it is still reasonable to conclude that the modification of family life and school experiences holds some promise for addressing delinquency even if the exact causal sequences in everyday life have yet to be untangled.

Summary

Social scientists have long regarded the influences of family, school, and peer groups as particularly crucial to understanding delinquency. However, theories vary on the importance of each and the specific ways they influence delinquency. Studies of family structure and interaction in relation to delinquency suggest a number of generalizations:

1. Children from homes with a biological mother and father present are less likely to appear in police, court, and institutional statistics, and most studies using self-report data indicate a small association with delinquency. Several studies suggest that homes with a stepfather or new companion for the mother generate the highest rates of problem behavior.

2. Intact households characterized by conflict generate rates of delinquency comparable to broken or single-parent households, supporting the view that the nature of relationships between children and parents is more relevant to explaining delinquency than is the broken or intact nature of the home. Warm, caring, solicitous families appear to be critical in socializing children to be law-abiding citizens.

3. The greater the reciprocal communication and mutual bonds between parent and child, the less the involvement in delinquency.

4. The extremes of permissiveness and overly strict discipline are more often associated with higher rates of delinquency than is a mild emphasis on discipline administered according to standards that appear fair and equitable to children.

5. The quantity of time a parent spends with a child is not as critical as the quality of the interaction between parent and child.

6. While violence is a significant aspect of American family life, it appears to be declining. However, the degree of violence in some homes is still disturbingly high.

7. Experiencing family violence is correlated with violence outside of the family and increases the odds that a youth will acquire a record in the future.

There has been far more speculation than actual research on the specific aspects of school that are relevant to an understanding of delinquency. The following observations seem justified in view of the research to date, with the same reservations about cause and effect expressed for family influences:

1. The higher a student's academic achievement or performance, the lower the involvement in delinquency. Some theorists attribute this correlation to the inhibiting impact of a youth's investments in conformity while others believe it to be a function of self-control established at an early age.

2. The stronger the bond between students and teachers and the more favorable the attitudes of students toward school, the less the involvement in delinquency.

3. Students in remedial or noncollege "tracks" have higher probabilities of delinquent involvement than students in college "tracks," regardless of IQ scores, father's occupation, or grade-point average.

4. The lower the performance on IQ tests, the poorer a student's school performance, and the poorer the school performance, the greater the probability of delinquent involvement.

We have noted that there is some controversy over the nature of the relationship between delinquent peers and a youth's involvement in delinquency. There seems to be common agreement that the acquisition of delinquent companions has a strong impact on involvement in delinquency. However, the view that teenagers have interests and attitudes that set them apart from the adult world and the view that a general orientation toward peers is conducive to delinquency are both subject to debate. The following observations are consistent with research findings:

1. Delinquent friends consistently emerge as critical in the explanation of delinquency, but the acquisition of delinquent associates is influenced by the degree of attachment to the family and success in or attachment to school.

2. Delinquency is most often a form of group behavior and typically occurs spontaneously in ordinary teenage peer groups.

3. While girls are less likely to engage in delinquency than boys, when they do so it is at least as likely to occur while with peers.

4. Peer groups with gang characteristics account for a disproportionate share of crime and delinquency but are not the typical form of peer group delinquency.

5. Peer groups with gang characteristics range in degree of organization and structure from loosely structured "near groups" to more enduring institutionalized gangs ("corporate" gangs).

7. The attitudes of teenagers in general toward the law, delinquent activities, and goals are primarily conventional, differing according to degree of approval and disapproval from adults.

8. Teenagers are quite commonly concerned about maintaining autonomy and resisting adult control, and those most involved in activities that facilitate such freedom have higher probabilities of involvement in delinquency.

Experiences in each setting—family, school, and peer groups—are interrelated and affect one another. The exact sequence of events differs among theorists but most research suggests that family and school experiences increase the odds of delinquency among youth by increasing their involvement with similarly situated peers.

Discussion Questions

1. Positive relationships with parents are typically thought to discourage a youth's involvement in delinquency. What does such a belief imply about the behavior and attitudes of parents? Use ideas from social learning theory to make other predictions.

2. What is a "broken home"? Do you think some types of broken homes are more conducive to delinquency than others? Draw on research to back up your answer.

3. What types of intervening mechanisms might generate a relationship between family size and delinquency? What possible mechanisms have been studied? Propose some new mechanisms for further research.

4. Most of us have heard statements to the effect that a good old-fashioned "whipping" might set kids straight and discourage delinquency. Discuss this traditional folklore in terms of actual research. Are there any theories that would lead to contrary expectations about punishment?

5. Why should we expect to find a relationship between intelligence-test performance and delinquency? Does this mean that delinquent youth are biologically inferior to nondelinquent youth? Develop several possible explanations.

6. Should youth who are on the verge of dropping out of school be encouraged to do so to avoid further frustration and school disruption? Discuss the pros and cons of such a proposal based on delinquency theory and research.

7. Gang delinquency is predominately a male problem. Does this mean that females do not engage in peer group delinquency when they do commit delinquent acts? Are girls more likely than boys to be loners or isolates when committing delinquent acts?

8. There are a variety of points of view about whether mothers should work outside the home, especially when their children are young. What bearing does research have on this argument?

9. Based on findings on the family, school, and peer groups, what could you do as a parent to discourage delinquency?

10. Most of you were in high school just a few years ago. Did you feel safer at school than on the streets or at home? Were you bullied, harmed, or victimized at school? What has been the general trend in school violence?

References

Agnew, R. 1983. "Physical Punishment and Delinquency: A Research Note." *Youth and Society* 15 (December):225–36.

———. 1992. "Foundation for a General Strain Theory of Crime and Delinquency." *Criminology* 30:47–87.

Ahrons, C. P. 1995. *The Good Divorce.* New York: Harper.

Amato, P. R. 1993. "Family Structure, Family Process, and Family Ideology." *Journal of Marriage and the Family* 55:23–38.

Amato, P. R., and B. Keith. 1991. "Parental Divorce and Adult Well-Being: A Meta-Analysis." *Journal of Marriage and the Family* 53:125–37.

Atlas, S. 1984. *Parents without Partners.* Philadelphia: Running Press.

Baker, K., and R. J. Rubel. 1980. *Violence and Crime in the Schools.* Lexington, MA: Lexington Books.

Batton, C., and G. F. Jensen. 2002. "Decommodification and Homicide Rates in the Twentieth Century United States." *Homicide Studies* 6:6–38.

Bell, R. R. 1983. *Marriage and Family Interaction.* 6th ed. Homewood, IL: Dorsey.

Berger, B. M. 1963. "Adolescence and Beyond." *Social Problems* 10 (Spring):394–408.

Blackman, A. 1994. "When Violence Hits Home." *Time* (4 July):18–25.

Boesel, D. 1978. *Violent Schools—Safe Schools: The Safe School Study Report to Congress.* Vol. 1. National Institute of Education. Washington, DC: GPO.

Boocock, S. S. 1978. "The Social Organization of the Classroom." In *Annual Review of Sociology—1978,* edited by R. H. Turner, J. Coleman, and R. C. Fox. Palo Alto, CA: Annual Reviews.

Bowlby, J. 1951. *Maternal Care and Mental Health.* Geneva: World Health Organization.

Bridgeland, J., J. Dilulio, and K. Morison. 2006. *The Silent Epidemic: Perspectives of High School Dropouts.* Washington, DC: Civic Enterprises.

Brittain, C. V. 1963. "Adolescent Choices and Parent-Peer Cross Pressures." *American Sociological Review* 28:385–91.

Bursik, R., and H. Grasmick. 1993. "The Use of Multiple Indicators to Estimate Crime Trends in American Cities." *Journal of Criminal Justice* 21:509–17.

Canter, R. J. 1982. "Family Correlates of Male and Female Delinquency." *Criminology* 20(2):149–67.

Cherlin, A., F. Furstenberg, L. Chase-Lansdale, K. Kierman, P. Robins, D. Morrison, and J. Tietler. 1991. "Longitudinal Studies of Effects of Divorce on Children in Great Britain and the United States." *Science* 252 (June):1386–89.

ChildStats.Gov. 2005. *America's Children.* Federal Interagency Forum on Child and Family Statistics.

ChildStats.Gov. 2004. *America's Children in Brief.* Federal Interagency Forum on Child and Family Statistics.

Chilton, R. J., and G. E. Markle. 1972. "Family Disruption, Delinquent Conduct and the Effect of Subclassification." *American Sociological Review* 37 (February):93–99.

Cloward, R. A., and F. F. Piven. 1979. "Hidden Protest: The Channeling of Female Innovation and Resistance." *Signs* 4 (November):651–69.

Cohen, J. 1980. "Adolescent Independence and Adolescent Change." *Youth and Society* 12:107–14.

Coleman, J. C. 1980. "Friendship and the Peer Group in Adolescence." In *Handbook of Adolescent Society,* edited by J. Adelson. New York: Wiley.

Coleman, J. S. 1961. *The Adolescent Society.* New York: Free Press.

Comaner, W. S., and L. Philips. 2002. "The Impact of Income and Family Structure on Delinquency." *Journal of Applied Economics* 5:209–32.

Conger, R. D. 1976. "Social Control and Social Learning Models of Delinquent Behavior." *Criminology* 14 (May):17–40.

Covington, J. 1982. "Adolescent Deviation and Age." *Journal of Youth and Adolescence* 11:329–44.

Curry, G. D., and S. H. Decker.1998. *Confronting Gangs: Crime and Community.* Los Angeles: Roxbury.

Davis, K. 1947. "Final Note on a Case of Extreme Isolation." *American Journal of Sociology* 52:432–37.

Dembo, R., G. Grandon, L. LaVoie, J. Schmeidler, and W. Burgas. 1986. "Parents and Drugs Revisited: Some Further Evidence in Support of Social Learning Theory." *Criminology* 24:85–104.

Durose, M., C. Harlow, P. Langan, M. Motivans, R. Rantala, and E. Smith. 2005. *Family Violence Statistics.* Washington, DC: U.S. Dept. of Justice.

Eder, D. 1981. "Ability Grouping As a Self-Fulfilling Prophecy: A Micro-Analysis of Teacher-Student Interaction." *Sociology of Education* 54:151–62.

Egley, A. 2002. *National Youth Gang Survey: Trends from 1996 to 2000.* Washington, DC: Office of Juvenile Justice and Delinquency Prevention.

Egley, A., and C. Ritz. 2006. *Highlights of the 2004 National Youth Gang Survey.* Washington, DC: Office of Juvenile Justice and Delinquency Prevention.

Elkin, F., and W. Westley. 1955. "The Myth of Adolescent Culture." *American Sociological Review* 20 (December):680–86.

Elliott, D. S. 1966. "Delinquency, School Attendance and Dropout." *Social Problems* 13 (Winter):306–18.

Elliott, D. S., and H. L. Voss. 1974. *Delinquency and Dropout.* Lexington, MA: Lexington Books.

England, R. 1960. "A Theory of Middle Class Juvenile Delinquency." *Journal of Criminal Law, Criminology, and Police Science* 50:535–40.

Erickson, M. L., and G. F. Jensen. 1977. "Delinquency Is Still Group Behavior!" *Journal of Criminal Law and Criminology* 68(2):262–73.

Esbensen, F., and D. Huizinga. 1993. "Gangs, Drugs and Delinquency in a Survey of Urban Youth." *Criminology* 31:565–87.

Eve, R. 1975. "Adolescent Culture: Convenient Myth or Reality? A Comparison of Students and Their Teachers." *Sociology of Education* 48 (Spring):152–67.

Fagan, J. 1989. "The Social Organization of Drug Use and Drug Dealing among Urban Gangs." *Criminology* 27:633–69.

———. 1990. "Social Processes of Delinquency and Drug Use among Urban Gangs." In *Gangs in America,* edited by C. R. Huff. Newbury Park, CA: Sage.

Farrington, D. 2005. "Childhood Origins of Antisocial Behavior." *Clinical Psychology and Psychotherapy* 12:177–90.

Farrington, D., and R. Loeber. 2000. www.ncjrs.gov/html/ojjdp/report_research_2000/findings.html. Accessed June 2006.

Felson, R., and J. Staff. 2006. "Explaining the Academic Performance-Delinquency Relationship." *Criminology* 44:299–320.

Finkelhor, D., S. Hamby, M. Straus, and D. Moore. 1997. "Sexually Abused Children in a National Survey of Parents: Methodological Issues." *Child Abuse & Neglect* 21:19.

Finkelhor, D., and L. Jones. 2004. "Sexual Abuse Decline in the 1990s: Evidence for Possible Causes." *Juvenile Justice Bulletin* NCJI99298:1–12.

Flynn, C. P. 1994. "Regional Differences in Attitudes toward Corporal Punishment." *Journal of Marriage and the Family* 56:258–68.

Frease, D. E. 1973. "Delinquency, Social Class, and the Schools." *Sociology and Social Research* 57 (July):443–59.

Gamoran, A. 1992. "Alternative Uses of Ability Grouping in Secondary Schools." *American Journal of Education* 102:1–22.

Gelles, R. J. 1974. *The Violent Home.* Beverly Hills: Sage.

Gelles, R. J. 2007. "Family Violence." In *The Cambridge Handbook of Violent Behavior and Aggression,* edited by D. J. Flannery, A. T. Vazsonyi, and I. D. Waldman, 403–17. New York: Cambridge University Press.

Gelles, R. J., and C. P. Cornell. 1985. *Intimate Violence in Families.* Beverly Hills: Sage.

Gold, M. 1970. *Delinquent Behavior in an American City.* Monterrey, CA: Brooks Cole.

Goldman, N. 1961. "A Socio-Psychological Study of School Vandalism." *Crime and Delinquency* 7:221–30.

Gottfredson, G. D., and D. C. Gottfredson. 1985. *Victimization in Schools.* New York: Plenum Press.

Gould, S. J. 1981. *The Mismeasure of Man.* New York: W.W. Norton.

Gove, W., and R. Crutchfield. 1982. "The Family and Juvenile Delinquency." *The Sociological Quarterly* 23 (Summer):301–19.

Hagan, J., J. Simpson, and A. R. Gillis. 1985. "The Class Structure of Gender and Delinquency: Toward a Power-Control Theory of Common Delinquent Behavior." *American Journal of Sociology* 90:1151–78.

———. 1987. "Class in the Household: A Power-Control Theory of Gender and Delinquency." *American Journal of Sociology* 92:788–816.

Hagedorn, J. M. 1988. *People and Folks: Gangs Crime and the Underclass in a Rustbelt City.* Chicago: Lakeview Press.

Hargreaves, D. 1968. *Social Relations in a Secondary School.* New York: Humanities Press.

Harlow, H., and M. Harlow. 1962. "Social Deprivation in Monkeys." *Scientific American* 207:137–47.

Hayes, C. D., and S. B. Kamerman, eds. 1983. *Children of Working Parents.* Washington, DC: National Academy Press.

Hill, C. R., and F. P. Stafford. 1979. "Parental Care of Children." *Journal of Human Resources* 15:219–39.

Hill, J. P. 1980. "The Family." In *Toward Adolescence,* edited by M. Johnson. Chicago: University of Chicago Press.

Hindelang, M. J. 1973. "Causes of Delinquency: A Partial Replication." *Social Problems* 21 (Spring):471–87.

Hirschi, T. 1969. *Causes of Delinquency.* Berkeley: University of California Press.

———. 1985. "Crime and Family Policy." In *Juvenile Delinquency: A Justice Perspective*, edited by R. A. Weisheit and R. G. Culbertson. Long Grove, IL: Waveland Press.

Hirschi, T., and M. J. Hindelang. 1977. "Intelligence and Delinquency: A Revisionist Review." *American Sociological Review* 42 (August):571–87.

Hopper, J. M. 1997. www.jimhopper.com/stats.

Ingrassia, M., and M. Berk. 1994. "Patterns of Abuse." *Newsweek* (4 July):26–33.

Jensen, G. F. 1976. "Race, Achievement and Delinquency: A Further Look at Delinquency in a Birth Cohort." *American Journal of Sociology* 82 (September):370–87.

Jensen, G. F. 2003. "Gender Variations in Delinquency: Self-Images, Beliefs, and Peers as Mediating Mechanisms." In *Social Learning and the Explanation of Crime*, edited by Ronald L. Akers and Gary F. Jensen. New Brunswick, NJ: Transaction Books.

Jensen, G. F., and D. Brownfield. 1983. "Parents and Drugs: Specifying the Consequences of Attachment." *Criminology* 21:543–54.

Jensen, G. F., and M. L. Erickson. 1978. "Peer Commitment and Delinquent Conduct." Unpublished manuscript.

Jensen, G. F., M. L. Erickson, and J. P. Gibbs. 1978. "Perceived Risk of Punishment and Self-Reported Delinquency." *Social Forces* 57 (September):57–78.

Johnson, R. E. 1979. *Juvenile Delinquency and Its Origins.* London: Cambridge University Press.

———. 1986. "Family Structure and Delinquency: General Patterns and Gender Differences." *Criminology* 24:65–84.

Juby, H., and D. Farrington. 2001. "Disentangling the Link between Disrupted Families and Delinquency." *British Journal of Criminology* 41 (Winter):22–41.

Kalmijn, M. 1994. "Mother's Occupational Status and Children's Schooling." *American Sociological Review* 59:257–75.

Kelly, D. H. 1974. "Track Position and Delinquency Involvement: A Preliminary Analysis." *Sociology and Social Research* 58 (July):380–86.

Kelly, D. H., and R. W. Balch. 1971. "Social Origins and School Failure." *Pacific Sociological Review* 14 (October):413–30.

Klein, M. W. 1995. *The American Street Gang: Its Nature, Prevalence, and Control.* New York: Oxford University Press.

Krohn, M., T. Thornberry, L. Collins-Hall, and A. Lizotte. 1995. "School Dropout, Delinquent Behavior, and Drug Use." In *Drugs, Crime, and Other Deviant Adaptations: Longitudinal Studies*, edited by H. Kaplan. New York: Plenum Press.

Lally, R. 1998. "Brain Research, Infant Learning, and Child Care Curriculum." *Child Care Information Exchange* 5:46–48.

Lees, J. P., and L. J. Newson. 1954. "Family or Sibship Position and Some Aspects of Juvenile Delinquency." *British Journal of Delinquency* 5:46–65.

Liska, A. E., and M. D. Reed. 1985. "Institutions and Delinquency." *American Sociological Review* 50 (August):547–60.

Loeber, R., and M. Stouthamer-Loeber. 1986. "Family Factors as Correlates and Predictors of Juvenile Conduct Problems and Delinquency." In *Crime and Justice: An Annual Review of Research,* edited by M. Tonry and N. Morris, Vol. 7. Chicago: University of Chicago Press.

Marcos, A. C., S. J. Bahr, and R. E. Johnson. 1986. "Test of a Bonding/Association Theory of Adolescent Drug Use." *Social Forces* 65:135–61.

Matza, D., and G. M. Sykes. 1964. "Juvenile Delinquency and Subterranean Values." *American Sociological Review* 26 (October):712–17.

Maxson, C. L., M. A. Gordon, and M. W. Klein. 1985. "Differences between Gang and Non-Gang Homicides." *Criminology* 23 (May):209–22.

Maxson, C. L., and M. W. Klein. 1995. "Investigating Gang Structures." *Journal of Gang Research* 3:33–42.

McCord, J. 1984. "Family Sources of Crime." Paper presented at the meeting of the International Society for Research on Aggression, Turku, Finland.

———. 1991. "Family Relationships, Juvenile Delinquency and Adult Criminality." *Criminology* 29: 397–417.

McCord, W., J. McCord, and A. Howard. 1961. "Familial Correlates of Aggression in Nondelinquent Male Children." *Journal of Abnormal Social Psychology* 62:79–93.

Menard, S., and B. J. Morse. 1984. "A Structuralist Critique of the IQ-Delinquency Hypothesis: Theory and Evidence." *American Journal of Sociology* 89:1347–78.

Merton, R. K. 1957. *Social Theory and Social Structure*. Rev. ed. New York: Free Press of Glencoe.

Miethe, T., and W. Recoeczi. 2004. *Rethinking Homicide*. Boston: Cambridge Univ. Press.

Miller, W. G. 1958. "Lower Class Culture as a Generating Milieu of Gang Delinquency." *Journal of Social Issues* 14:5–19.

———. 1980. "Gangs, Groups and Serious Youth Crime." In *Critical Issues in Juvenile Delinquency*, edited by D. Shichor and D. H. Kelley. Lexington, MA: Lexington Books.

Mott, F. L., L. Kowaleski-Jones, and E. G. Menaghan 1997. "Parental Absence and Child Behavior: Does a Child's Gender Make a Difference?" *Journal of Marriage and the Family* 59:103–18.

National Center for Education Statistics. 2007. *Violence in U.S. Public Schools: 2007 School Survey on Crime and Safety*. Washington, DC: U.S. Dept. of Education.

Nye, F. I. 1958. *Family Relationships and Delinquent Behavior*. New York: John Wiley.

Oakes, J. 1985. *Keeping Track: How Schools Structure Inequality*. New Haven: Yale University Press.

———. 1994. "More Than Misapplied Technology: A Normative and Political Response to Hallinan on Tracking." *Sociology of Education* 67:84–89.

Ogburn, W. F. 1938. "The Changing Family." *Family* 19 (July):139–43.

Patterson, G. R. 1980. "Children Who Steal." In *Understanding Crime: Current Theory and Research,* edited by T. Hirschi and M. Gottfredson. Beverly Hills: Sage.

Patterson, G. R., J. B. Reid, and T. J. Dishion. 1992. *Antisocial Boys.* Eugene, OR: Castalia.

Peterson, D., J. Miller, and F. Esbensen. 2001. "The Impact of Sex Composition on Gangs and Gang Members Delinquency." *Criminology* 39:401–10.

Phillips, J. C., and D. H. Kelly. 1979. "School Failure and Delinquency: What Causes Which?" *Criminology* 17 (August):194–207.

Piaget, J. 1929. *The Child's Conception of the World*. London: Paul, Trench, Trubner and Co.

Porter, M. 2006. *Early Brain Development*. http://www.educarer.com/brain.htm.

Power, M. J., P. M. Ash, E. Schoenerg, and E. C. Sirey. 1974. "Delinquency and the Family." *British Journal of Social Work* 4:13–28.

Pulkkinen, L. 1982. "Self-Control and Continuity from Childhood to Late Adolescence." In *Life-Span Development*, Vol. 4, edited by P. B. Baltes and O. G. Brim. New York: Academic Press.

Rankin, J. H., and R. Kern. 1994. "Parental Attachment and Delinquency." *Criminology* 32:495–515.

Rebellon, C. J. 2002. "Reconsidering the Broken Homes/Delinquency Relationship and Exploring its Mediating Mechanism(s)." *Criminology* 40:103–36.

Richards, L. 1988. "The Appearance of Youth Subculture: A Theoretical Perspective on Deviance." *Clothing and Textiles Research Journal* 6:56–64.

Rosen, L., and K. Neilson. 1982. "Broken Homes." In *Crime in Society*, edited by L. Savitz and N. Johnston. New York: John Wiley.

Rosenthal, R., and L. Jacobson. 1968. *Pygmalion in the Classroom*. New York: Holt, Rinehart, and Winston.

Rush, F. 1980. *The Best Kept Secret: Sexual Abuse of Children*. New York: McGraw Hill.

Rutter, M., and H. Giller. 1984. *Juvenile Delinquency: Trends and Perspectives.* New York: Gilford Press.

Sattler, J. M. 1982. *Assessment of Children's Intelligence and Special Abilities.* Boston: Allyn & Bacon.

Savitz, L. D., M. Lalli, and L. Rosen. 1977. *City Life and Delinquency—Victimization, Fear of Crime and Gang Membership.* Washington, DC: Law Enforcement Assistance Administration.

Schaefer, W. E., C. Olexa, and K. Polk. 1972. "Programmed for Social Class Tracking in High School." In *Schools and Delinquency,* edited by K. Polk and W. E. Schaefer. Englewood Cliffs, NJ: Prentice-Hall.

Shonkoff, J., and D. Phillips, eds. 2000. *From Neurons to Neighborhoods: The Science of Early Childhood Development.* Washington, DC: National Academy Press.

Short, J. F. 1990. *Delinquency and Society.* Englewood Cliffs, NJ: Prentice-Hall.

Short, J. F., and F. L. Strodtbeck. 1965. *Group Process and Gang Delinquency.* Chicago: University of Chicago Press.

Simons, R. L., C. Johnson, and R. D. Conger. 1994. "Harsh Corporal Punishment versus Quality of Parental Involvement as an Explanation of Adolescent Maladjustment." *Journal of Marriage and Family* 56:591–607.

Simons, R., L. Simons, and L. Wallace. 2004. *Families, Delinquency and Crime: Linking Society's Most Basic Institution to Antisocial Behavior.* Los Angeles: Roxbury.

Smeja, C. M., and D. G. Rojek. 1986. "Youthful Drug Use and Drug Subcultures." *The International Journal of Addictions* 21:1031–50.

Smith, C., and T. P. Thornberry. 1995. "The Relationship between Childhood Maltreatment and Adolescent Involvement in Delinquency." *Criminology* 33:451–81.

Snow, R. 1969. "Unfinished Pygmalion." *Contemporary Psychology* 14:197–99.

Spivack, G., and N. Cianci. 1987. "High-Risk Early Behavior Pattern and Later Delinquency." In *Prevention of Delinquent Behavior,* edited by J. D. Burchard and S. N. Burchard. Beverly Hills: Sage.

Steffensmeier, D. J. 1983. "Organizational Properties and Sex-Segregation in the Underworld: Building a Sociological Theory of Sex Differences in Crime." *Social Forces* 61 (June):1010–32.

Steinmetz, S. K. 1987. "Family Violence." In *Handbook of Marriage and the Family,* edited by M. B. Sussman and S. K. Steinmetz. New York: Plenum Press.

Steinmetz, S. K., and M. A. Straus. 1973. "The Family as Cradle of Violence." *Society* 10:119–28.

Stouthamer-Loeber, M., K. B. Schmaling, and R. Loeber. 1984. "The Relationship of Single Parent Family Status and Marital Discord to Antisocial Child Behavior." Unpublished manuscript. Department of Psychiatry, University of Pittsburgh.

Straus, M. A. 1991. "Discipline and Deviance: Physical Punishment of Children and Violence and Other Crime in Adulthood." *Social Problems* 38:133–54.

———. 1994. *Beating the Devil Out of Them.* New York: Lexington Books.

———. 2001. *Physical Aggression in the Family: Prevalence Rates, Links to Non-Family Violence, and Implications for Primary Prevention of Societal Violence.* Durham: University of New Hampshire, Family Research Laboratory.

Straus, M. A., and R. J. Gelles. 1986, 1990. "Societal Change and Change in Family Violence from 1975 to 1985 as Revealed by Two National Surveys." In *Violence: Patterns, Causes and Public Policy,* edited by N. A. Weiner, M. A. Zahn, and R. J. Sagi. San Diego: Harcourt Brace Jovanovich.

Straus, M. A., R. J. Gelles, and S. K. Steinmetz. 1980. *Behind Closed Doors: Violence in the American Family.* Garden City, NY: Anchor.

Straus, M. A., D. B. Sugarman, and J. Giles-Sims. 1997. "Spanking by Parents and Subsequent Antisocial Behavior of Children." *Archives of Pediatric and Adolescent Medicine* 151:761–67.

Sutherland, E. H., and D. R. Cressey. 1974. *Criminology.* 9th ed. Philadelphia: J. B. Lippincott.

Taylor, C. S. 1990. "Gang Imperialism." In *Gangs in America,* edited by C. R. Huff. Newbury Park, CA: Sage.

Taylor, T., D. Peterson, F. Esbensen, and A. Freng. 2007. "Gang Membership as a Risk Factor for Adolescent Violent Victimization." *Journal of Research in Crime and Delinquency* 44:351–80.

Thornberry, T. P., and J. H. Burch II. 1997. *Gang Members and Delinquent Behavior.* Juvenile Justice Bulletin, Washington, DC: Office of Juvenile Justice and Delinquency Prevention.

Thornberry, T. P., A. Lizotte, M. Krohn, M. Farnworth, and S. Jang. 1991. "Testing Interactional Theory: An Examination of Reciprocal Causal Relationships among Family, School and Delinquency." *Journal of Criminal Law and Criminology* 82:3–25.

Thornberry, T. P., M. Moore, and R. L. Christenson. 1985. "The Effect of Dropping Out of High School on Subsequent Criminal Behavior." *Criminology* 23:3–18.

Thorndike, R. L. 1968. "Review of R. Rosenthal and L. Jacobson, Pygmalion in the Classroom." *American Educational Research* 5:708–11.

Toby, J. 1983. "Crime in the Schools." In *Crime and Public Policy,* edited by J. Q. Wilson. San Francisco: Institute for Contemporary Studies.

Tolan, P., D. Gorman-Smith, and D. Henry. 2006. "Family Violence." *Annual Review of Psychology* 57:557–83.

U.S. Census Bureau. 1975. *Historical Statistics of the United States.* Washington, DC: GPO.

———. 1996. *Statistical Abstract of the United States: 1995.* Washington, DC: GPO.

———. 2004. *America's Families and Living Arrangements: 2003.* Washington, DC: GPO.

———. 1970–2000 Issues. *Statistical Abstract of the United States.* Washington, DC: GPO.

———. 2005. *Current Population Survey.* Washington, DC: GPO.

Van Voorhis, P., F. T. Cullen, R. A. Mathers, and C. C. Garner. 1988. "The Impact of Family Structure and Quality of Delinquency: A Comparative Assessment of Structural and Functional Factors." *Criminology* 26:235–61.

Vander Ven, T. M., and F. T. Cullen. 2004. "Impact of Maternal Employment on Serious Youth Crime." *Crime and Delinquency* 50(2):272–92.

VanderZanden, J. 1986. *Core Sociology.* New York: Alfred A. Knopf.

Warr, M. 1993. "Parents, Peers, and Delinquency." *Social Forces* 72(1):247–64.

West, D. J. 1982. *Delinquency: Its Roots, Careers and Prospects.* Cambridge: Harvard University Press.

West, D. J., and D. P. Farrington. 1973. *Who Becomes Delinquent?* London: Heinemann.

Wilson, W. J. 1987. *The Truly Disadvantaged.* Chicago: University of Chicago Press.

Wolfgang, M., R. M. Figlio, and T. Sellin. 1972. *Delinquency in a Birth Cohort.* Chicago: University of Chicago Press.

Wright, L., and F. Cullen. 2001. "Parental Efficacy and Delinquent Behavior: Do Control and Support Matter?" *Criminology* 39:677–705.

Yablonsky, L. 1959. "The Delinquent Gang as a Near Group." *Social Problems* 7:108–17.

eight

Contexts for Socialization
Religion, Media, and Guns

279

Hasn't anyone noticed that the worst criminals have been corrupted, since their infancy, by injurious reading? Hasn't anyone beheld them, in the course of their trials, confessing that it was sordid literature that dragged them onto the road which ended fatally at prison and at the gallows?

(E. Caron, Director of Education for the City of Paris, 1864)

Not only are crime comics a contributing factor to many delinquent acts, but the type of juvenile delinquency of our time cannot be understood unless you know what has been put into the minds of these children.

(Frederic Werthman, *Ladies Home Journal*, November 1953)

Long-term television viewing is one cause of violent or aggressive behavior in children and contributes substantially to childhood obesity, the American Academy of Pediatrics said yesterday.

(Chicago—Associated Press, 1990)

Introduction

When there are sudden outbreaks of violence involving the young, media pundits usually focus on one or more of three causes—the alleged demise of religion and related "moral values," exposure to violence in the media, and easy access to guns.

After the Columbine High School shootings, Pat Buchanan proclaimed that "if those kids had walked into schools with Bibles headed for a class, they would have been called to the principal's office" and attributed such events to Supreme Court challenges to school prayer and the barrier between religion and state-supported education. The implication of such arguments is that strengthening religious beliefs and values would help prevent delinquency and youth crime.

Another typical suspect is media violence in one form or another. Both President Clinton and Arkansas Governor Mike Huckabee attributed violence to video games, action movies, and popular music. Violence on television was one of the first concerns to be expressed in national newspaper editorials the day after the Columbine shootings. Of course, the tendency to attribute the transgressions of the young to popular culture and its contents has a long history, including children's penny "chapbooks" in the 1700s; "sordid literature" in the 1800s; comic books, music, and movies beginning in the early 1900s; television beginning in the mid-1900s; and video games and the Internet in the late 1900s. Indeed, as this chapter was being written, Congress was holding hearings on violence in video games, with numerous members claiming that such games lead to violence on the streets. Just as the young are singled out as the source of societal problems, anything that "entertains" them tends to be singled out as well.

A third suspect when addressing school shootings is the ease of access to guns. Michael Moore's award-winning documentary, *Bowling for Columbine*, keyed in on the American love affair with guns and indicted the National Rifle Association for its sustained opposition to further gun control. A conservative estimate is that there are over

200 million guns in America, and advocates of stronger gun control believe that the ready availability of firearms contributes to firearm violence among all age groups. Of course, youths involved in school shootings are likely to use guns acquired legitimately by their parents, relatives, or friends, which leads the NRA to counter that new controls would have no effect.

It should not be surprising that religion, media, and guns provoke heated debates since they each involve deeply held beliefs about fundamental rights of one form or another. Opponents of restrictions on firearms draw on their interpretation of the Second Amendment's right "to bear arms" and commonly state that "guns don't kill, people kill." Those concerned about restrictions on the content of mass media draw on deeply held commitments to free speech embodied in interpretations of the First Amendment and stress the responsibility of parents to regulate what their children watch. People concerned about restrictions on religious activities in schools tend to believe that Supreme Court interpretations have built too rigid a wall between church and state and that the attempt to maintain religious freedom now infringes on rights of religious expression.

Any attempt to present an objective assessment of the relevance of religion, media, and guns to juvenile delinquency and youth crime will upset one group or another, and criminologists are not necessarily trusted as objective scientists in adjudicating among these contending positions. However, this chapter will take that risk and attempt to summarize what criminologists have learned to date. We can propose tentative answers to a variety of questions about the relevance of religion, mass media, and guns to the explanation of delinquency and youth crime; however, we will also leave numerous questions unanswered. The statement that "further research is needed" is frustrating to students and the general public, but should be motivation for new generations of criminologists.

Religion and Delinquency

Religious variables have not been central to criminological theories, despite the fact that the founding fathers of sociology all included religion as an important force in understanding societies and human behavior. Although neither advocating its desirability nor endorsing any particular religion as necessary for social order, the most prominent general theorists in the historical development of sociology were all concerned with the nature and consequences of religion. Émile Durkheim (1897) viewed religion as a basic integrative mechanism in human society and felt that social order could be maintained only if people had common beliefs in something greater than themselves. The basic problem in the Western civilization of his time, he believed, was a trend toward "individualism" and the demise of shared values, norms, and beliefs. However, he also argued that high levels of "religious passion" among nations were associated with high rates of homicide. As will be discussed later, recent research reveals a complex relationship between religiosity and homicide rates.

Another grand master of sociology, Karl Marx, accorded religion a role in the prevention of crime, unrest, and revolution. For Marx, religion was the "opium of the masses" in that it directed their attention away from repressive, alienating economic systems. The powerless could find an illusion of happiness through religion and look to a future life filled with meaning and satisfaction. Religion was a force maintaining a status quo that Marx believed inevitably would be brought down by a revolution of alienated human beings. Religion was viewed as playing a role in the maintenance of social order, albeit a rather unflattering role.

Finally, a third grand master of sociology—Max Weber—felt religious institutions were intertwined with other institutions and with the economic development of society. Weber stimulated considerable sociological research on the role that Protestantism, Catholicism, and other religious beliefs play in facilitating or inhibiting economic development and achievement. Religion was an important social institution in his perspective, but he did not address crime.

The "sociology of religion" has been and remains a major specialty in sociology. However for much of the history of that field of study, those specializing in the sociology of religion paid little attention to its relationship to crime or delinquency. Although every delinquency text discusses the relevance of the family, school, and peers for understanding delinquency, it is quite rare to find a text that gives any consideration to religion. This neglect reflects the fact that religious variables were dismissed as irrelevant or unnecessary by some prominent criminologists (see Sutherland and Cressey, 1978) or were not specifically incorporated into other types of theories until quite recently. It also has been argued that religiosity was ignored because of irreligious or antireligious attitudes among sociologists (Stark, Kent, and Doyle, 1982). Of course, it may also be avoided because some group will be outraged no matter what the results of criminological research suggest.

Religious variables could have been incorporated quite readily into each of the major theories. For example, bonds to the church, a faith, or most sets of religious beliefs can be viewed as barriers to crime and delinquency since most religions encourage law-abiding conduct and respect for authority. In fact, recent research on religious variables has included them as a type of social bond within a social control theory framework.

Strain theories could encompass religious variables as well. For example, if religion directs attention away from the pursuit of worldly success, it would alleviate strain. Thus, theoretically, religion might inhibit delinquency by attenuating strain. It is also conceivable that involvement in religion could be an alternative response to strain or social rejection. In either case, religious variables would be relevant to explaining delinquency. As already noted, Karl Marx viewed religion as one force in the maintenance of social order, and its role in directing attention away from the contradictions and strains of capitalism was emphasized.

Historically, religion also has been a source of some degree of lawlessness. Some Mormons still believe in polygamy and a few have been arrested in recent years for practicing their beliefs. In fact, the leader of a Mormon sect was added to the FBI's ten "most wanted" list in April 2006 on grounds related to the practice of polygamy. In addition, some faiths do not believe in medical intervention to deal with health problems and proponents of that view have been prosecuted for neglect or abuse of sick children. The bombing of abortion clinics and the trashing of adult bookstores attest to the ways in which commitments to certain religious beliefs can produce violations of the law. The protection and transportation of political refugees in violation of immigration laws is another example. Acts considered criminal have been carried out in the name of religion throughout human history. On the other hand, charitable and life-saving acts are encouraged by religion as well.

One of the most prominent cultural conflict theorists, Donald Cressey, argues that "there is no specific evidence regarding the effect of religion, considered as something different from anticriminal values, on crime" (Sutherland and Cressey, 1978:234). Of course, if participation in or commitment to a religion were found to encourage commitment to anticriminal values, then it would have relevance to delinquency. The relevance would be indirect; that is, anticriminal values would be the intervening mechanism explaining the relevance of religion to delinquency. However, that is also the case for family, school, and peer group influences in a cultural conflict perspective. It is the impact of social institutions and arrangements on normative learning that distinguishes cultural conflict theory from other theories. The church is one context in which normative learning can occur.

Social learning theorists could encompass religious variables in a variety of ways. Differential association can readily encompass interaction in religious contexts and it is quite common for parents to invoke religiously founded normative standards when teaching conventional culture (normative socialization). In American society it is not difficult to delineate tenets of the Judaic-Christian tradition and common ethical standards embodied in both law and expressions of moral standards. Of course, as Durkheim argued, there may also be ways in which religious passions and beliefs can lead to violence as well. Social learning theory encourages consideration of countervailing mechanisms where religious variables can both inhibit and facilitate some forms of violence.

Research on Religion and Delinquency

Early research on religion in studies of labeled delinquents generated a hodge-podge of results: (1) delinquents were occasionally found to be more religious than nondelinquents (Middleton and Fay, 1941), (2) delinquents were found to be similar to nondelinquents in their attitudes toward religion (Kvaraceus, 1944; Mursell, 1930; Hightower, 1930; Hartshorne and May, 1930), and (3) nondelinquents were found to be more religious than delinquents in yet other studies (Healy and Bronner, 1936; Glueck and Glueck, 1950; Miller, 1965). However, no matter which of the three patterns researchers found, the actual differences reported were small.

Self-report research has yielded seemingly divergent findings as well. Some studies seem to suggest that church attendance is associated with lower rates of delinquency (Rhodes and Reiss, 1970; Nye, 1958), while Travis Hirschi and Rodney Stark (1969) reported no significant relationship. We will consider Hirschi and Stark's research here in some detail for two reasons. First, their study reinforced the common sociological opinion of the 1960s that organized religion was irrelevant to understanding delinquency. Second, their research stimulated a whole new line of inquiry, as evidenced by the flourish of research on religion and delinquency that began in the mid-1970s. Indeed, by 2001 a review of research on religion and crime concluded that "religious behaviors and beliefs exert a moderate deterrent effect on individuals' criminal behavior" (Baier and Wright, 2001:3).

Using data gathered from junior and senior high school students in Richmond, California, Hirschi and Stark investigated the relationship between church attendance and attitudes toward the law, the police, people in general, and supernatural beliefs (that is, a life after death and the existence of the devil). They found no significant relationship between church attendance and attitudes toward people and some weak, but significant, relationships between church attendance and positive attitudes toward police and the law. The strongest relationship was between church attendance and belief in supernatural sanctions. In turn, Hirschi and Stark found that positive attitudes toward people, the law, and the police were associated with low involvement in delinquency, while belief in the supernatural was unrelated to delinquency. In short, those attitudes that were *unrelated* or weakly related to church attendance were the most relevant for delinquency, and those beliefs that *were related* to church attendance were not related to delinquent behavior. In view of these findings, it is not surprising that Hirschi and Stark found no relationship between church attendance and delinquency. The results of this study appeared to further substantiate Glock and Stark's earlier observation in *Religion and Society in Tension*: "Looking at American society as a whole . . . organized religion at present is neither a prominent witness to its own value system nor a major focal point around which ultimate commitments to norms, values, and beliefs are formed" (1965:184). While the vast majority of Americans will confess to being religious or to a belief in a deity, such beliefs may not be reflected in actual behavior as compared to the irreligious. Moreover, our everyday secular life is so infused with religious notions (e.g., "in God we trust") paralleling traditional religious beliefs that even the irreligious may be committed to a type of "civil religion" (Bellah, 1967). The pervasiveness of religious notions in everyday life may keep formal religion from distinguishing people.

Variations by Type of Offense

Five years after the publication of Hirschi and Stark's study, Steven Burkett and Mervin White's "Hellfire and Delinquency: Another Look" appeared (1974). These authors argued that when secular values do not clearly define certain criminal or delinquent activities as wrong, then religious participation or beliefs may be relevant to understanding delinquent behavior. They suggested that offenses about which there is moral ambiguity in everyday life and offenses that run counter to religious traditions of self-control and self-denial might be inhibited by religiosity. Thus, they hypothesized that activities such as alcohol and marijuana use should be less common among the religiously active than among the inactive and less common among those who believe in the supernatural than among those who do not. Their findings were in large part consistent with their expectations. After analyzing questionnaire data from high school students in a city of about 170,500 in the Pacific Northwest, Burkett and White concluded that belief in the supernatural is only "slightly" related to the use of alcohol and marijuana, but that "a very definite relationship" exists between religious participation and the use of those substances. In comparison to Hirschi and Stark, Burkett and White reported stronger associations between religious participation and attitudes toward worldly authority and endorsement of conventional moral positions.

It also should be noted that before Burkett and White's study, Bruce Johnson (1972) had concluded that among college students, religious participation is one of four variables (the others being sex, political liberalism, and cigarette smoking) that are good predictors of marijuana use. In Johnson's study, 77 percent of regular church attenders reported never having used marijuana, while only 26 percent of nonattenders were complete abstainers. Church attenders were also less likely to be "regular" users. Similarly, in even earlier research, Middleton and Putney (1962) had proposed that the relationship between religion and delinquency was stronger for "anti-ascetic" offenses than "anti-social" offenses; that is, religion should be more consequential for actions which violate religious expectations for disciplined and sober conduct than actions which violate widely shared social norms.

Since the Burkett and White study, additional studies dealing with the relevance of religiosity to delinquency have appeared. Using self-report data from tenth-graders in Atlanta, Georgia, Paul Higgins and Stan Albrecht (1977) found a "moderate" relationship between church attendance and a wide variety of delinquent activities. They suggested that "church attendance in Atlanta might indicate a stronger commitment to general ethical and moral values than does church attendance in California." Albrecht, Bruce Chadwick, and David Alcorn (1977) collected data from Mormon teenagers in three western states and found that religious variables were greater inhib-

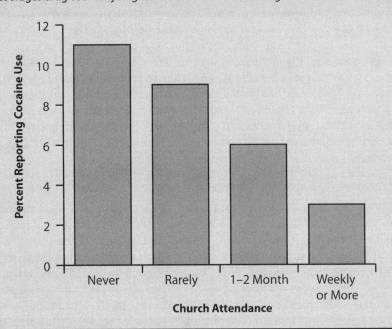

Box 8-1   Cocaine Use and Church Attendance

The graph below shows the percent of high school seniors who admitted having used cocaine in the prior twelve months (based on the 2003 MTF survey). Most research has shown measures of religiosity to be more relevant to inhibiting drug use than other types of delinquency. What issues discussed in chapter 5 would need to be addressed to make a case that involvement in religion discourages drug use? Why might it be more relevant to drug use than other offenses?

itors of victimless deviance (for example, drug use) than of deviance involving victims, and that a good prediction of deviance was possible when religious variables were combined with measures of peer and family relationships. In yet another study, Rick Linden and Raymond Currie (1978) reported that among their sample of youths aged 15 to 24 in Calgary, Canada, the greater the ties to the church, the lower the probability of drug use.

Gary Jensen and Maynard Erickson (1979) attempted a reconciliation of divergent findings by analyzing aspects of Hirschi and Stark's data, as well as data gathered from high school students in southern Arizona. The analysis of Hirschi and Stark's data on students in Richmond, California, showed that as church attendance increases, smoking, drinking, and truancy decline (the only victimless offenses on which data were available from the Richmond youths).

Finally, Burkett and Warren (1987) showed that the impact of religion on marijuana use was mediated by involvement with other users. Specifically, they found that

> youth with lowered religious commitment are vulnerable to progressive and more exclusive involvement with other users, and with that they are more likely to use marijuana. Religious youth, on the other hand, are likely to select as companions those who are similarly inclined both in attitude and behavior. (1987:127)

In other words, religion operates as a critical variable in the creation of peer groups and those peer groups have a vital impact on the use or nonuse of marijuana.

Variations by Measures of Religiosity

In addition to the elaboration of research to encompass different types of offenses, researchers have proposed that certain measures of religiosity are more likely to correlate with delinquency as well. Scholars studying religion have noted that there are multiple dimensions to what they refer to as **religiosity** (Glock and Stark, 1965), and church or Sunday School attendance is only one way in which a person can be religious. People vary in terms of more personal and private aspects of religiosity as well. For instance, people who attend church regularly may vary considerably in the extent to which their religious beliefs influence their everyday life. People who never attend church may have deeply felt religious beliefs. Variations in these personal measures of religiosity have been argued to be more relevant for delinquency than behaviors (such as regular church attendance) that may only reflect parental coercion. This argument has been substantiated in several studies (Hadaway, Elifson, and Petersen, 1984; Stark, Kent, and Doyle, 1982; Elifson et al., 1983).

Variations by Denomination and Moral Climate

While all recent studies indicate that religious participation is associated with some types of delinquency, there is no comparably consistent observation concerning religious affiliation and delinquency. Some studies have indicted lower delinquency rates for Jews than for Protestants and higher rates for Catholics than for Protestants (Goldscheider and Simpson, 1967; Rhodes and Reiss, 1970). In an analysis of arrest statistics, Roy Austin (1977) found that Jews had significantly lower rates than Catholics and this difference could not be explained solely by the social-class composition of the samples. Austin found no significant differences between Catholics and Protestants. In comparing Catholics, Protestants, and all "other" denominations, Burkett and White found no significant differences in self-reported delinquency. Similarly, Hirschi and Stark reported no significant differences by denomination.

Rather than considering denomination and church attendance as totally separate variables, Jensen and Erickson (1979) proposed that the meaning, or relevance, of religious involvement for behavior should be *variable* by denomination. Higgins and Albrecht (1977) suggested a similar possibility when they argued that religious variables appear more relevant to understanding delinquency in the South because of regional variation in the meaning of religion. Jensen and Erickson hypothesized that the denominational composition, rather than the regional composition, of the samples studied may have accounted for some of the variation in research findings.

Jensen and Erickson's findings were consistent with their hypothesis. In analyzing Hirschi and Stark's data, they found that church attendance was more relevant to delinquency in "fundamentalistic" or highly "ascetic" denominations (such as Church of Christ, Church of God, and Disciples of Christ). Among Baptists, the overall relationships turned out to be quite comparable to those reported in Higgins and Albrecht's study of Atlanta youth. Further evidence of the intertwining relevance of denomination and church attendance was found in Jensen and Erickson's analysis of southern Arizona data. Catholic, Protestant, and Mormon differences in delinquency were most prominent among regular church attenders. Attendance made the greatest difference among Mormons, particularly with regard to those activities strongly and distinctively prohibited by the Mormon Church (smoking, drinking, and drug use). In sum, it appears that there is considerable similarity in research results when analyzed in terms of similar offenses for similar groups and settings. Given the research available, the most plausible explanation of divergent findings and complicated inconsistencies may rest with the variable and complicated nature of our society.

Another line of theoretical development in the study of religion and crime stresses the importance of the **religious climate** for explaining the impact of religiosity on delinquency. Rodney Stark, Lori Kent, and David Doyle (1982) argue that religious variables are most likely to be relevant to variations in delinquent behavior in communities or contexts where religion is a salient feature of everyday life. In contrast, Stark and his colleagues argue that in "secular" communities, variations in religiosity make little difference for behavior. They support this interpretation with data for youths in schools that varied in the salience of religion in youths' lives, as well as through a comparison of studies in Seattle; Richmond, California; and Provo, Utah. While they do not address the possibility that variations in the relevance of religiosity for delinquency are due to denominational differences, subsequent analyses by other researchers (see Thompson and Brownfield, 1986) show that the variations in the relevance of religiosity between moral and secular school settings remains even when denomination is taken into account.

Is the Relationship Spurious?

Researchers studying religion and delinquency also have considered whether the association between measures of religiosity and some types of delinquency are due to other circumstances in youths' lives. The fact that measures of religiosity have been found to correlate with delinquency in a variety of studies does not necessarily mean that those variables inhibit delinquency, since variations in religiosity often go hand-in-hand with other variations as well. Youths who are religious also tend to have strong familial bonds and to do well in school (Elifson, Petersen, and Hadaway, 1983). Efforts to untangle the potential relevance of distinct but correlated characteristics of youth have not yielded any one simple generalization about the independent relevance of religion. Jensen and Erickson (1979) report that church attendance is associated with lower rates of drug use even when other characteristics of youth are taken into account. In contrast, Elifson and colleagues (1983) found that the relationship between religiosity and delinquency appeared to be due to other characteristics of the youths studied and concluded, "It appears that the relationship of religion to delinquency is so closely tied to the family and other influences that it has little influence that is statistically independent of other predictor variables" (1983:521). As noted earlier, Burkett and Warren (1987) found peer groups to be the key mediating force accounting for the relationship between religiosity and marijuana use. In short, while researchers have not yet fully untangled the relationships, religion may turn out to be consequential only because of its impact on other social relationships. This finding is quite consistent with Akers's social learning theory in that social learning theory identifies peer group variables as the key mechanisms through which parents and other social institutions influence delinquent behavior.

New Complexities

The most recent controversy surrounding the relevance of religion to crime does not focus on delinquency per se, but on the contribution of some forms of religiosity to violence. In contrast to the preventative argument, religious zeal has been cited as a source of national and international problems, ranging from homicide, hate crime, and terrorism to genocide and ethnic cleansing. Reflecting upon *When Religion Becomes Evil*, Charles Kimball (2003) proposes that religious belief systems can become destructive when they are characterized by absolute truth claims, notions of a cosmic struggle between God and the Devil (**cosmic dualism**), and rigid dichotomies between good and evil.

In an attempt to make sense of high rates of homicide and low rates of suicide in the American South, Luper, Hopkinson, and Kelly (1988) suggested that southern Protestant fundamentalism ascribes intentionality to people's actions, prompting people to react to a wide variety of situations as intentional attacks requiring a personal counter attack. Grasmick and colleagues (1992) have developed similar arguments to explain southern support for punitive sanctions, and Unnithan and coauthors (1994) have extended this line of argument by proposing, "Adherence to a fundamentalist doctrine would increase the chances of attributing the causes of one's failures to the malevolent acts of others, thus resulting in aggression being directed outward rather than inward."

Recent research on homicide rates among U.S. cities reports findings quite compatible with the religious passion argument. Among southern cities, Ellison, Burr, and McCall (2003) found the percent of evangelical Protestants to be a positive correlate of homicide rates when other relevant variables were controlled. As a type of social bond or a type of conventional activity, religion may inhibit a variety of crimes, but measures of religiosity that tap into religious passion, evangelical dualism, or belief in malevolent forces may have the opposite effect on homicide.

Gregory Paul (2005) has highlighted the view that religious variables can have negative consequences. In an analysis of eighteen prosperous nations, Paul reports positive relationships between a variety of measures of religiosity and homicide rates as well as other social problems. He concludes that nations lower in religiosity have lower homicide rates and less serious social problems than found in the United States, a nation high in religiosity.

In response to Paul's study, Jensen (2006) conducted a more elaborate analysis of international variations and found that it was only certain specific types of "religious cosmologies" that were conducive to homicide. The highest rates of homicide were found among nations (including the United States) characterized by cosmic dualism; that is, conceptions of religion as a struggle between dueling deities as expressed in high levels of belief in the Devil and Hell combined with belief in God and Heaven. Homicide rates were low among nations where people accept God and Heaven but do not accord significance to their malevolent counterparts. In other words, some **religious cosmologies** are associated with high levels of violence while others are associated with lower levels of violence.

These patterns were supported using nations as units of analysis and should not be used to reach conclusions about the characteristics of individuals and their involvement in violence. Yet, the findings certainly have implications for reasonable speculation about homicide at other levels of analysis. The findings are consistent with Ellison, Burr, and McCall's (2003) analysis of the strength of evangelical Protestantism and city homicide rates. It seems quite reasonable to hypothesize that the evangelical movement encourages high levels of passion and moral and/or religious dualisms. It is plausible to propose that religious and moral dualisms may coincide with other forms of dualism at the individual level. As Luckenbill and Doyle (1989) argue, homicide is one outcome of situated transactions where honor is at stake with a narrow range of options for responding and heightened sensitivity to what might appear to be minor affronts. Whether called a "culture of violence" or a "code of the street" (Anderson, 1999), disputes are easily triggered and there is little flexibility in acceptable responses. In short, other cultural or subcultural dualisms may help explain variation in behavior at the individual level. If a youth grows up in a world where there are rigid boundaries for attaining honor, a wide range of situations that are interpreted as disrespect, and limited cultural means for reestablishing honor, the range of situations generating interpersonal violence are enhanced.

The Maharishi Effect

Research on religion and crime has concentrated on conventional religious institutions and belief systems in the United States. New or imported forms of spirituality have received little attention. However, in 1986 Elaine and Arthur Aron published *The Maharishi Effect*, which summarized research on the effects of transcendental meditation (TM) on individuals' health and behavior and its alleged effect on the world around them. **Transcendental meditation** is a method for achieving an enlightened consciousness through techniques that include the use of a personal mantra. The most controversial claim involving the **Maharishi effect** was that when TM practitioners meditated collectively, such a collective effort brought "coherence" and peace to people in the wider system around them. Such coherence, so it is argued, leads to reductions in crime. Their claims have to be taken seriously since advocates of TM and "coherence theory" are planning a major expansion into other states. Moreover, the Maharishi University has been successful in gaining grants to conduct research bearing on the theory. In short, TM has become much more than a fad.

Because many of the advocates have advanced degrees in the sciences, numerous quantitative studies have been conducted and, on the surface, appear to support their argument. For example, Borland and Landrith (1976) matched cities with more than one percent of the population involved in TM with cities they considered comparable on other features and found lower crime rates for TM cities, controlling for a variety of variables. This same approach was taken in another study published in a peer-reviewed journal in criminal justice (Dillbeck, Landrith, and Orme-Johnson, 1981). Most of the research has been summarized in a work by Jay Marcus (1996) with the ambitious title, *The Crime Vaccine: How to End the Crime Epidemic.* TM techniques are argued to be the vaccine that can lower crime and delinquency in the United States.

It is difficult to assess this research for several reasons. The most serious problem is researchers' claim to have matched cities. When the TM vs. control cities are examined, there are significant differences in the educational level of the residents. For example, Chapel Hill, North Carolina, is a TM city in which nearly 70 percent of the population has four or more years of college education. In contrast, only 9 percent of the residents of the "matched" control city, Rocky Mount, North Carolina, has four or more years of college. In fact, considering all pairs of TM and control cities, TM cities have twice the proportion with four or more years of college. There are other significant contrasts as well (e.g., racial composition) and it is very questionable whether the cities have been properly matched.

A second problem with such research is its use of the total crime rate which, as seen in chapter 1, is primarily a larceny index. Hence, it is highly sensitive to variations in age composition as well as the size of transient populations. When crime is limited to murder, rape, and aggravated assault for TM and control cities used in the research, TM cities do not fare significantly better than control cities (author's own analysis). Furthermore, some of the pairs cannot be compared for the simple reason that some of the control cities have very little violence compared to TM cities. For example, Oshkosh, Wisconsin, had no violent acts in 1972, but six in 1973. In contrast, its TM "match" had 77 violent acts in 1972 and 53 in 1973. This pattern would support the argument that violence declined for the TM city and increased for the control city. But ask yourself which place would you consider to be safest? Oshkosh is not a good match city. Other cities used in the research exhibit the same problem (e.g., Moscow, Idaho). Finally, the years chosen can make a major difference for results, with fewer instances of the TM effect when comparing 1972 with 1974, 1975, or 1976. Overall, there are about as many pairs contrary to their argument as pairs that support it.

At present, the efforts of TM researchers cannot be totally dismissed, but there are sufficient problems to justify considerable skepticism. Their data typically include measures that are not available to outsiders attempting to replicate their arguments. For example, the Washington DC police could not provide the data needed to verify the results of one TM study of that city. Moreover, in their body of research there are many instances where data are substituted or cases dropped, which can affect the final results and preclude verification. There are sufficient uncertainties that it is safe to state that TM has not been shown to be a "vaccine" for crime. This situation could change with further "research," but that research should be available to nonbelievers for a critical assessment.

Mass Media and Delinquency

The **mass media** refer to impersonal instruments used to entertain or transmit written, oral, and visual material to a large audience of people. In contemporary society, the major forms of such transmission include television, radio, computers, records, tapes, books, motion pictures, newspapers, magazines and billboards, and video games. In terms of the prevalence and intensity of attention, television is the most pervasive of the mass media, reaching 98 percent of households. Time spent watching television ranks third behind sleeping and school as a childhood and juvenile activity in the United States, with the average teenager watching about 24 hours per week (World Almanac, 1990). With the proliferation of cable and satellite channels, video cassette recorders, and digital video recorders, the opportunity for exposure to violence has increased, prompting considerable concern about the role of television violence in the explanation of violent behavior among youth.

While television violence and pornography on the Internet are two recent targets of concern, several forms of mass media have been criticized at one time or another as possible sources of deviance. In the early 1700s, "penny histories" or "chapbooks" (short, inexpensive printed tales, ballads, and poems with woodcut illustrations) were popular with children as well as their parents, prompting religious critics to warn that they filled children's heads with foolish and dangerous ideas. In the 1800s, officials lamented that "sordid literature" led the worst criminals "onto the road which ended fatally at prison and at the gallows." In the early 1900s, the father of scientific criminology, Cesare Lombroso, condemned "really criminal newspapers, which spread abroad the virus of the most loathsome social plagues, simply for sordid gain, and excite the morbid appetite and still more morbid curiosity of the lower social classes" (1911:211). Similar concerns have been expressed about "flaming youth" in the silent film era of the 1920s (Gilbert, 1986). From the 1930s through the 1950s, crime comics were identified as a potential source of delinquency. In more recent years, media charged with encouraging some form of deviance include hard rock music as a cause of drug use, "rap" music as a cause of violence, and country western music as a cause of suicide. The Internet transmission of pornography to personal computers and violent computer games have been added to the list of media that some people believe encourage deviant behavior.

Despite the alleged influence of the media, the major theories of delinquency do not accord mass media a primary role. Edwin Sutherland contended that personal relationships were far more important than impersonal media in explaining crime and delinquency, a position that has been reaffirmed repeatedly in research. There are, however, ways in which the media could be specifically incorporated into these theories. For example, control theorists could argue that media content fosters values, norms, and beliefs that "free" a youth to commit delinquent acts, or that the media convey the "subterranean" aspects of American culture that facilitate delinquency.

Some forms of media activity might inhibit delinquency as well (e.g., going to movies or watching television with the family). Youths engrossed with television and the Internet are not in the streets. The fact that various medical associations warn that too much time engrossed in media contributes to obesity is actually contrary to the notion that such engrossment leads to violence on the streets. Media depictions of people as mean and untrustworthy may create barriers among people, contributing to community disorganization and crime. Time spent watching television is a negative correlate of school performance and may have indirect consequences through problems at school.

From a strain perspective, the media emphasis on advertising could be seen as facilitating strain by raising wishes and aspirations that cannot be met. Although no one has studied the issue, it is conceivable that television is a source of stress or feelings of anger and injustice, an argument that would be consistent with Agnew's general strain theory. Media images may reinforce distorted expectations about appearance, leading to eating disorders, steroid use, suicide, and other mental and behavioral problems. On the other hand, television, films, and other media might constitute escape mechanisms and means of attenuating frustrations. Of course, if both types of processes occur, they might counter-balance one another, yielding no relationship in the general population.

Cultural conflict theorists might argue that the media glamorize lawbreaking and present an excess of definitions favorable to lawbreaking. Mass media have been argued to exert an influence on deviance through several social learning processes that can affect behavior directly: (1) **imitation**, where people mimic actions they were exposed to in the media, (2) **desensitization**, where behaviors that originally prompted negative reactions no longer have an impact, (3) **normative socialization**, where the activities and attitudes portrayed come to be defined as socially acceptable, and (4) **vicarious reinforcement**, where perceptions of positive outcomes increase the probability that deviant behaviors will be viewed as rewarding. These mechanisms may facilitate pro-social behavior or antisocial behavior, depending on the content presented and the degree to which people identify with the people and situations represented.

Research on Media Effects

Although there are numerous mechanisms through which the media might influence deviance, scientific assessments of actual influence vary, depending on the medium studied, methods used, and the outcomes examined.

An Early Culprit: Comic Books

In the 1950s, psychiatrist Frederic Werthman (1954) argued that comic books were seducing the innocent and contributing to crime and delinquency by exposing the young to violence, sex, and sadism. These assertions were based on clinical experience rather than any rigorous scientific analysis. Two studies reported statistically significant relationships between time spent reading comic books and delinquency (Hoult, 1949; Hirschi, 1969), although the relationships were very weak and the associations observed could be spurious; that is, they could be products of other personal and social characteristics. Moreover, it was never established whether reading comic books preceded or followed involvement in delinquency (i.e., causal order was unknown).

Television

The relationship between televised violence, interpersonal aggression, and criminal or delinquent conduct has been the most common subject of scientific research. In 1972, Leonard Eron and his colleagues claimed to have "demonstrated that there is a probable causative influence of watching violent television programs in early formative years on later aggression" (Eron et al., 1972:263). Critics of this view argued that the relationship described by Eron and colleagues was spurious and that the important factor in shaping both viewing preferences and aggressive behavior is parental responses to aggression in a child's early years. A methodological critique suggested that the study by Eron and associates could actually support conclusions directly contrary to its authors' claims (Becker, 1972).

A three-year $1 million research project by the Surgeon General's Scientific Advisory Committee on Television and Social Behavior (1971) concluded that violence on television can induce mimicking in children shortly after exposure and that *under certain circumstances* television violence can lead to an increase in aggressive acts. The committee suggested that those children most responsive to television violence are likely to be predisposed to aggression or to respond with pleasure to violent content. The committee paid considerable attention to experimental work because it allows an assessment of causal order and eliminates arguments of spuriousness through random assignment of subjects to experimental and control groups.

A review of experimental research by Robert Kaplan (1972:969) found that the majority of experimental studies were consistent with the hypothesis that witnessing violence increases the probability of aggressive behavior. Another government overview a decade later (Pearl et al., 1982) concluded that the studies strongly suggest that viewing violent television programs contributes to aggressive behavior. Yet, the fact that mild forms of aggression can be instigated in laboratory experiments may have no bearing on a link between actual criminal violence (as opposed to aggression) and exposure to violence on television and in films.

One method for studying the relationship between exposure to television violence and criminal violence is the collection and analysis of survey data on these variables. In one study, researchers administered questionnaires to junior and senior high school students, asking them to specify their favorite television shows, total amount of time they spent watching television, and their perceptions of violent content in their favorite shows (Hartnagel, Teevan, and McIntyre, 1975). Other questions asked about the students' involvement in violence (fights and assaults) and their background characteristics. They found that when other characteristics of youth (e.g., age, grades, social class) which could affect rates of violence were taken into account, television violence made no difference for violence among males and was slightly correlated for females. In comparison to other background characteristics of youth, they deemed the impact of television violence to be "unimportant." Another survey study compared violent male prisoners to a control group of men without violent histories and reported a small, but statistically significant, relationship between adult violence and childhood exposure to televised violence when other characteristics that could affect violence were controlled (Kruttschnitt, Heath, and Ward, 1986). Survey studies suggest little or no significant relationship between past viewing habits and violent criminal or delinquent behavior.

Aimee Dorr (1986) has reviewed research on the impact of television on children, including panel studies carried out in 1972 and 1982. **Panel studies** gather data from a panel of people at different points in their life course, which allows consideration of changes in behavior over time. The 1972 study found a small relationship between mothers' reports of third graders' viewing habits and peer ratings of how aggressive a youth was. There was a relationship between violent content on a child's favorite show based on mother's report and peer ratings of aggression at subsequent points in time among boys, but not among girls. The 1982 study focused on peer nominations as aggressive, as well as reports of violent behavior and viewing habits, based on both the subject's and the mother's reports of favorite shows. When race and socioeconomic status were controlled, the 1982 study found little or no relationship between exposure to television violence and aggression and concluded that there was no evidence that television violence led to the development of aggressive behavior patterns. Dorr concludes that the studies of television and aggression "suggest that the effects of exposure to television violence are attenuated in everyday life as compared to the laboratory" and that effects on the individual over time "are particularly weak or even nonexistent" (1986:78).

In contrast to these negative assessments, Paik and Comstock (1994) reach a somewhat different conclusion in a **meta-analysis** (a quantitative summary and analysis of data reported in prior research) of the effects of television violence on "antisocial behavior." They note that findings of small relationships are sufficiently common across several types of studies to conclude that there is a small and statistically significant relationship between television violence and antisocial behavior, but the relationship is more prominent for aggression towards objects than people and is weakest for actual criminal violence. For criminal violence the amount of variance explained is somewhere between .004 and .02 percent. Since the studies reviewed vary in the degree to which other variables were controlled, the final conclusion is fairly similar to more conservative assessments. There is a very small positive relationship between television violence and illegal violence.

The Invention of Television

Widely cited research published in the *Journal of the American Medical Association* (JAMA) has supported the view that the presumed link between television violence and violent crime has a foundation in sound scientific research, and that a considerable amount of violence can be directly attributed to children's exposure to that medium. In an analysis of homicide rates in the United States, Canada, and South Africa, Brandon Centerwall concludes that the spread of television in the United States was followed ten to fifteen years later by an increase in homicide: "Following the introduction of television into the United States, the annual white homicide rate increased by 93 percent from 3.0 homicides per 100,000 white population in 1945 to 5.8 per 100,000 in 1974" (1992:3060). The rate increased in Canada during this span of time as well. In contrast, homicide decreased in South Africa where television broadcasting was banned. After the ban was lifted in South Africa in 1975, the homicide rate escalated

130 percent by 1983. The results of this "historical experiment" led Centerwall to conclude that "the introduction of television in the 1950s caused a subsequent doubling of the homicide rate, i.e., long-term exposure to television is a causal factor behind approximately one half of the homicides committed in the United States" (1992:3061).

This research has been cited by the American Medical Association as part of the basis for warning parents about the effects of television. However, it is seriously flawed research. For example, an attempt to approximate an experimental design would consider the magnitude of the murder rate before the introduction of television. If television can account for as much as one half of subsequent homicides, then we would expect that the homicide rate should be higher following its introduction than in prior spans of time. If we consider the entire span of years from 1900 to 1995, the average homicide rate is higher from 1900 to 1945 than from 1945 to 1995. Allowing for Centerwall's ten- to fifteen-year lag, the average homicide rate should be higher in the 1960s and 1970s than in the decades before the introduction of television. Yet, the average homicide rate for 1961 through 1975 is 7.1 per 100,000. This is a lower homicide rate than found for any decade prior to the introduction of television. When homicide rates before the introduction of television are considered, rather than limiting the analysis to the after phase, it appears that Americans were as prone to murder (if not more so) on average when their exposure to media violence was limited to dime novels, comic books, radio, and the movies.

Centerwall correctly points to a surge in homicide rates in the 1960s but, in addition to the fact that there were similar surges and higher averages prior to the invention of television, there were a variety of social and demographic changes during this same span of time that might explain that surge. An adequate assessment of variation in homicide rates over time requires a multi-variate analysis in which the impact of television is examined together with other potential correlates.

The end of World War II was accompanied by a short-lived surge in divorce rates as couples ended relationships and began new ones. However, family breakdown began to escalate in the late 1950s with a nearly 150 percent increase in the divorce rate between 1958 and 1979. Hence, increasing proportions of the youthful population were growing up in families characterized by conflict and breakdown. Of course, those two decades are the same decades encompassing the lagged effect of television in Centerwall's theory.

Another variable that could account for increases in murder rates is alcohol abuse. Whether measured by estimates of gallons of distilled spirits consumed per capita or cirrhosis death rates, alcohol use paralleled the pattern for divorce following World War II. Consumption surged in 1945–1946 and cirrhosis surged in close proximity between 1946 and 1948. Like divorce rates, both fell off and stabilized until the mid-1950s when they began moving upward—a trend that would be sustained for twenty years. Both cirrhosis death rates and estimates of consumption peaked between 1973 and 1975. Thus, the span of time in which the escalation in murder occurred was marked by a 150 percent increase in divorce, and a 50 to 60 percent increase in alcohol use/abuse. These changes could readily escalate murder rates regardless of the invention and distribution of television.

Jensen (2001) tested an alternative hypothesis that relationships involving primary groups are more important for understanding variations in homicide rates over time than the spread of television. This hypothesis was supported in analyses for the United States, Canada, and South Africa. The positive effect of television was reduced to statistical insignificance when measures of family breakdown and alcohol use were included in the analyses. In short, the alleged effect of television on murder rates highlighted by Centerwall appears to have been spurious due to its coincidental correlation with the course of family breakdown and alcohol use. Murder rates escalated during this span of time as a function of these social changes rather than as a function of the impact of television.

Homicide rates increased for juveniles from the mid-1980s to the early 1990s in the United States, and, once again, the surge in violence was attributed by many observers to media portrayals of violence. Of course, that rate peaked in 1993 and began to decline precipitously with no apparent change in television violence that would account for such a decline. An adequate theory of violence has to address both increases and decreases and to consider alternative explanations for variation. With no evidence that television content has changed, recent variations in juvenile murder are far more likely to be attributable to more volatile social conditions, such as short-lived increases in competition over crack cocaine markets in major urban areas, the proliferation of handguns in the possession of juveniles, and self-limiting waves of gang activity. The solution to those problems will not be found in warnings to parents about television.

Pornography

Another heated debate involving the media as a source of deviance involves the effects of pornography. This topic was the subject of considerable review and research by the President's Commission on Obscenity and Pornography in 1970. One of the commission's conclusions was that there was "no evidence to date that exposure to explicit sexual materials plays a significant role in the causation of delinquent or criminal behavior among youths or adults" (1970:32). Support for this observation came from (1) studies comparing delinquent and nondelinquent youth, (2) statistical studies of the relationship between availability of erotic materials and rates of sex crimes in both Denmark and the United States, and (3) comparisons of sex offenders with other adults.

In 1985 a second government study was undertaken under the auspices of Attorney General Edwin Meese. This commission had a budget of $500,000 (one-sixteenth that of the 1970 commission in adjusted dollars) and one year (compared to two in 1970) to complete its task. The second commission did not conduct any research and did not conduct a serious review of the scientific literature. Rather, it sponsored a series of public hearings in major cities and its report is essentially a compilation of the testimony of private individuals. The 1986 *Final Report* states, "We have found a causal relationship between sexually explicit materials featuring violence and these consequences, and thus conclude that the class of such materials, although not necessarily every individual member of that class, is on the whole harmful to society" (1986:329). The 1986 report emphatically undercut the 1970 report, suggesting that times had changed and that "there can be no doubt that we confront a different world than that confronted by the 1970 commission" (1986:286).

Several studies were carried out between the two commission reports. A study by Harold Kant and Michael Goldstein (1976) led them to conclusions similar to those reached by the 1970 commission. After comparing 60 molestation cases, 52 cases of "users of pornography," and 63 supposedly normal males, Kant and Goldstein concluded that sexual deviates have little exposure to erotica during adolescence. In fact, these researchers suggested that such adolescent exposure is associated with "adult patterns of acceptable heterosexual interest and practice." They noted that exposure to erotica appeared to be a quite common aspect of adolescence and that there was no evidence in their study that such exposure was associated with sex crimes. Their findings seemed to suggest the opposite—that is, that such exposure may be associated with acceptable sexual patterns.

Pornography that depicts violent sexual activity and abuse of women has been of particular concern, as is the use of children in pornographic media. As might be anticipated, given the uncertainty encountered in other areas of research, the picture is not altogether clear on this topic. For example, Malamuth and Check (1981) reported that college men who viewed pornography that coupled sex with violence reported being aroused by the idea of rape and showed less sympathy for rape victims than did men not shown such material. However, in a review of this research, Susan Gray (1982) notes that research on sexual arousal that measures activity in male sex organs does not show that such material is sexually arousing. After a review of relevant research, Gray concludes that "there is little evidence that exposure to hard-core pornography produces aggressive behavior in men." She also concludes that there is evidence that "levels of aggression in already angered men are increased by exposure to hard-core materials" (1982:387).

In a review of research on pornography and violence, Richard Felson concludes that "evidence does not support the hypothesis that exposure to nonviolent pornography leads to violence toward women. Most experimental studies show no difference in aggression toward women between subjects exposed to pornographic films and control groups" (1996:387). A major use of the Internet has been to gain access to pornography, but that surge in access has not been accompanied by increasing rates of sexual assault. In sum, there may be reasons to object to such content and the ease of access to such material, but there is no evidence that it has led to increases in delinquency or youth crime.

It is highly unlikely that there will ever be research providing clear-cut evidence on the subtle or long-term influences of the media. Current emphases and popular theory focus on negative consequences, which have not been clearly demonstrated. The various government investigations into the media have focused on such negative consequences because they are of concern to many people and organizations. However, the content and messages conveyed in the media are very complex, and negative outcomes may be balanced by positive outcomes. For example, the 1970 President's Commission on Obscenity and Pornography developed a list of "presumed consequences of exposure to erotica." The list of consequences, some of which are regarded as "beneficial," was compiled on the basis of all the arguments presented by various theories and parties to the pornography debate.

The Internet

When discussing traditional forms of media violence, we noted the tendency to introduce media effects when crime and delinquency are increasing, but to ignore them when crime and delinquency are decreasing. A new culprit has been added to the discussion—access to violent and pornographic materials over the World Wide Web. Use in households escalated as more and more people bought personal computers for the home, but was quite rare until the early to mid-1990s. As recently as 1997, only 19 percent of homes had Internet access. However, by 1998 it had increased to 26 percent and by the turn of the century 42 percent of homes had such access. By 2007 over 90 percent of households had such access.

Box 8-2   Juvenile Violence and Internet Access

The Internet is the latest technological innovation to be blamed for violence. Data on the percent of the population with access to the Internet is plotted below together with rates of juvenile assault and murder. Do these data support the hypothesis that increasing access to the Internet is associated with increases in juvenile violence? Are they consistent with the contrary hypothesis? What questions should be answered before proposing the notion that time spent on the Internet reduces the rates of juvenile violence?

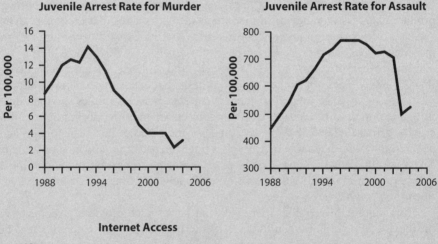

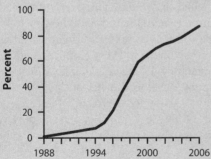

Source: Internet estimates are based on issues of the *Statistical Abstract of the United States,* U.S. Census Bureau. Arrest data are based on issues of the FBI's *Crime in the United States*. Arrest data have been normalized to allow display on the same graph.

We already noted the inconsistency in arguments by medical associations that television is making youths both obese and violent, and we have to raise some of the same issues here. In contrast to the emphasis on criminogenic effects, a case can be made that time spent in such activities in the home may lower real-world violence. In fact, if trends in Internet use are plotted against juvenile violence, we have to note that the impressive decline in youth violence beginning in the mid-1990s coincides with the equally impressive escalation of Internet use. It would be misleading to conclude that Internet use was a causal factor in the decline of juvenile violence, but it is even more implausible to imply that increases in Internet use are responsible for juvenile violence. Violence should have increased since the mid-1990s were the Internet as criminogenic as commonly argued. The fact that the two are trending in opposite directions cannot be ignored in the debate over media influences.

Firearms and Violence

We began the sections on religion and mass media by summarizing how they fit with various criminological theories. It is not a simple matter to do the same for gun violence, the third common target in attempts to make sense of episodes of senseless violence. Yet, we will see that a consideration of the relevance of such theories would have led to better research on issues involving firearms and violence than encountered thus far in the research literature.

The attempt to locate implicit theories in distinct theoretical traditions will guide us to consider a variety of topics that are clarified by such an effort. For example, Michael Moore's documentary on Columbine attacked the National Rifle Association and showed videos of the perpetrators "locking and loading" and treating firearms as toys. The underlying assumption is that personal grudges and anger would not have escalated into lethal violence without easy access to firearms and a willingness to use them against "enemies." The implication is that a reduction in access to guns might have prevented Columbine.

Both social learning theory and routine activities theories can encompass the availability of guns or access to firearms under the rubric of opportunity. At the individual level, the easier it is to acquire a gun, the greater the odds that "something" illegal will happen involving guns. Youths who committed school shootings did not have to go out of their way to find weapons. They were readily available in their households or at relatives' households. However, with estimates of at least 200 million guns available in the United States (see Wright, 1995), it is also obvious that millions of youth have access and do not commit offenses. One of the issues raised with regard to new attempts to control the proliferation of firearms is that firearms are so common that any attempt to reduce that number may have no effect. Philip Cook and Jens Ludwig refer to this point of view as the **futility hypothesis** (2004:30).

If a huge proportion of the young have access to guns, then other variables have to be introduced to make sense of firearms violence. Most people, including members of the NRA, would agree that children and teenagers should not have unfettered access to guns and that parents and relatives should keep weapons under lock and key. Parental monitoring, a variable central to social learning and social control theories, is certainly relevant. A youth determined to get a weapon may overcome a variety of constraints to do so, but, in general, social learning and social control theory lead us to expect that the odds of doing so are reduced by parental attempts to control guns.

Not only do parents play a major role in limiting access, but they are also key to the development of attitudes toward guns. As we noted earlier, the youths involved had to be willing to accept the use of guns as a means for resolving conflicts and establishing what they defined as justice. They had to be willing to use guns to kill or injure people they knew.

If we allow that such attitudes are differentially learned in different types of social settings, then it is clear that ideas central to cultural deviance, differential association, and social learning theories are relevant to understanding the "conventional" and "deviant" use of firearms. In fact, Moore interviewed Canadians on this topic and left viewers of his documentary with the impression that Canadians had access to guns comparable to Americans, but were less willing to shoot one another. He was incorrect with regard to comparable access for Canadians, but the contention that Americans and Canadians have different attitudes toward guns and their acceptable use is certainly plausible. Both social learning and cultural deviance theories imply that we have to consider definitions and attitudes about weapons use as distinct from access and the opportunity to use guns.

Research on Firearms and Violence

One of the ecological patterns stressed in versions of cultural deviance theory was the high rate of homicide in the American South compared to other regions, and one of the explanations stressed a "gun culture" that allegedly encouraged violence. It was assumed that the combination of available firearms with a subcultural willingness to use such weapons to resolve disputes generates a high rate of homicide. The support for this view was very indirect in that it was presumed that since economic and demographic characteristics of regions did not appear to fully explain the differences, the remainder must be due to something subcultural (see Dixon and Lizotte [1987] for a summary of such perspectives). In short, if regional patterns cannot be explained fully by economic and demographic variables, then there must be something "different" about the attitudes, values, norms, or beliefs of people in different regions.

However, when researchers attempted to measure such subcultural differences, the results were not as expected. When Jo Dixon and Alan Lizotte used survey data to more directly examine the attitudes of gun owners in different regions, they did not find gun ownership to be associated with attitudes conducive to initiating violence. They note that such findings do not challenge the existence of a "gun subculture" or a "subculture of violence," but that the two do not appear to overlap or to be unduly "southern."

One issue in ongoing debates about guns and violence involves the best way to measure the prevalence of guns. Researchers have used methods as widely varying as telephone surveys, NRA membership, subscriptions to *Guns & Ammo* magazine, suicides using firearms, gun permit registrations, stolen weapons as reported to the FBI, and hunting licenses. However, Jensen (2005) argues that these measures are not all "proxies" for the measurement of access, but measures of quite different aspects of the "firearms landscape." He proposes that NRA membership, subscriptions to gun magazines, hunting licenses, and retail gun stores are actually measures of a conventional gun culture that is not, itself, conducive to firearms violence and may, in fact, inhibit it. In contrast, other researchers have shown that the percentage of suicides committed with guns and telephone survey data estimates are highly correlated among states and are good prospects as measures of the actual prevalence of guns as distinct from a "gun subculture" (Azrael, Cook, and Miller, 2004; Kleck, 2004).

Box 8-3 illustrates the rationale for considering some of the "proxies" as measures of distinct features of the state firearms landscape which, paradoxically, are related to one another but have distinctively contrary relationships with firearm homicide. For example, estimated NRA membership is not a significant positive correlate of gun homicide despite the fact that it is highly correlated with measures of gun prevalence and that estimates of gun prevalence are positive correlates of gun homicide. In fact, NRA membership comes close to being a significant inhibiting variable for gun homicide. Moreover, when subjected to multivariate analysis, estimated NRA membership has a significant negative effect (i.e., the greater the membership, the lower the gun homicide rate of a state). In contrast, the prevalence of firearms is a significant positive correlate (i.e., the greater the prevalence, the higher the gun homicide rates). A legally oriented or conventionally organized gun culture is associated with low gun homicide rates, while the prevalence of guns in a state is a statistically significant positive correlate.

These distinctions are implied by Dixon and Lizotte's (1987) assessment of the independence of a "gun subculture" and a "subculture of violence" as well as the importance of differentiating between access and attitudes. It seems quite reasonable to propose that the more a gun culture involves norms for responsible and careful use (i.e., the more conventionally organized that culture is), the less likely it will generate high rates of gun homicide. However, to the degree that it encourages the proliferation of guns, such organization may have an indirect effect on gun homicide rates.

In *More Guns, Less Crime* (2000), John Lott proposed a very different theory about the effect of guns on crime. He proposed that offenders are deterred from committing offenses when the general population is perceived to be armed and when potential victims can defend themselves with guns. He shocked people by stating that had the teachers at Columbine been armed, the Columbine shootings may have had a very different outcome. Lott mounted a major study of variations in crime among counties that extended rights to carry weapons compared to those counties that did not and reported support for his theory.

This conclusion generated a great deal of criticism, and close inspections of the data led numerous criminologists to challenge Lott's argument. One critique and reanalysis indicated that the argument was dependent on results for only one state, Florida (Black and Nagin, 1998). Without Florida's counties in the analysis, the theory received no support. Of course, although that observation seriously weakens the argument, it may mean that the argument does apply to Florida.

However, other researchers have challenged whether the argument did apply to Florida. Kovandzic and Marvell (2003) examined rates of violence over time for 58 counties in Florida to assess the effect of a right-to-carry law that had been implemented in 1987. Instead of examining the applicability of the law, they examined the

Box 8-3   Guns and Gun Cultures

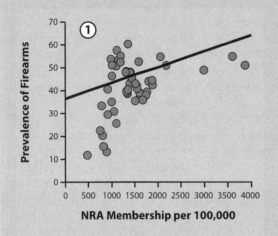

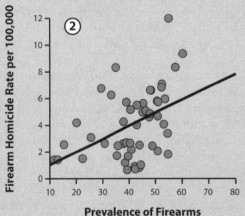

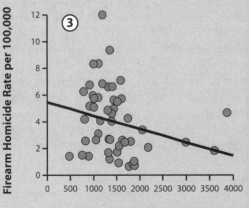

The graphs on this page show the relationship between (1) an estimate of the prevalence of firearms and estimates of NRA membership per 100,000, (2) the firearm homicide rate and prevalence of firearms, and (3) the firearm homicide rate and estimates of NRA membership.

There is a paradox here in that NRA membership per 100,000 is a positive correlate of the availability of guns among states, and the availability of guns is a positive correlate of firearm homicide. However, in a multivariate analysis, the independent effect of the NRA variable is strongly negative ($-.54$) while the prevalence of guns remains a strong positive correlate ($+.67$) of firearms homicide. How might the type of "gun culture" characterizing a state explain these patterns?

Source: Jensen, 2005. Estimates of prevalence of firearms are taken from Azrael, Cook, and Miller, 2004.

actual issuing of RTC permits. Prior studies had concentrated on the legal possibility of acquiring a permit rather than actual variation in the issuing of permits. Examining rates of valid handgun permits, they found no credible reductions in violence, including homicide. They note that few people actually pursued permits, that people may have been carrying concealed weapons without permits, or that RTC had both escalation and deterrent effects that counterbalanced one another. Moreover, it should be noted that it is the offender's belief that potential victims may be armed and may use weapons in self-defense that are central to Lott's theory and those underlying variables have not been measured.

Although it appears that right-to-carry laws have not led to an escalation in violence, there is little or no support for the view that they have had a deterrent effect either. Moreover, such research does not tell us whether or not more guns means less crime or more crime. If the "easy access" argument were correct, then we should expect that among states, the greater the prevalence of firearms, the higher the rate of firearm violence. If Lott's deterrence hypothesis were correct, then we would expect the exact opposite (i.e., more guns means less crime). By far, most research suggests a positive correlation between the prevalence of guns and gun homicide.

Another question involving the prevalence of guns is whether prevalence affects the probability of juveniles carrying weapons. If prevalence has no effect on teenagers carrying weapons, then availability of guns might be irrelevant to the problem of juvenile firearms violence. Cook and Ludwig (2004) note that in 1995 one in ten adolescent males indicated carrying a gun at least once a month. Moreover, among counties in the United States, the estimated prevalence of firearms is a significant correlate of gun-carrying among teens. The more guns available in a county, the more likely they were to report carrying a gun. Cook and Ludwig conclude that "supply-side" interventions are not inherently doomed to failure in that fewer guns meant fewer teenagers carrying guns.

A final issue to be considered is whether gun control laws and/or changes in the law have any bearing on firearms violence. Much of the gun control debate has involved the 1994 Brady Handgun Violence Prevention Act, which required purchasers to wait five days for a background check before being allowed to purchase a handgun from dealers licensed by the Bureau of Alcohol, Tobacco, Firearms and Explosives. The waiting period provision expired in 1998 and was replaced by a new "National Instacheck System" managed by the FBI.

The impact of the Brady Act would seem to be an easy issue to address. Did handgun violence decrease after implementation of the Brady Act? The decline in violence since the early to mid-1990s might be taken as evidence that it did. Yet, the decline was not limited to gun violence and may have been a product of other changes in society. Did handgun violence decrease more in states where the Brady Act made a real difference as compared to states that were exempted because they already had similar legislation? Cook and Ludwig (2000) compared 32 states that implemented the Brady Act as a new restriction with 18 states that already had their own Brady-type regulations. Examining variations over time in deaths involving firearms, they found no significant difference in temporal patterns between Brady states and control states.

One reason it is difficult to assess the impact of gun control laws is that states have a myriad of laws in place and any additions or changes may have little net effect in the context of existing laws. Hence, it might be wise to consider whether the *accumulated set* of gun regulations is related to variations in firearms homicide. One way to examine such a relationship is to use "gun grades" accorded states by the Brady campaign (2001).

States are "graded" based on types of legislation: (1) Is it illegal for a child to possess a gun without supervision? (2) Is it illegal to sell a gun to a child? (3) Are gun owners held responsible for leaving loaded guns easily accessible to children? (4) Are guns required to have child-safety locks, loaded-chamber indicators, and other child-proof designs? (5) Are there restrictions on unsafe "Saturday night specials"? (6) Do cities and counties have authority to enact local gun laws? (7) Are background checks required at gun shows and between private parties? (8) Is it legal to carry concealed handguns in public?

An analysis of the relation between gun grades and firearms homicide explains why the debate over gun control and firearms violence is so difficult to resolve (Jensen, 2005). There is no significant relationship overall between a state's gun grade and its gun homicide score. For example, Illinois and Maryland have among the highest firearms homicide scores, but also have among the highest gun-control grades. In contrast, at least nine states that received very low grades have very low rates of firearms homicide (Maine, Vermont, New Hampshire, Wyoming, Montana, Idaho, Utah, North and South Dakota). However, the story would be incomplete were it ended with that observation.

Jensen proposes that certain states have well developed conventional gun cultures associated with traditions of hunting and sporting use of guns, traditions that do not facilitate or may even inhibit high rates of firearms homicide. These states score high in NRA membership, retail gun outlets, hunting licenses, and subscriptions to gun-oriented magazines. In fact, when these states are removed from the analysis, there is a significant negative relationship between gun grades and firearms homicide (i.e., states with good grades have significantly lower firearms homicide rates).

Further analysis helped untangle a complex relationship. Relating firearms homicide to both a hunting culture and gun grades, both were found to be significant independent correlates of firearms homicide; that is, states with a conventional gun culture have lower rates of firearms homicide and, independent of that relationship, states with good gun grades have lower firearms homicide rates. Moreover, the reason that good gun grades are associated with lower rates is that they are a strong negative correlate of the prevalence of guns. In short, states scoring high in measures of an organized or conventional gun culture have low firearm homicide rates and gun legislation has an impact through its effect on the prevalence of guns. Of course, these data are "correlations" and do not clearly tell us the causal sequences involved. On the other hand, correlational data have been used by both sides of the debate and are used here to suggest a complex, but quite meaningful, pattern that shows some support for both sides.

Summary

The impact of religion, media, and guns on delinquency and youth crime has been of greater interest in popular discourse about surges and upward trends than in sociological theory and research. The family, school, and peer groups are viewed as the primary contexts for explaining variations in delinquency and the research literature is consistent with that view. However, there is sufficient research to propose some generalizations about each of the three topics in this chapter.

Research on religion and delinquency has shown that religiosity is more likely to be related to illegal drug use than to other delinquent offenses, is most relevant to drug use in denominations that prohibit such activity, is more relevant to delinquent offenses in general among ascetic or fundamentalistic denominations than among liberal denominations, and is more relevant to delinquency in moral than in secular settings. Moreover, measures of personal religiosity are more relevant to delinquency than measures such as church attendance. In addition, it appears that religiosity explains relatively little about delinquency when compared to the impact of more intimate social relationships and social bonds.

There are two new topics involving religion and crime that can be addressed as well, the impact of "religious cosmologies" on violence and the alleged effect of TM practices on crime rates. One line of research proposes that nations with a high level of religiosity have worse homicide rates than secular nations. However, a more precise differentiation of nations indicates that nations with dualist religious belief systems combining strong belief in God with strong belief in the devil ("dueling deities") have the highest rates of homicide. Research supportive of the crime-inhibiting effect of transcendental meditation practices has come entirely from advocates of a TM religious belief system, and it has proven difficult to fully assess their arguments. However, there is evidence that the TM cities and control cities in their research differ in too many ways to accord lower crime rates to TM practice.

The impact of the media on delinquency and crime has been examined in a considerable body of research. However, most of it has been criticized as either irrelevant or inadequate for assessing such relationships. The following observations reflect the current state of research and the qualifications that the criticisms demand:

1. Experimental studies have shown that exposure to televised content intended to arouse aggressive behavior increases the probability of interpersonal aggression in controlled situations where the opportunity for aggression is provided following exposure. However, these findings cannot be automatically generalized to the relationships between delinquent behavior and exposure to television outside the laboratory setting.

2. The more time a person spends watching television, reading comic books, or reading romance magazines, the greater the probability of involvement in delinquency, but arguments concerning the causal order and spuriousness of this relationship have not been eliminated. Moreover, research specifically examining preferences for violent programming in relation to self-reports of violence have found such programming to be only weakly correlated, if at all.

3. The conclusion of the 1970 President's Commission on Obscenity and Pornography still stands: scientific studies have not shown exposure to erotica to increase the probability of sex crimes or delinquent behavior.

4. Reactions to mass media are conditioned by other characteristics of consumers such that no simple, definitive conclusion about the impact (or lack thereof) of violence and/or pornography is possible at this time.

Once again we will state that we are focusing on regularities. There are undoubtedly people who are incited to commit a crime by something they have seen or read, but there are also people who may refrain from crimes as a result of such stimuli. *On balance*, there is no basis for concluding that television violence or erotic literature enhances the probability of delinquency.

Access to firearms has become a major topic in criminological research in the late twentieth and early twenty-first centuries. Such research has focused on identifying the "best" way to measure availability, ownership, or access to firearms and on specific issues involving gun legislation and crime. At present, most research suggests that the prevalence of firearms is associated with higher rates of firearms homicide, but that recent changes in laws have had little or no impact on homicide rates. However, attempts to differentiate among different proxies for access to guns have suggested that they are measuring different features of the firearms landscape and that measures of a conventional gun culture are negative correlates of firearms homicide while measures of the availability of firearms are positive correlates. This new approach may help reconcile competing perspectives on guns, gun cultures, and gun violence.

Discussion Questions

1. Did any of the major sociological theories accord religion an important role in delinquency causation? How might religious variables be incorporated into any one of the theories of delinquency summarized in chapter 6?

2. Why is it important to consider variations by type of offense, variations by measures of religiosity, and variations by denomination or moral climate to explain some of the variation in findings concerning religion and delinquency in different studies?

3. What are some of the "new complexities" that have to be considered to understand the relationship between religion and delinquency?

4. Do any of the major sociological theories accord the media a major role in the explanation of delinquency? How might media influences be incorporated into the theories of delinquency outlined in chapter 6?

5. Why is it important to examine homicide rates in the first half of the twentieth century when assessing arguments that the invention and rapid spread of television was responsible for the surge in homicide after World War II? What other changes in society at that time have to be considered?

6. Make a list of possible negative and positive consequences of television viewing. Based on your list, what would you predict about the relationship between time spent watching television and delinquent behavior?

7. Do any of the major sociological theories accord firearms a role in the explanation of delinquency? How might issues related to the firearms/violence relationship benefit from considering sociological theories?

8. One of the ecological patterns stressed in versions of cultural deviance theory was the high rate of homicide in the American South compared to other regions. Has that high rate been found to be a product of easy access to guns?

9. What are the two contrary positions on the relevance of gun availability for explaining variations in crime, especially violence? How might that disparity be resolved by considering different features of the firearms landscape in America?

10. Why is it difficult to assess the impact of gun control laws among states in the United States? How might a consideration of the "accumulated set of gun regulations" help resolve the issue?

References

Albrecht, S. L., B. A. Chadwick, and D. S. Alcorn. 1977. "Religiosity and Deviance: Application of an Attitude-Behavior Contingent Consistency Model." *Journal for the Scientific Study of Religion* 16(3):236–74.

Anderson, E. 1999. *The Code of the Streets: Decency, Violence, and the Moral Life of the Inner City.* New York: W. W. Norton.

Aron, E., and A. Aron. 1986. *The Maharishi Effect*. New York: E.P. Dutton.

Attorney General's Commission on Pornography. 1986. *Final Report.* Washington, DC: U.S. Department of Justice.

Austin, R. 1977. "Religion and Crime Control." Paper presented at American Society of Criminology convention, Atlanta, Georgia.

Azrael, D., P. J. Cook, and M. Miller. 2004. "State and Local Prevalence of Firearms Ownership: Measurement, Structure and Trends." *Journal of Quantitative Criminology* 20(1):43–62.

Baier, C. J., and B. R. E. Wright. 2001. "If You Love Me Keep My Commandments." *Journal of Research in Crime and Delinquency* 38:3–31.

Becker, G. 1972. "Causal Analysis in R-R Studies: Television and Aggression." *American Psychologist* 27:967–68.

Bellah, R. 1967. "Civil Religion in America." *Daedalus* 96:1–21.

Black, D. A., and D. S. Nagin. 1998. "Do Right-to-Carry Laws Deter Violent Crime?" *Journal of Legal Studies* 27(1):209–19.

Borland, C., and G. Landrith, III. 1976. "Improved Quality of City Life through the Transcendental Meditation Program: Decreased Crime Rate." In *Scientific Research on the Transcendental Meditation Program: Collected Papers,* Vol. 4, edited by D. W. Orme-Johnson and J. T. Farrow. Rhenweiler, W. Germany: MERU Press.

Brady Campaign to Prevent Gun Violence. 2001. "State Report Cards." www.bradycampaign.org/facts/reportcards.

Burkett, S., and B. Warren. 1987. "Religiosity, Peer Association and Adolescent Marijuana Use: A Panel Study of Underlying Causal Structures." *Criminology* 25:109–25.

Burkett, S., and M. White. 1974. "Hellfire and Delinquency: Another Look." *Journal for the Scientific Study of Religion* 13 (December):455–62.

Centerwall, B. S. 1992. "Television and Violence: The Scale of the Problem and Where to Go from Here." *Journal of the American Medical Association* 267:3059–63.

Cook, P., and J. O. Ludwig. 2000. "Homicide and Suicide Rates Associated with Implementation of the Brady Handgun Violence Prevention Act." *Journal of the American Medical Association* 284:585–91.

———. 2004. "Does Gun Prevalence Affect Teen Gun Carrying After All?" *Criminology* 42:27–54.

Dillbeck, M. C., G. S. Landith, III, and D. W. Orme-Johnson. 1981. "The Transcendental Meditation Program and Crime Rate Change in a Sample of 48 Cities." *Journal of Crime and Justice* 4:25–45.

Dixon, J., and A. J. Lizotte. 1987. "Gun Ownership and the 'Southern Subculture of Violence.'" *American Journal of Sociology* 93:383–405.

Dorr, A. 1986. *Television and Children*. Beverly Hills: Sage Publications.

Elifson, K. W., D. M. Petersen, and C. K. Hadaway. 1983. "Religiosity and Delinquency: A Contextual Analysis." *Criminology* 21 (November):505–27.

Ellison, C. G., J. A. Burr, and P. McCall. 2003. "The Enduring Puzzle of Southern Homicide: Regional Religious Culture the Missing Piece?" *Homicide Studies* 7:326–52.

Eron, L. D., L. R. Huesmann, M. M. Lefkowitz, and L. O. Walder. 1972. "Does Television Violence Cause Aggression?" *American Psychologist* 27:253–63.

Felson, R. B. 1996. "Mass Media Effects on Violent Behavior: Messages from Pornography." Part II in *Annual Review of Sociology*, vol. 22.

Gilbert, J. 1986. *A Cycle of Outrage: America's Reaction to the Juvenile Delinquent in the 1950s*. New York: Oxford University Press.

Glock, C. Y., and R. Stark. 1965. *Religion and Society in Tension*. Chicago: Rand McNally.

Glueck, S., and E. Glueck. 1950. *Unraveling Juvenile Delinquency*. Cambridge: Harvard University Press.

Goldscheider, C., and J. E. Simpson. 1967. "Religious Affiliation and Juvenile Delinquency." *Sociological Inquiry* 37 (Spring):297–310.

Grasmick, H. G., E. Davenport, M. B. Chamblin, and R. J. Bursik, Jr. 1992. "Protestant Fundamentalism and the Retributive Doctrine of Punishment." *Criminology* 30:21–45.

Gray, S. H. 1982. "Exposure to Pornography and Aggression towards Women: The Case of the Angry Male." *Social Problems* 29 (April):387–98.

Hadaway, C. K., K. W. Elifson, and D. M. Petersen. 1984. "Religious Involvement and Drug Use among Urban Adolescents." *Journal for the Scientific Study of Religion* 23(2):109–28.

Hartnagel, T. F., J. J. Teevan, and J. J. McIntyre. 1975. "Television Violence and Violent Behavior." *Social Forces* 54 (December):341–51.

Hartshorne, H., and M. A. May. 1930. *Studies in Deceit*. Vol. 1. New York: Macmillan.

Healy, W., and A. J. Bronner. 1936. *New Light on Delinquency and Its Treatment*. New Haven: Yale University Press.

Higgins, P. C., and G. L. Albrecht. 1977. "Hellfire and Delinquency Revisited." *Social Forces* 55 (June):952–58.

Hightower, P. R. 1930. "Biblical Information in Relation to Character and Conduct." *University of Iowa Studies in Character* 3:33–34.

Hirschi, T. 1969. *Causes of Delinquency*. Berkeley: University of California Press.

Hirschi, T., and R. Stark. 1969. "Hellfire and Delinquency." *Social Problems* 17 (Fall):202–13.

Hoult, T. F. 1949. "Comic Books and Juvenile Delinquency." *Sociology and Social Research* 33:270–84.

Jensen, G. F. 2001. "The Invention of Television as a Cause of Homicide." *Homicide Studies* 5:114–30.

———. 2005. "The Prevalence of Guns: A New Approach to Alternative Measures." Paper presented at the 2005 meeting of the Homicide Studies Working Group, University of Central Florida.

———. 2006. "Religious Cosmologies and Homicide Rates among Nations." *The Journal of Religion and Society* 8:1–13.

Jensen, G. F., and M. L. Erickson. 1977. "Delinquency and Damnation." Paper presented at Pacific Sociological Association Convention, San Francisco, California.

———. 1979. "The Religious Factor and Delinquency: Another Look at the Hellfire Hypothesis." In *The Religious Dimension: New Directions in Quantitative Research*, edited by R. Wuthnow. New York: Academic Press.

Johnson, B. 1972. *Social Determinants of the Use of Dangerous Drugs by College Students*. New York: John Wiley.

Kant, H. S., and M. J. Goldstein. 1976. "Pornography." *Psychology Today* 4(7):61–64.

Kaplan, R. M. 1972. "On Television as a Cause of Aggression." *American Psychologist* 27:968–69.

Kimball, C. 2003. *When Religion Becomes Evil.* San Francisco: HarperCollins.

Kleck, G. 2004. "Measures of Gun Ownership Levels for Macro-Level Crime and Violence Research." *Journal of Research in Crime and Delinquency* 41:3–36.

Kovandzic, T. V., and T. B. Marvell. 2003. "Right-to-Carry Concealed Handguns and Violent Crime: Crime Control through Gun Decontrol." *Criminology & Public Policy* 2:363–96.

Kruttschnitt, C., L. Heath, and D. A. Ward. 1986. "Family Violence, Television Viewing Habits, and Other Adolescent Experiences Related to Violent Criminal Behavior." *Criminology* 24:235–67.

Kvaraceus, W. 1944. "Delinquent Behavior and Church Attendance." *Sociology and Social Research* 28:284–89.

Linden, R., and R. Currie. 1978. "Religiosity and Drug Use: A Test of Social Control Theory." *Canadian Review of Anthropology and Sociology* 15:346–55.

Lombroso, C. 1911. *Crime: Its Causes and Remedies.* Boston: Little, Brown.

Lott, J. R., Jr. 2000. *More Guns, Less Crime: Understanding Crime and Gun-Control Laws.* Chicago: University of Chicago Press.

Luckenbill, D. F., and D. P. Doyle. 1989. "Structural Position and Violence: Developing a Cultural Explanation." *Criminology* 27:419–36.

Luper, M., P. J. Hopkinson, and P. Kelly. 1988. "An Exploration of the Attributional Styles of Christian Fundamentalists and Authoritarians." *Journal of the Scientific Study of Religion* 27:389–98.

Malamuth, N., and J. Check. 1981. "The Effects of Mass Media Exposure on Acceptance of Violence against Women: A Field Experiment." *Journal of Research in Personality* 15:436–46.

Marcus, J. B. 1996. *The Crime Vaccine: How to End the Crime Epidemic.* Baton Rouge, LA: Claitor's Law Books and Publishing Division.

Middleton, R., and S. Putney. 1962. "Religion, Normative Standards, and Behavior." *Sociometry* 25:141–52.

Middleton, W., and P. Fay. 1941. "Attitudes of Delinquent and Non-Delinquent Girls toward Sunday Observance, the Bible and War." *Journal of Educational Psychology* 32:555–58.

Miller, M. 1965. "The Place of Religion in the Lives of Juvenile Offenders." *Federal Probation* 29:50–54.

Mursell, G. R. 1930. "A Study of Religious Training as a Psychological Factor in Delinquency." Ph.D. dissertation, Ohio State University.

Nye, F. I. 1958. *Family Relationships and Delinquent Behavior.* New York: John Wiley.

Paik, H., and G. Comstock. 1994. "The Effects of Television Violence on Anti-Social Behavior: A Meta-Analysis." *Communication Research* 21:516–46.

Paul, G. S. 2005. "Cross-National Correlations of Quantifiable Societal Health with Popular Religiosity and Secularism in the Prosperous Democracies: A First Look." *Journal of Religion and Society* 7. [http://moses.creighton.edu/JRS/2005/2005-11.html]

Pearl, D., L. Bouthilet, and J. Lazar. 1982. *Television and Behavior.* Rockville, MD: National Institutes of Mental Health.

President's Commission on Obscenity and Pornography. 1970. *The Report of the Commission on Obscenity and Pornography.* New York: Bantam Books.

Rhodes, A., and A. Reiss, Jr. 1970. "The Religious Factor and Delinquent Behavior." *Journal of Research in Crime and Delinquency* 7:83–98.

Stark, R., L. Kent, and D. P. Doyle. 1982. "Religion and Delinquency: The Ecology of a Lost Relationship." *Journal of Research in Crime and Delinquency* 18(2):4–24.

Surgeon General's Scientific Advisory Committee on Television and Social Behavior. 1971. *Television and Growing Up: The Impact of Televised Violence.* Washington, DC: National Institute of Mental Health.

Sutherland, E. H., and D. R. Cressey. 1978. *Criminology.* 10th ed. Philadelphia: J. B. Lippincott.

Thompson, K., and D. Brownfield. 1986. "Religiosity and Delinquency in Moral and Secular Communities." Paper presented at the American Society of Criminology Convention, Atlanta, Georgia.

Unnithan, N. Prabha, L. Huff-Corzine, J. Corzine, and H. Whitt. 1994. *The Currents of Lethal Violence: An Integrated Model of Suicide and Homicide.* Albany: State University of New York Press.

Werthman, F. 1954. *Seduction of the Innocent.* New York: Holt, Rinehart and Winston.

Wright, J. D. 1995. "Ten Essential Observations on Guns in American Society." *Society* (March/April):63–68.

World Almanac and Book of Facts. 1990. New York: Pharos Books.

nine

Deterrence and Labeling

> People are governed in their daily lives by rewards and penalties of every sort. We shop for bargain prices, praise our children for good behavior and scold them for bad, expect lower interest rates to stimulate home building and fear that higher ones will depress it, and conduct ourselves in public in ways that lead our friends and neighbors to form good opinions of us. To assert that "deterrence doesn't work" is tantamount to either denying the plainest of facts of everyday life or claiming that would-be criminals are utterly different from the rest of us.
>
> (James Q. Wilson, *Thinking About Crime*, 1983)

Introduction

The most common public and political outcry to deal with problems of crime and delinquency is that we need to get tough—to do something more punitive and threatening than is currently being done. Declarations that the juvenile court is a "kiddies court" and that it is soft on crime reflect the view that the court ought to be a punitive agency assigning penalties with sufficient certainty, severity, and speed (celerity) to scare real and potential offenders straight. To many advocates this **deterrence** doctrine is so unquestionably true that only the naive and misguided would question it.

The idea that a primary aim of legal sanctioning or punishment is to deter offenders, as well as the general public, from future transgressions developed in the eighteenth century. It is associated with such philosophers as Cesare Beccaria (1738–1794) and Jeremy Bentham (1748–1832), who formulated a perspective on crime that came to be called the *classical school* of criminology. The classical view was rational and utilitarian, emphasizing that a punishment is just only if it contributes to the greatest happiness for the greatest number. The major justification for legal sanctioning was its presumed inhibiting effect on crime. For a punishment to serve such a purpose and contribute to the social good, there had to be a measure of equity between the crime and the punishment. Thus, Beccaria maintained that "for a punishment to attain its end, the evil which it inflicts has only to exceed the advantage derivable from the crime" (1767). For Beccaria, punishment should be as certain as possible and as harsh as necessary to deter potential offenders.

Bentham, basing his approach on utilitarian principles, argued that criminal activities were a product of free choices made by rational beings on the basis of a consideration of profit and cost. Consistent with this view, the function of criminal law and criminal justice was to design punishments that would deter, but that would do so without inflicting more pain than was necessary. Classical theorists attacked arbitrary and cruel practices found in many countries in Europe and focused instead on human reason and the perfectibility of social institutions as rational agencies dealing with rational beings.

Although the classical school's principles of deterrence became the philosophical foundation for our criminal justice system, they were attacked while the juvenile justice system was developing. The optimism of the classical school during the eighteenth century gave way to the reformatory movement of the nineteenth century, which sought to save youthful offenders from the perils of contemporary society. The function of the juvenile court was not to punish, nor was it to design and implement penalties that would deter. Rather the court was to find appropriate techniques for "treating" or "helping" troubled youths. The juvenile justice system was supposed to emphasize rehabilitation rather than deterrence.

In chapter 2 we summarized the arguments of social historians who assert that the primary motives behind the creation of the juvenile justice system were not so benevolent and that punishment and control of dangerous youth were central to the practices of the juvenile court. Indeed, the Supreme Court critique of the juvenile justice system that led to the extension of several rights of due process to juveniles in the 1960s emphasized the punitive nature of the system and its failure to serve the interests of children. The dominant orientation among sociologists at that time emphasized the failure of the system to rehabilitate or deter. Rather, the juvenile justice system was accused of turning youth into career offenders by labeling and stigmatizing them and treating temporary problems of youth as if they were criminal activities (see Schur, 1969).

While politicians have tended to advocate some version of a "get tough" approach, there are strong supporters of a less punitive approach as well. For example, Ira Schwartz, administrator of the Office of Juvenile Justice and Delinquency Prevention (OJJDP) under President Carter, advocated an "action agenda" that was in marked contrast to deterrence-based arguments. Among other things, he proposed (1) enacting laws that would prohibit the confinement of juveniles in adult jails, (2) closing all large training schools, (3) reducing predispositional detention, (4) raising the maximum age of juvenile court jurisdiction to 18 in all states, and (5) ending the use of detention as a "short, sharp shock" (1989). Schwartz's book is titled (*In)justice for Juveniles* to convey his view that a return to a deterrence orientation is a step backward rather than progress. Schwartz's views are in marked contrast to the administrator of the OJJDP under President Reagan, Alfred Regnery, who argued that juveniles are "Getting Away with Murder" (1985) and that "the deterrent approach should be the main focus of the justice system." There are strong advocates on both sides of the issue, just as there were when the system was being developed.

In this chapter we will review theory and research relevant to two contrasting positions on law enforcement and delinquency—deterrence theory and labeling theory. While they have varied in popularity, ideas central to both underlie continuing debate about how the problem of juvenile delinquency should be addressed. In chapter 11 we will examine programs that implement or reflect these different theories.

Deterrence Theory and Explanations of Delinquency

For much of the twentieth century, social scientists either ignored deterrence or deemed it irrelevant to understanding crime or delinquency. In his influential *Principles of Criminology*, Edwin Sutherland wrote that "control . . . lies in the group pressure, the recognition and response secured by lawful conduct rather than fear of punishment. Not the fear of legal penalties but the fear of loss of status in the group is the effective deterrent" (1924:374). Sutherland argued that the whole psychology underlying the classical school, with its emphasis on free will and the calculation of pleasures and pains, was questionable.

Of the major sociological theories of delinquency examined in chapter 6, none originally included deterrence in its explanation of delinquency. The most popular sociological theories have been motivational theories that focus on the social, cultural, and interactional forces that encourage or discourage lawbreaking. The emphasis has been on people as social and moral beings who make decisions on the basis of values, norms, and beliefs, rather than on the basis of rational calculations of losses and gains. Although social control theory, as an amotivational theory, could readily encompass legal sanctions as a potential barrier to crime and delinquency, only some formulations incorporated such notions (Minor, 1977). Social control theorists have instead focused on what are referred to as "informal" control mechanisms and "positive" social bonds (such as attachment, commitment, involvement, and acceptance of conventional beliefs).

Fear of punishment is a major source of social order in Marxist theory, but it is not viewed as an enduring or healthy basis of order in the long run. From a Marxist perspective, a true socialist order would not have to be maintained by force. However, when social and economic arrangements are not serving the interests and needs of sizeable segments of society, control over legal punishment is one means of keeping the masses in line. Hence, while the classical school and social control theories are often viewed as ideologically contrary to Marxist theory (the latter attacking the status quo and the former defending it), they share in common the belief that people can be constrained, at least in the short run, by actual and anticipated punishment.

Social learning theory focuses on both reward and punishment and can readily encompass any deterrent consequences of actual or threatened legal sanctions. However, the emphasis in social learning theory has been on peer group relationships and informal sanctioning processes. Such processes are viewed as far more important for the explanation of delinquent behavior than legal sanctions. In general, that assumption has proven to be correct.

Deterrence theory has been central to two additional perspectives in criminology, **rational choice theory** (Cornish and Clarke, 1986, 1998) and routine activities theory (Cohen and Felson, 1979; Cohen, Felson and Land, 1980; Felson, 1994). Both perspectives assume that offenders will exhibit some degree of rationality in the selection of targets and that variations in the degree to which potential targets are protected by "capable guardians" is relevant to variation in crime.

Although it had generally been ignored in traditional theories and had been questioned repeatedly by prominent criminologists, the study of deterrence emerged as a major research topic in the late 1960s and continued to grow in prominence in the 1970s. This growth in interest was stimulated in part by the development of the labeling perspective, which focused on how laws, law enforcement, and sanctioning played a role in magnifying, rather than reducing, social problems. From the labeling perspective, not only was deterrence questionable, but criminalization, stigmatization, and legal sanctioning were potential *sources* of the very problems they were supposed to solve. On the other hand, deterrence theory argued that reacting to deviance by imposing sanctions deterred individuals from deviance and helped solve problems. The two perspectives stressed contrasting outcomes. However, the development of the labeling perspective had the effect of shifting the emphasis from deviant behavior to *reactions* to deviance and, especially, the *consequences* of reactions to deviance. Thus, although labeling theorists attacked deterrence, the very fact that they did so (coupled with the surge of interest in reactions to deviance) helped to generate new interest in deterrence.

Distinctions in Deterrence Theory

Before we can examine the research literature on deterrence, we must deal with several conceptual matters. First, some deterrence theorists insist that a distinction be made between true deterrence and the **general preventive effects** of punishment. Jack Gibbs, one of the most prominent deterrence theorists, has defined deterrence as "the omission of an act as a response to the perceived risk and fear of punishment for *contrary* behavior" (1975:2). The omission of an act must be linked to assessments of risk and fear before a valid claim can be made that deterrence has occurred. Other circumstances or conditions may inhibit delinquency but not be instances of deterrence. For example, moral commitments and fear of social disapproval can inhibit delinquency (Grasmick and Green, 1980) but they are not directly relevant to deterrence theory.

From Gibbs's perspective, certain ways of preventing or inhibiting lawbreaking do *not* involve fear of punishment and therefore should be viewed as "preventive consequences of legal punishment" rather than deterrence. For example, executing people or locking people up may prevent further involvement in crimes against the public, but this preventive consequence is called **incapacitation** rather than deterrence. In addition, people may refrain from lawbreaking because they know and respect the law. If that knowledge and respect were influenced by punishment, it would be called an *enculturation* or *socialization* consequence of punishment. In this case, punishment would prevent crime through socialization rather than fear of punishment. Gibbs listed a total of ten preventive effects of punishment other than deterrence, but the important point here is that some theorists restrict the term *deterrence* specifically to the inhibiting effects of *fear of punishment*. On the other hand, Gibbs himself noted that we may never be able to isolate the effect of fear of punishment from other preventive effects of punishment (see box 9-1). Thus, the research we will summarize in the next section deals with the preventive effects of punishment but is generally phrased in terms of the study of deterrence.

Another very important conceptual matter in examining the research literature on deterrence (or preventive effects) is the distinction between specific deterrence and general deterrence. **Specific deterrence** refers to the omission of *further* criminal or delinquent acts by the individual who was punished. For instance, if a juvenile refrains from shoplifting because he or she was caught and fears being caught again, this would be an instance of specific deterrence. In contrast, **general deterrence** refers to the omission of criminal or delinquent acts as a result of anticipated or feared punishment among those who have not been punished. The two types of deterrence are distinct, and in this chapter we will focus most extensively on the general deterrence literature.

Another distinction of some importance for understanding the research literature on deterrence is the difference between two types of general deterrence: **absolute deterrence** and **restrictive deterrence**. Jack Gibbs has defined the two as follows:

Box 9-1   Deterrence and Preventive Consequences

Which of the "preventive consequences of legal punishment" does the woman in the cartoon likely have in mind when she proposes that the death penalty is not a deterrent? Which of them is reflected in the man's statement that the death penalty would cut down on repeat offenders?

© Steve Kelley, *The Times-Picayune*, New Orleans

The term "absolute deterrence" denotes instances where an individual has refrained throughout life from a particular type of criminal act because in whole or in part he or she perceived some risk of someone suffering a punishment as a response to the crime. Defined explicitly, "restrictive deterrence" is the curtailment of a certain type of criminal activity by an individual during some period because in whole or in part the curtailment is perceived by the individual as reducing the risk that someone will be punished as a response to the activity, even though no one has suffered a punishment as a consequence of that individual's criminal activity. (1975:32–33)

In short, if people never break the law as a result of fear of punishment, the deterrence process would be absolute. If people merely restrain themselves to some degree, then the process would be restrictive.

These conceptual distinctions are important for assessing the arguments for and against deterrence because parties to the debate may be referring to quite different issues. For example, someone might advance the following argument: "Sending people to prison does not deter crime but, instead, increases it. Look at the high recidivism rate among convicts. Obviously the prisons are not deterring." This particular argument focuses on specific deterrence. It has no bearing on whether the threat of imprisonment deters the *general* public. It would be possible for imprisonment to increase crime among the imprisoned and yet decrease crime among potential offenders. The net effect of an increase in the use of imprisonment might be a decrease in the crime rate (via general deterrence), even given an increase in recidivism (that is, a failure of specific deterrence). The main point is that we make certain we are talking about the same phenomenon when debating the issue of deterrence.

Another possible critique of deterrence might take the following form: "Most Americans drank during the Prohibition. Most adolescents have tried marijuana. Virtually all people break the law sometime during their lives. Obviously people are not deterred by the law." This type of statement focuses on *absolute* deterrence. It has no necessary bearing on whether people *restrict* their involvement in crime or delinquency as a result of fear of punishment. If everyone in a population violates a law sometime, then absolute deterrence does not exist. However, even then, the threat of punishment might restrict people's involvement to one or two transgressions on the average, rather than ten or twelve.

Debates about capital punishment can often confuse different preventive consequences of execution with deterrence as well. The central issue in the debate has been whether capital punishment has a deterrent effect on capital crimes. The grounds for advocating such a response shift whenever someone argues that capital punishment is effective because the people executed are no longer able to commit crimes. Execution is the ultimate form of incapacitation and arguing for it on those grounds is irrelevant to deterrence theory. Similarly, while execution might have an effect on crime through the message communicated about the moral gravity of certain crimes, this would be a socialization effect rather than deterrence.

Research on General Deterrence

Much of the research on deterrence does not deal directly with juveniles since it is based on crime rates for the general population and focuses on punishments that are more commonly meted out to adults than to juveniles. For example, many studies have attempted to measure the deterrent effect of capital punishment by analyzing homicide rates for states or for the total U.S. population. Homicide is actually quite rare among juveniles, as is the probability of being executed or sentenced to death. Prisoners under sentence of death tend to be young adults, and only a small percent of those prisoners are under the age of twenty.

Supreme Court cases relevant to the execution of juveniles were summarized in chapter 2. As recently as 1989 the Supreme Court had ruled that states had the authority to execute nonadults, although it ruled against the execution of the mentally retarded in 2002. In 2004 this exemption was extended to all persons under 18 years of age. There were 73 juvenile offenders under sentence of death in 2004 and 22 juveniles have been executed since the resumption of executions in 1976; 59 percent of them in the state of Texas (American Bar Association, 2004). The United States ranked first worldwide in the number of juvenile executions carried out between 1994 and 2004.

Capital Punishment

Several types of evidence have been brought to bear on the general deterrent effects of **capital punishment** over the years. In early analyses, one type of evidence was based on comparisons of capital crime rates for states with and without the statutory possibility of capital punishment. Such comparisons showed that states without the death penalty do not have higher capital crime rates than states with the death penalty. Similarly, rates in individual states before and after abolishment of the death penalty, as well as comparisons of those before and after statistics with data for states retaining capital punishment, failed to show a deterrent effect. These findings held true even when comparing similar or contiguous states (Bowers, 1974; Schuessler, 1952; Sellin, 1967).

Such research has been criticized, however, in that the statutory possibility of the death penalty does not mean that it is actually used or that those so sentenced are executed. Actually, during the period for which national statistics are available, the peak year for executions was 1938, when 190 prisoners were executed. By the 1950s the number had declined to less than 100 per year, and by 1960 there were 56. From 1968 to 1976 there were none. Between 1977 and 1983 only 11 prisoners were executed; however, beginning in 1984, there have been approximately 20 executions per year.

Does the actual occurrence of executions reduce capital crime rates? The safest answer to that question is that there is no consistent evidence of a deterrent effect. For example, Leonard Savitz (1958) examined the frequency of felony murders in Philadelphia (that is, murders committed in the act of committing another felony) several weeks before and after well-publicized executions and found no evidence of a deterrent effect. In contrast, research by Isaac Ehrlich (1975) claimed to show that executions had a deterrent effect on homicide rates. After analyzing homicide rates and executions from 1933 to 1969, Ehrlich concluded that each additional execution per year may have prevented seven or eight murders. The reason we indicate that he "claimed" to show a deterrent effect is because subsequent evaluations and replications of Ehrlich's analysis have challenged his conclusions. One of the problems is that after 1962 the homicide rate climbed rapidly, while the number of executions continued to decline as it had been doing for several decades (see box 9-2). These factors accounted for most of the association that Ehrlich observed. Moreover, further analysis of data from the 1960s (Forst, 1976) led to the same old conclusion: There is at present no scientifically acceptable support for the view that capital punishment is any more of a deterrent to capital crime than is imprisonment (Zeisel, 1976).

Some researchers have proposed that, contrary to deterrence theory, executions may increase the homicide rate (Bowers, Pierce, and McDevitt, 1984). They suggest that the state's use of lethal violence can have a **brutalization effect**, facilitating homicide rather than deterring it. Yet, a more recent study examined the impact of the resumption of executions on the homicide rate and concluded that contrary to both deterrence and brutalization theory, the resumption had no significant impact on homicide nationwide (Peterson and Bailey, 1988).

Another approach to the capital punishment issue has been to propose that the amount of publicity and drama surrounding executions might make a difference for the detection of deterrent effects. Initial studies suggested that publicity did make a difference. Steven Stack (1987) reported that executions that were publicized sufficiently to be reported in national information sources were followed by reductions in homicide rates. However, subsequent analysis of these same data found several errors in measuring the publicity of executions and reanalyzed the data in different ways. William Bailey and Ruth Peterson conclude that "the cumulative effect of capital punishment on homicides during the execution and subsequent months is essentially zero" (1989:722).

In a more recent analysis Bailey (1990) examined publicity about executions in television news from 1976 through 1987 in relation to monthly homicide rates. This research may be particularly important in the debate over capital punishment since

Box 9-2   Murder Rate and Execution Rate by Year, 1900–2005

The results of research on the impact of executions on murder rates vary, depending on the span of years chosen. Overall, there is no significant correlation between the two series graphed below when all 105 years of data are considered. Which span of time would you pick to make a case for a deterrent effect? Which span of time could you use to argue for a brutalization or escalation effect? Is it appropriate scientifically to be that selective in building your case?

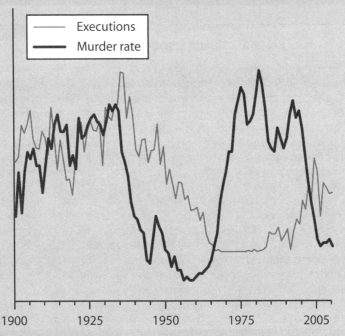

Source: Murder rates updated from Jensen, 2000. Execution data from ESPY file (www.icpsr.umich.edu/NACJD).

television news services have been pressing for permission to televise executions. The possibility of televised executions has generated considerable controversy with encouragement coming from both supporters and opponents of capital punishment (see box 9-3). Bailey found that the amount and nature of television publicity neither reduced (deterrence) nor increased (brutalization) homicide rates. Thus, while some advocates of televised executions cite Stack's research on the topic as empirical support for a possible deterrent effect, more recent analyses do not show publicity to enhance the deterrent effect of executions. Of course, the results of research on publicity cannot necessarily be generalized to preclude deterrent or brutalization effects from televised executions. All we can state is that there is no support for such a prospect in existing data.

A thorough assessment of data and research relevant to the effect of capital punishment on murder rates appeared in an article in the *Stanford Law Review* by John Donahue and Justin Wolfers (2005). First, they note that totally contrary positions can be supported by choosing certain spans of time, although overall there does not appear to be a relationship (see box 9-2). Second, since Canada basically abandoned capital punishment by the mid-1960s it can be examined as a comparison group when assessing patterns of homicide in the United States. Homicide rates are much lower in Canada than the United States, but their patterns over time are highly correlated. Donahue and Wolfers take that pattern as evidence against a deterrent effect. Moreover, your textbook authors have examined the patterns over time to assess whether

---

Box 9-3   Should Executions Be Televised?

Ernest van den Haag (1986), John Ohlin Professor of Jurisprudence and Public Policy at Fordham University, defends the use of the death penalty as "the ultimate punishment" available to society. However, he opposes televised executions because "The death even of a murderer, however well-deserved, should not serve as public entertainment. . . . Further, television unavoidably would trivialize executions, wedged in, as they would be, between game shows, situation comedies and the like." He also argues that televised executions would shift the focus from "the nature of the crime and the suffering of the victim" to the murderer as the victim. He states, "Far from communicating the moral significance of the execution, television would shift the focus to the pitiable fear of the murderer."

A person can oppose the death penalty and still advocate televised executions. For example, opponents of the death penalty might support televised executions on the grounds that the public should not be able to hide from state violence. Moreover, those who believe that the death penalty is justified only if it has a deterrent effect might support televised executions as a means to enhance deterrence. Richard Moran (1990), a sociologist at Mount Holyoke College, proposes that executions be televised on the grounds that it would (1) provide a test of the deterrence argument, (2) ignite public debate, and (3) allow a better evaluation of "the moral foundation of the death penalty." Of course, if van den Haag is correct, then the death penalty would lose its deterrent effect through such drama. If brutalization theorists are correct, then televised executions would backfire and Moran's proposed test would cost lives rather than save them.

Based on your own opinions, in which of the following categories do you belong? What are your reasons for that choice?

	Do you favor execution over life in prison for murder?	
	No	**Yes**
No		
Yes		

Do you favor televised executions?

the United States had lower than expected homicide rates compared to Canada during spans of time where the execution rates were high in the United States and can report that there is no consistent pattern in support of a deterrent effect. Third, Donahue and Wolfers found no support for a deterrent effect when examining variation in homicide rates over four decades for both abolitionist states and states with capital punishment nor when comparing patterns for states that changed their laws at various times. Finally, after examining each study that claims a deterrent effect, they found so many questionable decisions that had a great impact on the results that they were forced to reach the same conclusion as earlier research: There is no consistent evidence of either a deterrent or a brutalization effect of the use of the death penalty.

Certainty and Severity of Punishment

Although the effect of capital punishment on homicide rates remains a hot topic, beginning in the late 1960s social scientists turned to the more general issue of whether variations in the certainty and severity of arrest and imprisonment had a deterrent effect on crime rates. Since its inauguration in a study by Gibbs (1968), a common procedure in U.S. research has been to create measures of the certainty of punishment (for example, the number of admissions to prison for a certain offense relative to the number of such offenses known) and the severity of punishment (for example, the number of months served in prison for a certain type of offense) within the different states. If deterrence notions are to be supported, then states with a higher degree of certainty and severity of punishment for a certain offense should have a lower incidence of that offense than states in which the punishment is less certain and less severe. In general, the data have supported that hypothesis (although, as always, with some controversy). Research also has indicated some variations in deterrence by type of offense.

Atunes and Hunt (1973) noted that research results have been consistent with the conclusion that certainty of punishment "has a mild deterrent impact," but that severity of punishment appears to be relevant only to homicide. Their own analysis led them to similar conclusions. They found that the greater a state's certainty of punishment, the lower that state's crime rates, but that severity of punishment only made a difference for crime rates when certainty of punishment was high. If the chances of being punished are quite low, then it appears that the severity of the punishment does not matter.

Research by Charles Tittle and Allen Rowe (1974) also suggests that the effect of certainty of arrest on crime rates is strongest when a "threshold" in terms of probability of arrest is passed. Thus, certainty of arrest had its greatest impact after the probability of arrest exceeded 30 percent. When the certainty of arrest is very low, variations within that range do not appear to be important for explaining crime rates.

There are several major problems with deterrence research based on official statistics. Two of them are the same problems we have dealt with throughout this text: causal order and spuriousness. It is conceivable that states with high crime rates have low rates of certainty of punishment because of the overload on the criminal justice system. Hence, a relationship between low certainty and high crime rates could reflect the overload rather than deterrence. Moreover, any such relationship could be due to other factors, such as the moral climate or degree of social condemnation regarding particular types of offenses. When the populace is relatively intolerant of a certain crime, that crime may have both a high certainty of punishment and a low crime rate because of moral and social condemnation rather than because of deterrence (Erickson et al., 1977). Finally, a third major problem confronting such research is separating incapacitation effects from deterrence effects. If a state has a high rate of certainty of imprisonment, then the crime rate for that state may be low because heavy contributors to the crime rate are locked away. This would be an incapacitation effect, rather than a deterrence effect.

A study by Michael Geerken and Walter Gove (1977) attempted to assess which interpretation of the relationship between certainty of punishment and crime rates was most plausible—deterrence, overload, or incapacitation. After an analysis of data for all cities with a population of 500,000 or more, they concluded that predictions derived from deterrence theory receive more support than do those derived from interpretations based on overload or incapacitation. To reach this conclusion, Geerken and Gove tested the argument advanced by numerous deterrence theorists (for example, Chambliss, 1967; Andenaes, 1971; Zimring and Hawkins, 1973) that rational, "instrumental" crimes (such as stealing) are more readily deterred than emotional, "expressive" crimes (such as most murders). They posited that the deterrence model, being a rational model, should be most applicable to rational, property-oriented offenses directed at profit and least applicable to emotional crimes of interpersonal violence, such as murder and assault. Their findings (as well as some earlier research) were consistent with this hypothesis. They found that certainty of arrest had a strong impact on property crimes, a moderate association with rape, and little or no relationship to homicide or assault.

Research during the 1980s examining variations in crime and punishment over time has shown that support for the deterrence doctrine is much weaker than earlier research using official statistics suggested. For example, research on clearance rates in relation to crime rates over time for 1964 to 1970 failed to support deterrence theory; that is, changes in clearance rates did not explain variation in crime rates (Greenberg and Kessler, 1982). An analysis of imprisonment rates and crime rates between 1941 and 1978 also concluded that changes in imprisonment rates did not lead to changes in crime rates (Bowker, 1981). Both of these studies dealt with variations over time and, thus, attempted to address the issue of causal order.

Experimental Research on Deterrence

The ideal procedure for dealing with problems of causal order and spuriousness is an experimental model. By manipulating the certainty and severity of punishment and measuring the subsequent effects, the problem of causal order is solved, and by controlling other conditions, problems of spuriousness can be minimized. However, controlled experiments relevant to many deterrence issues are ethically impossible. To illustrate these problems, Hans Zeisel outlined some possible experiments with the death penalty:

> How morally and legally impossible such an experiment is can easily be seen if its details are sketched out. In one conceivable version a state would have to decree that citizens convicted of a capital crime and born on odd-numbered days of the month would be subject to the death penalty; citizens born on even-numbered days

would face life in prison. A significantly lower number of capital crimes committed by persons born on uneven days would confirm the deterrent effect. The date of birth here is a device of randomly dividing the population into halves by a criterion that we will assume cannot be manipulated.

The equally impossible experiment that would test the effect of differential frequencies of execution would require at least three randomly selected groups. In the first group everybody convicted of a capital crime would be executed. In the second, only every other such convict (again selected by lot) would be executed. In the third, nobody would be executed. (1976)

The deterrence experiments that have been done have been limited to such activities as classroom cheating, income tax evasion, and illegal hookups to television cable services. For instance, Tittle and Rowe (1973) carried out an experiment in which college students were allowed to grade their own exams. Students were initially reminded of their moral obligation to grade their exams honestly. Such an appeal had no effect. Later the students were told that spot checks of their accuracy in grading would be made and offenders punished. The threat of sanction did reduce cheating. It was less effective for males than for females and less effective for those experiencing disparity between earned grades and expected grades. Those who were dissatisfied with their grades were less likely to be deterred than those who were content with their grades.

With the cooperation of the Internal Revenue Service, Richard Schwartz and Sonja Orleans (1967) designed a field experiment in which sets of people were randomly assigned (1) to be interviewed and made aware of the penalties for income tax evasion, (2) to be interviewed and reminded of their moral obligation to pay taxes, (3) to be interviewed with neither of these messages, and (4) not to be interviewed at all. Subjects in both the moral-appeal and sanction-threat groups paid more taxes than either of the other two groups, with the moral appeal making the biggest difference.

Mark Stafford and colleagues (1986) designed a deterrence experiment in which college students could cheat in a computer-simulated game. However, they informed subjects about the chances of getting caught and the consequences in terms of points fined. They reported that certainty and severity of punishment each made a difference for cheating but that they magnified the effect of each other as well; that is, certainty of punishment had a much stronger effect at high levels of severity, and severity had a stronger effect at high levels of certainty. Since the same pattern was found in their analysis of homicide data, they believe that their results reflect processes that occur outside the laboratory setting.

Another experiment carried out in the field involved illegal hookups to Home Box Office services through unauthorized descramblers (Green, 1985). Cable thieves were sent a written legal threat and their reaction measured by reexamining cable hookups after the warning. The main reaction was an attempt to hide the violation. Two-thirds of violators removed descramblers and a few others reacted in other ways. Males, the youngest, and the richest were least likely to heed the warning.

In another study, the government filed a complaint for price-fixing against bakeries (Block, Nold, and Sidak, 1981). While the government threatened to take action, no litigation actually took place. Yet, the price of bread began to drop. Braithwaite and Geis (1982) suggest that deterrence is most evident for activities that are profit-oriented and where there is little commitment to the activity.

Although experimental studies can avoid the problems confronting statistical studies, experimental research has its own shortcomings. Cheating is not a crime, and the way people behave in regard to paying taxes and pirating cable TV may not be generalized to other types of behavior. Moreover, in the real world people may not perceive the threat of sanctions, whereas in experimental research the threat can be directly communicated. However, experimental research overcomes many of the limitations of other types of research and has consistently supported deterrence theory.

Survey Research on Deterrence

Several deterrence theorists have noted that deterrence theory is a psychological theory in that it makes certain assumptions about the perception of risk of apprehension or punishment (Jensen, 1969; Waldo and Chiricos, 1972; Erickson et al., 1977; Carmichael and Piquero, 2006). As a "perceptual" theory, deterrence theory presumes some public knowledge and awareness of legal sanctions. In fact, Jensen, Erickson, and Gibbs have argued that the central assertion of the deterrence doctrine is that "the more members of a population perceive the punishment for a type of offense as being certain, severe, and celeritous (swift), the lower the rate for that population" (1978:58). Thus, subjective or perceptual estimates of risk of punishment are viewed as more directly relevant to testing deterrence hypotheses than the probabilities reflected in official statistics

Although most of the research on perceptions of risk has been consistent with the deterrence doctrine, such research has not yielded a perfectly consistent set of conclusions. For example, in interviews with a sample of youths aged 13 to 16, Martin Gold (1970) asked: "Out of every ten kids who commit an offense, how many get caught?" Gold found very little difference between the delinquents and nondelinquents in such perceptions and concluded that his findings cast considerable doubt on deterrence theory.

A study of college students by Bailey and Lott (1976) also failed to support deterrence notions. Bailey and Lott gathered data from 268 college students enrolled in sociology courses and found no significant relationships between number of reported criminal offenses and perceived certainty of punishment (likelihood of arrest and conviction) or between number of reported criminal offenses and perceived severity of punishment.

In contrast to these two studies, numerous others have reported some degree of support for the deterrence theory when studying perceived certainty of punishment (Jensen, 1969; Waldo and Chiricos, 1972; Grasmick and Milligan, 1976; Kraut, 1976; Minor, 1977; Silberman, 1976; Tittle, 1977; Jensen, Erickson, and Gibbs, 1978; Jensen and Stitt, 1982; Montmarquette and Nerlove, 1985). Like objective deterrence research, survey research is more likely to support arguments regarding certainty of punishment than it is to support those regarding severity of punishment.

The key issue confronting perceptual research on deterrence is causal order. It has not been demonstrated that the perceived threat or fear of punishment *precedes* involvement in delinquency. Those who perceive low risk may be those who have violated the law already and have not been caught. Beliefs about punishment and delinquent behavior may be interrelated. Environmental responses to behavior may shape perceptions or beliefs about risk, and those beliefs in turn may affect the probability of future delinquency. Perceptual studies have only shown an association between perception of risk and delinquent behavior.

There have been some studies of people at different points in time and such research suggests greater support for the view that perceptions of risk are affected by successful deviance than for the view that perceived risk has deterrent consequences (Minor and Harry, 1982; Saltzman et al., 1982). However, such research has been based on undergraduates followed over a relatively short period of time and has focused on drug use and minor forms of theft. As one of those studies concludes, ". . . even after a decade of intensified perceptual deterrence research, very little is known about the relationship between perceptions and behavior" (Paternoster et al., 1985:430).

The most recent research on deterrence issues focuses on the link between law enforcement and perceptions of risk. Based on Colorado inmates, Stephanie Carmichael and Alex Piquero (2006) found that the more arrests inmates had experienced relative to their self-reported crimes, the greater the inmates' estimates that they might be caught for a crime. As the ratio of arrests to offenses increases, the inmates' perceived certainty of punishment increases. It is clear that individual sanction experiences can affect individual perceptions of certainty. However, Gary Kleck and his colleagues have investigated whether actual punishment levels as measured by official statistics are reflected in the general public's perceptions of the certainty, severity, and swiftness of punishment. They found "no detectable impact of actual punishment levels on perceptions of punishment" (Kleck et al., 2005:623). Thus, although inmates' personal experiences seem to affect their perceptions, there is little evidence that general public perceptions reflect the realities of law enforcement. In short, what people perceive may be related to their past experiences and future behavior, but does not appear to be a product of actual enforcement by the justice system.

Although each type of deterrence research has its shortcomings, the shortcomings vary from one type to another. Thus, perceptual research has not demonstrated causal order, but it has suggested an association between perceived risk and criminal or delinquent behavior in many different samples of the population. Experimental work solves the problem of causal order, but it has been limited to a narrow range of lawbreaking activities and its findings may not be generalizable to everyday situations. Deterrence research has been confronted with issues of spuriousness, incapacitation, overload, and all the problems stemming from the use of official statistics. At present, the whole body of research supports the *tentative* conclusion that stiffer law enforcement would likely reduce the extent of several forms of crime and delinquency. Although this hypothesis has not been proven conclusively, there appears to be more compatible than contrary evidence.

It is important to remember that such a statement neither requires nor necessitates a get-tough approach to delinquency prevention (see chapters 10, 11, and 12). The school, family, peer groups, beliefs about proper and improper conduct, and a variety of other social forces exert greater influences on behavior than fears or beliefs about legal punishment. Programs attempting to change experiences within these settings can be advocated as potentially more consequential than increasing the certainty, severity, or celerity of punishment. However, that view does not mean that legal sanctions make no difference for behavior.

Labeling Theory

Our criminal and juvenile justice systems are based on the assumption that laws that accord the state the right to regulate certain types of conduct are necessary for the prevention and control of undesirable or injurious behavior. Moreover, the enforcement of those laws is presumed to be necessary if they are to have their intended effects. Such assumptions, at one time taken for granted, have been challenged for several decades now by *labeling theorists*, who advocate examining the unanticipated, hidden, and negative consequences of law and law enforcement.

Labeling theorists have focused on three issues involving the law and law enforcement: (1) the creation of and changes in the legal categories applied to people and their behavior, (2) circumstances affecting the actual application of legal labels, and (3) the individual and societal effects of the labeling process. One of the most quoted statements in the sociology of deviance is Howard Becker's observation:

> Social groups create deviance by making rules whose infractions constitute deviance, and by applying those rules to particular people and labeling them as outsiders. From this point of view, deviance is not a quality of the act a person commits, but rather a consequence of the application of rules and sanctions to an "offender." The deviant is one to whom the label has successfully been applied; deviant behavior is behavior that people so label. (1963:9)

In **labeling theory** the focus is not on the causes and correlates of deviant acts but on the social and political construction of the rules defining acts as deviant and the labeling process involved in applying and enforcing those rules.

The basic thesis with regard to the laws defining criminal and delinquent conduct is that they represent the values and interests of those groups, organizations, and entrepreneurs who are able to organize resources and influence legislation. Whenever a new category of people or conduct is "criminalized" or an old one "decriminalized" we should expect, according to labeling theorists, that certain groups, organizations, or individuals were at work providing the moral entrepreneurship leading to changes in the law.

Labeling theorists challenge us to ask questions like the following:

1. Why is marijuana use illegal but tobacco legally available to most members of society?

2. Why is alcohol use acceptable but other, less serious, forms of drug use criminalized?

3. Why were status offenses included in definitions of delinquency and why are they now being separated from that category?

4. Why is youth crime dramatized when the most profitable crimes involve adults?

The answers to such questions can be found by studying the people, groups, and organizations involved in the creation and change of legal categories.

Labeling theorists also direct our attention to the application of labels and argue that those who are most likely to be labeled are those who lack the resources necessary to avoid such processes. They presume that since most people have engaged in activities for which they *could* have been caught and processed, it is not really the offense that determines reactions but other characteristics of the offender such as race, gender, and social status (see chapter 3).

Just as the nature of laws reflects the values and interests of people with the resources to shape legislation, the enforcement and application of laws is viewed as a reflection of power. Punishment is most certain and severe among those who lack the resources to avoid it. Thus, the labeling perspective approaches the explanation of laws and their application in much the same manner as Marxist and conflict theories (see chapters 2 and 6).

The most unique feature of labeling theory is its emphasis on the role that legislation and law enforcement can play in perpetuating or magnifying problems at both the societal and individual levels. In considering the deviance of individuals, labeling theorists emphasize the role that organizational processing plays in *engulfment* in deviant careers. In considering deviance on a societal level, they focus on the *secondary expansion* of social problems as a result of the legal reaction to them. Arguments that processing children as delinquent has the self-fulfilling consequence of encouraging further delinquency reflect the approach of labeling theorists to individual deviance, while arguments concerning the consequences of overcriminalization or overlegislation reflect their societal concern. In both instances, the emphasis is on the role that laws and law enforcement can play in compounding the problems they are intended to solve. We will consider arguments about the general consequences of criminalization (**general labeling effects**) first and then turn to arguments and research relevant to the effects of labeling on offenders (**specific labeling effects**).

Drug Legislation

An area in which labeling arguments have been particularly forceful is with regard to the prohibition of various kinds of drugs. The view that the criminalization of drugs contributes to the crime problem rather than reduces it was a popular argument in the late 1960s and early 1970s and was revived in political debates of the late 1980s and 1990s. While associated with liberal and radical politics in the first wave, the position has been embraced by a broad range of scholars and politicians in more recent times (see Trebach, 1988; Inciardi, 1986). The "war on drugs" mounted by President George Bush and Drug Czar William Bennett in the late 1980s prompted several counterproposals to decriminalize the activity as a means of lowering its profitability.

With regard to drug laws, Erich Goode has written that "ironically and tragically, it is the law and its enforcement that is principally responsible for the size of the addict population, for the recent increase in addiction, and for a majority of the most harmful features of drug use and the drug scene" (1972:181). However, in supporting such labeling arguments the emphasis tends to be on the way laws and their enforcement transform the drug problem *in general*, rather than on the way they affect the specifically targeted behavior. For example, Goode summarized data that suggested that the number of heroin addicts decreased but that addiction in general was transformed following the passage of the Harrison Act in 1914 and the establishment of the Bureau of Narcotics in 1930. With the passage of the Harrison Act, over-the-counter sale of narcotic preparations was outlawed. A deterrence theorist could legitimately argue that legislation had a general deterrent effect on heroin addiction. However, in attacking deterrence arguments, Goode shifted the focus to addiction in general. After noting the apparent deterrent impact of outlawing heroin, Goode argued:

> . . . what happened as a result of the Harrison Act was not a diminution of a once large addict population but the appearance of a totally different population altogether. Far from reducing a problem, legislation and enforcement practices on drugs appear to have *created a problem* out of whole cloth. The federal laws outlawing the sale of narcotics seem to have created three distinct groups from the existing addict population. The first of these represents the majority of the middle-class addicts, mostly women; when the supply of opium and morphine was discontinued for the nervous, distressed housewife, she eventually turned to the use of barbiturates, under the care of her physician. . . . The second group created by the narcotic laws consists of those addicts who discontinued use altogether. But it is likely that this segment comprised the least addicted of the turn-of-the-century addict population. . . . The third segment of the addict population constitutes the present group of "street" addicts. A certain proportion of the earlier addicts refused to discontinue the use of narcotics, and since they did not, or could not, obtain legally available drugs, they became dependent on an illegal supply and thus automatically joined the ranks of the criminal underworld. (1972:193–94)

In sum, the evidence mustered is not directly contrary to deterrence arguments. No data indicate that the outlawing of heroin led to an overall increase in the extent of heroin addiction. The arguments and evidence presented are more relevant to the shaping or transformation of the drug problem than to the inability of the legislation to deter the prohibited activity.

Even arguments concerning some of the secondary problems generated by the outlawing of heroin have been challenged. For instance, both Schur and Goode believed that drug legislation and law enforcement contributed to the creation of an addict subculture. Goode argued that before the passage of the Harrison Act there was "no addict subculture of any significance" and that "it was the criminalization of addiction that created addicts as a special and distinctive group" (1972:195). On the other hand, William McAuliffe argued that "there can be no doubt that there was a substantial subculture of drug users" before the outlawing of heroin (1975:225). In analyzing research published in 1928, McAuliffe found what he considered to be all the major features of a "criminal-addict subculture" *before punitive laws came into effect.* According to McAuliffe, the legislation did not cause the problem; rather the problem developed because of the absence of controls. Thus, punitive drug laws were a response to an already existing problem. Moreover, following the passage of the Harrison Act, the prevalence of heroin addiction in some settings declined (O'Donnell, 1967).

The argument that addicts are driven to commit secondary forms of crime as a result of the law has been criticized as well. McAuliffe claimed that "almost all heroin addicts are deviant prior to drug dependence and are not mere victims of an innocently acquired habit and unreasonable laws" (1975:228). James Q. Wilson argued along similar lines. He noted that we really do not know the extent to which other crimes would be affected if heroin were legalized because as many as three-fourths of known addicts have been found to have records for delinquent acts before their drug dependence. However, Wilson also noted that "heroin addiction does necessitate some degree of involvement in crime beyond that which would occur without addiction" (1975). In contrast, Greenberg and Adler (1974) have argued that criminal activity in general would be about the same regardless of addiction.

In a study of narcotic addicts admitted to the California Civil Addict Program, researchers found that addicts had a higher rate of property crime (both in terms of arrests and self-reports) during periods of addiction than at times when they were not using narcotics daily (McGlothlin, Anglin, and Wilson, 1978). In short, criminal activity does seem to be reinforced by addiction even though many addicts would have been involved in criminal activity despite their addiction. McGlothlin and his colleagues concluded that although policies that limit daily use of narcotics may not lead to total abstinence, they show promise of minimizing the social costs of addiction.

The Prohibition of Alcohol

Labeling theorists view laws as the outcome of activities by moral entrepreneurs and interest groups to get their point of view embodied in the law. The 1919 Volstead Act that prohibited the manufacture, sale, or transportation of liquor in the United States has been attributed to the activities of such groups as the "Anti-Saloon" League and the Women's Christian Temperance Union, who were defending the values of small-town and rural Protestants against the growing urban, Catholic population. Joseph Gusfield (1963) argues that Prohibition was a "symbolic crusade" in the sense that the prohibitionist legislation symbolically reaffirmed the points of view of a threatened group of people. It did not matter whether it would work or not in addressing alcohol problems. What was important was the symbolic victory of native Protestants threatened by immigration, urbanization, and industrialization.

It is commonly believed that Prohibition failed or actually made the alcohol problem worse. This conclusion is perpetuated in criminology texts with virtually no discussion of historical evidence on the topic (e.g., Siegel, 1989:378–80; Scarpitti and Andersen, 1992:154). The fact that this period is called "The Roaring Twenties" conveys the wild, carefree image of America during that time. Organized crime gained control over the supply of liquor. People made liquor at home. Illegal bars, or "speakeasies," flourished. Prohibition certainly did not stop alcohol use and transformed it in several ways.

However, it is not altogether clear that the prohibition of alcohol failed to affect the activity toward which it was directed, and, we can actually turn to a labeling theorist, Goode (1978), for a summary of evidence that Prohibition did attenuate some aspects of the "alcohol problem." Goode argued that the repeal of Prohibition was not a result of clear evidence of its failure to reduce alcohol consumption and related problems but, rather, reflected gains in political, organizational, and economic power by groups opposed to Prohibition. In short, the repeal of Prohibition was the product of yet another symbolic crusade with groups pursuing their interests and values regardless of actual evidence. Ironically, to strengthen the case for the repeal of Prohibition as a symbolic event, Goode argued that there was considerable evidence that the legislation had worked! It is ironic because in the course of defending one labeling argument, Goode supports the deterrent effects of prohibitionist legislation. He notes that estimates of alcohol consumption were lower for the Prohibition period, that alcohol-related traffic fatalities dropped, and that cirrhosis of the liver declined as well.

While the deterrent effects of Prohibition may seem only remotely related to juvenile delinquency, it is analogous to the failures of legislation that have provided the fuel for labeling arguments. The general emphasis is on how attempts at legal control backfire or boomerang. Yet, to argue that Prohibition was repealed because it did not work would imply a rational, reasonable response to reality—a position contrary to the emphasis on the symbolic, value-laden sources of legislative change. The most dramatic evidence of the "irrationality" of its repeal would be evidence that it worked. Hence, Goode's inadvertent defense of deterrence theory. In subsequent editions of his work, Goode (1989) recognized the implications of those findings and actually opposed legalization of many forms of illicit drugs on the grounds that the law does constrain use to some degree.

Evidence of the legislation's deterrent effect on some aspects of the alcohol problem does not mean that the overall consequences of Prohibition were positive. It may have contributed to other sorts of problems. It may have given organized crime an economic boost. It may have led to a black market and necessitated association with all sorts of undesirable characters in order to get a drink. Indeed, there is evidence that murder rates escalated because of competition over the illicit market despite the fact that lower alcohol use should have meant lower homicide rates (Jensen, 2000). As we noted for drug legislation, labeling theorists require a consideration of a wide range of secondary problems that may be generated in attempts to deal with the primary one. Yet, the development of secondary problems and the transformation of the nature of problems as a result of legislation do not rule out deterrent consequences.

It should also be noted that the apparent effect of prohibitionist legislation on cirrhosis death rates does not mean that prohibitionist legislation is the only force affecting alcohol use. In addition to the ever-present possibilities of spurious relationships, figure 9-1 shows that cirrhosis death rates began a long decline in the mid-1970s with no states prohibiting alcohol use. Yet, there has been an increase in prohibitionist activity of other types. There have been changes in laws governing the age required for alcohol consumption, the legal consequences of driving under the influence have been increased, and organizations such as Mothers Against Drunk Driving have provided considerable moral enterprise for regulating behavior relevant to alcohol use.

Specific Labeling Effects

Although it was rooted in earlier theories and some early works on crime, labeling theory emerged in the 1960s as a critique of the official processing of several forms of deviance. According to labeling theorists, sociolegal categories or typifications such as "delinquent," "retarded," or "mentally ill" are applied to only a fraction of the people to whom they could be applied (generally, those without the resources to resist such labeling). Those to whom such labels are applied are reacted to by others in terms of the label and are gradually "engulfed" in deviant roles. In the words of one of the earliest labeling theorists, "The person becomes the thing he is described as being" (Tannenbaum, 1938:20).

Edwin Lemert (1967), one of the major figures in the development of the labeling perspective, introduced a distinction between **primary deviance** and **secondary deviance** to distinguish between the initial acts of rule breaking which can result in labeling, and acts that reflect acceptance of a deviant role, identity, or career. One means

Figure 9-1   Death Rate per 100,000 (right axis) from Cirrhosis of the Liver and Number of Prohibitionist States (left axis)

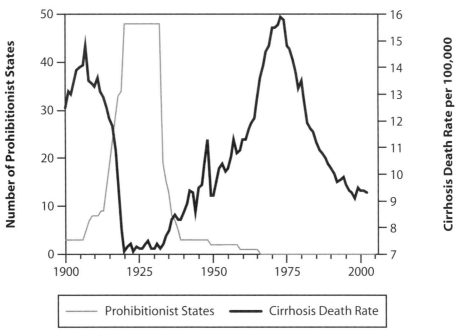

Source: Jensen, 2000.

by which primary deviance is transformed into secondary deviance is through labeling. While initially a youth might engage in a series of deviant acts that have little meaning ("I was just having fun," "We were just fooling around," etc.), the process of being caught and labeled can dramatize those events and the "roles" or "identities" associated with them. When those activities become a reflection of a career or acceptance of a particular role, then future rule breaking takes on new meaning and is called secondary deviance. Labeling theorists have been interested primarily in describing and explaining the creation of secondary deviance, and the labeling process is central to their explanation. The emphasis in the study of juvenile delinquency has been on the consequences of labeling for youth who are labeled.

Juvenile Justice and Labeling

The earliest statement of a labeling argument specifically relating to juvenile delinquency appeared in Frank Tannenbaum's *Crime and the Community* (1938). Tannenbaum argued that the tagging and processing of the young delinquent was a "dramatization of evil" that had self-fulfilling consequences.

> The process of making the criminal, therefore, is a process of tagging, defining, identifying, segregating, describing, emphasizing, making conscious and self-conscious; it becomes a way of stimulating, suggesting, emphasizing, and evoking the very traits that are complained of. If the theory of relation of responses to stimulus

has any meaning, the entire process of dealing with the young delinquent is mischievous in so far as it identifies him to himself or to the environment as a delinquent person. . . . The person becomes the thing he is described as being. Nor does it seem to matter whether the valuation is made by those who would punish or by those who would reform. (1938:19–20)

This line of argument has been extended to deviance in general (see Lemert, 1967) and to a variety of specific types of deviance (for example, mental illness). However, the basic logic is the same in each instance: official processing results in the application of labels to which others react in such a manner that they propel those so labeled into careers of crime and delinquency.

In the 1960s and 1970s it was labeling theorists who mounted the most vociferous criticisms of juvenile justice in the United States. Although the juvenile court was initially conceived as an experiment in the decriminalization of juvenile lawbreaking, labeling theorists tended to view the actual changes that the court wrought as minimal. Edwin Schur argued that despite the terminology employed in juvenile justice, the "adjudicated delinquent is in fact stigmatized, punished, and potentially criminalized" (1973:87). The focus in this statement, however, is on how being processed through the juvenile justice system affects the individual juvenile. This specific focus is in contrast to the labeling theorists' concern over the more general effects of drug legislation and consensual crimes. The labeling theorists' major criticism of the juvenile court has been the alleged impact of adjudication on those processed through the system, or what we call *specific labeling* (in contrast to *specific deterrence*).

Ideas about the general labeling effects of juvenile law and its enforcement are only hinted at in the literature. For example, the broad scope of juvenile delinquency statutes might promote a view among adolescents in general that laws are totally arbitrary and deserving of little respect. This possibility is suggested by Schur's argument that increased clarity, precision, and limits on the legal compass of juvenile law and juvenile court jurisdiction "would probably generate among young people greater respect for the legal system" (1973:169). An implicit assumption underlying such a statement is that juvenile law and its enforcement may have consequences for the attitudes of the juvenile population in general and not just for those who directly experience the system.

Research on the Specific Effects of Labeling

As we have just noted, the labeling theorists' major criticism of juvenile justice has been the possible deleterious consequences of official processing and adjudication for those juveniles who are netted by the system. In this view, juvenile processing does not deter further delinquency through fear of further apprehension and processing, nor does it prevent additional delinquency through rehabilitation of the offender. Rather, the labeling critique has emphasized the role that the juvenile justice system may play in facilitating further delinquent or criminal behavior.

In this section we will consider research that has focused on the consequences of official processing for future behavior and adolescent self-images. The latter topic is of most significance to the labeling theorists since they are interested in deviant behavior that represents or reflects a person's identity or self-image. A behaviorist would be most interested in the consequences of official processing for future *behavior* and would not feel it necessary to consider the effects of labeling on identity or self-image. These topics would be viewed by the behaviorist as hypothetical mental constructs that contribute little or nothing to understanding actual behavior. Most labeling theorists would find the focus on the consequences of official processing for subsequent rates of crime and delinquency as *relevant* to labeling theory but not necessarily *crucial*. From a labeling perspective, Schur has argued that sociologists have been challenged to study the self-concept of the deviating individual as a crucial dependent variable "to which we should pay more attention than to the deviating behavior itself" (1969:311). Of course, the value of such a viewpoint depends on the theoretical inclinations of different publics, and certainly a behaviorist (e.g., learning theorists such as B. F. Skinner) would not find such an emphasis crucial. Recognizing that there are divergent points of view, we will consider research on attitudes and self-conceptions, as well as future behavior. First, however, we will consider research that has attempted to determine whether official processing of juveniles has a specific deterrent or a specific labeling effect.

Specific Deterrence versus Specific Labeling

How can we tell if official processing by the juvenile justice system increases involvement in crime and delinquency? One answer might be to determine the relationship between adult crime and juvenile delinquency. Why not just look at the proportion of juveniles with a record who go on to acquire a record as adults? For instance, in a study of males and females born in 1949, Shannon (1976) reported the following progression of contacts with the police: of 677 white males, about 61 percent (414) acquired a record between the ages of 6 and 18. Of those 414, 326 acquired a record after age 18. In sum, of those white males labeled as juvenile delinquents, around 78 percent acquired a subsequent record. In contrast, of the white males who did *not* acquire a juvenile record, about 50 percent acquired a record as an adult. Thus, those labeled as delinquent as youths were more likely than those not so labeled to acquire records when they were older. *One* possible conclusion based on such a difference is that labeling when young increases the chances that further delinquent or criminal acts will be committed in the future.

However, there are other possible explanations. We have already encountered a number of social characteristics, experiences, and attitudes that are correlated with juvenile delinquency. These characteristics may account for involvement in lawbreaking activity over a period of time. Thus, a high-risk youth at age 13 may remain a high-risk person at 18, 21, and beyond, whether or not he or she is caught and labeled. In short, such a finding does not tell us whether the *labeling experience* increases the probability of future crime.

The scientifically ideal methodological procedure for assessing whether official processing of juveniles increases involvement in crime or delinquency would be an experiment in which youths were ignored or processed on a random basis. Under the right circumstances, the groups would be nearly the same on every conceivable characteristic *except* the one under experimental control (that is, being processed or labeled). Since such experiments are legitimately challenged on ethical grounds, the alternative is to examine the relationship between labeling and future delinquency among youths who are as similar as possible in terms of other characteristics. This procedure involves comparing "matched pairs" and was the basis for Martin Gold and Jay Williams's study of "the aftermath of apprehension" (1969). Gold and Williams's data included self-reports of delinquent activity, as well as police and court records. On this basis, they were able to compare youths involved in delinquency who had been caught with youths who had not been caught. Out of 847 cases, 74 youths had been apprehended. Gold and Williams were able to match 35 of these cases with boys who had committed similar offenses and who had other similar characteristics, but who had not been apprehended. Of the 35 pairs, apprehended youth had a higher subsequent delinquent involvement than the nonapprehended youth in twenty comparisons. On the other hand, in ten comparisons the youth who had been apprehended reported *less* involvement than the nonapprehended youth, and five pairs exhibited comparable involvement. The data are contrary to the view that apprehension reduces the chances of further delinquency and suggest that the opposite may be a more likely occurrence.

David Farrington reports similar results for working-class boys in London (1977). Farrington studied boys with similar degrees of involvement in delinquency at age 14 and examined the delinquency scores at age 18 for youths who had been determined guilty in court compared to youths who had not appeared in court. The delinquency of those labeled was greater by age 18, while delinquency had decreased for those not labeled. He could not find any other characteristic that would account for this difference other than the labeling experience itself.

Lloyd Klemke (1978) attempted to determine whether apprehension for shoplifting amplified shoplifting, as suggested by labeling theory, or terminated shoplifting, as suggested by deterrence theory. Among high school students he found that there were very few significant relationships between apprehension by store personnel or parents and shoplifting activity, although relationships were consistently in the direction suggesting higher rates for those caught than those not caught. Similarly, youth who were referred to the police had higher rates than those who were dealt with less formally. However, these results were statistically insignificant as well. Moreover, Klemke acknowledges that some of the shoplifting activity he measured could have occurred before youths were apprehended. There were also no controls for variables that might make the relationship spurious (i.e., variables related to the frequency of shoplifting and the chances of getting caught).

While these studies are typically cited as support for the labeling perspective, their meaning is actually quite ambiguous. For example, if the reason the youths who were caught had a higher subsequent rate of involvement in delinquency was because they realized that nothing much happened after being caught, then the results could support deterrence theory. In contrast, if the experience increased subsequent delinquency by either decreasing other opportunities, increasing association with other labeled youth, stigmatizing the youth, or leading to further social rejection, then the results could support labeling theory. Without evidence concerning the mediating processes or mechanisms affecting future behavior, the results could support either point of view.

In contrast to research in which one set of youths had experienced a legal reaction and the other set had experienced none, most of the research cited as relevant to labeling focuses on the effects of *different reactions* to crime. For example, comparisons have been made between juveniles who received a court hearing and those who were released short of any formal procedure (Meade, 1974). Other studies have compared youths who became wards of the court with youths who did not (McEachern, 1968). Terence Thornberry (1971) analyzed the subsequent offense records of youths in terms of the degree of severity of their original dispositions. In the study of deterrence, these comparisons would be viewed as relevant to establishing the *marginal deterrent efficacy* of a reaction to delinquency since the comparison is between or among *different possible reactions* (Gibbs, 1975:33). When assessing marginal deterrent effects, the question is what "margin" of delinquency is deterred by a particular reaction beyond that which would occur given an alternative reaction. Similarly, studies of different reactions cited as relevant to labeling theory are really dealing with *marginal labeling effects* (in that these studies attempt to determine the extent to which a more severe reaction leads to a higher subsequent rate of delinquency). Actually, the topics dealt with in the next two chapters (alternative reactions, imprisonment, "scared straight," diversion, and restitution) are all potentially relevant to issues of labeling effects and specific deterrence. In the remainder of this section, we will deal with research that has been cited or presented as relevant to labeling theory or that has been couched in labeling terms.

Labeling and Future Behavior

The three studies of marginal labeling effects previously mentioned (Meade, 1974; McEachern, 1968; and Thornberry, 1971) have generated findings that are both consistent and inconsistent with labeling arguments. For example, in a study of more than 2,000 youths in eight California counties, Alexander McEachern (1968) reported that those who were made wards of the court showed *less* subsequent involvement in delinquency than those dealt with less severely, but those probationers who had the most contact with their probation officers had the highest rates of subsequently detected offenses. The latter finding could mean that the risk of *detection* increases as contact with probation officers increases. Thus, the finding may not be evidence of a labeling effect. Thornberry's study (1971) of the delinquent careers of all boys born in Philadelphia in 1945 yielded similar equivocal results. He found that youth who had been institutionalized had a lower subsequent volume of delinquency and lesser involvement in terms of seriousness of the offenses committed than youth who had not been institutionalized. On the other hand, measures of the severity of disposition were associated with a *higher* volume of delinquency for *some* offenders. Among the white youths and the less serious offenders, severity of reaction was associated with higher subsequent delinquency. Finally, Meade's research (1974) indicated that youths who faced a court hearing had higher subsequent rates of detected delinquency than those dealt with less formally.

These results are so variable that we cannot reach a firm conclusion about the effect of labeling. Moreover, the findings are not clearly relevant to labeling theory to begin with, since they focus on alternative reactions *after* initial apprehension and labeling. In addition, studies that focus on subsequent delinquency activity *that is detected* (that is, recidivism rates derived from police data) do not have a clear bearing on the effects of labeling on *actual* subsequent behavior. As we will discover in chapter

10, some experimental programs appear to have low recidivism rates compared to the recidivism rates of available alternatives. The lower rates may reflect the unwillingness of more tolerant probation officers to officially recognize a subsequent offense for youths in an experimental program. Recidivism rates may not be accurate reflections of actual delinquent behavior. Thus, the results of recidivism research can be given a number of alternative interpretations that have little to do with either labeling or deterrence effects.

Labeling and Adolescent Attitudes and Self-Images

Another line of research relevant to labeling and delinquency has focused on the consequences of labeling in a youth's social environment or the potential impact of labeling on values, commitments, or self-images. The results of this type of research have been both consistent and inconsistent with labeling notions. For example, Foster, Dinitz, and Reckless (1972) interviewed boys in trouble with the law and found that very few perceived that their predicaments had generated any difficulties with family or friends. Sethard Fisher (1972) examined the school grade-point averages of probationers before and after being processed and found no demonstrable effect of that experience on school grades. Probationers were found to have lower grades on the average than other students both *before and after* acquiring that legal status.

David Matza (1964) has argued that violation of the commonly held expectations of adjudication gives rise to a "sense of injustice" and that sense of injustice in turn weakens "the bind of the law." In Matza's view, the actual operation of the juvenile court regularly violates "norms of fairness" or "due process," which confirms the delinquent's "conception of irresponsibility and feeds his sense of injustice."

Peggy Giordano (1976) has attempted to test such arguments in a study of juvenile reactions to the justice system. She interviewed youths who had (1) been reprimanded by the police and released, (2) proceeded as far as an intake hearing, (3) been placed on probation, (4) been placed on probation at least twice, or (5) had not been processed by the justice system at all. She found no significant difference in attitudes or behavior between the group with no contact and the contact groups. Among youths who had had some contact, the extent of system contact made no difference for attitudes toward police but was associated with positive attitudes toward probation officers and judges. Youths with more extensive contact judged police, probation officers, and judges as less "effective" than did those with less contact. However, there was no evidence that contact or adjudication generated a sense of injustice.

In contrast, in the study of working-class boys in London, Farrington (1977) found that hostility towards the police increased after conviction. Since they were able to examine attitudes before and after conviction as well as compare these boys with the nonlabeled youths at different points in time, their results are more meaningful than studies that compare youths with different degrees of labeling using data gathered after the experience alone (e.g., Giordano's study). The British research supports Matza's argument.

Gary Jensen (1972) examined the self-images of youths with police records and those without and found that the relationship was quite variable in different categories of junior and senior high school students. Among African-American males who had police records for one offense or two or more offenses, about 47 percent at least sometimes thought of themselves as delinquent, compared to 56 percent of the white males with a record for one offense and 72 percent of the white males with a record for two or more offenses. Among both African Americans and whites, about one-third of those without records at least sometimes thought of themselves as delinquent. Thus, in both groups, those with a record were more likely to think of themselves in terms of the label. However, the biggest differences between the labeled and unlabeled occurred among whites. Jensen also found that labeling differentiated most among youths who held fairly positive attitudes toward the law. His analysis was consistent with an earlier study by Leroy Gould (1969) in which Gould argued that if the label "delinquent" or "troublemaker" is commonly applied to a particular group, then the labeling process may have little personal relevance.

Suzanne Ageton and Delbert Elliott (1974) improved upon Jensen's study by examining changes in attitudes over time and by limiting their analysis to subjects who had no contacts with the police or court at the beginning of the study. They found that respondents with subsequent police contacts demonstrated "substantial" gains in measures of delinquent orientations as compared to respondents who had no such subsequent contacts. Moreover, neither controls for self-reported delinquency nor controls for delinquent friends altered this finding. However, further analysis revealed that police contact was related to increased delinquent orientations only for white youth. Thus, two separate studies based on large random samples of populations have yielded quite similar observations: labeling may be more consequential for whites than for African Americans.

John Hepburn (1977) gathered data from two samples: (1) 105 white males ages 14 to 17 with no record of police contact who were randomly selected from school enrollments, and (2) 96 white males ages 14 to 17 who had had formal contact with the municipal police. Hepburn found that official intervention was not significantly related to self-concept variables when other variables, such as self-reported delinquency, were taken into account. On the other hand, some measures of official intervention did have an impact on respondents' predictions of future delinquency, measures of "commitment to delinquent others," and attitudes toward the police. Hepburn suggested that the relationships between official intervention and measures of "self-satisfaction" or "delinquent identification" are spurious. He argued that the greater the involvement in delinquency, the greater the chances of being labeled and of developing a delinquent identity. However, according to Hepburn, official labeling or intervention itself has no impact on delinquent identity.

Once again, we are confronted with some consistent and some divergent findings. Data from Hepburn's study, as well as from Ageton and Elliott's, suggest that labeling affects the development of delinquent value orientations. The studies by Jensen, Ageton and Elliott, and Thornberry suggest that labeling effects are more prominent for whites than for African Americans. However, Hepburn found a spurious relationship between official intervention and measures of delinquent identity, whereas Jensen implied that official intervention did affect the degree to which an adolescent viewed himself in terms of the label.

The inconsistency may reflect differences in the samples studied by the researchers. Jensen (1980) found that youths who acquired a record were more likely to express delinquent self-evaluations than those without police records, even when the variable of self-reported delinquent behavior was controlled. Hepburn found that official intervention had no impact when self-reported delinquency was taken into account. However, Hepburn's sample was purposely designed to overrepresent delinquents with records. Jensen's sample included only those officially recorded delinquents who happened to be included in a representative sample of the junior and senior high school populations in the area studied. In short, Hepburn's sample included more labeled delinquents than Jensen's, and possibly more heavily involved delinquents as well. If labeling has different consequences depending on the extent to which the sample is involved in delinquency, then the apparently disparate findings of these two studies could be reconciled. In a further analysis of the issue, Jensen found that the differences in delinquent self-evaluations between the labeled and unlabeled are very slight among youths who report having committed several delinquent acts. However, among adolescents who are less involved in delinquency, differences between the labeled and unlabeled are more prominent. Along similar lines, Farrington (1977) reports that while convictions prior to age 14 increased delinquency, subsequent convictions did not intensify the difference. In view of such findings and those outlined previously, it appears that the effects of labeling may be quite variable from one group to another.

Strengths and Weaknesses of Labeling Theory

Throughout this summary we have referred to labeling as a "theory" and discussed it in contrast to deterrence theory. Deterrence theorists argue that variations and changes in the perceived risks of legal punishment will affect the probabilities of subsequent criminal and delinquent behavior. In contrast, labeling theorists generally claim that official reactions intended to inhibit delinquency "may" have the opposite effect. It is virtually impossible to falsify a claim that official reactions "may" propel youths into delinquent careers. Conceivably, the vast majority of youths might go straight for the remainder of their lives after being caught, processed, and labeled, and the statement would not be falsified. If translated into a more definitive claim such as "youths who spend time in detention will engage in more delinquent activity after that experience than they did prior to it," then the findings that would falsify or support the statement are clearer. Thus, while labeling theory helped "sensitize" the justice system to the potential harm of certain types of negative labeling, it did not develop into a set of testable propositions to be pitted against deterrence theory or other sociological theories.

In chapter 3 we summarized the literature on the role of extralegal variables on official labeling. That literature suggests that the frequency and seriousness of delinquent activity are primary determinants of labeling but that there are some differences by social background. Thus, labeling is not as arbitrary and discriminatory as claimed by labeling theorists. On the other hand, the data do not allow the dismissal of charges of bias. Unexplained differences by social background appear often enough to warrant continued investigation.

Finally, the labeling theorist's arguments may no longer apply to juvenile justice in numerous jurisdictions, partly because practitioners have become sensitive to negative labeling. Many of the treatment and prevention programs we will consider in subsequent chapters attempt to build positive self-images and to counter the types of negative labeling stressed by the theory. Some programs for treating drug and alcohol abuse actually include acceptance of a label as a first step in treatment. For example, in Alcoholics Anonymous admission that one is an alcoholic is viewed as a crucial step toward rehabilitation. However, in the process the meaning of the label is changed and it carries with it group beliefs that the individual can gain control of the problem. Such programs are actually trying to change the meaning of labels in positive directions. However, labeling theory suggests even programs that attempt to avoid dramatizing evil have to be wary of self-fulfilling prophecies and to assess whether acceptance of modified labels has positive or negative consequences. Enough programs have "boomeranged" to warrant continued concern about such prospects.

The Social Meaning of Sanctions

The observation that labeling and sanctions may reinforce, deter, or make no difference for subsequent behavior or self-images has stimulated theoretical attempts to specify the conditions under which sanctions or labels may have different consequences. For instance, Bernard Thorsell and Lloyd Klemke (1972) argued that the labeling process may be both a reinforcement and a deterrent. Its positive and negative consequences for future behavior depend upon several conditions that have yet to be studied. In addition to the stage in a person's deviant career when labels are applied, these conditions include: (1) whether the label is confidential, (2) whether the person labeled cares about or acknowledges the legitimacy or authority of the labeler, (3) whether the label can be easily removed, and (4) whether official labels generate a negative social response.

Other theorists (e.g., Tittle, 1975) have attempted to develop comparable lists of factors that might improve our knowledge of the conditions under which sanctions have different effects. However, very little research has been done in this area. We have seen evidence that perceived threat of punishment may deter some types of offenses more than it does others, but that observation is the only specification suggested thus far in research literature. The fact of the matter is that we know very little about such seemingly simple (but, in reality, complex) issues as the actual meaning of the labeling process or the threat of labeling to juveniles.

Eckland-Olson, Lieb, and Zurcher report that the relationship between perceived threat and behavior is exceedingly complex and depends on interpersonal relationships and a host of situational factors. For example, they propose that "persons rich in associations will fear sanctions more than loners, and those who expect that after a sanction their friends and associates will treat them as before will fear that sanction less than those who expect to be shunned" (1984:160). Based on field observations and interviews with drug dealers, the researchers found that fear of sanctions led drug dealers to restrict their network of relationships. This closure also decreased their opportunities to supply drugs. In this instance, fear of punishment inhibited criminal activity but not directly through fear-related avoidance of the behavior. Rather, restricted interpersonal relationships limited the market for drug dealing. The impact of feared sanctions was mediated by social relationships.

In research carried out among high school students in southern Arizona (Jensen and Erickson, 1978), students were asked to imagine that they had been caught and taken to juvenile court. They were then asked how much each of the following would worry them (their response choices were definitely yes, probably yes, uncertain, probably not, and definitely not): (1) the police might hurt you, (2) the judge might send you to a reformatory, (3) the judge might put you on probation, (4) how your parents might react, (5) a delinquent record might keep you out of college, (6) a record might keep you from getting a good job, (7) other teenagers might think badly of you, (8) your teachers might think badly of you, (9) you might think badly of yourself.

Nearly all the students indicated they would worry about their parents' reaction, and 83 percent indicated they would worry about a record keeping them from getting a good job. Sixty-nine percent would worry about a record keeping them out of college. It was quite common for students to indicate they might think badly of themselves. Relatively few students (34 percent) worried about the reactions of peers, and the least concern was expressed over the possibility of being hurt by the police. With regard to the reactions of significant reference persons or groups, parental reaction was of more concern than either teacher reaction or the reactions of other teenagers.

Jensen and Erickson report some interesting variations in these perceived ramifications of labeling. For each of the nine concerns, females were found to be significantly more concerned than males. Girls were especially more concerned than boys over parental reaction and over the possibility that they might think badly of themselves. Similarly, youths who wanted to go to college were obviously more concerned about jeopardizing their plans than were those who did not plan to go to college. Students who were doing well in school worried more about teacher reaction than students who were not faring well. Students with delinquent friends worried less about the reactions of other teenagers than did students with no delinquent friends. In short, the nature and degree of concern about the possible ramifications of labeling is related to a person's attachments, commitments, and beliefs. Furthermore, the study indicated that those who are not worried about such costs are the most likely to commit delinquent acts.

What relevance do such observations have for labeling and deterrence among juveniles? For one thing, it appears that those who anticipate stigmatic consequences as a result of official labeling are the least likely to engage in behavior that is liable to labeling. In contrast, those most likely to commit delinquent acts are those for whom labeling may be socially meaningless. Similarly, those most likely to be *persistently* or *repeatedly* involved in delinquency are the very youths for whom labeling or official processing generates relatively little concern. If this interpretation is correct, then we would expect that official labeling would *neither* specifically deter *nor* reinforce involvement in delinquency but would instead be a rather meaningless experience. Labeling does not constitute a "dramatization of evil" when there is no audience, no drama, and no shared definition of evil. Thus, if a study of the effects of labeling is based on a sample that includes a sizable proportion of youths who accord little significance to official labels, then the application of labels is likely to be of little consequence in the study. On the other hand, a sample that includes youths who accord legitimacy to official labels might find the experience traumatic and stigmatizing. Moreover, those who find the experience stigmatizing might actually be deterred from further delinquency to avoid further stigmatization.

The study of the social meaning of sanctions suggests a possible **labeling paradox:** those most likely to be affected by labels are those least likely to do things that make them liable to labeling; those who do accord stigmatic significance to labels but become the victims of labeling are likely to refrain from further acts to avoid further stigmatization. Such speculation does not rule out the possibility of labeling effects. For example, if a delinquent record is a source of status or reputation in a particular group or social setting, then labeling could lead to an increase in delinquent behavior through processes of social reinforcement (social learning theory). Similarly, if the labeling experience undermines tenuous "stakes in conformity," or becomes the "last straw" for already shaky bonds between a youth and parents or school, then it could increase the chances of further violations.

The study of the social meaning of sanctions may provide clues as to why some categories of youth are less likely than others to go on to adult crime. For example, the study of delinquent and criminal careers mentioned earlier (Shannon, 1976) revealed that 78 percent of white males who acquired records before age 18 acquired a record after that age. About 48 percent of the white females who had been labeled as juvenile delinquents subsequently acquired records as adults. Thus, the majority of white girls who were labeled did *not* go on to acquire records as adults. Why are girls less likely to acquire subsequent records than boys? As we noted earlier, the answer may have nothing to do with labeling or deterrent effects, but the hypothesis that females are more likely than males to be deterred by labeling is at least tenable. At the very minimum, we should be studying the variable meaning of sanctions or labels in different groups as the possible source of answers concerning the effects of different reactions to delinquency.

Jensen and Erickson's findings regarding the meaning of the labeling process for high school students also are relevant to the study of general deterrence and to some of the sociological positions taken on that issue. At the beginning of this chapter, we cited Sutherland's claim from more than half a century ago that "not the fear of legal penalties but the fear of loss of status in the group is the effective deterrent." For adolescents, that statement should be revised: Apprehension, adjudication, and legal penalties are feared most when they are perceived to entail loss of status, opportunity, and self-respect. Fear of loss of status and loss of opportunity are important barriers to delinquency. It is when such losses are perceived to result from being caught and labeled that the justice system may have its greatest impact.

John Braithwaite's theory of reintegrative shaming (1989) builds on observations about the variable impact of punishment and has prompted renewed interest in the impact of labeling. Braithwaite proposes that **disintegrative shaming**, where offenders are excluded from interaction with the nonoffending populace and suffer loss of opportunity to redeem themselves, increases the odds of further crime. In contrast, **reintegrative shaming** involves efforts to reintegrate the offender with the community and allow personal redemption and forgiveness. He applies the theory to variations among societies as well as among groups within societies. America is considered to be a society that emphasizes disintegrative shaming, where offenders are segregated and stigmatized in perpetuity with little chance for redemption. Several Asian and European nations attempt to avoid imprisonment as a solution to the crime problem and emphasize reconciliation and restitution. Such policies are growing in popularity in the United States (e.g., victim-offender reconciliation programs) but the predominant response to offenders is punitive rather than reintegrative. Labeling theory predicts that most punitive responses to delinquency will backfire because such responses dramatize the offender as evil, isolate and concentrate similarly stigmatized and alienated offenders together, and insist that records of evil continue to have costs for the remainder of an offender's life. These are the characteristics of institutions of disintegrative shaming in Braithwaite's perspective and, in his view, help to explain high rates of crime and recidivism in the United States.

Summary

In this chapter we examined labeling theory and deterrence theory—two divergent points of view about the impact of the law on the social problems the law is intended to solve. From a deterrence perspective, the criminalization of an activity is supposed to reduce the involvement of those punished (specific deterrence) and inhibit involvement in the rest of the populace (general deterrence). Labeling theorists have challenged such notions, arguing that criminalization can transform minor problems into major ones by creating new dimensions of the problem (general labeling effects) and by increasing the criminal involvement of those labeled or punished (specific labeling effects).

Research on issues of general deterrence has progressed from the study of capital punishment to the study of the relationship between perceived risk of punishment and self-reported delinquent behavior to field observation and experiments. At present, there is still no evidence that capital punishment has a general deterrent impact on criminal homicide or on other capital crimes. However, research of several different types (laboratory, field, and natural experiments; analysis of police, court, and corrections statistics for states; and survey studies) has tended to support the conclusion that the greater the threat of punishment for crime and delinquency, the lower the involvement in crime and delinquency. Several issues concerning that relationship (causal order, spuriousness, variations by offense, mediating or intervening processes) have yet to be resolved. However, there is evidence of an *association* of the type predicted by the deterrence perspective.

Labeling theorists are often unclear about whether the law and its enforcement increase the magnitude of the specific activity toward which they are directed or add new dimensions to the total problem. Their arguments seem to apply best to the latter possibility, although even arguments about the secondary effects of drug legislation have been challenged by critics of the labeling perspective. Since arguments about secondary effects are often matters of historical conjecture based on impressionistic evidence, we may never arrive at a resolution to the debate. We can say that there is evidence that property crime is greater for narcotic addicts than for nonaddicts and that it is greater during periods of daily narcotics use than at other times. It appears that addiction reinforces criminal involvement, although many addicts would have been involved despite their addiction. However, the larger issues of the impact of the law and its enforcement on the total crime problem, the delinquency problem, and even problems involving so-called victimless crimes are still subject to debate.

The situation is comparably complex and confusing when we consider issues of specific deterrence versus specific labeling effects. There are bits and pieces of research consistent with both arguments. Clarification of the impact of labeling may evolve from greater attention to a variety of issues concerning the social meaning of sanctions. Both labeling theorists and deterrence theorists have suggested that the consequences of labeling vary depending on characteristics of the authority applying labels, the meaning of such experiences in the social world of different youths, and a variety of other circumstances that shape the relevance of legal sanctions in different environments.

Discussion Questions

1. What role did fear of legal sanctions play in major sociological theories of crime and delinquency? Explain how deterrence could be incorporated into any two theories in this textbook.

2. Edwin Sutherland wrote that "not the fear of legal penalties but the fear of loss of status in the group is the effective deterrent." Based on the material summarized in this chapter, how should that statement be revised?

3. Develop a theory explaining how executions might *increase* rather than decrease homicide rates and contrast it with deterrence theory. What outcome would you expect in regard to executions if both theories were true?

4. Based on the research summarized in your text on publicity of executions, discuss the view that live television coverage could enhance their deterrent impact.

5. What would be the ideal procedure for studying the deterrent effect of capital punishment? Why has such a procedure not been used?

6. Discuss the common view that the prohibition of alcohol during the 1920s and early 1930s failed to curb drinking or made the alcohol situation worse. In what sense was it a failure or a success?

7. It is commonly assumed that heroin addiction leads people to commit property crimes. What other point of view has been advanced concerning the link between the two types of offenses? Is there any evidence to support the common opinion?

8. Findings that apprehended youth have higher subsequent delinquency rates than those not caught has been accepted as support for labeling theory. How might it be interpreted as support for deterrence theory? What would we have to know about the consequences of being caught to consider the results as support for either theory?

9. In your opinion, what characteristics of youth or their social environments affect the meaning and consequences of official labeling? Relate your ideas to the notion of a "labeling paradox" discussed in the text.

10. What would you fear most about acquiring a criminal or delinquent record? How do your concerns compare to those of the youth discussed in the text?

References

Ageton, S. S., and D. S. Elliott. 1974. "The Effects of Legal Processing on Delinquent Orientations." *Social Problems* 22 (October):87–100.

American Bar Association. 2004. "Cruel and Unusual Punishment: The Juvenile Death Penalty." Fact Sheet, March 16, 2004.

Andenaes, J. 1971. "Deterrence and Specific Offenses." *University of Chicago Law Review* 38:537–53.

Atunes, G., and L. Hunt. 1973. "The Impact of Certainty and Severity of Punishment on Levels of Crime in American States: An Extended Analysis." *Journal of Criminal Law and Criminology* 64(4):486–93.

Bailey, W. C. 1990. "Murder, Capital Punishment, and Television: Execution Publicity and Homicide Rates." *American Sociological Review* 55:628–33.

Bailey, W. C., and R. P. Lott. 1976. "Crime, Punishment and Personality: An Examination of the Deterrence Question." *Journal of Criminal Law and Criminology* 67 (March):99–109.

Bailey, W. C., and R. Peterson. 1989. "Murder and Capital Punishment: A Monthly Time-Series Analysis of Execution Publicity." *American Sociological Review* 54 (October):722–43.

Beccaria, C. 1767. *On Crimes and Punishments*. Translated (1963) by H. Paolucci. Indianapolis: Bobbs-Merrill.

Becker, H. 1963. *Outsiders*. New York: Macmillan.

Block, M., F. Nold, and J. Sidak. 1981. "The Deterrent Effect of Anti-Trust Enforcement." *Journal of Political Economy* 89:429–45.

Bowers, W. J. 1974. *Executions in America*. Lexington, MA: D. C. Heath.

Bowers, W. J., G. Pierce, and J. McDevitt. 1984. *Legal Homicide: Death as Punishment in America, 1864–1982*. Boston: Northeastern University Press.

Bowker, L. 1981. "Crime and the Use of Prisons in the United States: A Times Series Analysis." *Crime and Delinquency* 27(2):206–12.

Braithwaite, J. 1989. *Crime, Shame and Reintegration*. Cambridge: Cambridge University Press.

Braithwaite, J., and G. Geis. 1982. "On Theory and Action for Corporate Crime Control." *Crime and Delinquency* 28:292–314.

Carmichael, S. E., and A. R. Piquero. 2006. "Deterrence and Arrest Ratios." *International Journal of Offender Therapy and Comparative Criminology* 50:71–87.

Chambliss, W. J. 1967. "Types of Deviance and Effectiveness of Legal Sanctions." *Wisconsin Law Review* (Summer):703–19.

Cohen, L. E., and M. Felson. 1979. "Social Change and Crime Rate Trends: A Routine Activity Approach." *American Sociological Review* 44:588–608.

Cohen, L. E., M. Felson, and K. C. Land. 1980. "Property Crime Rates in the United States: A Macrodynamic Analysis, 1947–1977; with ex Ante Forecasts for the Mid-1980s." *American Journal of Sociology* 86:90–118.

Cornish, D., and R. V. Clarke, eds. 1986. *The Reasoning Criminal*. New York: Springer-Verlag.

———. 1998. "Understanding Crime Displacement: An Application of Rational Choice Theory." In *Criminology Theory Reader,* edited by S. Henry and W. Einstadter. New York: New York University Press.

Donahue, J. J., and J. Wolfers. 2005. "Uses and Abuses of Empirical Evidence in the Death Penalty Debate." *Stanford Law Review* 58:789–846.

Eckland-Olson, S., J. Lieb, and L. Zurcher. 1984. "The Paradoxical Impact of Criminal Sanctions: Some Microstructural Findings." *Law and Society Review* 18:159–78.

Ehrlich, I. 1975. "The Deterrent Effect of Capital Punishment: A Question of Life and Death." *American Economic Review* 65:397.

Erickson, M. L., J. P. Gibbs, and G. F. Jensen. 1977. "Deterrence and the Perceived Certainty of Legal Punishment." *American Sociological Review* 42 (April):305–17.

Farrington, D. P. 1977. "The Effects of Public Labeling." *British Journal of Criminology* 17:112–25.

Felson, M. 1994. *Crime and Everyday Life*. Thousand Oaks, CA: Pine Forge Press.

Fisher, S. 1972. "Stigma and Deviant Careers in School." *Social Problems* 20 (Summer):78–83.

Forst, B. 1976. "The Deterrent Effect of Capital Punishment: A Cross-State Analysis of the 1960s." Mimeographed.

Foster, J. D., S. Dinitz, and W. C. Reckless. 1972. "Perceptions of Stigma Following Public Intervention for Delinquent Behavior." *Social Problems* 20 (Fall):202–9.

Geerken, M., and W. R. Gove. 1977. "Deterrence, Overload and Incapacitation: An Empirical Evaluation." *Social Forces* 56 (December):424–47.

Gibbs, J. P. 1968. "Crime, Punishment and Deterrence." *Southwestern Social Science Quarterly* 48 (March):515–30.

———. 1975. *Crime, Punishment and Deterrence.* New York: Elsevier.

———. 1986. "Deterrence Theory and Research." In *Law as a Behavioral Instrument*, edited by G. Metton. Lincoln: University of Nebraska Press.

Giordano, P. C. 1976. "The Sense of Injustice: An Analysis of Juveniles' Reactions to the Justice System." *Criminology* 14 (May):93–112.

Gold, M. 1970. *Delinquent Behavior in an American City.* Belmont, CA: Brooks Cole.

Gold, M., and J. R. Williams. 1969. "National Study of the Aftermath of Apprehension." *Prospectus* 3:3.

Goode, E. 1972. *Drugs in American Society.* New York: Alfred A. Knopf.

———. 1978. *Deviant Behavior: An Interactionist Approach.* Englewood Cliffs, NJ: Prentice-Hall.

———. 1989. *Deviant Behavior: An Interactionist Approach.* 3rd ed. Englewood Cliffs, NJ: Prentice-Hall.

Gould, L. C. 1969. "Who Defines Delinquency? A Comparison of Self-Reported and Officially Reported Indices of Delinquency for Three Racial Groups." *Social Problems* 16 (Winter):325–36.

Grasmick, H. G., and D. Green. 1980. "Legal Punishment, Social Disapproval and Internalization as Inhibitors of Illegal Behavior." *Journal of Criminal Law and Criminology* 71:325–35.

Grasmick, H. G., and H. Milligan, Jr. 1976. "Deterrence Theory Approach to Socioeconomic Demographic Correlates of Crime." *Social Science Quarterly* 57 (December):608–17.

Green, G. S. 1985. "General Deterrence and Television Cable Crime: A Field Experiment in Social Control." *Criminology* 23 (November):629–45.

Greenberg, D. F., and R. C. Kessler. 1982. "The Effects of Arrest on Crime: A Multivariate Panel Analysis." *Social Problems* 60 (March):771–90.

Greenberg, S. W., and F. Adler. 1974. "Crime and Addiction: An Empirical Analysis of the Literature, 1920–1973." *Contemporary Drug Problems* 3:221–69.

Gusfield, J. R. 1963. *Symbolic Crusade: Status Politics and the American Temperance Movement.* Urbana: University of Illinois Press.

Hepburn, J. R. 1977. "The Impact of Police Intervention upon Juvenile Delinquents." *Criminology* 15 (August):235–62.

Inciardi, J. 1986. *The War on Drugs.* Palo Alto, CA: Mayfield.

Jensen, G. F. 1969. "'Crime Doesn't Pay': Correlates of a Shared Misunderstanding." *Social Problems* 17 (Fall):189–201.

———. 1972. "Delinquency and Adolescent Self-Conceptions: A Study of the Personal Relevance of Infraction." *Social Problems* 20 (Summer):84–103.

———. 1980. "Labeling and Identity: Toward a Reconciliation of Divergent Findings." *Criminology* 18:121–29.

———. 2000. "Prohibition, Alcohol and Murder: Untangling Countervailing Mechanisms." *Homicide Studies* 4 (February):18–36.

Jensen, G. F., and M. L. Erickson. 1978. "The Social Meaning of Sanctions." In *Crime, Law and Sanctions: Theoretical Perspectives*, edited by M. Krohn and R. Akers. Beverly Hills: Sage.

Jensen, G. F., M. L. Erickson, and J. P. Gibbs. 1978. "Perceived Risk of Punishment and Self-Reported Delinquency." *Social Forces* 57 (September):57–78.

Jensen, G. F., and B. G. Stitt. 1982. "Words and Misdeeds." In *Deterrence Reconsidered*, edited by J. Hagan. Beverly Hills: Sage.

Kleck, G., B. Sever, L. Spencer, and M. Gertz. 2005. "The Missing Link in General Deterrence Research." *Criminology* 43:623–59.

Klemke, L. W. 1978. "Does Apprehension for Shoplifting Amplify or Terminate Shoplifting Activity?" *Law and Society Review* 12 (Spring):391–403.

Kraut, R. E. 1976. "Deterrent and Definitional Influences on Shoplifting." *Social Problems* 23 (February):358–68.

Lemert, E. M. 1967. *Human Deviance, Social Problems, and Social Control.* Englewood Cliffs, NJ: Prentice-Hall.

Matza, D. 1964. *Delinquency and Drift.* New York: John Wiley.

McAuliffe, W. 1975. "Beyond Secondary Deviance: Negative Labeling and Its Effects on the Heroin Addict." In *The Labeling of Deviance,* edited by W. Gove. New York: John Wiley.

McEachern, A. W. 1968. "The Juvenile Probation System." *American Behavioral Scientist* 11(3):1.

McGlothlin, W. H., M. D. Anglin, and B. D. Wilson. 1978. "Narcotic Addiction and Crime." *Criminology* 16 (November):293–315.

Meade, A. C. 1974. "The Labeling Approach to Delinquency: State of the Theory as a Function of Method." *Social Forces* 53 (September):83–91.

Minor, W. 1977. "A Deterrence-Control Theory of Crime." In *Theory in Criminology: Contemporary Issues,* edited by R. F. Meier. Beverly Hills: Sage.

Minor, W., and J. Harry. 1982. "Deterrent and Experiential Effects in Perceptual Deterrence Research: A Replication and Extension." *Journal of Research in Crime and Delinquency* 19 (July):190–215.

Montmarquette, C., and M. Nerlove. 1985. "Deterrence and Delinquency: An Analysis of Individual Data." *Journal of Quantitative Criminology* 1:37–58.

Moran, R. 1990. "The Case for Public Executions." Newsletter of the Crime, Law and Deviance Section of the American Sociological Association (Spring).

O'Donnell, J. A. 1967. "The Rise and Decline of a Subculture." *Social Problems* 15(1):73–84.

Paternoster, R., L. Saltzman, G. P. Waldo, and T. Chiricos. 1985. "Assessments of Risk and Behavioral Experience: An Exploratory Study of Change." *Criminology* 23 (August):417–36.

Peterson, R., and W. C. Bailey. 1988. "Murder and Capital Punishment in the Evolving Context of the Post-Furman Era." *Social Forces* 66 (March):1973–84.

Regnery, A. S. 1985. "Getting Away with Murder: Why the Juvenile Justice System Needs an Overhaul." *Policy Review* 34 (Fall):65–68.

Saltzman, L., R. Paternoster, G. P. Waldo, and T. G. Chiricos. 1982. "Deterrent and Experiential Effects: The Problem of Causal Order in Perceptual Deterrence Research." *Journal of Research in Crime and Delinquency* 19 (July):172–89.

Savitz, L. 1958. "A Study of Capital Punishment." *Journal of Criminal Law, Criminology and Police Science* 49:338.

Scarpitti, F. R., and M. L. Andersen. 1992. *Social Problems.* 2d ed. New York: HarperCollins.

Schuessler, K. F. 1952. "The Deterrent Influence of the Death Penalty." *Annals of the American Academy of Political and Social Science* 284 (November):54–62.

Schur, E. 1969. "Reactions to Deviance: A Critical Assessment." *American Journal of Sociology* 75 (November):309–22.

———. 1973. *Radical Non-Intervention: Rethinking the Delinquency Problem.* Englewood Cliffs, NJ: Prentice-Hall.

Schwartz, I. M. 1989. *(In)justice for Juveniles.* Lexington, MA: D.C. Heath.

Schwartz, R. D., and S. Orleans. 1967. "On Legal Sanctions." *University of Chicago Law Review* 34 (Winter):274–300.

Sellin, T. 1967. *Capital Punishment.* New York: Harper & Row.

Shannon, L. 1976. "Predicting Adult Careers from Juvenile Careers." Paper presented at Pacific Sociological Association annual meeting, San Diego.

Siegel, L. 1989. *Criminology.* 3d ed. St. Paul, MN: West.

Silberman, M. 1976. "Toward a Theory of Criminal Deterrence." *American Sociological Review* 52:532–40.

Stack, S. 1987. "Publicized Executions and Homicide, 1950–1980." *American Sociological Review* 52:532–40.

Stafford, M. C., L. N. Gray, B. A. Menke, and D. A. Ward. 1986. "Modeling the Deterrent Effects of Punishment." *Social Psychology Quarterly* 49:338–47.

Sutherland, E. 1924. *Principles of Criminology.* Philadelphia: J. B. Lippincott.

Tannenbaum, F. 1938. *Crime and the Community.* New York: Columbia University Press.

Thornberry, T. P. 1971. "Punishment and Crime: The Effect of Legal Dispositions on Subsequent Criminal Behavior." Ph.D. dissertation, University of Pennsylvania.

Thorsell, B. A., and L. W. Klemke. 1972. "The Labeling Process: Reinforcement and Deterrent." *Law and Society Review* 7 (Spring):372–92.

Tittle, C. R. 1975. "Deterrents or Labeling?" *Social Forces* 53 (March):399–410.

———. 1977. "Sanctions, Fear and the Maintenance of Social Order." *Social Forces* 55 (March):579–96.

Tittle, C. R., and A. R. Rowe. 1973. "Moral Appeal, Sanction Threat and Deviance: An Experimental Test." *Social Problems* 20 (Spring):488–98.

———. 1974. "Certainty of Arrest and Crime Rates: A Further Test of the Deterrence Hypothesis." *Social Forces* 52:455–62.

Trebach, A. S. 1988. *Law Enforcement News*, 30 April.

Van den Haag, E. 1986. "The Ultimate Punishment: A Defense." *Harvard Law Review* 7 (May):99.

Waldo, G. P., and T. G. Chiricos. 1972. "Perceived Penal Sanction and Self-Reported Criminality: A Neglected Approach to Deterrence Research." *Social Problems* 19 (Spring):522–40.

Wilson, J. Q. 1975. *Thinking about Crime.* New York: Basic Books.

———. 1983. *Thinking about Crime.* Rev. ed. New York: Basic Books.

Zeisel, H. 1976. "The Deterrent Effect of the Death Penalty: Facts v. Faiths." In *The Supreme Court Review*, edited by P. Kurland. Chicago: University of Chicago Press.

Zimring, F. E., and G. Hawkins. 1973. *Deterrence: The Legal Threat in Crime Control.* Chicago: University of Chicago Press.

ten

Imprisonment and Alternatives

TALLULAH, Louisiana (AP)—The allegations began soon after the prison opened for business: teenage inmates beaten by guards, beating each other, running loose on the rooftops of the barracks-like dorms. Ten years later, Louisiana is shutting down its toughest juvenile prison, a move that child welfare advocates see as an admission of failure. The closing comes after years of investigations—by the U.S. Justice Department, human rights advocates and others—called the lockup a place of chaos and brutality. "Tallulah became known as one of the worst, if not the worst, juvenile facility in the country," said Mark Soler, head of the Youth Law Center, an advocacy group in Washington. Advocates said the adult-style prison—with individual cells inside cell blocks behind fences and razor wire—created an atmosphere unlikely to rehabilitate the teens. They said the teens were more likely to commit far worse crimes when they got out.

(*CNN.com*, May 27, 2004)

Imprisonment: The Continuing Controversy

As noted in chapter 2, one of the rationales for creating the juvenile justice system was to avoid imprisoning youth with adults and to emphasize rehabilitation over punishment. Probation and treatment were to be the hallmarks of the new system, and "child savers" of the time hoped to minimize the use of prison-like settings to warehouse juveniles. In general, the public still supports those goals for the majority of youths. Even during one of the surges in juvenile violence in the late 1980s and early 1990s, 78 percent of adults surveyed indicated they thought the main purpose of the juvenile court was treatment and rehabilitation rather than punishment (Schwartz, Guo, and Kerbs, 1991). However, when asked about juveniles charged with serious felonies, the public was likely to want such offenders dealt with in the adult criminal justice system. Yet within the juvenile system it has proven necessary to maintain secure facilities for a sizeable number of offenders who are waiting for hearings (detention) or whose disposition calls for some type of facility (residential placement).

The latest comprehensive national report from the Office of Juvenile Justice and Delinquency Prevention (OJJDP) reveals a one-day count of 109,225 juveniles in 2,861 public or private juvenile justice facilities in the United States in 2003 (Snyder and Sickmund, 2006). Although only a small proportion of the juvenile population is in custody at a given point in time (307 per 100,000 in 2003), many more youths are admitted and released from these facilities within a given year. With a median stay of between 105 days for public facilities and 121 days for private facilities, a conservative estimate is that more than two to three times as many cases are admitted as are resident on a specific day. With a median stay of about two weeks in detention centers, as many as thirty times more youths may pass through detention centers. Some will pass through the system more than once, so it is difficult to specify the percent of the juvenile population that will experience some form of confinement in a given year, but it is safe to estimate that it is between 2 and 3 percent of the juvenile population. By the time juveniles fall under the jurisdiction of the adult system, that small annual percent may have accumulated to encompass a sizeable percentage of youth.

One reason to keep confinement at a minimum is simply cost. The average cost of confining a youth for a year ranges between $23,000 and $64,000 with an average of about $43,000, a figure that often surprises people. This amount is about the same as the cost of tuition and living expenses at an elite private university. Moreover, these figures do not include the cost of building facilities. Were such figures added, the cost per case would be considerably higher. Of course, confinement may be necessary to satisfy and protect the public, but any call for massive increases in its use will have to acknowledge the fact that it is very costly.

Given the high cost of imprisonment as a response to juvenile delinquency, we need to carefully assess its use and compare it to alternatives. First, we have to put imprisonment in historical perspective. In historical context, imprisonment has been viewed as a benevolent advancement over corporal (bodily) and capital punishment. Many forms of confinement that we might today define as "cruel and unusual" were the progressive ideas of one era or another. Responses to delinquency that were criticized at one time may later regain popularity. Second, we have to consider whether we are getting our money's worth. How do we determine the benefits of imprisonment relative to alternatives? Finally, we need to consider the fit between correctional programs and criminological theories. In general, the most promising correctional treatments will be those that take into account the best substantiated criminological theories, and those that fail or boomerang will be found to have done so because they violate principles of those theories.

Development of the Prison

The use of imprisonment as a tool for correcting, deterring, or punishing offenders was itself an aspect of various reform efforts. One review of corrections in America described the use of confinement or incarceration as a phase in "the continued search for alternatives to brutality" (Carter, McGee, and Nelson, 1975). Until the 1800s the major means of punishment took the form of flogging, mutilation, branding, torture, banishment, removal to penal colonies, or some form of restitution for the damage or harm done to the victim and the state. Imprisonment was a prelude to the actual punishment, not the punishment itself. It was also used as a penalty for political prisoners of high rank and as a means of coercing payment of debts (Johnston, 1973). Today, youths in some societies may be subject to whippings with canes as a form of punishment, but this response would not pass modern interpretations of cruel and unusual punishment in the United States.

In twelfth-century England, jails were used to detain the accused while they awaited trial and to punish offenders (Schrag, 1971). Beginning in the sixteenth century, houses of correction and workhouses were established in Europe for minor offenders, beggars, and vagabonds. Such institutions were widespread by the seventeenth century. Such houses were not specifically designed to deal with criminals but were repositories for an assortment of minor offenders, the destitute, and the unemployed (Sykes, 1978). Execution, corporal punishment, and banishment were the preferred methods for handling serious criminals (Fox, 1972).

Box 10-1   Spare the Rod?

The history of corrections and juvenile justice in America has involved a shift away from corporal (bodily) punishments. In contrast, numerous societies still use whipping and other forms of corporal punishment for juveniles and adults. In 1994, an 18-year-old American student attending school in Singapore was charged with spray painting cars and acts of vandalism. A judge sentenced him to be beaten by a rattan cane, serve four months in jail, and pay a $2,230 fine. The sentence to be caned (whipped) caused an uproar in the United States. Do you think whipping or caning should be acceptable punishments for youths committing acts of vandalism in the United States? Why or why not?

In the American colonies, jails and houses of correction were erected along European lines. Jails were used primarily to house individuals awaiting trail, and houses of correction were institutions for drunkards and vagrants. The conditions in early American jails (and in their European counterparts) were deemed appalling. The following is an account of the conditions in the Walnut Street Jail in Philadelphia shortly after the Revolutionary War:

> It is represented as a scene of promiscuous and unrestricted intercourse, and universal riot and debauchery. There was no labor, no separation of those accused, but yet untried, not even of those confined for debt only, from the convicts sentenced for the foulest crimes; no separation of color, age or sex, by day or night; the prisoners lying promiscuously on the floor, most of them without anything like bed or bedding. As soon as the sexes were placed in different wings, which was the first reform made in the prison, of thirty or forty women confined there, all but four or five immediately left it; it having been a common practice, it is said, for women to cause themselves to be arrested for fictitious debts, that they might share in the orgies of the place. Intoxicating liquors abounded, and indeed were freely sold at a bar kept by one of the officers of the prison. Intercourse between the prisoners and those without was hardly restricted. Prisoners tried and acquitted were still detained till they should pay jail fees to the keeper; and the custom of garnish was established and unquestioned; that is the custom of stripping every newcomer of his outer clothing, to be sold for liquor, unless redeemed by the payment of a sum of money to be applied to the same object. It need hardly be added, that there was no attempt to give any kind of instruction and no religious service whatsoever. (Gray, 1847:15–16)

The conditions of jails and houses of correction in both Europe and America prompted reform efforts, which in America led to the creation of the **penitentiary** in the late 1700s. English prison reformer John Howard (1726–1790) published an influential book, *State of Prisons,* which led to prison reform in Europe and the United States. The very word that Howard used, "penitentiary," is a clue to the religious origins of the institution. The Walnut Street Jail just described became the first institution to incorporate the Quaker idea that restraint and isolation would lead inmates to contemplate the error of their ways and to do penance for their sins. Rather than flogging, physically branding, or inflicting pain, imprisonment itself was to be both punishment and a means to interpersonal reform. In Quaker philosophy, sin and crime were synonymous. Life in an austere and disciplined environment, meditation, and Bible reading would strengthen the moral and spiritual fibers of the inmates. To facilitate penitence, inmates were kept in single cells, were not allowed contact with other inmates, and were required to carry out their assigned work in isolation. This conception of the penitentiary as a method of correction came to be known as the **Pennsylvania system**.

A second school of corrections emerged in New York State in the early 1800s and became known as the **Auburn system**. The hallmark of the Auburn system was not total isolation but, rather, silence. Inmates worked together during the day but were kept in solitary confinement at night. Although there was contact, rules requiring silence were strictly enforced. Prisoners worked in common workshops and ate in a common dining hall but were not allowed to communicate. The Auburn system became the dominant penal system in America, primarily because it was economical and secondarily because of concern over the psychological impact of isolation. The Pennsylvania system called for individual confinement, which entailed the construction of separate living quarters for each inmate. The Auburn system's architectural design was more economical, requiring only common work areas and small solitary cells for sleeping. Prisons such as Sing Sing, built in 1825, followed the Auburn model. The Pennsylvania system was ultimately abandoned in the United States, although European penologists who studied the two systems preferred the Pennsylvania model for prisons in their countries (Fox, 1972).

Although proponents of each of these systems cast aspersions on the other, both were based on a similar philosophy. Both emphasized rigid discipline, restraint, isolation, and work as the means to personal reform. At about the same time, a somewhat different correctional philosophy was being implemented in Australia, Austria, Spain, and Ireland (Sykes, 1978; Sutherland and Cressey, 1978). In Australia, Alexander Maconochie, superintendent of a penal colony, devised the **mark system**. Under this system, inmates had to earn their release through hard work and good behavior. Prisoners could work for a *ticket of leave*, similar to parole. If the prisoner successfully completed the parole period, he was granted a conditional pardon and, finally, transported back to England as a free man. This progressive method of liberation was imported to Ireland where it became known as the **Irish system**. The Irish system was characterized by the use of an indeterminate sentence (i.e., length of confinement dependent on progress made by the inmate) and the "mark" whereby prisoners could gain their release. Marks were awarded for good behavior and, after earning a set number of such marks, the prisoner was eligible for parole. The system embodied the features of contemporary behavior modification programs which will be discussed later in this chapter.

The Irish system was hailed in this country as the most progressive penal model to date. Its philosophy became the underlying correctional philosophy of prison organization in the United States. In 1870 the National Prison Association was founded under the leadership of Enoch Wines, considered the foremost authority on prisons in the latter part of the nineteenth century (Platt, 1969). Out of the reform efforts of Wines and his organization, a new penal system emerged. Elmira Reformatory, established for offenders between the ages of 16 and 30, opened in New York in 1876. The

Elmira Reformatory combined the central features of the Irish system with a strong emphasis on rehabilitation through education and trade training. The goal was not punishment, but treatment and reform. However, according to Sutherland and Cressey (1978), the "treatment" at Elmira was so severe and the use of corporal punishment so frequent that convicted offenders pleaded with judges to be sentenced to the outmoded Auburn Prison rather than the Elmira Reformatory.

The Society for the Prevention of Pauperism was formed in 1817 for the purpose of finding "a practical measure for the cure of pauperism and the diminution of crime" (Dean and Reppucci, 1974). New York City was particularly beset with pauperism and its associated problems. Immigrants coming to this country were often stranded in New York City, and the children of destitute families were seen as prime candidates for crime. The Society for the Prevention of Pauperism selected the problem of juvenile delinquency as its major focus.

In 1825 the New York House of Refuge opened as a full-time residence for delinquent, dependent, and neglected children. It was the first attempt to provide separate facilities for young offenders and thereby remove them from the contaminating influence of adult prisons. In 1826 the House of Reformation in Boston was established, followed in 1828 by the opening of the Philadelphia House of Refuge. These early institutions, which were supported by private funds, developed many of the principles of treatment and rehabilitation that would characterize the philosophy of the juvenile court as it emerged at the start of the twentieth century. Despite the rhetoric of the early house of refuge movement, the administrators of these institutions utilized two basic models: one drawn from the public school system, which called for education and discipline, and the other based on the state penitentiary system, which utilized a strict regimen, physical labor, and corporal punishment (Schlossman, 1977). In institutions for juveniles—variously known as houses of refuge, reformatories, industrial schools, and training schools—coercion, restraint, and discipline became an integral part of "treatment." The enlightened ideology of the reformatory movement gave way to the stark reality of overcrowding, inadequate resources, mismanagement, and disillusioned staff. The distinction between juvenile institutions and adult prisons became extremely tenuous.

The house of refuge actually came to parallel the adult penitentiary, as did the Elmira Reformatory. These products of the reform movement came under attack in the 1850s by "anti-institutionalists" such as Charles Loring Brace and Samuel Gridley Howe, who felt the best means of reform was the family. The family, according to Brace, was "God's reformatory." The anti-institutionalists' critiques and proposals facilitated the development of the **family reform school**, an organizational model that was growing in popularity in Germany and France. The family reform school actually represented a compromise between the anti-institutionalists' ideas and the realities of an already existing "institutional establishment" (Schlossman, 1977:49). Steven Schlossman has described the system as follows:

> To Americans the essence of the family design was a format whereby anywhere from one to three dozen inmates with similar personality were placed in separate small homes or cottages under the supervision, ideally, of a surrogate father and mother. Each family lived, worked, and attended school together, meeting with other inmates only on infrequent ceremonial occasions. This residential arrange-

ment contrasted sharply with the Jacksonian refuge, where children of different ages and dispositions slept in cells or barracks-like dormitories, performed identical tasks according to a uniform schedule, and possessed no close authority figure to appeal to for personal assistance or comfort. (1977:49)

Following the development of the family reform school, the next major phases in the evolution of juvenile justice and corrections were the Progressive Era and the juvenile court movement. As we noted in chapter 2, there has been considerable debate about whether the accomplishments of that era were in fact progressive. Analyses of the juvenile court movement in Canada (Hagan and Leon, 1977) and the United States (Schlossman, 1977; Finestone, 1976) tend to agree that the most central and significant aspect of the movement was its emphasis on probation. Confinement in reformatories persisted as a response to problem youth, but treatment of youths and their families within the community was a major philosophical emphasis.

It is not clear whether the progressive ideology had any real consequences for the probability that a youth might be imprisoned. For instance, in his historical analysis of the juvenile court movement in Chicago (Cook County), Anthony Platt argued that "Cook County juvenile court's early records show that institutional confinement was a basic tenet of the child-saving philosophy" (1969:140). He notes that one-third of all juveniles charged with delinquency were sent to a state reformatory. Platt also contends that institutional confinement was increasingly used to deal with delinquency. In contrast, Schlossman's analysis of the juvenile court system in the neighboring state of Wisconsin led him to the following conclusions:

> Probation accounted for the great majority of dispositions . . . with the model period of supervision running about one and a half years. The heavy reliance on probation, especially for male delinquents, is confirmed by records showing a rather small number of commitments to the state reform school at Waukesha during this period. . . . Between 1905 and 1916, the average number of youths committed each year was only thirty. Moreover, although the number of reformatory committals varied from year to year, it clearly did not increase at a rate proportional to rising intake in the court. Indeed, if anything, it decreased. For example, in 1906, 55 boys were committed to the reformatory, out of 536 new delinquency cases; in 1911, 15 boys were committed out of 705. To sum up, the odds of being committed to a reformatory for boys charged with delinquency in the Progressive Era were rather small. Despite increases in intake, the court's reliance on long-term committals actually diminished after 1905. (1977:155)

Schlossman warns us that these observations do not necessarily mean that the use of *confinement* declined, since large numbers of children were held in detention centers before, during, and sometimes after their hearings. The proportion of persons detained actually increased during that time. Schlossman argued that detention centers developed into children's jails that allowed institutional control and incapacitation in a system that emphasized probation.

The Progressive Era of the early 1900s was also characterized by dramatic increases in resources invested in public reformatories for girls. Schlossman and Wallach (1982) note that twenty-three new facilities for girls opened between 1910 and 1920 compared to only five between 1850 and 1910. These reform schools were generally small facilities compared to such institutions as the New York House of Refuge, which held over 1,000 males. Based on their historical research, Schlossman and Wallach found that female juvenile delinquents were viewed as "fallen women," and a major concern in the juvenile courts and reformatories was to control their sexual precociousness and promiscuity. Girls were to be isolated from males, kept long enough to insure marriageability after release, and taught the skills necessary for a domestic future. The Victorian emphasis on sexual purity and growing concern about biological and mental degeneration of society led to increased confinement of girls at a time when anti-institutionalists were challenging the use of institutions for boys. Girls were actually viewed as less amenable than boys to change through probation and home treatment, and incarceration was deemed necessary to control female sexuality. Schlossman and Wallach conclude that the expansion of female reformatories was "part of a larger cultural reaction, an attempt to revitalize Victorian morality and to punish women—prostitutes and sexually promiscuous girls alike—who impeded attainment of that goal" (1982:70).

Thus, by the early 1900s four basic dimensions of juvenile justice and institutional confinement had been established: (1) prison-like reform and training schools, (2) family-cottage reform schools, (3) probation, and (4) detention facilities for the short-term confinement of youthful offenders. Moreover, the use of confinement for females who violated sexual mores and for boys who violated criminal laws developed in this period. The incarceration of female status offenders would not come under serious attack for another half century.

The Contemporary Scene

Since the establishment of a separate juvenile justice system there has been a proliferation in the types of juvenile facilities available. In addition to training schools and detention centers, a significant number of youths may spend time at ranches, forestry camps, farms for delinquent youth, wilderness survival programs, boot camps, or in halfway houses and group homes. Ranches, camps, and farms for children in custody are not as restrictive as training schools and detention centers, but do maintain security and isolate youths by virtue of their location. Halfway houses and group homes maintain control over youth but allow structured and monitored contact with the wider community. Youths may live in such homes while attending school or even working at a job but are subject to rules established and enforced by people acting as their custodians.

There are other facilities for children under state custody, such as shelter care homes, which are used primarily for dependent and neglected children but also provide care for young offenders and status offenders who do not constitute security risks. Youth may spend some time in reception and diagnostic centers as well. Such centers are facilities for evaluating delinquent youths and their circumstances before an ultimate disposition is made.

Juvenile Facilities

With the dramatic drop in juvenile offense rates beginning in the mid-1990s, we would expect a comparable drop in youths held in detention and committed to residential placement. Such a pattern can be noted, although it appears that the downward trend in confinement has lagged behind the decrease in juvenile offense rates. The peak year for detention or commitment was 1999, and the trend since then has been downward through the latest year in available data (2003). Between 1999 and 2003 there was a 10 percent decline in juvenile offenders in residential placement as compared to a 27 percent increase between 1991 and 1999 (Snyder and Sickmund, 2006).

Variations in rates of confinement or imprisonment may reflect the availability of facilities at different points in time as well as shifts in juvenile justice philosophy. As arrest rates and court cases rose dramatically from the 1960s through the 1980s the number of youths confined increased, but not nearly as rapidly as youth crime was increasing. The justice system, in essence, could not keep up with crime and delinquency. When juvenile crime leveled out and began to decline, the juvenile justice system began to "catch up" in terms of facilities and resources available. However, once sufficient facilities were developed, confinement became a more likely option than when the system was more seriously overburdened. Moreover, consistent with the growing conservatism of public and political sentiment, juvenile justice officials grew more enamored with "setting things right" with victims; that is, scaring potential offenders and incapacitating repetitive offenders. Incapacitation, deterrence, and restitution developed into key issues among justice scholars and professionals during the 1980s and early 1990s.

Two patterns have been noted in recent years by the OJJDP (Snyder and Sickmund, 2006). Minority youth constituted about 60 percent of the youth committed to juvenile facilities in 2003, but this percent represents a decline from 64 percent since 1997. The decline is consistent with the decline in minority violence noted in earlier chapters.

The second pattern involves females. As plotted in figure 10-1, the ratio of males to females in juvenile facilities has declined from nearly 10 to 1 in 1991 to just over 6 to 1 in 2003. This decline parallels the decline noted in self-reports of serious violence summarized in chapter 4. However, it is important to note that one of the reasons that ratio is declining is because there has been a greater decline for males than females. Females are constituting an increasing share, but males still greatly outnumber females (see figure 10-2).

The increase in females in juvenile facilities has led some criminologists to note that we need programs in juvenile facilities that recognize differences in the circumstances that may have led girls to imprisonment compared to boys. The most notable difference is the prevalence of sexual abuse in girls' backgrounds (Chesney-Lind and Shelden, 1998). Moreover, numerous critics of the treatment of girls in the system argue that approaches developed for boys do not necessarily work for girls. For example in *Justice by Gender*, a joint assessment by the American Bar Association and the National Bar Association, the authors argue that "of the limited programs that currently exist for girls, most are modeled after programs that serve males. Consequently, girls, and especially minority girls, increasingly are being placed in programs that fail to meet their unique developmental, physiological, and emotional needs" (2001:22). Koons and colleagues (1997) argue that victimization and self-esteem issues are central to the development of effective programs for girls.

Figure 10-1   Ratio of Male Delinquents to Female Delinquents in Juvenile Facilities

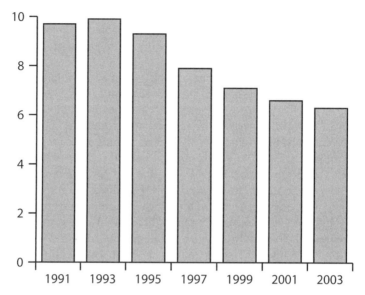

Source: Based on Snyder and Sickmund, 2006.

Figure 10-2   Number of Males and Females in Juvenile Facilities

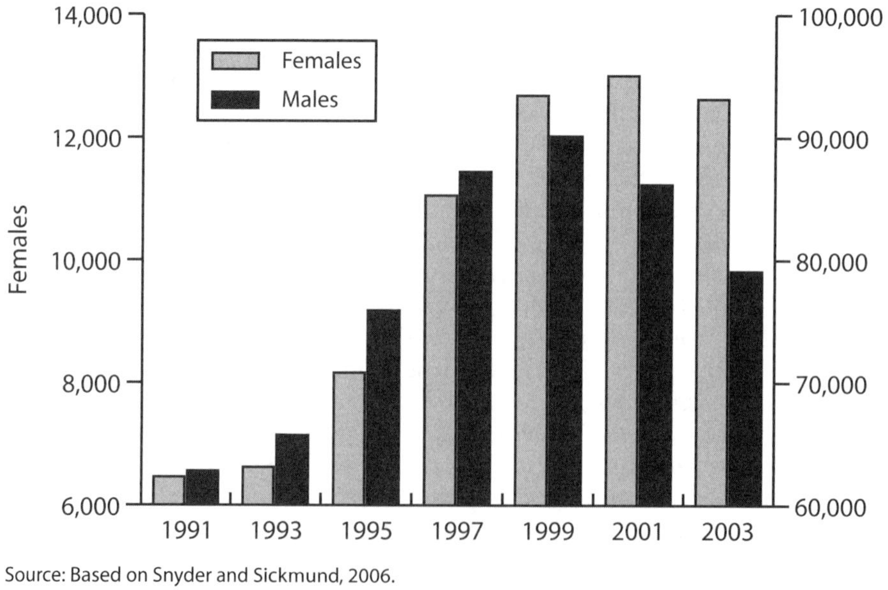

Source: Based on Snyder and Sickmund, 2006.

The Privatization of Juvenile Justice

One of the most notable trends in juvenile justice in the United States has been the **privatization** of juvenile correctional programs; that is, the creation of juvenile institutions run not by state or local government but by private agencies or individuals. In 1950 about 22 percent of youths confined in a long-term facility were in private rather than public or government-owned facilities. However, this figure began climbing in the early 1970s and by 1974 about 50 percent of youths under correctional supervision were in a private facility. The figure has increased to approximately 60 percent at the present time. However, because private facilities tend to handle smaller caseloads, they encompass about 38 percent of juveniles in residential placement.

Ironically, the proliferation of private facilities was facilitated by the movement to **deinstitutionalize** status offenders and to provide community-based alternatives for minor offenders as reflected in government legislation in 1968 (the Omnibus Crime Control and Safe Streets Act) and 1974 (the Juvenile Justice and Delinquency Prevention Act). The alternatives to public training schools and existing forms of long-term confinement were new long-term and short-term programs developed in the private realm. Presently there are 1,682 private juvenile facilities in the United States and 1,170 public juvenile facilities. In 1979 private facilities handled a total of 69,000 admissions and by 1991 this grew to 140,000—an increase of 101 percent. Conversely, public juvenile facilities handled 568,000 admissions in 1979 and this grew at a much more modest rate of 20 percent to 683,000. The trend toward privatization has slowed somewhat in recent years, with the number of private facilities peaking at 1,795 in 1999 while the number of public facilities peaked in 2001 at 1,197 (Snyder and Sickmund, 2006).

Private correctional enterprise was encouraged by the government and moved rapidly to provide new alternatives. Such enterprise was consistent with the commonly held view that the private sector could provide services more economically than government bureaucracies. However, it has proven difficult to determine the relationship between cost and recidivism. For one, the National Report on Juvenile Offenders and Victims (Snyder and Sickmund, 2006) does not differentiate between for-profit and nonprofit, privately run facilities nor between state and county-run programs. A study of programs in Florida found higher recidivism rates for the for-profit enterprises than for state, county, or nonprofit facilities (Bayer and Pozen, 2005). However, the cost per "case released" was lower for the for-profit and the county facilities than for the state or nonprofit programs. Second, despite efforts to control for a wide range of characteristics that might have explained the lower cost for for-profit and county programs, the fact remains that some types of facilities are more expensive to run than others. For example, a meta-analysis of private versus publicly owned prisons for adult males found that variables such as age of the facility, security-level, and economies of scale (e.g., larger caseloads may be cheaper per case) explained variations in cost, and there was no significant advantage for private prisons when those characteristics were considered (Pratt and Maahs, 1999). Third, the results of research on this issue are highly variable, depending on sources of funding for the research. All studies funded by agencies or corporations that benefit from privatization have concluded that privatization saves the public money, while studies carried out independent of such funding sources have found either no difference or a complex pattern such as that noted above for Florida. The most startling instance of bias involved a professor at Florida who had made at least $3 million as a consultant or board member of the largest for-profit correctional enterprise in the nation.

It is surprising that some studies show lower costs per "case released" because one difference between private and public facilities is median days in placement. The median for status offenders in private facilities is close to twice that for public facilities (117 days versus 65). In general, the disparity is lower for the most serious offenses (e.g., 124 days versus 106 for crimes against persons as compared to 142 days versus 111 for public order offenses). In short, there is a tendency for private programs to keep youths longer despite the fact that they are dealing with less serious offenders. One reason some programs may be cheaper per case is lower costs for personnel and greater employee turnover, two characteristics that have been found to be more characteristic of private facilities than public ones.

Although it does not differentiate between youths in nonprofit versus for-profit programs, the OJJDP report does reveal differences in the characteristics of youths held in public and private settings. Private facilities are more likely to house status offenders (3,262 versus 1,548 in residential facilities in 2003) while public facilities house the more serious offenders (e.g., 23,499 personal offenders versus 9,671 in 2003). A greater proportion of juveniles in private facilities are female. Private facilities held about 36 percent of all female offenders in 2003 as compared to about 31 percent of male offenders, and for categories such as "ungovernable" private facilities housed 84 percent of females held. In sum, public facilities and private facilities handle a different clientele—another possible reason for variation in cost. Moreover as Howard Snyder and Melissa Sickmund (2006) note, many female offenders require special programming because of issues of sexual abuse. Juveniles in custody often have backgrounds of abuse, but it is more likely to have a sexual component for girls than boys. Hence, higher costs may reflect the need for special programming for females and status offenders.

The privatization of juvenile justice has been associated with a growing segregation of offenders by race and ethnicity. As Snyder and Sickmund note, "Minority youth are not distributed evenly across facility types" (2006:212). Historically, African Americans and Hispanics have constituted an increasing proportion of youths in secure, public long-term facilities (Shover and Einstadter, 1989) while white youth have been diverted to alternative programs to a greater degree than minority youth. Scholars may debate which is the more positive or negative experience for youth, but it does appear that correctional experiences in the public versus the private realm are differentially distributed by racial or ethnic status. Such segregation is partially a reflection of the types of interpersonal violent offenses that are overrepresented among minority youth, but there also is precedent to propose biases in dispositions as part of the explanation as well. Neal Shover and Werner Einstadter state that "some part of this inequity is due to systematic discrimination" (1989:107).

Depending on the laws of each particular state, some youths also end up in adult jails and correctional facilities. Between 1990 and 1999, juveniles serving time in adult jails increased from about 2,200 to about 9,500, but fell to just over 7,000 by 2003. They constitute about 1.4 percent of the state jail population. New admissions to state prisons of youth under 18 increased from about 5,000 to around 7,500 in 1995–1996 and have declined to about 4,100 in 2003. In 2003, there were 2,225 youth under 18 serving sentences of life without parole, most of them in adult prisons. The number of new admissions for such sentences increased from about 60 in 1990 to about 150 by 1996, but had fallen to below 60 by 2003.

The National Council on Crime and Delinquency (Hartney, 2006) argues that most of the impacts of processing youths in the adult system are negative for the youths. Of course, since the primary motive for increases in such processing was to assure that "the punishment met the crime" (retributive justice) or deterred other young offenders, such outcomes are not surprising. The Council states that youth tried as adults get harsher sentences, youth convicted as adults get little or no rehabilitative programming, they cannot expunge their record and start over, they are at greater risk of victimization in adult jails and prisons, they may be disenfranchised and denied military service, and that they have higher recidivism rates than offenders remaining in the juvenile system. For those who serve their sentences or are paroled, the net effect on future crime may outweigh whatever deterrent effect or retributive justice that may have been anticipated by moving youths to the adult system.

The death rate for the general population of juveniles in the United States is about 2.5 times greater than the same rates for juveniles in facilities. In 2002 there should have been about 62 deaths for juveniles in facilities were they to parallel societal rates, but there were only 26 (10 suicides, 2 homicides, and 12 through illness or accident). Most facilities evaluate youth for risk of suicide and establish procedures to minimize such events.

The Prison Rape Elimination Act of 2003 requires the Bureau of Justice Statistics to track sexual violence in both juvenile and adult facilities, including youth-on-youth nonconsensual acts, youth-on-youth abusive acts, staff-on-youth misconduct, and staff-on-youth harassment. In 2004 there were 2,821 allegations, 59 percent youth-on-youth and 41 percent staff-on-youth incidents. Two-thirds of incidents involving youth-on-youth were deemed to be "nonconsensual." The rate per 1,000 beds was 22.6 per 1,000 in state-operated facilities and 16.5 in locally or privately operated facilities. In contrast to suicide and death rates, these figures are greater than would be expected using general statistics on victimization. The overall victimization rate of about 18.1 per 1,000 beds is many times greater than the victimization rate for similar age groups using the National Crime Victimization Surveys or Uniform Crime Reports. Rates are even higher for girls in confinement: 34 percent of victims are female but they constitute only 11 (public) or 17 (private and local) percent of the custody population. Either such victimizations are more common among youth in custody or they are more likely to be reported and processed than in the general population.

The Training School

The proliferation of different types of facilities for juveniles is reflected in reports from the Bureau of Justice Statistics that categorize facilities as (1) public or private, (2) long-term or short-term, and (3) institutional or open. The traditional **training school** falls in the long-term, institutional category and most of them are public facilities. In 2003, about 45 percent of committed offenders were in secure, long-term facilities. Group homes held about 11 percent, another 11 percent were in shelter facilities,

Box 10-2   Correctional Goals and Prison Design

Juvenile training schools can take many forms and vary greatly in the types of treatment programs offered. Some look much like adult prisons and others are like small school campuses.

If you were starting from scratch and designing an institution to serve just one of the goals below, what would it be like in terms of architecture, separation from the outside world, programs, use of corporal punishments, and other characteristics:

if rehabilitation were its only goal?
if general deterrence were its only goal?
if specific deterrence were its only goal?
if incapacitation were its only goal?
if retribution were its only goal?

Source: Photo by author.

and 7 percent were in boot camps. Four percent were in wilderness camps. It should be noted that two-thirds of the training school facilities are public while between 60 and 80 percent of the shelter, group, boot camp, and wilderness camps are private.

While training schools are likely to be viewed by juveniles as the most severe form of incarceration, they take a variety of forms and, ideally, are supposed to provide treatment and education while maintaining security. In 1975 the Children's Bureau described the functions of such schools as follows:

> The prime function of a training school is to re-educate and train the child to become a responsible, well-adjusted citizen. . . . The training schools must be essentially treatment institutions with an integrated professional service wherein the disciplines of education, casework, group work, psychology, psychiatry, medicine, nursing, vocational rehabilitation and religion all play an important role. Through such an integrated program the child is expected to learn self-discipline, to accept responsibility, and act and react in a more socially acceptable manner. (1975:3)

Although this philosophy calls for a dynamic, resocializing environment, several overviews of training schools in the 1960s suggested they were like miniature prisons, exacerbating rather than attenuating the delinquency problem. In its criticism of traditional juvenile institutions, a Presidential Task Force in the late 1960s stated:

Mass handling, countless ways of humiliating the inmate in order to make him subservient to rules and orders, special rules of behavior designed to maintain social distance between keeper and inmates, frisking of inmates, regimented movement to work, eat, play, drab prison clothing and similar aspects of daily life, all tend to depersonalize the inmate and reinforce his belief that authority is to be opposed, not cooperated with. (President's Commission on Law Enforcement and Administration of Justice, 1967:142)

Such descriptions of juvenile institutions suggested that they did not differ significantly from adult prisons. For instance, in his study of a cottage-type residential treatment center in New York, Howard Polsky (1962) found a stratification system based on toughness and manipulative abilities. The social hierarchy was so pervasive and the code of conduct so strongly enforced that Polsky concluded that the cottage system was culturally and organizationally "delinquency bound." Polsky's research suggested that the cottage lifestyle tends to sabotage the system's treatment programs and that juvenile institutions may suffer from the same type of prisonization effects as adult penitentiaries. **Prisonization** refers to the oppositional inmate code adopted by prisoners as a result of socialization by other inmates. Such prisonization is viewed as a barrier to treatment and reintegration into conventional society.

Barry Feld (1981) reached similar conclusions about juvenile institutions in Massachusetts in the early 1980s. Youths in ten cottages in two institutions appeared to come into the institutions with negative attitudes and these were compounded by an inmate culture that developed within the cottages. However, such prisonization was more evident in the punitive and custodial-oriented cottages than in treatment-oriented cottages.

Many training schools have made a concerted effort to move away from a custodial approach where security and discipline are foremost concerns to a treatment orientation like that advocated by the Children's Bureau. The success of such a move depends on the integration of treatment goals and custodial concerns and the degree of cooperation among the staff.

The Office of Juvenile Justice and Delinquency Prevention issued a research report entitled "Conditions of Confinement: Juvenile Detention and Corrections Facilities" in 1994. It examined private and public facilities and found that 75 percent of juveniles were confined in facilities whose populations exceeded their design capacity or slept in rooms that did not meet national standards. Security practices to prevent escapes or to provide for a safe environment were lacking in 80 percent of the juvenile facilities. Suicidal behavior was a serious problem. The research report cited 11,000 juveniles who had engaged in 17,000 incidents of suicidal behavior in one year. Health care also was a serious problem with untrained staff administering health care. The report went on to cite the lack of educational services, the lack of emergency preparedness, and a lack of restraint on staff discretion (room searches and strip searches). The authors of this report found that in many instances these deficiencies were in fact increasing rather than being addressed.

The Impact of Correctional Efforts

Have any efforts to save, treat, rehabilitate, or deter youths from further offenses been successful? Does confining youth alleviate the delinquency problem? Such questions are far more difficult to answer than most people initially anticipate. In box 10-3, the key issues or questions are summarized, including the purpose of a response, the limits on responses within a given culture, the outcomes chosen, the measures used, and the basis for comparison. Most correctional research uses some form of official statistics to measure the impact of a response on offenders using one or more existing forms of correctional response as a basis for comparison. The focus tends to be on changes in individual behavior brought about by a particular response.

The most common variable in evaluating the effectiveness of juvenile incarceration or institutionalization has been **recidivism**. Recidivism refers to the further commission of offenses after release from a program or facility and, typically, it is measured by the percentage who are rearrested. It is extraordinarily difficult to find any tabulations of recidivism rates at the local, state, or federal level. A wealth of information is available regarding how many get arrested, for what crime, how the case is disposed in juve-

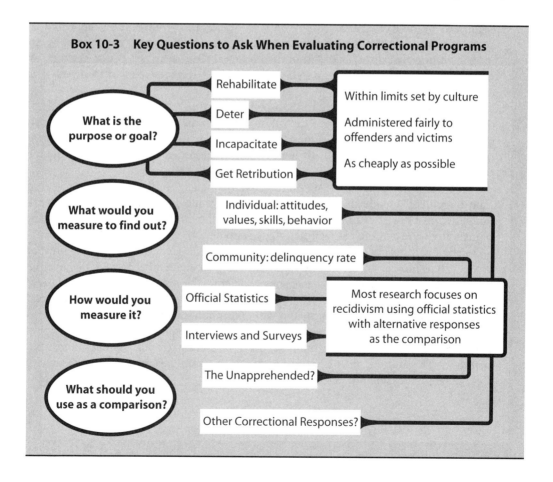

Box 10-3   Key Questions to Ask When Evaluating Correctional Programs

What is the purpose or goal?
- Rehabilitate
- Deter
- Incapacitate
- Get Retribution

Within limits set by culture
Administered fairly to offenders and victims
As cheaply as possible

What would you measure to find out?
- Individual: attitudes, values, skills, behavior
- Community: delinquency rate

How would you measure it?
- Official Statistics
- Interviews and Surveys

Most research focuses on recidivism using official statistics with alternative responses as the comparison

What should you use as a comparison?
- The Unapprehended?
- Other Correctional Responses?

nile court, and how many are in custody, but nowhere will a simple table appear showing how many juveniles get rearrested after having been institutionalized. Recidivism rates are the basic indicator of whether the juvenile justice system is accomplishing its goals, and whether different treatment strategies are more successful or less successful than doing nothing. Billions of dollars are spent annually to run the juvenile justice system, but a basic recidivism rate is not computed. A study that comes close to supplying a plausible recidivism rate was conducted by the FBI in the late 1980s (Beck and Shipley, 1987). A group of young adult offenders who were paroled in 1978 were followed for six years and their rearrest, reconviction, and reincarceration rates were computed. While these were not strictly juvenile offenders, they were only slightly older. What the FBI found was that after six years, 68 percent of these offenders were rearrested, 52 percent were reconvicted, and nearly 50 percent were reincarcerated.

Do such recidivism rates indicate failure of the correctional system? The answer to that question requires a basis for comparison. One relevant comparison would be the repetitive delinquency rate of offenders who have *never* been caught and punished. It is conceivable that the repetitive offense rate for those never caught could be greater than the high recidivism rates for youth released from institutions. If that were the case, then *relative to no response*, imprisonment would not be considered a total failure. In most attempts to evaluate the impact of different reactions to delinquency, the comparison is between offenders released from institutions and youths in alternative programs. These sorts of comparisons tell us something about the impact of one reaction compared to another, but not the impact of any reaction compared to no reaction.

We will learn more about the impact of training schools relative to alternative programs when we summarize research on correctional experiments later in this chapter. We have already encountered some information relative to the success or failure of training schools in chapter 9. Terence Thornberry's (1971) study found that youths who had been institutionalized had lower subsequent involvement in delinquency than youths who had received less severe dispositions. A second study is noteworthy here because, as Richard Lundman states, ". . . its findings fly in the face of the near consensus among social scientists and others that institutionalization is an ineffective method of controlling delinquents" (1984:199).

In a study called *Beyond Probation* (1979), Charles Murray and Louis Cox compared 317 serious and repetitive juvenile offenders who had been sent to the St. Charles Training School or Valley View Training School in Illinois with youths sentenced to community-based alternatives. Rather than focusing on the proportion of youths who were caught offending after intervention, Murray and Cox studied the "reduction" in the volume of delinquent offenses. While a youth who had been caught, punished, released, and then reoffended would be a recidivist and, traditionally, considered a "failure," Murray and Cox argued that such a stringent definition of failure does not tell us whether the odds of delinquency were reduced more by one program than another. If youths processed through one program were committing five offenses per month before that experience and only one per month after intervention while another program reduced delinquency to three offenses, the former would be the more successful program in terms of the "suppression" of delinquency.

Of course, some changes in delinquency might occur due merely to aging or maturational reform and, hence, data on reductions in delinquency are useful for comparing alternative interventions rather than assessing the actual reduction in delinquency compared to no response. Thus, their study is relevant to the *comparative suppression of delinquency* among alternative interventions. This point is important to remember because summaries of *Beyond Probation* can give the impression that a reduction in delinquency after intervention means that the intervention "worked." For example, with regard to the Illinois research, Lundman states that "everything worked to suppress involvement in delinquency" (1984:206). In fact, all that can be said is that delinquency declined regardless of the type of intervention. Whether those declines were a result of the interventions would require data for youths where no intervention occurred at all.

For example, the 2006 national report on *Juvenile Offenders and Victims* reveals that 40 percent of youths with no prior referrals never returned to the juvenile court (Snyder and Sickmund, 2006:235). If lack of subsequent referrals is a measure of success, then 40 percent might be the overall "success" rate. For youths 13 years of age at first referral, about 57 percent return. For 14-year-old youth, the figure is 53 percent. For 15-year-old youth, it is 45 percent. It drops to 33 percent for 16-year-olds and 16 percent for 17-year-olds. Taking "eligibility" to return, these figures might be interpreted as indicating that about 16 percent of youths return for each year of eligibility (e.g., the return rate is 16 percent with one year eligibility, 33 percent for two years, and 45 percent for three).

What were the comparative suppression rates for alternative reactions in the Murray and Cox study? Youths sent to the training schools committed 68 percent fewer offenses in the first twelve months after their release than in the twelve months prior to intervention. This figure represents a greater reduction than nonresidential programs and most other alternatives. While some programs did as well or better, the data are contrary to the view that institutions or training schools make youths worse either in an absolute or a comparative sense.

In short, the view of institutions as schools of crime is no better substantiated than a view of imprisonment as a specific deterrent or as a setting for reform. Advocacy of a particular point of view appears to be more a function of ideology than of evidence. Regardless of its basis in fact or fiction, the view of confinement in institutions as an inappropriate, expensive, and counterproductive force has generated considerable correctional experimentation. As we have already noted, assessing the success or failure of any particular type of intervention is no easy matter, and such is the case for measuring the success of correctional experiments.

Evaluating Correctional Experiments

There are numerous criteria for evaluating correctional programs but the two most common are *effectiveness* and *efficiency*. Program effectiveness refers to the attainment of goals or objectives, while efficiency refers to the resources expended in attaining objectives. Both are important when making decisions about the investment of resources because they do not necessarily coincide. Expenditures may not appear justified in terms of payoff either in an absolute sense or in comparison to alternatives. For example, James Q. Wilson (1975) has recounted the efforts of the New York City Police Department to curb subway robberies. In 1965 the New York police increased patrols of subways and assigned police to every subway train and station during peak hours for felony offenses. Robberies immediately dropped and in terms of effectiveness the program was a success. Yet, the cost of each felony prevented was about $35,000. Whether this was an efficient use of resources depends on the cost of alternatives.

The same issue is involved when evaluating community-based alternatives to training schools. One type of intervention may do no better or worse than another but, if one expends fewer resources, it may be the preferred response. We use the word "may" because there are other grounds for evaluating the total impact of an intervention other than goal attainment and comparative efficiency. For one, if the focus is on the behavior of offenders after release, a particular intervention may be as effective and efficient as any other but have other consequences that could make it undesirable. For example, some people advocate imprisonment because while the youth is confined citizens are not being victimized. If the number of crimes prevented during imprisonment exceeds the number prevented after participation in a less-restrictive alternative, then confinement might come out ahead in terms of total impact. If confinement of some youths deters others from committing offenses for fear of the same consequences, then confinement might be the more effective program in terms of total impact on the delinquency rate in a community. In sum, while evaluation research has concentrated on recidivism of youths processed through a particular program in comparison to alternatives, there are broader considerations of total impact that could affect the relative merits of alternatives.

Of course, the focus on effectiveness and cost reflects the utilitarian approach to program evaluation even if expanded to include consideration of incapacitation and deterrence. If an intervention does not seem appropriate given public evaluations of the offenders or offenses involved, then demonstrations of effectiveness and efficiency may fall on deaf ears. Similarly, a particular intervention might be preferred because it is judged more humane than another. Paul Lerman has suggested that when two alternatives are similar in terms of effectiveness and cost, the most humane response should be chosen (1968:63). Thus, issues of morality and justice may enter into the assessment of correctional alternatives with contrasting conclusions depending on the values and points of view involved.

Even if the focus were exclusively on recidivism, a researcher should deal with a variety of methodological issues before making any claims about demonstrated program effectiveness. One simple, but often ignored, requirement is to establish a basis for comparison. We have already noted that what may seem like a very high recidivism rate in an absolute sense may be low relative to alternative interventions. Such alternatives provide a basis for comparison.

Sometimes offenses by the experimental subjects before intervention are compared with offenses after intervention and, in that sense, the "experimental" group is compared with itself. Such comparisons may be meaningful if repeated numerous times and if other possible causes of change (such as aging or maturational reform) are taken into account. However, ideally, a comparison of before-and-after delinquency among youths subject to alternative interventions and no intervention at all would make the results far more meaningful.

A common problem in correctional experimentation is that the composition of youths in a particular program can make a program look successful when, in fact, it merely had "better" subjects. A true experimental design attempts to solve this problem by assigning subjects to different groups or conditions through a random process. If different groups are created by the "luck of the draw" or some other random process and the number of youths in each group is large enough, then we can have some confidence that the groups are comparable on all sorts of characteristics that might bias the results. As simple as random assignment sounds, there are serious ethical questions involved in implementing it. Most conceptions of justice are based on the presumption that the response to an offender should be based on characteristics of the offense and the circumstances surrounding its commission. Responses to offenders are not supposed to be random either for the benefit of society and/or the offender. Hence, the only circumstances where random assignment is likely to occur is for trivial offenders or for minor variations in response where issues of justice are not a serious problem.

LaMar Empey and Maynard Erickson (1972) have described the difficulty of implementing an experimental design in the study of a nonresidential treatment approach. Their experiment in Provo, Utah, called for random assignment of boys either to a traditional institutional setting or a probation alternative. In the interest of science, the juvenile court judge initially expressed willingness to participate in the experiment. However, once the program got underway, the judge was reluctant to commit boys to institutions. The judge believed institutions to be harmful and preferred to divert youths. From a scientific perspective, the effects of institutions and alternatives need to be studied and analyzed. However, from a legal and ethical perspective, the random assignment of a youth to an institution or to probation is a violation of the delinquent's civil rights.

Correctional research must also overcome questions of how outcomes are to be measured and evaluated. Stated another way, what constitutes a success or a failure? Lerman (1968) examined the California Youth Authority's Community Treatment Project and found that youths in the experimental and comparison groups were reacted to differently by probation workers. Boys placed in community treatment who committed a new offense were often given a "second chance," whereas subjects in the comparison groups who broke the law were more likely to have their probation revoked. The criterion for failure was different for the two categories of youth and therefore biased results in favor of the experimental youths.

Several reviews of correctional treatment literature have commented on both the quality and the results of such studies. By far the most controversial review was a report submitted to the Governor's Special Committee on Criminal Offenders in New York in the mid-1970s (Lipton, Martinson, and Wilks, 1975). In a search for available reports on attempts at rehabilitation from 1945 through 1967, these researchers found 231 studies that met a minimum set of standards for a methodologically adequate study. Perhaps the most telling statement about the methodological adequacy of such research is Robert Martinson's observation in a report titled "What Works?" that "it is just possible that some of our treatment programs *are* working to some extent, but that our research is so bad that it is incapable of telling" (1974:48). This comment was merely a cautionary note to Martinson's more substantive conclusion that the best studies available

> give us very little reason to hope that we have in fact found a sure way of reducing recidivism through rehabilitation. This is not to say that we have found no instances of success or partial success; it is only to say that these instances have

been isolated, producing no clear pattern to indicate the efficacy of any particular method of treatment. (1974:49)

Martinson's report came to be the foundation for claims that "nothing works," a conclusion that was not totally correct. For purposes of formulating policy, Martinson concentrated on methods of treatment. For a treatment program to have policy implications, he believed it should be generally applicable, amenable to implementation in new settings, and should rely on something other than "exceptional" personnel. Martinson did cite some specific programs that appeared to be effective. However, he noted that the determinants of success for those programs did not seem to be the method of treatment per se, but the coincidence of exceptional personnel, subjects amenable to treatment, and enthusiasm for the program. To recommend that exceptional people be hired to do "something" with enthusiasm to subjects ready to change did not strike him as a policy for treatment.

Reaffirmation of Rehabilitation

The notion that "nothing works" was a gross oversimplification of the research. Many programs had not been evaluated and many had been successful. In fact, in a review of Martinson's report by Ted Palmer he noted that 48 percent of the studies reviewed yielded positive results (1976). However, the lament that nothing works fit the political climate at that time. As Francis Cullen (2005) observes, the report came out "in the midst of a broader assault on the legitimacy of criminal justice and corrections" by critics from both the left and right. Radical critics viewed correctional institutions as repressive tools of government and the programs within them as making offenders worse. Conservative critics had always challenged the notion that people could be changed through treatment, viewing punishment and security as the legitimate and primary goals of corrections.

Although support for rehabilitation programs waned, numerous critics of Martinson's report (see Cullen and Gilbert, 1982; Cullen and Gendreau, 1989; and Cullen, 2005) sought to save rehabilitation. A major development accelerating that defense was the application of meta-analysis to treatment programs. Mark Lipsey (1992) compiled data from more than 400 delinquency treatment programs, coded their characteristics and "effect sizes," and used multivariate statistical techniques to identify what worked and what did not. He was able to control for variations in methodology and variation in risk based on background and prior offenses.

Lipsey later examined data on over 500 studies conducted between 1950 and 1995, attempting to answer the question: Can intervention rehabilitate serious delinquents? His answer is that "well-designed rehabilitative strategies do reduce recidivism" (1999:142). However, as with the "nothing works" research, the number of studies that could be used to provide an answer was reduced to 200 after imposing a small set of rules for inclusion. A total of 117 studies involved noninstitutionalized offenders and 83 involved institutionalized juveniles. Most of the noninstitutionalized offenders were on probation or parole.

Lipsey found several interventions that appeared effective, but their effectiveness varied among noninstitutionalized and institutionalized offenders. For example, among noninstitutionalized youth, programs classified under "individual counseling" were deemed to be highly effective. One involved citizen volunteers who were matched on several characteristics with juvenile probationers and provided individual counseling. A second involved "reality therapy" with female graduate students counseling youth on steps required to gain self-control over their lives. A third involved a "youth or family" and focused on "cognitive processes."

Seven programs that Lipsey examined involved either interpersonal skills, behavioral programs involving offenders and their families, or multiple services ranging from recreation to vocational placement. All of these programs included some form of work with families, and/or teachers, and/or groups. In sum, eight of ten programs judged to be exemplary involved groups or group processes and/or interventions where some attempt was made to alter the external environment.

Lipsey reports several types of programs that were ineffective or associated with increased recidivism among noninstitutionalized offenders. This set included wilderness programs, early release, shock incarceration (see chapter 11), and reduced caseloads for probation or parole officers.

There was some overlap for programs involving institutionalized juveniles in that the most effective programs involved training in interpersonal skills and types of behavioral modification, and multiple services. Two additional forms of successful intervention were "community residential" programs and "teaching-family homes." All of these interventions modify the institutional environment by breaking down barriers with the surrounding community or creating a new family or group environment.

Meta-analysis has challenged the "nothing works" doctrine and can serve as a guide to promising approaches. However, there is still considerable analysis to be done before the most salient dimensions of effective programs can be conclusively identified. Although classified under "interpersonal skills," "teaching-family home," and "behavioral programs," the effective programs involved a community home school, training in groups, role-playing, teaching parents, community-based group homes, discussion groups, and peer counseling.

Focus and Locus

Correctional experiments can be classified along a variety of dimensions and one of them is the specific focus of the treatment effort. Some correctional efforts are directed specifically at the *individual* offender and attempt to deal with specific individual problems through counseling or individual casework techniques. Other programs work through and with *groups*. Sometimes such group-oriented treatment may be nothing more than counseling or discussion in group sessions. However, it may also involve guiding the development of groups in a way that can be used to gain control of members' behavior in positive ways and in a wide range of circumstances. Finally, while the ultimate goal is to change the behavior of individuals, modification of the wider social environment is the central focus of some correctional experiments as well. It is also the basis for the teaching-family program (which provides a surrogate family, with house parents serving as role models) and related behavior modification or **token economy** programs. When extended beyond the confines of the institutional setting, such environmental approaches are the most global and ambitious of the forms of treatment because they call for a restructuring of relationships between offenders and the wider community.

In addition to the focus of treatment efforts, a second dimension for classifying forms of correctional experimentation is the degree to which they isolate offenders from the community or the degree of confinement involved. Some programs are totally residential with youths living within the confines of an institution, while others are community-based with variable degrees of control over the everyday lives of subjects. They may be nonresidential with youths living at home or semiresidential with youths attending school, working, and participating in recreational activities in the wider community but, otherwise, living within program facilities.

Individualized Treatment in an Institutional Context

Research on the recidivism rates of youths receiving some form of individualized treatment within an institutional context has yielded confusing and unpromising results. The California Youth Authority's Community Treatment Project used personality assessment techniques in setting up treatment plans geared specifically to the needs of individual offenders. A study of a California treatment program that used psychodynamically oriented individual counseling found no improvement in recidivism rates (California Department of Corrections, 1958). Evaluations of psychotherapy for young male offenders (Guttmann, 1963) and female offenders (Adams, 1959; 1961b) in California institutions produced the same findings. Two studies have suggested, however, that subjects who are deemed amenable to individual psychotherapeutic treatment have lower recidivism rates than nontreated subjects, but that the recidivism rates of subjects who are nonamenable to treatment are higher than the rates of nontreated subjects (Adams, 1961a). In yet another study, Karl Jesness (1970) classified delinquents into "maturity types" such as asocial, conformist, manipulative, and neurotic. He then randomly assigned one group to an experimental program that formulated a specific treatment according to the needs of the individual and the other group to a traditional institutional program. After both groups of juveniles were released back into the community, Jesness found their recidivism rates virtually identical. Moreover, traditional individual and group counseling methods appear to be no more promising with adults (Kassebaum, Ward, and Wilner, 1971) than they are with juveniles (Martinson, 1974).

With the perception that juveniles were becoming more crime prone in the early 1980s, there was increasing concern that the juvenile justice system was too lenient and what was needed was a "get-tough" policy. More than 40 states amended their juvenile codes to facilitate the transfer of juvenile offenders to adult criminal courts (Feld, 1988). The net effect of these legislative changes has been a dramatic increase of juvenile offenders in adult courts and the assumption that tougher sanctions imposed by the criminal courts will reduce juvenile crime. Donna Bishop and her colleagues (1996) looked at the impact of sending juveniles to adult court and found that harsher punishment produced higher recidivism rates. Despite being incarcerated for longer periods of time, youths transferred to adult courts had a higher reoffending rate than those who were not transferred to adult court. Harsher punishment may have produced a greater sense of alienation from society, lower self-esteem, and possibly a sense of anger and resentment.

Group-Oriented Approaches in an Institutional Context

One of the earliest alternatives to the traditional institutionalization of juvenile offenders was "therapeutic" treatment through carefully guided group processes. The goal of this type of group therapy is to help deviant groups uncover their problems and develop strategies for resolving their problems through legitimate means. The setting for such a treatment program has usually been a small residential institution, which could also be regarded as a therapeutic milieu. This type of group therapy experience is referred to as **guided group interaction** (GGI). Such programs see the group as the crucial factor in adolescent rehabilitation. According to the Center for Studies of Crime and Delinquency:

> GGI programs involve the delinquent in frequent and intensive group discussions of their own and other members' current problems and experiences. Based on the theory that antisocial youth behavior receives the support and approval of the delinquent peer group, and that substituting acceptable norms for delinquent values and attitudes also requires the support of the peer group, these programs encourage the development of a group culture and the acceptance by members of responsibility for helping and controlling one another. As the group culture develops and the group begins to accept greater responsibility, the staff group leader allows the group a greater degree of decision-making power. Over time, the group's responsibility may extend to decisions involving disciplinary measures imposed on a member or determination of a member's readiness for release. (Public Health Service, n.d.:3)

The best-known residential GGI program is Highfields, which began in 1950 in New Jersey. The Highfields program provides a highly supervised setting. It is limited to serving approximately twenty boys, age 16 and 17, who have not been previously committed to a correctional institution. During the day, the boys work at a nearby mental hospital as orderlies. They are not permitted to attend school. In the evening, two groups of ten boys each meet for guided group interaction sessions. Highfields has a short-term treatment approach that normally does not exceed three months.

The Highfields program was first evaluated by McCorkle, Elias, and Bixby (1959), who reported that the recidivism rate for Highfields "graduates" was only 18 percent, compared to a 33 percent rate for reformatory inmates. Ashley Weeks (1963) compared a sample of reformatory parolees with Highfields parolees and found the recidivism rate for the reformatory group to be 63 percent, compared to 47 percent for the Highfields group.

On the surface, the Highfields program seemed to be a successful treatment approach. However, critical examinations of the data have shown the program's results to be far less convincing than originally concluded. For example, Lerman (1968) noted that 18 percent of the cases from Highfields were "in-program" failures who did not complete the program. That is, some adolescents were discharged from the program for not adhering to the rules. When these internal failures were added to the external failures—those who completed the program but were rearrested—the promising results of the Highfields program were reduced, although a difference still existed. The results of the Highfields program appear promising, but adolescents were selected for the program based on certain criteria, such as no drug problems, and they were dismissed from the program for not following the rules.

Guided group interaction techniques have been used successfully to reduce conflicts within large institutions as well. In 1968 Harvey Varruth at the Minnesota Training School (Redwing) for boys adapted the GGI program to a large institutional setting of more than 600 juveniles. At that time the institution had been having severe discipline problems and seemed on the verge of explosion. The new approach was received with great enthusiasm, and the internal conflict subsided. It has also been claimed that recidivism and inmate behavioral problems declined while staff morale improved. Of course, it is important to remember that these claims merely suggest that the introduction of a new set of procedures into an explosive situation can have beneficial consequences.

Sarason and Ganzer (1973) reported on a project (Cascadia) in Washington State that uses a variety of techniques, including group discussion, modeling, and role-playing, to teach youths the skills necessary for avoiding peer pressure, applying for jobs, and planning their futures. For some groups staff "acted out" certain behaviors that the subjects could use as models for their own performance and role playing. Others participated in group discussions relevant to these same problems and skills. The researchers collected data on recidivism for a period of thirty-three months after discharge and then again after five years. The recidivism rate was lower for both experimental groups for both periods and especially low for those involved in group discussions. The rate after five years was less than one-half that found for the control group.

In sum, group-oriented approaches seem to show greater promise than individual counseling or psychotherapy for institutionalized youth. Such approaches also may be successful with noninstitutionalized offenders as suggested by Lipsey's analysis. Another name for GGI is "attack therapy," which means that adolescents are encouraged to vent their problems in a confrontational style. For some adolescents who are not verbal or who are thin-skinned, the experience with GGI can be extremely distasteful. However, the possibility that the effects are real may be as conclusive as correctional experimentation ever gets and may be a satisfactory basis for advocating such techniques.

Changing Environments in Institutions

Current environmentally oriented programs in totally residential settings tend to be based on **behavior modification** techniques derived from Skinnerian operant conditioning theory and, more recently, from social learning theory (see chapter 5). A major characteristic of behavior modification programs is the systematic manipulation of the environment to create a potential for changing behavior. For example, Cohen and Filipczak (1971) reported on a "new learning environment" (CASE) for boys in an institution that included a special environment aimed at expanding the social and academic repertoires of the residents and a token economy that rewarded the boys for academic competence and punished them for academic lethargy. The result of this treatment approach was a significant increase in grade level as measured by the Stanford Achievement Test. There was also a mean increase of 12.5 points in IQ scores after ten months in the program.

A second example of a behavioral program in an institutional setting is Project ACE (Applied Contingency Environment) at the Maryland Training School for Boys. This institution provides cottage housing and a school program for about 300 delinquent youths. Project ACE was introduced in two cottages that housed the institution's most belligerent inmates. The project involved identifying target behaviors (breaking windows or chairs, assaultive behavior, poor school performance) and establishing a "point economy" system. Subjects could earn points through appropriate behavior and spend them in a "spending room" for such tangible goods as candy, soda, and grooming articles. They could also use them for admission to a game room. The program was effective in controlling the behavior of boys within the institution.

Robert Ross and H. Bryan McKay (1978) reviewed twenty-four behavior modification/token economy programs within institutions and found only three that provided follow-up data on juveniles, including Cohen and Filipczak's. A follow-up of twenty-seven boys suggested lower recidivism at one and two years but no difference at three years. However, the adequacy of the control group was questionable since there was no random assignment. Another study by Jesness and others (1972) suggested a lower parole violation rate for youths in a token economy experiment than for control groups, while a third study involving females reported higher recidivism rates for experimental subjects (Ross and McKay, 1976). Such variation in results and doubts about pre-intervention comparability of experimental and control groups led Ross and McKay to state, "We can conclude with confidence that behavior modification is not the panacea it was touted as when it was introduced to corrections" (1978:289). However, the implications of such experiments for institutional management are more impressive and more conclusive: "In each of the programs . . . a behavioral approach was found to be successful in either reducing antisocial behavior in the institution" or in enhancing the offender's achievement or industrial productivity (1978:289). Ross and McKay remind us once again that rehabilitation "is only one goal of corrections" and in terms of influence on targeted behavior within institutions, token economies appear to work. The problem is measuring the institutional impact on the everyday lives of youth when they return to the community and encounter a new or even contradictory learning environment.

Halfway Houses

The **halfway house** is a temporary residence for offenders and is usually located within a community. The residents are generally given freedoms that are not possible in a totally residential program. These freedoms include access to community-based employment, education, and recreation. Private charitable organizations began operating halfway houses for offenders in the nineteenth century, and governmental agencies began establishing such programs in the 1950s. One of the purposes of the halfway house is to provide a transitional setting that will reduce recidivism, which tends to be inordinately high during the early stages after release. Thalheimer has described the purpose of a halfway house in the following manner:

> The very name halfway house suggests its position in the corrections world; halfway-in, a more structured environment than probation and parole; halfway-out, a less structured environment than institutions. As halfway-in houses they represent a last stop before incarceration for probationers and parolees having faced revocation; as halfway-out houses, they provide services to probationers and parolees leaving institutions. Halfway houses also provide a residential alternative to jail or outright release for accused offenders awaiting trail or convicted offenders awaiting sentencing. (1975:1)

Depending on the particular halfway house in question, treatment may consist of an informal family-like atmosphere, formalized group therapy (such as guided group interaction), or individual counseling. Because of the diversity of programs and a lack of good follow-up data, it is difficult to assess the effectiveness of halfway houses per se, and the effectiveness of individual therapy within such settings is unknown.

A variation of the halfway house is home confinement with electronic monitoring. The juvenile must wear a transmitter on the ankle, neck, or wrist that is either an active or passive tracking system. The active system sends a constant signal that permits virtually round-the-clock monitoring and the passive system requires the youth to send an electronic signal in response to a computer-activated call. Thus, the juvenile is permitted to reside at home but confined to his or her home unless attending school or engaged in work or some other legitimate activity. While this is an intriguing application of technology to juvenile corrections, there are strong reservations about electronic monitoring. The ease of electronic monitoring might lead to its overuse and abuse. Does this represent an invasion of privacy and a "big brother" atmosphere that is overly invasive? Finally, does turning the home into a prison and the parents into guards destroy the efficacy of the home environment? The potential uses of electronic monitoring are great, but so is the potential for its abuse.

Group-Oriented Techniques in a Semiresidential Setting

The best known experiment with group-oriented techniques in a semiresidential setting is the Silverlake Experiment. The Silverlake Experiment was conducted by Empey and Steven Lubeck (1971) between 1964 and 1968. At Boy's Republic, a private residential treatment facility for delinquent boys in Los Angeles, some boys were randomly assigned to a special community-based program, while others were placed in the regular institutional regimen. The experimental group, which consisted of no more than twenty boys, lived in a residential home located in a middle-class neighborhood during the week and returned home on weekends. The boys attended high school and had the assistance of a tutor. They also attended daily group meetings that were conducted along the lines of guided group interaction. The experiment lasted three years, with an additional year devoted to the collection of follow-up data.

The overall results indicated no significant difference between the experimental and control group in relative frequency of arrest during the twelve months following release. During that period, there was a 73 percent reduction in the volume of delinquency committed by experimental subjects and a 71 percent reduction in the volume of delinquency committed by the control group. This reduction might mean that both programs were successful, but without other bases of comparison we cannot reach such a conclusion. Although the Silverlake program failed to show positive results compared to another program, the experiment remains one of the most careful and sophisticated studies of community-based treatment.

The Teaching-Family Model

The image of training schools as prisons for juvenile offenders has given way in many settings to smaller, family-like living quarters without barbed-wire fences, bars, cells, or armed guards. A dramatic example of this change is Boys' Town and Girls' Town. Boys' and Girls' Towns are based on a **teaching-family model**, which attempts to reproduce a home-like environment for learning new skills and behaviors. The "family" is composed of a husband and wife, who are known as teaching parents, and five to ten adolescents. The youths and the teaching parents live together for approximately one year. Depending on a youth's needs, the parents attempt to instill new academic, vocational, social, and family-living skills. The system for establishing and maintaining new behaviors is based in part on a token economy. Individuals earn points for behaviors deemed desirable and may exchange accumulated points for goods and privileges. As a youth progresses in the teaching-family program, these motivational aids are gradually reduced.

A similar attempt to design a new learning environment and to remove barriers between the program and the outside world is Achievement Place. Achievement Place provides residential group care for delinquents and is organized similarly to Boys' Town. Youth in this program continue to attend school, visit parents, and may even earn stays at home. A token economy is used within a family-like environment with teaching parents. Youths are encouraged to work their way out of the token system by demonstrating that they can perform well on their own merits. When they are able to return home, parents are given instruction on maintaining appropriate behavior. Thus, the program is based on principles of behavior modification but goes beyond a token economy in the attempt to encourage trustworthy behavior in settings where rewards and punishments are not as explicit or forthcoming as in a token system.

The authors are aware of no evaluative data relevant to recidivism rates for Boys' and Girls' Town, but there has been some evaluation of Achievement Place. As was the case for behavior modification techniques within more confining institutional settings, such techniques are highly successful in bringing about change in targeted behavior. However, the impact on subsequent delinquent behavior is unclear since nonrandom control groups are used as a comparison. Over a one-year follow-up period, 19 percent of sixteen Achievement Place youths had been committed to an institution compared to about 53 percent of youths in the control group (Phillips et al., 1971). Over a two-year follow-up period, 56 percent of eighteen Achievement Place youths were found to still be in school compared to 33 percent of controls matched as "comparable" to these youths by a probation officer. Their recommittal rate was 22 percent compared to 47 percent for the matched control as well. While these results are suggestive, the same issues of preintervention comparability have to be raised.

Wilderness Survival

Lipsey's meta-analysis identifies the teaching-family model as one of the most effective alternatives to secure, residential placement. The teaching-family model attempts to create a new learning environment by gaining control over reward and punishment and restructuring relationships with the community. A quite different approach with a similar goal is central to a variety of wilderness survival and back-to-nature programs in the United States and Canada. Such programs attempt to build confidence and skills through activities that are believed to be inherently rewarding and conducive to the development of problem-solving skills.

Two such programs in the United States are Outward Bound and Vision Quest. Outward Bound provides challenges such as backpacking, rock climbing, sailing, and route-finding, which are supposed to develop a sense of competence and accomplishment as well as cooperation and leadership. The program uses existing environments and offers activities that are presumed to be challenging, rewarding, and rehabilitative in themselves. In a follow-up study in Massachusetts, Outward Bound graduates were found to have a significantly lower recidivism rate after one year than a control group of matched juveniles handled through regular channels. However, the advantage was not significant after five years.

An analysis of a wilderness experience program for probationers in eastern Canada (Winterdyk and Roesch, 1982) yielded less promising results. The Canadian program was based on the Outward Bound philosophy and provided the same sorts of activities to minor or first-time offenders. Data on psychological traits and attitudes that were supposed to be affected by the experience were "inconclusive" and both the experimental youths and control youths were found to have a reconviction rate of about 20 percent. There was some indication that the experimental groups' offenses were less severe but the differences were too small to be statistically significant.

Vision Quest is a more diverse program than Outward Bound but embodies much of the same philosophy. It is a private, for-profit treatment program for delinquent and troubled youth and has headquarters in Arizona and Pennsylvania. The program has grown to provide home-based treatment, group homes, and learning centers in addition to wilderness experiences. It is best known for its "wagon train" that makes regular appearances in parades throughout the country. The Vision Quest program also has drawn considerable critical attention (and is the subject of civil lawsuits) for deaths that occurred during one of its sailing ventures. In addition to building self-respect through challenging activities, the program also is known for its use of confrontational techniques in which inappropriate behavior is immediately addressed by a staff member and youth are forced to accept responsibility for their behavior. The technique has drawn some criticism since it may involve excessive force and pressure in order to immediately confront the problem. The program publicizes itself as successful and has been applauded by numerous corrections personnel, but it has not been carefully evaluated in comparison to alternative responses.

Peter Greenwood and Susan Turner (1987) of the Rand Corporation examined the effectiveness of Vision Quest and found that the probation department in the San Diego Juvenile Court strongly opposed the program. It was alleged that adolescents were placed in potentially dangerous activities, that the staff of Vision Quest resented oversight by the probation staff, and Vision Quest staff wanted to determine when youths would be released from the program. The most serious criticisms involved the use of confrontational tactics in solving problems and what some termed as abusive disciplinary action. The sea-going version of Vision Quest, called Ocean Quest, was temporarily discontinued after a boating accident that resulted in nine deaths. A Coast Guard investigation found no evidence of misconduct but cited the crew's lack of experience and the fatigue of the persons on board who had been at sea for some forty hours.

Nonresidential Experiments

One of the most highly acclaimed rehabilitation experiments is the Community Treatment Program in California (Warren and Palmer, 1966; Palmer, 1971). Youths who otherwise would have been sent to California Youth Authority training schools were assigned to an experimental program and returned to their community for intensive treatment. Each member of the experimental group was diagnosed and classified on a scale of "interpersonal maturity." Within each maturity level, or "I-level classification," there were further subclassifications based on measures of the way a delinquent responded to or perceived the world. Categories within the I-levels were based on whether responses were passive or aggressive, conforming or manipulative, neurotic, acting out, or culturally identifying. The comparison or control group was comprised of youths assigned to one of the existing institutions of the California Youth Authority.

The initial reports from this project purportedly demonstrated greater success than traditional confinement. After fifteen months in the community, the experimental subjects had a parole violation rate of 28 percent, compared to 52 percent for the control subjects. However, in a critical analysis of this project, Lerman (1975) concluded that the most dramatic finding was that the project changed *parole officers' behavior* rather than the youths' behavior. Lerman found that the reported *number of offenses* for the two groups was approximately the same, if not higher for the experimental group, but that the *reactions* of officials were different. Parole officers for juveniles who were in the experimental group recommended fewer parole revocations than for members of the control group. Youths in the community treatment program were more likely to be given additional chances to reform even though the experimental subjects had committed an average of 2.8 offenses in the follow-up period compared to 1.6 for the control group. This unexpected difference may reflect greater interaction with parole officers for experimental subjects, increasing the chances that a parole officer would be aware of their misbehavior. Such differences make it difficult to draw definite conclusions about either the success or failure of the program. It would appear that California's Community Treatment Program succeeded in changing the behavior of adult parole officers rather than adolescent parolees.

The basic principles of the Highfields project (GGI) were expanded upon in a nonresidential setting in Provo, Utah, beginning in 1959 (Empey and Erickson, 1972). Each day, following work or school, boys assigned to the experimental program went to a center for guided group interaction sessions. The control groups were to be a random selection of adjudicated youths placed on probation in the community and youths committed to the state training school. However, once the program was underway, the juvenile judge decided against randomly committing boys to the training school, and a new comparison group of youths committed to the training school from other Utah counties had to be used for comparison.

Analysis of the program showed that the experimental group did not have a significantly higher success rate than the probationers. After the first year of the program, the recidivism rate for both groups was approximately 50 percent and the differences did not change appreciably over the next four years. After four years the recidivism rate for both groups was around 60 percent. However, both the experimental group and probationers did better than youths committed to a training school. After one year, 60 percent of training school youths had recidivated and by the end of four years about 80 percent had done so. Thus, confinement was less effective than two noninstitutional alternatives. Since the training school comparison group was not randomly created from the same population of youth as the probationers and experimental subjects, caution must be exercised in interpreting these findings.

A small-scale experiment in Hawaii called the Buddy System used nonprofessional volunteers to provide a new social relationship for youths in their natural environment. Based on the same philosophy as Big Brother or Big Sister programs, youths with school problems were assigned a "buddy" to serve as a role model, monitor, and confidant. In essence, youths entered into a small-group relationship with an older, conventional buddy. An evaluation of Buddy System programs in two cities in Hawaii (Fo and O'Donnell, 1974) found that youth with truancy problems who were referred to the program by schools were truant less often, especially when the volunteer buddy controlled a small amount of money that was used as a reward contingent on the performance of the youth.

The objective in nonresidential, environmentally oriented programs is to alter the communal or social relationships of the offender. Some alterations have been relatively minor while others have involved major changes in neighborhoods. The Chicago Area Project (Kobrin, 1959), instituted in the 1930s by Clifford Shaw, is the most notable example of an attempt to alter the environment on a rather large scale. The project had the dual objectives of rehabilitating parolees and preventing delinquency in neighborhoods with high crime rates. The core aim of the project was the revitalization of neighborhood identity and pride through local self-help enterprises. Parolees were expected to have a better chance of avoiding future crime if the neighborhoods to which they returned were organized in ways that would increase bonds between offenders and conventional organizations, people, and institutions. Solomon Kobrin has cited evidence that the program did reduce delinquency, and an assessment by Schlossman and Sedlak (1983) suggests that the arrest rate may have been halved in one of the project neighborhoods compared to no reduction of the arrest rate in a comparable nonproject neighborhood.

Project New Pride in Denver, Colorado, is a difficult program to classify because it involves rather comprehensive attempts to alter the relationship between a youth and the community environment, but working primarily through the offender. It does not attempt to reorganize the environment in the sense that the Chicago Area Project did, but it does address nearly every aspect of a youth's interaction with the community. It is a nonresidential, community-based program for repetitive and fairly serious offenders. Based on the belief that youths who do not want help are not likely to be helped, the program prefers voluntary enrollment and handles about sixty new enrollees per year. The project includes an alternative school and a learning disabilities center and provides intensive counseling, behavioral modification, and contracting and job placement. A follow-up study of New Pride youths found them to have a slightly lower recidivism rate (27 percent) than a control group (32 percent) with some of the success attributable to job placement and re-enrollment in school (Blew et al., 1977). However, it is important to remember that the New Pride youths were volunteers and may have differed motivationally prior to treatment compared to control youths.

Family Intervention

Another approach to altering the problem behavior of youth without confinement attempts to alter the behavior of parents in relation to their children. Extensive research on such **family intervention** techniques has been carried out by researchers at the Oregon Social Learning Center (see Patterson et al., 1973; Patterson, 1980;

Patterson and Fleischman, 1979). Parents of delinquent youth and aggressive children are taught noncoercive techniques of control and how to interact more positively with their children. The emphasis is on establishing stronger bonds between parents and children, improving parental monitoring, and insuring appropriate reactions to approved and disapproved behavior. One study of youths who had committed theft showed impressive reductions in stealing—from .83 events per week to only .07 per week immediately following treatment (Patterson, 1981, 1982). A subsequent study, however, found that after a year the youths had returned to their original rate (Moore et al., 1979). The family intervention approach has been used with some success to change aggressive behavior and such results appear to be more enduring than the change produced in the study of theft.

Overview

The correctional experiments summarized in the previous section support several observations. First, meta-analyses suggest that numerous programs are effective, and the most effective programs are those that provide several services, minimize prisonization by breaking down barriers to community life, and attempt to modify numerous dimensions of the social environment by guiding peer group interaction and reproducing family life. Second, token economies and behavior modification are effective tools for the management of offenders, the control of contrary behavior *within* a program, and the enhancement of educational, vocational, and other skills. Third, it is extremely rare for a correctional experiment to make offenders worse and most have done no worse than training schools and many have done better.

Lundman (1993) concluded his examination of efforts in the prevention and control of juvenile delinquency, including many of the programs we have summarized, with several recommendations for policy. One recommendation is that routine probation be retained as the first and most frequent sentencing option for moderately delinquent juveniles convicted of index crimes against property (1993:247). This recommendation was supported by the Provo Experiment, where routine, haphazard supervision by probation officers with large caseloads was just as effective as intense, community-based services. Lundman also recommends that community-based treatment, including intensive supervision programs, be permanently expanded to accommodate nearly all chronic property offenders currently sentenced to juvenile correctional facilities (1993:252). This recommendation is advocated on the grounds that community treatment does no worse than confinement, is often less expensive, and is more humane than incarceration. Finally, Lundman recommends that institutionalization be reserved for juveniles adjudicated delinquent for index crimes against persons (1993:255). Cheaper and more humane alternatives are available for the vast majority of offenders but imprisonment may be justified when an offender constitutes a continuing threat to the community.

Such recommendations stem from available research but it is important to note that they are based primarily on evidence concerning recidivism. Martinson noted that the emphasis on rehabilitating offenders has overshadowed other criteria for evaluating programs such as *general deterrence* and *incapacitation*. A particular treatment program might generate lower recidivism rates and yet contribute to a community's crime rate by allowing free movement of offenders and reducing fear of punishment among nonoffenders. Such possibilities are the basis for growing criticism of studies that use recidivism as the sole criterion for evaluating the effects of treatment programs (Martinson, 1976; Wilson, 1975).

Summary

In this chapter we have summarized the history and current status of the imprisonment of juvenile offenders. While the risk of apprehension for a delinquent offense is quite low and the proportion of delinquents who are sent to correctional facilities is modest, the use of imprisonment as an appropriate reaction remains a key controversy in juvenile justice. Ironically, imprisonment itself was originally viewed as a humane alternative to physical punishment. Moreover, the imprisonment of offenders came to be viewed as a means of changing, or "reforming" people, rather than as simply a means of punishment. The reformatory emerged as a symbol of a new correctional philosophy but soon generated criticism from anti-institutionalists. While the emergence of a separate juvenile justice system was characterized by arguments for probation and home treatment rather than reformatories, such institutions were not abolished and, in fact, a new form of short-term confinement, the detention center, was invented. The need for secure, custodial institutions for juveniles is still under attack, although countered in recent years by arguments for imprisonment as a means of incapacitation, retribution, and general deterrence.

The results from hundreds of correctional experiments allow us to reject the claim that the data compiled show that "nothing works." There are systematic variations and many programs do better than others. On the other hand, we cannot conclusively claim that doing "something" is typically better than doing nothing. That fact has led some critics to challenge the notion that experimentation with more of the same is the best direction for addressing problems of juvenile delinquency. In the 1970s radical critics advocated policies of minimal intervention, tolerance, and basic social change. In the 1980s and 1990s critics with a more conservative bent advocated a return to an emphasis on the potential deterrent, incapacitative, and retributive functions of imprisonment. Approaches reflecting these different points of view are reviewed in the next chapter, where we consider programs that attempt to divert youths, to scare them straight, to assure that they set matters right with victims, or that subject them to the rigors of military discipline.

Discussion Questions

1. Is concern about imprisonment as a response to delinquency a recent or a long-standing issue? How does the public line up on the issue in recent times?

2. One of the earliest correctional models emphasized solitary confinement and minimal interaction with other prisoners. Discuss the pros and cons of such a model.

3. In what ways are private programs advocated as a better investment than public programs? Discuss the evidence for such arguments. What are the potential hazards of privatization?

4. What criteria other than recidivism rates might be used for evaluating the total impact of a correctional program?

5. If offenders released from one institution have lower recidivism rates than offenders released from another, can we conclude that one had a greater rehabilitative effect than the other? Justify your answer, taking into account the meaning of rehabilitation.

6. Why is it not possible to glibly and unquestionably accept the argument that all training institutions are "schools for crime"?

7. What was the conclusion of the controversial report on the effectiveness of correctional treatment submitted by Lipton, Martinson, and Wilks to the Governor's Committee in New York? Were any programs considered successful? Why were these successes considered to have no clear policy implications?

8. What is "meta-analysis" and how has it affected the "nothing works" doctrine?

9. Describe how any one of the specific correctional programs in the "Focus and Locus" section of the chapter fits with any of the theories in chapter 6.

10. Which programs do you think appeal to people with conservative political leanings and which appeal to people with more liberal leanings? Are there any programs that both might find appealing?

References

Adams, S. 1959. "Effectiveness of the Youth Authority Special Treatment Program: First Interim Report." Research report no. 5. Sacramento: California Youth Authority.

———. 1961a. "Effectiveness of Interview Therapy with Older Youth Authority Wards: An Interim Evaluation of the PICO Project." Research report no. 20 (January 10). Sacramento: California Youth Authority.

———. 1961b. "Assessment of the Psychiatric Treatment Program: Phase 1, Third Interim Report." Research report no. 21 (January 31). Sacramento: California Youth Authority.

American Bar Association and National Bar Association. 2001. *Justice by Gender: The Lack of Appropriate Prevention, Diversion and Treatment Alternatives for Girls in the Justice System.*

Bayer, P., and D. Pozen. 2005. "The Effectiveness of Juvenile Correctional Facilities: Public versus Private Management." *Journal of Law and Economics* 48(2):549–90.

Beck, A. J., and B. E. Shipley. 1987. *Recidivism of Young Parolees.* Washington, DC: U.S. Dept. of Justice.

Bishop, D., et al. 1996. "The Transfer of Juveniles to Criminal Court: Does It Make a Difference?" *Crime and Delinquency* 42:171–91.

Blew, C. H., D. McGillis, and G. Bryant. 1977. *Project New Pride.* Washington, DC: GPO.

California Department of Corrections. 1958. "Intensive Treatment Program: Second Annual Report." Prepared by H. B. Bradley and J. D. Williams (December 1). Sacramento: California Dept. of Corrections. Mimeographed.

Carter, R. M., R. A. McGee, and E. K. Nelson. 1975. *Corrections in America.* Philadelphia: J. B. Lippincott.

Chesney-Lind, M., and R. Shelden. 1998. *Girls, Delinquency, and Juvenile Justice.* 2nd ed. Belmont, CA: Wadsworth.

Children's Bureau. 1975. *Institutions Serving Delinquent Children.* Washington, DC: GPO.

Cohen, H. D., and J. Filipczak. 1971. *A New Learning Environment.* San Francisco: Jossey-Bass.

Cullen, F. T. 2005. "The Twelve People Who Saved Rehabilitation: How the Science of Criminology Made a Difference." *Criminology* 43:1–41.

Cullen, F. T., and P. Gendreau. 1989. "The Effectiveness of Correctional Rehabilitation: Reconsidering the 'Nothing Works' Debate." In *American Prisons: Issues in Research and Policy,* edited by Lynne Goldstein and Doris MacKensie. New York: Plenum.

Cullen, F. T., and K. E. Gilbert. 1982. *Reaffirming Rehabilitation.* Cincinnati, OH: Anderson.

Dean, D. W., and N. D. Reppucci. 1974. "Juvenile Correctional Institutions." In *Handbook of Criminology,* edited by D. Glaser. Chicago: Rand McNally.

Empey, L. T., and M. L. Erickson. 1972. *The Provo Experiment.* Lexington, MA: Lexington Books.

Empey, L. T., and S. G. Lubeck. 1971. *The Silverlake Experiment.* Chicago: Aldine.

Feld, B. C. 1981. "A Comparative Analysis of Organizational Structure and Inmate Subcultures in Institutions for Juvenile Offenders." *Crime and Delinquency* 27 (July):336–63.

———. 1988. "*In re Gault* Revisited: A Cross-State Comparison of the Right to Counsel in Juvenile Court." *Crime and Delinquency* 34:393–424.

Finestone, H. 1976. *Victims of Change.* Westport, CT: Greenwood Press.

Fo, W. S. O., and C. R. O'Donnell. 1974. "The Buddy System: Relationship and Contingency Conditions in a Community Intervention Program for Youth with Non-Professionals as Behavior Change Agents." *Journal of Consulting Clinical Psychology* 42:163–69.

Fox, V. 1972. *Introduction to Corrections.* Englewood Cliffs, NJ: Prentice-Hall.

Gray, F. C. 1847. *Prison Discipline in America.* London: J. Murray.

Greenwood, P. W., and S. Turner. 1987. *The Vision Quest Program: An Evaluation.* Santa Monica, CA: Rand Corporation.

Guttmann, E. S. 1963. "Effects of Short-Term Psychiatric Treatment on Boys in Two California Youth Authority Institutions." Research report no. 36 (December). Sacramento: California Youth Authority.

Hagan, J., and J. Leon. 1977. "Rediscovering Delinquency: Social History, Political Ideology and the Sociology of Law." *American Sociological Review* 42 (August):587–98.

Hartney, C. 2006. "Youth Under Age 18 in the Adult Criminal Justice System." National Council on Crime and Delinquency Fact Sheet, June.

Jesness, K. F. 1970. "The Preston Typology Study." *Youth Authority Quarterly* 23 (Winter):26–38.

Jesness, K. F., et al. 1972. *The Youth Center Research Project.* Sacramento: California Youth Authority.

Johnston, N. 1973. *The Human Cage: A Brief History of Prison Architecture.* New York: Walker.

Kassebaum, G., D. Ward, and D. Wilner. 1971. *Prison Treatment and Parole Survival: An Empirical Assessment.* New York: John Wiley.

Kobrin, S. 1959. "The Chicago Area Project: A 25-Year Assessment." *Annals of the American Academy of Political and Social Science* 322 (March):20–29.

Koons, B., J. D. Burrow, M. Morash, and T. Bynum. 1997. "Expert and Offender Perceptions of Program Elements Linked to Successful Outcomes of Incarcerated Women." *Crime and Delinquency* 43:512–32.

Lerman, P. 1968. "Evaluative Studies of Institutions for Delinquents: Implications for Research and Social Policy." *Social Work* 13 (July):55–64.

———. 1975. *Community Treatment and Social Control.* Chicago: University of Chicago Press.

Lipsey, M. W. 1992. "Juvenile Delinquency Treatment: A Meta-Analytic Inquiry into the Variability of Effects." In *Meta-Analysis for Explanation: A Casebook,* edited by T. D. Hooker, H. Cooper, D. S. Cordray, H. Hastmann, L. V. Hedges, R. J. Light, T. A. Louis, and F. Mosteler, pp. 83–127. New York: Russell Sage Foundation.

——— 1999. "Can Intervention Rehabilitate Serious Delinquents?" *Annals of the American Academy of Political and Social Science* 564:142–66.

Lipton, D., R. Martinson, and J. Wilks. 1975. *The Effectiveness of Correctional Treatment: A Survey of Treatment Evaluation Studies.* New York: Praeger.

Lundman, R. 1984. *Prevention and Control of Juvenile Delinquency.* New York: Oxford University Press.

———. 1993. *Prevention and Control of Juvenile Delinquency.* 2nd ed. New York: Oxford University Press.

Martinson, R. 1974. "What Works?—Questions and Answers about Prison Reform." *Public Interest* 35 (Spring):22–54.

———. 1976. "California Research at the Crossroads." *Crime and Delinquency* (April):180–91.

McCorkle, L. W., A. Elias, and F. L. Bixby. 1959. *The Highfields Story.* New York: Holt, Rinehart and Winston.

Moore, D. R., P. Chamberlain, and L. H. Mukai. 1979. "Children at Risk for Delinquency: A Follow-Up Comparison of Aggressive Children and Children Who Steal." *Journal of Abnormal Child Psychology* 7:345–55.

Murray, C. A., and L. A. Cox. 1979. *Beyond Probation: Juvenile Corrections and the Chronic Offender.* Beverly Hills: Sage.

Office of Juvenile Justice and Delinquency Prevention. 1994. *Conditions of Confinement: Juvenile Detention and Corrections Facilities.* Washington, DC: U.S. Dept. of Justice.

Palmer, T. B. 1971. "California's Community Treatment Program for Delinquent Adolescents." *Journal of Research in Crime and Delinquency* 8 (January):74–92.

———. 1976. "Martinson Revisited." In *Rehabilitation, Recidivism and Research*, edited by M. Matlin. Hackensack, NJ: National Council on Crime and Delinquency.

Patterson, G. R. 1980. "Treatment for Children with Conduct Problems: A Review of Outcome Studies." In *Behavior Change: Biological and Social Processes*, edited by S. Feshbach and A. Fraczek. New York: Praeger.

———. 1981. "Some Speculations and Data Relating to Children Who Steal." In *Theory and Fact in Contemporary Criminology*, edited by T. Hirschi and M. Gottfredson. Beverly Hills: Sage.

———. 1982. *Coercive Family Processes.* Eugene, OR: Castalia.

Patterson, G. R., J. A. Cobb, and R. S. Ray. 1973. "A Social Engineering Technology for Retraining the Families of Aggressive Boys." In *Issues and Trends in Behavior Therapy*, edited by H. E. Adams and I. P. Unikel. Springfield, IL: Chas. C. Thomas.

Patterson, G. R., and M. J. Fleischman. 1979. "Maintenance of Treatment Effects: Some Considerations Concerning Family Systems and Follow-Up Data." *Behavior Therapy* 10:168–85.

Phillips, E. L., E. A. Phillips, D. L. Fixen, and M. M. Wolf. 1971. "Achievement Place: Modification of the Behaviors of Pre-Delinquent Boys within a Token Economy." *Journal of Applied Behavioral Analysis* 4:45–59.

Platt, A. 1969. *The Child Savers.* Chicago: University of Chicago Press.

Polsky, H. W. 1962. *Cottage Six.* New York: Russell Sage Foundation.

Pratt, T., and J. Maahs. 1999. "Are Private Prisons More Cost-Effective Than Public Prisons? A Meta-Analysis of Evaluation Research Studies." *Crime and Delinquency* 45:358–71.

President's Commission on Law Enforcement and the Administration of Justice. 1967. *Task Force Report: Corrections.* Washington, DC: GPO.

Public Health Service. n.d. *Community Based Correctional Programs: Models and Practices.*

Ross, R. R., and H. B. McKay. 1976. "A Study of Institutional Treatment Programs." *International Journal of Offender Therapy and Comparative Criminology* 20:165–73.

———. 1978. "Behavior Approaches to Treatment and Corrections: Requiem for a Panacea." *Canadian Journal of Criminology* 20(20):279–95.

Sarason, I. G., and V. J. Ganzer. 1973. "Modeling and Group Discussion in the Rehabilitation of Juvenile Delinquents." *Journal of Counseling Psychology* 20:442–49.

Schlossman, S. L. 1977. *Love and the American Delinquent.* Chicago: University of Chicago Press.

Schlossman, S. L., and M. Sedlak. 1983. *The Chicago Area Project Revisited.* Santa Monica, CA: Rand Corporation.

Schlossman, S. L., and S. Wallach. 1982. "The Crime of Precocious Sexuality: Female Juvenile Delinquency and the Progressive Era." In *Women and the Law: The Social Historical Perspective*, edited by D. Kelley Weisberg. Cambridge, MA: Scherlman.

Schrag, C. 1971. *Criminal Justice: American Style.* Washington, DC: GPO.

Schwartz, I. M., S. Guo, and J. Kerbs. 1992. "Public Attitudes toward Juvenile Crime and Juvenile Justice: Implications for Public Policy." In *Exploring Delinquency: Causes and Control*, edited by D. G. Rojek and G. F. Jensen. Los Angeles: Roxbury.

Shover, N., and W. J. Einstadter. 1989. *Analyzing American Corrections*. Belmont, CA: Wadsworth.

Snyder, H. N., and M. Sickmund. 2006. *Juvenile Offenders and Victims: 2006 National Report*. Washington, DC: U.S. Dept. of Justice.

Sutherland, E. H., and D. R. Cressey. 1978. *Criminology*. 10th ed. Philadelphia: J. B. Lippincott.

Sykes, G. 1978. *Criminology*. New York: Harcourt, Brace, Jovanovich.

Thalheimer, D. J. 1975. *Cost Analyses of Correctional Standards: Halfway Houses*. Vol. 2. Washington, DC: Law Enforcement Assistance Administration.

Thornberry, T. P. 1971. "Punishment and Crime: The Effect of Legal Dispositions on Subsequent Criminal Behavior." Ph.D. dissertation, University of Pennsylvania.

Warren, M. Q., and T. B. Palmer. 1966. *The Community Treatment Project after Five Years*. Sacramento: California Youth Authority.

Weeks, H. A. 1963. *Youthful Offenders at Highfields*. Ann Arbor: University of Michigan Press.

Wilson, J. Q. 1975. *Thinking about Crime*. New York: Basic Books.

Winterdyk, J., and R. Roesch. 1982. "A Wilderness Experiential Program as an Alternative for Probationers." *Canadian Journal of Corrections* 24 (January):39–50.

Recent Themes
From Diversion to Boot Camps

Does clubbing a man reform him? Does brutal treatment elevate his thoughts? Does handcuffing him fill him with good resolves? Stop right here, and for a moment imagine yourself forced to submit to being handcuffed, and see what kind of feelings will be aroused in you. Submission to that one act of degradation prepares many a young man for a career of crime. It destroys the self-respect of others, and makes them the easy victim of crime.

(John P. Altgeld, *Our Penal Machinery and Its Victims*, 1884)

Introduction

In the last chapter we summarized a large volume of literature on corrections and correctional experiments of various kinds. This chapter will be more narrow in focus. We will address five themes in juvenile justice that emerged as new and innovative approaches in the past several decades and which have dominated discussions of delinquency control for some time. In the 1970s the major emphasis was on diverting offenders who had not committed serious offenses to community-based programs. This major programmatic theme became known as **diversion**. However, the concern about protecting some offenders from the presumed trauma of traditional court processing was paralleled by a growing concern for protecting the rights of victims. Matters had to be set right with the victims of crime, and offenders had to play an active role in that process. This victim-orientation was reflected in programs requiring that offenders pay back their victims and/or society through their own labor. **Restitution** emerged as a programmatic emphasis in the 1980s.

Public, political, and social scientific opinion grew more conservative during the 1970s and 1980s. The emerging victim-orientation was accompanied by an increasing commitment to get tough with juvenile offenders. Youths needed to be dramatically confronted with the potential costs of their transgressions. If adolescents could not be corrected by the system, then maybe they could be **scared straight** by direct exposure to the hazards of prison life, an approach also known as "shock therapy." Along similar lines a highly structured, militaristic approach called boot camp was a dominant theme in the 1990s. **Boot camps** are a type of "shock incarceration" where strict discipline, physical training, drills, and physical labor are viewed as central to reforming the juvenile delinquent.

Finally, the most recent approach, **restorative justice**, attempts to make the offender aware of the hardship he or she created and to provide the victim with an opportunity to participate in helping to dramatize the harm caused by the offense. Diversion, restitution, shock therapy, boot camps, and restorative justice have each been promoted as a new way to deal with the age-old problem of juvenile delinquency. They have intuitive appeal as plausible alternatives to traditional processing of juvenile offenders, but, as with all "new and improved" products, we must examine them with a critical eye.

Diversion

Although diversion was a key theme in juvenile justice philosophy in the 1970s and 1980s, its underlying philosophy was anything but new. The basic notion that juvenile offenders should be protected from the harshness of the adult criminal justice system was the precise rationale for the creation of a separate juvenile justice system. One of the first attempts at diversion was the very creation of the juvenile court in Cook County, Illinois, in 1899. In the quote heading this chapter, Governor Altgeld was condemning the lack of special consideration for juveniles in the criminal codes of the nineteenth century. In a popular pamphlet published in 1884 entitled "Our Penal Machinery and Its Victims," Governor Altgeld described the criminal justice system as a "crushing process." His forceful indictment of the inhumane treatment of offenders was a catalyzing force in the development of the juvenile court in Illinois. Similarly, in a treatise on prisons, Enoch Wines (1880), a nineteenth-century penologist, stated that "human justice is a clumsy machine and often deserves the punishment which it inflicts." Wines advocated a reformatory system for juveniles that would reflect the conditions of home life rather than the harsh and punitive aspects of the penitentiary. The advent of the juvenile justice system may have represented certain regressive and politically motivated social policies, as Anthony Platt's (1969) study of the juvenile court contends (see chapter 2), but there also is evidence that the emergence of the juvenile court represented a perceived need to divert juveniles from the adult criminal justice system with its institutional modes of treatment (see Hagan and Leon, 1977; Schlossman, 1977).

Therefore, although the juvenile court was originally created as part of a diversion movement in the nineteenth century, in the latter stages of the twentieth century attempts were being made to divert youthful offenders from this initial diversion project. By the late 1960s criticism of the juvenile justice system solidified in a concert of arguments to the effect that many youthful offenders needed to be deflected from juvenile processing. In the words of one scholar, the juvenile court had become a "dumping ground" for all youthful offenders that families, schools, and other agencies could not handle (Emerson, 1969). Some criminologists specifically challenged the scope of the court and of juvenile delinquency statutes. Edwin Lemert (1971) advocated a philosophy of "judicious nonintervention," arguing that the juvenile court should be an agency of last resort for children, to be used only when all other remedies have been exhausted. In devoting time and attention to relatively petty behavioral problems, the juvenile court was less able to deal with far more serious matters.

By the end of the 1960s, disillusionment with the scope of the juvenile court was widespread and the call for diversion and new alternatives developed into a set of policy recommendations. The 1967 report of the President's Commission on Law Enforcement and Administration of Justice was highly critical of the juvenile justice system. It called for the utilization of alternative programs so that contact with the juvenile justice machinery could be minimized:

> The formal sanctioning system and pronouncement of delinquency should be used only as a last resort. In place of the formal system, dispositional alternatives to adjudication must be developed for dealing with juveniles, including agencies to provide and coordinate services and procedures to achieve necessary control with-

out unnecessary stigma. Alternatives already available, such as those related to court intake, should be narrowed, with greater emphasis upon consensual and informal means of meeting the problems of difficult children.

This commission advocated limiting the jurisdiction of the juvenile court to criminal cases involving juvenile offenders.

Theoretical Precedents

When the members of the President's Commission advocated diversion, they made specific reference to the dangers of stigmatization and contamination believed to be inherent in the labeling and legal processing of juvenile offenders. In doing so, they were drawing on two prominent sociological perspectives on delinquency—*labeling* and *differential association*. According to the tenets of labeling theory, juveniles who are processed through the juvenile justice system become stigmatized as delinquents and in the process become what they are labeled. Diversion policies would presumably avoid or minimize the stigma of being labeled a delinquent by diverting less serious juvenile offenders out of the court system.

Similarly, advocates of differential association theory assume that crime, like other behavior, is learned in social interaction. By associating with persons whose attitudes favor law violation, an individual comes to learn those attitudes and gradually becomes a lawbreaker himself. From the perspective of differential association theory, the juvenile justice system creates more delinquency by introducing novice delinquents to the infectious values of hard-core delinquents. Differential association theorists would lobby for diversion in order to prevent any fraternization of "predelinquents" with "hard-core law violators."

Juvenile Rights and Due Process

Another underlying theme in the development of a diversion philosophy in the 1960s and 1970s was concern for the clarification of children's rights and the extension of guarantees of due process of law to juveniles. Several critics of juvenile justice had argued that the denial of certain rights of due process and the processing of juveniles for trivial and often unspecified transgressions might contribute to a "sense of injustice" (Matza, 1964) and undermine respect for the legal system (Schur, 1973). A concern for juvenile rights and due process was central to the idea of judicious nonintervention or what Edwin Schur termed "radical nonintervention" in the lives of the young. Schur's rallying theme became "leave kids alone wherever possible" (1973:155).

The Attack on Detention

A major concern among the advocates of diversion was to keep as many juveniles as possible out of detention or jail. Juvenile detention is the practice of holding juveniles in secure custody pending court disposition for offenses that range from abandonment by parents, incorrigibility, and running away from home to such serious offenses as homicide, rape, burglary, and aggravated assault. Youths involved in the less serious offenses are often referred to as "PINS," "MINS," or "CHINS," which translate into persons, minors, or children in need of supervision. Many who are designated as PINS are dealt with informally but are in need of some temporary care until suitable placement can be found. Those juveniles charged with criminal acts may also be placed in a detention facility as a measure of public protection and to prevent the offender from absconding before the juvenile court can review the case. Thus, adolescents in need of temporary custodial care can range from a first-time status offender to a hard-core, chronic delinquent.

According to the Office of Juvenile Justice and Delinquency Prevention, 25,019 juveniles were detained for serious delinquency offenses prior to adjudication or disposition, and another 1,250 were detained for status offenses (Snyder and Sickmund, 2006). Between court referral and case disposition, another 329,800 or 21 percent of all delinquency cases in 2000 resulted in detention (Puzzanchera et al., 2004). This represents an increase of 41 percent from 1985 when 224,500 youths were detained for delinquency cases. In some local jurisdictions where no juvenile detention facilities exist, youths may be held in detention by being placed in a separate section of the local jail. Howard Snyder and Melissa Sickmund (2006) report that on a typical day about 7,000 persons younger than 18 were inmates in jails. Although the federal government has repeatedly sought to have juveniles removed from adult jails, this has not been completely successful. The Juvenile Justice and Delinquency Prevention Act states that "juveniles will not be detained or confined in any institution in which they have contact with adult inmates" (Snyder and Sickmund, 2006:236), but there is provision for "sight and sound separation" which states that brief stays are permitted. Similarly, there are exceptions to jail lockups where juveniles can be held provided that adults and juveniles cannot see each other.

In addition to the practice of using adult jails in those locales where no juvenile detention facility exists, a second difficulty with detention is the fact that, unlike adults, bail is not used with juveniles. According to Snyder and Sickmund (2006), juveniles placed in detention facilities had an average stay of fifteen days. However, this average is misleading because the actual distribution of days in detention clusters either at one day or several weeks. Detention is supposed to be used prior to a juvenile court hearing to hold youths who are a danger to themselves or to others, but it is often used as a type of unofficial punishment (Sarri, 1983). Thus, removing juveniles from detention, particularly when the placement is for inappropriate reasons, has been a major objective of diversion advocates.

Economics

Depending on the type of diversion program implemented, removing even a small percentage of noncriminal offenders from the juvenile justice system could save millions of dollars. A Bureau of Justice Statistics Bulletin (Hughes, 2006) reports that federal, state, and local expenditures for criminal justice amounted to $185.5 billion in 2003, an increase of 418 percent from 1982. The average cost for a one-year stay per resident now varies from a low of $35,000 in South Dakota to a high of $80,000 in Rhode Island. Further, of those juveniles who are held in residential placement facilities, only 34 percent are violent offenders (Snyder and Sickmund, 2006). The rest are property, status, public order, or drug-related offenders or probation violators. By removing even a fraction of these less serious offenders from the juvenile correctional system, diversion might serve the lofty ideals of human justice, as well as the practical need for economic retrenchment.

The Meaning of Diversion

The exact meaning of diversion is ambiguous in that it has been used to refer to policies as diverse as doing nothing to programs indistinguishable from existing juvenile justice practices. It can refer to the simple act of deflecting juveniles away from the juvenile justice system. However, in many other instances, it implies the development of alternative strategies or programs for dealing with juveniles outside of the formal processing mechanisms of the juvenile court. These alternative strategies range from informal, "field adjustment" strategies to sophisticated treatment programs. To make matters even more confusing, some juvenile justice agencies use the term "diversion" to refer to formal actions taken by the juvenile court that attempt to "minimize penetration into the juvenile justice system" (Cressey and McDermott, 1973). In this instance, the "diverted" juvenile actually remains within the formal system, but attempts are made to reduce the offender's exposure to the juvenile court process. This type of diversion may take the form of an official or semiofficial program in which the standard procedures of the juvenile justice system are somewhat modified. In 1974, when Congress passed the Juvenile Justice Delinquency Prevention Act, the concept of diversion was quite clear: remove status offenders from formal juvenile court processing. However, diverting status offenders from the juvenile justice system inadvertently involved referring them to something else, and diversion became conceptually confused with referral to other programs or services. Thus, as simple as the word "diversion" may be, the actual implementation of diversion may entail radically different alternatives (Rojek, 1986).

In the broad sense of the term, diversion may occur within the police department after a juvenile has been taken into custody. Police do not necessarily refer juveniles to the juvenile court. A sizeable percentage of juveniles are never brought to the attention of the juvenile court. Police may instead refer youths to a welfare organization, to some other police agency, or handle them within the police department and release them (Federal Bureau of Investigation, 2005). Thus, the police exercise a significant amount of discretion not only in deciding whether to take a juvenile into custody, but also determining how the juvenile is to be dealt with after the apprehension occurs.

Of the 1.6 million delinquency cases referred to the juvenile court in 2000, 42 percent were nonpetitioned or allowed to bypass the formal court process. The remaining 58 percent were petitioned, but 310,300 or 33 percent were nonadjudicated cases and, in a sense, also allowed to bypass a formal court appearance. Of the original 1.6 million cases, 630,000 cases (waived and adjudicated) or 38.5 percent had a formal court appearance and the remaining 61.5 percent were processed more informally. Further, of those who were actually adjudicated, 149,200 or 24 percent were actually placed in a formal juvenile facility. As seen in figure 11-1, of the 1.6 million delinquency cases, 90 percent of all referrals to the juvenile court result in something other than formal placement, and only 10 percent are either waived to the adult court or placed in a juvenile facility. This would suggest that the juvenile court sends the vast majority of its referrals back to the community and in a sense diverts them from the formal court process.

In an attempt to clarify a muddled concept, Malcolm Klein (1976) has suggested that the term "diversion" should refer only to the process of turning alleged juvenile offenders away from the formal juvenile justice system. According to this definition, diversion does not require that specific alternatives be prescribed, only that the juvenile not enter the official system. The term "referral" is used to describe the process by which a juvenile who is diverted from the formal system is placed in a program that is not directly related to the juvenile justice system. Much confusion exists regarding the precise meaning of the term "diversion" and while in some instances it may represent a new and innovative approach for dealing with delinquency, in other instances it may be nothing more than bringing the juvenile offender in the side door rather than the front door. Finally, diversion may also refer to the discretionary judgment exercised by the police and juvenile court officials. In other words, diversion may refer to the option of simply having a wider latitude in dealing with youth.

Figure 11-1   Flowchart of Juvenile Processing

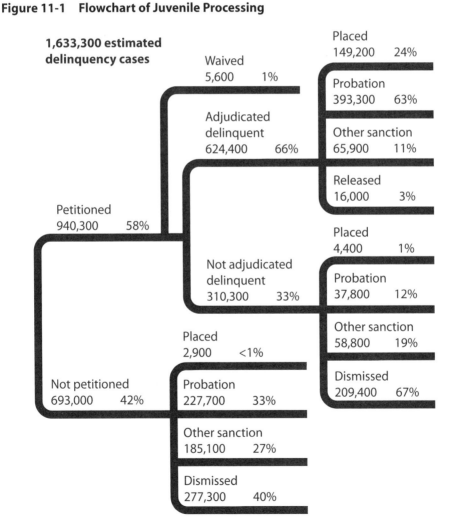

Source: Puzzanchera et al., 2004.

Evaluation of Diversion Programs

The ambiguities with the concept of diversion make it difficult to summarize evaluation studies of diversion programs (Rojek and Erickson, 1982b). For some, the success or failure of diversion is simply the removal of juvenile offenders from the formal juvenile justice process. For others, it means that offenders are dealt with in a manner that is less formal and less bureaucratic. For yet others, diversion means referring a juvenile to some form of community treatment. Furthermore, can we equate informal and unstructured diversion that occurs outside the official system with official diversion that occurs within the juvenile justice system? Some juvenile courts operate diversion programs but these may be more structured and coercive than the informal and less supervised diversion programs that are operated in the community. Research is handicapped by an absence of precise operational definitions and clear operational concepts of how these programs supposedly function.

Research Findings

In a previous edition of this text (Jensen and Rojek, 1998) we noted that research findings on the impact of diversion did not support any one conclusion. Some programs may have had their intended impact, minimizing future involvement of diverted youths with the juvenile justice system, while others appeared to make no difference or to do worse than traditional court responses. A national evaluation of diversion programs in different regions of the nation suggests that diversion is no better or worse than ordinary court responses. Selke (1982) pointed out that diversion programs are highly vulnerable to selection bias, more commonly called **creaming**, where the subjects selected for the program are low-risk offenders. Diversion programs must be carefully examined to be certain that characteristics of the system, such as arrest practices or court intake procedures, are not biasing the outcomes.

Published evaluations based on programs in Arizona (Rojek and Erickson, 1982a, 1982b), Connecticut (Rausch and Logan, 1983), Illinois (Spergel et al., 1981), Florida (Frazier and Cochran, 1986), and California (Lundman, 2001) have been quite consistent. Youths diverted into programs created as alternatives to ordinary court practices do no better or no worse than youths dealt with by traditional means. Moreover, with the implementation of such alternatives, police appear more willing to bring youth in for processing. Reports from England (see Rutter and Giller, 1985) suggest a similar outcome. Efforts to lessen the severity of juvenile processing tend to result in more cases being processed. Rather than narrowing the range of candidates for intervention, diversion has been charged with "widening the net" (Esbensen, 1984; Klein, 1979).

Given the unexpected outcome of diversion, some critics question whether the results justify the lax attention to issues of due process that may accompany processing. Richard Lundman (2001) argues that diversion can result in large numbers of youth receiving "treatment without trial" and a widening of the net to include youth who would have previously been ignored. Moreover, once created, the existence of diversion agencies depends on cases being assigned to them for service. Dean Rojek and Maynard Erickson (1982b) found programs in the county they studied competing for status offenders, suddenly a scarce "resource," and accepting any kind of offender into their program to justify its existence. Youths in diversion were a mixed bag of offenders rather than youths who had only committed status offenses. The existence of a "pure status offender," a juvenile who committed only status offenses and nothing else, was overly simplistic. It was discovered, for example, that diversion programs created for status offenders were not only accepting youths who had committed property, drug, and violent offenses, but also nonoffenders.

Rojek (1986) examined the issue of inappropriate referrals to diversion agencies. Specialized programs had been established under the auspices of diversion to deal with juveniles who had specific problems. However, diversion agencies found that they had vacancies and needed to recruit juveniles to their programs in order to fill all available slots. What invariably occurred was a mismatch between services provided and a juvenile's specific needs. For example, runaway facilities were dealing not only with runaways but also with truants, curfew violators, drug violators, and often nonoffenders. Although it might be alleged that some service is better than no service at all, it was found that in those instances where diverted youth were receiving inappropriate "treatment" from a specialized agency, the youth were less well-adjusted after completing the program. Some juveniles who were indiscriminately placed in treatment programs simply to fill openings experienced increased frustration and anger.

While these reports challenge some of the rationales for diversion, it is important to note that some diversion programs appear to be more successful than others. For example, a review of diversion projects in California found that in three of eleven programs studied, youths who were diverted into special community-based programs did significantly better than comparison youths dealt with through routine procedures (Palmer and Lewis, 1980). Of course, youths in eight of eleven diversion programs did not do significantly better than comparison youths. Moreover, the lower recidivism rates for the diverted youths did not extend to first-time offenders or youths who had several prior offenses. Palmer and Lewis suggested that diversion may work for youths with slight prior involvement with the justice system and when the programs have the following characteristics: (1) minimal personal distance between workers and youths, (2) high levels of personal concern and acceptance of youth, and (3) high frequency of contact. They also note that the programs that significantly reduced recidivism were more costly on the average than those that had no effect.

Randall Shelden (1999) reports on a program that appeared to work in San Francisco. The Detention Diversion Advocacy Project (DDAP) offered community-based supervision using people from outside of the justice system, user-friendly facilities, and very low caseloads. The program diverted youths who would have been detained and, thus, did not "widen the net." Controlling for a variety of characteristics that might account for differences between the experimental and control groups, the experimental group had significantly lower recidivism rates. However, the differences were found primarily among males, with few significant differences for females. Shelden suggests that the combination of characteristics incorporated in the DDAP may explain why this program appears to have worked, but could not explain why the positive results were limited to males. Much more research on the specific problems and needs of female offenders is needed to explain these differences.

However, a recent evaluation of a program for status offenders by Steven Patrick and Robert Marsh (2005:59) summarized the results as follows:

> In a three-year longitudinal study of first-time juvenile status offenders assigned at random to three treatment groups and a control group, no significant differences were found in recidivism rates among the groups. A total of 398 juveniles in this study were cited for offenses of tobacco or alcohol in a medium-sized metropolitan northwest city. The offenders were assigned at random to four groups: a traditional magistrate court, a traditional youth court diversion program, a new nonjudicial-diversion program, and a control group. None of the groups, including the control group, showed a significant difference in recidivism rates. It was determined from the evaluation of all groups that the diversion program offered the most cost-effective program intervention to provide more services to potentially troubled teens.

In short, diversion had no effect on recidivism, but, in this instance, was cost effective compared to other responses that had comparable results.

The overall assessment of diversion varies. For those who believe that diversion is supposed to reduce the involvement of government agencies in youths' lives, diversion has turned out to be particularly disturbing because it often leads to greater involvement. Arnold Binder and Gilbert Geis (1984) note that while critics of diversion point to increases in the range and number of youth dealt with as an undesirable side effect of diversion, increased attention to problems of youth can be defined as a positive consequence. If organized community attention to youth addresses real needs and problems that would not go away by ignoring them, then the infusion of resources into new programs may be worthwhile. Thus, for those who believe that providing a greater range of programs to a wider range of youth is the rationale for diversion, then diversion may have succeeded.

Although Binder and Geis defended diversion, they did note that there were more negative findings than positive ones. Kenneth Polk sees a much more sinister side to diversion. He argues:

> The net-widening effects observed with these apparent efforts at "destructuring" are not illustrations of "good ideas gone astray." The widening of the net of social control that results from much of diversion or from such programs as "community treatment" or "community corrections" instead should be seen as a logical consequence of the ideas within which the programs were initially conceived and defined. The persons who controlled the implementation of these efforts, whether they were top-level bureaucrats or line-level staff, were explicitly—and from the beginning—in the business of expanding the treatment or rehabilitative resources of the community. (1987:375–76)

In other words, diversion was supported with the explicit view of bringing more clients into community service organizations. As with any new program, funds were made available to a wide range of community treatment agencies, and this meant a new source of revenue. As stated by Polk, "Less meant more precisely because that was what was intended" (1987:377). Daniel Curran (1988) found that a bifurcated system exists in the United States, with public facilities responsible for institutionalized offenders and the private sector concentrating on diverted juvenile offenders. The existing public juvenile institutions have been maintained at the same level as before the advent of diversion, with most of the major changes occurring in the private sector. Rausch and Logan, in supporting this contention, assert:

In essence, the diverted population was drawn from a pool of offenders who, prior to the implementation of diversion programs, would probably have been released or left alone. The effect of such a policy has been to expand control over a larger, less seriously involved sector of the juvenile population. (1983:21)

Some programs avoid these problems, and Binder and Geis (1984) argue that sociologists rejected diversion prematurely because of their basic distrust of police, their overidentification with underdogs, and their cynicism about the criminal justice system. Polk, on the other hand, asserts that "it would be easier to take the comments of Binder and Geis more seriously if they had paid closer attention to the empirical record available on diversion" (Polk, 1987:360). Clearly, diversion is a policy that evokes strong sentiment on both sides of the debate. After close to four decades of proliferation of diversion strategies, the evidence is still lacking that diversion is the panacea originally intended. As Shelden notes, there are some promising results, but no "magic bullets" (1999).

Juvenile Restitution

A second and more recent theme in dealing with delinquency is restitution. Unlike diversion, where the objective is to protect the juvenile, restitution represents a significant shift to a policy of juvenile accountability. As a sanction imposed by the court, restitution requires the offender to make payment, either in monetary terms or by performing service to the victim or the community. Alfred Regnery of the Office of Juvenile Justice and Delinquency Prevention noted:

No program in juvenile justice has met with greater enthusiasm from courts and communities across the nation than restitution. Perhaps because restitution offers an element of "common sense" to juvenile justice that other approaches seem to lack, it is especially adaptable to a wide variety of program goals and methods. (Juvenile Justice Bulletin, 1985:2)

Because this approach is simple, victim oriented, and reasonably inexpensive, restitution programs are currently enjoying increasing popularity in the adult and juvenile court systems. Anne Schneider (1986) points out that in 1977 there were only fifteen formal juvenile restitution programs in the United States; currently they exist in nearly every state.

In 1992 the Office of Juvenile Justice and Delinquency Prevention announced the introduction of Balanced and Restorative Justice (BARJ) for juvenile court. BARJ is based on the concept that the juvenile offender "incurs an obligation to restore the victim—and by extension the community—to the state of well-being that existed before the offense" (Bilchik, 1996). This approach emphasizes the need for the offender to actively pursue restoration of the victim by paying restitution or performing community service. The BARJ model emphasizes juvenile accountability and restructures the role of juvenile justice staff from being office-based to community-based. That is, juvenile justice personnel become involved in community work and competency development for offenders so that they can pursue legitimate endeavors after release. Such personnel also oversee victim-offender mediation as part of the restorative process. In 1997 Congress allocated $16.5 million to support local programs that "ensure that juveniles are subject to accountability-based sanctions for every act for which they are adjudicated delinquent" (Matese, 1997).

Historical Basis of Restitution

The concept of restitution dates back to ancient civilizations. Some aspect of restitution is found in the code of Hammurabi, the Torah, Greek law, and Roman law. Interestingly, restitution was required in many early societies as a way of protecting the offender from aggressive retaliation by the victim or the community. Anglo-Saxon codes required that a specified amount of "blood money" be paid as a substitute for retaliation (Martin, 1981). Under the Anglo-Saxon code, the offender made one payment to the victim and another to the king for having broken "the king's peace." However, under the Common Law, this early Anglo-Saxon tradition of payment to the victim eroded as the monarchy gained strength. Payment to the crown took a larger and larger share of the final settlement. Eventually, the state replaced the victim and when any crime took place it was considered a violation against all of society. In the process, the concept of compensation or payment of damages to the victim gradually disappeared from criminal codes in the Common Law. Thus, the system of justice on which the American court system was based called for offenders to be punished for their crimes, but the concept of restoring to the victim what was lost or damaged, or compensation for a personal injury, was not a consideration.

Presently, a victim of a criminal act who seeks some type of compensation must turn to the civil code and file charges for tort action. Under the Common Law, such litigation is distinct from the criminal process and usually takes a back seat while the state actively pursues the prosecution of the offender. Even if the state proves that the offender committed the act, there is no provision in criminal law for the victim to receive compensation other than the satisfaction of sending the offender to prison. Thus, an offender may have caused serious physical and/or psychological injury and, upon being found guilty, may be sent to prison—but the victim receives no compensation.

Many countries operating under a Civil Law system (such as European or Asian countries) rather than the Common Law system inherited from England tend to place the rights of victims above the rights of the state. For example, in the People's Republic of China, the issue of victim compensation is of tantamount importance. In an assault trial in Shanghai attended by one of the authors, an individual was accused of attacking another person with a knife. To the amazement of the Western observers, the victim himself brought in a bag that contained all of the evidence. The victim proceeded to show the judge each article of clothing that was stained with blood, several towels that were blood stained, plus the bicycle tire that had a hole in it. Under the procedures governing criminal law in the United States, such evidence could not be casually brought in by the victim and then presented to the judge. However, in China the trial judge encouraged the presentation of such evidence, carefully examined such items, determined their value, and tallied the damages. At the conclusion of the trial, the offender agreed to buy the victim all new clothing, new towels, replace the bicycle tire, pay for medical bills and, finally, pay the victim for the one day of lost wages. The judge gave the offender one year of probation and required him to apologize to the victim.

In the United States, we define justice as the offender being found guilty and sentenced to prison. The victim seems to stand in the shadows of the court proceeding and receives no compensation for the financial loss that the offender caused. Justice seems to have embraced the notion of vengeance by punishing the offender, with little effort to compensate the victim. At the conclusion of a criminal trial the victim could file a lawsuit in civil court for damages, but the criminal justice system does not play a role in this matter and the victim is responsible for hiring an attorney and the cost of filing charges (Van Ness and Strong, 2002).

Types of Restitution

Restitution can assume several different forms. For example, one arrangement requires offenders to compensate the victim with monetary payment. A second type of restitution involves monetary payments made by the offender to a community agency such as a hospital or a service agency, a third party such as an elderly citizen who is in need of assistance, or the community at large (for example, purchasing trees for a city park or purchasing playground equipment). Often, these kinds of restitution arrangements occur when the victim cannot be located or when the "victim" is the public at large. A third type of restitution requires the offender to personally repair whatever damage he or she committed. A fourth type of restitution, often referred to as symbolic restitution, requires offenders to provide a service to the community. Typically the offender has to work a certain number of hours in a social service facility like a community mental health agency or a neighborhood recreation program, or address youth groups on the dangers of drug abuse.

Figure 11-2 (on the following page) is an example of a restitution agreement used in the District of Columbia. The juvenile offender agrees to provide direct services to the victim, make monetary restitution, or perform community service. As long as the juvenile honors this agreement, he or she will remain on probation; any violation of the restitution agreement may result in the revocation of probation.

The Goals of Restitution

Restitution can serve multiple purposes as outlined by Schneider (1985). First and foremost, it gives some consideration to victims' rights as a legitimate part of the process. In the strictest sense, it does not matter whether the offender, the offender's family, or even the state compensates the victim. The victim suffered a loss and, for justice to be served, it is imperative that the victim's loss be restored. A second purpose of restitution is rehabilitation. Many restitution programs are organized around the notion that by compensating the victim, the offender is undergoing a type of treatment and learns that crime does not pay. By varying the amount and type of restitution, the juvenile court can offer a treatment program that will serve the needs of the juvenile offender. A third rationale for restitution is accountability. Unlike the *parens patriae* basis of the juvenile court, which tends to excuse juvenile offenders for not being totally responsible for their actions, restitution purportedly "reflects a shift in thinking about youth; one that emphasizes juveniles' individual responsibility and therefore, accountability for their actions" (Schneider, 1985:7). It is argued that by holding the youth accountable, recidivism is reduced and public confidence in the juvenile justice system is increased. Finally, for some, restitution can be seen as a form of punishment because the juvenile court is imposing a sanction and the offender must pay a price for his or her transgression. Others might argue that restitution is not

Figure 11-2   Sample Restitution Agreement

Superior Court of the District of Columbia

Social Services Division   Family Branch

Restitution Agreement
Juvenile Community Service Program

Superior Court of the District of Columbia
Social Services Division—Family Branch

I, _____, agree to participate in the Juvenile Restitution Program. I agree to all the requirements listed below under the checked paragraphs.

DIRECT SERVICE TO VICTIM. _____was a victim of this offense. I will work directly for   him   her   for a total of _____ hours in the following manner:

MONEY RESTITUTION. As a result of my offense _____ suffered monetary damages. I agree to repay him her for the total sum of $_____ to be paid in the following manner:

COMMUNITY SERVICE. I agree to pay the community for my offense by performing _____ hours of community service. I will perform this service in the following manner:

_____
_____
_____
_____
_____
_____

I agree that this agreement will become a condition of my probation and I further recognize that if I break this agreement, the Social Services Division may request that the Court revoke my probation and commit me to the Department of Human Services. I also recognize that I must fulfill other conditions in order to participate on probation in the Restitution Program. These conditions are:

_____
_____
_____
_____

PROBATIONER'S SIGNATURE:

ATTORNEY FOR DEFENDANT: DATE:

COMMUNITY WORKER: DIVISION OF SOCIAL SERVICES:

CORPORATION COUNSEL: VICTIM:

MEDIATOR:

punishment in the traditional sense because the offender is merely repaying a debt. Strictly speaking, punishment means not merely the repayment of a debt but a sanction that exceeds the proportionality of the debt.

A theoretical basis for restitution is **equity theory**. When someone commits a criminal act, both the victim and the offender find themselves in an inequitable situation. Offenders can overcome that inequity by justifying or excusing the victimization (a "psychological" equity) or they can restore actual equity by compensating the victim. The use of restitution as a sanction may restore the balance that existed prior to the criminal act. According to equity theory, direct restitution from the offender to the victim produces the most psychologically satisfying results. Stephen Schafer states that restitution "is something an offender does, not something done for him or to him and as it requires effort on his part, it may be especially useful in strengthening his feelings of responsibility" (1970:125). Similarly, Susan Martin (1981) suggests that restitution can be devised in such a fashion as to allow the harm-doer the opportunity to neutralize the damage that was done and to become reintegrated into society by doing something positive. The equity rationale avoids the notion of the offender as "sick" or in need of treatment. "Restitution gives victims a voice that is often denied them in traditional justice practices" (Fields, 2003).

Research Findings

One of the problems in evaluating restitution programs is that restitution is typically added to other consequences. For example, in addition to being placed on probation, the juvenile offender is also required to repay the victim for the harm that occurred. A youth may succeed in one regard and fail in the other. The terms of probation may be met but the add-on stipulation may or may not be met satisfactorily. Researchers found that when restitution is the sole sanction rather than an add-on to probation, youths are more likely to successfully abide by the court order and less likely to commit a new offense (Schneider, Griffith, and Schneider, 1982). However, in this research, low-risk offenders were found to be given restitution as a sole sanction more often than high-risk offenders. Hence, we do not know whether restitution had an impact or whether low-risk offenders are less likely to recidivate.

Schneider also examined the outcomes of four studies where juvenile offenders were randomly assigned into restitution or into traditional juvenile court programs, such as detention on weekends or incarceration (1986). In the first study, she found that the restitution group had fewer subsequent offenses than the control group, but the difference was not large. In the second study, Schneider found the restitution group to have lower recidivism scores, but again the difference was slight. The third study produced results that were supportive of restitution rather than probation. Finally, in the fourth study, the restitution group tended to reoffend slightly more than the probation group. Schneider concluded that the "results from the experiments regarding the effect of restitution on recidivism should be viewed as quite encouraging" (1986:549). While restitution groups had a slightly lower recidivism rate than the control groups in three comparisons, the magnitude of the differences was quite small, varying between 3 and 10 percent. Whether such differences are "quite encouraging" is a matter of interpretation.

Current Assessment of Restitution

As was the case with diversion, restitution makes eminently good common sense and, theoretically, both of these approaches ought to be successful. The arguments in favor of restitution are quite appealing. Unlike incarceration, restitution is relatively inexpensive, the victim is compensated for losses incurred, the negative effects of incarceration are avoided by allowing uninterrupted schooling or employment, reparation might have a rehabilitative effect, and the community becomes an integral part of the overall program. On the other hand, restitution can become just another sanction applied to an increasing range of problems. As with diversion, there is the potential for restitution to be used in a discriminatory manner. For example, upper-class youth may have far more financial resources than lower-class youth. Staples (1986) argued that unemployment rates, coupled with the burden of "being in trouble with the law," may make it difficult for juveniles to find employment and therefore to make monetary restitution. There have been alleged instances of work or service programs that are inadequately supervised and undocumented. In other cases, there have been criticisms of work time assigned that is so excessive as to be self-defeating. After a lengthy review of restitution, Martin concluded: "Like diversion and probation, restitution is a broad concept with theoretical promise, popular appeal, and unsystematic empirical support that indicates that it is a potentially effective sentencing alternative for use with certain types of offenses and offenders" (1981:492). Some judges are reluctant to use restitution in lieu of traditional institutionalization on the grounds that the judge may appear to be "soft" on youthful offenders (Fields, 2003).

Victim-Offender Mediation

A more recent version of restitution brings together the victim and the offender in a face-to-face meeting with a trained mediator, to negotiate the type or amount of restitution. Hughes and Schneider (1989) sought to identify victim-offender mediation programs at the juvenile court level and found 171 such programs in the United States. In attempting to assess the effectiveness of these programs, they found that in most cases both the victim and the offender expressed satisfaction with the outcome, although the offender was less satisfied than the victim. The outcome of the mediation was generally monetary restitution to the victim, but in a few instances community service was required or some type of behavioral change in the offender was proposed, such as improved school attendance or grades. Another study found that in the few restitution/mediation programs that had been evaluated at that time, the victims were highly satisfied with the outcome and indicated they would participate again (Coates and Gehm, 1985). Unfortunately, because victim-offender mediation in juvenile justice is relatively new and has not been properly evaluated, little can be said about the overall success of these types of programs. Though reports indicate that the outcome is viewed favorably by the participants and the community, the suggestion that mediation also produces a lower recidivism rate requires much more careful research. David Karp and colleagues found that many youthful offenders "made only monosyllabic responses or said nothing during their panel meeting" (2004:204). Further, they argue that many of the apologies were not always voluntary and had to be drawn out. Youthful offenders felt sorry for what they had done but their remorse was not directed toward the victim.

Shock Therapy

The two types of institutional alternatives already discussed in this chapter have not made for exciting reading in the popular press and it is conceivable that most individuals have little awareness of these programs. However, the third "new" approach that we will examine has received enormous publicity and is enthusiastically supported by the public at large. In one sense, shock therapy is both an application of deterrence theory (discussed in chapter 9) and a prevention approach (discussed in chapter 12). But it can also be a form of community-based treatment. Central to the notion of deterrence is the assumption that any rational individual can be deterred from committing a crime if that person is convinced that dire consequences are likely to follow (Lundman, 2001). Shock therapy such as a Scared Straight type of program, which entails intensive verbal confrontation between adult prisoners and juveniles, sends a simple message: "Mess around with the law and you are going to spend time in prison, and prison life ain't pretty."

Punishment Rather Than Treatment

During the 1980s, a pronounced shift took place—from the "velvet glove approach" to the "clenched fist." Throughout the 1970s there had been growing concern for the rights of status offenders, but little attention was paid to the problem of rehabilitating serious juvenile offenders. However, in 1984 the National Advisory Committee for Juvenile Justice and Delinquency Prevention recommended that grants which supported programs aimed at the deinstitutionalization of status offenders be discontinued, and a more punitive orientation be adopted in the juvenile courts. "Law and order" became a popular slogan, and several state legislatures began to revise their juvenile codes to reflect a more punishment-oriented stance. Indeed, juvenile incarceration rates increased 50 percent between 1975 and 1991 (National Center for Juvenile Justice, 1997).

There is a clear indication of a get-tough approach in juvenile reform legislation calling for mandatory and determinate sentencing of juveniles, as well as the lowering of the upper age of the juvenile court's jurisdiction (Ohlin, 1983). In 1977 the state of Washington was the first state to revise its juvenile code in order to clearly endorse punishment as its primary objective and to step back from the traditional goal of rehabilitation. Incarceration was made mandatory for certain offenses, with the length of incarceration varying according to the seriousness of the offense. New York and Colorado also require mandatory periods of incarceration, and other states may soon follow. Many more states are beginning to restrict the exclusive jurisdiction of the juvenile court and require particular types of offenses to be turned over to the jurisdiction of the adult court. Some states lowered the age for waiver to adult court, others excluded certain serious offenses from juvenile court jurisdiction, and still other states permit concurrent jurisdiction of the juvenile court and adult court for serious offenses. It was out of this national frustration, anger, and allegation of "mollycoddling" of juvenile offenders that the Scared Straight program emerged.

The Rahway Prison Project

In September 1976 a group of inmates who were serving long prison sentences at Rahway State Prison in New Jersey organized a Juvenile Awareness Project. These inmates, who became known as the Lifers' Group, began to "counsel" juveniles who were becoming more and more involved in delinquent behavior. The basic approach of the Lifers' Group was to expose these juveniles to the harsh realities of prison life and to scare these adolescents into going "straight." Over time, these sessions developed into extremely harsh confrontations and the experience was termed *aversion therapy.*

This program was first briefly discussed in a *Reader's Digest* article. A television producer who read the article conceived the idea of producing a documentary film on the Juvenile Awareness Project (Finckenauer and Gavin, 1999). A documentary film was produced in 1978 entitled *Scared Straight* and was aired in Los Angeles for a local audience. This show received such a phenomenal response that in March of 1979 it was broadcast from coast to coast. *Scared Straight* received virtually every award possible for a documentary film, including an Oscar and an Emmy. Soon after the film was shown, thirty-eight states started or initiated plans for juvenile awareness programs (Cavender, 1981).

Evaluation of Scared Straight

The documentary film entitled *Scared Straight* shows a small group of juveniles being escorted into Rahway State Prison where they will have a confrontational encounter with the Lifers. While Peter Falk narrates, the camera shows seventeen streetwise and cocky adolescents casually walking into the prison. Falk points out that these kids represent the dregs of adolescent society. They have been arrested for every conceivable offense and clearly they are headed for adult prison. One of the girls in the group points out how much fun it will be to watch these "burn-outs" in prison and see what "losers" they are. Upon entering the prison, the juveniles see crowded cells, hear the jarring sound of steel prison doors opening and closing, and walk the prison corridors listening to the verbal taunts of prisoners making sexual overtures. In the actual confrontation with Lifers, the language is crude, crass, and vulgar. The inmates unleash a verbal barrage of the horrors of prison life including sexual assaults, beatings, and even murder. The Lifers take turns haranguing these adolescents and taunting them with the notion that they are "losers and dummies" for whom prison is inevitable. After nearly two hours of verbal abuse, the adolescents are then brought back to the waiting bus and taken home. Falk states that three months after this visit, sixteen of the seventeen adolescents have gone straight. Over 13,000 juveniles attended these intensive confrontation sessions and the documentary claims that 90 percent of these have gone straight. The program is powerful and gripping. By the time *Scared Straight* ends, the average viewer is convinced that the problem of juvenile crime can be solved. Once again, we confront a simple solution to a complex problem.

James Finckenauer and Patricia Gavin (1999) investigated the making of the film along with the policy implications of Scared Straight programs and have written a devastating critique. First of all, they point out that the Lifers did not keep very good records. Precisely how they determined that 90 percent of adolescents went straight is somewhat of a mystery. Further, it is not clear how the producer of this documentary arrived at the conclusion that the seventeen youngsters used in the film were hard-core delinquents. These adolescents were recruited for the filming and were told to be somewhat arrogant going into the prison and somber coming out. No concrete evidence was actually gathered to prove that, in fact, sixteen of the seventeen went straight. Of the 13,000 adolescents who were subjected to this shock treatment, most were recruited from local high schools and the students were under the impression they were going on a field trip. Again, there is no concrete evidence to suggest that these youngsters were delinquent. Most likely they were straight before they went to Rahway State Prison.

The key question is why ninety minutes of abusive language and scare tactics should reform a person for life. This approach assumes juveniles are totally responsible for their behavior and ignores social factors that may play a role in the onset of delinquency. No follow-up services were provided to the adolescents once they left the prison setting. In this sense, Vito and Tewksbury (1998) suggest that Scared Straight was hardly a program. It was an effort by a group of inmates with good intentions who had no clear intervention strategy, no theory, no data, and no follow-up procedures.

Finckenauer and Gavin (1999) conducted an experiment of the Scared Straight program with an experimental group of adolescents who were exposed to a confrontation session at Rahway State Prison and a control group that was not exposed to the Scared Straight experience. They report that attending intensive confrontation sessions did not alter juveniles' perceptions of the severity of punishment, and 59 percent of the youngsters who went through the Rahway Scared Straight program had not been charged with an offense in the six months following the "rap" session. However, 89 percent of the control group who did not participate in the program remained free from delinquent activity during the same period. Not only did the program fail to have the expected impact, it may have boomeranged and made things worse. On this basis, Finckenauer and Gavin (1999) questioned the credibility of the film and argued that the Juvenile Awareness Project failed to reduce delinquency.

The State of New Jersey investigated the net worth of the project at Rahway Prison and concluded that the warden needed to be transferred and the program itself drastically changed. A "showtime mentality" had developed at the prison, with two sessions being held each day, five days a week. Further, there were hints of excessive abuse and sexual advances. Lundman (2001) states that these confrontation sessions went beyond verbal taunts and threats. Some adolescents were fondled, kissed, and literally assaulted. Scared Straight programs have since been restructured to something more like a prison tour, sometimes including a discussion with some inmates. But inmates no longer run the program. Lundman concludes:

> At best, taking juveniles to prisons for intensive confrontation sessions does not deter. At worst, intensive confrontation sessions make children more rather than less delinquent. I had said it twice before and I say it once again. It is time to get out and stay out of the business of trying to scare juveniles straight. (2001:202)

Other Shock Therapy Programs

One of the longest running juvenile awareness programs in the United States is the Squires Program at San Quentin in California. The Squires Program is similar to the modified Scared Straight approach. That is, juvenile offenders are brought in for a prison tour and a discussion session with the inmates, but scare tactics and abusive language are not used. Lewis (1983) evaluated this program using an experimental and control group, and followed these subjects over a twelve-month period. Lewis's results were quite similar to those reported by Finckenauer and Gavin (1999): the experimental group actually had a higher recidivism rate than the control group, although the differences were not statistically significant.

An evaluation of the Stay Straight program in Hawaii found that the experimental group had a higher number of subsequent arrests but the authors could not attribute this higher failure rate to the Stay Straight program. They concluded, "It is unrealistic to expect that any single experience, no matter how profound, would have a significant and long-lasting impact on a problem so complicated and intractable as juvenile delinquency" (Buckner and Chesney-Lind, 1983:245).

There were numerous other programs created in the wake of Scared Straight, including JOLT (Juvenile Offenders Learn Truth at the State Prison of Southern Michigan), The Insiders Juvenile Crime Prevention Program (Virginia State Penitentiary), STYNG (Save the Youth Now Group, Milhaven Penitentiary, Ontario, Canada), and JAIL (Juvenile Awareness of Institutional Life, Idaho State Penitentiary). Many of these programs started around the time of Scared Straight, but by the early 1980s they were terminated. The Scared Straight philosophy even made its way to Norway in the early 1990s, but because of strong opposition and allegations of "Gestapo methods" the program was terminated in 1997 (Finckenauer and Gavin, 1999). Most of these programs failed to gather any data, instead using correspondence or testimonials as follow-up information. In the few instances where they were evaluated, no evidence could be found demonstrating program effectiveness.

The Scared Straight approach is a classic example of the bandwagon effect—it captured the attention of the public but had little substance. As Cavender states, it was a "media-generated phenomenon" (1981). The proposed solution to crime was superficial, based on distorted facts and exaggerated claims. There was little structure to the program, no attempt to alter the social situation in which these youth lived, and no aftercare service. Lundman (2001) warns that simply scaring adolescents is no solution to delinquency and may even exacerbate the problem. It is important to recognize that the initial Scared Straight program essentially tried to use the threat of crime and violence *within* institutions as a deterrent to juvenile crime. Thus, in supporting such a program, the justice system was in essence admitting that it could not control the problem even within its own secure institutions.

Boot Camps

The various forms of shock therapy programs just discussed are often referred to as **shock probation**. Youthful offenders are required to visit a prison as part of their probation sentence but typically they are released to the care and custody of their parents. A more extreme form of the shock therapy approach is a boot camp. In some jurisdictions this is called **shock incarceration**. The first boot camp appeared in December 1983 in Georgia in response to a federal takeover of the state's overcrowded prison system. Boot camps were originally designed to siphon off certain types of offenders from prison to reduce the prison population. David Hayeslip (1996) predicted that because of prison crowding, every state would eventually jump on the boot camp bandwagon.

Boot camps tend to target young, nonviolent, first-time offenders who have not committed major felonies. Normally speaking, these offenders would be sent to a juvenile institution but are given the option of being committed to a boot camp where the average length of stay is approximately ninety days. Because the atmosphere of a boot camp reflects intense discipline, precision military drills, and physical labor, most boot camps accept only males. MacKenzie and Herbert offer the following description of military boot camps:

> In the military, boot camps represent an abrupt, often shocking transition to a new way of life. Discipline is strict; there is an emphasis on hard work, physical training, and unquestioning obedience to authority. The new recruit is told when to sleep, when to get up, when to eat; he marches with his fellows everywhere he goes, to meals, to training; orders must be obeyed instantly; personal liberty is almost nonexistent. By the end of boot camp, the young recruit has become a different person. (1996:4)

The hope is that the model of military boot camps, which transform civilians into soldiers, would divert young offenders to a life of law-abiding behavior. However, the assumption that because boot camps work for the military they also will work for juvenile corrections is problematic. At times the objective of boot camps in the juvenile justice setting becomes stretched to the point of incredulity. Consider, for example, the rationale of juvenile boot camps as stated in a National Institute of Justice report:

> Embedded in boot camp theory are the twin themes of discipline and development. The implicit hypothesis is that external discipline fosters the self-discipline needed to engage in, and benefit from, program treatment and development components. The hypothesized logic chain begins with uniformed drill instructors carefully selected and trained to give offenders strict military-like discipline and supervision. Drill instructors who brook no nonsense from program participants and consistently enforce prescribed manners of behavior are instrumental in establishing the boot camp's structured environment. Program participants exposed to this environment will learn self-discipline, resistance to peer pressure, and commitment to traditional values. Over time, these personal changes will enhance feelings of self-worth and reinforce socially desirable behaviors such as seeking and holding jobs, continuing education, and resisting criminal activities. (Bourque et al., 1996:11–12)

Screening

Because of the rigors associated with living in a boot camp, offenders typically are required to volunteer for the boot camp program and to sign a legal document indicating that they chose the boot camp option as opposed to traditional institutionalization. This is viewed as a protection against liability should an offender later argue that the rigors of boot camp resulted in some physical harm. Critics argue that this is hardly voluntary since an offender's choice is limited to two different types of confinement. Generally speaking, participants must be in relatively good health, have committed relatively minor felonies, usually are first-time offenders, have no mental impairments, have not committed violent or sex crimes, and are not addicted to drugs.

Thus, boot camps are viable options only for relatively low-risk offenders. In considering the success or failure of boot camps it needs to be emphasized that a certain element of creaming occurs, which ought to increase the chances of success for boot camp participants.

Some critics argue that boot camps discriminate against females, disabled inmates, and older offenders. "If eligible male inmates are given a chance to shorten their prison terms in a boot camp, similar females should have the same opportunity" (Zachariah, 1996:15). Similarly, mentally and physically disabled inmates are not given the alternative to participate in a boot camp and thereby shorten their period of incarceration. Finally, older offenders also are excluded from such programs because of the physical training and hard labor that is part and parcel of a boot camp. Many boot camps are limited to individuals who are under 30 years of age. In states such as Florida, Kansas, Colorado, Arizona, and Michigan, the upper age limit is 25. It would seem difficult to consider a 26-year-old too old for boot camp.

Program Emphasis and Objectives

Sentences to boot camps are relatively short compared to the sentences that participants would normally serve. The length of time spent in boot camps ranges from a low of 30 days in some programs to a high of 240 days. However, the vast majority of programs are in the range of 90 to 120 days. After successfully completing the program, the participant is allowed to return home, subject to certain conditions of parole or supervision.

All programs emphasize a daily regiment of military drills, discipline, and physical conditioning. They live in spartan surroundings, have reduced contact with the outside world, and are expected to keep themselves and their bunks clean and orderly. Participants may be subject to summary discipline such as having to do push-ups for minor infractions and typically encounter intimidation tactics by drill-sergeant-type instructors. Other features include:

1. A platoon structure of ten to thirteen youths who enter the program every four to six weeks, and are expected to graduate together.

2. An intense daily routine that begins at 5:30 AM and ends with lights out at 9 or 10 PM.

3. Military-style uniforms for youths and drill instructors and use of military jargon, customs, and courtesies.

4. Emphasis on precision drill and calisthenics.

5. Hard physical labor such as clearing land, constructing sidewalks or retaining walls, and grounds maintenance.

6. Educational programs, but often this is limited to basic literacy skills.

Outcomes

The General Accounting Office (GAO) examined boot camps and concluded that "there is no evidence that boot camps significantly reduce recidivism" (General Accounting Office, 1993:25). However, recidivism data are not easy to come by. In Georgia, the GAO found that sixty months after release 51.5 percent of boot camp participants had recidivated compared to 57 percent of short-term prison inmates and 58 percent of long-term prison inmates (1993:29). The GAO also found that the recidivism rate for offenders put on regular probation was 34.1 percent (that is, no special services or programs, no incarceration, no form of boot camp). Similarly, Peters (1996) found that while there were no significant differences in recidivism between juveniles placed in boot camps compared to youth committed to traditional residential programs, he did find that boot camp youth recidivated sooner than those youth sent to a traditional institution. There is some suggestion in the literature that boot camp participants "go wild" after the rigors of a boot camp sentence and the finding of faster recidivism supports this observation.

The GAO found that boot camps cost less than standard institutionalization because offenders generally spend ninety days at a boot camp and considerably longer at a typical juvenile institution. However, the daily costs of a boot camp are higher because of the special program requirements, including uniforms and higher salaries paid to the drill instructors. Doris MacKenzie and Alex Piquero (1994) found that because many boot camp participants would have normally been placed on probation but were instead sent to a boot camp, there was no reduction in prison populations and the overall cost to the correctional system increased because of boot camps. As with juvenile diversion, boot camps can contribute to the "widening-of-the-net" phenomenon.

The state of California conducted a randomized experiment with long-term follow-up to evaluate the effectiveness of its boot camps. The results are summarized by Bottcher and Ezell:

> The boot camp model became a correctional panacea for juvenile offenders during the early 1990s, promising the best of both worlds—less recidivism and lower operating costs. Although there have been numerous studies of boot camp programs since that time, most have relied on nonrandomized comparison groups. The California Youth Authority's (CYA's) experimental study of its juvenile boot camp and intensive parole program (called LEAD)—versus standard custody and parole—was an important exception, but its legislatively mandated in-house evaluation was prepared before complete outcome data were available. The present study capitalizes on full and relatively long-term follow-up arrest data for the LEAD evaluation provided by the California Department of Justice in August 2002. Using both survival models and negative binomial regression models, the results indicate that there were no significant differences between groups in terms of time to first arrest or average arrest frequency. (2005: 309)

While the common-sense rationale of boot camps appealed to many politicians and segments of the public, Morash and Rucker argue that the very idea of using physically and verbally aggressive tactics in an effort to train people to act in a prosocial manner is fraught with contradictions (1990:216). The argument is whether promoting the military's emphasis on macho, masculine aggressiveness and male stereotypes is the appropriate model for instilling anticrime characteristics. It is ironic that both boot camps and Scared Straight programs emphasize crude, verbally assaultive, and insulting language in order to bring out warm, caring, affectionate responses from the program participants. Morash and Rucker suggest that such experiences can increase aggression and result in negative outcomes. Moreover, brutality-related criminal charges and/or civil lawsuits have arisen in several states (Schnurer and Lyons,

Box 11-1   Faulty Logic?

Boot camps were the panacea of the 1990s, but many criminologists doubted that they would produce better results than alternatives. How would you explain their rather dismal performance? What learning theory processes (see chapters 5 and 6) might lead to a prediction that boot camps could make kids worse?

"If I can't make a kid puke or piss in his pants on his first day, I'm not doing my job."
A youth trainer at a juvenile facility

"Boot camp youth dies of thirst after forced exercise; 8 indicted."
KSLA News 12, May 24, 2006

"Tape released showing teen beaten at boot camp. Video shows guards restraining, punching boys."
WPBF News.com, February 17, 2006

"Teen dies 3 hours after being admitted to military-style lockup."
Carol Mill and Mary Klas, *Miami Herald,* January 11, 2006

"Camp death leads to murder charges—boy dies after being restrained by counselors."
Craig Schneider, *The Atlanta Journal Constitution,* July 19, 2005

"Lawsuit: Youth claims camp counselors broke his arms."
Barbara Stack, *Pittsburgh Post-Gazette,* May 3, 2005

2006). Ironically, youths in boot camps more frequently reported feeling in danger from staff rather than from other residents (MacKenzie et al., 2001).

One of the major problems that boot camps face is that drill instructors (DIs), who are often recruited from the military, are highly susceptible to "burnout" (Bottcher and Ezell, 2005). DIs may become disillusioned with the low pay that normally is associated with being a correctional officer, but more importantly are often dismayed at the lack of respect and lack of maturity on the part of juvenile offenders. Clearly, there is a significant difference between a military recruit who is being trained to ultimately join an elite fighting unit and a juvenile offender who sees boot camp as a means of avoiding imprisonment. Peters (1996) reports that tension often develops between the DIs—who embrace military structure and discipline—and boot camp directors who are more interested in therapy. DIs often have little understanding of the needs and background characteristics of juvenile offenders. MacKenzie and others (1989) found overzealous DIs who became overly abusive, both physically and verbally, and had to be dismissed from the program. Thus, with high staff turnover, boot camps often do not achieve the desired level of stability and run the risk of being staffed with untrained personnel.

The potential for abuse in boot camps is a very real problem. MacKenzie and Herbert state:

> Policymakers may need to consider that . . . boot camps operate very close to the line of unconstitutionality. The verbal and physical aspects of the program (the same aspects that appeal to much of the public) do not have to deteriorate very far to reach the point of illegality. Camp operations must be supervised very carefully to avoid this deterioration. (1996:33)

In conjunction with the military rigor and discipline found in boot camps, the dropout rate at some facilities is quite high. Some boot camps are very selective and as a result have a difficult time keeping their programs filled. For example, in South Carolina, out of 8,542 candidates for boot camp only 723 were admitted (Hayeslip, 1996). In addition, of the limited number who get accepted, a significant proportion will drop out for medical, personal, or disciplinary reasons. Hayeslip (1996) reported that in Louisiana 43 percent of those admitted dropped out. Bourque and colleagues (1996) found the dropout rate to range from 4 to 20 percent in the boot camps they examined. Thus, some juveniles opted for standard institutionalization rather than boot camps despite having to be confined for a substantially longer period of time.

Finally, the aftercare services provided to "graduates" of boot camps are often nothing more than standard parole or probation. "Without the 24-hour surveillance and regimentation of boot camp, youths soon reverted to old patterns of behavior" (Bourque et al., 1996:7). Bourque, Han, and Hill examined fifty-two boot camps and their aftercare programs. They found that "of the fifty-two boot camp programs surveyed, only thirteen programs have developed aftercare programs specifically targeted to the boot camp population. . . . This means that for most boot camp graduates, boot camp ends upon graduation" (1996:21).

While the results of boot camps are dubious at best, Hayeslip (1996) notes that boot camps are still popular and Lundman (2001) suggests that boot camps make "good theater." Politicians are impressed by the image that boot camps convey, and this fits the "get-tough" mentality of the present time. Further, boot camps enjoy "favorable media coverage" and "make for good copy, conveying powerful visual images well suited to the electronic media" (Hayeslip, 1996:3). Because the juvenile and criminal justice systems typically do not engage in scientific evaluations of their programs, the relative success or failure of boot camps may remain a subject of controversy. Hence, programs tend to continue despite their shortcomings or even negative outcomes.

Restorative Justice

A new approach emerged in the 1990s that viewed crime not as an act committed against the state with a singular focus on the offender but as an act that involved victim, offender, and the community.

> Instead of viewing the state as the primary victim in criminal acts and placing victims, offenders, and the community in passive roles, restorative justice recognizes crime as being directed against individual people. It is grounded in the belief that those most affected by crime should have the opportunity to become actively involved in resolving the conflict. (Umbreit et al., 2005)

John Braithwaite published the seminal work in this area, *Crime, Shame and Reintegration* (1989), in which he argued that **community shaming** was more effective in crime control than traditional forms of punishment. Punishment erects barriers between the offender and the community whereas shaming maintains a bond between the offender and the community that can ultimately lead to his or her reintegration. "A shaming ceremony followed later by a forgiveness and repentance ceremony more potently builds commitment to the law than a shaming ceremony alone" (Braithwaite, 1989:81). Howard Zehr (2002) provides a simple conceptualization differentiating conventional criminal justice and restorative justice:

Criminal Justice	Restorative Justice
• Crime is a violation of the law and the state.	• Crime is a violation of people and relationships.
• Violations create guilt.	• Violations create obligations.
• Justice requires the state to determine blame (guilt) and impose pain (punishment).	• Justice involves victims, offenders, and community members in an effort to put things right.
• **Central focus:** offenders getting what they deserve.	• **Central focus:** victim needs and offender responsibility for repairing harm.

Thus, restorative justice involves the victim, the offender, and the community in resolving the conflict. The ultimate goal is to restore harmony between victims and offenders. Perhaps the fundamental emphasis in restorative justice is empowering victims to participate in the concept of justice and providing opportunities for dialogue between victims and offenders. The ultimate objective is to encourage collaboration and reintegration of the offender rather than engendering alienation, hostility, and anger—that is, hallmarks of traditional criminal justice.

In 1994 the American Bar Association endorsed victim-offender mediation. In 1995 the National Organization for Victim Assistance endorsed the principles of restorative justice (Umbreit et al, 2005). Suddenly, restorative justice policies and programs began to emerge in nearly every state and in countries throughout the world. These programs include victim-offender mediation, restitution and repayment of damages, rehabilitation, and ultimately reintegration back into the community. "The goal here is not to punish or exclude, but to restore relationships and to assist the offender to take a more responsible role in society" (Fields, 2003:48).

Currently there are myriad forms of restorative justice programs that hold juveniles accountable for their delinquent acts. Juveniles typically are released back into the community, where they receive needed services in counseling, education, and vocational training (Rodriquez, 2005). One form of restorative justice became known as **Victim Impact Panels** (VIPs), popularized by Mothers Against Drunk Driving as a way to expose DUI offenders to the potential harm caused by drunk driving (Rojek et al., 2003). The objective of VIPs was to provide a forum for DUI victims to share their pain and suffering with DUI offenders. Rather than condemning DUI offenders, the VIPs approach was to elicit testimony from victims about the tragedy and trauma of drunk driving. Shaming of DUI offenders, particularly juvenile DUI offenders, was seen to be more effective in reducing DUI offenses than traditional court proceedings. An evaluation of a juvenile restorative justice program in Canada found that restitution and community service were positively related to reductions in recidivism (Bonta et al., 2002). Mark Umbreit and colleagues reviewed myriad restorative justice programs and conclude:

> The restorative justice movement is having an increasing impact upon criminal justice system policymakers and practitioners throughout the world. . . . By drawing up many traditional values of the past, from many different cultures, we have the opportunity to build a far more accountable, understandable, and healing system of justice and law that can lead to a greater sense of community through active victim and citizen involvement in restorative initiatives. (2005:304)

There are however, numerous drawbacks associated with restorative justice programs. Some victims may not want to participate in a victim-offender mediation session. In fact, Umbreit and colleagues refer to the "re-victimization" of victims who confront their offenders and experience anger, fear, and trauma (2005). Others note that young offenders may refuse to participate in any sort of a dialogue with the victim, and the mediation session may become more of a confrontation rather than a dialogue (Karp et al., 2004). Rodriguez (2005) found that the relative success of restorative justice programs is highly contingent on community characteristics. For example, race and ethnicity divisions, unemployment rates, poverty levels, and the degree of social stratification can influence the outcome of restorative justice. Black and Latino juveniles were less likely to be placed in restorative justice programs than whites. Roberts and Stalans (2004) suggest that public support for restorative justice programs declines as the seriousness of the offense increases. Violent offenders and chronic recidivists may not be suitable candidates for restorative justice programs. Gordon Bazemore suggests that "restorative justice seems to work best for communities and individuals that need it the least" (2005:138). Citizen apathy, weak community ties, fractured communities, and racially/ethnically divided communities may be unable to facilitate an environment conducive to restorative justice programs. Finally, an often-seen pattern in the history of juvenile justice is that what is new is seen as progress, and what is old is discarded. We need much more research on restorative justice programs before they can become fully integrated into the juvenile justice system.

Summary

We have examined five current and popular responses to juvenile delinquency and found many of them to be less than promising. There is some potential in restitution and diversion but their impact on delinquent behavior has yet to be convincingly demonstrated. Scared Straight and boot camp programs appear to be ineffective and even counterproductive. Restorative justice is a fresh approach that has some demonstrated success.

Juvenile diversion arose out of the criticism of the juvenile justice system as a stigmatizing and self-depreciating experience. Diversion programs attempt to deflect juveniles from the traditional system and in those instances where youth need special help, to generate a community-based response.

A review of the literature suggests that:

1. More rather than less juveniles get processed, and many of the diverted youth are petty rather than hard-core offenders.

2. Community competition for clients can result in inappropriate services and a frenzied recruitment of clients.

3. There are several conflicting points of view about the nature of diversion, and evaluations of its success or failure vary depending on underlying conceptions of what constitutes diversion (e.g., "leave them alone" versus "give them more programs").

4. Diversion may represent an instance of treatment without trial, where the protection of individual rights tends to be ignored.

5. Some programs reduce recidivism but the reason some work and most do not has yet to be determined.

Restitution programs arose during the onset of disillusionment with juvenile diversion. Restitution has intuitive appeal, combining concern for the rights of victims with acceptance of responsibility on the part of offenders. Our review of the existing literature suggests the following:

1. The research literature dealing with restitution programs is quite sparse.

2. Many restitution programs are add-ons to traditional probation. There is a need for research on programs that are exclusively restitution-oriented.

3. There is a danger that the stipulations of a restitution program can be excessive.

4. Restitution can place severe demands on lower-class youth but be nothing more than a slap on the wrist for upper-class youth.

5. The research findings to date are inconclusive, suggesting some small differences in recidivism.

6. Participants in restitution/mediation programs expressed satisfaction with the outcome, but evidence suggesting reduced recidivism is slight.

The third approach we examined was shock therapy, or, more specifically, the Scared Straight type of program. Some of these programs are merely prison tours, while others have used aversive shock techniques. Our review of the literature revealed:

1. The *Scared Straight* documentary film made exaggerated, ill-founded claims.

2. A follow-up study found that an experimental Scared Straight group had higher recidivism rates than a control group. It is not clear whether this is simply an artifact of small data sets or whether exposure to prison life encourages delinquent activity.

3. While these shock programs initially appeared in a majority of states, they have been drastically cut back or eliminated. In those instances where the programs are still operational, there appears to be some concerted effort to work only with delinquents and not the general population of adolescents.

4. The Scared Straight philosophy flows from changing orientations in the Supreme Court, state legislatures, and public opinion calling for a more punitive response to juvenile delinquency.

The fourth approach we examined was the emergence of boot camps. This panacea gained popularity in the mid-1990s as a response to prison overcrowding. The objective was to siphon off first-time, nonviolent offenders into short-term, military-style boot camps predicated on the notion that such training would instill a sense of self-esteem, self-confidence, and self-discipline. The evaluation of boot camps reveals that:

1. Recidivism rates for boot camp participants and regular prison inmates are virtually identical. There is no evidence that boot camps reform or rehabilitate a juvenile offender.

2. Because boot camp programs tend to run 90–120 days, the cost of sending a juvenile offender to boot camp is less than traditional institutionalization. However, the daily cost of running a boot camp program is higher than regular institutionalization.

3. Boot camps have been accused of skimming off those offenders who are most amenable to treatment: the first-time, nonviolent offender. Some see an element of discrimination in establishing eligibility requirements for boot camps.

4. The potential for verbal and physical abuse in a boot-camp setting is high. The drill instructors (DIs) tend to come from military backgrounds and assume the juvenile offender is similar to the raw military recruit. Antagonism between DIs and offenders can be problematic.

5. The regimen of a boot camp—predicated on physical exercise and military drill—does not seem to transfer to the civilian world. These "get-tough" approaches have popular appeal but little payoff for the juvenile offender.

6. Some states have closed boot camps or are considering closing boot camps because of the potential for abusive treatment.

Restorative justice is the newest approach in juvenile justice and such programs have appeared in virtually every state and every nation. It is a move away from traditional retributive and rehabilitative responses to a more restorative function for juvenile justice. Current research suggests that:

1. There is some evidence that restorative justice has a positive impact on reducing delinquency but many of the evaluations lack scientific rigor.

2. Restorative justice brings the victim and the community into the determination of what constitutes justice, and the elevation of victims' rights is of paramount importance.

3. The concept of reintegration into the community for juvenile offenders is a more efficacious approach than punishment, which can engender alienation and hostility.

4. Victim-offender mediation sessions might be reflective of reintegration into the community but these sessions can also be counterproductive.

5. Community characteristics can be directly related to the success or failure or restorative justice goals.

6. Restorative justice appears to work best with nonviolent offenders and least effective with chronic recidivists and violent offenders.

Discussion Questions

1. In what way could one argue that current diversion programs are merely a case of reinventing the wheel? That is, is diversion really new? Justify your answer.

2. In the 1970s Edwin Schur proposed a policy of radical nonintervention consisting of the simple principle: "Leave kids alone whenever possible!" Discuss the diversion programs of the 1970s and 1980s in terms of his proposal.

3. Elaborate two distinct theoretical rationales for a diversion philosophy.

4. What types of offenders are typically assumed to be good candidates for diversion? Do you think that they should be separated from youth charged with more serious crimes? Why?

5. The idea that militaristic boot camps could straighten out youth was very popular in the 1980s and 1990s, and such boot camps still exist around the United States. Have they worked? Can you think of reasons they might not work?

6. Use at least two of the theories discussed in chapter 6 to develop a rationale for restitution programs.

7. Why do restitution programs appeal to both conservatives and liberals?

8. Develop two lists: (1) reasons why restitution should reduce recidivism and (2) reasons why it might not.

9. What type of theory was implicit in the Scared Straight program? Can you think of any alternative theories that could be used to predict possible boomerang effects?

10. Do you think that juvenile courts should continue to develop diversion, Scared Straight, or restitution programs? Base your answer on research generated to this date.

References

Altgeld, J. P. 1884. *Our Penal Machinery and Its Victims.* Chicago: Jansen and McClurg.

Bazemore, G. 2005. "Whom and How Do We Reintegrate? Finding Community in Restorative Justice." *Criminology & Public Policy* 4:131–48.

Bilchik, S. 1996. *Balanced and Restorative Justice Project.* Fact Sheet no. 42 (July). Washington, DC: Office of Juvenile Justice and Delinquency Prevention.

Binder, A., and G. Geis. 1984. "Ad Populum Argumentation in Criminology: Juvenile Diversion as Rhetoric." *Crime and Delinquency* 30:309–33.

Bonta, J., S. Wallace-Capretta, J. Rooney, and K. McAnoy. 2002. "An Outcome of a Restorative Justice Alternative to Incarceration." *Contemporary Justice Review* 5:319–39.

Bottcher, J., and M. Ezell. 2005. "Examining the Effectiveness of Boot Camps: A Randomized Experiment with a Long-Term Follow Up." *Journal of Research in Crime and Delinquency* 42:309–32.

Bourque, B., R. Cronin, D. Felker, F. Pears, M. Han, and S. Hill. 1996. "Boot Camps for Juvenile Offenders: An Implementation Evaluation of Three Demonstration Programs." U.S. Dept. of Justice, Research in Brief.

Bourque, B., M. Han, and S. Hill. 1996. "A National Survey of Aftercare Provisions for Boot Camp Graduates." U.S. Dept. of Justice, Research in Brief.

Braithwaite, J. 1989. *Crime, Shame and Reintegration.* Cambridge: Cambridge University Press.

Buckner, J. C., and M. Chesney-Lind. 1983. "Dramatic Cures for Juvenile Crime: An Evaluation of a Prisoner-Run Delinquency Prevention Program." *Criminal Justice and Behavior* 10:227–47.

Cavender, G. 1981. "Scared Straight: Ideology and the Media." *Journal of Criminal Justice* 9:431–39.

Coates, R. B., and J. Gehm. 1985. *Victim Meets Offender: An Evaluation of Victim-Offender Reconciliation Programs.* Valparaiso, IN: PACT Institute of Justice.

Cressey, D., and R. McDermott. 1973. *Diversion from the Juvenile Justice System.* Ann Arbor, MI: National Assessment of Juvenile Corrections.

Curran, D. J. 1988. "Destructuring, Privatization, and the Promise of Juvenile Diversion: Compromising Community-Based Corrections." *Crime and Delinquency* 34:363–78.

Emerson, R. M. 1969. *Judging Delinquents.* Chicago: Aldine.

Esbensen, F. A. 1984. "Net Widening? Yes and No: Diversion Impact Assessed Through a Systems Processing Rates Analysis." In *Juvenile Justice Policy*, edited by S. H. Decker. Beverly Hills: Sage.

Federal Bureau of Investigation. 2005. *Crime in the United States, 2005.* Washington, DC: U.S. Dept. of Justice.

Fields, B. 2003. "Restitution and Restorative Justice." *Youth Studies Australia* 22:44–51.

Finckenauer, J. O., and P. Gavin. 1999. *Scared Straight: The Panacea Phenomenon Revisited.* Long Grove, IL: Waveland Press.

Frazier, E. E., and J. K. Cochran. 1986. "Official Intervention, Diversion from the Juvenile Justice System, and Dynamics of Human Services Work: Effects of a Reform Goal Based on Labeling Theory." *Crime and Delinquency* 32:157–75.

General Accounting Office. 1993. "Prison Boot Camps: Short-Term Prison Costs Reduced, but Long-Term Impact Uncertain." Washington, DC: U.S. General Accounting Office.

Hagan, J., and J. Leon. 1977. "Rediscovering Delinquency: Social History, Political Ideology and the Sociology of Law." *American Sociological Review* 42 (August):587–98.

Hayeslip, D. W. 1996. "The Future of Boot Camps." In *Correctional Boot Camps: A Tough Intermediate Sanction*, edited by D. L. MacKenzie and E. E. Herbert. NIJ Report.

Hughes, K. A. 2006. *Justice Expenditure and Employment in the United States, 2003.* Washington, DC: Bureau of Justice Statistics.

Hughes, S. P., and A. L. Schneider. 1989. "Victim-Offender Mediation: A Survey of Program Characteristics and Perceptions of Effectiveness." *Crime and Delinquency* 35:217–33.

Juvenile Justice Bulletin. 1985. "Introducing RESTTA." U.S. Dept. of Justice.

Karp, D., M. Sweet, A. Kirshenbaun, and G. Bazemore. 2004. "Reluctant Participants in Restorative Justice? Youthful Offenders and Their Parents." *Contemporary Justice Review* 7:199–216.

Klein, M. W. 1976. "Issues and Realities in Police Diversion Programs." *Crime and Delinquency* 22 (October):421–27.

———. 1979. "Deinstitutionalization and Diversion of Juvenile Offenders: A Litany of Impediments." In *Crime and Justice*, edited by M. Norris and M. Tonry. Chicago: University of Chicago Press.

Lemert, E. M. 1971. *Instead of Court: Diversion in Juvenile Justice*. Rockville, MD: National Institute of Mental Health.

Lewis, R. V. 1983. "Scared Straight—California Style: Evaluation of the San Quentin Squires Program." *Criminal Justice and Behavior* 10:227–47.

Lundman, R. J. 2001. *Prevention and Control of Juvenile Delinquency*. 3rd ed. New York: Oxford University Press.

MacKenzie, D., L. Gouy, L. Riechers, and J. Shaw. 1989. "Shock Incarceration: Rehabilitation or Recitation?" *Journal of Offender Counseling Services and Rehabilitation* 14:25–40.

MacKenzie D., A. Gover, G. Armstrong, and O. Mitchell. 2001. *A National Study Comparing Environment of Boot Camps with Traditional Facilities for Juvenile Offenders*. Research in Brief. Washington, DC: National Institute of Justice.

MacKenzie, D., and E. Herbert. 1996. *Correctional Boot Camps: A Tough Intermediate Sanction*. NIJ Report.

MacKenzie, D., and A. Piquero. 1994. "The Impact of Shock Incarceration Programs on Prison Crowding." *Crime and Delinquency* 40(2):222–49.

Martin, S. E. 1981. *New Directions in the Rehabilitation of Criminal Offenders*. Washington, DC: National Academy Press.

Matese, M. A. 1997. *Accountability-Based Sanctions*. Washington, DC: Office of Juvenile Justice and Delinquency Prevention.

Matza, D. 1964. *Delinquency and Drift*. New York: John Wiley.

Morash, M., and L. Rucker. 1990. "A Critical Look at the Idea of Boot Camp as a Correctional Reform." *Crime and Delinquency* 36:204–22.

National Center for Juvenile Justice. 1997. *Juvenile Court Statistics, 1994*. Pittsburgh, PA: NCJJ.

Ohlin, L. E. 1983. "The Future of Juvenile Justice Policy and Research." *Crime and Delinquency* 29:463–72.

Palmer, T., and R. V. Lewis. 1980. *An Evaluation of Juvenile Diversion*. Cambridge, MA: Oelgeschlager, Gunn, and Hain.

Patrick, S., and R. Marsh. 2005. "Juvenile Diversion: Results of a 3-Year Experimental Study." *Criminal Justice Policy Review* 16:59–73.

Peters, M. 1996. *Evaluation of Impact of Boot Camps for Juvenile Offenders*. Washington, DC: Office of Juvenile Justice and Delinquency Prevention.

Platt, A. 1969. *The Child Savers*. Chicago: University of Chicago Press.

Polk, K. 1987. "When Less Means More: An Analysis of Destructuring in Criminal Justice." *Crime and Delinquency* 33:358–78.

President's Commission on Law Enforcement and Administration of Justice. 1967. *Task Force Report: Juvenile Delinquency and Youth Crime*. Washington, DC: GPO.

Puzzanchera, C., A. Stahl, T. Finnegan, N. Tierney, and H. Snyder. 2004. *Juvenile Court Statistics, 2000*. Pittsburgh, PA: National Center for Juvenile Justice.

Rausch, S. P., and C. H. Logan. 1983. "Diversion from Juvenile Court: Panacea or Pandora's Box?" In *Evaluating Juvenile Justice*, edited by J. R. Kluegel. Beverly Hills: Sage.

Roberts, J., and L. Stalans. 2004. "Restorative Sentencing: Exploring the Views of the Public." *Social Justice Research* 17:315–34.

Rodriquez, N. 2005. "Restorative Justice, Communities, and Delinquency: Whom Do We Reintegrate?" *Crime and Public Policy* 4:103–30.

Rojek, D. G. 1986. "Juvenile Diversion and the Potential of Inappropriate Treatment for Offenders." *New England Journal of Criminal and Civil Confinement* 12:329–47.

Rojek, D., J. Coverdill, and S. Fors. 2003. "The Effect of Victim Impact Panels on DUI Rearrest Rates: A Five-Year Follow-Up." *Criminology* 41:1319–40.

Rojek, D. G., and M. L. Erickson. 1982a. "Delinquent Careers: A Test of the Career Escalation Model." *Criminology* 20:5–28.

———. 1982b. "Reforming the Juvenile Justice System: The Diversion of Status Offenders." *Law and Society Review* 16:241–64.

Rutter, M., and H. Giller. 1985. *Juvenile Delinquency: Trends and Perspectives.* New York: Guilford Press.

Sarri, R. C. 1983. "The Use of Detention and Alternatives in the United States since the *Gault* Decision." In *Current Issues in Juvenile Justice,* edited by R. R. Corrado, M. LeBlanc, and J. Trepanier. Toronto: Butterworth.

Schafer, S. 1970. *Compensation and Restitution to Victims of Crime.* Montclair, NJ: Smith Patterson.

Schlossman, S. L. 1977. *Love and the American Delinquent.* Chicago: University of Chicago Press.

Schneider, A. L. 1985. *Guide to Juvenile Restitution.* Washington, DC: U.S. Dept. of Justice.

———. 1986. "Restitution and Recidivism Rates of Juvenile Offenders: Results from Four Experimental Studies." *Criminology* 24:533–52.

Schneider, P. R., W. R. Griffith, and A. L. Schneider. 1982. "Juvenile Restitution as a Sole Sanction or Condition of Probation: An Empirical Analysis." *Journal of Research in Crime and Delinquency* 17:47–65.

Schur, E. M. 1973. *Radical Non-Intervention: Rethinking the Delinquency Problem.* Englewood Cliffs, NJ: Prentice-Hall.

Schnurer, E., and C. Lyons. 2006. "Juvenile Boot Camps: Experiment in Trouble." www.cnponline.org.

Selke, W. L. 1982. "Diversion and Crime Prevention: A Time-Series Analysis." *Criminology* 20:395–406.

Shelden, R. G. 1999. *Detention Diversion Advocacy: An Evaluation.* Washington, DC: Office of Juvenile Justice and Delinquency Prevention.

Snyder, H. N., and M. Sickmund. 2006. *Juvenile Offenders and Victims: 2006 National Report.* Washington, DC: Office of Juvenile Justice and Delinquency Prevention.

Spergel, I. A., F. G. Reamer, and J. P. Lynch. 1981. "Deinstitutionalization of Status Offenders: Individual Outcome and System Effects." *Journal of Research in Crime and Delinquency* 18:34–46.

Staples, W. G. 1986. "Restitution as a Sanction in Juvenile Court." *Crime and Delinquency* 32:177–85.

Umbreit, M., B. Voss, R. Coates, and E. Lightfoot. 2005. "Restorative Justice in the Twenty-First Century: A Social Movement Full of Opportunities and Pitfalls." *Marquette Law Review* 89:251–304.

Van Ness, D., and H. Strong. 2002. *Restoring Justice.* 2nd ed. Cincinnati: Anderson Publishing.

Vito, G. F., and R. Tewksbury. 1998. *The Juvenile Justice System: Concepts and Issues.* Long Grove, IL: Waveland Press.

Wines, E. C. 1880. *The State of Prisons and of Child-Saving Institutions in the Civilized World.* Cambridge: Harvard University Press.

Zachariah, J. K. 1996. "An Overview of Boot Camp Goals, Components, and Results." NIJ Report.

Zehr, H. 1990. *Changing Lenses: A New Focus for Crime and Justice.* Scottsdale, PA: Herald Press.

— twelve —

Prevention
Dilemmas of Choice, Change, and Control

421

> Today, we continue to attempt to change the behavior of juvenile delinquents and their parents because it is so inconvenient for us to attempt to change larger social conditions. Yet ultimately those conditions are the origin of the problem of delinquency, and changing them is the only way to solve that problem.
>
> (Thomas J. Bernard, *The Cycle of Juvenile Justice*, 2006)

Introduction

The last several chapters have concentrated on theory and research relevant to deterrence, labeling, and correctional experimentation, including popular programs to divert nonserious offenders, scare others straight, and set matters right with victims. Some responses to delinquency appear promising while others either make no difference or make offenders worse. A different approach to addressing the delinquency problem is to focus on prevention. Efforts to correct and rehabilitate focus on changing the offender "after the fact" in comparison to **prevention**, which focuses on changing conditions thought to be conducive to delinquency in general before youths have a chance to become offenders. The conditions emphasized when prevention is the goal can range from individual skills, attitudes, and perceptions to major modifications in the social environment. Advocates of prevention generally differentiate between changes in law enforcement and positive changes in youths and social environments that inhibit crime and delinquency, limiting prevention to the latter.

An important issue to be addressed before we begin exploring prevention research is whether the public supports such interventions. Given the strong advocacy of get-tough approaches by many politicians, it would be easy to conclude that the public would more readily support investments in imprisonment than spending more money on treatment or prevention. However, a recent study of the willingness of the general public to support the investment of funds in either (1) extra time in prison (2) treatment, or (3) prevention revealed that investments in prevention have the most public support. Daniel Nagin and his colleagues asked a random sample of adults in Pennsylvania households about their willingness to pay for certain policy changes. Contrary to the expectation that the public would allocate the most additional funding to punishment, respondents were actually more willing to pay for prevention in the form of nurse visits to households. There was considerable support for home visits by nurses to young mothers to encourage healthy behaviors, with the anticipated outcome to be reflected in the behavior of their children in the future. Additional rehabilitation was second and additional prison time was third. Although Pennsylvanians may not be representative of Americans in general, these findings do suggest support for prevention (Nagin et al., 2006).

Peter Greenwood acknowledges that "there is general agreement among many policy makers and the wider public that delinquency and crime prevention are important activities," but warns that "there is little agreement concerning which agencies of government should direct them, or what these efforts should consist of, or how they should be run" (2006:5). He continues:

Crime prevention is a field that cries out for rigorous definitions and precision in its terminology, especially at a time when simplistic sound bites and slogans prevail. It is a field in which rigorous evaluation is absolutely essential but rarely applied. (2006:25)

Greenwood further argues that much of delinquency prevention has been "driven largely by fads and wishful thinking rather than careful research and analysis" (2006:27).

Greenwood asserts that as crime rates fell in the 1990s, "public officials tried to make the case that their tougher sentencing policies were responsible for the decline, [however] tougher sentencing was not the primary cause of the decline" (2006:4). Rather, a constellation of social events converged and ultimately led to a dramatic reduction in crime and delinquency; for example, a strong economy, an older population, a decline in cocaine use, and low unemployment rates. In other words, changes in social conditions had a greater impact on crime rates than did specific crime-control policies.

Researchers interested in delinquency prevention point to the success of **risk-focused approaches** to the prevention of health problems. Smoking cessation, regular exercise, healthy diets, alcohol reduction, and early intervention were targeted by public health officials as ways to reduce one's risk of cardiovascular disease. Similarly, certain risk-focused approaches to preventing juvenile crime have been identified. According to David Farrington (1998), the risk-factor prevention paradigm popularized in medicine and public health slowly emerged in delinquency research and practice in the 1990s. This emergence, notes James Howell (2003), was the result of efforts by criminologists and policy makers in the 1990s to reassess the role of delinquency prevention.

Prevention Revisited

The term "prevention," like the terms "rehabilitation," "deterrence," and "diversion," has no single, unambiguous, agreed-upon definition. At one time or another, virtually all attempts to inhibit the delinquent activity of offenders or potential offenders have been referred to as prevention programs. For example, a review of literature revealed that of 350 research reports using the words "delinquency prevention" (or their equivalent), a large number were actually programs involving juvenile court probation and parole techniques (Wright and Dixon, 1977). In a review of 443 evaluations of prevention and rehabilitation programs, Mark Lipsey (1992) found serious methodological flaws in the evaluations, including a lack of random assignments, no control groups, failure to follow-up, and most critically, conceptual ambiguity differentiating prevention from rehabilitation.

An orientation toward prevention is by no means new. It has been proposed periodically for centuries. A prevention philosophy has been central to social reform movements throughout American history, although with considerable variation in views about what needed to be reformed and how change should be accomplished. It also has been central to sociological positions on crime and delinquency. Consider, for example, the following paragraphs from Edwin Sutherland's 1924 edition of *Principles of Criminology*:

Two methods of reducing the frequency of crimes have been suggested and tried. One is the method of treatment, the other is the method of prevention. The conventional policy has been to punish those who are convicted of crimes, on the hypothesis that this both reforms those who are punished and deters others from crimes in the future. Also, according to this hypothesis crime rates can be reduced by increasing the severity, certainty, and speed of punishment.

Methods of reformation have been suggested and tried, also. These have been in the form of probation, educational work in prisons, and parole supervision. These methods, like the methods of punishment, have not been notably successful in reducing crime rates.

Prevention is a logical policy to use in dealing with crime. Punishment and other methods of treatment are, at best, methods of defense. It is futile to take individual after individual out of the situations which produce criminals and permit the situations to remain as they were. A case of delinquency is more than a physiological act of an individual. It involves a whole network of social relations. If we deal with this set of social relations we shall be working to prevent crime. It has become a commonplace in medicine that prevention is better than cure. The same superiority exists in the field of crime. (1924:613–14)

Treatment programs are reactive in that they are implemented after a juvenile has been apprehended. Prevention is proactive and anticipatory in that it focuses on the future. The goal is to stop delinquency before it occurs. Treatment programs focus on individuals who have violated community standards, whereas prevention programs seek to change the social conditions that facilitate deviant behavior. Clearly prevention is a much more ambitious undertaking, more expensive, and more indirect.

Many criminologists have attempted to identify key life-course experiences and circumstances that lead to or inhibit delinquency and crime, and much of the theory and research summarized in earlier chapters is potentially relevant to prevention. For example, the emphasis on mass media content as a target for significantly lowering delinquency rates has little support when data on variations in crime and variations in media content are examined. Were it possible to drastically change the content of media it would have minimal consequences for crime and delinquency. On the other hand, there is considerable consistency in research on the importance of family variables, school experiences, and peer group associations. For example, Robert Sampson and John Laub (1993) identified three sets of factors that significantly influence the odds of becoming a delinquent. The first set was called "early childhood effects" and included such measures as being a difficult child and exhibiting troublesome behaviors. The second set was called "family structure" variables and included family size and crowded family dwelling units. The third set was called "social process" variables and included erratic parental discipline, delinquent peers, and attachment to school. Were it possible to alter these correlates at key points in youths' lives, then some portion of the delinquency problem could be prevented.

Prevention Experiments

As we've already noted, the phrase "delinquency prevention" is ambiguous. Some correctional experiments, such as those discussed in chapter 10, are included in comprehensive reviews of the prevention literature. Such reviews suggest that the vast majority of reports on programs that aspire to delinquency prevention provide no data on program effectiveness. Steven Lab (1988) surveyed the literature on prevention and found much confusion on the type of subjects, types of crime, intervention strategies, and outcome measures. Similarly, of the 350 research reports examined by William Wright and Michael Dixon, only 96 contained any type of empirical data.

More recent reviews have emphasized positive rather than negative results, and, in fact, led the OJJDP (1995) to conclude that "delinquency prevention works." For example, Richard Mendel (1995) concludes his analysis of youth-oriented anticrime programs with the statement:

> Clearly, prevention can curb crime and delinquency. If programs target high-risk children and their parents early in life, and if they provide intensive and extended (2 years or more) counseling, education, and parental assistance via highly skilled youth development professionals, prevention efforts yield powerful reductions in later aggressiveness, delinquency, and criminal behavior.

In short, as was the case for correctional experiments, some prevention programs "can" work and others may show promise. On the other hand, it would be accurate to state that most prevention programs have yielded rather disappointing results and that it is possible that some prevention programs are indeed working but that poor evaluation research techniques may be distorting their real impact. Moreover, some social programs that are not considered "delinquency prevention" experiments may have delinquency prevention as one of many long-term goals (e.g., Head Start). We will review several important studies in the history of delinquency prevention research with the aim of identifying likely sources of failure as well as possible reasons for success.

Early Identification and Intensive Treatment

In a discussion of delinquency prevention several decades ago, Jackson Toby (1965) observed that one argument concerning delinquency prevention that often strikes people as "breathtakingly plausible" involves **early identification and intensive treatment**. According to this argument, delinquency can be prevented by developing techniques to identify those who are headed for trouble and providing some form of treatment that would prevent such an unfolding of events. Such a prevention approach has been the dream of social control agencies.

One of the proposed uses of the personality tests discussed in chapter 5 has been the early identification of potential offenders. For example, the Minnesota Multiphasic Personality Inventory (MMPI) was developed in the 1940s as an aid in the diagnosis of personality disorders. It was initially administered to hospitalized psychiatric patients and to a group of "normal" individuals. A series of subscales were then created that purported to measure specific personality problems such as depression, schizophrenia, hysteria, and paranoia. It was suggested that the MMPI could be an important tool in predicting delinquency. Some degree of success was found by using the schizophrenia subscale, on which delinquents scored somewhat high. However, it was found that there was a 76.2 percent error in predicting delinquency four years after testing (Lundman, 2001). Various subscales were combined to increase the accuracy of the MMPI, but even with this improvement there was still a 65.5 percent error rate. Researchers concluded that no personality test can predict delinquency.

The most famous early identification and treatment program was the Cambridge-Somerville Youth Study first begun in 1937. The original goal was for teachers and police officers to identify two groups of boys: "difficult boys," who were viewed as potential delinquents, and "average boys," who were viewed as having no predisposition toward delinquency. By a random process, about half of the predelinquent boys were assigned to an experimental group, while the other half were assigned to a control group. The experimental group received family guidance, individual counseling, tutoring, medical care, and recreational services. The control group received no special treatment. World War II forced a premature end to the study (which was to have lasted ten years) when both counselors and adolescent subjects were drafted into military service. However, during the project's eight years it provided some test of the effect of intensive counseling and academic tutorial services for youth who were "headed for trouble." An evaluation five years after the end of the project revealed little positive effect. In a thirty-year follow-up conducted in 1975 using court, mental health, and alcoholism treatment records, Joan McCord found that "none of the . . . measures confirmed hopes that treatment had improved the lives of those in the treatment group" (1978:289). One of the lessons learned from the Somerville project was the inability to foresee national events like World War II, which essentially crippled the research study. A good prevention strategy calls for long-term intervention, but unanticipated events like war, environmental disasters such as hurricanes and floods, disease, or even a change in government officials can impact or seriously negate a long-term study.

Community and Neighborhood Experiments

Sociologists have quite commonly attributed the failure of psychiatrically and individually oriented prevention strategies to their focus on the individual rather than the social environment. John Martin (1961) argued that the basic flaw with "individual-centered techniques" is that "such efforts fail to come to grips with the underlying social and cultural conditions giving rise to delinquency." Similarly, Edwin Schur maintained that "our overall crime picture massively reflects conditions that require collective social solutions" and that "social reform, not individual counseling, must have the highest priority in our program to reduce crime problems" (1969:15).

Somewhere between the two poles of individual treatment and basic social reform are action programs that attempt to strengthen or reorganize certain social relationships in neighborhoods or areas of a city. This type of prevention program tries to overcome factors in the youth's immediate environment that are seen as contributing to delinquent behavior in the neighborhood or community.

Perhaps the best-known prevention program focusing on the social environment is the **Chicago Area Project**. Developed by Clifford R. Shaw in the 1920s and still operating in some parts of Chicago, the project was based on social disorganization theory (see chapter 6). It attributed delinquency to a lack of neighborhood cohesiveness and advocated that the key to prevention was self-help enterprises on the part of residents of areas with high crime rates. Indigenous community leaders were tapped to serve as conventional role models for youngsters in such areas in the hope of facilitating the growth of an antidelinquent culture. The remedy for delinquency was the creation of self-help community comities that were concerned with recreational programs, neighborhood improvement, and youth gangs. Shaw "firmly believed that people could be motivated to help themselves and especially their children" (Lundman, 2001:108). This project remains as a marvelous example of local self-help community intervention.

> The CAP (Chicago Area Project) developed after-school recreation programs and built weekend camping facilities to attract the participation of youth; volunteers developed contacts with all youth that had any contact with the police. Volunteers were trained to provide "curbside counseling" to gang-involved youth. They were also trained to act as mediators for neighborhood youth who were having troubles in school or who became involved with the police, were on probation, or were paroled. In this latter capacity, CAP developed an ambitious version of what we would today call a "reentry" program. It kept track of all local youth sentenced to Illinois corrections facilities and maintained contact with the youth and their families. CAP interceded with the parole board to help set the conditions of release and worked with youths after they returned to the community to help them get back in school or acquire jobs. (Greenwood, 2006:22)

However, measuring the effectiveness of a program like the Chicago Area Project is extremely difficult—if not impossible. Shaw made no effort to evaluate the success of his project and since the project had no control groups, no comparison community, its findings were inconclusive. However, the program did pay sufficient attention to the organization, development, and implementation of the area projects to provide some clues as to the conditions under which a total community strategy might be feasible. Richard Lundman concludes, "Unless one is willing to accept the subjective assessments of persons associated with the project, there is no method of determining whether the Chicago Area Project accomplished its announced goal of preventing delinquency" (2001:112).

It is important to note that while design problems precluded a definite claim of success, the Chicago Area Project may have had significant impact. As noted in chapter 10, a reassessment of the evidence by Steven Schlossman and Michael Sedlak (1983) suggests that the declines in delinquency were far greater than would be expected given delinquency statistics for comparable, nonproject neighborhoods. Nevertheless, a promising prevention program was seriously flawed because of a simple lack of a comparison group.

Although the Chicago Area Project could not claim to have demonstrated a preventive impact on delinquency, it did stimulate many ideas on how to develop grassroots organizations in a community. For example, natural leaders and the human resources of neighborhoods were sought out with the intent of building from the bottom up rather than the top down. Programs were not imposed on neighborhoods; rather, highly differentiated, flexible, and experimental projects were devised. Community improvement campaigns were created to instill a sense of pride in local neighborhoods. Recreation was central to the project because it served as a springboard for eliciting adult participation, counseling, employment opportunities, and ultimately the supervision and involvement of youth in conventional activities. Schlossman and Sedlak (1983) suggest that the Chicago Area Project remains as an exemplary model of community organization designed to get at the roots of delinquency.

The ideas originally developed in the Chicago Area Project were implemented in several subsequent projects. One such project was a "total community" delinquency program carried out in a lower-class district of Boston from 1954 to 1957 (Miller, 1962). Known as the **Midcity Project**, it was concerned with developing and strengthening local citizens' groups and organizing relationships among agencies and institutions involving youth by using professional agencies and delinquency experts. The project also provided an intensive program of psychiatrically oriented casework for "chronic problem families" and assigned professionally trained adults to work with street gangs in certain areas of the city. The workers' goal was to help the street gang move in the direction of conventional, rather than delinquent, activities. Workers also acted as intermediaries between adult institutions and gang members. The project used psychiatric clinics, family service agencies, and group therapy sessions when cases or situations were felt to require such a response. Organizers felt that using a variety of techniques would be valuable for testing what Walter Miller called the **synergism concept**—the idea that the application of a diverse set of procedures in concert might be more effective than distinct programs operating individually (1962:189). According to Lundman (2001), the major difference between the Midcity Project and the Chicago Area Project was that the latter was unique in its faith that the residents of inner-city neighborhoods could deal with their own problems rather than bringing in "experts."

Given the Midcity Project's intensity and diversity of programs, the ultimate conclusions concerning delinquency prevention generated by this project were surprising. The evaluation of the project, which used a variety of different measures of delinquency, concluded that there was no significant inhibition of either illegal or immoral behavior resulting from this prevention program. In the words of Miller, "All major measures of violative behavior . . . provide consistent support for a finding of 'negligible impact'" (1962:187). As a qualification to this finding, Miller observed that the project, which had been instituted in response to concern over "rampant gang violence," did appear to mollify those fears and to calm the adult community. Moreover, the project did establish new local organizations that survived the project. Miller further noted that there was considerable variability in the responses of different neighborhood groups.

Another community delinquency prevention program, the **Mobilization for Youth Project**, was created in 1961 in Manhattan's lower east side. This program was built on Richard Cloward and Lloyd Ohlin's opportunity theory, and attempted to improve access primarily for Puerto Rican and African-American youth in the areas of education, employment, and social services. Employment assistance included job-training programs, subsidized work, and vocational-guidance programs for unemployed, out-of-school youth. Educational programs included a "homework helper" project, tutorial programs, increased parent-school contacts, and curriculum revision geared to help minority students. Recreational programs were developed; a **detached worker program** sent adults into the streets to mingle with street gangs; a coffee house was established to provide an alternative meeting place for young people. In sum, the Mobilization for Youth Project was a comprehensive, multidimensional prevention program that received substantial funding and widespread support. Unfortunately, while it enjoyed some limited success, it did not have a dramatic impact on delinquency in New York City. Some administrative irregularities were uncovered and the program suddenly lost the support of public officials. The program became involved with struggles over the distribution of power and resources, and New York City officials charged that the program was "riot-producing, Communist-oriented, left-wing and corrupt" (Weissman, 1969:25). Many supporters of this program argued that progress was being made, but the strategy of the program assumed that social conflict was necessary to alleviate the causes of delinquency, and the program lost credibility.

In 1962 a smaller-scale project designed to prevent delinquency among "high-risk" African-American youths was implemented in Seattle's central area. Whereas the Midcity Project worked with existing gangs, the workers in the **Seattle Delinquency Control Project** were each assigned a set of youths whom they subsequently attempted to organize into groups. The caseworkers, who were trained male social workers, worked with the boys, their families, and the schools. Berleman and Steinburn (1967) evaluated the impact of the program by comparing an experimental group of high-risk boys with a control group of high-risk boys. Cases had been randomly assigned to either group. They also compared the experimental and control groups with boys who refused to participate and with a set of "low-risk" boys. One interesting finding was that at all points in time examined, boys who refused to participate had the highest scores in terms of combined indexes of school and police disciplinary records. There were no significant differences between the experimental (treatment) group and the control group. Disciplinary scores for the treatment group appeared to decrease over time compared to increases in the other groups, but the differences were too small to be reliable. The treatment group's improvement disappeared after termination of service.

Community-oriented projects have been implemented in Canada as well. David Turner (1984) reported on the Blanshand Community Project in a subsidized housing project that had been the source of a serious delinquency problem. The Blanshand program brought professionals together with people in the community, established "talk groups" for mothers to improve parenting skills, made an apartment into a community center, developed a recreation program, and encouraged the development of a community response to juvenile justice issues. A "rent-a-kid" program also was developed to help integrate youths into the community by providing employment opportunities. Turner reported a decline in delinquency complaints from seventy in 1972 to only seventeen by 1976. The housing project dropped from first among such housing projects in delinquency to fifth. Again, while the data do not allow definite claims of preventive success, the decline appears unusual and greater than in comparable projects.

Another type of community prevention program is called **community policing**. Community policing is an example of an informal effort to develop closer ties between the police and local neighborhoods. Police establish storefront centers, hold neighborhood meetings, and distribute information on crime in local neighborhoods. While couched in terms of community prevention, it is not clear whether such programs are designed to reduce crime through processes of general deterrence or by building neighborhood ties. If the emphasis is on strengthening ties between youth and the law or strengthening communal bonds, then the theory behind community policing would be similar to some of the other prevention projects we have discussed. Such deterrence-oriented programs have become quite popular in many cities. Lawrence Sherman (1986) reviewed many of these programs and found that they tend to be more successful when there is *less* citizen involvement. Sherman found that citizen involvement increases the fear of crime and often creates an exaggerated perception of the crime problem. Numerous community policing programs have been evaluated and some have produced positive evaluations of the police by residents—but little evidence of reducing crime in the community (Adams, Rohe, and Arcury, 2002).

Another popular crime prevention strategy is the **neighborhood watch** program. Residents of a particular neighborhood meet with a police representative to discuss the crime problem in their immediate area, discuss ways to prevent crime, and devise ways to supervise the neighborhood and report suspicious activity to the police. Such neighborhoods proudly display prominent "neighborhood watch" signs in their homes and on street signs. Dennis Rosenbaum (1987) found that neighborhood watch programs in middle-class, culturally homogeneous neighborhoods can be reasonably successful. However, in lower-class, culturally heterogeneous neighborhoods where residents hold conflicting views, subscribe to different norms, and display varied family styles, these programs do not work well. Even in those neighborhoods where these programs are accepted with great enthusiasm, researchers found that with the passage of time, interest in the program declines rapidly (Lindsay and McGillis, 1986). In sum, low-income neighborhoods where crime is more prevalent are typically less organized, and residents tend to feel less in control over what happens in their neighborhood and typically receive little outside support to do much about crime.

Youth Service Bureaus and the Neighborhood Youth Corps

A third type of prevention strategy includes a broad range of services for juveniles. The 1967 report of the President's Commission on Law Enforcement and Administration of Justice recommended the creation of **youth service bureaus** to reduce the role of the juvenile court and to act as central coordinators of various community services for juveniles. The concept of youth service bureaus is not totally clear or precise, but basically they act as brokers of all community services for young people. Originally they were to be diversion agencies for arrested children, but most youth service bureaus received referrals from nonlegal and nonjudicial agencies. The true potential of youth service bureaus as an alternative to formal juvenile court intervention was never realized because Congress cut funds for the program in the early 1970s. Those youth service bureaus that did not close were incorporated into the juvenile court structure and the program was greatly reduced.

The **Neighborhood Youth Corps**, operated under the Department of Labor, employs youngsters living in low-income families and provides them with income, work experience, counseling, and remedial education. Gerald Robin summarized the rationale for Neighborhood Youth Corps programs as follows:

> The dialogue supporting such programs has increasingly emphasized their contribution toward reducing delinquency and youth crime by inculcating more positive and socially acceptable attitudes and values in the youths and by constructively occupying leisure time through employment activities, thereby reducing the inclination and opportunity of its recipients to engage in behavior which would make them objects of law enforcement attention. (1969:323)

Robin reported on evaluations of two such programs. One was a Neighborhood Youth Corps program in Cincinnati that provided jobs to students from poor families. Participants were allowed to work up to fifteen hours per week during the school year and thirty-two hours per week during the summer, earning the minimum wage. The work projects were generally sponsored by school boards and educational institutions. The participants were directed by a work supervisor and assigned to counselors who were to help with any problems. Since there was a large waiting list of equally qualified applicants, the researchers were able to select enrollees randomly, thus creating a control group "of unassailable quality" (Robin, 1969:323). The experimental group was comprised of actively enrolled youths, and the control group consisted of eligible youths who had not been accepted into the program. The other program evaluated was a Neighborhood Youth Corps project in Detroit.

Robin examined offense records for the control group and for enrollees both during and after participation in the program. His findings illustrate the importance of having a control group for comparison. During participation in the Cincinnati Neighborhood Youth Corps program, there was a 33 percent reduction in the proportion of year-round male enrollees who had contact with the police. This is a type of finding that could easily be reported to the public and funding agencies as evidence of success. However, the presence of a control group allowed a comparison with those youths who did not make it into the program. The startling finding was that for the control group, the reduction was 39 percent. Comparisons of the program enrollees with the control groups indicated that participation in the Neighborhood Youth Corps in Cincinnati and Detroit neither reduced delinquency during the program relative to nonparticipation nor prevented subsequent delinquency. These findings were true for both males and females. Robin concluded:

> Assuming that police contacts are a valid index of variation in illegal behavior, then the putative importance of antipoverty programs that consist largely of the creation of work opportunities in reducing criminality among juveniles and young people may be more illusive than real. (1969:331)

Johnson and Goldberg (1982) examined a vocational rehabilitation program in Massachusetts and came to a similar conclusion: providing occupational opportunities for youth had little impact on delinquency. These programs do not address the underlying problems of poverty, school dropouts, dysfunctional families, crime-ridden neighborhoods, or gang-related problems. Further, the type of jobs that are made available are typically low paying, manual labor with limited career advancement opportunities.

School-Based Programs

Schools in the United States are critical gatekeepers to what might be called "the good life." School dropouts are destined to become members of lower-class society with little or no opportunity for career advancement. The relationship between dropping out of school and criminal behavior has been well documented (Thornberry, Moore, and Christenson, 1985). Potential school dropouts have higher levels of delinquent activity, and after dropping out of school their criminal activity not only continues but actually increases.

> Dropping out of high school was found to have a positive long-term effect on criminal behavior. Throughout the early 20s, dropouts have consistently higher rates of arrests than do graduates, and it is not unit the mid-20s that the rates for the two groups begin to converge. These findings are also observed for minority

group subjects and those from blue-collar backgrounds. . . . Finally, dropout status was also found to have a significant positive effect on crime when postschool experiences of marriage and employment are controlled. In general, therefore, results of this analysis are quite consistent with the theoretical expectations of social control theory—dropping out of school has a positive effect on subsequent arrest even when age and postschool experiences are controlled. (Thornberry, Moore, and Christenson, 1985:17)

In 1980 the Office of Juvenile Justice and Delinquency Prevention established an "Alternative Education Initiative" based on the theory that delinquency can be reduced by increasing youths' bonds to school and education and their sense of competence and belonging (see chapters 6 and 7). Seventeen programs were funded under this initiative and evaluations suggest that such an approach does have some merit (see Gottfredson and Gottfredson, 1986).

Denise Gottfredson reported on one of the school-based programs in detail (1986). Project **PATHE (Positive Action Through Holistic Education)** was carried out between 1980 and 1983 in three high schools and four middle schools within a public school system. Gottfredson describes the rationale for the program as follows:

> The program assumed that delinquency and low attainment have multiple causes. Approaches targeting only selected aspects of the environment would be ineffective, according to this view, because the nontargeted negative forces in the environment would swamp any progress made in the targeted area. Approaches attempting to change the behavior of delinquency-prone individuals without attention to the features of the environment that elevate these students' risk for engaging in delinquent activities would also be ineffective. These ideas are reflected in the program's comprehensive approach. It targeted several aspects of the environment for change, and it simultaneously attempted to ameliorate the academic and social deficits of delinquency-prone students and to alter environmental cues, rewards and punishments, and structural arrangements in the school in ways intended to make undesired behavior less likely to occur. (1986:707)

The PATHE program combined prevention techniques aimed at high-risk youth with more basic changes in the school environment as a whole.

These changes were planned and accomplished through a team structure involving staff, students, administrators, parents, and members of the community. Both curriculum and school discipline were addressed and teachers were provided training in innovative teaching and classroom management. Students were involved in the establishment of both classroom and school rules. Mini-courses were developed, student learning teams were created, and a "school pride" campaign was mounted together with an expansion of extracurricular activities and the development of peer counseling or "rap" sessions. Career-oriented interventions included a career exploration program and a job-seeking skills program. About 10 percent of the students were eligible for direct services based on academic and behavioral problems. Specialists established behavioral objectives for this high-risk category, provided counseling and academic services, and monitored their progress.

Data on both school-level and individual-level outcomes were collected, including self-reported delinquency, suspensions, and school punishment as well as official school and court records. Researchers also measured academic progress, attachment to school, attendance, educational expectations, self-concepts, and perceptions of general school climate, morale, and discipline. PATHE schools were compared to nonintervention schools, and targeted high-risk students were compared to other high-risk students who did not receive direct services. The treatment and control high-risk groups were created through random assignment.

Gottfredson reports that, based on both self-reports and official data, the program brought about "a small but measurable reduction in delinquent behavior and misconduct" (1986:705). School climate and students' sense of belonging improved as well. In contrast, the provision of services to high-risk youths did not reduce their delinquency although they did appear to have lower dropout rates, higher chances of graduation, and improved achievement test scores. However, targeted students in the only school where high-risk students received the planned intensity of personal service did engage in significantly less delinquency. Overall, it appeared that organizational-level change relevant to the experiences of all students is more promising than treatment programs aimed specifically at high-risk populations.

Another preventive effort centering on schools is an aggressive law enforcement approach called **Drug-Free School Zones** (DFSZ). The objective of this national effort is to pass legislation in every state that establishes drug-free zones around a 1,000-foot school perimeter, school property, school buses, bus routes, and bus stops. Anyone caught in this zone using, distributing, manufacturing, selling, or trafficking in illegal substances is subject to increased criminal and civil penalties than are normally charged against offenders outside the drug-free zone. Public service advertisements are posted in the community warning people of the significance of a drug-free zone (see figure 12-1). Some states are expanding drug-free zones to include public parks, libraries, and swimming pools. The objective of this legislation is not necessarily the eradication of drugs in the community but the creation of drug-free havens in those areas frequented by school-aged children.

Early Childhood Programs

A review of research on crime prevention notes that most programs "target late childhood and adolescence rather than early childhood" and that prevention programs that focus on (1) the improvement of cognitive and social skills in children, and (2) parenting skills and well-being of parents can have some beneficial short-term and long-term consequences (Yoshikawa, 1995:51–75). For example, compared to nonparticipants, children who participate in **Head Start** preschool education programs appear to experience a short-term advantage in terms of IQ test performance and long-term advantages in avoiding "being held back," assignment to special education classes, and appearances in the justice system (Barnett, 1995). Since nonparticipants catch up in terms of IQ test performance, it is believed that the advantage may stem from greater confidence in school and greater educational motivation and/or parental support throughout the school years.

The Perry Preschool Project in Ypsilanti, Michigan, is an example of a program that combined preschool experiences with home visits by teachers. It involved 123 three- and four-year-old African-American children. The kids attended preschool for two and one-half hours each day, five days per week, combined with weekly, ninety-minute home visits by teachers. The project was conducted for a two-year period.

Figure 12-1   Sample of a Drug-Free School Zone Warning

Hirokazu Yoshikawa summarizes the results as follows: "The project decreased rates of self-reported delinquency at age 14, official chronic delinquency at age 19 and, in the most recent follow-up at age 27, adult criminality" (1995:59). Yoshikawa proposes that these reductions, together with the results of other program evaluations, stemmed from positive effects on cognitive skills, verbal ability, and parenting. While costly in the short-run, economic analyses suggest a considerable savings over the life-course of the child. For example, the Perry Preschool Project cost about $12,000 per family but saved about $108,000 in the long-run due to savings for the justice system and potential victims. At present there is reason to believe that a combination of family support and early education services can reduce the odds of future delinquency at considerable savings to society.

The evidence is overwhelming that academic failure is a high risk factor for the onset of delinquency and the escalation of delinquent behavior (Howell, 2003). Interventions that improve children's academic performance early in their educational career have been shown to reduce delinquency (Maguin and Loeber, 1996). For example, **Fast Track** is a program that targets kindergarten children who have conduct problems at home and at school. The program attempts to instill a sense of problem-solving skills and self-control (Herrenkohl et al., 2001). At the end of the first grade, children in the Fast Track program showed improvements in prosocial behavior and problem solving, decreases in aggression, and improvements in behavior at home and school. Other components of the program included parental involvement, conflict resolution skills at home and at school, home visitation, and child tutoring (Greenberg and Kusché, 1993).

The **Second Step** program is a violence prevention approach for the early elementary grades (Herrenkohl et al., 2001). The program is designed to address anger management, impulse control, and empathy. These young children are introduced to techniques of anger management and the resolution of interpersonal disputes. Similarly, **PeaceBuilders** is a program for children in kindergarten through fifth grade that attempts to develop prosocial behavior and change the conditions that lead to aggression. Activities are designed to improve the interactions of the children, teachers, staff, and parents. "The children were taught five basic principles: praise people, avoid put-downs, seek wise people as advisors, notice and correct hurts, and right wrongs" (Howell, 2003:184). The evaluation of this program found a significant improvement in anger management, fewer visits to the school nurse for injuries resulting from fighting, and increased prosocial behavior. Anger management programs in schools have been found to reduce school violence in meta-analysis of such programs as well (Wilson, 2000).

The apparent success of these and other school-based programs raises an important issue in evaluation research. Programs that succeed in keeping youth in school, that reduce the rate of out-of-wedlock births, that improve parenting and other skills in both parents and children, that address anger management skills, and reduce aggressive behavior may have an impact on rates of delinquency many years down the road. If evaluations were carried out over lengthy periods of time with randomly assigned experimental and control groups, many programs that were not specifically designed for delinquency prevention might prove to have such an effect.

An Overview

The National Institute of Justice issued a research bulletin entitled "Preventing Crime: What Works, What Doesn't, What's Promising" (Sherman et al., 1998). This report compiled a list of programs that have demonstrated evidence of success based on a systematic review of scientific crime prevention practices (see table 12-1). Of those programs that work, it is significant that most are early intervention programs. Conversely, those programs that do not work such as DARE, neighborhood watch, and electronic monitoring are popular programs but have produced no scientific evidence to support their claims. Numerous studies show that the antisocial careers of male juvenile offenders begins, on average, at age 7—not at age 14, which is the average age of first court contact.

Table 12-1   Preventing Crime: What Works, What Doesn't, What's Promising

What Works

For infants
- frequent home visits by nurses and other professionals

For preschoolers
- classes with weekly home visits by preschool teachers

For delinquent and at-risk preadolescents
- family therapy and parent training

For schools
- organizational development for innovation
- communication and reinforcement of clear, consistent norms
- teaching of social competency skills
- coaching of high-risk youth in "thinking skills"

What Doesn't Work
- Gun buyback programs
- Drug Abuse Resistance Education (DARE)
- Summer jobs or subsidized work programs
- Neighborhood watch programs
- Home detention with electronic monitoring
- Arrests of juveniles for minor offenses
- Storefront police offices
- Scared Straight programs for at-risk youth
- Shock probation
- Residential programs for juvenile offenders using challenging experiences in rural settings

What's Promising
- Gang monitoring by community workers
- Community-based after school recreational programs
- Schools within schools that group students into smaller units
- Moving urban public housing residents to suburban homes
- Improved classroom management and instructional techniques
- Training or coaching in "thinking" skills for high-risk youth

Source: Sherman et al., 1998.

Problems in Implementation, Cooperation, and Finance

Some prevention programs show promise and several have had a positive impact on the attitudes and morale of people living in a community. Yet, why have so many experiments failed to reduce delinquency? If we consider the observations of prevention researchers themselves, we can find some common themes regarding experimental failures. One recurrent theme is: "The theory is still good, but we need to do what we did with more resources, greater intensity, and for a longer period of time." The Boston Midcity Project was no casual, haphazard program; yet it had no significant impact. An early school-based experiment carried out by Walter Reckless and Simon Dinitz (1972) was based on the notion that boys' self-image is a critical determinant in explaining delinquent behavior. Teachers were trained to be positive role models, strong emphasis was placed on improving reading ability, and students were sensitized to respect the rights of others. The program ran for three years with strong support from both teachers and students. Yet, despite the program's rigorousness and widespread support, there was no discernable impact on reducing delinquency. Reckless and Dinitz concluded that one of the lessons they learned from their prevention program was that they needed to develop more effective methods of presenting role models and of training effective project teachers. Thus they wrote, "There is a reason to suspect that the exposure to role-model internalization was not intensive enough" (1972:158). The McCords (1959) felt the same way in their reevaluation of the Cambridge-Somerville Youth Study. However, it is hard to imagine creating more intensive prevention programs than those already attempted. Robin found the lack of preventive effect in the Neighborhood Youth Corps programs a "somewhat unexpected finding if for no reason other than that the program utilized approximately 1,000 hours of what would otherwise have been leisure time and therefore opportunity for misbehavior" (1969:327). Unless the researchers' own descriptions of their programs are misleading, it is hard to believe that more of the same in bigger doses will make the difference.

If the failure of these programs is a problem of intensity, then we have to face the fact (or propose some way to overcome it) that there are political, social, and cultural forces that limit the implementation of prevention programs of any greater intensity than those already described. In fact, the circumstances that limit more intense intervention are quite commonly mentioned as problems in implementing several of the programs that have been tried. In evaluating the Minnesota Youth Advocate Program, Higgins (1978) observed that the funding for and ultimate demise of this program was determined by lobbying efforts and conflicts between advocates and school principals, rather than by any evidence of the program's success or failure. Advocates were "going to bat" for youths whom some school principals did not particularly want to see back in school. However, when advocates began encouraging their clients to enroll in private schools, they generated complaints that funds for public schools were being threatened. Very few school principals supported the program.

It often appears that delinquency persists because of the reluctance of many people, groups, and organizations to accommodate changes that might reduce delinquency. Some action programs require a redistribution of power—the "haves" yielding some decision-making power to the "have-nots." It is at this juncture in implementing a new policy that change falls short. For instance, some years ago one of this text's authors was involved in a Head Start program for Mexican-American children. One of the fundamental goals of the program was to involve parents in the education of their children. Not only would the children receive a preschool "head start" in the educational arena, but also, and more importantly, parents were to become involved in a group similar to a PTA (Parent-Teacher Association). This group was to include parents, teachers, and school officials, and was to act as an advisory board in running the program. One problem that arose involved the daily diet of "Anglo" food for Mexican-American children who were unaccustomed and unreceptive to this type of food. The advisory council recommended that the children be gradually introduced to new foods lest they refuse to eat altogether. However, the school administration decreed that the Mexican-American preferred food was too high in starches and unwholesome. Even though many of the children were not eating their "nutritious" school meals because they were unfamiliar with such foods, the administration refused to yield on this point. The issue was recast into a power struggle between "professional" school administrators and "ill-informed" or uneducated parents.

A second confrontation between the advisory board and the school administration concerned the employment of Spanish-speaking teachers who lacked a few credit hours for state certification. It was suggested by the advisory board that teachers be employed who could speak Spanish even if they only had provisional teaching certificates. However, the school administration asserted that only fully certified teachers could be hired even though they could not speak Spanish. It was argued that even though these teachers could not communicate with their students, they met the qualifications of the school system.

Eventually the advisory council fell into performing perfunctory chores and never achieved the decision-making role it was initially intended to have. The school administration was so recalcitrant that even the slightest suggestion was viewed as a threat to its power. Delinquency prevention programs commonly confront this same dilemma: addressing the delinquency problem may require some redistribution of power or sharing of resources. Invariably this proves to be too threatening to the power structure, and ultimately nothing is changed.

In addition, internal problems in the implementation of a prevention program may reflect the fact that the program is operating as a small unit in a hostile bureaucratic milieu. For example, with regard to the Chicago Area Project, Harold Finestone observed that some community committees began to distance themselves from the delinquency issue and some committee members did not want to associate with people with delinquent or criminal backgrounds (1976:137). Miller (1958) found that a major impediment to delinquency prevention in the Midcity Project was conflict among the program participants. Miller wrote that the executive board became a battleground for different groups, organizations, and agencies over conflicting causes of crime, disposition of offenders, organizational style, and the hiring of personnel. Miller concluded that such conflict is a major source of difficulty in implementing and carrying out delinquency prevention programs. Similarly, program sponsors, whether they are public or private organizations, have specified orientations and goals that cannot be threatened by funded programs. For example, a delinquency prevention program that encouraged any form of abortion counseling for pregnant teenagers would be in danger of losing its funding. Oftentimes delinquency prevention advocates must be reminded to "work within the system," which means supporting the status quo. Unfortunately, it may be the status quo that exacerbates or creates the problem in the first place. The very nature of a true prevention approach suggests modifying some basic component in the social environment, but this can threaten the established order.

On the other hand, we also need to question some of the underlying assumptions of delinquency prevention programs. We have already cited the rationale behind the Neighborhood Youth Corps programs—that the services provided would take up time, as well as inspire new attachments, commitments, or attitudes. However, as we noted in chapter 6, merely occupying a youth's time does not appear to be an important barrier to delinquency. In general, delinquent activities are episodic, situational, and require very little time. Moreover, it may be that the types of activities provided by the Neighborhood Youth Corps do not inspire "more positive and socially acceptable attitudes and values" as intended. Too often the work opportunities provided are for "busy work" that serves no real purpose. For example, one of the authors was called upon to provide work for Neighborhood Youth Corps enrollees on a research project where extra help was not really needed. However, the Youth Corps staff was desperate for placements. This in turn prompted the youths in the program to view the money they received as a gift that would be awarded regardless of the quantity or quality of their work.

What is ironic about this prevention program is that research has shown that having spending money is related to many types of delinquency (see Cullen, Larson, and Mathers, 1985). Gary Jensen (1979) found that students who were in the top half of their high school in terms of spending money were significantly more likely to report alcohol and marijuana use, experimentation with more serious drugs, and a variety of "hell-raising" activities, such as joyriding, dragging, and vandalism. Moreover, this effect persisted regardless of parental social status. No matter what the parents' social standing, the adolescent with more spending money was freer to engage in delinquent activity than the adolescent with less money. As we noted in chapter 7, having a car also appears to increase the freedom to commit delinquent acts. The point here is not that paying disadvantaged youths is bad or wrong. Given the larger economic system and the larger social world of a program's participants, any delinquency prevention program would probably flounder at the outset without monetary incentives. However, it should be recognized that some aspects of a program may increase the probability of some forms of delinquency.

Overall it appears that the major limitation on both the implementation and potential effectiveness of prevention programs is that the wider system—the real world—will have its way. It might generate optimism and make us feel better to argue (1) that prevention strategies purporting to be comprehensive must be directed at fairly massive kinds of environmental change, and (2) that rather than focusing on individual delinquents or potential delinquents, delinquency prevention must call for an alteration of those factors in the environment that contribute to delinquent behavior. However, the fact of the matter is that if delinquency programs opting for small-scale change have met strong resistance, it is doubtful that large-scale prevention programs will ever be mounted successfully.

Evaluation Research

The total amount of money spent for the criminal justice system for 2005 is a staggering $204 billion dollars (Justice Expenditure and Employment Extracts, 2005). Of that amount, the federal government spent $35 billion, the states spent $65 billion, and local governments spent $104 billion. As seen in figure 12-2, these expenditures rose steadily for each governmental jurisdiction. While many might assume that the federal government pays the highest portion of the criminal justice tab, it in fact pays the smallest portion, 17 percent, while states pay 32 percent and local governments pay 51 percent. In 1985 the total criminal justice expenditure was $48.5 billion. By 1995 it more than doubled to $112.8 billion, and ten years later it had nearly doubled again to $204 billion. The second chart in figure 12-2 breaks down the criminal justice system costs by function. The police generate most of the expenditure, $94 billion or 46 percent; the correctional system cost $65 billion or 32 percent of all expenditures; and the judiciary cost $44 billion or 22 percent of all expenditures.

What is most disturbing is that there is no possible way of ascertaining what this $204 billion accomplishes because there is very little scientific research conducted in the area of criminal justice. For example, we have crude estimates of recidivism rates but no concerted research is conducted on improving policing, the judicial system, or the corrections system. There is a dire need for scientific evaluation of programs, but the criminal justice system seems to have a low regard for research. Police departments, judicial agencies, and correctional agencies need to consistently gather data and evaluate their objectives, but few of these agencies have any evaluation component; thus knowledge of what works is seriously lacking.

Figure 12-2   Direct Expenditures by Level of Government and Criminal Justice Function, 1982–2005

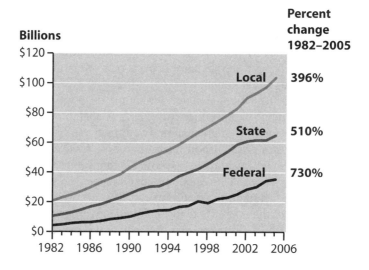

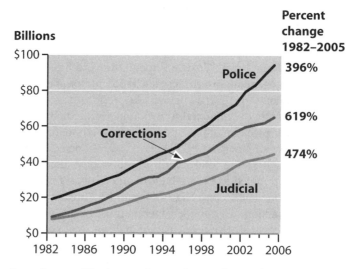

Source: Justice Expenditures and Employment Extracts, Bureau of Justice Statistics, 2005.

Lipsey and Wilson (1998) argue that evaluation of juvenile justice programs needs to go beyond studies of individual programs to what they call meta-analyses, or the combination of multiple program evaluations. By combining multiple program evaluations, Lipsey and Wilson were able to identify intervention techniques that were not readily apparent in previous studies because of low numbers in the control and experimental groups. Lipsey (1992) argues that many delinquency treatment programs were more successful than originally thought because the individual evaluation programs had flaws, but by examining a collection of treatment techniques across programs, the results were stronger. The most effective programs employed some form of behavior modification. Lipsey suggests that it is not a matter of whether the treatment of delinquency works but of defining those necessary conditions that maximize the effectiveness of various proven intervention strategies.

Choices: Assessing Our Own Values, Beliefs, and Commitments

Despite the intuitive appeal of listing a series of recommendations from research findings or critics of the juvenile justice system, we need to consider our own stake in this matter. Obviously, there are any number of alternatives that could be selected for a nationwide delinquency prevention program. However, overcoming personal bias, prejudice, or even ignorance while we collectively fashion a plan of action that may ultimately fail is no simple matter. Furthermore, any set of far-reaching proposals that calls for a significant alteration of the social structure very quickly becomes an intensely personal matter. The price of eradicating crime and delinquency may be too painful for us to bear. It is relatively simple to suggest changes in the lives of other people, but far more difficult to alter our own lifestyles. Before we commit society to a plan of action, we need to judiciously assess our own contribution to the problem and consider how much we are willing to sacrifice in order to find a solution. Grappling with choices is what delinquency prevention is all about and why it is so radical, and ultimately, why it is so difficult to implement.

> Too often juvenile justice officials have put forward a single program as the panacea for curing juvenile offenders. . . . it is not really plausible that one single therapeutic programmatic approach will be effective for the wide range of needs of the young people who come into the juvenile justice system. (Krisberg, 2005:152)

Personal Reform

Adults, particularly parents, serve as critical role models for children and adolescents. Our values and attitudes, political orientations, language, behavioral mannerisms, and even tastes were strongly influenced by key adult role models as we were growing up. Adults and parents can subtly influence not only law-abiding behavior but also law-violating behavior. It is one thing for adults to bemoan the fact that adolescents are committing all forms of crime, but then again these same adolescents are confronted with endless examples in the daily news of bank fraud, income tax cheating, embezzlement, political corruption, savings and loan scandals, insider trading, property crime, and every conceivable form of violence against persons. If parents and adults can dabble in criminal activity, why can't adolescents?

Personal apathy is very likely a major contributor to the failure of prevention efforts. Victimization reports show that nearly two-thirds of personal and household victimizations are not reported to the police. Similarly, we hear stories of bystanders who watched a crime take place and took no action. Even more distressing are accounts of assault, rape, and child abuse that occur because no one intervenes. Since anonymity facilitates crime and delinquency, we need to work to reduce distance between ourselves, our neighbors, and our children. Locked doors and security devices do reduce the risk of victimization, but excessive social isolation can contribute to juvenile crime as well.

Early Intervention

Many children are born into high-risk environments where delinquency is virtually inevitable. Children who live in family environments where violence, poverty, chemical dependency, and mental health issues are rampant need immediate care. Home-visitation programs that provide support for at-risk mothers have been shown to be effective (U.S. Department of Health and Human Services, 2001). Programs that train registered nurses as home visitors have consistently demonstrated significant long-term improvements in the mothers' childcare abilities and social skills development (Greenwood, 2006). A fifteen-year follow-up of the **Prenatal/Early Infancy Project** demonstrated that nurse home visits greatly reduced child abuse and neglect, and there were significant declines in arrest rates for the mother and the child (Olds et al., 1997). But funding for such programs is problematic and local communities are cutting out such "frill" programs in an effort to balance budgets.

Education and Schools

Early education and parenting programs show promise of reducing future delinquency and yielding savings several times greater than their cost. Not only is there evidence that they work, but such evidence is consistent with well-substantiated theories of delinquency (especially social learning and social control theories). Additional educational programs that target specific skills that affect success throughout the school years and help secure stable jobs for program participants after school should have similar beneficial consequences for delinquency. For example, George Farkas (1997) has found that reading ability is the major key to academic success and, ultimately, occupational achievement and that "elementary school interventions hold the greatest promise of reducing this reading failure" (1997:9). Furthermore, successful interventions to improve reading involve one-on-one instruction, and the most cost effective strategies involve large-scale training, deployment, and supervision of hourly-paid tutors. Farkas's program, **Reading One-on-One**, operates out of the University of Texas at Dallas and has been found to result in considerable net gains in reading levels for students in the program. The one-on-one tutoring program with hourly wages for part-time tutors (generally students) serves four times the number of clientele dealt with in programs involving highly paid experts at the same cost. Of course, that fact has also generated opposition to the program from organizations representing those professionals. As Farkas notes, "The principal obstacles to successfully deploying this intervention are political and bureaucratic" (1997:23). His analysis of a variety of reading programs suggests that they are all fairly effective but that the problem of reading deficits is so massive that large-scale, low-cost alternatives must be pursued to have any significant impact on the problem.

Law Enforcement

Most liberals are likely to emphasize reforms of specific social institutions or limited redistributions of wealth within the existing system as steps in the amelioration of social problems. People of a more conservative political orientation tend to focus on stricter laws and increases in the certainty, severity, and celerity (speed) of enforcement and punishment as the most realistic and reasonable approaches to the control of crime and delinquency. As was summarized in chapter 9, there is quite a bit of evidence consistent with the point of view that stiffer law enforcement might reduce delinquency. Such findings are the basis for advocating that the juvenile justice system has to include some consequences certain and severe enough to have general deterrent effects. Moreover, regardless of deterrent effects, some form of imprisonment is necessary for a limited set of offenders who constitute serious risks to the community.

However, the failure of Scared Straight programs to inhibit delinquency should generate reservations about carrying the deterrence philosophy too far. When the state begins to use the threat of exposure to illegal violence and problems within prisons that it cannot control as part of the "threat" of punishment, then it is admitting defeat and its own inefficacy in coping with crime. Indeed, the tendency of youth processed through such programs to do worse than those who are not exposed suggests that such an approach is counterproductive. The use of the system's failures as threats may be alienating and disillusioning in the long run. Policies aimed at increasing the threat of sanctions within the limits of the law and with appropriate concern for due process hold more promise for inhibiting delinquency.

We have to recognize that in addition to the limitations of support for deterrence theory summarized in chapter 9, experiences at school, in the family, and in peer groups are far more strongly related to delinquency than anticipated punishment by the legal system. Such a finding does not mean that law enforcement is unimportant in the control of delinquency but it does require that we put enforcement in perspective. There is some foundation for the belief that youth may make different choices if they perceive legal punishment to be certain and severe. Policies enhancing such beliefs might reduce their delinquent choices. However, there is also evidence that it is anticipated costs to relationships and aspirations in other contexts that gives the legal system its clout. It is doubtful that the threat of legal sanctions can have much of an effect on delinquency if people do not accord the law legitimacy and its agents respect and authority.

Religion and Faith-Based Initiatives

One of the themes advocated by conservatives after the Columbine shootings was that such offenses would not occur if there were greater support for prayer in the schools and less emphasis on separation of church and state. Research on religiosity and delinquency does suggest that youth with strong religious bonds are less likely to use drugs. However, such religious characteristics are established by familial and religious institutions and have their effect in a context where schools are and have been relatively secular. Moreover, bonds to parents and to school inhibit delinquency regardless of students' and parents' religiosity. Relatively irreligious parents can and do encourage good citizenship and adherence to basic societal norms. It is very doubtful that the expansion of religious institutions and faith-based initiatives would have a significant effect on the most serious forms of juvenile delinquency. Indeed, forms of religiosity that encourage dualistic, good-versus-evil conceptions of the world may encourage some forms of violence.

Gun Control

Our analysis in chapter 8 showed that the prevalence of firearms within a state does affect the magnitude of firearm homicide, but also showed that the strength of a conventional gun culture might be a negative correlate of firearm homicide. These findings suggest that responsible firearm management and training may discourage use of firearms to harm others. However, activities or values associated with that culture tend to increase the prevalence of firearms, an indirect positive correlate of homicide rates. Hence, we should support policies that encourage responsible acquisition and use of firearms, but also encourage policies that reduce the overall prevalence of firearms. Among states that have relatively weak conventional gun cultures, there is a very prominent relationship between gun control grades and firearm homicide. State and local policies that encourage the careful management of guns are likely to yield lower rates of firearm homicide.

The Failure of Militaristic Approaches

The feeling that "we've got to do something!" often occurs in the context of a so-called crisis, and the response to such national panics in America has been a "war on drugs" or a "war on crime." Alarmist approaches tend to draw on a militaristic belief system and a characterization of the problem as involving an enemy that must be attacked through coercive, emergency action. Of course, the only changes that can be made quickly involve tougher laws and increases in imprisonment. When critics of such approaches argue that we need to remedy some of the early problems that facilitate crime through increased support of early education and reading tutorials, they are labeled "liberals" or "do-gooders" and their arguments are often dismissed. Because reading programs and the like do not directly address crime and may realize their potential ten or fifteen years later, they are not thought of as crime-control programs. Indeed, proponents of social programs are labeled as "soft on crime" and their opposition to an overreliance on imprisonment as the best solution leads to charges of being more concerned about offenders than victims. Yet, any approach that can be shown to reduce the odds of future delinquency and crime or to ameliorate the social problems that are intimately correlated with delinquency and crime is a victim-oriented approach. But because the potential effects are realized ten or fifteen years later, such approaches do not appeal to people who expect a "quick fix."

John Sutton (1988) concluded his study of the American juvenile justice system by stating that "juvenile justice reforms are best understood as symbolic efforts to dramatize an ideal vision of social order rather than instrumental attempts to control children's misbehavior" (1988:239). He goes on to call many reformers "socially marginal cranks" or "on-the-make professionals" who enjoy reveling in a nostalgic vision of the moral order. The theme that has been repeated throughout this book is that children are by definition immature and subject to the whims of adult society. One way of dealing with the inadequacy of contemporary society is to blame it all on our recalcitrant youth.

In short, our responses to delinquency and crime are not necessarily objective, based on the actual magnitude and nature of the problem. When we stand back and take an objective look at ourselves, our institutions, and our society, we discover that the very problem we abhor and want to do "something" about may be embedded in our society, institutions, and ultimately ourselves.

> Strong criminal and juvenile justice sanctions possess a natural, intuitive appeal. They permit politicians to talk with macho bravo without being held accountable for the poor results of these programs. Given the enormous fiscal and human investments and human consequences of these approaches, it is scandalous that our research base is so slender. It is as if contemporary policies have adopted a "hear no evil, speak no evil, see no evil" strategy. In particular, policies to increase the use of secure confinement or to place more youths in prison are not supported by scientific evidence, but are informed by anecdotes, jingoes (Do the Crime, Do the Time), and media popularized fads. Our elected officials go from Tough Love to Scared Straight, from boot camps to chain gangs. It is not surprising that many of our young people have become very cynical about a public policy process that squanders so much money on unproven policies and programs. (Krisberg 2005:178)

Summary

Delinquency is shaped and facilitated by aspects of the social world that each of us helps to create and sustain. We may not do so consciously or intentionally since we are each also constrained by the social world. However, an understanding of the forces that shape delinquency and of reactions to delinquency should help us understand ourselves and our own role in the problem. Such understanding does not provide clear and certain answers to the choices we must make, which is why this chapter is subtitled "Dilemmas of Choice, Change, and Control."

If we choose to view delinquency as a serious problem and want to advocate doing something about it, then it is important to learn what has been tried and to consider alternatives in view of past failures. If previous prevention designs did not work because they were not intensive enough or because of vested interests and political limitations, then we will have to overcome such limitations and try these designs again. If they failed because they did not change society sufficiently, then we may choose to alter the system radically and hope for the best. There will be risks and costs involved and no scientific research to tell us with certainty what the rewards and costs of alternative utopias will be. If our actions or inactions contribute to the problem, then we can certainly change ourselves. If we feel we need to know more before deciding what to do, then let's pursue such knowledge and support others in that pursuit. Existing knowledge is a risky and uncertain guide. It can help narrow the options, but it also leaves us in the age-old human position of making choices with no guarantee of success.

Discussion Questions

1. People often become enthusiastic about "preventing" delinquency as opposed to dealing with delinquent youth after they have already offended. Is this idea new? Justify your answer.

2. Can you think of reasons why some programs that identify youth who are predicted to be headed for trouble might "boomerang"? What theory discussed in the text can account for such unintended effects?

3. Delinquency prevention programs are often based on implicit assumptions that need to be made explicit if we are to understand their success or failure. Discuss the assumptions behind the Neighborhood Youth Corps program and comment on their validity.

4. Based on research discussed in this textbook, suggest two ways that important social institutions (e.g., family, school, religion, gun culture) might be changed in an attempt to prevent delinquency.

5. How might changes in our own behavior affect the delinquency problem?

6. What forms of early intervention are most promising for reducing future rates of violence in the United States?

7. What theories discussed in chapter 6 are reflected in the PATHE school-based programs? Why might changing attachment to school and community be more effective than programs directed at high-risk youth alone?

8. The evaluation of the Neighborhood Youth Corps program in Cincinnati reported a 33 percent reduction in police contacts for youth in the program. Does this mean that the program was successful? Discuss the methodological requirements for deeming a program a success.

9. This textbook has been fairly critical of militaristic approaches to either preventing or treating delinquency. What is the basis of that criticism? If you were to modify that approach, what features would you retain?

10. Chapter 8 discussed the "usual suspects" blamed when there is a well-publicized episode of violent crime. How would you address these "usual suspects" to reduce juvenile violence? Be specific and pay attention to the research on these topics.

References

Adams, R., W. Rohe, and T. Arcury. 2002. "Implementing Community-Oriented Policing: Organizational Change and Street Officer Attitudes." *Crime & Delinquency* 48:399–430.

Barnett, W. S. 1995. "Long-Term Outcomes of Early Childhood Programs: Analysis and Recommendations." *The Future of Children* 5:6–24.

Berleman, W. C., and T. W. Steinburn. 1967. "The Execution and Evaluation of a Delinquency Prevention Program." *Social Problems* 14 (Spring):413–23.

Bernard, T. J. 2006. *Serious Delinquency: An Anthology.* Los Angeles: Roxbury.

Bureau of Justice Statistics. 2003. *Sourcebook of Criminal Justice Statistics.* Washington, DC: U.S. Dept. of Justice.

Cullen, F. T., M. T. Larson, and R. A. Mathers. 1985. "Having Money and Delinquency Involvement: The Neglect of Power in Delinquency Theory." *Criminal Justice and Behavior* 12 (June):171–92.

Farkas, G. 1997. "Ten Propositions about Schooling, the Inheritance of Poverty, and Interventions to Reduce This Inheritance." *Research in Social Problems and Public Policy* 6:125–69.

Farrington, D. P. 1998. "Explaining and Preventing Crime: The Globalization of Knowledge." *Criminology* 38:1–24.

Finestone, H. 1976. *Victims of Change*. Westport, CT: Greenwood Press.

Gottfredson, D. C. 1986. "An Empirical Test of School-Based Environmental and Individual Interventions to Reduce the Risk of Delinquent Behavior." *Criminology* 24(4):705–31.

Gottfredson, D. C., and G. D. Gottfredson. 1986. *The School Action Effectiveness Study: Final Report*. Center for Social Organization of Schools. Baltimore: The Johns Hopkins University.

Greenberg, M., and C. Kusché. 1993. *Promoting Social and Emotional Development in Deaf Children: The PATHS Project*. Seattle: University of Washington Press.

Greenwood, P. W. 2006. *Changing Lives: Delinquency Prevention and Crime-Control Policy*. Chicago: University of Chicago Press.

Herrenkohl, T., B. Huang, R. Kosterman, D. Hawkins, J. Catalano, and R. Smith. 2001. "A Comparison of Social Development Processes Leading to Violent Behavior in Late Adolescence for Childhood Initiators and Adolescent Initiators of Violence." *Journal of Research in Crime and Delinquency* 38:45–63.

Higgins, P. S. 1978. "Evaluation and Case Study of a School-Based Delinquency Prevention Program." *Evaluation Quarterly* 2 (May):215–34.

Howell, J. C. 2003. *Preventing and Reducing Juvenile Delinquency*. Thousand Oaks, CA: Sage.

Jensen, G. F. 1979. "Final Report: Delinquency in a Middle-Class High School." Washington, DC: National Institute of Mental Health.

Johnson, B., and R. Goldberg. 1982. "Vocational and Social Rehabilitation of Delinquents." *Journal of Offender Counseling Services and Rehabilitation* 6:43–60.

Justice Expenditure and Employment Extract. 2005. *Bureau of Census Annual Government Finance Survey and Annual Survey of Public Employment*. Washington, DC: U.S. Dept. of Justice.

Krisberg, B. 2005. *Juvenile Justice: Redeeming Our Children*. Thousand Oaks, CA: Sage.

Lab, S. P. 1988. *Crime Prevention: Approaches, Practices and Evaluations*. Cincinnati: Anderson.

Lipsey, M. W. 1992. "Juvenile Delinquency Treatment: A Meta-Analytic Inquiry into the Variability of Effects." In *Meta-Analysis for Explanation*, edited by T. D. Cook et al. New York: Russell Sage.

Lipsey, M., and D. Wilson. 1998. "Effective Interventions with Serious Juvenile Offenders: A Synthesis of Research." In *Serious and Violent Offenders: Risk Factors and Successful Interventions*, edited by R. Loeber and D. Farrington, pp. 313–45. Thousand Oaks, CA: Sage.

Lindsay, B., and D. McGillis. 1986. "Citywide Community Prevention: An Assessment of the Seattle Program." In *Community Crime Prevention: Does It Work?*, edited by D. P. Rosenbaum. Beverly Hills: Sage.

Lundman, R. J. 2001. *Prevention and Control of Juvenile Delinquency*. 3rd ed. New York: Oxford Press.

Maguin, E., and R. Loeber. 1996. "Academic Performance and Delinquency." *Crime and Justice* 20:145–64.

Martin, J. M. 1961. "Three Approaches to Delinquency Prevention: A Critique." *Crime and Delinquency* 7 (January):16–24.

McCord, J. 1978. "A Thirty-Year Follow-Up of Treatment Effects." *American Psychologist* 33:284–89.

McCord, J., and W. McCord. 1959. "A Follow-Up Report on the Cambridge-Somerville Youth Study." *Annals of the American Academy of Political and Social Science* 322 (March):89–98.

Mendel, R. A. 1995. "Prevention or Pork? A Hard-Headed Look at Youth-Oriented Anti-Crime Programs." Washington, DC: American Youth Policy Forum.

Miller, W. B. 1958. "Inter-Institutional Conflict as a Major Impediment to Delinquency Prevention." *Human Organization* 17 (Fall):20–23.

———. 1962. "The Impact of a 'Total Community' Delinquency Control Project." *Social Problems* 10 (Fall):168–91.

Nagin, D. S., A. R. Piquero, E. S. Scott, and L. Steinberg. 2006. "Public Preferences for Rehabilitation versus Incarceration of Juvenile Offenders: Evidence from a Contingent Valuation Survey." *Criminology and Public Policy* 5:301–26.

Office of Juvenile Justice and Delinquency Prevention. 1995. *Delinquency Prevention Works.* Washington, DC: U.S. Dept. of Justice.

Olds, D., J. Eckenrod, J. Henderson, H. Kizman, J. Powers, R. Cole, K. Sidor, P. Morris, L. Pettit, and D. Luckey. 1997. "Long-Term Effects of Home Visitation on Maternal Life Course and Child Abuse and Neglect." *Journal of the American Medical Association* 278:637–43.

Reckless, W. C., and S. Dinitz. 1972. *The Prevention of Juvenile Delinquency: An Experiment.* Columbus: Ohio University Press.

Robin, G. D. 1969. "Anti-Poverty Programs and Delinquency." *Journal of Criminal Law, Criminology and Police Science* 60 (Fall):323–31.

Rosenbaum, D. P. 1987. "The Theory and Research behind Neighborhood Watch: Is It a Sound Fear and Crime Reduction Strategy?" *Crime and Delinquency* 33:103–34.

Sampson, R. J., and J. H. Laub. 1993. "Structural Variations in Juvenile Court Processing: Inequality, the Underclass, and Social Control." *Law & Society Review* 27:285–312.

Schlossman, S., and M. Sedlak. 1983. *The Chicago Area Project Revisited.* Santa Monica, CA: Rand Corporation.

Schur, E. 1969. *Our Criminal Society.* Englewood Cliffs, NJ: Prentice-Hall.

Sherman, L. W. 1986. "Policing Communities: What Works?" In *Communities and Crime,* edited by A. J. Reiss, Jr., and M. Tonry. Chicago: University of Chicago Press.

Sherman, L., D. Gottfredson, D. MacKenzie, J. Eck, P. Reuter, and S. Bushway. 1998. *Preventing Crime: What Works, What Doesn't, What's Promising.* Washington, DC: National Institute of Justice.

Sutherland, E. 1924. *Principles of Criminology.* Philadelphia: J. B. Lippincott.

Sutton, J. R. 1988. *Stubborn Children: Controlling Delinquency in the United States, 1640–1981.* Berkeley: University of California Press.

Thornberry, T., M. Moore, and R. Christenson. 1985. "The Effect of Dropping Out of High School on Subsequent Criminal Behavior." *Criminology* 23:3–16.

Toby, J. 1965. "An Evaluation of Early Identification and Intensive Treatment Programs for Predelinquents." *Social Problems* 13 (Fall):160–65.

———. 1984. "Toby Releases Study on School Violence." *The Criminologist* 9:304.

Turner, D. 1984. "The Probation Officer and Community Delinquency Prevention: The Shift Out of Reactive Casework." *Canadian Journal of Criminology* 26 (January):75–96.

U.S. Department of Health and Human Services. 2001. *Youth Violence: A Report of the Surgeon General.* Rockville, MD: U.S. Dept. of Health and Human Services.

Weissman, J. 1969. *Community Development in the Mobilization for Youth.* New York: Association Press.

Wilson, S. J. 2000. *Effectiveness of School Violence Prevention Programs.* PhD dissertation, Vanderbilt University.

Wright, W. E., and M. C. Dixon. 1977. "Community Prevention and Treatment of Juvenile Delinquency." *Journal of Research in Crime and Delinquency* 14 (January):35–67.

Yoshikawa, H. 1995. "Long-Term Effects of Early Childhood Programs on Social Outcomes and Delinquency." *The Future of Children* 5:51–75.

Glossary

absolute deterrence (9)—when individuals refrain throughout life from a particular type of criminal act because they perceive some risk of suffering a punishment as a response to the crime; in other words, people who never have broken the law because they fear punishment.

adjudicated (2)—judicially determined to be a delinquent, status offender, or dependent/neglected.

adjudication hearing (2)—hearing to determine whether a child should be adjudicated.

adolescence (2)—a term that came into use in the nineteenth century to denote the interim status between childhood and adulthood.

advisory hearing (2)—a preliminary hearing to determine what subsequent actions are necessary.

alienation (6)—in criminology this term has been used to refer to lack of commitment to conventional institutions and the values, norms and beliefs associated with those institutions.

amotivational theories (6)—those that attempt to explain delinquency by focusing on barriers; that is, the absence or breakdown of mechanisms that discourage delinquent behavior.

association (5)—when two variables co-vary in a systematic fashion.

Auburn system (10)—the preferred prison model in the United States in the early 1800s, emphasizing group work coupled with silence and solitary confinement at night.

aversion therapy (11)—exposing juvenile offenders to the harsh realties of prison life through intense, verbal confrontations with inmates.

behavior modification (10)—type of treatment program in residential settings in which the environment is manipulated in order to create the potential for changing behavior; that is, placing delinquents in a new environment that expands their social and academic skills and rewards them for academic competence.

boot camps (11)—short-term sentence for delinquent offenders at camps that mirror a military boot camp.

broken home (7)—generally defined as a home with children where parents have separated or divorced.

broken windows theory (6)—Wilson and Kelling's theory attributing the escalation of crime over time and space to the proliferation of observable signs of social disorder.

brutalization effect (9)—the proposition that when the government inflicts lethal violence, e.g. capital punishment, such state-sanctioned violence actually increases homicide rates rather than reduces them.

capital punishment (9)—the execution of offenders by the state.

case histories (1)—intense examination and documentation of the life experiences of specific offenders or types of offenders.

causal order (5)—the assumption that variation in one variable or circumstance leads to (temporally precedes) variations in another variable or circumstance.

449

Chicago Area Project (12)—community-wide delinquency prevention program emphasizing self-help enterprises on the part of residents of areas with high crime rates; focused on recreational programs, neighborhood improvement, and working with youth gangs.

child savers (2)—influential women who began a campaign in the late nineteenth century to establish a juvenile court that would be distinct from the adult criminal court.

classical conditioning (5)—learning theory popularized by Ivan Pavlov which asserts that a particular signal or cue can, over time, produce an involuntary, conditioned response. As applied to criminology, some have argued that learning experiences when we are very young affect the probability of later delinquency; in particular, negative reactions to rule breaking early in life can condition a child to avoid bad, i.e. delinquent, behavior.

classical school (5)—in the early development of criminology, the school of thought that believed that laws and justice should be based on a view of humans as rational, thinking beings who would choose actions that give pleasure and avoid those that give pain.

code of the street (6)—Anderson's theory that disadvantaged youth develop a code for survival on the streets that encourages violence.

collective efficacy theory (6)—theory introduced by Sampson and various colleagues in the social disorganization tradition; they attribute variations over time and space to shared feelings of empowerment in controlling the surrounding neighborhood.

community policing (12)—an informal effort to develop closer ties between the police and local neighborhoods.

community shaming (11)—a form of psychological punishment whereby the community chastises an offender.

concordance rate (5)—a statistic indicating the probability that one twin has a trait when the other twin has the same trait.

conflict gangs (6)—Cloward and Ohlin's theory that disadvantaged youth form conflict-oriented gangs when there are no organized adult criminal subcultures in an area.

contraculture (6)—a system of values that is in opposition to dominant standards and in fact is the result of problems experienced in trying to obtain status while abiding by such conventional standards.

control-balance theory (6)—Tittle's theory attributing the motivational impetus for crime to the desire to escape deficits and attain surpluses of power. The outcome of that motivation is determined by a variety of facilitators and constraints.

co-offending (3)—committing offenses with someone else.

corporal punishment (7)—inflicting physical punishment, e.g., spanking, slapping, or the use of such implements as belts or paddles.

cosmic dualism (8)—conception of religion as a struggle between the dueling deities of God and the Devil.

creaming (11)—selecting the lowest risk offenders for a particular program.

crimes known to the police (3)—refers to events that have been processed to the stage where police decide that a crime has occurred.

criminal atavism (5)—Lombroso's theory that criminals exhibit traits of earlier primitive stages of human or animal evolution.

criminal gangs (6)—Cloward and Ohlin's theory that disadvantaged youth form instrumentally oriented gangs when there are organized adult criminal subcultures in an area.

criminology (1)—the scholarly tradition that encompasses the scientific study of the processes of making laws, breaking laws, and reacting to the breaking of laws.

defiant individualism (6)—Sanchez-Jankowski's theory that a distinct type of social character develops among youth in competition for scarce resources. That social character is distinguished by a high sense of competitiveness, mistrust, self-reliance, social isolation, and an emphasis on survival.

deinstitutionalization (10)—the movement to provide community-based alternatives for status offenders and minor offenders.

delinquency (2)—acts or conduct in violation of criminal law.

delinquency as a pickup game (7)—the spontaneity of juvenile group behavior that mimics the development of a street game of basketball.

delinquent act (2)—an act committed by a juvenile for which an adult could be prosecuted in a criminal court, but when committed by a juvenile is within the jurisdiction of the juvenile court.

delinquent gang (6)—refers to a group of youth who engage in delinquent activities together and are defined by themselves or others as members of a gang.

dependent variable (5)—a variable whose value or state depends on other variables.

dependent/neglected (2)—those cases covering neglect or inadequate care on the part of the parents or guardians. They include lack of adequate care or support resulting from death, absence, or physical or mental incapacity of the parents; abandonment or desertion; abuse or cruel treatment; and improper or inadequate conditions in the home.

desensitization (8)—in discussions of media influences it refers to a decline in emotional reactions to observations of harm to others as a result of continued exposure.

detached worker program (12)—sending adults into the streets to monitor and supervise juveniles.

detention (2)—temporary incarceration of a child who requires secure custody for his/her protection or protection of the community.

detention hearing (2)—hearing to determine whether a child is in need of secure detention.

deterrence (9)—the theory that delinquency is inhibited by fear of punishment; that is, when penalties are sufficiently certain, severe, and speedy, real and potential offenders are deterred from criminal behavior.

differential association theory (5)—first presented by Edwin Sutherland as a theory of criminal behavior, the position that deviant behavior is not the product of unconscious drives or biological facts, but simply behavior that is the product of social interactions that define lawbreaking in favorable and unfavorable terms.

differential association (6)—the process through which delinquency is learned by youth within a social system whose standards of right and wrong are in conflict with those embodied in the law.

differential reinforcement theory (5)—as formulated by Burgess and Akers, the position that involvement in delinquency can be explained by the reinforcing or punishing consequences in the environment.

discrimination (3)—in juvenile justice the concept refers to differential treatment of youth based on criteria deemed to be inappropriate or unjust.

disintegrative shaming (9)—also called stigmatic shaming; forms of shaming that isolate and magnify rejection from the group and society.

disposition (2)—definite action taken or a treatment plan decided upon or initiated regarding a particular case.

disposition hearing (2)—a hearing held to determine what should be done after a child has been adjudicated.

diversion (11)—refers to attempts to avoid formal court processing of juveniles, typically by sending youth to community-based programs.

dizygotic (5)—refers to twins that developed from two separate fertilized ova.

drift theory (6)—Matza's theory that delinquent youth are committed to neither conventional nor deviant values but drift between the two.

Drug-Free School Zone (12)—law-enforcement approach in which 1,000-foot perimeters are established around schools and related property; anyone caught using or dealing drugs within the zone is subject to stiffer penalties than would normally be the case.

early identification and intensive treatment (12)—the contention that delinquency can be prevented by developing techniques to identify potential offenders and by providing them with intense treatment of various kinds.

ectomorphy (5)—a body type characterized by a predominance of neural tissues (long and thin).

ego (5)—in Freud's psychoanalytic theory, the ego is the aspect of the human personality that is in close contact with social reality. The ego develops as the child grows and counteracts the urges of the id and directs behavior in a way that is consistent with physical and social reality.

egoism (6)—Bonger's term for the dominance of self-centered interests over social and moral commitments to others (altruism).

endomorphy (5)—a body type characterized by a predominance of digestive viscera (round, heavy, and fat).

equity theory (11)—underlying philosophy of restitution and restorative justice; i.e. restoring balance to relationships.

ethnographies (1)—studies of the culture and social relationships of a people generally living in a specific territory.

etiology (1)—the study and determination of causes of a phenomenon.

eugenics (7)—a social movement in the late 1800s and early 1900s that advocated improving the genetic characteristics of the population through government controls on fertility and breeding.

family intervention (10)—nonresidential treatment strategy that involves professional guidance of families and their problem youth to recognize and solve problems through regularly scheduled family discussion. The focus is on altering the behavior of parents in relation to their children.

family reform school (10)—a type of residential placement developed in the 1850s by anti-institutionalists. Inmates were grouped in cottages under the supervision of surrogate parents and lived, worked, and studied as a family unit.

Fast Track (12)—a program that targets kindergarten children who have conduct problems.

feminist theory (6)—in criminology, feminist theories focus on dimensions of the female world and female experiences that affect offending, victimization, and the relationship between the two.

feral children (7)—children who have been raised by animals or kept in nearly total isolation by parents or relatives.

focal concerns (6)—Miller's theory that disadvantaged people develop attitudes conducive to lawbreaking and pass these attitudes on through normal processes of socialization.

formal control processes (1)—when used in criminology the concept refers to organized law enforcement and judicial machinery charged with processing lawbreakers.

functional gang member (7)—an individual who belongs to a group that gets into fights with other groups and expects fighting of its members.

futility hypothesis (8)—used to refer to the hypothesis that guns are so widely available that attempts to control guns will have little or no effect.

general deterrence (9)—refers to the omission of criminal or delinquent acts as a result of anticipated or feared punishment among those who have not been punished.

general labeling effects (9)—labeling theory analog to general deterrence; it encompasses the escalating consequences of criminalization and law enforcement in a society.

general preventive effects (9)—Gibbs's concept encompassing all ways in which punishment can lower offense rates (general and specific deterrence, incapacitation, and socialization).

general strain theory (6)—Robert Agnew's version of structural strain theory that focuses on disparities between individual expectations and experiences related to those expectations.

general theory of crime (6)—Gottfredson and Hirschi's theory attributing all forms of crime to variations in opportunity and self-control.

guided group interaction (10)—a type of group treatment provided in an institutional context that involves frequent and intensive group discussions of members' current problems and experiences. The goal is to help delinquents become part of a group culture that advocates solving problems through legitimate means.

halfway house (10)—a temporary residence for offenders that usually is located within a community and which generally offers freedoms to residents that are not available in a totally residential program.

Head Start (12)—a preschool program that attempts to prepare children for kindergarten or first grade.

houses of refuge (2)—prison-like schools for juvenile offenders and impoverished children; established by private philanthropists in the 1820s who were concerned about increasing numbers of poor, urban immigrant children.

id (5)—according to Freud's psychoanalytic theory, the id is the force within the human personality that is concerned with immediate gratification; it is the only force that is functioning at birth.

imitation (8)—a learning process where the behavior and characteristics of others are copied.

in loco parentis **(2)**—doctrine that asserts that school officials and/or teachers act in place of parents and thus can claim immunity from Fourth Amendment protections against unreasonable search and seizure.

incapacitation (9)—when an offender is locked up or executed, any resultant decrease in that offender's criminal acts by constraining opportunity is said to be due to incapacitation.

incorrigible (2)—a juvenile law categorization in some jurisdictions encompassing youth who are repeatedly in conflict with authority.

independent variables (5)—variables used to explain the variation in other, dependent variables.

informal adjustment (2)—subject to court approval, after investigation in a delinquent or unruly referral, the designated court officer concluded that a child is within the jurisdiction of the court and undertakes to remedy the situation by giving counsel and advice to the parties with a view toward informal adjustment of the case. If the informal adjustment is not successful, the court officer may terminate the informal adjustment and file a petition.

infracultural (subterranean) values (6)—typically unacknowledged but widely shared values that are conducive to crime and delinquency (e.g., stylish and clever lawbreaking).

innovation (6)—one of Merton's deviant responses to disparities between aspirations to conventional goals and prospects of realizing those goals characterized by adoption of new ways to achieve those goals (e.g., theft).

institutional anomie theory (6)—Messner and Rosenfeld's theory attributing variations in serious crime to breakdowns in social institutions brought about by the combination of economic, materialist goals with variations in opportunity to realize those goals.

intake officer (2)—probation officer who first reviews a referral and makes a recommendation on proper court action in a case.

intake services (2)—unit at juvenile court center where referrals are initially processed.

integrated strain-bond theory (6)—Elliott's type of strain-frustration theory in which failure to achieve conventional goals provides the motivational impetus toward delinquency with the outcome explained by variations in social bonds.

interactionist theory (6)—Thornberry's version of life-course theory; it integrates social control and social learning theory and posits that the specific etiological forces vary by age and stage in a delinquent career.

intervening mechanisms (5)—the processes that link independent and dependent variables.

interview or self-administered questionnaire (4)—the two methods used to gather data on individual offending. The direct interview is preferred for assuring accuracy and overcoming reading problems, while the questionnaire checklist allows for greater anonymity.

IQ score (7)—short for "intelligence quotient"; based on tests designed to measure mental skills.

Irish system (10)—a form of the mark system revised in Ireland and characterized by indeterminate sentences, an initial period of solitary confinement, and congregate work. By accumulating marks inmates could progress to less restrictive correctional facilities and, eventually, earn parole and release.

Italian positivism (5)—school of thought associated with Cesare Lombroso (1835-1909) that promoted the application of scientific methods to determine the causes of crime.

jurisdictional age (2)—the age *below which* a person is subject to juvenile court jurisdiction.

juvenile court (2)—any court which has jurisdiction over matters involving juveniles.

Kleinfelter's syndrome (5)—a complex of characteristics in males with an extra X chromosome.

labeling paradox (9)—refers to circumstances where (1) youth who accord the most stigmatic meaning to sanctions are most likely to avoid offending, and (2) those who accord little stigma are most likely to offend.

labeling theory (9)—when applied to delinquency, the theory that labeling youth can increase their involvement in delinquency as a result of changes in identity, opportunity, and social interaction.

latchkey child (7)—child whose parent or parents work and who is unsupervised after school.

law-violating youth groups (7)—Miller's term to encompass any group of youth who violate laws, including gangs and more casual groups.

life-course/informal control theory (6)—Sampson and Laub's theory attributing age-graded variations in crime and delinquency to age-graded variations in convention-inducing social bonds.

life-course/social learning theory (6)—Warr's theory that explains age-graded variations in delinquency by age-graded variations in peer group processes as well as convention-inducing social bonds.

Maharishi effect (8)—the belief that the collective meditation of those who practice transcendental meditation has a calming effect on the wider community, thus leading to reductions in crime.

marginality (6)—a sociological term referring to people who lack the opportunity or resources to achieve widely shared social goals.

mark system (10)—a correctional model originating in Australia that allowed inmates to earn their "ticket of leave" (parole) through hard work and good behavior. If the offender succeeded on parole, he could be pardoned and return to freedom in England.

Marxist theory (6)—emphasizes capitalism and variations in advantage as causes of lawbreaking and variation in laws and their enforcement.

mass media (8)—impersonal instruments used to entertain or transmit written, oral, and visual material to a large audience of people.

maternal deprivation hypothesis (7)—based on the theory that a mother's engagement in activities outside of the home contributes to the delinquency of her children.

maturational reform (1)—concept used to refer to declines in offending that stem from age-graded changes in contrast to treatment or punishment effects.

mesomorphy (5)—a body type characterized by a predominance of muscular tissue (large bones, solid).

meta-analysis (8)—a quantitative summary and analysis of data reported in prior research.

Midcity Project (12)—a "total community" delinquency prevention program concerned with developing and strengthening local citizens' groups and organizing relationships among programs and institutions involving youth by using professional agencies.

Mobilization for Youth Project (12)—community delinquency prevention program in New York City that attempted to help minority students succeed in school and find jobs.

Monitoring the Future (4)—annual self-report survey conducted by the Institute for Social Research at the University of Michigan. The survey administers questionnaires about offenses and victimizations and a wide range of other characteristics of youth using samples of 10,000 high school seniors.

monozygotic (5)—refers to twins that developed from the same fertilized ovum.

moral panic (6)—a sociological concept referring to overreactions and exaggerations of the threat of specific problems in a society.

National Crime Victimization Survey (NCVS) (4)—the best known of the victimization surveys; administered by the Bureau of Justice Statistics, with annual interviews conducted by the Census Bureau.

near groups (6)—Yablonsky's conception of gangs as falling between loosely organized mobs and tightly knit peer groups. They are characterized by diffuse role definitions, limited cohesion, impermanence, minimal normative consensus, shifting membership, disturbed leadership, and limited expectations for membership.

neighborhood watch (12)—residents supervise their own neighborhoods and report suspicious activity to the police.

Neighborhood Youth Corps (12)—a federal program that attempts to provide employment, counseling, and remedial education for needy youth.

normative (or cultural) conflict (6)—a type of criminological theory attributing crime and delinquency to values and norms that conflict with those embodied in legal codes of a social system.

normative socialization (8)—social learning of values, norms, and beliefs.

official statistics (3)—used to refer to data or statistics compiled by personnel working in an official capacity within the law enforcement system.

operant conditioning (5)—learning theory associated with B.F. Skinner, who asserted that learning is voluntary and takes place through trial and error, as opposed to being an involuntary, conditioned reaction.

ordinal position (7)—birth order; subject of periodic interest in research on the family and delinquency.

organized gang (7)—a gang with clear leadership and membership.

overcriminalization (1)—the view that too many types of behavior are treated as crimes. For some, this is a partial explanation for the extent of our "crime problem."

panel studies (8)—method of inquiry that gathers data from a panel of people at different points in their life course, which allows consideration of changes in behavior over time.

parasympathetic nervous system (5)—part of the autonomic (or involuntary) nervous system; the parasympathetic nervous system is activated following a sympathetic nervous system response and induces a state of quiescence and relaxation.

parens patriae **(2)**—the right of the state to care for minors and others who cannot legally take care of themselves. This concept, which originated in fifteenth-century English Common Law, was used as a theoretical and legal justification for the development of the American juvenile court.

part I offenses (3)—the eight crime-index offenses (including arson) listed by the FBI for persons arrested; generally considered felony offenses.

part II offenses (3)—the remaining 21 offenses listed by the FBI for persons arrested; generally speaking, most are misdemeanor offenses.

party gang (7)—group activities that do not entail serious delinquent activity but foster a party atmosphere; often includes drinking.

PATHE (12)—positive action through holistic education; a school-based prevention program targeting change in the school environment and among high-risk students.

PeaceBuilders (12)—program for kindergarten through 5th grade students that focuses on prosocial behavior and reducing aggression.

peer group (6)—people of similar age and social characteristics who regularly engage in activities together.

penitentiary (10)—first developed in the U.S. in the late 1700s by prison reformer John Howard, this type of institution employed the Quaker principles of restraint and isolation in the belief that an austere and disciplined environment would lead inmates to contemplate the error of their ways and do penance for their sins. Also known as the **Pennsylvania system**.

penology (1)—that branch of criminology concerned with the punishment and treatment of offenders and the administration of correctional programs and institutions.

petition (2)—a document filed in juvenile court alleging that a juvenile is a delinquent, a status offender, dependent or abused, or for a special proceeding (i.e., child support, legitimation) and asking that the court assume jurisdiction over the juvenile or asking that an alleged delinquent be transferred to criminal court for prosecution as an adult.

placing out (2)—system developed by Charles Loring Brace in the mid-1800s by which poor and vagrant urban children were sent via orphan trains to be placed with farm families in the Midwest.

power-control theory (7)—Hagan, Simpson, and Gillis's theory that links the gender difference in delinquency to the power status of mothers and fathers in the household.

Prenatal/Early Infancy Project (12)—a program of nurse home visits to improve mothers' prenatal and postnatal health as well as infant health; appears to have also reduced abuse and violence in the home.

prevention (12)—proactive attempts to reduce delinquent behavior before it starts.

primary deviance (9)—Lemert's concept referring to casual involvement in rule-breaking behavior that does not link to a person's identity.

prisonization (10)—oppositional inmate code adopted by prisoners as a result of socialization by other inmates and which serves as a barrier to treatment and reintegration into conventional society.

privatization (10)—the trend toward the creation of juvenile institutions that are not operated by state or local governments but by private agencies or individuals, both for profit and nonprofit.

proactive policing (3)—police activity initiated by the police as opposed to reactions to complaints.

Progressive Era (2)—period from about 1880 to 1920 when the United States experienced increased urbanization and immigration, along with increasing labor violence, technological advances, and the concentration of wealth in the hands of a few.

psychopath (5)—individual who is unsocialized, irresponsible, unable to feel guilt, and unable to learn from experience or punishment.

Pygmalion effect (7)—used to refer to situations where labeling, defining, or categorizing a person has a self-fulfilling effect.

rational choice theory (9)—refers to theories that assume that people and offenders make deliberative decisions based on assessments of costs and rewards.

reaction formation (6)—the psychological process introduced in criminology by Albert Cohen to encompass the rejection of initial values and the embracement of their opposite.

reactive policing (3)—police activity that is a reaction to calls or complaints.

Reading One-on-One (12)—a one-on-one reading improvement program involving paid part-time tutors.

rebellion (6)—one of Merton's deviant responses to disparities between aspirations to conventional goals and prospects of realizing those goals; characterized by creation of new goals and ways of achieving those goals (e.g., hippies).

recidivism (10)—the further commission of offenses after release from a program or facility, typically measured by the percentage who are rearrested.

reciprocal causation (5)—when two variables affect each other, operating as both independent and dependent variables.

reconstructed families (7)—general term referring to the re-creation of a family unit after a disruption, with a variety of parents, children, and others functioning in family roles with no necessary biological relationship.

referral (2)—the filing of a complaint by a law enforcement officer; the child's parents, guardians, or custodians; the school system; a social service agency; or other individuals or agencies requesting the court to exercise its authority.

reformatories (2)—state-supported institutions for the care of young offenders. The first of these appeared in Massachusetts in the mid-1800s.

reintegrative shaming (9)—Braithwaite's concept in which forms of shaming that concentrate on maintaining and strengthening ties rather than excluding or isolating the offender have preventive effects.

reliability (4)—a measurement technique is presumed to be reliable when repeated measurements yield consistent results.

religiosity (8)—a multidimensional concept used to refer to the ways in which individuals are involved in and committed to religious values, norms, beliefs, and practices.

religious climate (8)—term used to refer to the centrality of religious institutions, values, norms, and beliefs by people in a shared territory.

religious cosmologies (8)—beliefs about the supernatural and sources of authoritative knowledge anchored in religious traditions and institutions.

representative sample (4)—when a sample is determined to represent the characteristics of interest in the total population.

resocialization (6)—learning new norms, values, beliefs, and techniques when conformity to earlier standards is not rewarded.

restitution (11)—in contemporary juvenile justice it refers to programs that require offenders to compensate the victims and/or community in some fashion.

restitution (2)—plan requiring offender to return property, make monetary compensation, or provide service to the victim and/or community to compensate for harm inflicted by the offender.

restorative justice (11)—a form of justice that involves the community and restores the relationship between the offender and society.

restrictive deterrence (9)—when individuals curtail a certain type of criminal activity during some period because the curtailment is perceived as reducing the risk that they will be punished as a response to the activity; in other words, people who merely restrain themselves to some degree.

retreatism (6)—one of Merton's deviant responses to disparities between aspirations to conventional goals and prospects of realizing those goals; characterized by abandonment of those goals (e.g., drug use).

retreatist gangs (6)—Cloward and Ohlin's theory that disadvantaged youth retreat into drug use when there is no adult criminal subculture and youth are ill-equipped for conflict.

risk-focused approach (12)—a public health model of prevention that has been adapted to delinquency prevention; such an approach attempts to identify risk factors that need to be addressed to reduce delinquency.

ritualism (6)—one of Merton's deviant responses to disparities between aspirations to conventional goals and prospects of realizing those goals; characterized by purposeless and rigid conformity (e.g., bureaucratic personalities).

routine activities (6)—Cohen and Felson's theory attributing variation in crime and delinquency over time and among territories to variations in the availability of unprotected targets.

sampling bias (4)—when a sample overrepresents or underrepresents certain categories of people in a population.

Scared Straight (11)—program developed at Rahway Prison that attempted to scare juveniles into going straight by exposing them to harsh verbal confrontations with inmates.

scientific method (1)—method of inquiry employed to discover and explain orderly patterns or regularities through the systematic collection of data or evidence that can be verified by others.

scientific theory (5)—a theory constructed in a manner that allows specification of the findings that would *disconfirm* the theory.

Seattle Delinquency Control Project (12)—a program that assigned social workers to a set of youth whom they organized into groups for various treatment efforts.

Second Step (12)—violence prevention program for elementary children that targets anger management, impulse control, and empathy.

secondary deviance (9)—Lemert's concept referring to the repetitive involvement and engulfment in rule-breaking behavior that reflects an identity established through the experience of labeling.

self-control theory (6)—Gottfredson and Hirschi's theory attributing variation in crime and delinquency to individual variations in learned impulse control assumed to be established at an early age and constant over the life course.

self-derogation theory (6)—Kaplan's version of strain-frustration theory in which failures to attain or maintain self-esteem through conventional behavior provides the motivational impetus for attaining self-esteem through criminal and delinquent conduct.

self-report surveys (4)—one of the two major alternatives to official police statistics on juvenile crime; they attempt to measure juvenile offense behavior through interviews or questionnaires.

sensory-deprived environment (7)—an environment where a child experiences very restricted interaction with others.

serious delinquent gang (7)—a gang that is involved in criminal activities.

serious-crime index (1)—the crimes for which data are provided in the Uniform Crime Reports category designated as "crimes known to the police." These include homicide, forcible rape, robbery, aggravated assault, burglary, larceny, and motor vehicle theft. Arson was added to the list of "crimes known" but does not enter into the index.

shock incarceration (11)—a form of incarceration that is demanding and harsh, like a boot camp.

shock probation (11)—refers to a condition of probation that requires offenders to attend a Scared Straight type of presentation.

social constructionism (6)—in criminology this term refers to a general perspective on social problems emphasizing the roles played by various groups in defining problems and shaping reactions to those problems.

social control theory (6)—a criminological theory attributing individual lawbreaking to the weakness, breakdown, or absence of those social bonds or socialization processes that are presumed to encourage law-abiding conduct.

social disorganization theory (6)—a type of criminological theory attributing variation in crime and delinquency over time and among territories to the absence or breakdown of communal institutions (e.g., family, school, church, and local government) and communal relationships that traditionally encouraged cooperative relationships among people.

social gang (7)—a gang that serves a social function for its members but does not entail serious delinquent behavior.

social learning theory (5)—in criminology, the theory formulated by Ronald Akers that variations in deviant behavior can be explained by four learning processes: normative socialization, imitation, differential reinforcement, and differential association. The opportunity to commit an act must also be present.

social structure social learning (SSSL) theory (6)—Aker's theory that variations in lawbreaking among categories of people can be explained by variations in social learning processes.

social support theory (6)—Cullen's type of social control theory emphasizing variations in conventional social support as the central force inhibiting crime and delinquency.

sociology (6)—the scientific study of patterns and changes in relationships among people, communities, and societies.

somatotype (5)—body type; William Sheldon (1898-1977) proposed that there would be differences between the somatotypes of delinquent boys and the somatotypes of the rest of the population.

source of referral (2)—the agency or individual filing a complaint with intake (which initiates court processing).

specific deterrence (9)—refers to the omission of further criminal or delinquent acts by an individual who was punished.

specific labeling effects (9)—labeling theory analog to specific deterrence; it encompasses the escalation of delinquent and criminal activity as a consequence of the labeling and processing of offenders.

specification (5)—identification of the circumstances or conditions under which variables are related.

spurious (5)—a relationship between two variables that is the product of (1) coincidental connections, or (2) shared connections with other variables that cause both.

status frustration (6)—the unpleasant state experienced when attempts to achieve or sustain positive self-evaluations fails.

status offense (2)—behavior which is considered an offense only when committed by a juvenile (for example, running away from home).

stepfamilies (7)—families with children where one of the parents is not the biological parent but functions in such a capacity due to marriage.

structural gang member (7)—an individual who belongs to a group with acknowledged leadership, a common meeting place, and a territory or turf within which the gang feels safe and where entry by others may provoke the group to violence.

structural strain theory (6)— a criminological theory attributing variations in crime and delinquency over time and among territories to disparities between learned cultural goals and realistic possibilities of attaining such goals.

subcultural socialization (6)—learning of norms, values, beliefs, and skills of specific subgroups.

subculture (6)—as applied to the study of delinquency, youth with shared traditions or value systems that are passed from one generation to another and which facilitate lawbreaking.

subterranean beliefs (6)—another term for infraculture.

superego (5)—the last element of personality development, according to Freudian psychoanalytic theory; the superego represents the conscience, which attempts to restrain the urges of the id and achieve balance.

sympathetic nervous system (5)—part of the autonomic (or involuntary) nervous system; the sympathetic nervous system is activated when an individual experiences anger, fear, or anxiety and influences heart rate, blood pressure, sweating, and changes in the saline content of perspiration.

synergism concept (12)—the idea that employing multiple techniques in combination will be more effective than distinct programs operating individually.

taken into custody (3)—the stage at which legally authorized persons assume temporary control of a juvenile.

teaching-family model (10)—treatment milieu that attempts to reproduce a home-like environment in which residents can learn new skills and behaviors.

techniques of neutralization (6)—Sykes and Matza's theory that specific learned excuses for breaking laws encourage delinquency and crime.

testosterone (5)—the hormone regulating the development of male sexual characteristics and sexual functioning in both males and females, produced by the testes in men and in smaller amounts by the ovaries in women.

token economy (10)—correctional model where offenders can earn and lose points for specified positive and negative behaviors; those points can be exchanged for goods and privileges.

tracking (7)—method of curriculum assignment that places students in educational programs based on scores on intelligence tests and levels of academic achievement.

training school (10)—long-term, institutional type of facility with the goal of helping offenders develop skills that are supposed to lower recidivism after release.

transcendental meditation (8)—a form of meditation developed by Maharishi Mahesh Yogi for achieving an enlightened consciousness using a variety of techniques and repetition of a personal mantra to aid in reaching that state.

transfer hearing (2)—hearing to determine whether a case should be remanded or waived to the criminal justice system.

Uniform Crime Reports (3)—FBI's annual report on crime in the United States; contains four sections: crimes known to the police, persons arrested, crimes cleared (solved), and numbers of law enforcement personnel by state.

validity (4)—a measure is considered to have validity when it can be shown that it measures what it is suppose to measure.

vicarious reinforcement (8)—social learning through observation of the consequences of others' behavior.

victimization surveys (4)—one of the two major alternatives to official police statistics on juvenile crime; household members are asked about their experiences as victims of crime through interviews or questionnaires.

victimology (4)—the study of victims and the processes of victimization.

VIPs (11)—victim impact panels; where DUI offenders are exposed to the pain and suffering of DUI victims.

XYY syndrome (5)—a complex of characteristics in males with an extra Y chromosome.

youth service bureaus (12)—created to reduce the role of the juvenile court and to act as central coordinators of community services for juveniles.

Author Index

Subject Index